306.0973 S
Smith-Rose
This violent empire

P9-CFL-321

JUL 2010

The Birth
of an
American
National
Identity

CARROLL SMITH-ROSENBERG

This Violent Empire

Published for the Omohundro Institute
of Early American History and Culture,
Williamsburg, Virginia, by the
University of North Carolina Press,
Chapel Hill

The Omohundro Institute
of Early American History
and Culture is sponsored
jointly by the College of
William and Mary and the
Colonial Williamsburg
Foundation. On November
15, 1996, the Institute adopted
the present name in honor
of a bequest from Malvern
H. Omohundro, Jr.

© 2010 The University of
North Carolina Press
All rights reserved

Designed by
Jacquline Johnson
Set in Adobe Caslon
by Keystone Typesetting

Manufactured in the
United States of America

Library of Congress Cataloging-in-Publication Data
Smith-Rosenberg, Carroll.
This violent empire : the birth of an American national
identity / Carroll Smith-Rosenberg.
p. cm.
Includes bibliographical references and index.
ISBN 978-0-8078-3296-7 (cloth : alk. paper)
1. National characteristics, American—History—18th century.
2. United States—Civilization—1783–1865. 3. Men, White—
United States—Attitudes—History—18th century.
4. Difference (Psychology)—Political aspects—United States—
History—18th century. 5. Political culture—United States—
History—18th century. 6. Violence—United States—History—
18th century. 7. Racism—United States—History—18th
century. 8. Paranoia—United States—History—18th century.
9. Sexism—United States—History—18th century.
10. Marginality, Social—United States—History—18th
century.
I. Omohundro Institute of Early American History &
Culture. II. Title.
E164.S64 2010
973.2'5—dc22
2009039481

The paper in this book meets the guidelines for permanence
and durability of the Committee on Production Guidelines
for Book Longevity of the Council on Library Resources.

The University of North Carolina Press has been a member
of the Green Press Initiative since 2003.

"You've Got to Be Carefully Taught" by Richard
Rodgers and Oscar Hammerstein II. Copyright
© 1949 by Richard Rodgers and Oscar Hammerstein II.
Copyright renewed. International copyright secured. All
rights reserved. Used by permission.

"Shall We Dance?" by Richard Rodgers and Oscar Hammerstein II. Copyright © 1951 by Richard Rodgers and
Oscar Hammerstein II. Copyright renewed. International
copyright secured. All rights reserved. Used by permission.

"Oklahoma" by Richard Rodgers and Oscar Hammerstein
II. Copyright © 1943 by Williamson Music. Copyright re-
newed. International copyright secured. All rights reserved.
Used by permission.

14 13 12 11 10   5 4 3 2 1

FOR

Alvia Grace Golden

with love

You've got to be taught to hate and fear
You've got to be taught from year to year,
It's got to be drummed in your dear little ear—
You've got to be carefully taught!

OSCAR HAMMERSTEIN II, South Pacific

PREFACE

*Violence has been the American daily bread since we have heard of America. This violence . . .
is not merely literal and actual but appears to be admired and lusted after, and the key to the
American imagination.* —JAMES BALDWIN, "Here Be Dragons"

Suspicion! Fear! Rage! As the twenty-first century takes form, these emotions have become pressing realities in American life. A war against terrorism ensnares the nation. Enemies from without and within menace our cities and transportation systems. Dark-visaged foreigners alarm us. Our own citizens are not above suspicion. Government agents search through immigrant communities, scrutinize private citizens' phone calls, internet communications, fiscal records—even library visits. Nor are terrorists the only fear. Illegal immigrants penetrate our borders. English no longer stands as our unquestioned national tongue. Filled with foreign speakers, the poor, criminals, our once-heralded "melting pot" cities are now seen as sites of vulnerability and danger, alien threats to the pure American heartland. Even that most basic of institutions, marriage, is threatened as state after state legalizes gay marriage and women demand the right to abortion.

Responding in anger, our government, with great popular support, leveled preemptive strikes against regimes perceived as hostile, repudiated the Geneva Convention, set up secret prisons and torture chambers, violated citizens' time-honored guarantees to privacy, due process, and habeas corpus. Private militias patrol our borders and scour rural villages. Even after the 2008 election promised a reversal of these policies, we remain loath to relinquish our extraconstitutional military tribunals or grant accused terrorists due process of the law. Our prisons remain filled with black and Latino youth.[1]

1. See James Baldwin, "Here Be Dragons," in Baldwin, *The Price of the Ticket: Collected Nonfiction, 1948–1985* (New York, 1985), 677–690, esp. 678. The 2007 prison population was in excess of two million (U. S. Department of Justice, Office of Justice Programs, Prison Statistics, Summary Findings).

Is this a unique moment in U.S. history? Emphatically, no. The fear of alien attacks, the need to violently exclude Others seen as dangerous or polluting has formed a critical component of the United States' national identity from the Alien and Sedition Acts of the 1790s through Joseph McCarthy's war on domestic Communists to the present. To fear and dehumanize alien Others, to ruthlessly hunt them down, is truly American. *This Violent Empire: The Birth of an American National Identity* traces the origin of these fears and the violent responses they provoke to the very beginnings of U.S. history—to the founding moments of the new nation and the debates over the ratification of the Constitution. The roots of American paranoia, racism, and violence lie in the instability of Americans' national sense of self. A violent and sudden revolution gave birth to the new United States. Before—indeed, for decades after—that revolution, the states, far from united, were an uncertain amalgam of diverse peoples, religions, cultures, and languages. No common history, no governmental infrastructure, no shared culture bound them together. Certainly no shared culture welcomed social outcasts—African Americans, free and enslaved, the poor and geographically marginal. Only a history of murderous usurpation explained the presence of European settlers on the American continent. Nor did any single, unquestioned system of values and beliefs help unify the founding generation. Rather, a host of conflicting political discourses, religious beliefs, and social values further destabilized the new nation's image of itself as a unified whole.

Seeking to constitute a sense of national collectivity for the motley array of European settlers who had gathered at the nether side of the North Atlantic, the new nation's founding generation not only had to create a mythic heritage of bravery and love of liberty for those residing in the new republic to embrace. They had to imagine themselves arrayed against an expanding series of threatening Others whose differences from the settlers overshadowed the divisions that distinguished the settlers from one another. The creation of these Others was designed to give European Americans a sense of national coherence that the reality of their lives did not support. Difference perceived as dangerous, disdained as polluting, demanding expulsion, formed a critical component of America's new national identity.[2]

---

2. "Identity's constitution," Stuart Hall reminds us, "is always based on *excluding* something and establishing a violent hierarchy between the two resultant poles. . . . Identities can function as points of identification and attachment only because of their capacity to exclude, to leave out, to render 'outside,' abjected" (Hall, "Introduction: Who Needs 'Identity'?" in Hall and Paul Du Gay, eds., *Questions of Cultural Identity* [London, 1996], 1–17, esp. 5). Susan Stanford Friedman agrees. "Identity is . . . unthinkable without some sort of imagined or literal

What was true at the nation's beginning remains true today. As a nation, we continue to be a motley array of immigrants and the descendants of immigrants, an uneasy composite drawn from every corner of the world, every language, religion, and culture. To mold this composite into a cohesive whole, those who embrace our normative national culture must not only imagine a romanticized national past; they must continue to call forth a host of Others, domestic and foreign, to represent all that we true Americans do not wish to be. Poor, dark, and disorderly, speaking foreign tongues, these Others establish the boundaries that define what it is to be an American. They constitute "a site of dreaded identification," against which we relentlessly struggle, consolidating our uncertain sense of self. Depicting these Others as abject, deformed, and dangerous, we reaffirm the need to dehumanize them, expel them from the American body politic, guard the nation's borders against them.[3]

But the nation's Others cannot be so easily expelled. They are our own fantasized creations, our discursive and psychological doubles, projections of our most feared and hated qualities. To paraphrase Pogo, they are us. At the same time, figures of the forbidden and dangerous, they fascinate and intrigue us. A tortured ambivalence thus lies at the heart of America's relation to its Others. To keep these Others at bay, to maintain "the foreclosures . . . we prematurely call identities," requires the increasingly enraged enactments of their exclusion, enactments that have found expression throughout the United States' long history of racism, xenophobia, and sexism.[4]

On the pages that follow, *This Violent Empire* will explore the complex processes by which a national identity first emerged on the pages of the new nation's public print culture and the complex interaction of "us" and "them" that lies at the heart of that story. Further, *This Violent Empire* will examine the uncertainties, contradictions, and insecurities that characterize America's national identity—its unsettled trajectory, its repeated production of Others who threaten our sense of national coherence and security and the frustration, rage, and violence those threats give rise to. Dread and desire, the need to exclude and the inability to exclude, lie at the heart of our national identity. They were

---

boundary" (Friedman, *Mappings: Feminism and the Cultural Geographies of Encounter* [Princeton, N.J., 1998], 3).

3. Judith Butler, *Bodies That Matter: On the Discursive Limits of "Sex"* (New York, 1993), 3.

4. Ibid., 22. Racial and racist concerns render national identities infinitely more complex. As Ania Loomba explains, "Ambivalence is fundamental to dominant imperial and colonial discourses that are heterogeneously composed [and] unevenly imposed" (Loomba, *Gender, Race, Renaissance Drama* [Manchester, 1989]). See, as well, Mechal Sobel, *Teach Me Dreams: The Search for Self in the Revolutionary Era* (Princeton, N.J., 2000), 5–6.

critical at the moment of our beginning. They shadow our actions today. They are the subject of *This Violent Empire*.

In this preface, I use the terms "true Americans," "the nation," "our," and "we" almost interchangeably. Does my doing so mean that I embrace a national identity that I have just described as paranoid, racist, and violent? No. But I do see myself as a product of that culture. While recognizing that many Americans do not see themselves as part of that culture, that large numbers of citizens have been excluded from it, and that many of both the included and excluded envision a quite different, all-inclusive America, those of us who see ourselves as its product must not simply distance ourselves by calling it "theirs." We must acknowledge our resisted connectedness to that culture and its exclusions. As part of the problem, we have a responsibility to point out the existence of that problem and to work to unravel its mystique.

Having begun my argument with a quote from James Baldwin, let me end with one from Bob Marley: "Four hundred years / And it's the same— / The same philosophy / I've said it's four hundred years."[5]

5. Bob Marley and Peter Tosh, "400 Years," *Catch a Fire*, Island Records, Kingston, Jamaica, 1973.

ACKNOWLEDGMENTS

T he path between my previous book, an examination of gender and sexuality in nineteenth- and early-twentieth-century America *(Disorderly Conduct: Visions of Gender in Victorian America)* and *This Violent Empire,* an exploration of the violence that lies at the heart of America's national identity, has been long and arduous. As I sought to understand the ways the founding generation constituted an American national identity, I found traditional historical narrative structures and forms of evidence insufficient to the task. Increasingly, I turned to literary critical practices (close readings, rhetorical analysis) and to poststructural and postcolonial theory for ways to penetrate the maze of contradictions and instabilities that enveloped the founding generation's efforts to create a national sense of self. Slowly, I came to think of national identities as compilations of conflicting discourses, to see our new republic as simultaneously the first modern postcolonial nation and as an "infant Empire," heir to Britain's vast North American holdings. I explored the ways the founding generation sought to obscure the contradictions between these self-images as well as those between the Declaration of Independence's celebration of man's inalienable rights and the Constitution's protection of chattel slavery. I came to see national identities as dynamic performances of memories imperfectly repressed. And always I sought to position these theoretical approaches within dense political and economic contexts.

In writing *This Violent Empire,* I had, as well, to explore the ways the founding generation invented such critical aspects of political modernity as the modern republic, the republican citizen, the political representative, and the capitalist state. I had, in short, to engage in a vigorous project of analytic retraining—as well as learn to weave through the labyrinth of historical disputes about the nature of the American Revolution, the ratification of the new constitution, and the impact of commercial and fiscal capitalism on the new nation's economy and society.

I was only able to do so with the constant support, admonitions, and suggestions of a host of scholarly friends and associates. My progress began years ago, while I was on the faculty of the University of Pennsylvania. Here dear friends, especially those associated with the modestly entitled faculty discussion group, the Diversity of Language and the Structure of Power, first guided me in the intricacies of poststructural theory and literary analysis: Houston Baker, Farah Griffin, Anne R. Jones, Maureen Quilligan, Robert St. George, Elaine Scarry, Jerry Singerman, Peter Stallybrass, Lilianne Weissberg—and Michael Malone, who taught us to laugh at our own seriousness and sense of self-importance. I am especially grateful to two wonderful historians at Penn, Mary Berry and Evelyn Brooks Higginbotham, who have added greatly to this book. And, above all, I am indebted to Mary, Lucienne Frappier Mazur, Phyllis Rackin, and Gabrielle Spiegel, who read many of my early essays on these new modes of analysis, chided, disagreed, and greatly improved my efforts. To all these old friends, I offer my heartfelt gratitude.

Within the powerfully stimulating intellectual atmosphere of the University of Michigan, I continued my progress toward developing new historical approaches. I am particularly indebted to the members of the university's Atlantic Studies Initiative: Fernando Coronil, Philip Deloria, Mamadou Diouf, Greg Dowd, Laurent Dubois, Frieda Ekotto, Lorna Goodison, Dena Goodman, Linda Gregerson, Sandra Gunning, David Hancock, Jean Hébrard, Martha Jones, Arlene Keizer, Mary Kelley, Steven Mullaney, Ifeoma Nwankwo, Marianetta Porter, Sonya Rose, Julius Scott, Rebecca Scott, Julie Skurski, Valerie Traub, and Gustavo Verdesio. My work is far richer for their influence and example. Philip Deloria and Greg Dowd inspired and guided my analyses of Native American/European American relations. Philip's *Playing Indian* and Greg's *War under Heaven* have cast long shadows over *This Violent Empire*. Teaching with Arlene Keizer, Sonya Rose, and Mamadou Diouf offered stimulating and enriching exchanges. Dena Goodman is a remarkable and challenging reader. Mary Kelley's extraordinary contributions to *This Violent Empire* are too many and too great to be listed. Mamadou Diouf, Jean Hébrard, and Martha Jones know how they have reshaped my thinking. My indebtedness to them is great and ongoing. Nor can I forget Brendan O'Malley, a wonderful young scholar completing his dissertation at the Graduate Center, City University of New York, whose scholarly and editing expertise contributed significantly to the final stages of this volume.

Some friends span time and institutions—Sue-Ellen Case, Blanche Cook, Clare Coss, Toby L. Ditz, Susan Foster, Sally Gordon, Marianne Hirsch, Jean Howard, Linda K. Kerber, Rogers Smith, Domna Stanton, Leo Spitzer, Sterling Stuckey, Susan Sturm—and continents: Françoise Ducrocq, Cristina Giorcelli, Karen Hagerman, Catherine Hall, Yasmine Hoffman, Michel Imbert, Rhys Isaac, Rada Ivekoviæ, Dominique Marcais, Viola Sacks, and Bill Schwartz. Sadly, some passed away before I could publicly acknowledge their impact on my thought, in particular that generative figure in American Studies, Emory Elliott. Others have influenced me powerfully through their writing as well as their conversations. Stuart Hall's nuanced understanding of the interplay of race, power, and the state has shaped my thinking, as have his essays on national identity formation. I am equally grateful to Joseph Roach, who knows how thoroughly indebted I am to his brilliant analysis of performance, memory, and identity formation in his monumental *Cities of the Dead*, and in particular to his vision of a circum-Atlantic culture built around incomplete forgetting of the Atlantic holocaust (slavery, the slave trade, and the genocide of Native Americans). Their work, fused in my mind with M. M. Bakhtin's vision of the heteroglossic dynamism of language and meaning, constitutes the foundation blocks with which *This Violent Empire* was constructed.

Thank you, as well, to Susan Douglas, T. R. Durham, Rick Hills, Deb Labelle, Brenda Marshall, Maria Montoya, Philip Pochoda, Abby Stewart, Ed West, Kate West, and David Winter for hours of idea-expanding conversation. And, for profound emotional support through years of nattering on about my work: Joan Berner, Martha Boethel, Tish Romer, and Cathy Warren. Nina Hauser brought a unique graphic imagination to discussions of my book. Roni Moncur offered psychological insights and encouragement essential to the book's completion.

A number of scholars encouraged the publication of early versions of some of the material that ultimately made up *This Violent Empire*. These articles include "Domesticating 'Virtue': Coquettes and Revolutionaries in Young America," in Elaine Scarry, ed., *Literature and the Body: Essays on Populations and Persons* (Baltimore, 1988), 160–184; "Dis-covering the Subject of the 'Great Constitutional Discussion,' 1786–1789," *Journal of American History*, LXXIX (1992), 841–873; "Subject Female: Authorizing an American Identity," *American Literary History*, V (1993), 481–511; "Federalist Capers: Reflections on the Nature of Political Representation and the Empowerment of the Political Subject," unpublished paper, 1994; "Political Camp or the Ambiguous Engendering of the American Republic," in Ida Blom, Karen Hagemann, and Catherine Hall, eds., *Gendered Nations: Nationalisms and Gender Order in the Long Nineteenth Century* (Oxford, 2000); "The Republican Gentleman: The Race to Rhetorical Stability in the New United States," in Stefan Dudink, Karen Hagemann, and John Tosh, eds., *Masculinities in Politics and War: Gendering Modern History*, 61–76 (Manchester, 2004); "Black Gothic: The Shadowy

Origins of the American Bourgeoisie," in Robert Blair St. George, ed., *Possible Pasts: Becoming Colonial in Early America* (Ithaca, N.Y., 2000), 243–269; "Surrogate Americans: Masculinity, Masquerade, and the Formation of a National Identity," *Proceedings of the Modern Language Association*, CXIX (2004). I am most grateful to all these scholars.

Clearly, institutional support is critical to any scholarly endeavor. While working on *This Violent Empire*, I received invaluable support from a number of scholarly foundations: the Institute for Advanced Study, Princeton; the American Council of Learned Societies; the Guggenheim Foundation; the Rockefeller Foundation Bellagio Center; the Center for Ideas and Society, University of California, Riverside; and the University of Michigan Humanities Fellowship Program.

No scholar can function without the support of research librarians, whose knowledge and generosity underpin all historical endeavor. I have been particularly fortunate in the assistance I have received from two of the great American research libraries, the Library Company of Philadelphia and the William L. Clements Library of the University of Michigan. I want particularly to thank James N. Green, Phil Lapsansky, Cornelia S. King, and Nicole Joniec of the Library Company of Philadelphia and Clayton Lewis, Barbara DeWolfe, and Brian Dunnigan of the Clements Library for their expertise, patience, and generosity, without which *This Violent Empire* would never have been possible. These libraries constitute two of this country's premier scholarly resources.

A number of individuals associated with the Omohundro Institute of Early American History and Culture made this volume a shared enterprise. From the first, Fredrika J. Teute embraced this project at the same time as she worked assiduously to improve it, as did Mendy C. Gladden. I am especially grateful to Fredrika for securing such tough and discerning readers as Michael Meranze and Steven Shapiro, who brought their quite distinctive expertise to the reading and improvement of my manuscript. Every scholar imagines an ideal copyeditor. In Kathy Burdette, I was blessed with one of the sharpest-eyed, most creative, and most patient. My gratitude is boundless. In short, I am delighted that Omohundro embraced this project and is publishing this book.

Friends, foundations, libraries, and editors have been crucial in my progress, but so, too, have been family. My daughter, Leah Reade Rosenberg, has taught me far more than a daughter should by rights teach a mother. Her grasp of postcolonial theory, her nuanced understandings of the ways national identities took form in the Caribbean, and the sophisticated ways she interweaves literary texts and historical contexts have been a model for my efforts in this volume. Above all, I want to thank my partner of nearly thirty years, Alvia Golden, who has been with me every step of this long way—supporting, encouraging, and, at times, threatening the most dire punishments. Without her astute criticism and deep belief in the value of this project, *This Violent Empire* would not have been possible. In all things, in all ways, I am in her debt.

CONTENTS

Preface ix

Acknowledgments xiii

List of Illustrations xxi

INTRODUCTION "What Then Is the American, This New Man?" 1

SECTION ONE THE NEW AMERICAN—AS—REPUBLICAN CITIZEN

Prologue One The Drums of War / The Thrust of Empire 47

   CHAPTER ONE Fusions and Confusions 55

   CHAPTER TWO Rebellious Dandies and Political Fictions 88

   CHAPTER THREE American Minervas 136

SECTION TWO DANGEROUS DOUBLES

Prologue Two Masculinity and Masquerade 191

   CHAPTER FOUR Seeing Red 207

   CHAPTER FIVE Subject Female: Authorizing an American Identity 250

SECTION THREE THE NEW AMERICAN—AS—BOURGEOIS GENTLEMAN

Prologue Three The Ball 291

   CHAPTER SIX Choreographing Class / Performing Gentility 309

   CHAPTER SEVEN Polished Gentlemen, Troublesome Women,
   and Dancing Slaves 365

   CHAPTER EIGHT Black Gothic 413

Conclusion 465

Index 469

ILLUSTRATIONS

PLATE ONE Bookcase, c. 1780–1800 24

PLATE TWO Title page of *Bannaker's Almanac, or Ephemeris,* 1795 25

PLATE THREE Annis Boudinot Stockton 147

PLATE FOUR Mercy Otis Warren 148

PLATE FIVE Joseph Brant 221

PLATE SIX Ballroom, Powel House 324

PLATE SEVEN Bedroom, Graeme Park 325

PLATE EIGHT Writing desk, c. 1801–1805 326

PLATE NINE Mrs. Daniel Hubbard 330

PLATE TEN Mary (Finch), Viscountess Andover 331

PLATE ELEVEN Isaac Royall 334

PLATE TWELVE Office, Powel House 337

PLATE THIRTEEN Wallpaper design, "Wallpaper Depicting Captain John Cook" 342

PLATE FOURTEEN Anne Willing Bingham 346

PLATE FIFTEEN *An Unfinished House in Chestnut Street* 356

PLATE SIXTEEN Mary and Elizabeth Royall 396

PLATE SEVENTEEN Reverend Richard Allen 432

PLATE EIGHTEEN Reverend Absalom Jones 434

PLATE NINETEEN Title page, *A Narrative of the Proceedings of the Black People* 436

PLATE TWENTY *Revenge Taken by the Black Army for Cruelties Practised on Them by the French* 448

PLATE TWENTY-ONE *The Mode of Exterminating the Black Army as Practised by the French* 452

PLATE TWENTY-TWO *Dragon, (Haïti)* 457

This Violent Empire

"What Then Is the American, This New Man?"

Identities are never unified . . . never singular but multiply constructed across different, often intersecting and antagonistic discourses, practices and positions. They are . . . constantly in the process of change and transformation. . . . They arise from the narrativization of the self, but the necessarily fictional nature of this process in no way undermines its discursive, material or political effectivity.—STUART HALL, Questions of Cultural Identity

Analysts . . . should seek to explain the processes and mechanisms through which what has been called the "political fiction" of the nation . . . can crystallize, at certain moments, as a powerful, compelling reality.—FREDERICK COOPER, Colonialism in Question

Though we live in a time of global capitalism and interlocking economies, our world remains organized around nation-states, their right to protect their borders against foreign invasions, unwanted immigrants, and terrorists, their responsibility for protecting—and policing—their peoples. Despite multinationals' economic power, individuals continue to swear allegiance to their nations, patriotically promise to kill and be killed for them. Nationalism continues to pose one of the greatest threats to world peace and prosperity. It behooves us, therefore, to explore the ways nations and national identities take form and why they continue to constitute such an essential aspect of an individual's sense of self. Most especially, we must seek to understand the tie between nationalism and violence, between the pleasures of being included within a nation and the drive to violently exclude others.

We do not usually turn to the United States when studying nationalism and violence. Yet, in many ways, American nationalism provides an ideal case study. Few nation-states or national identities are as artificially constructed. Few have been more successful in imbuing generation after generation of immigrants with a deep sense of national belonging. And few are as renowned for their

I

proclivity for violence. What the formation of the U.S. nation-state can teach us about the violence that lies at the heart of national identities is the focus of *This Violent Empire*.[1]

IN THE BEGINNING

America's declaration of independence from Great Britain presented the new nation's founding generation with significant challenges. It had to constitute a new nation. That nation, for the first time in modern history, would be an independent republic, built upon the radically new and untried principles of popular sovereignty and universal equality. Citizens for that republic had to be imagined—"invented" would be the more appropriate word. Although they would be endowed with inalienable rights, the most fundamental being the right to self-government, the exact form that self-governance would take was hotly contested. The citizen's rights and responsibilities in relation to his new republic, his fellow citizens, and his political representatives had to be delineated. Most especially, who among the new nation's diverse inhabitants could claim the rights of full, active citizenship had to be decided.[2]

With equal urgency, the new Republic's founding generation had to envision a cohesive national identity, one that would bind together the varied inhabitants of the newly united states. In doing so, they had to imagine a new American whom citizens as diverse as Maine fishermen, Philadelphia merchants, western squatters, and South Carolinian planters could identify with, wish to become, boast that they were. They had to teach their fellow European

1. See J. Hector St. John de Crèvecoeur, *Letters from an American Farmer* (New York, 1904), letter 3, 54; Stuart Hall, "Introduction: Who Needs 'Identity'?" in Hall and Paul Du Gay, eds., *Questions of Cultural Identity* (London, 1996), 5; Frederick Cooper, *Colonialism in Question: Theory, Knowledge, History* (Berkeley, Calif., 2005), 63.

2. European Americans were not alone in exploring the nature of that radical new construction, the modern republican citizen. The concept of man as citizen, Étienne Balibar tells us, was a defining characteristic of the Age of Revolution. Rather than being seen, as he always had been, as subject to the law of God and king, man emerged as an active citizen, defined as he who "makes the law" and is "accountable for the consequences, the implementation and non-implementation of the law he has himself made." "What is new," Balibar continues, "is the sovereignty of the citizen . . . this sovereignty must be founded on a certain concept of man, or, better, on a new concept of man." Balibar, of course, is thinking of the French Revolution. But the invention of the U.S. republican citizen preceded the emergence of the French citizen by some twenty years (Balibar, "Subjection and Subjectivation," in Joan Copjec, ed., *Supposing the Subject* [London, 1994], 1–15, esp. 10–12; Balibar, "Citizen Subject," in E. P. Connor and J. L. Nancy, eds., *Who Comes after the Subject?* [New York, 1991], 40–41).

Americans to embrace that mythic figure as their own, true self and, in the process, bring the new nation into being.

These were daunting challenges—and daunting times. For the previous century and a half, Britain's mixed monarchy had brought European American settlers many benefits. It had guaranteed them the right to political representation and freedom from unwarranted searches, the right to a trial by jury and habeas corpus. It had also brought them relative political stability grounded on a hierarchical social order. Would all that change now? A republic without a king and a hereditary aristocracy to maintain stability and order, eighteenth-century political writers had long warned, could easily descend into the chaos and excesses of democracy—demands by the poor and uneducated for a voice in their own governance, attacks on private property. Many cast nervous glances back to the confusions of Cromwell's Commonwealth. With even greater anxiety, they observed events unfold in western Massachusetts, where rebellious farmers forced state courts to close, or along the Ohio frontier, where squatters defied land speculators and battled federal troops sent to drive them from the land. Without a king, what was to prevent every ragtag person— apprentices, day laborers, men without a penny in their pocket or a wit of learning in their heads—from declaring all government oppressive and themselves in a "state of nature"? How popular could popular sovereignty become before anarchy ensued? These questions had troubled political thinkers since the Ranters and the Levelers had first challenged parliamentary authority. At this moment of imperial rupture, popular uprisings, and unforeseeable futures, observers contemplated them with growing alarm.

Especially since, at the moment of Independence, the thirteen states were far from united. No overarching institutions, no long history, no ingrained sense of community—in short, no "we"—bound the states and their inhabitants together. Local experiences and identities far outweighed national ones in their immediacy.[3] The new Republic was an ill-sorted collection of far-from-united

---

3. It was rare even for elite European American travelers to visit colonies remote from their own. The erudite Annapolis physician Alexander Hamilton is the exception that proves the rule. He traveled from Annapolis to Boston in the 1750s. Yet Hamilton had no network of friends and associates whose houses formed the spine of his trip. Rather, he entered each town as a stranger, making social contacts at gentlemen's coffeehouses. See Richard L. Bushman, "American High-Style and Vernacular Cultures," in Jack P. Greene and J. R. Pole, eds., *Colonial British America: Essays in the New History of the Early Modern Era* (Baltimore, 1984), 345–383, esp. 359. See, as well, Bushman, *The Refinement of America: Persons, Houses, Cities* (New York, 1992), 79; and Michael Warner, *The Letters of the Republic: Publications and the Public Sphere in Eighteenth-Century America* (Cambridge, Mass., 1990), 133.

states; it was not until the ratification of the Constitution that the term "united states" was routinely capitalized. Indeed, a cadre of political leaders, sharing a national vision and working together across state and regional lines to constitute a strong federal government, did not emerge until the exigencies of war and the pressing needs of a wartime army convinced those revolutionaries of the high price the independent states paid for their political autonomy and economic rivalries. Still, large numbers of the new Americans continued to fear these leaders' national and cosmopolitan vision. Was that vision driven by elite economic interests? Would common people lose the rights and powers they had forged through revolution?[4]

Fear of change took many forms. Until the Revolution, European Americans had thought of themselves primarily as British subjects resident in North America. Britishness, for them, was an expansive identity, enveloping all white settlers who claimed a British heritage wherever they resided within the empire —England, Scotland, Ireland, the Caribbean, North America, African slave forts, or the Indian subcontinent. Throughout the eighteenth century, British settlers had ardently supported Britain's imperial wars. British heroes were their heroes, British enemies, their enemies—and, they fervently believed, their enemies were Britain's enemies.[5] They traced their most prized political rights back to the Magna Charta, to the parliamentary revolutions of the seventeenth century, and to English common law. When they began to protest British imperial regulations, they thought of themselves as protecting time-honored British freedoms. That is, until the American Revolution turned the world upside down. Until then, Europeans commonly used the word "American" to refer, not to British or European settlers in North America, but to America's indigenous peoples.[6] White settlers' seizure of the name "American" was as revolutionary an act as engaging the British at Lexington and Concord. In

4. Saul Cornell, "Politics of the Middling Sort: The Bourgeois Radicalism of Abraham Yates, Melancton Smith, and the New York Antifederalists," in Paul A. Gilje and William Pencak, eds., *New York in the Age of the Constitution, 1775–1800* (Madison, N.J., 1992), 151–175.

5. On European Americans' sense of Britishness, see T. H. Breen, "Ideology and Nationalism on the Eve of the American Revolution: Revisions *Once More* in Need of Revising," *Journal of American History*, LXXXIV (1997), 13–39, esp. 27–28; Rhys Isaac, *Landon Carter's Uneasy Kingdom: Revolution and Rebellion on a Virginia Plantation* (New York, 2004); and Brendan McConville, *The King's Three Faces: The Rise and Fall of Royal America, 1688–1776* (Chapel Hill, N.C., 2006).

6. For explorations of images of America entertained by Europeans, see, for example, Susan P. Castillo, *Colonial Encounters in New World Writing, 1500–1786: Performing America* (London, 2006); Karen Ordahl Kupperman, ed., *America in European Consciousness, 1493–1750* (Chapel Hill, N.C., 1995).

hindsight, it may have been more so. Asserting themselves as Americans, European Americans firmly established their separateness from Britain. They asserted, as well, their rightful possession of the North American continent. Contradictions and ironies marked the birth of the new nation, contradictions and ironies that continue to this day. Is the United States the world's first postcolonial nation, the bold defender of democracy and self-determination around the world, or is it the world's most powerful empire? Which identity would be—is—dominant? The founding generation saw no reason to choose between them. In 1776, the new Americans boasted, they had taken up arms to resist British imperial tyranny, vanquished an army long thought invincible, and constituted themselves an independent republic. Those same actions proclaimed them the rightful inheritors of Britain's North American empire. As the British had before them, European Americans believed themselves called by God to civilize and rule the vast continent and its indigenous peoples. Without any sense of irony, they proclaimed their republic an "infant empire" and America's indigenous peoples their colonized wards. As none other than George Washington insisted,

> The citizens of America, placed in the most enviable condition, as the sole *lords and proprietors* of a vast tract of continent, comprehending all the various soils and climates of the world and abounding with all the necessaries and conveniences of life, are now, by the late satisfactory pacification, acknowledged to be possessed of absolute freedom and independency. They are from this period to be considered as actors on a most conspicuous theatre, which seems to be peculiarly designed by providence for the display of human greatness.[7]

7. "A Circular Letter from His Excellency General Washington, Commander in Chief of the Armies of the United States of America, Addressed to the Governors of the Several States, on Resigning His Command, and Retiring from Public Business," *American Museum*, I (1787), 388 (emphasis added). The Great Seal of the United States similarly fused American Independence and American imperialism. "The escutcheon or shield is borne on the breast of an *American* eagle, without any other supporters, to denote, that the united states of America ought to rely on their own virtue," the designers explained. "The eagle itself," they continued, reinforcing their adoption of a well-known Roman symbol, "is a symbol of empire." "The device of the Armorial Atchievement [*sic*], appertaining to the United States . . . which . . . forms the Great Seal for the United States, in Congress assembled" (*Columbian Magazine*, I [1786], 33–34). See, as well, Dr. Ladd, "Extracts from an Oration Delivered before His Excellency the Governor of South Carolina . . . ," *American Museum*, II (1787), 332–336, esp. 333. From being acknowledged the sovereign possessors of American lands with whom Europeans negotiated sovereign treaties, Native Americans became "wards" of the new, white Republic. The status of "ward" for Native

Tellingly, Washington's letter positioned European Americans as imperialists first and independent republicans second. Facing east, toward Great Britain, European Americans called themselves Sons of Liberty, true heirs of Augustan republicanism and the Scottish Enlightenment. Facing west, they declared themselves "lords and proprietors of a vast continent."

Privileged by race, European Americans were, nevertheless, rendered uncertain by their geographic location. A small band of white settlers clinging to the edge of a red continent, they feared that their newly won separation from England had cast them off from all they considered civilized. No longer part of the proud British Empire, would they still be able to distinguish themselves from those other Americans, the "savage" tribes that inhabited vast stretches of the American continent? Defensively, they insisted that Britain's culture was their culture, Britain's literature, their literature. Sharing racial and cultural identities with their former colonizers, distinguishing themselves racially from those other (Native) Americans, eighteenth-century European Americans embodied a complex form of postcoloniality. Existing between, and thus outside of, the Enlightenment's stabilizing categories of metropole and native, European and savage, they could claim but an uncertain sense of self. In the face of such multiple and deeply conflicted identities, who could help them constitute a stable national identity?

The leadership that worked to create a strong new nation was as new as the nation itself. With Independence, the colonial elite—its royal officeholders, military officers, representatives of great British commercial houses, and tory sympathizers—had gone "home" to England, leaving a critical void in European American political and social hierarchies. This void was less noticeable in the South, where leading tidewater planter families continued to rule, but in the North, it appeared simultaneously cavernous and inviting. Although some of the older northern elite had embraced Independence, many had left, opening the field for ambitious men seeking to assume their predecessors' authority and legitimacy. Prominent among these new men were wealthy northern merchants, land speculators, and entrepreneurs—Robert Morris, James Wilson, and John Nicholson, among others. Less wealthy but more politically promi-

---

Americans became official U.S. policy with John Marshall's decision in *Cherokee Nation v. Georgia*, 1831, in which Marshall stated, "Indians . . . occupy a territory to which we [the Federal government] assert a title independent of their will . . . they are in a state of pupilage. Their relation to the United States resembles that of a ward to his guardian" (see Charles F. Hobson, ed., *The Papers of John Marshall*, XII [Chapel Hill, N.C., 2006], 58). The term "ward" appeared in Federal legislation throughout the nineteenth century and into the twentieth.

nent were the lawyers and physicians who had taken a leading role in orchestrating the Revolution—John Adams and James Warren in Boston, Benjamin Rush in Philadelphia, Alexander Hamilton and John Jay in New York. Before the war, most of these men had occupied subordinate positions within the older colonial social and political structures. Though they were men of remarkable talent and bold vision, their claims to new authority were shaky and often bitterly resented by their social inferiors. To keep their toehold in the uncertain social and political order, to legitimate their newly won prominence and authority, proved challenging.[8]

The Revolution did more than eliminate the upper echelon of the colonial elite and elevate ambitious new leaders. It reached down into the minds and hearts of ordinary citizens, breeding a desire for political enfranchisement and power. Frontier farmers, urban mechanics, and petty shopkeepers demanded—and, at times, gained—a voice in the nation's political development.[9] Of course, their voices jarred, violently at times, both with one another and more strenuously still with the more refined tones of the new urban and would-be urbane elite. A cacophony of political, social, and cultural voices emerged as European

8. For discussions of the political and social ambitions of these men and their social insecurities, see, among others, Thomas M. Doerflinger, *A Vigorous Spirit of Enterprise: Merchants and Economic Development in Revolutionary Philadelphia* (Chapel Hill, N.C., 1986), esp. chap. 1; Gordon S. Wood, *The Radicalism of the American Revolution* (New York, 1993), esp. 271; Bernard Friedman, "The Shaping of the Radical Consciousness in Provincial New York," *JAH*, LVI (1970), 781–801; Joanne B. Freeman, *Affairs of Honor: National Politics in the New Republic* (New Haven, Conn., 2001); Gary J. Kornblith and John M. Murrin, "The Making and Unmaking of an American Ruling Class," in Alfred F. Young, ed., *Beyond the American Revolution: Explorations in the History of American Radicalism* (DeKalb, Ill., 1993), 27–79, esp. 45–52.

9. Saul Cornell, "Aristocracy Assailed: The Ideology of Backcountry Anti-Federalism," *JAH*, LXXVI (1990), 1148–1172; Cornell, *The Other Founders: Anti-Federalism and the Dissenting Tradition in America, 1788–1828* (Chapel Hill, N.C., 1999). Others certainly support Cornell's view. See, for example, Gary B. Nash, *The Urban Crucible: Social Change, Political Consciousness, and the Origins of the American Revolution* (Cambridge, Mass., 1979); Young, ed., *Beyond the American Revolution;* Paul A. Gilje, *The Road to Mobocracy: Popular Disorder in New York City, 1763–1834* (Chapel Hill, N.C., 1987), sect. 2, and Gilje's more recent *Liberty on the Waterfront: American Maritime Culture in the Age of Revolution* (Philadelphia, 2004), chap. 5; Dirk Hoerder, *Crowd Action in Revolutionary Massachusetts, 1765–1789* (New York, 1977), 92–94, 271, 280; Charles S. Olton, *Artisans for Independence: Philadelphia Mechanics and the American Revolution* (Syracuse, N.Y., 1975). For the impact of Revolutionary rhetoric on African Americans, see Mechal Sobel, *Teach Me Dreams: The Search for Self in the Revolutionary Era* (Princeton, N.J., 2000), 7–9; Nash, *Forging Freedom: The Formation of Philadelphia's Black Community, 1720–1840* (Cambridge, Mass., 1988), 220–247; and John Wood Sweet, *Bodies Politic: Negotiating Race in the American North, 1730–1830* (Baltimore, 2003), chap. 5.

Americans, urban and rural, refined and rough, northern and southern battled over what form the Republic and republican citizenship would take. What powers, what authority would the new citizen be able to claim in constituting a new political identity? This early in the struggle, no answer was available. No group could claim the unquestioned right to leadership. None offered unqualified deference. All was in process, in formation.

Not limited to the political, change and uncertainty encompassed the economic sphere as well. Throughout the long eighteenth century, North America's role in the British mercantile system had steadily expanded. European American–made and –owned ships carried American agricultural products to West Indian plantations and British cargoes from African slave forts to the Caribbean and then on to Liverpool. As a result of the trade, the riches of the world increasingly found their way onto the wharves of Philadelphia, Boston, and New York—Chinese silks and porcelains, Caribbean sugar, Brazilian chocolate, Indian calicoes, and British manufactures. From there, carried by coastal ships, overland wagons, and peddlers' saddlebags, they made their way to smaller port towns, inland agricultural villages, and isolated farms. By the mid-eighteenth century, Britain's consumer culture was thoroughly at home in North America as a "vernacular culture" spread from America's entrepôts to inland villages and farms. Carole Shammas estimates that farming families expended one-quarter of their income on consumer items brought from outside the community. "These were not precapitalist farmers sullenly submitting to the market," T. H. Breen adds. "They welcomed economic change." The cautious capitalist values of "a penny saved is a penny earned," classic republican admonitions against extravagant lifestyles, and the anti-materialism of self-sufficient farming families—until now, apparently content with homespun and crude country pottery—struggled against growing desires for new comforts and pleasures.[10]

10. Carole Shammas, *The Pre-industrial Consumer in England and America* (Oxford, 1990); T. H. Breen, "An Empire of Goods: The Anglicization of Colonial America, 1690–1776," *Journal of British Studies*, XXV (1986), 467–499, esp. 484–485. See also Breen, *The Marketplace of Revolution: How Consumer Politics Shaped American Independence* (New York, 2004); Bushman, "American High-Style and Vernacular Cultures," in Greene and Pole, eds., *Colonial British America;* Arthur L. Jensen, *The Maritime Commerce of Colonial Philadelphia* (Madison, Wis., 1963); Doerflinger, *Vigorous Spirit of Enterprise;* Cathy D. Matson, *Merchants and Empire: Trading in Colonial New York* (Baltimore, 1998), esp. chaps. 6, 7; David S. Shields, *Civil Tongues and Polite Letters in British America* (Chapel Hill, N.C., 1997). These patterns of consumerism and production would escalate rapidly as the new century commenced. But it is important to see their steady increase in significance from the mid-eighteenth century on. It is interesting that a

As desires for new goods fused with desires for upward mobility, time-honored social practices and economic relations began to dissolve. The newly desiring farming families of the middle Atlantic colonies and New England, needing income to pay for consumer purchases, not only turned with increased energy to the production of surplus agricultural goods for commercial markets; they began to dedicate the long winter months to cottage industry, churning out cheap shoes, pantaloons, and shirts. European Americans' consumer economy and plantation slavery abetted one another, as local shopkeepers and more distant putting-out merchants funneled these manufactures into the provision trade to the West Indies, where they clothed and shod enslaved Afro-Caribbean workers.[11] To further these new manufacturing goals, by the late 1780s, factories began to spring up along the fast-running streams of Rhode Island, southeastern Pennsylvania, and Delaware, areas able to draw upon an "excess population" of poor white women and children. In towns and cities, wage labor began to replace apprenticeship arrangements. The tightly knit artisanal social units of masters and resident apprentices began just so slightly

---

consumer economy had come to the western frontier of the Susquehanna and Ohio Valleys as early as the 1750s and 1760s.

11. Doerflinger, *Vigorous Spirit of Enterprise,* 115–116, 151–154, 174; Carole Shammas, "Changes in English and Anglo-American Consumption from 1550 to 1800," in John Brewer and Roy Porter, eds., *Consumption and the World of Goods* (London, 1993), 177–205; and Shammas, "Consumer Behavior in Colonial America," *Social Science History,* VI (1982), 67–86, rpt. in Peter Charles Hoffer, ed., *American Patterns of Life: Selected Articles on the Provincial Period in American History* (New York, 1987). See, as well, James T. Lemon, *The Best Poor Man's Country: A Geographical Study of Early Southeastern Pennsylvania* (Baltimore, 1972); Robert D. Mitchell, *Commercialism and Frontier: Perspectives on the Early Shenandoah Valley* (Charlottesville, Va., 1977); Joyce Appleby, "Commercial Farming and the 'Agrarian Myth' in the Early Republic," *JAH,* LXVIII (1982), 833–849; Bettye Hobbs Pruitt, "Self-Sufficiency and the Agricultural Economy of Eighteenth-Century Massachusetts," *William and Mary Quarterly,* 3d Ser., XLI (1984), 333–364; Winifred B. Rothenberg, "The Market and Massachusetts Farmers, 1750–1855," *Journal of Economic History,* XLI (1981), 283–314; Rothenberg, "The Emergence of Farm Labor Markets and the Transformation of the Rural Economy: Massachusetts, 1750–1855," *JEH,* XLIII (1988), 537–566. James Henretta has offered an alternative view—that western farmers clung to a precommercial, family-centered way of life. See Henretta, "Families and Farms: *Mentalité* in Pre-industrial America," *WMQ,* 3d Ser., XXXV (1978), 3–32; Henretta, "Wealth and Social Structure," in Greene and Pole, eds., *Colonial British America,* 262–289. For a late-eighteenth-century comment on the rise of domestic manufacturing in farming families during the winter, see "American Intelligence," *American Magazine,* I (1788), 678–680, esp. 679. For a slightly later elaboration of the tensions between old and new ways, see Robert E. Shalhope, *A Tale of New England: The Diaries of Hiram Harwood, Vermont Farmer, 1810–1837* (Baltimore, 2003).

to fray.[12] But with an extremely weak fiscal infrastructure and a striking shortage of hard currency, the new commercial/consumer economy was far from stable. Political independence notwithstanding, European American merchants and their subsidiaries (urban and rural shopkeepers, would-be commercial farmers/consumers) remained heavily dependent on British credit and, consequently, vulnerable to credit contractions driven by imperial events far removed from American shores and European American control. Booms and busts destabilized the United States economy far into the nineteenth century. Merchants, shopkeepers, artisans, and commercial farmers never knew when the specter of bankruptcies and farm foreclosures would strike.

At the same time, possibilities never before conceived of captured the popular imagination. New roles multiplied—not only that of citizen in contrast to monarchical subject or, far more radically, of a white rather than a "savage" American, but those of entrepreneur, manufacturer, stock speculator, retail clerk, fashionable consumer, wage and factory laborer, pieceworker, and, yes, freedman, as manumissions and emancipation gradually spread through the northern

12. Cynthia J. Shelton, *The Mills of Manayunk: Industrialization and Social Conflict in the Philadelphia Region, 1787–1837* (Baltimore, 1986); Philip Scranton, *Proprietary Capitalism: The Textile Manufacture at Philadelphia, 1800–1835* (New York, 1983); Anthony F. C. Wallace, *Rockdale: The Growth of an American Village in the Early Industrial Revolution* (New York, 1978). See, as well, Gary Kulik, "Pawtucket Village and the Strike of 1824: The Origins of Class Conflict in Rhode Island," *Radical History Review*, XVII (1978), 5–37; Gary Kulik, Roger Parks, and Theodore Z. Penn, eds., *The New England Mill Village, 1790–1860* (Cambridge, Mass., 1982); Jonathan Prude, "The Social System of Early New England Textile Mills: A Case Study, 1812–40," in Michael H. Frisch and Daniel J. Walkowitz, eds., *Working-Class America: Essays on Labor, Community, and American Society* (Urbana, Ill., 1983), 1–36.

For a discussion of factors effecting the substitution of free wage labor for indentured and slave labor after the mid-eighteenth century, see Nash, *Urban Crucible*, 206. For a discussion of the shift from hand-weaving to factory production, see Adrienne D. Hood, *The Weaver's Craft: Cloth, Commerce, and Industry in Early Pennsylvania* (Philadelphia, 2003). Economic and urban historian Elizabeth Blackmar has described the impact this change had in terms of shifting urban residential patterns: "As the household labor system and slavery gave way to the free labor market at the end of the eighteenth century, domestic and trade quarters became two distinct arenas of economic activity, and New Yorkers who earned cash wages began to pay 'domestic rents.' Manhattan's eighteenth-century merchant rentiers had opened the channels for the accumulation of local wealth from *ground* rents, but it was a new entrepreneurial class of landowners that extended the real estate market's reach by capitalizing on housing" (Blackmar, *Manhattan for Rent, 1785–1850* [Ithaca, N.Y., 1989], 42, and see chap. 2). For shifts in the economic structure along with the rise of banks, stock speculation, and consumerism, see Doerflinger, *Vigorous Spirit of Enterprise*, esp. chap. 7. For emancipation efforts, especially in Philadelphia, see Alice Felt Tyler, *Freedom's Ferment: Phases of American Social History to 1860* (Minneapolis, 1944), esp. chap. 3; and Sweet, *Bodies Politic*.

states. In the mouths of new speakers, old words assumed new meanings. The most sacred beliefs broke free from traditional moorings. Authoritative languages lost their power to impose order. This was a world increasingly cut off from the old—old identities and loyalties, connections and cultures, values and practices. Endless possibilities danced before the eyes of the daring and ambitious. Bravado became their second language. But the fear of loss and the desire to remain connected to what had once seemed sure and uncontested shadowed heady expectations. These conflicting emotions wove in and out of European Americans' proclamations of new beginnings and exciting potential.[13]

Change and uncertainty posed one set of challenges. Diversity and contention posed others. Each new state was a mosaic of social differences and ethnic and religious antagonisms. New York State alone counted among its inhabitants hardworking Dutch farmers, proud of their language, culture, and Reform Protestantism; successful Dutch and British merchants who strove to establish vast landed estates along the Hudson; and poor New England Congregationalist and Baptist farming families, also drawn to the Hudson Valley's rich farmlands and deeply resentful of the quitrents imposed by the landed classes. To this contentious agricultural mix were added the flotsam and jetsam of the peoples wafted to New York City on the winds of trade—Huguenots fleeing repression following the Edict of Nantes, Sephardic Jews, white creoles from both the Anglophone and Francophone Caribbean, enslaved and free Africans and Afro-Caribbeans, skilled European artisans and unskilled Irish laborers, French dancing masters, German and Italian musicians, and British actresses and playwrights. Nor can we forget that, until the century's end, the Iroquois claimed most of New York as their home. From New York Harbor to Glimmerglass, New York was a composite of peoples and religions, enmities and desires.[14]

13. The new order, in short, fractured the old ways. Yet it could only exist in relation to the old social and economic order, when it stood surrogate for that order. As Joseph R. Roach argues, to write of the new is to invoke memories of the old—New and old England, New and old York. But memories of the past are, as often as not, misrememberings, the imposition of present desires upon that past. Their memories of the past, consequently, complicated the new Americans' understandings of the present and their hopes for the future. Roach cites Ralph Ellison's comment: "That which we remember is, more often than not, that which we would like to have been, or that which we hope to be." New World memories of Old World pasts evoked thoughts of past connections, of shared cultures now cut off (Roach, *Cities of the Dead: Circum-Atlantic Performance* [New York, 1996], chap. 2).

14. Each group brought its own religious practices and cultural memories: Jews, Dutch Reform, Huguenots, Congregationalists, Presbyterians, Episcopalians, Roman Catholics, African Muslims, Methodists, Baptists, and, just as the Revolutionary War was about to break out, a

An even greater blend of peoples, religions, and cultures characterized Pennsylvania: Quakers, Anglicans, Presbyterians, Jews, Catholics, and even Muslims (as slaves transported from Africa in the years preceding Independence brought their Muslim faith, and even a rare Koran, with them). By mid-century, Philadelphia was rapidly becoming a multiethnic and polyglot city, home to Africans and African Americans as well as a growing number of European immigrants. Yoruba and Igbo were heard in its slave quarters and freedman's homes. Street signs appeared in both German and English. By the 1790s, newspapers began to carry ads in French to accommodate those fleeing the Haitian Revolution.[15]

---

stalwart band of British Shakers, following their messianic leader, Mother Anne Lee. For New York City, see, among others, Thelma Wills Foote, *Black and White Manhattan: The History of Racial Formation in Colonial New York City* (New York, 2004); Edwin G. Burrows and Mike Wallace, *Gotham: A History of New York City to 1898* (New York, 1999); Carl Bridenbaugh, *Cities in Revolt: Urban Life in America, 1743–1776* (New York, 1955). For an examination of eighteenth-century New York City, Isaac Newton Phelps Stokes's *Iconography of Manhattan Island*, 6 vols. (New York, 1915–1928), is indispensable. For a study of New York commerce, see Matson, *Merchants and Empire*. See also David M. Ellis et al., *A Short History of New York State* (Ithaca, N.Y., 1957); Nash, *Urban Crucible;* Patricia U. Bonomi, *A Fractious People: Politics and Society in Colonial New York* (New York, 1971); Bonomi, *Under the Cope of Heaven: Religion, Society, and Politics in Colonial America* (New York, 1986); Aaron Spencer Fogleman, *Jesus Is Female: Moravians and the Challenge of Radical Religion in Early America* (Philadelphia, 2007). For contemporary comments, see, among others, W. Winterbotham, *An Historical, Geographical, Commercial, and Philosophical View of the American United States . . .* , 2 vols. (London, 1795); and William Alexander Duer, *Reminiscences of an Old Yorker* (New York, 1867).

15. See, for example, Russell F. Weigley, Nicholas B. Wainwright, and Edwin Wolf, eds., *Philadelphia: A 300-Year History* (New York, 1982); Billy G. Smith, ed., *Life in Early Philadelphia: Documents from the Revolutionary and Early National Periods* (University Park, Pa., 1995). Roger W. Moss's *Historic Houses of Philadelphia: A Tour of the Region's Museum Homes,* with photographs by Tom Crane (Philadelphia, 1998), presents a very useful pictorial history of the city. For the standard history of Quaker Philadelphia, see Frederick B. Tolles, *Meeting House and Counting House: The Quaker Merchants of Colonial Philadelphia, 1682–1763* (Chapel Hill, N.C., 1948). For a history of Philadelphia Jews, see Edwin Wolf and Maxwell Whiteman, *The History of the Jews of Philadelphia from Colonial Times to the Age of Jackson* (Philadelphia, 1957). For contemporary commentary, see Benjamin Franklin's description of his life among youthful artisans in eighteenth-century Philadelphia (Franklin, *Autobiography and Other Writings,* ed. Kenneth Silverman [New York, 1986], 28–77). See, as well, Elaine Forman Crane, ed., *The Diary of Elizabeth Drinker: The Life Cycle of an Eighteenth-Century Woman* (Boston, 1994); Catherine L. Blecki and Karin A. Wulf, eds., *Milcah Martha Moore's Book: A Commonplace Book from Revolutionary America* (University Park, Pa., 1997). See also Nash, *Forging Freedom,* chap. 1. For newspaper ads directed to creole planters fleeing the opening years of the Haitian Revolution, see *General Advertiser,* Philadelphia, August–September, December 1793.

Diversity was not limited to the banks of the Delaware. Far to the west, William Penn's generous land policies had attracted large numbers of Irish and Scotch-Irish settlers along with pietists from Germany and Switzerland. Scotch-Irish immigrants savagely engaged with the Delawares and Shawnees for possession of Pennsylvania's western lands, often encouraged by the acts of unscrupulous land speculators in Pennsylvania, Connecticut, and Virginia. In contrast, Mennonite settlers sought to transform Native Americans into pious Christian farming families, enraging their Scotch-Irish neighbors. Philadelphia's alarmed Quaker and Anglican elites struggled to contain the violent potential of this mixture at the same time as their speculation in western lands agitated both western settlers and the western tribes.[16]

New Jersey and Delaware mirrored the diversity of their larger neighbors. From its founding, Rhode Island had welcomed all whom trade and religious persecution carried to their shores. The Scotch-Irish settling the western reaches of Virginia and the Carolinas brought ethnic and religious heterogeneity to those southern states. While the plantations dotting the Georgia coast mixed blacks and whites, the Creeks and Cherokees controlled the rich lands stretching west. If these disparate peoples shared any memory, it was of antagonism and persecution. Throughout the colonial period, from Puritan New England to the Carolina frontier, they had battled and murdered, exiled and executed one another in the name of religious purity, ethnic memories, and questionable land claims.[17]

16. See, for example, Eric Hinderaker, *Elusive Empires: Constructing Colonialism in the Ohio Valley, 1673–1800* (Cambridge, 1997); Gregory H. Nobles, *American Frontiers: Cultural Encounters and Continental Conquest* (New York, 1997); William A. Pencak and Daniel K. Richter, eds., *Friends and Enemies in Penn's Woods: Indians, Colonists, and the Racial Construction of Pennsylvania* (University Park, Pa., 2004). For a discussion of Native American presence, see Amy C. Schutt, *Peoples of the River Valleys: The Odyssey of the Delaware* (Philadelphia, 2007); and Gregory Evans Dowd, *War under Heaven: Pontiac, the Indian Nations, and the British Empire* (Baltimore, 2002), esp. map, 24. For a lengthier discussion of the Pennsylvania and Ohio Valley frontier, see Chapter 4, below.

17. Gabrielle M. Lanier, *The Delaware Valley in the Early Republic: Architecture, Landscape, and Regional Identity* (Baltimore, 2005); Barry Levy, *Quakers and the American Family: British Settlement in the Delaware Valley, 1650–1765* (New York, 1988); Carol E. Hoffecker et al., *New Sweden in America* (Newark, N.J., 1995); C. A. Weslager, *The English on the Delaware, 1610–1682* (New Brunswick, N.J., 1967); James P. Byrd, Jr., *The Challenges of Roger Williams: Religious Liberty, Violent Persecution, and the Bible* (Macon, Ga., 2002); Jay Coughtry, *The Notorious Triangle: Rhode Island and the African Slave Trade, 1700–1807* (Philadelphia, 1981); Edwin S. Gaustad, *Liberty of Conscience: Roger Williams in America* (Grand Rapids, Mich., 1991); Perry Miller, *Roger Williams: His Contribution to the American Tradition* (Indianapolis, 1953); Edmund Sears Mor-

Economic divisions made demographic differences even more contentious, especially those between an increasingly commercialized East Coast and a still largely self-sufficient agrarian West. Commerce, the new consumerism, and fiscal capitalism brought with them the demands of a cash economy—banks and compound interest, debt foreclosures and debtors' prisons. Substituting banknotes for book debts, expanding the flow of credit, and providing a stable, if privately controlled, currency, banking revolutionized mercantile and fiscal practices in the postwar years, making fluid what had been illiquid, accelerating mercantile growth and stimulating the economy. Banks also issued stock. Other corporations soon followed—as did a wild wave of speculation in commercial paper and then in western lands. By the mid-1790s, millions of western acres were in the hands of speculators at home and abroad. Much of the Ohio Valley was in the hands of eastern venture capitalists. Millions of acres in New York State had been sold to European land speculators. Henry Knox, Washington's military and political ally, had bought up much of Maine.[18]

Self-sufficient western farmers viewed these changes with alarm. They had not fought the Revolution to replace the tyranny of Parliament with the tyranny of taxes, courts, land speculators, and eastern surveyors. Priming their muskets, they determined to protect their Revolutionary freedoms from commercial incursions. Barely a state escaped sporadic frontier violence as backwoods farmers battled eastern land speculators and their surveyors, tax collectors and absentee landholders. Eastern alarm escalated responsively.[19]

Diversity and conflict existed not only on the economic and demographic register but on the discursive plane as well. Heterogeneous societies are polyglot societies, in the multiple meanings of the word "polyglot." Not only did German, Dutch, French, Spanish, Yiddish, Ladino, Yoruba, Igbo, and a number of Native American languages engage one another on the crowded streets of America's seaports and in settlements along the frontier; so did multiple divergent, at times warring, political, social, and economic discourses: republicanism grounded in Aristotle's *Politics;* Machiavelli's sixteenth-century rereading of Aristotle and the British gentry's rereading of Machiavelli; seventeenth-century continental Pietism; British parliamentary theory; Lockean liberalism;

gan, *Roger Williams: The Church and the State* (New York, 1967). See, as well, Rhys Isaac, *The Transformation of Virginia, 1740–1790* (1982; rpt. Chapel Hill, N.C., 1999); Isaac, *Worlds of Experience: Communities in Colonial Virginia* (Williamsburg, Va., 1987); Kenneth A. Lockridge, *The Diary, and Life, of William Byrd II of Virginia, 1674–1744* (Chapel Hill, N.C., 1987).

18. See, for example, Doerflinger, *Vigorous Spirit of Enterprise,* esp. 7–8, 11–69, 283–364.

19. For a discussion of frontier/urban conflict, see Chapters 2 and 4, below.

Puritan tribalism; the language of the sympathies; the discourses of commercial and, increasingly, of fiscal capitalism; the dictates of politesse and gentility, consumerism and fashion. During these troubled and changing times, divergent speakers battled over the meaning of even such basic political terms as "independence," "republican virtue," "citizenship," and "popular sovereignty."[20]

Discursive discord seemed particularly threatening once Britain's governing class was no longer present to contain the discursive flux.[21] Would-be governing groups (Federalists and Antifederalists, the bourgeois elite, tidewater planters, the new professional classes) advanced warring claims to space in the new republican public sphere and to political, social, and discursive authority. Agricultural forces, both commercial farming families and western settlers/squatters, often warring among themselves, also fought to have their voices heard in the new legislative halls. Each of the various groups developed its own image of what the nation should look like, how it should be governed, and who could claim the identity of a true American. As the eighteenth century drew to

20. My vision of this cacophony of conflicting discourses is informed by M. M. Bakhtin's concept of heteroglossia, his insistence on the dynamic and dialogic nature of language, and the complex and shifting nature of meanings.

> At any given moment of its evolution, language is stratified not only into linguistic dialects in the strict sense of the word (according to formal linguistic markers) . . . , but also—and for us this is the essential point—into languages that were socio-ideological: languages of social groups, "professional" and "generic" languages, languages of generations and so forth. Alongside the centripetal forces, the centrifugal forces of language carry on their uninterrupted work; alongside verbal-ideological centralization and unification, the uninterrupted processes of decentralization and disunification go forward. The processes of centralization and decentralization, of unification and disunification, intersect in the utterance; the utterance not only answers the requirements of its own language as an individualized embodiment of a speech act, but it answers the requirements of heteroglossia as well; it is in fact an active participant in such speech diversity. And this active participation of every utterance in living heteroglossia determines the linguistic profile of the utterance.

See Bakhtin, *Dialogic Imagination: Four Essays*, ed. and trans. Michael Holquist, trans. Caryl Emerson (Austin, Tex., 1996), 271–272, 274–288, 291–299.

21. Mark R. Patterson, in his *Authority, Autonomy, and Representation in American Literature, 1776–1865* (Princeton, N.J., 1988), 17, remarks that, by 1784, the new Republic "had settled into chaotic bickering of regional and political factions, each seeking a voice and order in the new nation." The Republic was characterized by "disorder and lack of imitable power." Gordon S. Wood makes the same argument, calling post-Independence European American society "a precariously maintained social hierarchy, sensitive to the slightest disturbance" (Wood, *The Creation of the American Republic, 1776–1787* (1969; rpt., Chapel Hill, N.C., 1998), 16.

a close, no clearly dominant group had emerged.[22] Rather, multiple dissident social and economic groups began to invest words with ever more radical meanings. Newly freed African Americans applied Thomas Jefferson's ringing phrase "All men are created equal" to themselves.[23] Socially and politically marginalized sailors, day laborers, and hill-town and frontier farmers seized the arguments John Adams and John Hancock had deployed against Parliament to empower themselves in relation to Boston's new bourgeois elite that had first introduced those concepts to American parlance. Women began to contemplate the meanings "life, liberty, and the pursuit of happiness" might promise them.[24] Some among the educated classes, the youthful novelist Charles Brock-

22. Nor would one emerge for decades to come as the Age of the Common Man, Evangelical revivalism, and industrial capitalism followed one another in rapid succession. The Civil War would come and go before America would see the reemergence of what Bakhtin called a "unitary language," meaning an ideological and rhetorical hegemony. The term "unitary language" is ubiquitous throughout Bakhtin's *Dialogic Imagination;* for a precise definition, see 270.

23. For examples of African American insistence on their right to a place in the public sphere and a voice in the public print culture, see Absalom Jones, *A Thanksgiving Sermon, Preached January 1, 1808, in St. Thomas's, or the African Episcopal, Church, Philadelphia: On Account of the Abolition of the African Slave Trade, on That Day, by the Congress of the United States* (Philadelphia, 1808); Richard Allen and Absalom Jones, *The Life, Experience, and Gospel Labours of the Rt. Rev. Richard Allen* . . . (Philadelphia, 1833). For a white application of liberal principles to African Americans, see John Parrish, *Remarks on the Slavery of the Black People* . . . (Philadelphia, 1806). See, as well, Peter H. Wood, "'Liberty Is Sweet': African-American Freedom Struggles in the Years before White Independence," in Young, ed., *Beyond the American Revolution,* 149–184; Sweet, *Bodies Politic;* Foote, *Black and White Manhattan,* chap. 7. Nash's *Forging Freedom* offers a detailed account of African American resistance in Philadelphia, the city with the largest free African American population. For the beginnings of an organized effort by northern African Americans to end slavery, see Roy E. Finkenbine, "Belinda's Petition: Reparations for Slavery in Revolutionary Massachusetts," *WMQ,* 3d Ser., LXVI (2007), 95–105.

24. See, for example, W. J. Rorabaugh, "'I Thought I Should Liberate Myself from the Thraldom of Others': Apprentices, Masters, and the Revolution," 185–217, and Alan Taylor, "Agrarian Independence: Northern Land Rioters after the Revolution," 221–245, both in Young, ed., *Beyond the Revolution.* See, as well, Olton, *Artisans for Independence;* Bruce Laurie, *Working People of Philadelphia, 1800–1850* (Philadelphia, 1980); Sharon Salinger, *"To Serve Well and Faithfully": Labor and Indentured Servants in Pennsylvania, 1683–1800* (Cambridge, 1982); David Montgomery, "The Working Classes of the Pre-industrial American City, 1780–1830," *Labor History,* IX, no. 1 (Winter 1968), 3–22; Billy G. Smith, *The "Lower Sort": Philadelphia's Laboring People, 1750–1800* (Ithaca, N.Y., 1990); Peter Linebaugh and Marcus Rediker, *The Many-Headed Hydra: Sailors, Slaves, Commoners, and the Hidden History of the Revolutionary Atlantic* (Boston, 2000), esp. chap. 7; Linda K. Kerber, *Toward an Intellectual History of Women: Essays* (Chapel Hill, N.C., 1997), 100–131; and Kerber, *Women of the Republic: Intellect and Ideology in Revolutionary America* (Chapel Hill, N.C., 1980), chaps. 7, 8; Susan Branson, *These*

den Brown, for example (we will discuss Brown at length later), feared that rhetorical violence would lead to actual violence. Others gloried in the new freedom of self-expression. With European Americans so politically, economically, and socially divided, how could a coherent national identity ever emerge?[25]

This may be the moment to pause and ask what we mean by the term "identity." Informed by feminist, poststructuralist, and postcolonial theories, scholars no longer think of identity as an organically coherent phenomenon. Rather, we see identities as discursive constructions taking form within rich material, economic, and social contexts. Identities are multiply layered, fluid, changing, often contradictory, their forms dependent on where and in relation to whom they are constituted. As we have just seen, when facing east, European American patriots proclaimed themselves as anti-imperialists dedicated to the defense of Independence and liberty. But, when they faced west, they, without hesitation, assumed the role of imperialists staking claims to a vast empire and its subject peoples. If we focus more precisely on the nation's emerging bourgeoisie, we see again that, facing west, they presented themselves as polished gentlemen, in contrast to the frontier's rude and illiterate settlers. But, if they looked east to Europe's great metropoles, they knew themselves to be struggling tradesmen, as economically uncertain as they were unsure of their claims to civility and social polish. Composites of diverse and shifting personas, of the gentleman and the hardworking tradesman, the

Fiery Frenchified Dames: Women and Political Culture in Early National Philadelphia (Philadelphia, 2001); Rosemarie Zagarri, *Revolutionary Backlash: Women and Politics in the Early American Republic* (Philadelphia, 2007); Fredrika J. Teute, "Reading Men and Women in Late Eighteenth-Century New York," paper presented at the annual meeting of the American Society for Eighteenth-Century Studies, March 12, 1994; Teute, "'A Wild, Desolate Place': Life on the Margins in Early Washington," in Howard Gillette, Jr., ed., *Southern City, National Ambition: The Growth of Early Washington, D.C., 1800–1860* (Washington, D.C., 1995), 47–101; Teute, "Roman Matron on the Banks of the Tiber Creek: Margaret Bayard Smith and the Politicization of Spheres in the Nation's Capital," in Donald R. Kennon, ed., *A Republic for the Ages: The United States Capitol and the Political Culture of the Early Republic* (Charlottesville, Va., 1999), 89–121; Teute and David S. Shields, "The Confederation Court," paper presented at the Eighteenth-Century Studies Seminar, University of Michigan, Winter 2001; Sobel, *Teach Me Dreams*, 5; Crane, ed., *Diary of Elizabeth Drinker*, 163.

25. See Peter Kafer, *Charles Brockden Brown's Revolution and the Birth of American Gothic* (Philadelphia, 2004); Fredrika J. Teute, "A 'Republic of Intellect': Conversation and Criticism among the Sexes in 1790s New York," in Philip Barnard, Mark L. Kamrath, and Stephen Shapiro, eds., *Revising Charles Brockden Brown: Culture, Politics, and Sexuality in the Early Republic* (Knoxville, Tenn., 2004), 149–181; Christopher Looby, *Voicing America: Language, Literary Form, and the Origins of the United States* (Chicago, 1996), 147–148.

Lockean liberal and the slaveholder, the classic republican and the fiscal capitalist, identities in the new Republic were dynamic productions informed by their social location and interactions.[26]

How does this fluid but generalized understanding of identity fit in with current understandings of national identities, those mythic visions of a national collective self?

NATIONAL SUBJECTS: FRAGMENTED AND UNSTABLE

Nations need subjects, men and women who identify passionately with their nation and are dedicated to its service. Indeed, as Étienne Balibar tells us, "a social formation only reproduces itself as a nation to the extent that, through a network of apparatuses and daily practices, the individual is instituted as *homo nationalis*." Otherwise the nation would exist only as "an arbitrary abstraction; patriotism's appeal would be addressed to no one." For a nation to live, its heterogeneous, often contentious, inhabitants must experience themselves as integral parts of a collective "We, the People." Rhetoric, images, and words lie at the heart of the daily practices that create that collective national identity. Homo nationalis and the nation he enacts are products of that rhetoric, those images. But, as nations need citizens, so, too, do citizens need nations. Becoming a homo nationalis breaks down the individual citizen's sense of isolation. It gives him a share in his nation's history—in its mythic past and its promise of future greatness. National identities "stabilize, fix . . . guarantee an unchanging oneness or cultural belongingness," Stuart Hall explains. They provide citizens with a sense of "history and ancestry held in common. . . . [a sense of] some common origin or shared characteristics," no matter how artificial, how fictional that sense of belongingness.[27]

26. Susan Stanford Friedman presents an interesting analysis of identity formation and its debts to feminism, poststructuralism, and postcoloniality. See her *Mappings: Feminism and the Cultural Geographies of Encounter* (Princeton, N.J., 1998), esp. introduction and chap. 1. See, as well, Patricia Yaeger, ed., *The Geography of Identity* (Ann Arbor, Mich., 1996); Kathleen M. Kirby, *Indifferent Boundaries: Spatial Concepts of Human Subjectivity* (New York, 1996); Seyla Benhabib, *Situating the Self: Gender, Community, and Postmodernism in Contemporary Ethics* (London, 1992); James Clifford, *Routes: Travel and Translation in the Late Twentieth Century* (Cambridge, Mass., 1997); and, of course, Homi K. Bhabha, *Nation and Narration* (London, 1990).

27. Johann Fichte, *Reden an die deutsch Nation* (Leipzig, n.d.), cited by Étienne Balibar, "The Nation Form: History and Ideology," trans. Immanuel Wallerstein and Chris Turner, *Review*, XIII (1990), 329–361, esp. 345–351; Hall, "Who Needs 'Identity'?" in Hall and Du Gay, eds., *Questions of Cultural Identity*, 4. Chantal Mouffe agrees, pointing out that "politics is about the

A discursive fabrication, national identities are stitched together out of the narratives of national greatness and identity that we read about in newspapers, magazines, and history books, learn in school, hear from pulpits, celebrate on national holidays, and enact through festivals, parades, patriotic rituals, and songs. National identities are scripts that take form and feel natural as a result of repetitive, ritualized enactments—as when, as children, we pledge allegiance to the flag or, as adults, stand for the national anthem. To feel American, one must imagine oneself connected in some mythical way to the Puritans landing at Plymouth Rock, Paul Revere riding to Lexington and Concord, frontiersmen boldly striding across the vast continent. Thinking of such heroic figures, our hearts beat just a bit faster. But these feelings are not grounded in common experiences. How many of us, after all, have family memories that extend back to Plymouth Rock, the Revolution, or the Civil War? Even family memories of Ellis Island have begun to fade as millions of new immigrants arrive for whom Ellis Island is a museum, not a point of arrival, interrogation, and possible deportation. To borrow a bitter phrase from Richard Rodgers and Oscar Hammerstein's *South Pacific,* citizens are actors who have "to be carefully taught" what it is to be an American. Taught and taught again, for it is their performances that produce the individual as homo nationalis and thus produce the nation.[28]

Of course, no performance precisely enacts the foundational script. Nor does any one performance precisely mirror any other. Variation, change, and, often,

---

constitution of a political community. . . . The political community . . . [is] where 'we' is constituted." See Mouffe, "Democratic Politics and the Question of Identity," in John Rajchman, ed., *The Identity in Question* (New York, 1995), 33–46, esp. 36. See, as well, Mouffe, ed., *Dimensions of Radical Democracy: Pluralism, Citizenship, Community* (London, 1992). For the multitude of discourses played out on the local level, see John L. Brooke, *The Heart of the Commonwealth: Society and Political Culture in Worcester County, Massachusetts, 1713–1861* (Cambridge, 1989), 151–152. I am indebted to my colleague Martha Jones for reminding me that Britishness was as much an invention as Americanness—and that the meanings European Americans projected onto "Englishness" were rapidly changing, especially in these years immediately after political independence but of continued cultural dependence.

28. Richard Rodgers and Oscar Hammerstein II, *South Pacific* (New York, 1949). I am grateful to Michael Meranze for stressing the link between these performances and the production of the nation (personal communication). As Benedict Anderson argued years ago, nations are imagined communities, fictions born of political need, bureaucratic convenience, ethnic fears, and fantasies. As nations are imagined, so, too, are national identities (Anderson, *Imagined Communities: Reflections on the Origin and Spread of Nationalisms* [London, 1983]). Of course, Anderson's vision of national formations has been challenged by many scholars—though the image of the nation as "an imagined community" remains very suggestive.

resistance become part of the performative process of national identification. Difference, dissonance, and instability creep into our performances, rendering identities multiple, contradictory, uncertain. Yet, because we internalize our national identities as we perform them, we always also experience them as intensely real, as our own true self. We need this sense of surety. Not to be a national subject is to experience oneself as marginal, as excluded from a larger, collective world. It is to be "a man without a country." This is why it is so important that national identities both appear and feel coherent. They must give their citizen-actors the sense of an internally unified self.[29]

Of course, national identities are anything but internally coherent. Not only do they shift in response to differing geopolitical positions and social relationships; they emerge at the confluence of the multiple discourses that proliferate in heterogeneous societies. These discourses are themselves internally contradictory—they change constantly as the world in which they take form changes, are often at war with one another. It is only through the production of a series of constituting Others that the contradictions produced by these dis-

29. Which is not to say that all residents of a country share a common national identity. Located differently along class, racial, gender, religious, and regional lines, different groups within modern heterogeneous nations may well generate different, at times quite disruptive, national histories and myths. Nor did all Americans choose to participate in these nation-building processes, especially those already on the cultural, economic, or racial margins of this brave new world. Western hunters and trappers, often of mixed European and Native American ancestry, are one example. So are their geographic counterparts, the men of the sea, especially African Americans. Sailors lived and worked among men gathered from the four corners of the world and were often far more at home in the Antilles, South America, Africa, or the Pacific than in the continental United States. For a discussion of the world of the eighteenth-century western trapper/hunter, see, for example, Richard White, *The Middle Ground: Indians, Empires, and Republics in the Great Lakes Region, 1650–1815* (Cambridge, 1991); or, more picturesquely, James Fenimore Cooper's many novels about Natty Bumppo and his world: *The Deerslayer; or, The First War-Path* (New York, n.d.); *Last of the Mohicans; or, A Narrative of 1757* (Boston, n.d.); *The Pathfinder; or, The Inland Sea* (Boston, n.d.); *The Pioneers; or, The Sources of the Susquehanna . . .* (New York, n.d.); and *The Prairie: A Tale* (Philadelphia, n.d.). For the world of the sea, few books could be more revealing than Herman Melville, *Moby-Dick; or, The Whale* (New York, 1851). For historical analyses, see Linebaugh and Rediker, *Many-Headed Hydra;* W. Jeffrey Bolster, *Black Jacks: African American Seamen in the Age of Sail* (Cambridge, Mass., 1997); Julius Sherrard Scott III, "The Common Wind: Currents of Afro-American Communication in the Era of the Haitian Revolution" (Ph.D. diss., Duke University, 1986). On variation in the performative process of national identification, see Judith Butler, *Bodies That Matter: On the Discursive Limits of "Sex"* (New York, 1993), x, 2. The commonplace usage "man without a country" was originally derived from Edward Everett Hall's short story of the same name; see Hall, "The Man without a Country," *Atlantic Monthly,* XII (1863), 665–680.

parate discourses, positions, and relationships can be papered over, that the national subjects they produce can begin to assume the appearance of inner cohesion and stability. By their overshadowing otherness, fabricated Others are designed to render insignificant the differences and contradictions that divide us as national subjects. They mark the boundaries of our belonging.

But boundaries marking our identity are deceptive, uncertain things. Within their confines, we bond with other national subjects, confirming our similarities, no matter how imaginary those similarities may be. Outside these boundaries, Others hover, threatening to penetrate and pollute our sense of national identity and unity. Seen thus, boundaries and Others are oppositional forces. Yet these very boundaries also connect us to our Others. They are liminal borderlands, spaces of fluidity, hybridity—and transgression. Within these borderlands, our Others beckon to us. Emblems of the proscribed, they point to forbidden possibilities, tempt us down prohibited paths. Consciously or unconsciously, we seek to incorporate them, at times, in response to deep-rooted fears of isolation and loss, at other times, for qualities we imagine their having and long to make our own. At still other times, we turn from them in disgust, for, as often as not, they are imaginative projections of our own worst qualities, of what we wish to expel from our consciousness and our country.[30] They become our mirror images, our own dark reflections. The borders dividing us from them are illusionary. Caught in an intimate—sometimes deadly—embrace, we cannot separate from Others we simultaneously dread and desire. In the chapters that follow, time and again, we will see our carefully constituted Others re-fuse the differences we impose on them, penetrate the borders of our newly constructed selves, destabilize our hoped-for sense of national inner cohesion. To resolve these often unbearable tensions, we turn upon our Others with rhetorical and literal violence.

Are these tensions greater within the United States than in other nations? That is hard to answer, since it depends on which nations and what times we speak of. *This Violent Empire* will argue that the need to artificially produce a sense of national cohesion for a people with no common heritage—deeply divided along racial, regional, and religious lines and beset by the ideological disjuncture between the United States' promise of universal equality and the realities of slavery and, later, of racial and gender discrimination—exacerbates

---

30. For lengthy discussions of the psychology of self/Other relations, see Jessica Benjamin, *The Bonds of Love: Psychoanalysis, Feminism, and the Problem of Domination* (New York, 1988), esp. chap. 2; and Benjamin, *Like Subjects, Love Objects: Essays on Recognition and Sexual Difference* (New Haven, Conn., 1995).

the tendency to exclusion, violence, xenophobia, and paranoia all national identities harbor within themselves.

PERFORMING THE NEW AMERICAN /
ENACTING THE NEW NATION

Where did newly independent European Americans first learn to play the role of the new American? Where did they begin to fine-tune their performances? Recently, historians have focused on the role street theater, parades, and other public celebrations, along with the art of public oratory, played in the production of the Republic's new national identity. David Waldstreicher, Simon P. Newman, and Sandra M. Gustafson, among others, have subjected Revolutionary street theater, along with the grand parades and public tableaus of the post-Revolutionary period, to analytic scrutiny, seeing them as central to the national identity that emerged in the closing years of the eighteenth century.[31] But of equal importance because of its relentlessly repetitive nature was the Republic's emerging public print culture, its newspapers, political and literary magazines, broadsides, and, increasingly, its fiction. As John Tomlinson argues, the " 'lived reality' of national identity" lies "in representations—not in direct communal solidarity." Looking at the emergence of a British national identity in the eighteenth century, Kathleen Wilson concurs. "The newspaper press was instrumental in structuring national and political consciousness, binding ordinary men and women throughout . . . to the processes of state and empire building." What was true of Britain was equally true of the United States.[32]

31. David Waldstreicher, *In the Midst of Perpetual Fetes: The Making of American Nationalism, 1776–1820* (Chapel Hill, N.C., 1997), 29, 30–35; Simon P. Newman, *Parades and the Politics of the Street: Festive Culture in the Early American Republic* (Philadelphia, 1997), 90–94, 187–188; Sandra M. Gustafson, *Eloquence Is Power: Oratory and Performance in Early America* (Chapel Hill, N.C., 2000). Some cultural analysts, Jay Fliegelman and Christopher Looby, for example, insist that late-eighteenth-century America was an oral, not a print, culture, and we should focus our principal attention on popular public performances. See Fliegelman, *Declaring Independence: Jefferson, Natural Language, and the Culture of Performance* (Stanford, Calif., 1993); and Looby, *Voicing America*. Most continue to be fascinated by print culture, though not in isolation from oral culture.

32. John Tomlinson, *Cultural Imperialism: A Critical Introduction* (Baltimore, 1991), 83–84. Kathleen Wilson insists, "Newspapers were central instruments in the social production of information. Both representing and verifying local experience, they refracted world events into socially meaningful categories and hierarchies of importance, bestowing order on the disordered and coordinating the imagination of time and space." Newspapers, she adds, worked to create a sense of national belonging—and of citizenship. "Literacy becomes the test of citizenship and the

No European American institution played a more essential role in constituting the new nation and its new citizens than its press. The one institution that
spanned the colonies, it had introduced colonial readers to republican political
principles—love of liberty, selfless devotion to the general good, the evils of tyranny, the virtue of resistance. On the pages of colonial newspapers and pamphlets, European Americans parsed the rights of Englishmen and debated Parliament's right to tax the colonies. There, they first learned of the social contract
and of man's inalienable rights.[33] There, they first honed an identity as freedom-
loving, independent political actors. As protests against British colonial policies
escalated during the 1760s and early 1770s, the press undertook the critical work
of representing local political protests and street theater to larger audiences, thus
creating a sense of national connectedness among distant readers. Reporting
public demonstrations against the Stamp Act, pledges to boycott British goods,
the dumping of tea in Boston Harbor to readers in distant towns, cities, and
colonies—and framing those acts in a Revolutionary political vocabulary—the
press made these events news. Newspaper after newspaper then disseminated
that news from city to town, county to county, and colony to colony. In this way,
local political protests were transformed into a national—and a textual—movement. "The press and the rituals of revolution," Waldstreicher explains, "fed one
another. . . . Learning to use the press to publicize their community's actions, . . .
local revolutionary leaders . . . communicate[d] across regional divides and even
more critically, local readers learned to think of themselves as 'Americans.'"[34]

---

instrument of political subjectivity itself and through print culture both the subject's right to
monitor the state and his potential for citizen activism were fulfilled" (Wilson, *The Sense of the
People: Politics, Culture, and Imperialism in England, 1715–1785* [Cambridge, 1998], 40, 41, 43, 160).

33. Warner insists on the importance of the public print culture in creating both the Revolution
and the new nation, arguing that the press "articulated and helped to mobilize an intercontinental
and proto-national public" *(Letters of the Republic,* chaps. 1, 2, esp. 67–72). See, as well, Bernard
Bailyn, *The Ideological Origins of the American Revolution* (Cambridge, Mass., 1967); and Bailyn
and John B. Hench, eds., *The Press and the American Revolution* (Worcester, Mass., 1980).

34. Waldstreicher, *In the Midst of Perpetual Fetes,* 29. Eighteenth-century scholars have long
insisted on the importance of the press in building a sense of national unity. Bailyn points out
that "every medium of written expression was put to use" *(Ideological Origins,* 1–2). See, as well,
Robert A. Ferguson, *The American Enlightenment, 1750–1820* (Cambridge, Mass., 1997), chap. 4.
Other scholars stress the interplay between popular performative culture (street theater, protests, and parades) and the press. Simon Newman argues, "The rites and festivals of the new
republic and the expansion of popular print culture . . . went hand-in-hand. Festive culture
required both participants and an audience, and by printing and reprinting accounts of July
Fourth celebrations and the like newspapers contributed to a greatly enlarged sense of audience"
(Newman, *Parades,* 3).

PLATE ONE Bookcase, American, c. 1780–1800. This bookcase, crafted from mahogany, maple, tulipwood, and glass, was from the library of Robert Waln (1765–1836), a Philadelphia merchant. Some speculate that it was fashioned by the Scottish-born craftsman and publisher John Aitken. Philadelphia Museum of Art: Bequest of R. Wistar Harvey, 1940, 40–16–21

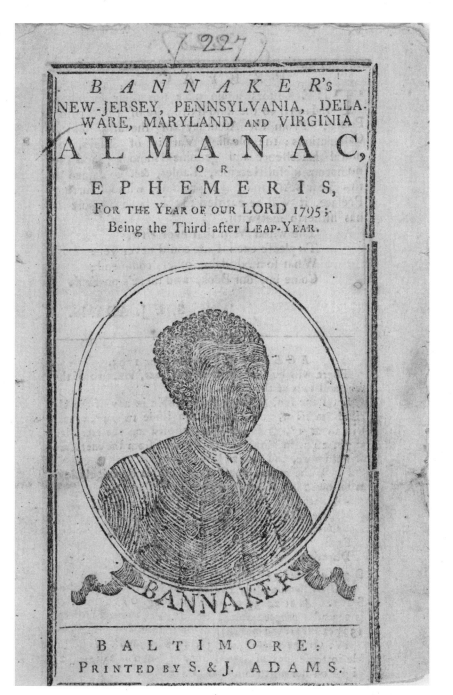

B A N N A K E R's
NEW-JERSEY, PENNSYLVANIA, DELA-
WARE, MARYLAND AND VIRGINIA
A L M A N A C,
O R
E P H E M E R I S,
FOR THE YEAR OF OUR LORD 1795;
Being the Third after LEAP-YEAR.

BANNAKER

B A L T I M O R E:
PRINTED BY S. & J. A D A M S.

PLATE TWO Title page of *Bannaker's New-Jersey, Pennsylvania, Delaware, Maryland, and Virginia Almanac, or Ephemeris* (Baltimore, 1795). The Library Company of Philadelphia

The press not only helped to make colonial subjects into Revolutionary Americans. It sought to make the American Republic a reading republic and its citizenry a community of readers. As resistance to British policies escalated, familiarity with the political primers Revolutionary leaders adopted from Britain—*Cato's Letters,* Locke's *Treatises,* Hume's *History*—became the bedrock upon which political virtue was perceived to rest. The new American that the new print culture imagined and worked to produce would be sophisticated enough to enjoy reading such volumes and wealthy enough to afford them. To all who were not, the urban print culture denied full membership in the national body politic. Thus access to print culture came to mark race, class, and, consequently, national identity as thoroughly as did wealth, dress, and manners. Most African Americans received little or no education and, although a few African Americans (Richard Allen and Absalom Jones in Philadelphia, Prince Hall in Boston) did enter the public prints to protest the horrors of chattel slavery and the injustice of racism, the venues through which those few could address public issues—and be read by European Americans—were hard to come by. In contrast to the marginalization of African American voices, Gustafson has shown that Native American oratory had a strong impact upon European Americans throughout much of the eighteenth century—especially on those engaged in diplomatic negotiations. But, again, the vast majority of Native Americans lacked access to Enlightenment texts while poverty, rural isolation, and cultural norms barred many of the European American rural and urban poor—or positioned them on the reading community's bottom rungs.[35]

Books were pricey items in eighteenth-century America, "part of a symbolic culture of regulated luxury." Their possession marked one as a (white) gentleman and a scholar, as a participant in an Enlightenment culture that stretched out from London and Paris to Boston and Philadelphia. As the exigencies of revolution faded in the 1780s and 1790s, the press increasingly became the voice of the urban literate classes. Of course, theirs was not the only vision

---

35. This is not to suggest that there were no educated African Americans or that Native Americans had no access to Enlightenment texts. See Elizabeth McHenry, *Forgotten Readers: Recovering the Lost History of African American Literary Societies* (Durham, N.C., 2002). For discussions of Native American oratory, see Jane T. Merritt, "Metaphor, Meaning, and Misunderstanding: Language and Power on the Pennsylvania Frontier," in Andrew R. L. Cayton and Fredrika J. Teute, eds., *Contact Points: American Frontiers from the Mohawk Valley to the Mississippi, 1750–1830* (Chapel Hill, N.C., 1998); and Gustafson, *Eloquence Is Power.* Rural New Englanders, imbued from childhood with the ringing phrases of the King James Bible, along with the less-melodic rhetoric of Puritan sermons, possessed a literacy other westerners— Scotch-Irish in the Ohio Valley, for instance—had not mastered.

of the new nation and the republican citizen, nor were they the only actors in the new public and political spheres. Frontier squatters, New England hill-town farmers, tidewater planters, women (white and black, urban and farming), African Americans (freed and enslaved), Jews, and Quakers all entertained their own images of the new nation and performed the role of new American in their own ways. The nation's stage was crowded with radically diverse actors. But not the pages of the new political magazines. These were the creation of an emergent bourgeoisie and its middling social and political allies.[36]

And it is on these magazines, their contributors and readers, that *This Violent Empire* focuses. The reasons are threefold. First, the bourgeoisie and its middling allies were key players in writing the new constitution, securing its ratification, and establishing a federal government that could impose law and order on the unruly Republic. How, I wondered, did those European Americans who worked so assiduously to put the new government in place imagine the new American who would be subject of and to the new government?

Second, the emerging bourgeoisie and its allies are of particular interest because they represented the voice of modernity and cosmopolitanism. They were the engine of economic change, introducing their fellow European Americans to the complexities of commerce and the new ways of fiscal capitalism. Though a minority voice within an agricultural republic, a variation of their imagined new American, made more inclusive along class and ethnic lines, would eventually emerge as the model of what all Americans should strive to become. Without question, their new American's virility, whiteness, and social respectability would remain core components of what it meant to be a true American—from their day to ours.[37]

Lastly, I am particularly intrigued with their new journalistic construction—the political magazine, which captured the clamor of conflicting visions and discourses that epitomized the new world of urban America and the complex ways roles are enacted. I will begin by laying out the history of the early political magazines, explaining in greater detail why I find them so fascinating. I will then discuss that radical new urban conglomerate—the bourgeois/middling classes—and the role I see them playing as magazine contributors and consumers in the production and enactment of the new national identity.

36. Warner, *Letters of the Republic,* 27.

37. Over the years, the image of George Washington would morph into that of John Wayne by way of images of Daniel Boone, Natty Bumppo, Andrew Jackson, and Teddy Roosevelt's aristocratic Rough Riders.

Political magazines were the innovative offspring of the Revolution and of efforts to constitute a strong federal union. The *Pennsylvania Magazine,* virtually the first Anglophone American magazine, began publication in 1775, with Thomas Paine as editor. Four years later, another ardent republican patriot, Hugh Henry Brackenridge, founded the patriotically named *United States Magazine.* The exigencies of war and scarcity of capital made both short-lived ventures. The return of peace and of political controversies in the mid-1780s, however, revived interest in political magazines. In the years immediately preceding and following the Constitutional Convention, six new magazines were founded in key U.S. cities, specifically to urge ratification of a strong Federal constitution. Thus, even before delegates to the Constitutional Convention began to arrive, Philadelphians had founded two new political magazines, Mathew Carey's politically influential *American Museum* and the lavishly illustrated *Columbian Magazine.* Both were highly critical of the Articles of Confederation. Both advocated ratification of the proposed constitution. Carey's *American Museum* printed the proposed constitution almost as soon as it was made public, surrounding it with numerous essays warning of the Articles' weaknesses and urging ratification.[38] In New York City, editor and publisher Noah Webster, timing his venture to coincide with the beginnings of the ratification debates in New York State, published the first issue of his *American Magazine* in December 1787. (As New York's ratification debates intensified, Webster used the *American Magazine* to publish the *Federalist Papers.* Indeed, even though Pennsylvania had already ratified the Constitution, Carey also reprinted the Federalist Papers in an effort to influence the New York vote.) A year and a half earlier, as the first stirrings of Shays's Rebellion were heard, Isaiah Thomas transformed his pro-Independence newspaper, the *Massachusetts Spy,* into the *Worcester Magazine,* well positioned to comment acerbically upon growing agrarian unrest. After a year in Worcester, however, Thomas

---

38. *American Museum,* II (July–October 1787). For a general survey of early American magazines, see Frank Luther Mott, *A History of American Magazines, 1741–1850,* 3 vols. (Cambridge, Mass., 1938), I, esp. 13–30. Respecting Mathew Carey, Mott writes, "Carey was the greatest of eighteenth-century magazine editors: he had the qualities necessary for editorial success—versatility and wide interests, personal magnetism, industry, and optimism. The *[American] Museum* is perhaps the most important American magazine file of its century: it is invaluable for a study of the society, economics, and politics of 1787–92, and it is far more American in materials than most of its contemporaries" (Mott, *A History of American Magazines, 1741–1930,* 5 vols. [Cambridge, Mass., 1957–1968], I, 54, 57, 60–64, 104–107).

returned to Boston to begin publication of the _Massachusetts Magazine,_ its goal to inform the political vision and refine the manners of Boston's bourgeoisie and middling readers. Even New Brunswick, New Jersey, briefly supported the _New Jersey Magazine._ New Brunswick was an influential Quaker enclave, and New Jersey, lying between Philadelphia and New York, was fully aware of the power of the written word in the performance of the new national identity. Certainly, urban and urbane Federalists saw the magazines as critical to their ratification campaign.[39]

Ties between the bourgeoisie and the new political magazines were economic as well as ideological and political. Unlike early-eighteenth-century British magazines and European American newspapers, which received a significant portion of their income from commercial advertisers (the pages of the _Spectator,_ like the pages of Boston and Philadelphia newspapers, were dotted with ads for the imported finery of the empire), America's new magazines were financially dependent upon subscriptions. Subscription fees were, as a consequence, high, well beyond the means of independent artisans and small shopkeepers. (Rates ranged from $2.50 to $3.33 per annum.)[40] Not surprisingly, the magazines listed among their readers successful overseas merchants,

39. During the Revolution, nearby Princeton had sheltered the Continental Congress after its members fled British-occupied Philadelphia. Princeton had also been home to America's first Revolutionary salon, presided over by the refined Annis Boudinot Stockton, sister of Elias Boudinot, president of the Continental Congress (Teute and Shields, "Confederation Court," esp. 5). As Waldstreicher tells us, "Federalists' seizure of the primary spaces for symbolic action [public parades and celebration in the press] . . . did precisely what it was intended to: increase the attractiveness and seeming inevitability of the Constitution, influence ratification in the key states of Massachusetts and New York, and make Federalism look more popular than it probably was" (Waldstreicher, _In the Midst of Perpetual Fetes,_ 93).

40. The geography of magazine publishing was centered in Philadelphia and Boston, from the middle till the end of the eighteenth century. No magazine was published south of Philadelphia until 1793 (and then only as far south as Baltimore), and none west of Philadelphia until the nineteenth century. Mott contrasts the cost of a magazine to a mechanic's average daily wage of $1. Even a Congregational minister (average salary $500 a year in Connecticut) might think twice about subscribing. On the other hand, the magazines' influence was far greater than the number of their subscribers might suggest. As Mott tells us, "Reading matter was not a commonplace of every man's daily mail, and we can depend upon it that every page of every copy of every magazine was usually read with care by a number of people" _(History of American Magazines_ [1938], I, 33–34, 67). See as well, Richard D. Brown, _Knowledge Is Power: The Diffusion of Information in Early America, 1700–1865_ (New York, 1989); Carol Sue Humphrey, _The Press of the Young Republic, 1783–1833_ (Westport, Conn., 1996); Carol Lynn H. Knight, _The American Colonial Press and the Townshend Crisis, 1766–1770: A Study in Political Imagery_ (Lewiston, N.Y., 1990).

bankers, stockbrokers, and speculators (the country's new fiscal capitalists), along with European-educated (or well-married) doctors, lawyers, and clergymen. In Philadelphia, the ambitious Mathew Carey proudly listed among the *American Museum*'s subscribers the new nation's political leaders (Washington, Jefferson, Franklin, and numerous delegates to the Constitutional Convention), commercial and financial leaders (Robert Morris, William Bingham, Thomas Willing, some of the new Republic's richest merchants), and members of the American Philosophical Society, planters from Maryland and Virginia, and merchants from as near as Delaware and as far away as New England. Nor can we forget the wives, sisters, and daughters of these men, many of whom were already avid readers of literary and fashion magazines imported from London. The new political magazines explicitly courted such women. At the same time, lesser merchants, shopkeepers, aspiring clerks, and artisan entrepreneurs also either subscribed to the political magazines or read them in coffeehouses and taverns. Although dedicated to the interests of the Federalist bourgeoisie, the magazines reached out to a broad swath of middling readers, women as well as men. Thus, although urban, literate, and white, the magazine's audience was far from monolithic in its social interests and perspectives.[41]

Fiercely nationalistic, the new magazines nevertheless modeled themselves on the British press. Not only did they pirate British essays and novels; they adopted the form and, at times, the actual content of London's fashionable magazines—the *Gentleman's Magazine,* for example, or the *London Magazine.* A subscription to their new magazines, they promised, would reconnect would-be urbane European Americans to elite British society and help them present themselves as cultured gentlemen and ladies. The magazines, devoted simultaneously to serving the political and cultural needs of their bourgeois readers, thus would permit those readers to assert both their political authority in the newly formed Republic and their cultural equality with the former metropole—something America's emergent bourgeoisie longed to do.

In these varied ways, the magazines played a key role in establishing the new

41. Breen, *Marketplace of Revolution;* Shields, *Civil Tongues,* chaps. 2, 4; Sarah E. Fatherly, "Gentlewomen and Learned Ladies: Gender and the Creation of an Urban Elite in Colonial Philadelphia" (Ph.D. diss., University of Wisconsin, Madison, 2000), 27. See also Noah Webster's invitation to "fair readers" *(American Magazine,* I [1787], 3). Carey listed the names of his subscribers on the opening pages of early volumes of the *American Museum.* For initial subscribers, see *American Museum,* I (1787), v–xv. For the relation of class and print culture, see, as well, George W. Boudreau, "Highly Valuable and Extensively Useful: Community and Readership among the Eighteenth-Century Philadelphia Middling Sort," paper presented to the Philadelphia Center for Early American Studies, Oct. 20, 1995.

Federal government and instructing citizens in the ways of polite European society. But there is still one other aspect of the new magazines that we must explore. Far from insignificant, the word "magazine" says it all. Derived from the Arab "khozana," meaning "to store up," and presumably entering English through commercial interactions with Muslim merchants in the Middle East and North Africa, the word "magazine" originally referred, literally, to "a place where goods are laid up; a storehouse or repository for goods or merchandise; a warehouse, depot." This meaning continued into the 1820s and 1830s. The other term frequently used to describe eighteenth-century magazines was "miscellany." How appropriate both words are. The early political and literary magazines were just that—warehouses of randomly collected items, jumbles of news, commentary, political essays, poetry, travel accounts, snippets from novels, descriptions of scientific inventions and medical oddities. Their contents were often pirated not only from British or French magazines but from one another. They were never the work of a single hand (not even those founded by such strong-minded editor/publishers as Carey or Webster). Rather, they were warehouses of the contending political, economic, and cultural discourses that circulated among their disparate readers. In a single issue, indeed, on a single page (as we will see time and again), visions and voices met discordantly. Inconsistencies abounded, offering readers a hodgepodge of conflicting roles, the fusion of which would come to constitute a new American.[42]

Another aspect of the political magazines is even more significant in terms of the production of a national identity. The magazines were sites of productive performativity—not only for their editors and contributors but for their readers. Here, alone in their imaginations or through conversations with friends (since eighteenth-century magazines were often read collectively and were displayed and discussed, making them occasions for polite sociability), readers studied the divergent roles that abounded on the magazines' pages, played at being cosmopolitan readers, patriotic republicans, liberal gentlemen, abolitionists, or, alternatively, racists. Reading and discussing the magazines, urban readers learned to perform a new American identity (though, as we know, this identity was never static or unified). It was through these acts that they finetuned their opposing performances.

Who were those new readers, those agents of economic and political change, whose resources were sufficient to permit them to subscribe to a political magazine? At the upper echelon we find those American historians usually refer to as the new national elite, men of wealth, gentility, and political ambi-

42. *Oxford English Dictionary*, s.v. "magazine," "miscellany."

tion. However, I prefer the term "bourgeoisie." It is not just their wealth that I find significant but their deep-seated connections to commerce and urban life that the name "bourgeois" conjures up. America's leading merchants and bankers were not simply rich men. They were rich men whose lives revolved around trade.[43] Trade turned their faces outward—to Europe, the Caribbean, and Africa. It enriched them, elevating them far above the status of shopkeeper or artisan. But, at the same time, commerce subjected them to the harsh uncertainties of distant markets, storms at sea, a life built upon credit and haunted by fears of debtors' prison. By British standards, North American commerce was shockingly underfinanced. A "merchant prince" in North America had little more capital than a shopkeeper in London or Liverpool and was at far greater risk. To counteract these dangers and uncertainties, European American merchants labored tirelessly. Early morning found them in their counting rooms or tromping through mud or dust to inspect ships and cargoes. Evening saw them in coffeehouses and taverns studying newspapers for information about foreign markets, trade disrupted by war, harvests destroyed.[44]

Though numbered among North America's richest inhabitants, these men held uncertain claims to the status of gentleman, especially from the perspective of Britain's country gentry—and Britain's gentry set the norm for gentility around the North Atlantic. There, a gentleman's status rested on his possession of landed estates, protected by entail and primogeniture, on his disdain for labor and his life of leisure. Judged by these standards, European American merchants sadly failed. Royal officeholder Cadwallader Colden's description of

43. My use of the term "bourgeois" reflects C. B. MacPherson's understanding of "bourgeois" in his *Political Theory of Possessive Individualism: Hobbes to Locke* (Oxford, 1962), 162: "Bourgeois society . . . I take to be a society in which the relations between men are dominated by the market; in which . . . land and labour, as well as movable wealth and goods made for consumption, are treated as commodities to be bought and sold and contracted for with a view to profit and accumulation, and where men's relations to others are set largely by their ownership of these commodities and the success with which they utilize that ownership to their own profit."

44. Doerflinger, *Vigorous Spirit of Enterprise*, chap. 1; Matson, *Merchants and Empire;* Matson and Peter S. Onuf, *A Union of Interests: Political and Economic Thought in Revolutionary America* (Lawrence, Kans., 1990); Onuf, *Jefferson's Empire: The Language of American Nationhood* (Charlottesville, Va., 2000); Arthur L. Jensen, *The Maritime Community of Colonial Philadelphia* (Madison, Wis., 1963); and Jacob M. Price, "Economic Function and the Growth of American Port Towns in the Eighteenth Century," *Perspectives in American History,* VIII (1974), 123–186; Gary B. Nash, "Social Development," 233–261, and Henretta, "Wealth and Social Structure," 262–289, both in Greene and Pole, eds., *Colonial British America;* Henretta, "Economic Development and Social Structure in Colonial Boston," *WMQ,* 3d Ser., XXII (1965), 75–92.

mid-eighteenth-century colonial society in New York not surprisingly reflects the British gentry's perspective. The "first class," Colden proclaimed, were the great landed proprietors. "Gentlemen of the Law" constituted the "second class," especially if such "gentlemen" were connected to the proprietors through marriage. (In post-Revolutionary New York, Alexander Hamilton, married to Elizabeth Schuyler, exemplified this second class.) Only then did Colden consider merchants who, he declared, constituted a third social rank, coldly remarking that these men not infrequently had risen from the "lowest rank"—that is, mechanics and farmers.[45]

But, although commerce compromised the European American merchants' claims to gentility, it broadened their vision far beyond that of America's village dwellers or commercial farmers. Commerce exposed them to new ideas, made them familiar with racial diversity and social complexity. They had to become aware of how others saw them—from the perspective of Asians and Africans, as white men and Christian gentlemen, though probably as less powerful than European traders; from the perspective of Europe, as struggling provincials; from the perspective of their less elevated neighbors, as great men possessed of wealth and power. Commerce also made them improvisers, pragmatists, members of the eighteenth century's new class of economic, fiscal, and social risk-takers. The European American bourgeoisie pioneered new foreign markets and founded the nation's first banks, insurance companies, and stock markets.[46] They pioneered, as well, the role of liberal republican citizen. They learned to manipulate the press to their political advantage. They formed political fac-

45. Colden's remarks were printed in "London Documents, XXXVIII: Mr. Colden's Account of the State of the Province of New-York," in E. B. O'Callaghan, ed., *Documents relative to the Colonial History of the State of New-York . . .* , 15 vols. (Albany, N.Y., 1853–1887), VII, 795. They are quoted in both Stuart M. Blumin, *The Emergence of the Middle Class: Social Experience in the American City, 1760–1900* (Cambridge, 1989), 17; and Bernard Friedman, "Shaping of the Radical Consciousness," *JAH*, LVI (1970), 781–901. See, as well, Kornblith and Murrin, "Making and Unmaking," in Young, ed., *Beyond the American Revolution*, 27–79. The evolution of the gentleman, first in Great Britain and then in North America, will be discussed at great length in Section 3, below.

46. Doerflinger, *Vigorous Spirit of Enterprise*, chaps. 2, 7, 70–114, 283–334; Pauline Maier, "The Revolutionary Origins of the American Corporation," *WMQ*, 3d Ser., L (1993), 51–84; Breen, "An Empire of Goods," *Journal of British Studies*, XXV (1986), 467–499; Bushman, *Refinement of America*; Lorinda R. B. Goodwin, *An Archaeology of Manners: The Polite World of the Merchant Elite of Colonial Massachusetts* (New York, 1999); Cary Carson, Ronald Hoffman, and Peter J. Albert, eds., *Of Consuming Interests: The Style of Life in the Eighteenth Century* (Charlottesville, Va., 1994).

tions and legislative alliances. They rallied voters to their cause. Of greatest importance, they founded a republic and fathered its constitution. But, all along, they worried about their lack of Old World culture and civility.[47]

Creatures of commerce, the bourgeoisie were also creatures of cities. Cities embedded the European American bourgeoisie in dense, polyglot communities drawn from the four corners of the world. Cities made them habitués of a newly emerging public sphere of coffeehouses, bookstores, libraries, and theaters. They became participants in the Republic's proliferating print culture. It was within this world that they studied and performed their roles as hardworking merchants, polished gentlemen, liberal philanthropists, and new republican citizens.[48]

Of course, the bourgeoisie were not alone in America's cities nor alone as consumers of the new urban print culture. Below the bourgeoisie's elevated ranks stretched the cities' amorphous middling ranks: smaller merchants,

47. For a discussion of such worries, beginning in the early eighteenth century, see Shields, *Civil Tongues*, 61–79. See, as well, David W. Conroy, *In Public Houses: Drink and the Revolution of Authority in Colonial Massachusetts* (Chapel Hill, N.C., 1995); Bushman, *Refinement of America*, xv; and Wood, *Creation of the American Republic*, 16; Warner, *Letters of the Republic*, chaps. 1, 2; Jeffrey L. Pasley, *"The Tyranny of Printers": Newspaper Politics in the Early American Republic* (Charlottesville, Va., 2001); Pasley, Andrew W. Robertson, and David Waldstreicher, eds., *Beyond the Founders: New Approaches to the Political History of the Early American Republic* (Chapel Hill, N.C., 2004); Cornell, *Other Founders*, 19–21; Richard R. John, *Spreading the News: The American Postal System from Franklin to Morse* (Cambridge, Mass., 1995); John K. Alexander, *The Selling of the Constitutional Convention: A History of News Coverage* (Madison, Wis., 1990), 16; Bailyn and Hench, eds., *The Press and the American Revolution*; Arthur M. Schlesinger, *Prelude to Independence: The Newspaper War on Britain, 1764–1776* (New York, 1953); Brown, *Knowledge Is Power*; Brown, *The Strength of a People: The Idea of an Informed Citizenry in America, 1650–1870* (Chapel Hill, N.C., 1996); Joanne B. Freeman, *Affairs of Honor: National Politics in the New Republic* (New Haven, Conn., 2001); Walt Brown, *John Adams and the American Press: Politics and Journalism at the Birth of the Republic* (Jefferson, N.C., 1995); Julie Hedgepeth Williams, *The Significance of the Printed Word in Early America: Colonists' Thoughts on the Role of the Press* (Westport, Conn., 1999). See, as well, papers from the Deference in Early America Conference, Philadelphia, 2004, including Alison Gilbert Olson, "Political Humor, Deference, and the American Revolution," and Barbara Clark Smith, "Beyond the Vote."

48. Warner, *Letters of the Republic*, chaps. 1, 2; Shields, *Civil Tongues*; John Dizikes, *Opera in America: A Cultural History* (New Haven, Conn., 1993), 45–47; Shields, "Anglo-American Clubs: Their Wit, Their Heterodoxy, Their Sedition," *WMQ*, 3d Ser., LI (1994), 293–304; Peter Thompson, *Rum Punch and Revolution: Taverngoing and Public Life in Eighteenth-Century Philadelphia* (Philadelphia, 1999); Goodwin, *Archaeology of Manners*; John F. Kasson, *Rudeness and Civility: Manners in Nineteenth-Century Urban America* (New York, 1990). For further descriptions of genteel urban life at the end of the eighteenth century, see Section 2, below.

many involved in inland trade; shopkeepers, some newly come from country towns; American-educated lawyers and doctors; tavern and coffeehouse owners; artisan/entrepreneurs ambitious to succeed in manufacturing; aspiring printer/publishers.[49] Although subscribing to a magazine might tax their budgets, many of these men chose to do so, seeking political information and, miming their social betters, to play the gentleman. Cities were home, as well, to a mélange of newly arrived political refugees, many well educated by American standards but desperately short of capital and connections (their numbers sharply increasing first with the French and then the Haitian Revolutions): small-scale artisans, journeyman printers, young farm boys who had managed to learn a fine hand at some country school and now sought jobs as clerks in hopes of upward mobility. These last men, especially, were far more likely to read newspapers and magazines within coffeehouses and taverns, where they might also rub shoulders with their betters and pick up bits of knowledge and gossip. This had to do for the present. Their overriding ambition, however, was to rise socially until they, too, could afford a magazine subscription, a fine drawing room in which to read it, an elegant wife to read it with, and, ideally, a

49. Blumin, *Emergence of the Middle Class,* chap. 2; Doerflinger, *Vigorous Spirit of Enterprise,* chap. 1; Blackmar, *Manhattan for Rent;* Matson, *Merchants and Empire;* Matson and Onuf, *Union of Interests;* Breen, *Marketplace of Revolution;* Kornblith and Murrin "Making and Unmaking," in Young, ed., *Beyond the American Revolution,* 43–52; Cornell, "Politics of the Middling Sort," in Gilje and Pencak, eds., *New York in the Age of the Constitution,* 151–175; Howard B. Rock, Paul A. Gilje, and Robert Asher, eds., *American Artisans: Crafting Social Identity, 1750–1850* (Baltimore, 1995); Sharon V. Salinger, *Taverns and Drinking in Early America* (Baltimore, 2002); S. D. Kimmel, "Philanthropic Enterprise: The Imperial Contradictions of Republican Political Economy in Philadelphia during the Era of Lewis and Clark," in Robert S. Cox, ed., *The Shortest and Most Convenient Route: Lewis and Clark in Context* (Philadelphia, 2004), 52–101. We must remember that the middling ranks were far from exclusively male. "Lady" boardinghouse owners, milliners, tailoresses, and smaller, less well-capitalized shopkeepers purveying food, ribbons, and other notions added a female component to the cities' middling ranks. However, it is not likely that these women would have subscribed to the new magazines. For women participants in the eighteenth-century urban economy, see, for example, Joan Gundersen, *To Be Useful to the World: Women in Revolutionary America, 1740–1790* (New York, 1996), esp. chap. 4; and Ellen Louis Hartigan-O'Connor, "The Measure of the Market: Women's Economic Lives in Charleston, S.C., and Newport, R.I., 1750–1820" (Ph.D. diss., University of Michigan, 2003). Below the middling ranks stretched the laboring classes. For descriptions of their lives, see Gilje, *Liberty on the Waterfront;* Billy G. Smith, "Poverty and Economic Marginality in Eighteenth-Century America," *Proceedings of the American Philosophical Society,* CXXXII (1988), 85–118; Howard B. Rock, *Artisans of the New Republic: The Tradesmen of New York City in the Age of Jefferson* (New York, 1984); Nash, *Forging Freedom;* Foote, *Black and White Manhattan,* esp. chaps. 2, 6, 7.

liveried black servant to deliver it to them. As we know, class associations are grounded as often in aspiration and desire as in the economic reality of the moment.[50]

Certainly, the magazines were one site where alliances, imaginative and real, could be made up and down the social scale. Children of commerce and the city, the bourgeois elite and the aspiring middling ranks together comprised the voice of American modernity. Whether as elite subscribers or tavern readers, venture publishers or artisan printers, they collectively produced the new nation's political print culture—and it was upon the pages of that print culture that a new American identity first emerged. Readers are critical, but, to understand the print culture and the new American that culture figured, we must also understand the publishers and editors who produced him.

THE MEN BEHIND THE MASTHEADS

The publishers and editors of the new political magazines mirrored the diversity of their readers. Mathew Carey, founder and publisher of the nation's premier political magazine, the *American Museum,* was an Irish political refugee who had fled to Philadelphia in the 1780s. His radical past made him a friend of Benjamin Franklin (whom he met earlier when a political exile in France in 1780), Thomas Jefferson, and the Marquis de Lafayette. Later on, Carey would become a leader of Philadelphia society, a philanthropist, and a social reformer and critic of note. (Interesting parallels exist between Carey's career and that of Benjamin Franklin.) Nevertheless, throughout much of his early career, Carey remained a struggling entrepreneur, hovering on the brink of bankruptcy. During the six years that he published the *American Museum,* he later wrote, "I was in a state of intense penury." Indeed, to finance the first issue, Carey had had to borrow funds from his butcher. Noah Webster, founder of the *American Magazine,* New York City's first political magazine, was a far more secure member of the nation's middling ranks—a Yale graduate, a well-published educator, and an ardent Federalist closely connected to Connecti-

---

50. A psychologically nuanced presentation of such ambitious young men can be found in the late-eighteenth-century fiction of Charles Brockden Brown. See, for example, *Arthur Mervyn; or, Memoirs of the Year 1793* (1799–1800; Kent, Ohio, 1980). Nor can we forget that at the periphery of this white world stood free African American communities who included in their ranks successful entrepreneurs and skilled artisans. Certainly, many in these communities were regular newspaper readers. Still, it is unlikely that they would have been interested in subscribing to magazines that largely ignored their existence.

cut's Federalist elite.[51] Isaiah Thomas was far less comfortably positioned. The founder of both the *Worcester Magazine* and the *Massachusetts Magazine,* a Revolutionary War patriot and an advocate of a national American literature, Thomas had begun his career as a poor apprentice and then as a journeyman printer. Only in later life would he emerge as a critical shaper of European American intellectual life. Lastly, the *Columbian Magazine,* the new nation's most elegant political and literary magazine, was published by a consortium of the intellectual elite—a signer of the Declaration of Independence, an important poet—and artisan printers (Francis Hopkinson, John Trenchard, William Spotsworth, and Charles Cist). Significantly, no single one of these men had the resources to finance publication. At the same time, however, it tells us a great deal about the important political role the new magazines were seen as playing that their editors were able attract contributions from the likes of Benjamin Franklin, Benjamin Rush, Thomas Jefferson, J. Hector St. John de Crèvecoeur, and such Yale-educated Hartford Wits as Timothy Dwight and Joel Barlow.[52]

51. Mathew Carey, "Letter IV," in Carey, *Autobiography* (Brooklyn, N.Y., 1942), 22. See, as well, Edward Carlos Carter II, "The Political Activities of Mathew Carey, Nationalist, 1760–1814" (Ph.D. diss., Bryn Mawr College, 1962); and Earl Bradsher, *Mathew Carey, Editor, Author, and Publisher: A Study in American Literary Development* (New York, 1912). Before founding his *American Magazine,* Webster had already published a widely distributed spelling book and numerous political essays. See Luisanna Fodde, *Noah Webster: National Language and Cultural History in the United States of America, 1758–1842* (Padova, 1994); Richard M. Rollins, *The Long Journey of Noah Webster* (Philadelphia, 1980); Rollins, ed., *The Autobiographies of Noah Webster from the Letters and Essays, Memoir, and Diary* (Columbia, S.C., 1989); Rollins, "Words as Social Control: Noah Webster and the Creation of the *American Dictionary,*" *American Quarterly,* XXVIII (1976), 415–430.

52. For information about Isaiah Thomas, see David D. Hall, "On Native Ground: From the History of Printing to the History of the Book," *Proceedings of the American Antiquarian Society,* XCIII (1983), 313–336; James David Moran, "Preserving All Others: A New One-Act Play about Isaiah Thomas," ibid., CIX (1999), 289–308; Marcus A. McCoirson, "Isaiah Thomas, the American Antiquarian Society, and the Future," ibid., XCV (1981), 27–37; Richard Walser, "Boston's Reception of the First American Novel," *Early American Literature,* XVII (1982), 65–74. Mott calls the *Columbian Magazine* "one of the best of the eighteenth century magazines" (*History of American Magazines,* I, 94). For biographical sketches of the consortium members, most of whom were printers, see 94–99, esp. 94–95. One member, however, Francis Hopkinson, was a highly respected member of the new nation's bourgeois elite. He was a signer of the Declaration of Independence, a poet, a writer, and the first European American to compose operas (Dizikes, *Opera,* 46). For other discussions of Hopkinson, see Angela René Hand, "Francis Hopkinson: American Poet and Composer" (Ph.D. diss., University of Texas, Austin,

The new political magazines provide invaluable insights into the founders' vision of an ideal American, his gendered, racial, and class characteristics. But, at the same time, the late-eighteenth-century political press was a tricky and uncertain instrument not well designed to produce a national hegemony. The issues the press had to deal with—citizens' political rights and responsibilities, who among North America's diverse peoples should be admitted to full citizenship, how the new Republic would accommodate the needs of the new fiscal capitalists—were too new for the emerging bourgeoisie to have created a consensus upon, especially since the bourgeoisie and the urban middling ranks were still unsure of their social standing and their political authority. Certainly, neither the bourgeoisie nor the middling ranks spoke with one voice. As a consequence, their new American was a man of multiple, often inharmonious parts. He assumed the appearance of inner cohesion only when the political magazines contrasted him to those they held up as his opposing—or constituting—Others. Both foreign and home-grown figures, these Others were themselves multiple: tyrannical monarchs and effete aristocrats (the villains of Revolutionary War rhetoric), impoverished and rebellious farmers (the villains of Shays's Rebellion), vain and foolish matrons (stock figures in eighteenth-century political discourses), and bestial Africans and savage Indians (increasingly important characters in the late eighteenth century's emergent racist discourses).[53]

2000); Dixon Wecter, "Francis Hopkinson and Benjamin Franklin," *American Literature*, XII (1940), 200–217; Elizabeth R. Waara, "'Franklin's Ingenious Friend' and Scientific Heir," *Proceedings of the American Philosophical Society*, CXVIII (1974), 315–320; George E. Hastings, "Francis Hopkinson and the Anti-Federalists," *American Literature*, I (1930), 405–418. For material on John Trenchard, see Annie Mitchell, "A *Liberal* Republican 'Cato,'" *American Journal of Political Science*, XLIX (2004), 588–603; Gary L. McDowell, "The Language of Law and the Foundations of American Constitutionalism," *WMQ*, 3d Ser., LV (1998), 375–398; Heather Elizabeth Barry, "'So Many American Cato's': John Trenchard and Thomas Gordon's Work in Eighteenth-Century British America" (Ph.D. diss., State University of New York, Stonybrook, 2002). For Charles Cist, see Boyd Childress, "Charles Cist: Philadelphia Printer," *Papers of the Bibliographic Society of America*, LXXXV (1991), 72–81.

53. Sobel, in her study of the late-eighteenth-century European American unconscious, *Teach Me Dreams*, notes that, within American society, "gender and race (often in combination) became the central focuses of alterity and identity." "White males increasingly defined themselves as not-black and not-female, while women increasingly recognized the male as the alien other. Blacks recognized whites as their enemy other" (5). Although *This Violent Empire* focuses primarily upon these others as rhetorical figures, the racial, gender, and class categories those

How are we to uncover the discursive and psychological complexities that unsettled this imagined new American? A close reading of the incongruities that dotted virtually every page of the new political magazines offers one route—but, by itself, a difficult one. A didactic, opinion-shaping genre, the political magazines struggled to mask their contradictions and slippages. Early European American novels and romances did not. Thriving on contradiction and ambivalence, intrigued by secret desires, they plumbed the unconscious to lay bare the hidden. Though their moralistic endings ultimately affirmed the normative, their complex plots made readers familiar with the forbidden and the dangerous. As important, the political was never far from the surface of their pages.[54] Their preferred topic was the internally troubled new American. The conflicts that divided him, his uncertain claims to virtue, and his efforts to understand his evolving new world were their meat and drink. Not only were the novels' protagonists confused—and confusing—they were surrounded with

---

figures represented were, in very real ways, excluded not only from the imagined new national body politic but from the exercise of active citizenship. As Rogers M. Smith points out: "Large portions of the population were for long stretches of time literally not seen or heard in the halls of power in America. Those exclusions mattered precisely because they severely limited the capacities of large numbers of Americans to shape their collective civic fates through the exercise of potent political agency." "Through most of U.S. history," Smith continues, "lawmakers pervasively and unapologetically structured U.S. citizenship in terms of illiberal and undemo-cratic racial, ethnic, and gender hierarchies, for reasons rooted in basic, enduring imperatives of political life" (Smith, *Civic Ideals: Conflicting Visions of Citizenship in U.S. History* [New Haven, Conn., 1997], 1, 7).

54. That was certainly true of the early novels of Charles Brockden Brown, proclaimed "father of the American novel." And it was not only Brown who focused on the political. Ardent nationalist Hugh Henry Brackenridge, publisher of the nation's second (and short-lived) politi-cal magazine, focused his multivolumed American picaresque, *Modern Chivalry: Containing the Adventures of a Captain and Teague O'Regan, His Servant* . . . (Pittsburgh, 1819), on issues of political representation—Could the masses ever be trusted to rule wisely? How could the elite maintain moral sway over those masses? In its second volume, the *Columbian Magazine* pub-lished excerpts from *Amilia*. A romance set against the backdrop of the American Revolution, *Amilia* pitted a virtuous republican father against a villainous redcoat. For explorations of early American literature that focus on its political content, see, for example, Cathy N. Davidson, *Revolution and the Word: The Rise of the Novel in America* (New York, 1986); Kerber, *Women of the Republic;* Joseph J. Ellis, *After the Revolution: Profiles of Early American Culture* (New York, 2002); Emory Elliott, *Revolutionary Writers: Literature and Authority in the New Republic, 1725–1810* (New York, 1982); Elliott, ed., *The Cambridge Introduction to Early American Literature* (Cambridge, 2002); Larzer Ziff, *Writing in the New Nation: Prose, Print, and Politics in the Early United States* (New Haven, Conn., 1991). For a major exploration of the eighteenth-century British novel, see Nancy Armstrong, *Desire and Domestic Fiction: A Political History of the Novel* (New York, 1987).

a cast of equally confusing secondary characters, all of whom, Susan Freidman points out, "move[d] through narrative space and time occupy[ing] multiple and shifting positions in relation to each other and to different systems of power relations." The early American novel existed at the vortex of the discursive contestations that destabilized the new national identity. Their failed closures, silences, and ellipses reinscribed the contradictions of their times in far more accessible forms than the magazines did.[55]

The nature of the novel as a highly popular literary genre only increases its appeal to cultural analysts, since it was ideally designed to attract new, unsophisticated readers—and writers. Certainly, the late-eighteenth-century novel was an attractive and accessible vehicle for bourgeois and middling women readers and writers. Indeed, the novel was virtually the only socially acceptable genre in which they could publicly express their feelings and perspectives, especially on political issues. Novels, consequently, offer a window into the overt and covert opinions (and desires) of the new Republic's growing population of literate women.[56]

Counterpointing male- and female-authored novels to one another and to the political magazines, socially and politically contextualized readings give a clearer sense of the discursive and ideological discord that existed beneath the surface of the political magazines and, even more tellingly, of the subterranean tensions existing between the idealized new American and his troubling Others. This is especially true if we are careful not to privilege gender as the writer's preeminent identity but focus, rather, on the interplay of gender, race, and class

55. Friedman, *Mappings*, 28. The late twentieth and early twenty-first centuries, in particular, have seen a number of scholars turning to the late-eighteenth-century novel for insights into the conflicts and concerns troubling the new Republic. See, for example, Looby, *Voicing America*; Julia A. Stern, *The Plight of Feeling: Sympathy and Dissent in the Early American Novel* (Chicago, 1997); Elizabeth Barnes, ed., *Incest and the Literary Imagination* (Gainesville, Fla., 2002); Patterson, *Authority, Autonomy, and Representation*; Warner, *Letters of the Republic*; Kafer, *Charles Brockden Brown's Revolution*; Jeffrey H. Richards, "The Politics of Seduction: Theater, Sexuality, and National Virtue in the Novels of Hannah Foster," in Della Pollock, ed., *Exceptional Spaces: Essays in Performance and History* (Chapel Hill, N.C., 1998), 238–257; Donna R. Bontatibus, *The Seduction Novel of the Early Nation: A Call for Socio-political Reform* (East Lansing, Mich., 1999). For an exploration of British women writers during this same time period, see Eleanor Rose Ty, *Unsex'd Revolutionaries: Five Women Novelists of the 1790s* (Toronto, 1993).

56. The number of works exploring women's fiction in the early national period has exploded in the past decades, beginning with Davidson's *Revolution and the Word* and Kerber's *Women of the Republic*. See, among others, Stern, *Plight of Feeling*; Bontatibus, *Seduction Novel of the Early Nation*; Mary Kelley, *Learning to Stand and Speak: Women, Education, and Public Life in America's Republic* (Chapel Hill, N.C., 2006), esp. chap. 4.

that informs each text. Bearing these admonitions in mind, *This Violent Empire* will draw the discursive ambivalences of the period into relief.[57]

WHERE DO WE GO FROM HERE?

To capture as fully as possible the multiple facets of the new American and the complexities that marked his birth, *This Violent Empire* is divided into three sections. Each section explores a central aspect of the imagined new American identity. Section 1 begins where the founders began. Focusing on the new political magazines, it explores the figure of the European American as a republican citizen, tracing the multiple contradictory political discourses that simultaneously constituted and destabilized him. It then turns to the two principal constituting Others the political magazines deployed to veil these contradictions. The first was the rebellious farmers of western Massachusetts whom the press presented as embodying all the evils democracy threatened. The second was women. Eighteenth-century political discourses agreed, women, lacking reason, independence, and physical strength, constituted the virtuous republican citizens' ultimate contrasting Other. Consequently, women must be excluded from the pure republican body politic. But would these constituting Others remain reassuringly other, confirming the new republicans' coherent identity? Or would they fracture the gendered distinctions that marked the republican citizen as manly, resolute, and self-controlled? Each, in its own way, did precisely that—representations of wild-eyed Shays rebels rendered manliness artificial and performative, whereas women's fiction appropriated a Revolutionary male voice to assert women's equal right to life, liberty, and happiness in the new Republic. The readings for this section concentrate on magazines and novels published between 1786 and 1797.

Section 2 explores European/Native Americans' complex interactions as a dangerous fusion of desire, dread, and hatred. Denigrating Native Americans as cruel savages, denying them any right to an American identity (or land), European Americans nevertheless were unable to separate themselves from their (Native) American twin, unable to deny Native Americans a central place in the American *imaginaire*. Rather, Native and European Americans emerged as dangerous doubles. Readers of the popular press had to ask, Which one was

57. Attempting to capture some of these complexities, *This Violent Empire* will explore novelists from a variety of different social locations: the wife of a New England clergyman (Hannah Foster), a Philadelphia Quaker–become–New York sophisticate (Charles Brockden Brown), a British American actress, playwright, and novelist (Susanna Rowson), and "A Philadelphia Lady" (Leonora Sansay, the mistress of Aaron Burr).

the true savage, which the true American—the white settler, the indigenous "red"? Dismayed by the wild excesses of frontiersmen they thought of as "white Indians," bourgeois Americans and their popular print culture could not decide. Thus, as gender and class had destabilized the new American–as–republican citizen, so race and culture problematized European Americans' claim to an American identity. Section 2 engages in contextualized readings of political magazines, Indian captivity narratives (a best-selling genre pirated by the political magazines), and two novels: Charles Brockden Brown's canonical *Edgar Huntly* and a text uniformly ignored by literary critics but which I find very revealing—Susanna Rowson's *Reuben and Rachel*. Both novels focus on the instability of Native/European American difference. The texts examined span the period 1786 to 1801.

Section 3 explores the ways economic changes born of the Revolutionary War further compromised the American republican's rhetorical cohesion. Again questions of class enter the picture. How did the magazines represent the American as a man of economic and social standing? Was he a frugal, industrious exemplar of the Protestant work ethic, the ideal middle-class citizen, or a cosmopolitan gentleman with aspirations to fashionable urbanity? Did the magazines model him on Poor Richard or seek to inscribe him as an elegant British gentleman? If it were the latter, given classic republican suspicion of luxury and display, was the very term "republican gentleman" an oxymoron? Questions of gender and race reenter in the form of two surprisingly contrasting constituting Others—the refined American woman and the enslaved African American. As with the other sections, this will focus on the political magazines read in dialogue with novels, in this case Charles Brockden Brown's *Arthur Mervyn* and Leonora Sansay's *Zelica*, the latter an exploration of race and civic virtue during the Haitian Revolution.

Underscoring what I see as the performative nature of national identities, each section begins, like an eighteenth-century play, with a prologue depicting a theatrical event that captures the instability of that particular aspect of the emerging new identity. Section 1 commences with Timothy Dwight's valedictory address to the Yale graduating class of 1776, Section 2 with New York Tammany Society members, bedecked in ersatz Indian costumes, greeting a delegation of Creek warriors at the beginning of Washington's presidency, and Section 3 with a ball given by the French ambassador to celebrate the birth of the new Republic and the birthday of the dauphin.

One last caveat. Examining the relation of the idealized European American subject and his constituting Others is not a simple examination of contrasting binaries. A complex pattern of triangulation emerges. We find the new nation's obstreperous Others engaged in intense dialogue not only with the white male that comprised the center of the magazines' emerging American identity but with one another. In the new popular press, boundaries became liminal borderlands, distinctions uncertain. Gender, no longer biologically grounded, became a theatrical performance. Rugged western farmers assumed feminine characteristics, women masculine traits. Nor was race any surer a marker than gender, as distinctions between free and slave labor blurred and the clear differences between white matron and enslaved African disintegrated—on the pages of both the political magazines and the late-eighteenth-century novel. Nor does it seem that the European American could ever distinguish himself from his Native American (br)other. For, if he did, what then would become of his claim to be American? But if he did not, could he ever establish his claim to civility and Enlightenment culture?

This Violent Empire focuses on failure—on the ways differences collapse and efforts to solidify identities falter. It asks how and why the dark and polluting figures existing at the borders of the new American self continually "trouble and unsettle the foreclosures we prematurely call identity." Identities are not organic entities, the individual's own true, hidden self. Always in flux, always subject to transformation, they are experiences in the process of becoming. Susan Stanford Friedman thinks of identities as "historically embedded site[s], . . . crossroads of multiply situated knowledges . . . axial intersections of different positionalities, and the spaces of dynamic encounter." "Contingent and precarious," without centers or clear borders, identities will always be experienced as endangered by the Others they cannot dislodge from their imaginaire. As a consequence, across time and space, national subjects repeatedly turn with violence on their relentlessly threatening—and desired—Others.[58]

58. Butler, *Bodies That Matter,* 22; Friedman, *Mappings,* 19; Henretta, "Wealth and Social Structure," in Greene and Pole, eds., *Colonial British America,* 262–289; Matson, *Merchants and Empire.* The phrase "contingent and precarious" is Chantal Mouffe's. Concurring with Friedman, Mouffe argues that identity formation involves the "constant subversion and overdetermination of one [subject position] by one of the others." "We have to conceive of the history of the subject as the history of his/her identifications. . . . There is no concealed identity to be rescued"—or, I would add, detected. See Mouffe, "Democratic Politics," in Rajchman, ed., *Identity Question,* 33–44, esp. 34.

The New American–as–Republican Citizen

The Drums of War / The Thrust of Empire

Daring Dwight the epic muse sublime
Hails her new empire on the western clime

. . . .

His voice divine revives the promised land
The heav'n taught leader, and the chosen band

—JOEL BARLOW, The Vision of Columbus

Yale's class of 1776 graduated two weeks after the Continental Congress formally announced America's independence from Great Britain. These were times of exhilaration. These were times that tried men's souls. Most of the new states lacked formal constitutions, tax structures, or courts of law. The Continental Congress was a self-authorized gathering of attainted rebels. The document authorizing their meetings, the Articles of Confederation, would not be ratified for another five years. The Continental army was a ragamuffin collection of local militias; the United States Navy, four fishing boats to which a few cannon had been hastily added. The campaign to invade Canada had just failed ingloriously. Thirty-two thousand British troops, supported by the British fleet and one hundred fifty transport ships, were massed on Long Island. Within weeks, New York City would fall, as would much of Westchester and New Jersey. Within the year, the British army would seize the rebel capital of Philadelphia.[1]

Notable among the festivities marking Yale's commencement exercises that July afternoon was a valedictory address presented by the youthful Reverend Timothy Dwight. The grandson of Jonathan Edwards, Dwight was a promi-

1. [Thomas Paine], *The American Crisis,* no. 1 (Norwich, Conn., 1776). Congress did not officially proclaim independence from Great Britain until July 9, 1776.

nent member of New England's intellectual elite. He would soon be appointed a chaplain in the Continental army. Later, he would win fame as a Hartford Wit, an epic poet of national standing, the president of Yale, and, most especially, the "pope" of Connecticut Federalists. By the century's end, Dwight would become a leading opponent of the French Revolution, Thomas Jefferson, and, more generally, Deistic principles in religion and politics. His *Triumph of Infidelity* (1788) comprised a bitter attack upon the Enlightenment and its celebration of man's reason, progress, and perfectibility. *"You* will find all men . . . naturally ignorant," Dwight thundered from his Yale pulpit in the years following the French Revolution and the election of Jefferson. Political revolution and popular sovereignty would lead inevitably to disorder and mobocracy.[2]

In July 1776, however, all that lay in Dwight's future. That afternoon, young Dwight espoused a radically different vision of revolution, the future of the newly born nation, and, yes, the perfectibility, if not of all mankind, at least of his fellow New Englanders. Refuting the hard realities weighing so heavily upon the new nation, he urged Yale's graduates to soar with him on the wings of patriotic rhetoric, to willingly suspend their disbelief and imagine their politically divided and war-torn composite of states as "the greatest empire the hand of time ever raised up to view." In a paean to progress, Dwight proclaimed that God had delayed the birth of the new nation (and infant empire) until that special moment "when every species of knowledge, natural and moral, is arrived to a state of perfection, which the world never before saw." Now, "human greatness will find a period." "Here will be accomplished . . . the last thousand years of the reign of time. . . . a glorious Sabbath of peace, purity and felicity." How, Dwight demanded, could Yale's graduating class fail to leap to the defense of so mighty, so blessed a land? Embracing a millennial vision of republican political possibilities, he exhorted, "When you remember that your lot is cast in that land, which, in such a multitude of circumstances, is evidently the favorite of heaven; when you remember, that you live amongst the most free, enlightened and virtuous people on earth; when you remember that your labors may contribute to the hastening of that glorious period when nations shall be spiritually born in a day; with what zeal, with what diligence, with

2. Timothy Dwight, "On the Duties Connected with a Professional Life," in Dwight, *Sermons,* 2 vols. (New Haven, Conn., 1828), I, 303, quoted by Colin Wells, *The Devil and Doctor Dwight: Satire and Theology in the Early American Republic* (Chapel Hill, N.C., 2002), 17. Wells presents a detailed discussion of Dwight's political vision, especially his opposition to Deism, Jefferson, and the French Revolution.

what transport must you be inspired!" Passionately, he urged Yale's graduates to answer their country's call, "act . . . on the extended stage" of republican history, there to lay "the foundations of American greatness." "Enlarge your minds, expand the grasp of your benevolence, ennoble all your conduct," he cried, "and [you will be] crown[ed] with wreaths which cannot fade."[3]

"Innumerable must be the Actors in so vast a plot, and infinitely various the parts they act," Dwight continued. "Every character" was necessary. Given the critical moment in which Dwight spoke, the first and most obvious role Yale's new graduates must assume was that of classic republican warrior, battling for liberty. Yale's young men must act as "brave, generous and hardy soldiers." With "heroic firmness," "exalted disposition," and "divine patriotism," they must "strike terror into their enemies, and brighten the glory of their country." Of course, to guide the ship of state, the new Republic also needed selfless statesmen who, "with unwearied attention," would "facilitate the execution of justice, . . . establish universal good order, . . . stamp infamy on political corruption, . . . refine our manners, . . . increase our naval and military strength, and . . . fix on an immoveable basis, civil and religious Liberty." With these rhetorical flourishes, Dwight called on Yale's graduates to assume the role of the virtuous republican citizen, selflessly dedicated to the common good, a figure Aristotle had called a *zoon politikon*.[4]

The new states, however, produced few zoon politikons. From a classic republican perspective, it was only the inheritance of secure landed wealth, leisure, and a classic education that permitted the zoon politikon to serve his nation without thought of self-interest or compensation. Members of Yale's graduating class, Dwight acknowledged, were far more likely to be the sons of men who had labored hard to send them to college. Most would serve their country, in peace and war, by entering the world of commerce or by following one of the professions. Indeed, Dwight deployed the ringing cadences of classic republican rhetoric to represent roles such men could play in the new nation. As adventuresome merchants, they would bring it "inconceivable wealth and power." As manufacturers, they would "astonish" the world with their inventiveness. As lawyers and doctors, they would battle disease and fight for social justice. Brave warriors, selfless statesmen, hardworking merchants, doctors,

3. [Timothy Dwight], "A Valedictory Address to the Young Gentlemen, Who Commenced Bachelors of Arts, at Yale College, July 25th, 1776," *American Magazine*, I (1787), 42–47, and I (1788), 99–103 (hereafter cited as Dwight, "Address").

4. Ibid., 44, 46, 99, 102; J. G. A. Pocock, *The Machiavellian Moment: Florentine Political Thought and the Atlantic Republican Tradition* (Princeton, N.J., 1975).

and lawyers—all, Dwight proclaimed, would bring the new Republic ever closer to that "state of perfection which the world never saw before."[5]

Dwight's script for national greatness called for one more character to stride forth—a classic Enlightenment liberal, a man of reason who "despise[d] the shackles of custom, and the chains of authority" and worked to "diffuse . . . light and knowledge." Equally useful to the new Republic, the Enlightenment liberal, unlike the brave warrior or noble statesman, was not found in the political arena. Rather, as a private gentleman, he would act in the "important scenes of private life." "Your ceaseless endeavors will be exerted . . . to improve and refine the morals of mankind, . . . to defuse happiness . . . to dry the tears of the orphan, to spare the blushes of needy merit." Not political zeal but benevolence and the sympathies were his lodestars.[6]

To readers in the twenty-first century, Dwight's list may well seem a realistic representation of the variety of roles patriotic European Americans played during the Revolution and the years that followed. But Dwight's eclecticism might well have troubled his eighteenth-century audience. In the course of his address, Dwight had interwoven fragments of Calvinist orthodoxy, Puritan exceptionalism, the Enlightenment's vision of man as rational and noble, classic republicanism's celebration of the heroic citizen/warrior, commercial republicanism's praise of industry, whig commitment to progress and materialism, and liberalism's suspicion of the state and celebration of the private sphere. Dwight's new American was part zoon politikon, part hardworking member of the bourgeoisie, part Enlightenment gentleman. Each discourse, each figure warred with all the others—and, of course, with the anti-Enlightenment vision Dwight would shortly unveil in his sermons and satiric poetry. Dwight's rhetorical fusions suggest that ideological confusion lay just beneath the surface of his address and in the minds of many of his fellow new Americans.

To mask the eclectic, divided nature of the national subject his rhetoric

5. Dwight, "Address," 43–44. In this way, he exonerated America's doctors from the criticism of money-grabbing and quackery so frequently leveled at physicians in Britain and on the Continent. Dwight was fully conscious of those denigrations. Thus he urged those graduates headed for a medical career to avoid the behavior that rendered physicians the butt of bitter satire. If they did so, "we shall not have the pain of seeing you . . . rush forth into the world, and under the thick covering of long unintelligible terms, a frozen hypocritical phiz, a blustering advertisement of cures you never performed . . . delude the ignorance, empty the purses, and end the lives of your fellow creatures. Your minds will not be narrow enough to form *nostrums* of your own, nor weak enough to venture hastily upon the hidden poison of those, which have been formed by others" (ibid., 100).

6. Ibid., 45, 46, 100.

inscribed, Dwight insisted on the new Republic's homogeneity. In the face of Americans' ethnic, linguistic, and cultural diversity, Americans were a united, homogeneous people who shared "the same religion, the same manners, the same interests, the same languages . . . and principles." "This is an event," he boasted, "which, since the building of Babel, till the present time, the sun never saw. . . . [It] is indeed a novelty on earth." Such homogeneity was the hand-maiden of harmony and the mother of greatness. "A sameness in these impor-tant particulars cannot fail to produce the happiest effects. It wrought miracles in the minute, microscopic states of Greece. What may we not expect from its benign influence on the vast regions of America?"[7]

Difference, on the other hand, would divide and destroy.

> Differences in religion always produce persecutions and bloodshed. Differ-ence of manners . . . cannot but occasion coldness, contempt and ill-will. Contending interests ever exist with disputes, and end in war. Without sameness of language, it would be impossible to preserve that easiness of communication, that facility and dispatch in the management of business, which the extensive concerns of a great empire indispensably require. Essen-tially various forms, and unlike principles of government . . . are . . . the parents of endless contests, slaughter and desolation.

Dwight was thus one of the first architects of a self-image that denied Ameri-cans' actual heterogeneity. The Great Seal of the United States would promise E Pluribus Unum—from many, one. But Dwight's flight of fancy went further. It denied the initial diversity, the plurality from which American unity, the American "one," would be formed.[8]

The celebration of sameness implies a celebration of exclusion. Dwight's insistence that all virtuous Americans shared one common religion and culture and common interests expelled from the category "virtuous Americans" all who did not—among them Native Americans, African American Muslims, Jews, Catholics, and, increasingly, Dwight would claim, Deists and political radicals such as Thomas Paine and Thomas Jefferson. The list of roles Dwight called upon Yale's graduates to play further reinforced the exclusionary rhetoric of his address. His heroic warrior, wise statesman, successful merchant, and dedicated lawyer or physician represented both the career projections of Yale

---

7. Ibid., 45.

8. Ibid., 45. We see here Dwight both challenging Michel de Montaigne's insistence that republics must be tiny city-states, any larger unit promising political corruption, and at the same time embracing that vision as he warned against diversity.

graduates and the leadership of the First and Second Continental Congresses. But where, in the list Dwight drew up for his largely bourgeois audience, were Boston and New York's black and white mechanics and laborers whose threats of street violence had helped enforce nonimportation agreements? Where were the sailors who battled British naval officers to stop the impressment of liberty-loving Americans? Where were western Massachusetts's hardscrabble farmers who declared Massachusetts returned to a state of nature and capable of self-governance and thus precipitated the Revolution? Where were the women who bravely soldiered on at home, maintaining social order and agricultural production while fathers and husbands went to war? By insisting on the sameness of all virtuous Americans, Dwight barred from that category all who did not fit the profile of his fellow Yale men. How stable, how cohesive could a national identity be if it excluded the vast majority of those who had produced and were reproducing the new nation? Dwight's ringing cadences produced not a coherent but a fractured and divided national subject, comprised of the God-chosen few and the many who did not fit his vision.[9]

Dwight's national subject needed a series of constituting Others to provide him with the semblance of an inner cohesion that he lacked. Although in future sermons he would excoriate Deists, Jeffersonian Republicans, and French radicals, on this summer afternoon, Dwight presented Yale's graduates with only one significant constituting Other. A distinctive group of people, Dwight warned his listeners, cast a dark shadow across America's triumphant progress from "east to west." To the south of the new American empire lay a rival empire: Mexico. Stretching from the Yucatán to the northern reaches of California, Mexico occupied a far vaster expanse of land than the thirteen states. Conquerors of wealthy indigenous empires, resident in the Americas since the beginning of the sixteenth century, Mexicans boasted a rich and urbane culture. Their cities, universities, libraries, and churches were larger, older, and far more established than any in the thirteen states. As such, Mexico threatened Dwight's representation of the new states as the rightful, virtuous rulers of the vast North American continent—the last, greatest empire on earth.[10]

Dwight made the rhetorical conquest and elimination of Mexico and Mexicans the grand conclusion of his address. His Mexicans were not "Americans" as he defined that term. They were a degenerate people, a threat to true,

9. Dirk Hoerder, *Crowd Action in Revolutionary Massachusetts, 1765–1789* (New York, 1977); Gary B. Nash, *The Urban Crucible: Social Change, Political Consciousness, and the Origins of the American Revolution* (Cambridge, Mass., 1979), chap. 6.

10. Dwight, "Address," 46.

virtuous Americans. Long subject to a "tyranny rendered ten times more horrible by the infernal domination of an abandoned priesthood," they had no affinity for liberty and could claim only the most perverted form of Christianity. Going further, Dwight suggested that Mexicans were a mixed, inferior "race." "The southern and western parts of North-America . . . are peopled with as vicious, luxurious, mean-spirited and contemptible a race of beings, as any that ever *blackened* the pages of infamy." "Generally descended from the refuse of mankind," they lived in a "hot, wealthy and plentiful country" and were "educated from their infancy under the most shocking of all governments." Coming from a true New England Calvinist, Dwight's imagery connects Mexicans to the devil, "the prince of darkness," and his torrid kingdom. A decade later, Dwight would report that, even before "war's alarming clarion ceas'd to roar," the devil had taken up his dwelling in the new Republic. And where he resided, "the world grew dark." But Dwight's association of Mexicans with hot lands and dark superstitions suggests, as well, another "torrid" land and superstitious people: Africa and heathen Africans.[11]

In these varied ways, Dwight represented Mexicans as his brave new Americans' ultimate negative Other, the antithesis of republican virtue and honor. They must be eliminated, he insisted in a show of bravado that would become a characteristic of much later U.S. foreign policy. "The moment our interest demands it," he predicted, Mexico's "extensive regions will be our own." "The present race of inhabitants will either be entirely exterminated, or [a less likely possibility in Dwight's opinion] revive to . . . human dignity, by the . . . influence of just laws and rational freedom." In either case, Mexico's inhabitants would cease to exist as "Mexicans." Only true Anglo-Saxon, Protestant "Americans" would inhabit Dwight's glorious empire. As the address concluded: "A distinction . . . between them and ourselves . . . will [then] be useless and impertinent." "American" homogeneity would shine forth unblemished and intact. An image of the United States as a righteous, God-blessed, and violent empire was born.[12]

DWIGHT SPOKE AT A key moment in the birth of the new United States: a time of fear and boundless hope. Twelve years later, more sober European

11. Ibid., 44; Dwight, *The Triumph of Infidelity* (1788), lines 4, 15, rpt. in Wells, *Devil and Doctor Dwight*, 183–209 (emphasis added). Nor can we ignore the substantial numbers of enslaved and free Africans and Afro-Mexicans residing in seventeenth- and eighteenth-century Mexico. See, for example, Herman L. Bennett, *Africans in Colonial Mexico: Absolutism, Christianity, and Afro-Creole Consciousness, 1570–1640* (Bloomington, Ind., 2003).

12. Dwight, "Address," 44.

Americans gathered in Philadelphia to examine the flaws many felt marred their confederation. At that moment, another Yale graduate, educator, entrepreneur, and editor Noah Webster, republished Dwight's "Valedictory Address" in the premier issue of the political magazine he founded specifically to help secure New York State's ratification of the Constitution, the *American Magazine*. Webster was an ardent nationalist, a conservative New England Federalist, and thus a supporter of the later, more conservative Dwight. Webster had graduated from Yale two years after Dwight delivered his address. Perhaps he had been present that July afternoon, imbibing and internalizing Dwight's vision. That Webster chose Dwight's words to initiate his new magazine suggests that Webster shared Dwight's youthful vision of the new American nation as an infant and God-protected empire. Certainly, Dwight's address introduced many of the arguments that Webster and his fellow nationalist publishers and editors would later develop in their efforts to secure ratification of the new Federal constitution and constitute the new American as the rightful possessor of the American continent. Would they be able to avoid the ideological confusions, the rhetorical slippages that confused and fractured Dwight's new American? Or would their new America and its empire continue to be the offspring of unresolved ideological conflicts and discursive contradictions?

CHAPTER ONE

Fusions and Confusions

American citizenship . . . has always been an intellectually puzzling, legally confused, and politically charged and contested status. — ROGERS SMITH, Civic Ideals

From Maine taverns to Charleston mansions, citizens joyfully celebrated George Washington's defeat of General Cornwallis at Yorktown. British military might had been vanquished, freedom secured. Bells rang and cannons fired as people toasted liberty, Independence, and the united thirteen states. Peace was nigh, and with peace, European Americans assured themselves, prosperity would quickly salve the wounds of war.[1]

Popular joy was short-lived, however. Economic and political uncertainties soon destabilized the new Republic. Within a year, the commercial boom that had followed the war's end collapsed. Unsold cargoes rotted on wharves in Philadelphia and New York. Bankruptcy toppled merchant princes and threatened small country shopkeepers. Domestic manufacturing, which had thrived during the war, stagnated. Farming families struggled against high taxes and farm foreclosures. Rhode Island hovered on the brink of fiscal anarchy—at least from the perspective of Boston's and New York's propertied elite.[2] Eco-

1. See Rogers M. Smith, *Civic Ideals: Conflicting Visions of Citizenship in U.S. History* (New Haven, Conn., 1997), 14. For discussions of such popular celebrations, see David Waldstreicher, *In the Midst of Perpetual Fetes: The Making of American Nationalism, 1776–1820* (Chapel Hill, N.C., 1997), esp. 24–52; and Simon P. Newman, *Parades and the Politics of the Streets: Festive Culture in the Early American Republic* (Philadelphia, 1997), 11–43.

2. Cathy D. Matson, ed., *The Economy of Early America: Historical Perspectives and New Directions* (University Park, Pa., 2006); Ronald Hoffman et al., eds., *The Economy of Early America: The Revolutionary Period, 1763–1790* (Charlottesville, Va., 1988); Paul A. Gilje, *The Making of the American Republic, 1763–1815* (Upper Saddle River, N.J., 2006); John J. McCusker and Russell R. Menard, *The Economy of British America, 1607–1789* (Chapel Hill, N.C., 1985); Edwin J. Perkins, *The Economy of Colonial America,* 2d ed. (New York, 1988). For studies that

nomic unrest flared into political conflict. The Continental Congress fled to Princeton as Continental army troops, long unpaid and demanding redress, marched on Philadelphia. Massachusetts farmers rose in arms against the state's high taxes, forcing the state's courts to close and sending shockwaves through the nation. Independence, it seemed, had opened the floodgates to political chaos. It "was a frightened age," "a dangerous time," one "that left many insecure, even those who thought they wanted revolutionary change of one kind or another."[3]

Would-be post-Revolutionary elites North and South blamed the Articles of Confederation and the Continental Congress for the new nation's problems. An irresolute and ineffective instrument, they railed, the Continental Congress remained deadlocked as political crises succeeded economic crises. George

---

focus on postwar economic crises and political unrest, see, as well, Thomas M. Doerflinger, *A Vigorous Spirit of Enterprise: Merchants and Economic Development in Revolutionary Phila-delphia* (Chapel Hill, N.C., 1986), 261–267; Gordon Carl Bjork, "Stagnation and Growth in the American Economy, 1784–1792" (Ph.D. diss., University of Washington, 1963); Robert A. Gross, ed., *In Debt to Shays: The Bicentennial of an Agrarian Rebellion* (Charlottesville, Va., 1986); David P. Szatmary, *Shays' Rebellion: The Making of an Agrarian Insurrection* (Amherst, Mass., 1980); Philip L. White, *The Beekmans of New York in Politics and Commerce, 1647–1877* (New York, 1956).

In 1786, Rhode Island farmers, represented by the Country Party, voted out the more conser-vative, commercially oriented Mercantile Party and passed a series of agrarian-oriented acts. The legislature set up a land bank, issued £100,000 in paper money, and fined creditors who would not accept payment in paper. State creditors were then ordered to present their securities and receive but one-quarter of the principal in paper money. Judges who refused to enforce the new laws were removed from office. All such legislation alarmed commercial interests from Boston to Philadelphia. See Leonard L. Richards, *Shays's Rebellion: The American Revolution's Final Battle* (Philadelphia, 2002), 83–84. Pennsylvania's Revolutionary War constitution, with its unicameral legislature, widespread suffrage, and routine review of legislation in its turn threatened political democracy.

3. Mark R. Patterson, *Authority, Autonomy, and Representation in American Literature, 1776–1865* (Princeton, N.J., 1988), 61; Mechal Sobel, *Teach Me Dreams: The Search for Self in the Revolutionary Era* (Princeton, N.J., 2000), 165. The classic, and much revised, study of these troubles is John Fiske, *The Critical Period of American History, 1783–1789* (London, 1888). For more recent evaluations, see Gordon S. Wood, *The Creation of the American Republic, 1776–1787* (New York, 1972), 303–429, esp. 393–396; Peter S. Onuf, "Anarchy and the Crisis of the Union," in Herman Belz, Ronald Hoffman, and Peter S. Albert, eds., *To Form a More Perfect Union: The Critical Ideas of the Constitution* (Charlottesville, Va., 1992), 272–302; and Gary B. Nash, *The Unknown American Revolution: The Unruly Birth of Democracy and the Struggle to Create America* (New York, 2005). For the political magazines' response, see Camillus [Fisher Ames], "Obser-vations on the Late Insurrection in Massachusetts . . . Letter I," *American Museum*, II (1787), 315–318. Chapter 2 will discuss Shays's Rebellion at length.

Washington warned that, if the Articles of Confederation were not altered, "thirteen sovereignties . . . all tugging at the fœderal head; will soon bring ruin on the whole." Charles Pinckney, one of South Carolina's most prominent planters, denounced Congress as "weak and contemptible." Without a strong national government, the youthful Noah Webster complained, "each State is jealous of its neighbor . . . at the hazard even of our federal existence." Mobilizing across state lines and regional divides, these critics organized a series of conventions, culminating in Philadelphia in the summer of 1787.[4]

To augment their efforts, they turned to the urban press, orchestrating a deluge of newspaper articles that reached a crescendo as the opening of the Philadelphia convention drew near. Seeking to swing votes in key northern states, ardent advocates of change also founded political magazines designed to attract the attention of the northern bourgeoisie and the middling urban classes. Vociferously, these magazines denounced the Articles of Confederation for providing a "weak, imperfect, and distracted government." Congress, under the Articles, was shamefully disorganized and ineffectual. "Where the supreme power is said to be lodged," Philadelphia's *American Museum* noted, "we . . . are represented by thirteen voices." What the Republic needed, the urban press insisted, was a forceful new government, one that would provide firm, manly leadership. True to eighteenth-century rhetorical style, the press enriched its political attacks with sexual and gendered innuendos, scorning Congress as effeminate, indeed, feminine. "If any thing can be added to this description of the impotence of our federal government," one correspondent complained, "it must be a total want of authority over its own members." "Like the weak commands of a superannuated matron," said another, "the more [its laws] are attempted to be executed, the deeper they sink into contempt."[5]

4. Charles Pinckney, speech at the South Carolina Convention, May 14, 1788, in Jonathan Elliot, ed., *The Debates in the Several State Conventions on the Adoption of the Federal Constitution, as Recommended by the General Convention at Philadelphia, in 1787* . . . (Philadelphia, 1891), IV, 331; George Washington to James Madison, Nov. 5, 1786, *Documentary History of the Constitution of the United States*, 5 vols. (Washington, D.C., 1894–1905), IV, 33–35; and Noah Webster, "Remarks on the Manners, Government, and Debt of the United States" (Philadelphia, 1787), in *A Collection of Essays and Fugitive Writings* (New York, 1790), 82.

5. Harrington, "To the Freemen of America," *American Museum*, I (1787), 491–495, esp. 495; A Bostonian, "A View of the Federal Government of America; Its Defects, and a Proposed Remedy: Letter I," ibid., 294–298, esp. 295, 296; "Letter II: On the Same Subject," ibid., 298–303; "Letter III: Same Subject Continued," ibid., 303–306, esp. 303. See also "Account of a Deputation from Congress to the Assembly of New Jersey," ibid., II (1787), 48–55. The press, with hardly an exception, attacked Congress under the Articles of Confederation and supported Federalist efforts to form a new government. Editors warned that the new Republic was "bedeviled" with

The magazines called for a government endowed with "vigour [and] energy," by which they meant the swift repayment of the Revolutionary War debt along with government support of commerce and manufacturing. Such a virile government required not only forceful new structures but citizens renowned for their "ardent zeal for . . . honour and prosperity." A republic could only be as strong and virtuous as its citizens. The object of government, John Adams reminded his fellow Americans, was to produce citizens known for their "Strength, Hardiness Activity, Courage, Fortitude and Enterprise." Adams contrasted such folk to the effete, sybaritic, and deferential subjects of a monarchy—effeminate men known for their "Taste and Politeness. . . . Elegance in Dress. . . . Musick and Dancing." Heralded by these demands, the ideal new American began to emerge as forceful, energetic, and masculine—an image that would form the cornerstone of a new national identity.[6]

The eighteenth century provided the new magazines with three highly divergent, indeed warring, political discourses with which to conceptualize a virtuous republic and virtuous republican citizens: classic republicanism, commercial republicanism, and liberalism. Each of these discourses had originally developed in Britain. Each entertained a unique understanding of critical concepts: civic virtue, liberty, and independence. Each projected a distinctive

---

problems that, if not addressed, would soon overwhelm it. The *American Museum* called the Articles of Confederation feeble and "so injudiciously constructed, as to be not only incapable of executing those [powers] they at present possess, but to be a very unsafe deposit of such further authorities as are required by the system under their consideration" ("Account of a Deputation," 52). "We have gradually declined into feebleness, anarchy, and wretchedness, from that period in which the several states began to exercise [usurped] the sovereign and absolute right of treating the recommendations of congress with contempt" (Z., "On the Philadelphia Convention," ibid. [1787], 420–423, esp. 421). The *Albany Gazette* and the *New-Hampshire Spy* warned of British plots to invade. Philadelphia newspapers rivaled one another in the ardor with which they called for a new, stronger central government. From the distance of several hundred years, the process seems carefully orchestrated, with May 14, 1787—the day the Philadelphia convention was scheduled to open—noteworthy for the number of major newspaper articles published that day praising the convention and demanding the adoption of a new constitution. See Patterson, *Authority, Autonomy, and Representation,* 50–53, esp. 53; John K. Alexander, *The Selling of the Constitutional Convention: A History of News Coverage* (Madison, Wis., 1990), 3–4, 16, 21–30.

6. "Political Œconomy: Part of Judge Pendleton's Charge to the Grand Jurors of Gagetown . . . in the State of Carolina," *American Museum,* I (1787), 483–487, esp. 487; A Bostonian, "View of the Federal Government, Letter I," ibid., 295; John Adams to Mercy Otis Warren, Jan. 8, 1776, in *Warren Adams Letters: Being Chiefly a Correspondence among John Adams, Samuel Adams, and James Warren,* I, *1743–1777,* Massachusetts Historical Society, *Collections* (Boston, 1917), 201–203, esp. 201. For an example of such lecturing, see M. W., "On a Liberal Education: Some New Remarks, from Experience," *Columbian Magazine,* I (1787), 263–267, esp. 263.

vision of the new republican citizen. More to the point, each was contradictory and inconsistent, "replete with alternatives, conflicts, and confusions," as J. G. A. Pocock put it. Transported to the New World, these conflicts and confusions came alive on the pages of newspapers and political magazines, during discussions in coffeehouses, artisan shops, and village taverns—all with an intensity not seen within the relative stability of eighteenth-century British political thought and social relations.[7]

It was out of these clashing discourses that the Revolutionary generation had to constitute an American identity. Just as the founding generation could not wait for the slow accumulation of precedent and tradition to constitute a government—the British model that Edmund Burke so proudly celebrated—so they could not wait for the gradual weaving together of the disparate peoples that inhabited the thirteen states. As a new constitution had to be written, so a new national identity had to be imagined, disseminated, and performed by citizens across the country. Only then could one say that a new nation was coming into being. Nothing was settled or coherent about this new identity as it tentatively took form on magazine pages and during public discussions. A bricolage of contentious political discourses, it was held together more by images of the enemies it struggled against than by any sense of rhetorical or ideological cohesion. To better understand the new American who emerged in the new urban magazines and the national identity he embodied, we must explore these political discourses as they struggled for ascendancy on magazine pages and within the minds of the new urban readers.[8]

BRAVE SONS OF LIBERTY

As freedom-loving and loyal citizens of the British Empire, eighteenth-century European Americans cut their political teeth on the hard biscuit of

7. J. G. A. Pocock, *The Machiavellian Moment: Florentine Political Thought and the Atlantic Republican Tradition* (Princeton, N.J., 1975), 446. See, as well, Étienne Balibar, "Subjection and Subjectivation," in Joan Copjec, ed., *Supporting the Subject* (London, 1994), 1–15, esp. 7, 9; and Chantal Mouffe, "Democratic Politics and the Question of Identity," in John Rajchman, ed., *The Identity in Question* (New York, 1995), 35–46; Smith, *Civic Ideals*, 14.

8. My concern in this study is to focus largely on the fault lines within the discourses and values that the northern bourgeoisie spoke, wrote, and attempted to impose upon their fellow citizens. At the same time, of course, ideological conflicts between those readers and other groups— Antifederalists, frontier farmers, urban artisans, freed African Americans, women from both middling and working ranks—were even more stark and in their turn contributed to the instability of the new national identity.

classic republican rhetoric. It incited them to resist British tyranny and corruption, helped them face the dangers and hardships of war, inspired them to think of themselves as fearless warriors willingly sacrificing their lives, their fortunes and their sacred honor for freedom's sake.[9] In the difficult years following the war's end, the new Americans again turned to classic republican discourses, generating a mythic heritage of virtue and sacrifice around which to weave an emerging national identity.

The classic republican citizen the magazines held up for their readers' emulation was first and foremost a virile figure. Modeled after Roman heroes—Cincinnatus, the Gracchi, Cato the Elder—he dedicated his life to serving his republic as a warrior, statesman, and legislator. Valuing liberty above life itself, he battled fearlessly to preserve his own and his country's freedom and independence. Disdaining commerce's soft comforts as effeminizing and corrupting, he was Spartan in the rigor of his life, his disdain for ostentatious display, his military prowess, his fierce leadership in times of crisis. He was, in short, the quintessential political and martial animal, in Aristotle's phrasing, a zoon politikon. Not for him the private domestic scene, the pleasures of leisure and accumulating wealth. He lived on the heroic plane of political crises met, battles bravely fought, tyranny and corruption vanquished. He was a man of passion—passion for liberty, passion for his nation's honor—but always, of

9. In doing so, they turned frequently to classic British republican texts. Julie K. Ellison reminds us that Patrick Henry's immortal "Is life so dear or peace so sweet as to be purchased at the price of chains and slavery?" as well as Nathan Hale's dying words ("I only regret that I have but one life to lose for my country") were inspired by Joseph Addison's *Cato: A Tragedy,* a play frequently performed in America in the years immediately preceding the Revolution (Ellison, *Cato's Tears and the Making of Anglo-American Emotion* [Chicago, 1999], 68). On a considerably more earthy level, a contributor to the *Pennsylvania Packet* of 1777 invoked the spirit of classic republicanism's celebration of the politically courageous citizen—and, at the same time, the sexual implications of that rhetoric. "Let them call me rebel, and welcome, I feel no concern from it," he wrote at the war's beginning, "but I should suffer the misery of devils where I to make a whore of my soul by swearing allegiance to one, whose character is that of a sottish, stuped, stubborn, worthless, brutish man." See "The American Crisis, no. 1," *Dunlap's Pennsylvania Packet; or, The General Advertiser,* Jan. 4, 1777, an essay that sought to stir patriotic feelings by arguing, "The heart that feels not now, is dead: The blood of his children shall curse his cowardice, who shrinks back at a time when a little might have saved the whole." "'Tis the business of little minds to shrink," the essay continued, "but he whose heart is firm, and whose conscience approves his conduct, will pursue his principles onto death." Throughout the 1770s, the *Pennsylvania Packet* continued to deploy such classical republican rhetoric and arguments. See, for example, *Pennsylvania Packet and the General Advertiser, supplement,* Feb. 3, 1772; and *Pennsylvania Packet; or, The General Advertiser,* Jan. 11, Feb. 18, 1777.

course, passion governed by manly reason and moderation. Service tied to responsibility was his guiding mantra.

A man of courage, self-sacrifice, and resolution, the classic republican must also be a man of absolute political independence. Neither his sword, his pen, nor his vote could be corrupted. But political independence rested on economic independence. And true economic independence must be grounded on land. Only secure landed estates would enable a man to rise above self-interest, a righteous leader of his republic. A man whose wealth and status were tied to commerce and speculation would be blown about by the winds of chance. Such a man could not aspire to true republican virtue.[10]

Magazines played a critical role in forging this identity. Recalling European Americans' proud wartime heritage, they transformed the courage and sacrifices of the Revolutionary generation into a patriotic myth of military heroes purified by the trials of battle. "Ye martial bands! Columbia's fairest pride!" enthused a 1782 poem written to celebrate "the armies of the united states of America" and republished five years later in one of the *American Museum's* earliest issues.

> *To toils inur'd, in dangers often try'd—Ye gallent youths! whose breasts for glory burn*
>
> .   .   .   .
>
> *Ye who, unmov'd, in the dread hour have stood,*
> *And smil'd, undaunted, in the field of blood.*

Other contributors concurred, celebrating those who fought for Independence as "forceful," "commanding," "self-reliant," and "freedom loving." These brave warriors had "disdained . . . the united efforts of lawless power and oppression" and defeated the world's most powerful empire. "We have broken

---

10. Pocock's *Machiavellian Moment* has long been considered the definitive study of classic republican thought in eighteenth-century Britain. See, as well, Pocock's *Virtue, Commerce, and History: Essays on Political Thought and History, Chiefly in the Eighteenth Century* (Cambridge, 1985), 37–50. The list of scholars tracing classic republicanism's influence on America's revolution against Great Britain reads like a Who's Who of leading historians. See, among others, Wood, *Creation of the American Republic;* Bernard Bailyn, *The Ideological Origins of the American Revolution* (Cambridge, Mass., 1967); Edmund S. Morgan, *The Birth of the Republic, 1763–1789,* rev. ed. (Chicago, 1977); Lance Banning, *The Jeffersonian Persuasion: Evolution of a Party Ideology* (Ithaca, N.Y., 1978). For an older but still highly respected study of classic republicanism in Britain, see Caroline Robbins, *The Eighteenth-Century Commonwealthman . . .* (Cambridge, Mass., 1959).

the shackles, which the oppressive hand of tyranny had prepared for us," effused "An Old Soldier," writing in Philadelphia's *American Museum*. "We have become a free people." Self-governance and self-determination were their "birthrights," another writer announced, rights "we have vindicated with our swords."[11]

Of course, none exemplified such virtues with greater authority than George Washington, the brightest star in its galaxy of patriotic heroes, the new nation's Cincinnatus. "By his example, his activity his energy," "[his] manly boldness," "penetration," "and judgment," magazine contributors assured their readers, he "knew how to govern freemen in peace, and by his example . . . taught them to love glory and danger." But, though first in peace as he had been in war, Washington did not stand alone. The new magazines surrounded him with a host of other military heroes: General Nathaniel Greene, celebrated for "the ardent spirit of liberty with which his bosom glowed"; the "fallen hero" Lieutenant Colonel John Laurens, who "unit[ed] the bravery and . . . talents of a great officer, with the knowledge of . . . a scholar, and the engaging manners of a well-bred gentleman"; and the Marquis de Lafayette, "an Intrepid Soldier, a Skilful Commander, an Ardent Lover of Liberty, a Disinterested Patriot, and A True Philanthropist."[12]

Military heroes were not the only exemplars the magazines held up for the readers to emulate. Now that the Revolution had been won, virtuous republicans must turn their attention to the peaceful contributions they could make to the Republic. "A good husband—a good father—and a good master, are proper characters for a monarchy, where selfishness reigns in proportion to the degrees

11. Columbus [St. George Tucker], "Reflexions on the Policy and Necessity of Encouraging the Commerce of the Citizens of the United States of America . . . ," *American Museum*, II (1787), 263–274, esp. 265; "Address to the Armies of the United States of America . . . ," ibid., I (1787), 230–240 (this poem was followed by a second, classic republican celebration of Revolutionary soldiers, "A Poem on the Happiness of America . . . ," 240–263); An Old Soldier, "Essay on Paper-Money," ibid., II (1787), 34–36, esp. 36; "On Public Faith," ibid., I (1787), 405–408, esp. 407; "The Evil Consequences of Party Spirit," ibid., 185–186.

12. "Portrait of General Washington," *Columbian Magazine*, I (1787), 227–229, esp. 228. For similar praise of Washington, see "Major George Washington's Journal . . . ," *Massachusetts Magazine*, I (1789), 346–351; and Rev. Jedidiah Morse, "Memoirs of General Washington," ibid. (1789), 286–290; "Sketch of the Life of the Late Nathaniel Greene," *Columbian Magazine*, I (1786), 1–3, esp. 3. See, as well, an essay printed the following year: William Hillhouse, Esq., "An Oration in Commemoration of Major-General Nathaniel Greene . . . ," *American Museum*, II (1787), 337–343; and see David Ramsay, "Review of the History of the Revolution of South Carolina . . . ," *Columbian Magazine*, I (1786), 22–25; "Character of Lieutenant-Colonel John Laurens," ibid., 24–25, esp. 25; dedication and frontispiece of *American Museum*, II (1787), iii.

of tyranny," the *American Museum* stated. "A good citizen is the highest character for a man in a republic. The first duty we owe is to God—the second to our country—and the third to our families. The man who inverts the gradation of these duties, breaks in upon the order of nature, established by God for the happiness and freedom of the world." Ironically, given later political antagonisms, the magazines held up Thomas Jefferson as the model of selfless devotion to the Republic in peace as in war. The magazines praised him as the fearless author of the nation's declaration of independence from Great Britain, wartime governor of Virginia, and diplomat extraordinaire. He was a statesman, a scientist, an architect, an inventor, and a litterateur. Never had he hesitated to respond to his nation's call. Willingly, he had neglected his own economic interests, impoverished his estate, sacrificed his comfort. At all times, he had brought his remarkable intellect and broad reading to serve his nation's needs. He was, in the words of Philadelphia's elegant *Columbian Magazine,* "a senator of America, who sat for two years in the famous Congress which brought about the Revolution." The reach of his knowledge "was universal."[13]

As a model republican gentleman, Jefferson was, above all, a landed gentleman. Indeed, this was true of all the republican heroes the magazines held up: Washington, Laurens, Greene, and Jefferson. Moreover, like Athenians and Romans before them, these men derived their wealth and status from a slave labor economy. It was their ability to exploit other men's labor that enabled them to devote themselves so selflessly and dispassionately to the preservation of their own personal freedom, the good of their Republic, and the glory of their nation.[14] If one could not be like them (because one lacked independent

13. Sidney, "Maxims for Republics," *American Museum,* II (1787), 80–82, esp. 81; "Characters, Mr. Jefferson," *Columbian Magazine,* I (1787), 555–556. Ten years earlier, at one of the darkest moments during the war, "Junius" had made very similar remarks in the *Pennsylvania Packet:* "Next to the duty we owe the supreme Being, we lie under the most indispensable obligations to promote the welfare of our country. . . . In nothing, says Cicero, do we bear a stronger resemblance to the divinity" (Junius, "To the King," *Dunlap's Pennsylvania Packet; or, The General Advertiser,* Jan. 11, 1777). See, as well, *Pennsylvania Packet and the General Advertiser,* Dec. 23, 1771.

14. Even Greene, though a northerner at the time of the Revolution, can be included in this list. Immediately after the war, Greene invested heavily in the purchase of southern land and slaves, emerging as a significant planter and slaveholder.

It is here that we are reminded of classic republicanism's indebtedness to Aristotle's political vision—most notably his vision of the virtuous republican citizen as a landed slaveowner and his belief that some individuals were "naturally" slaves. See Sir Ernest Barker, ed., *The Politics of Aristotle* (Oxford, 1946); Nicholas D. Smith, "Aristotle's Theory of Natural Slavery," *Phoenix,* XXXVII (1983), 109–122; Julie K. Ward, "*Ethnos* in the *Politics:* Aristotle and Race," in Julie K. Ward and Tommy L. Lott, eds., *Philosophers on Race: Critical Essays* (Oxford, 2002), 14–37; Bat-

wealth, classical education, and freedom from the need to labor), then one should subject oneself to their guidance and rule, for, all classic republicans understood, only those free from the need to labor for their living could aspire to truly virtuous, disinterested citizenship.[15]

And so we come to the conservative underbelly of eighteenth-century classic republicanism. Its association with the American Revolution notwithstanding, classic republicanism was an elite political philosophy, one the magazines repeatedly reinscribed for their bourgeois and would-be bourgeois readers. These were troubled times, magazine subscribers were warned, especially now that sovereignty rested with the people. The western frontier from Maine to the Carolinas was an economic and political tinderbox threatening to reignite the flames of rebellion. If not carefully guarded against, "mobocracy" would prove an even greater threat to liberty and virtue in the new Republic than British tyranny and corruption had been in the colonies. Citizenship carried as many responsibilities as it did rights. Essay after essay warned urban readers not to become intoxicated with the promises of radical popular sovereignty. The most extreme cases of tyrannical oppression alone justified open rebellion. In all other cases, virtuous citizens must submit to the direction of their propertied and educated leaders.[16]

In issuing such warnings, the new political magazines reiterated an old script. British classic republican texts such as *Cato's Letters* had been standard reading matter for educated European Americans since the mid-eighteenth century. Such texts not only called on their readers to love liberty above life itself and dedicate their lives to public service; they warned their readers of the dangers that would follow if the wrong people were allowed to become active members of the body politic. Britain's republican gentry envisioned the virtuous republic as a homogeneous community of landed gentlemen united by family ties, serving their country as justices of the peace, officers in the county militia, and members of Parliament.[17]

Ami Bar On, ed., *Engendering Origins: Critical Feminist Readings in Plato and Aristotle* (Albany, N.Y., 1994), esp. Elizabeth V. Spelman, "Who's Who in the Polis," 99–126, and Eve Cole Browning, "Women, Slaves, and 'Love of Toil' in Aristotle's Moral Philosophy," 127–144.

15. Jefferson, Adams, and others wanted to think of themselves as a "natural aristocracy" far superior to Europe's corrupt hereditary aristocracy.

16. "Select Fragments," *Columbian Magazine*, I (1787), 818–819; "Evil Consequences of Party Spirit," *American Museum*, I (1787), 185–186; Doctor Plainsense, "To the Editor of the Columbian Magazine," *Columbian Magazine*, I (1787), 805–806, esp. 805.

17. John Trenchard and Thomas Gordon, *Cato's Letters*, 4 vols. (London, 1723–1724); Adam Ferguson, *Essay on the History of Civil Society*, ed. Duncan Forbes (Edinburgh, 1966); David

Homogeneity was the key. The country gentry was convinced that "a highly homogeneous citizen body is a necessary condition of . . . stable republics," David F. Ericson explains. "In the absence of social homogeneity, there can be no public good." Homogeneity depended on exclusion. All who were different, who did not belong to the orderly world of manor houses and country gentlemen, endangered the Republic and must be shut out. Most obviously, the poor and the propertyless must be barred from political participation. They lacked the virtuous republican's education and independence. So did most artisans and petty shopkeepers. Not only were they dependent on custom and patronage, their votes and voices easily commanded by others, their vision rarely extended beyond their last or shop door. The British gentry went further, barring from virtuous citizenship all who worked, no matter how socially elevated. Even great London merchants and wealthy industrial entrepreneurs were suspect. The lines between those included and those excluded in the classic republican polis were broadly drawn and must be carefully policed.[18]

The exclusion of merchants and entrepreneurs brings us to another key aspect of British classic republicanism—its fear of change and modernity, most especially the economic and social changes brought on by the relentless sweep of commercial and fiscal capitalism. Combined, the country gentry insisted, these two ills had created an urban and industrial world driven by unrestrained desires for wealth and its ensuing power and pleasures. Not landed gentlemen but a bourgeoisie of merchants, fiscal capitalists, and entrepreneurs governed this world, a bourgeoisie that grew steadily in size, wealth, and power. Of all these new men, the most dangerous were the fiscal innovators and speculators, "stock jobbers," in eighteenth-century parlance. Unconnected to the solid world of lands planted and traditions preserved, they traded in fantasy, banked on appearances, and indulged in ostentatious display. Blinded by self-interest, they were anathemas to the liberty-loving Republic.[19]

Merchants, though they worked long hours and lacked the solid indepen-

---

Mallett, ed., The *Works of the Late Right Honorable Henry St. John, Lord Viscount Bolingbroke,* 5 vols. (London, 1754).

18. David F. Ericson, *The Shaping of American Liberalism: The Debates over Ratification, Nullification, and Slavery* (Chicago, 1993), 13. Patterson concurs. The gentry imagined a world in which "all ranks and degrees were organically connected"—and, of even greater importance, hierarchically structured. "Political authority corresponded to social power," Patterson explains, "enabling the leaders to define the underlying cultural and social rules" *(Authority, Autonomy, and Representation,* 23, 24). See also Pocock, *Machiavellian Moment,* 462–505, and for a discussion of the gentry's attitude toward land, see 423–461.

19. Pocock, *Machiavellian Moment,* chap. 13.

dence only landed estates could secure, occupied a more ambivalent position within classic republican discourses. Commerce was productive. A source of riches and of national strength, it increased scientific and ethnographic knowledge, refined taste, and polished manners. But trade was also seductive, threatening to entrap citizens in a web of fashionable display, indebtedness, and corruption. "New acquisitions bring new wants; and imaginary wants are as pungent as real ones," *Cato's Letters* warned, "so that there is the same end of wishing as of living, and death only can still the appetites." The appetites, unrestrained by reason, would render men like women, and women had no place within the pure confines of a model republic. Trade further depended upon credit, which hung upon opinion, rumor, and the passions of hope and fear. Slippery and irrational, often inflated, credit (and hence commerce) was the epitome of all that was dangerous in the seductive new economy. Classic republicans viewed the new men of trade and speculation with the deepest suspicion.[20]

However, the insistence that only those with landed estates could be truly virtuous was ill-suited to a world that depended on trade for its very existence. Highly selective in their transcriptions of classic republican principles, the magazines glossed over classic republicanism's suspicions of trade and fears of speculation. They chose to stress, rather, the classic republican association of patriotic virtue with gentlemanly status and the politics of deference. These were soothing words for troubled bourgeois ears. But many of the magazines' readers were too well versed in the classic texts to live easily with the magazines' effacements. America's new bourgeoisie needed a positive American identity that would resonate with their experiences—the long hours they worked, the commercial and fiscal risks they faced, their fears of financial ruin. They needed one that celebrated their productivity, talents, and contributions to the Republic.

INDUSTRIOUS MERCHANTS AND SELF-MADE MEN

So it was that, on the pages of the same magazines that held up Washington, Laurens, and Jefferson as models of republican virtue, readers met with an alternative set of republican characters who were far more representative of their economic and social lives. A modified form of republicanism had emerged in the eighteenth century, one historians refer to as commercial republicanism.[21]

---

20. Trenchard and Gordon, *Cato's Letters*, II, 42; Pocock, *Machiavellian Moment*, 462–477.

21. For discussions of commercial republicanism in both British and European American thought, see Isaac Kramnick, *Republicanism and Bourgeois Radicalism: Political Ideology in Late*

Commercial republicanism validated the economic changes the commercial and fiscal revolutions had brought, celebrated individual industry, productivity, and talent. Employing its strong cadences, magazines' contributors insisted that America's independence and genius were best represented, not by leisured gentlemen, but by the new Republic's self-reliant and productive men of trade and manufacturing. Such men did not fritter away their capital on fashionable display but, intelligent and judicious, reinvested in productive and profitable ventures. Through their industry and talent, they enriched themselves and made America great. In this way, men of trade and manufacturing stepped forth on magazine pages as exemplars of republican virtue and virility. "How respectable is he, who, trusting with a manly confidence to the efficacy of his own exertions," the struggling young publisher/entrepreneur Mathew Carey assured his readers, "encounters, with a due sense of energy, the various difficulties of life—and has no reproaches to make himself for a spiritless neglect of his concerns." Thinking perhaps of his own financial struggles, Carey continued, "Such men . . . through timely industry . . . are enabled to defy the ill-nature of what is called *fortune*—a word," he added, "often used by the indolent and undeserving, to screen their . . . want of application."[22]

Eighteenth-Century England and America (Ithaca, N.Y., 1990); and Marvin B. Becker, *The Emergence of Civil Society in the Eighteenth Century: A Privileged Moment in the History of England, Scotland, and France* (Bloomington, Ind., 1994). See, as well, Pocock, *Machiavellian Moment*, 432. Kramnick takes a quite critical view of some of Pocock's analyses, in particular his failure to note that a "city" vision of political economy coexisted with the country gentry's republicanism as part of the anti-court political philosophy of eighteenth-century Britain. For discussions of the involvement of such literary giants as Alexander Pope, Daniel Defoe, Joseph Addison, and Henry Fielding in the political and economic debates of the eighteenth century, see, for example, Patrick Brantlinger, *Fictions of State: Culture and Credit in Britain, 1694–1994* (Ithaca, N.Y., 1996); Edward A. Bloom and Lillian D. Bloom, *Joseph Addison's Sociable Animal: In the Market Place, on the Hustings, in the Pulpit* (Providence, 1971); James Thompson, *Models of Value: Eighteenth-Century Political Economy and the Novel* (Durham, N.C., 1996); Nancy Armstrong, *Desire and Domestic Fiction: A Political History of the Novel* (New York, 1987). The journal literature on this subject is voluminous. See, for example, Lois A. Chaber, "Matriarchal Mirror: Women and Capital in *Moll Flanders*," *Proceedings of the Modern Language Association*, XCVII (1982), 212–226; James Cruise, "Fielding, Authority, and the New Commercialism in Joseph Andrews," *English Literary History*, LIV (1987), 253–276.

22. "On the Advantage of Depending upon Our Own Exertions," *American Museum*, I (1787), 154 (emphasis added); Doctor Plainsense, "To the Editor of the Columbian Magazine," *Columbian Magazine*, I (1787), 805–806, esp. 805. We should note that Carey, when praising men of commerce, deployed the classical republican understanding of "fortune," as in "Fortuna," meaning the dangers change and commerce posed to civic *virtu*. Political discourses are multilayered and conflicted tools with which to constitute a unified and coherent political subject. A word

Whereas military heroism and diplomatic skills had won the war, the magazines assured their urban readers, commerce would win the peace, restore prosperity, and secure political stability. Magazine contributors pointed to American ships crisscrossing the seven seas, opening new trade routes and markets in the Mediterranean and Africa, China and the East Indies. Trade, they reminded their readers, deposited the wealth of the world on American wharves and created markets for the Republic's farming families, enabling them to purchase the goods trade had brought. "History records but two ways which nations have taken to raise themselves to any degree of opulence and power," an essayist in Carey's *American Museum* noted. "The first is by conquest, laying waste countries, murdering the inhabitants, and seizing the spoil. . . . This is wading or rather swimming to riches through a sea of blood." "The other method," he continued, "is by encouraging agriculture, manufactures and commerce." In direct contrast with classic republicanism's fear of commerce as effeminizing and corrupting, another essay assured urban readers that "a CIVILIZED nation, without commerce, is a solecism in politics." This was especially true of republics, since liberty and commerce went hand in hand.[23]

Warehouses of divergent discourses, the magazines presented their readers with a confusion of new republican roles. In the very issue of the *American Museum* in which Mathew Carey had praised the classic republican as "the highest character for a man in a republic," he heaped praise upon industrious merchants. In another issue, one essayist condemned the hardworking merchant for meddling in politics because he lacked the leisure and economic independence to devote himself selflessly to public service, whereas other writers insisted that the merchant's self-reliance and ambition strengthened the Republic and promoted the general good.[24]

---

carrying a particular meaning within one political discourse, when transposed to a second political discourse, acquires additional meanings, which, layered onto the original, gives the word a different resonance—an additional, often contradictory "spin."

23. American, "Essay on the Advantages of Trade and Commerce," *American Museum*, II (1787), 328–332; "The True Interest of the United States, and Particularly of [Pennsylvania?], Considered," ibid. (1787), 23. Merchants, manufacturers, and farmers, working in harmony, would create a powerful new nation ready to compete for commercial and imperial preeminence. Essays praising commerce were commonplace in the years leading up to Independence and later in the new magazines. See *Pennsylvania Packet and the General Advertiser,* Feb. 17, 1772, and *Dunlap's Pennsylvania Packet; or, The General Advertiser,* Jan. 17, 1777; A Plain but Real Friend to America [Benjamin Franklin], "On American Manufactures: Letter I," *American Museum*, I (1787), 16–19; [Franklin], "Comfort for America, or Remarks on Her Real Situation, Interests and Policies," ibid., 5; "On the Origin of Commerce," *American Magazine*, I (1788), 713–714.

24. "Essay on Money as a Medium of Commerce . . . ," *American Museum*, II (1787), 47; St.

The magazines' praise of manufacturing and manufacturers added still another layer of complexity. Although Britain's classic republican scripts might, on rare occasions, include an exceptional merchant among their cast of virtuous republican citizens, they never included hardworking manufacturers or leather-aproned artisans. In sharp contrast, the European American commercial republican script cast resourceful manufacturers and entrepreneurs as worthy contributors to the Republic.[25] Editors and writers wrapped domestic manufacturing in the cloak of patriotism, associating it with the nonimportation agreements that had played so critical a part in opposing Britain's imperial policies during the war years. "When the minds of the people of America were really *virtuous* at the beginning of the late [Revolutionary] contest," one essayist argued, "every man was convinced of the necessity of our encouraging manufactures and employing our own people, that we might be truly *independent*." Having helped defeat British tyranny, manufacturers would now increase America's prosperity and sustain her independence.[26] (We must note

---

George Tucker, "Reflections on the Policy and Necessity of Encouraging the Commerce of the Citizens of the United States of America . . . ," ibid., 263–274; "Extract of a Letter from His Excellency Thomas Jefferson, Minister Plenipotentiary at Paris . . . ," ibid., 492–493.

25. [Benjamin Franklin], "Causes of a Country's Growing Rich," *American Museum*, I (1787), 13; Sylvius, "Letter IV: Further Remarks on Tender Laws—Necessity of Encouraging American Manufactures . . . ," ibid., II (1787), 117–121; William Barton, "Plan of the Pennsylvania Society for the Encouragement of Manufactures and the Useful Arts," ibid., 167–169; "Address to an Asssembly of the Friends of American Manufactures . . . ," ibid., 248–255; "The Utility of Manufactures," ibid., 256–257; Samuel Miles, "Address of the Board of Managers of the Pennsylvania Society for the Promotion of Manufactures and Useful Arts," ibid., 360–362.

26. Not surprisingly, former artisan and entrepreneur Benjamin Franklin insisted that, if Americans were to maintain their political and economic autonomy, they must "work up . . . their native commodities, to the last degree of manufacture," emulate Revolutionary resolve by wearing their own manufactures, invest in American industry, and export as many of their manufactures as possible. "Our governments must . . . promote the introduction of useful manufactures and trades among us; and protect such as are already instituted," William Barton urged. "Thus we shall employ and enrich our own citizens; accelerate the population of an extensive and valuable country; and increase our national strength, dignity, and independence." "There is no branch of political economy, that more deserves the attention of a wise and prudent government," the *Columbian Magazine*'s "Americanus" insisted, "than that which tends to promote a spirit of industry amongst the people, and at the same time to maintain a *favorable commerce* with other nations." Southerners, as well as northerners, concurred. In an entry signed "Charleston, 1786," "America," echoing Montesquieu, argued that "trade and manufacturing, more than agriculture or conquest, [are] the source of national wealth and power." See [Franklin], "Causes of a Country's Growing Rich," *American Museum*, I (1787), 13; Barton, "Essay on the Promotion of American Manufactures," ibid. (1787), 257; Americanus, "On American Manufactures," *Columbian Magazine*, I (1786), 25–29 (emphasis added).

that, even as they praised manufacturing, the urban magazines never applauded journeymen and day laborers whose riots from the Stamp Act on had helped precipitate the Revolution. Manufacturers passed muster in the new bourgeois magazines, but not the wage- or even skilled laborers manufacturers employed.)[27]

No one celebrated domestic manufacturing's contributions to American welfare with more zeal than the former printer/publisher Benjamin Franklin. Indeed, Franklin went further, urging the government to actively support domestic manufacturing. Building up the nation's infant manufacturing sector, Franklin argued, the government would not only employ more European Americans at home; it would encourage skilled and productive foreigners to settle in the new Republic. Of perhaps even greater importance, such support would slow down the westward flight of many large and industrious families. To illustrate this latter point, Franklin deployed a story of a farmer who had numerous sons but a limited amount of cultivated land. If manufactures were not encouraged, such a farmer, a prosperous and productive member of his community, would sell his land and move his large family of energetic sons to the frontier, where land was cheap but life primitive. There, the farmer would clear a field and begin planting. But, as his farm lay far from any commercial center, he lacked easy access to transportation and could not engage in commercial agriculture. "He therefore raises little more than what the wants of his family call for," Franklin warned, "and thus the state derives little or no advantage from him and his family." Far from markets, churches, and schools, the farmer's ambition would evaporate. His family would cease to value education, becoming slovenly and idle. Illiteracy and irreligion would follow. If, on the other hand, the government encouraged manufacturing, fathers, sons, and their wives and children would remain in more densely populated areas, where they would pay taxes and purchase domestic manufactures—among them the newspapers and almanacs Franklin had made his reputation and his fortune publishing. As a result, "there would be employment for all, and our country would be more thickly settled, and increase in strength." Then America would begin to resemble the profitable and well-populated agrarian areas of England and the Continent. (As we see later, Franklin and his fellow bourgeois spokes-

27. It is important to note than many Antifederalists praised hardworking artisans, yeoman farmers, and small shopkeepers. See, for example, Saul Cornell, "Politics of the Middling Sort: The Bourgeois Radicalism of Abraham Yates, Melancton Smith, and the New York Antifederalists," in Paul A. Gilje and William Pencak, eds., *New York in the Age of the Constitution, 1775–1800* (Madison, N.J., 1992), 82.

men had no romantic vision of the American frontier and American fron-tiersmen.) Government support for manufacturing would also provide em-ployment for the urban poor, "deliver[ing] them from the curse of idleness," encouraging household economy, and preventing social disorder. The self-interest of manufacturing entrepreneurs benefited all: what was good for man-ufacturing was good for the country.[28]

Nevertheless, Franklin, along with many of his contemporaries, cautioned that the capitalist self-interest had its limits. Commercial republicans remained republicans, acknowledging their responsibility to work diligently to advance the interests of their fellow citizens and the honor and well-being of their Republic. Franklin pointed to his own long career of public service and to the host of positions of public trust he had held. Working with other public-spirited businessmen, Franklin had helped found America's first secular uni-versity (the College of Philadelphia, later the University of Pennsylvania), its first public hospital (Pennsylvania Hospital), and its premier scientific orga-nization (the American Philosophical Society). However, Philadelphia's fire companies best exemplify Franklin's approach to practical and self-interested civic virtue. The fire companies were private, volunteer organizations that brought citizens together to save their own and their neighbors' homes and thus to serve their city by preventing major urban conflagrations. From volun-tary, collective self-interest, all profited.[29]

As the magazines held up George Washington as a model classic republican, so they celebrated Franklin, artisan/printer-turned-inventor-turned-scientist-turned-diplomat and statesman, as the model of virtuous and productive com-mercial republicanism. None agreed more ardently than fellow printer and publisher Noah Webster. Franklin's long career, Webster argued, demonstrated that one did not have to be well born and well connected to be a virtuous republican. When national crises demanded it, "this man, who for many years carried on the business of a printer at Philadelphia," strode forth a "powerful engine . . . [who shook] a great empire, and erect[ed] a congeries of republics from its dismembered parts." Joel Barlow's representation of Franklin was even more graphic than Webster's.

28. A Plain but Real Friend to America [Franklin], "On American Manufactures: Letter I," *American Museum*, I (1787), 18, and "On American Manufactures: Letter II," ibid., 116–119.

29. Benjamin Franklin, *The Autobiography of Benjamin Franklin* (New York, 1984), 96, 128, 135, 148, 150; Albert H. Wurth, Jr., "The Franklin Persona: The Virtue of Practicality and the Practicality of Virtue," in Richard K. Mathews, ed., *Virtue, Corruption, and Self-Interest: Politi-cal Values in the Eighteenth Century* (Bethlehem, Pa., 1994), 76–102, esp. 85–89.

See on yon darkening height bold Franklin tread,
Heaven's awful thunders rolling o'er his head;
See the descending streams around him burn,
Glance on his rod and with his guidance turn.
He bids conflicting heavens their blasts expire,
Curbs the fierce blaze and holds the imprison'd fire.[30]

In the Federalist press, Franklin stepped forth the equal of such classic republican warriors and statesmen as Washington, Laurens, and Jefferson. He, as much as they, had defeated imperial Britain, secured American Independence, and helped establish the new Republic as one of the world's great empires. And more—"his rod," ablaze, had conquered the very heavens. Invoking this image of Franklin, the magazines rescued the commercial republican's virility and power.[31]

Imagining Franklin as a model American, however, brought its own problems. One of the most troubling was the stress Franklin placed on performativity. Repeatedly in his newspaper and almanac writings and in his *Autobiography*, Franklin suggested, using his own experiences as examples, that the appearance of diligence, honesty, and public-spiritedness was as important—perhaps more so—than actually being diligent, honest, and public-spirited. Franklin's advice thus strongly countered classic republicans who associated civic virtue with absolute transparency.[32]

Franklin's repeated celebration of the self-interested individual further troubled European Americans brought up on classic republican principles. "The Franklin persona," Albert Wurth points out, "embodies an inescapable tension between its explicit defense of the individual pursuit of self-interest (reflected in Franklin's rise to prominence) and an implicit anxiety about the adequacy of self-interest as a model of the virtuous citizen. . . . Complementing but under-

30."Monthly Miscellany: Anecdotical Notices of Dr. Franklin," *American Magazine*, I (1788), 810–811; Joel Barlow, "The Columbian Parnassiad. . . . Extract from the Seventh Book, or the Progress of Arts in America . . . ," *Columbian Magazine*, I (1787), 443–444.

31. In this epic inscription of Franklin, we find a refiguring of the man of commerce as a phallic figure, indeed, as a figure renowned for his burning rod. Whether in celebration or in satire, Franklin seemed to call out phallic images.

32. Benjamin Franklin, *The Autobiography*, rpt. in Walter Isaacson, ed., *A Benjamin Franklin Reader* (New York, 2003), esp. 454–455, 459; Patterson, *Authority, Autonomy, and Representation*, 10. Patterson points out that Franklin's *Autobiography* is comprised of quite different segments, reflecting the very different lives he lived. The question eighteenth-century republicans would ask, however, is, Can you trust a man whose life was so self-consciously discontinuous?

cutting one another, these two themes pull in different directions." In the short run, Franklin's writings permit an association of self-interest with virtue. But, in the long run, "the Franklin persona emerges as problematic, an ambiguous but revealing legacy . . . anticipating liberalism's inherent dilemmas." This was especially true given Franklin's repeated ruptures of family ties (refusing his older brother's authority, breaking his apprenticeship) and his notorious philandering. Along with his embrace of self-interest and performativity, these behaviors threatened traditional republican associations of social order with community cohesion and patriarchal family order. Could one really trust the self-interested, performative subject?[33]

Even Franklin admitted that it was only his personal sense of civic responsibility and the personal pleasure he took from serving his city and his state that led him to devote himself to public service later in life. And even then, questions arose. As he served his country, how well had he simultaneously served himself? While Franklin coyly assumed the persona of Poor Richard or, under the guise of a letter to his (illegitimate) son, detailed his early economic travails, many found him elitist in his ambitions, dishonest in his political practices, and opposed to the interests of middling and poor Philadelphians. Years of political activity in Pennsylvania proved Franklin no democrat. Even among those as elitist as Franklin himself, his egotism proved troubling. Not the least among the annoyed was John Adams. In a letter to Benjamin Rush (a letter whose humor satirizes Barlow's patriotic representation of the phallic Franklin), Adams complained that Franklin, through his adept manipulation of the political press, had so puffed up his own political importance that "the History of our Revolution will be that Dr. Franklin's electric Rod smote the earth and out sprang General Washington." "That Franklin electrised him with his rod, and thence-forward these two conducted all the policy, negotiations, legislatures and war."[34]

33. Wurth, "Franklin Persona," in Mathews, ed., *Virtue, Corruption, and Self-Interest*, 76–102, esp. 76, 96. Wurth reads Franklin's *Autobiography* as a "systematic and thoroughgoing destruction of the claims of traditional authority. . . . Virtually all authority is suspect. Franklin confronts and systematically rejects the claims of family, church, community." This was a radical and disturbing message for eighteenth-century Americans (77–78, 86). Indeed, for all the patriotic myths that have grown up around Franklin, he was at best a very controversial figure in eighteenth-century Philadelphia. He certainly had his enemies, especially among Philadelphia's Quakers but also among many other groups. See Robert Middlekauff, *Benjamin Franklin and His Enemies* (Berkeley, Calif., 1996).

34. Middlekauff, *Franklin and His Enemies*, esp. chaps. 3 and 4; John Adams, quoted by Robert A. Ferguson, *The American Enlightenment, 1750–1820* (Cambridge, Mass., 1997), 2. For

Commercial republicanism, especially as exemplified by Franklin, wedded abashed self-interest and self-advancement to selfless dedication to the general good. Could these two opposing visions of republican virtue live in harmony? Would European American readers be able to meld them into a coherent self and national image, one that they could then perform and thereby become?

THE MANY FACES OF LIBERALISM

The same political magazines that alternatively applauded the virtuous republican's unselfish dedication to public service and his ambitious self-interest introduced their readers to yet another divergent and even more complex figure—the new American—as—liberal citizen. "The genius" of liberalism, Nancy Stepan proclaims, was its conceptualization of man as a *"universal individual* . . . the bearer of equal political rights . . . unmarked by . . . myriad specificities."* Where republicanism had grounded a man's claim to civic virtue and active citizenship in his actions and position in society, liberalism declared all men, by the mere right of birth, possessed of the inalienable right to freedom. The disembodied representative of "a common . . . political humanity," the liberal subject "opened the door to the modern polis."[35] The font of political sovereignty, the liberal subject was the heroic protagonist of the mythic

---

background to the quote, see Middlekauff, *Franklin and His Enemies,* chap. 7, esp. 185. The sexual implications embedded in the statement are hard to ignore.

35. Such, certainly, was how the foundational document of the new United States, the Declaration of Independence, presented him. Stripping the new American of all modifying social characteristics, endowing him with equality and inalienable natural rights, celebrating his reason and independence, it proclaimed him every political man. Representative republican government rested on his consent. Commenting on this Revolutionary aspect of liberalism, Carole Pateman calls it "the emancipatory doctrine *par excellence*" (Pateman, *The Sexual Contract* [Stanford, Calif., 1988], 39). See also Nancy Leys Stepan, "Race, Gender, Science, and Citizenship," in Catherine Hall, ed., *Cultures of Empire: Colonizers in Britain and the Empire in the Nineteenth and Twentieth Centuries* (New York, 2000), 61–86, esp. 63. "Human nature, in the glorious exercise of its own powers, under governments chosen as the object of great deliberation, and under a perfect conception of its inestimable rights and faculties," William Vans Murray declared shortly after Pennsylvania's ratification of the new constitution, "demands nothing but the enjoyment of itself." In such a situation, under such a government, "the noblest truths are unfolded by the improvement of his reason; his rights are ascertained; and the virtues of his heart become meliorated and multiplied" (Murray, "Political Sketches," *American Museum,* II [1787], 220–248, esp. 230). Isaiah Thomas's *Massachusetts Magazine* quickly joined in. "The term *man,*" it assured Bostonians, "comprizes and conveys the idea of something excellent" ("The Philanthropist, no. VI," *Massachusetts Magazine,* I [1789], 337–338).

social contract. He had contracted the modern republican state into existence to protect his personal liberties and, most critically, his private property. That accomplished, the liberal subject was then free to follow his self-interest wherever it might lead. The only qualification was that his self-interest not interfere with the rights and freedoms of other citizens. The liberal citizen thus emerged on the pages of the political magazines as a self-interested private man, the antithesis of the virtuous republican.

In conflict with both classic and commercial republicanism, liberalism was itself an inharmonious composite of divergent discourses and ideologies. From Voltaire, Montesquieu, and Condorcet, liberalism garnered a vision of universal brotherhood. Hugo Grotius, Pufendorf, and Beccaria added natural rights to the mix. From Voltaire's writings, liberals parsed religious skepticism—and acquired a fascination with science and technology. Rousseau envisioned the liberal as an independent citizen, as, in very different ways, did John Locke. To see how this multilayered political subject took form within the new American Republic, let us return to the political magazines.[36]

From continental Enlightenment writers, the magazines appropriated an idealized image of man as rational, human nature as "glorious," and mankind as perfectible. The antithesis of an earlier Calvinist image of man as a sinner, the new American—as—liberal subject belonged to a universal brotherhood that "unite[d] all men of sense, knowledge, and worthy qualities . . . by the great principle of virtue." Sameness in nature and in rights connected all, an essayist in Carey's *American Museum* noted. "Men are not to be essentially distinguished by the difference of tongues which they speak, of the clothes which they wear, of countries which they inhabit. The whole world is no other than one great republic, of which each nation is a family, and each individual a child." Here we find continental liberalism at its most inclusive.[37]

"The Trifler," a regular contributor to the *Columbian Magazine,* was even more audacious in his transcription of French Enlightenment concepts. Reflecting French philosophes' criticisms of religious orthodoxy in a way that undoubtedly shocked many of his readers, he attacked religion for "promot[ing]

---

36. Ferguson, *American Enlightenment,* 35–36.

37. Embracing a vision of universal perfectibility, the essay continued that, if all virtuous men embraced the Masonic vision, "the interest of the fraternity might become that of the whole human race; . . . all nations might increase in knowledge; and . . . every subject of every country, might exert himself without jealousy, live without discord, and embrace mutually, without forgetting, or too scrupulously remembering, the spot in which he was born" ("The Influence of Free Masonry upon Society, Philosophically Enquired Into: With an Account of the Institution," *American Museum,* I [1787], 545–550).

animosities and persecutions." As a consequence, men must be allowed perfect freedom of thought and expression. Religious opinions were dangerous because they "divide the world into sects and factions." The Trifler then urged Philadelphians to found an "Order of Merit," modeled on the Masonic order, its goal to "[excite] men to contemplate their duty . . . [and] inform their judgments in right or proper actions." The society would strike a medal for each member. On one side would be an engraving of public virtue and the motto *Quique fui mers alios secere merendo;* on the reverse, the image of the Good Samaritan and the motto *Miseris succurrere.* A true liberal, the Trifler had no need of the state. Free men, united in private voluntary organizations, could perfect the world.[38]

Despite his egalitarian rhetoric, however, the Trifler's society would be an elite institution rich enough to create a medal for each of its members, who, in their turn, were sufficiently erudite to read and derive pleasure (and perhaps social status?) from Latin engravings. The Trifler's society leads one to wonder where, on the pages of the new magazines, was the disembodied, unmarked figure Stepan celebrates as "the genius . . . of liberalism"? The magazines' representation of the liberal subject carried a thick set of social credentials: wealth, education, the time and resources to engage in philanthropic ven-

---

38. The Trifler, "No. V," *Columbian Magazine,* I (1787), 628–630, esp. 629. On one level, of course, the Trifler's espousal of cosmopolitanism, his commitment to universal brotherhood, and his religious skepticism represent the serious embrace of European Enlightenment values. Still, the Trifler's choice of a nom de plume deserves our attention. Why did the magazine's editors introduce such weighty matters under the title "Trifles"? Why did the essayist inscribe himself a trifler? Were the editors and the author attempting to camouflage their inscriptions of bold, Deistic sentiments as "trifling," using humor to cloak serious intellectual criticism? On the other hand, if the Trifler was suggesting that his religious criticisms were mere trifles, then were political liberty and brotherly love, which he espoused so eloquently, trifles also? The Trifler was not the only essayist to question religious orthodoxy—nor was the urbane *Columbian Magazine* alone in its willingness to publish such essays. Noah Webster included a similarly unorthodox essay, "A Rhapsody: Par Mons Abridgement of the Laws of Nature," in his *American Magazine.* This time, the criticism of religious orthodoxy appeared, not under the pseudonym "Trifler," but as part of a romantic paean to "Nature." (This essay was undoubtedly pirated from a liberal British journal, which in its turn might have translated an essay found in a European publication. Like commerce, the late-eighteenth-century press connected the far corners of the Atlantic.) The essay began with a challenge. "Thou dupe of superstition, return to nature," it counseled; "she will console thee; she will expel from thy heart the fears which oppress thee. Cease to contemplate the future—live for thyself—for thy kindred beings. I approve thy pleasures, which, without annoying thyself, will not injure thy brethren." Such expressions of Continental-inspired liberalism pushed the limits of European Americans' urbane tolerance ("A Rhapsody: Par Mons Abridgement of the Laws of Nature," *American Magazine,* I [1788], 131–133).

tures. These were precisely the credentials that, Uday Singh Mehta argues, served as "preconditions for the actualization" of liberalism's promised rights—preconditions that made class, race, and gender critical to individuals' claims to freedom, equality, and inalienable rights.[39]

But while the voices of European liberalism echoed across the pages of the new magazines, the liberal subject who appeared there most frequently was a creation of the Scottish Enlightenment and, most specifically, of Locke's writings. Far from seeing himself as a zoon politikon, selflessly devoted to the state, the new American–as–Lockean liberal was a private man who sought pleasure and happiness in developing his talents and accumulating capital. The state, he was sure, existed to protect and serve him, not he the state. As William Vans Murray wrote, "The office of government is to protect. . . . Every addition of restraint [is] a departure from natural liberty."[40]

The sanctity of private property was a central Lockean tenet, one that the magazines embraced. In so doing, they transformed classic republicans' understanding of liberty. Rather than standing for a man's right to participate in the governance of the Republic, liberty was refigured as the fundamental right to accumulate private property—and property as an absolute good in its own right. As one magazine expressed it, "Among the senses inherent in the nature of man, the sense of property is eminent." The right to private property incorporated the right to acquisition and accumulation—for the benefit and pleasure of the self. What a contrast to classic republican admonitions! It was with these words that the editors of the *Columbian Magazine* introduced an essay by Henry Home, Lord Kames (a leading liberal writer). This essay appeared at a critical moment, November 1787, a month after the Continental Congress submitted the new Federal constitution to the states for their examination and the very same month that the Pennsylvania legislature began to debate the new constitution's ratification, just a few blocks from where the *Columbian Magazine* was printed.[41]

39. Uday Singh Mehta, "Strategies: Liberal Conventions and Imperial Exclusions," in Mehta, *Liberalism and Empire: A Study in Nineteenth-Century British Liberal Thought* (Chicago, 1999), 46–72, esp. 49.

40. Murray, "Political Sketches," *American Museum*, II (1787), 220–231. Individual freedom, Locke insisted in his *Two Treatises of Government*, rested on a man's ownership of his own body, his labor, and the products of his labor. "Every Man has a Property in his own Person," Locke stated. "The Labours of his Body and the *Work* of his Hands . . . are properly his" (Locke, *Second Treatise of Government*, in Locke, *Two Treatises of Government*, ed. Peter Laslett (Cambridge, 1965), II, 27).

41. [Henry Home], Lord Kaims, "On the Progress of Mankind, with respect to Property,"

Far from apologizing for man's acquisitive nature or seeing it as a source of corruption, Lord Kames proclaimed acquisitiveness not only as a private right but as a social good. "The appetite for property is not bestowed upon us in vain," he insisted; "it has given birth to many useful arts, and to almost all the fine arts . . . without private property, what place would there be for benevolence or charity? Without private property there will be no industry, and without industry men would remain savages for ever." Of course, Kames adds, the desire for property can become excessive, producing its own form of human savagery. But, if guided by moderation and enabled by industry, it opens the door to pleasure and gaiety. "The beautiful productions of industry and art, rousing the imagination, excite a violent desire of fine houses, ornamented gardens, and of every thing gay and splendid." Lord Kames's essay provided America's bourgeoisie and emerging middling classes with a vigorous justification for self-interest, self-advancement, and, yes, ostentatious consumerism. Men who did not embrace self-interest and consumerism, who did not own "fine houses and ornamental gardens," were little better than "savages" (a highly racialized aspersion).[42]

In so many ways, republicanism and liberalism were mirror opposites— republicanism celebrating the zoon politikon, liberalism, the private citizen; republicanism, Spartan asceticism and dedication to the general good, liberalism, and self-interested capitalist acquisition. Classic republican rhetoric represented the republic as vulnerable, threatened by corruption and requiring its heroic citizens' vigilant support. For liberals, the state had become a threat to the individual's enjoyment of his private property. Classic republicanism condemned the private man as unheroic and unmanly, the private world as a distraction from man's noble engagement in the political. From a classic republican perspective, the liberal citizen appeared dangerously like the figure Carey's *American Museum* had condemned as "a proper character in a monarchy where selfishness reigns in proportion to the degrees of tyranny." Under his facade of natural rights, republicans asked, was the liberal little more than a self-absorbed, private figure, driven by self-interest, concerned first with the preservation of his property and his independence and only secondarily—if at all—with promoting the general good? In contrast, liberalism warned that classic republicanism sacrificed individual liberty to the good of the state. On the surface, commercial republicanism and liberalism appear to have more in

Columbian Magazine, I (1787), 813–816, esp. 813. It is worth noting that Lord Kames was one of Benjamin Franklin's frequent correspondents.

42. Ibid., 815.

common. The commercial republican script recognized the importance of the private economic sphere and of man's right to pursue his own interests. Still, it argued, commercial actors (merchants, manufacturers, scientists, and doctors) were virtuous members of the public, not because they had accumulated personal wealth and learning, but because, in serving themselves, they served the common good. In contrast to Lord Kames, commercial republicans condemned extravagant display and celebrated frugality as an economic virtue redounding to the good of the whole. "Violent desire" was not part of their rhetoric.

Even more fundamentally, liberalism's focus on the self-interested individual threatened both classic and commercial republicanism's sense of community. It escalated the threats to traditional systems of authority and social order at which Franklin's self-presentations as the autonomous, self-made man had merely hinted. To eighteenth-century men, an individual without strong ties to family, traditional institutional structures, and his community seemed remarkably like a man caught in a Hobbesian state of nature, engaged in a ruthless war of all against all, driven by fear and savagery. How were social order, stability, and civic virtue to be maintained if society was composed of such self-involved and isolated figures?[43]

Eighteenth-century Scottish liberalism mediated its vision of the intensely isolated individual by envisioning him as inhabiting a world governed by the sentiments and benevolence. By midcentury, a faith in the social efficacy of individual sentiments, governed always by reason and moderation, was commonplace among liberal thinkers. Sympathetic feelings, Locke, David Hume, and Adam Smith argued, would bind individuals to one another and to society in a highly personal and affective manner. The liberal individual, observing another person in pain or sorrow, would identify with the feelings the sufferer displayed. At the same time, he would be observed by other feeling individuals. The first observer's sympathetic feelings would inspire equally deep feelings in

43. Republican discourses insisted that the object of society was to connect the individual to his fellow citizens and to the collective good. Only then would the individual act as an ethical member of the collective body politic. If the raison d'être of national identities was to give the individual a sense of being part of a national "we," how could that need be satisfied by an identity derived from liberal concepts of individualism, autonomy, and privacy? Rogers M. Smith argues that liberalism, with its emphasis on the isolated individual and its suspicion of both the state and the community, did not provide the emotional or rhetorical substance to build a national identity around. I will discuss Smith's arguments at greater length later in this chapter (Smith, "'One United People': Second-Class Female Citizenship and the American Quest for Community," *Yale Journal of Law and the Humanities*, I [1989], 229–293, esp. 229).

those observing him. An ever-expanding network of sympathies would knit observers and the observed together—even across class, racial, and gendered divides. Social connections would multiply. This circulation of feelings among people would create a new—and totally apolitical—form of social bonding (not unlike the benefits that would result from the circulation of goods and money). Hume explained in his much-read *Treatise of Human Nature,* "As in strings equally wound up, the motion of one communicates itself to the rest; so all the affections readily pass from one person to another, and beget correspondent movements in every human creature." For Hume, the sympathies comprised a central component of modern structure in social relations, leading not only to social cohesion but to the amelioration of poverty and the soothing of unhappiness. Thus social cohesion and the general good would be accomplished, not in the public arena by zoon politikons sacrificing their self-interest for the general good, but in the private sphere by feeling individuals who dispensed charity with delicacy and accepted it with gratitude. It was a world in which noblesse oblige evoked deference and rewarded dependency. It was a world of spectators and spectacles.[44]

Such was the vision espoused by the anonymous author of "Affecting Anecdote of the Late CHARLES CHURCHILL," an essay Noah Webster reprinted in one of the first issues of his *American Magazine.* (Since the author had also written *The Adventures of a Guinea,* it would appear he was at home with both liberal and imperialist discourses.) As the tale began, New York readers were presented with the picture of Churchill, a youthful and well-to-do gentleman, "staggering

44. David Hume, *A Treatise of Human Nature,* ed. P. H. Nidditch (Oxford, 1978), 576, cited by Adela Pinch, *Strange Fits of Passion: Epistemologies of Emotion, Hume to Austin* (Stanford, Calif., 1996), 24. For general discussions of eighteenth-century stress upon the importance of the sympathies, see, among others, Janet Todd, *Sensibility: An Introduction* (London, 1986); G. J. Barker-Benfield, *The Culture of Sensibility: Sex and Society in Eighteenth-Century Britain* (Chicago, 1992); Bloom and Bloom, *Addison's Sociable Animal;* John Dwyer, *Virtuous Discourse: Sensibility and Community in Late Eighteenth-Century Scotland* (Edinburgh, 1987); John Mullan, *Sentiment and Sociability: The Language of Feeling in the Eighteenth Century* (Oxford, 1988). A significant shift in the sympathies' social function occurred between the seventeenth and eighteenth centuries. In the seventeenth century, the sympathies were seen as a noble male emotion that connected men within the same class, even if they differed by nation. In the eighteenth century, the sympathies were seen much more as facilitating bonding across class, between the wealthy philanthropist and the pathetic object of his concern. For a detailed analysis of earlier republican sympathies, see Ellison, *Cato's Tears.* Laura Brown's *Ends of Empire* provides a bridge connecting these two forms of the sympathies. For a variant on Ellison's understanding of the social and ideological work the sympathies performed, see Julia A. Stern, *The Plight of Feeling: Sympthy and Dissent in the Early American Novel* (Chicago, 1997).

home late one night from a party with some of his *libertine* companions." Rounding a London corner, Churchill came upon a young girl with "something in air and manner . . . different from those outcasts of humanity who offer themselves to casual prostitution in the streets." Viewing her "with silent compassion for some moments," he offered her a few coins. When she fell to her knees, praying heaven to reward him for his generosity, the dissipated Churchill was deeply touched. "Rais[ing] her tenderly from the ground," Churchill asked the young supplicant, "Can humanity feel greater wants than those under which you are sinking?" Tearfully, she begged him to aid her aged father and her starving mother and siblings. Churchill visited the family, offered them a modicum of relief, and was rewarded by their elaborate expressions of Christian gratitude and social deference. "When the moment he entered the room," he found "the whole family . . . upon their knees to thank him." Churchill continued to assist the family until the father found employment and patriarchal authority was restored within this laborer's domestic circle.[45]

By either classic or commercial republican standards, Churchill could make few, if any, claims to civic virtue. His libertine past (and future, for all the reader knows), his evident lack of employment or a profession, and the private nature of his actions disqualified him. Patronage and largesse, dependency and gratitude all signaled political corruption, tyranny, and feminized domestic space. Sympathy and gratitude were emotions appropriate to relations between masters and servants, patrons and dependents, husbands and wives—not those between equal, independent citizens. They would corrupt the political agora. In contrast, the spontaneity of his sympathetic response to the beggar girl/ prostitute and her family, his efforts to reestablish her family's domestic stability, and the fact that all was done in a private and affecting manner (with many tears on both sides) proved Churchill capable of sincere feelings that led him to alleviate human suffering. A failed republican, Churchill emerged a paradigm of sentimental liberal virtue.

The "Affecting Anecdote" underscores the very different worlds republicans and liberals imagined. Republicanism despised dependency and spectacular

---

45. [Charles Johnstone], "Affecting Anecdote, of the Late Charles Churchill: Written by the Author of 'The Adventures of a Guinea,'" *American Magazine*, I (1788), 109–113 (emphasis added). In all probability, Webster reprinted "Affecting Anecdote" from a British periodical. See also An Adept [Johnstone], *Chrysal; or, The Adventures of a Guinea, Wherein Are Exhibited Views of Several Striking Scenes, with Curious and Interesting Anecdotes of the Most Noted Persons in Every Rank of Life, Whose Hands It Passed through in America, England, Holland, Germany, and Portugal* (London, 1760). It is interesting to note that *Adventures of a Guinea* was reprinted in Baltimore, a slave city, in 1815.

displays of deference. Moreover, especially in its classic manifestations, re-publicanism paid little attention to the apolitical and to those whom classi-cal republicans did not consider worthy of citizenship—women, those who worked, and especially the poor and the illiterate. Liberalism, on the other hand, concerned itself with domestic space and a broad spectrum of apolitical social relations, those between the rich and the poor, men and women, parents and children. The "Affecting Anecdote" also reveals divisions within liberal ideology itself. Although liberalism in its political mode appeared to embrace a radical, universalistic vision of freedom and equality—the unmarked political Everyman—as actually inscribed on the pages of the new press, it celebrated private property, highly stratified class and gender relations, and patronage and deference. There, the liberal body was anything but unmarked. We must note, as well, that liberalism's new form of social bonding, always dependent on the outward display of feelings, was highly theatrical and audience-dependent. It required the sufferer to perform suffering sympathetically and spectators to respond appropriately. It thus warred with both classic and commercial repub-licanism's insistence on transparency and condemnation of self-conscious the-atricality and artifice.

And so we return to our original question: working with these contrary views of republican citizenship and society, could the political magazines fashion a coherent political subject and a coherent national identity?

PRAGMATIC VERSUS FRACTURED IDENTITIES

The discordant civic discourses and fractured political subjectivities, so sug-gestive of political and psychological instability, have failed to trouble many U.S. historians. In the long run, these scholars argue, the United States's heritage of ideological diversity and multiple possibilities neither fragmented European Americans' national identity nor destabilized their political beliefs. Rather, ideological diversity produced a pragmatic, eclectic, and flexible peo-ple, as capable of harmonizing divergent political discourses and ideologies as they were of incorporating new territories and ethnic groups. With a touch of national pride, David Ericson argues that the historian cannot expect to find pure political philosophy in the United States. European Americans, he ex-plains, have too much common sense to strive for ideological purity; they are too empirical. Martin Diamond, praising the "Framers'" statesmen-like pragmatism, similarly argues that "men of principle may properly make com-promises when the compromises adequately preserve fundamental principle."

Commenting on the "profusion and confusion of political tongues among the founders," Isaac Kramnick remarks wryly that the founders "lived easily with . . . clatter; it is we, two hundred and more years later, who chafe at their inconsistency."[46]

Political scientist Rogers Smith is perhaps the most articulate advocate of this eclectic position. Although Smith traces Americans' idealism and their commitment to democracy and human rights to liberalism, by itself, he argues, "the individualism, competitiveness, privatism, and inequalities of liberal societies work against strong feelings of community." "Even liberalism's attractive insistence on at least a minimum of respect for all persons, inside and outside one's political community," Smith continues, "is in tension with a vivid belief in the importance of one's particular civic membership, one's citizenship." Neither was classic republicanism, by itself, sufficient to the task, being too elitist and too hostile to the new commercial world to stand by itself. Only by fusing liberal and republican discourses could a new national identity emerge. To focus on discursive dissonance, from Smith's perspective, is to miss the essence of the dynamic pragmatism that lies at the heart of America's national identity.[47]

Such arguments are persuasive—and are corroborated, at least in part, by a number of essays in new urban magazines that overtly praise American pragmatism and flexibility. These essays, however, are more notable for their singularity than for their frequency. Indeed, their singularity leads me to question the concept of dynamic constructionism so many political historians and philosophers have embraced. Did the founders truly "live easily" with ideological "confusion" and discursive "clatter"? Or do the assertions of Smith, Kramnick, and Diamond slide too quickly over the bitter ideological conflicts that rent the new nation and destabilized its national identity?[48]

46. Ericson, *Shaping of American Liberalism*, 2–5; Martin Diamond, *The Founding of the Democratic Republic* (Itasca, Ill., 1981), 35; Kramnick, *Republicanism and Bourgeois Radicalism*, 261.

47. Smith, " 'One United People,' " *Yale Journal of Law and the Humanities*, I (1989), 229–293, esp. 230. See, as well, his *Civic Ideals*, chap. 1.

48. The "new American," one author proclaimed, was a man of all trades, political principles, and economic perspectives. Americans "turn their hands to everything," he boasted. "Their situation obliges them to do so." Another essayist celebrated the United States as a mosaic of regional diversities. New England had been settled by the proud descendants of Puritan forefathers, famed for resisting "the arbitrary power of . . . monarchs . . . [and] the double tyranny of despotism and intolerance." New Yorkers, the descendants of the thrifty, home-loving Dutch, boasted of their "domestic œconomy" and dedication to "their families." Charlestonians, in their turn, were famed for their cosmopolitanism, their "love [of] pleasure, the arts, and society." Only Pennsylvanians received criticism. They, it seemed, were too tolerant of difference and not

Political philosophers remind us that neither republican nor liberal discourses have demonstrated much tolerance for conflict and contradiction. Republicanism requires a tightly knit political community united in its values. As we have already seen, it tolerates neither diversity nor divisions. Robert Ferguson tells us that liberal Enlightenment thought was similarly suspicious of diversity. "Assum[ing] a unified answer to central problems," Ferguson says, "it could never encompass . . . ultimate disagreement. . . . Most Americans, in consequence, have had just two rhetorical recourses in conflict: *either* you misunderstand *or* you have turned your back on the truth for malicious reasons. Where misunderstanding ends, the politics of anger begins." The violent factional rhetoric of the political battles of the 1790s, culminating in the Alien and Sedition Acts and heated Federalist attacks on Thomas Jefferson (which continued at least until the Hartford Convention), suggests tolerance and heterodoxy found fewer advocates in the new Republic than among consensus historians of the twentieth and twenty-first centuries. Federalists and Antifederalists, radicals and conservatives, Calvinists and Evangelicals, classic republicans and liberal humanists, with few exceptions, viewed faction and difference with alarm—as they did opinions that differed from their own.[49]

Fears of faction appear much more frequently on the magazines' pages than praise of diverse opinions or origins. Heterodoxy and civic virtue were oxymorons. "The Spirit of Party is a Spirit of enmity," a writer in the *American Sentimental Magazine* declared; "it has always been hostile to the peace, and obnoxious to the virtue of mankind. . . . When it has prevailed, the private peace of society has been disturbed, and domestic felicity interrupted." We will recall that the Trifler lamented that "opinions divided the world into sects and parties." Nor can we forget Timothy Dwight's denunciation of diversity. "Contending interests ever exist with disputes and end in war," Dwight proclaimed. "Unlike principles of government . . . are consequently the parents of endless contests, slaughter and desolation." Virtually every Founding Father agreed. *The Federalist Papers* are filled with condemnations of difference and division. "A zeal for different opinions concerning religion, concerning government, . . . as well of speculation as of practice," Alexander Hamilton warned, "have . . . divided mankind into parties, inflamed them with mutual animosity, and rendered them much more disposed to vex and oppress each other than to co-

---

sufficiently committed to political and moral principles. "The Analogy between the Respective Forms of Government, and the Origins of the Several States of North America, Taken from the Entertaining Travels of the Marquis de Chastellux," *Columbian Magazine*, I (1787), 477–478.

49. Ferguson, *American Enlightenment*, x.

operate for their common good." James Madison heartily concurred. Criticism of the Articles of Confederation stressed their failure to contain diversity and to ensure harmony.[50]

Creating a viable republic and a cohesive national identity were not abstract concerns in the Revolutionary 1770s, the troubled 1780s, or the violent 1790s. They were desperate needs that many of the founding generation felt precluded philosophical tolerance, ideological diversity, and political discord. On the other hand, caught in the dialogic interaction of the long eighteenth century's multiple political and economic discourses, the political magazines were no more able to fuse the various conflicting scripts they had inherited from Augustan and Enlightenment Britain into a coherent identity than Timothy Dwight had been. On their pages, unresolved differences battled relentlessly. "Liberty," "virtue," and "Independence" assumed multiple conflicting meanings. Heaping equal praise upon such deeply contrary personas as heroic gentlemen and hardworking producers, zoon politikons and liberal philanthropists, disinterested statesmen and self-interested entrepreneurs, the magazines called upon their readers to play multiple parts and assume contradictory identities. A fusion of opposites, the figure of the new American they held up to their readers was divided and self-contradictory. Could repeated performances meld such deep-seated differences?

Two unifying themes did emerge on the pages of the new bourgeois magazines. The first was the insistent fusion of manliness and empowered citizenship, a vision the Latinized word *virtu*—derived from *vir*, "man"—captures.[51] Eighteenth-century political discourses agreed, citizenship was a male pre-

---

50. "On Party Spirit," *American Moral and Sentimental Magazine*, I (1797), 216–218; [Timothy Dwight], "A Valedictory Address to the Young Gentlemen, Who Commenced Bachelors of Arts, at Yale-College, July 25th, 1776," *American Magazine*, I (1787), 42–47, and I (1788), 99–103, esp. 44. For examples of criticisms that the Articles of Confederation failed to contain diversity, see Alexander Hamilton, no. 9, and James Madison, no. 70, in Isaac Kramnick, ed., *The Federalist Papers* (London, 1987), 124, 404. Political philosopher Robert A. Ferguson concurs: "Disputation," he points out, "is . . . the major source of evil in Franklin's autobiography." He continues: "The recurring early republican nightmare was of chaos and dissention. Anger and doubt compound the primal goal of consensus. In response, the representative texts of the period distort the nature of conflict to create order and clarity. . . . The founders struggle to make their signs, symbols and literary personae at once familiar, dominating and inclusive" (Ferguson, *American Enlightenment*, 15–16).

51. Pocock emphasizes the significance of Machiavelli's use of the term *virtu* and its centrality to republican rhetoric. *Virtu*, he points out, fuses *vir* (Latin for male) and *virtue*. He stresses classic republicans' celebration of manly fortitude and their disdain for the effeminate *(Machiavellian Moment,* chaps. 13–15).

rogative. Only men could claim the judgment, moderation, and love of liberty that citizenship required. Only men had the courage and strength to defend their republic, the productivity and talent to contribute to its wealth and secure its well-being. Civic virtue without virility was impossible, classic republicans insisted, the fusion of virtue and virility embodied by the resolute warrior and the noble statesman. Commercial republicans, accused of effeminacy by classic republicans, were equally determined to affirm their own version of manliness, insisting on the manly qualities of productivity and hard work. The rights-bearing liberal citizen was theoretically unmarked by gender, race, or class. Yet to any eighteenth-century observer, the liberal citizen's claims to independence and inalienable rights, to reason, education, and property were unquestionable markers of masculinity. The second point eighteenth-century political discourses agreed upon was that the republican citizen had to be economically independent, educated, and cultured. He had, that is, to belong to the middling or elite ranks. Day laborers, illiterate agricultural laborers, and frontier squatters were deemed unqualified and barred from voting by property qualifications. The unfree—slaves and indentured servants—by their very servitude defined both freedom and citizenship. But even middling shopkeepers, artisans, and small family farmers were suspect—at least on the pages of the new bourgeois press. Their citizenship, the magazines insisted, must be of a deferential sort. They must consent to be governed by their betters.

Were these two common characteristics sufficient to constitute a core around which the political magazines and their readers could build a national identity? Dotting the magazine pages we find images of two constituting Others, whose differences were designed to obscure the rhetorical and ideological divisions that threatened to destabilize the slowly emerging European American identity.

The first constituting Others we will examine were the participants in Shays's Rebellion, the riotous farmers of western Massachusetts who rose up against New England's mercantile elite in the summer of 1786. Wishing to solidify an image of an orderly and stable republic and of judicious, moderate republicans, the political magazines held up Shays's Rebellion as republicanism gone mad, the embodiment of "democratic excesses" and "mob rule." Brutish, violent, and irrational, the rebels were represented as the propertied citizen's dark and disturbing Other. In contrast to such wild men, the rhetorical and ideological contradictions that afflicted the magazines' virtuous republican paled. But they did not disappear. The magazines' representation of these rowdy men dangerously destabilized eighteenth-century understandings of manliness and virility, undercutting a key characteristic around which a unifying national identity could be imagined.

To recuperate a "naturalized" understanding of manliness, the political magazines turned to women. Whatever their other disagreements, eighteenth-century political discourses concurred—women were incapable of civic virtue and political judgment. By their very presence, they threatened to corrupt men's pure political state. More threatening still, unless governed wisely by fathers and husbands, women, by their seductive arts, threatened to make republican citizens like themselves—passionate, irrational, and dependent.

At first glance, these Others appear as unlike one another as they were unlike the magazines' vision of the virtuous citizen. The unruly farmer, musket primed, the extravagant lady at her tea table—what two figures could be more distinctive and more unlike the reasonable, upright new American? What is fascinating, however, is the frequency with which the differences among these Others dissolved. Time and again, on the pages of the new magazines, the republican citizen, the rebellious farmer, and the fashionable lady triangulated in a dizzying progression of interdependences until the boundary lines between the good citizen and his dangerous Others became permeable. To identify with the resultant figure was to internalize fundamentally destabilizing contradictions, to leave the newly figured white, male American identity uncertain, in search of more stabilizing Others against which European Americans could define themselves.

Let us explore the role these two Others played in the political magazines' efforts to confirm the cohesion and virtue of their new republican citizen—and the success of these efforts.

CHAPTER TWO

Rebellious Dandies and Political Fictions

The focus on the vulnerability of property necessarily bred a fear and, perhaps, contempt of the propertyless, who were to be the vast bulk of the people. The "people" as such—not in the sense of the society as a whole, but in the sense of the ordinary people, those not members of the propertied elite—were the threat that had to be contained. —JENNIFER NEDELSKY, Private Property and the Limits of American Constitutionalism

We are to look further than to the Bulk of the People, for the Greatest wisdom, firmness, consistency and perseverance. —THEOPHILUS PARSON, Essex Resolves

The American Revolution threw wide the door of radical political promise. Political authority no longer resided in the will of the king. "The People," having declared themselves free, equal, and endowed with inalienable rights, had become the ultimate source of political authority. A national identity built around the image of the new American–as–republican citizen began to take form. But what precise form would this new citizenship assume?

Enveloped in an aura of unlimited possibilities as citizens of the first modern republic, European Americans faced momentous—and bitterly contested—decisions. They had to resolve which rights and responsibilities citizenship bestowed and who could claim the right to self-governance. Until a hegemony could be built around these issues, the new national identity would remain uncertain and unstable. As we have seen, the ideological and rhetorical tools European Americans had to build such a hegemony were contradictory and discordant. Complicating matters, different social and economic groups within the far-from-unified new Republic, appropriating and reinterpreting words and concepts, relentlessly contested meanings and resisted resolutions.

America's emerging would-be political elite—northern whig lawyers like John Adams, Alexander Hamilton, and James Wilson; merchant princes and fiscal speculators like John Hancock, Robert Morris, and William Bingham; the ruling families of tidewater Virginia and the Carolinas—were determined not to open the door of radical possibilities too wide. True, they had disseminated radical Revolutionary political concepts throughout the colonies. Nevertheless, they were certain that a chasm separated virtuous republics from dangerous democracies, respectable citizens from howling mobs. Seeing their world divided between a minority of the propertied and a majority of the propertyless, the eastern elite, North and South, strove to ensure that, at the war's end, property qualifications and a politics of deference would confine political participation to the wise, well-born, and well-educated—that is, to themselves, as America's "natural aristocracy." All others must consent to be governed by their betters. If such consent was not forthcoming, then force would be both necessary and legitimate.

Revolutionary whig rhetoric, however, had captured the imagination of many others—hill-town farmers who, muskets primed, declared themselves returned to a state of nature and subject to no governance but their own; mechanics and small shopkeepers who forced themselves onto Philadelphia's and New York's Committees of Safety and Correspondence; African Americans who sued for freedom and reparations because Massachusetts's Revolutionary constitution declared all men free and endowed with inalienable rights; sailors, white and black, who had rioted against impressments and spread the news of revolution from port to port.[1] Initially directing their cries for freedom

1. The term "whig," which I have not used before, refers first and on the most general level to British critics of the increasingly imperial government—to its large state debts, standing army, large professional bureaucracy, and, as well, to long-standing Parliaments and their independence from voters. The term "Radical Whig" denominated those critics who saw government always as a battle between would-be tyrannical rulers and "the People." They celebrated liberty, insisted that sovereignty resided in the People, and called for frequent parliamentary elections and political representatives subject to their constituents' instructions. European Americans drew heavily upon Radical Whig rhetoric in framing first their opposition to British imperial regulations and then in calling for revolution and independence. Patriots, especially during the 1760s and early 1770s, called themselves whigs. See Gordon S. Wood, *The Creation of the American Republic, 1776–1787* (New York, 1972), chap. 1.

For discussions of the Revolution's impact in terms of radicalizing the "lower orders," see, for example, Alfred F. Young, ed., *Beyond the American Revolution: Explorations in the History of American Radicalism* (Dekalb, Ill., 1993); Paul A. Gilje, *The Road to Mobocracy: Popular Disorder in New York City, 1763–1834* (Chapel Hill, N.C., 1987); Gilje, *Liberty on the Waterfront: American Maritime Culture in the Age of Revolution* (Philadelphia, 2004); Saul Cornell, *The Other Founders: Anti-Federalism and the Dissenting Tradition in America, 1788–1828* (Chapel Hill, N.C., 1999); Gary B. Nash, *Forging Freedom: The Formation of Philadelphia's Black Community, 1720–*

against Britain's Parliament and royal officeholders, these others soon began to attack the eastern bourgeoisie as would-be aristocrats, predatory and tyrannical. While war still raged, common soldiers demanded the right to elect their own officers and Philadelphia militiamen rioted against their city's mercantile elite. Common laborers in New York demanded the vote, and farmers North to South asserted their right to instruct their representatives on how to vote. Even women began to ask what they might gain from the Revolution, and at least one educated "lady," adopting whig rhetoric she had helped parse at her breakfast table, warned that "we [women] are determined to foment a Rebellion and will not hold ourselves bound by any Laws in which we have no voice, or Representation."[2]

1840 (Cambridge, Mass., 1988); Peter Linebaugh and Marcus Rediker, *The Many-Headed Hydra: Sailors, Slaves, Commoners, and the Hidden History of the Revolutionary Atlantic* (Boston, 2000), esp. 211–247. For the role of black sailors in spreading the word of revolution around the Atlantic, see Julius S. Scott, "Crisscrossing Empires: Ships, Sailors, and Resistance in the Lesser Antilles in the Eighteenth Century," in Robert L. Paquette and Stanley L. Engerman, eds., *The Lesser Antilles in the Age of European Expansion* (Gainesville, Fla., 1996), 183–186; Scott, "The Common Wind: Currents of Afro-American Communication in the Era of the Haitian Revolution" (Ph.D. diss., Duke University, 1986).

2. See Thomas M. Doerflinger's description of the battle of Fort Wilson, during which the Philadelphia militia besieged between twenty and forty of the city's leading merchants, including Robert Morris, in James Wilson's house until the elite cavalry arrived to rescue the merchants (Doerflinger, *A Vigorous Spirit of Enterprise: Merchants and Economic Development in Revolutionary Philadelphia* (Chapel Hill, N.C., 1986), 257. See, as well, John K. Alexander, "The Fort Wilson Incident of 1779: A Case Study of the Revolutionary Crowd," *William and Mary Quarterly,* 3d Ser., XXXI (1974), 599–612, esp. 601. "Foment a rebellion": cited by Robert A. Ferguson, in *The American Enlightenment, 1750–1820* (Cambridge, Mass., 1997), 152–153. For discussions of northern popular political unrest, see Jesse Lemisch, "Jack Tar in the Streets: Merchant Seamen in the Politics of Revolutionary America," *WMQ,* 3d Ser., XXV (1968), 371–407; Charles S. Olton, *Artisans for Independence: Philadelphia Mechanics and the American Revolution* (Syracuse, N.Y., 1975); Dirk Hoerder, *Crowd Action in Revolutionary Massachusetts, 1765–1780* (New York, 1977); Edward Countryman, *A People in Revolution: The American Revolution and Political Society in New York, 1760–1790* (Baltimore, 1981); Gilje, *Road to Mobocracy;* Howard B. Rock, *Artisans of the New Republic: The Tradesmen of New York City in the Age of Jefferson* (New York, 1984); Peter H. Wood, "'Liberty Is Sweet': African-American Freedom Struggles in the Years before White Independence," in Young, ed., *Beyond the American Revolution,* 149–184; W. J. Rorabaugh, "'I Thought I Should Liberate Myself from the Thraldom of Others': Apprentices, Masters, and the Revolution," ibid., 185–217; Bernard Friedman, "The Shaping of the Radical Consciousness in Provincial New York," *Journal of American History,* LVI (1970), 781–801. For discussions of agrarian unrest, see, among others, Alan Taylor, "Agrarian Independence: Northern Land Rioters after the Revolution," in Young, ed., *Beyond the American Revolution;* Marjoleine Kars, *Breaking Loose Together: The Regulator Rebellion in Pre-Revolutionary*

From the moment the "shot heard round the world" was fired, the visions entertained by eastern bourgeois whigs and these clamorous others collided. This was a political and constitutional battle that would determine the meaning of citizenship and the power of political representatives in the first modern republic. At given moments, it was simultaneously a military and a rhetorical battle between western farmers and bourgeois elites who controlled both the nation's military establishments and political press. In the end, it would be on the pages of that press that the elite would win its most decisive victory.

At the center of this debate lay the issue of manliness. Choosing those who most immediately challenged their vision of an orderly, property-protecting republic, the magazines represented them as the antithesis of the virile and virtuous new American. Representations of these Others, their differences and failings, obscured the discursive and ideological contradictions that destabilized the magazines' vision of a new national identity and their idealized new American. With both the virtuous republican citizen and the property-owning liberal citizen coded "male," their Others had to be coded "effeminate," or, even worse, as women—no matter how counterintuitive that coding appeared.

ENTER THE SAVAGE SHAYSITE REBELS

In the summer of 1786, self-sufficient family farmers from the hill towns of western Massachusetts rose up in rebellion. They protested ruinous land taxes, poll taxes so high that many small landholders could not vote, and a wave of debt foreclosures that threatened to reduce many to tenancy. The Revolution had been betrayed, the farmers cried. It was time for America's true Sons of Liberty to strike back.[3] Thousands marched on the Massachusetts Supreme

---

North Carolina (Chapel Hill, N.C., 2002); Alan Kulikoff, "The Revolution and the Making of American Yeoman Classes," in Kulikoff, ed., *The Agrarian Origins of American Capitalism* (Charlottesville, Va., 1992).

3. The term "Sons of Liberty" itself provoked controversy. Originally used to refer to those among Boston's artisans, day laborers, and sailors who participated in riots against the Stamp Act in the fall and winter of 1765, by 1769, the phrase had been appropriated by Boston's whig elite to represent those invited to a formal dinner held annually in Roxbury (far removed from the homes of the actual rioters) to celebrate the riots and establish these men's respectability. As Hoerder explains: "By making the Boston celebration of 14 August a social rather than a political event, Samuel Adams and James Otis succeeded in drawing a large number of usually inactive members of the community to the side of the Whigs." Or, as the *Boston Post-Boy* put it, the dinners "established the sacred character, that the Enemies to *usurpation* and *oppression* are the great Exemplars of *Order* and *Decency*." Efforts to break this monopoly "remained unsuccessful" (*Crowd Action*, 140).

Court in Springfield, sending judges and tax collectors fleeing and bringing farm foreclosures to a halt. Then, following footsteps that in 1774 had led many of these same men to Lexington and Concord, they turned east, toward Boston. A second American Revolution seemed about to begin.[4]

The farmers called their armed uprising the Regulator Movement. Its object was to curb the greed and corruption of eastern merchants, speculators, and politicians. Merchants and creditors named it Shays's Rebellion, after one of the movement's prominent leaders. Under either name, it sent shockwaves through the nation. Did Shays's Rebellion prove European Americans incapable of self-government? alarmed eastern commercial interests wondered. Had their glorious Revolution been but the first step in America's rapid descent into anarchy and tyranny? At the very least, the Massachusetts uprising confirmed the inadequacy of the Articles of Confederation and a Congress incapable of maintaining domestic order. They called for the rebellion's violent suppression and intensified their demands for a radical restructuring of the national government. The new political magazines rallied to the cause. From the summer of 1786 through the debates over ratification—indeed, into the 1790s—attacks on the riotous behavior of western farmers and calls for an empowered new government fused on their pages.[5]

THE VOLCANO OF AGRARIAN DISCONTENT

Shays's Rebellion was not an isolated incident. From the 1740s to the early nineteenth century, frontier farmers everywhere, banded together under such vivid names as "Wild Yankees," "Black Boys," "Ely's Rebels," "Liberty Men," "Green Mountain Boys," and "Regulators," had repeatedly taken up arms against eastern-controlled legislatures and landed interests—often with great success.[6] To their contemporaries, these bands of propertyless westerners epito-

---

4. For studies of Shays's Rebellion, see Leonard L. Richards, *Shays's Rebellion: The American Revolution's Final Battle* (Philadelphia, 2002); Robert A. Gross, ed., *In Debt to Shays: The Bicentennial of an Agrarian Rebellion* (Charlottesville, Va., 1993); John L. Brooke, *The Heart of the Commonwealth: Society and Political Culture in Worcester County, Massachusetts, 1713–1861* (Cambridge, 1989); and David P. Szatmary, *Shays' Rebellion: The Making of an Agrarian Insurrection* (Amherst, Mass., 1980). For a discussion of agrarian radicalism during the Revolutionary War, which the Shays rebels frequently referred to, see Hoerder, *Crowd Action*.

5. Richards, *Shays's Rebellion*, chaps. 6, 7; Michael Lienesch, "Reinterpreting Rebellion: The Influence of Shays's Rebellion on American Political Thought," in Gross, ed., *In Debt to Shays*, 161.

6. It is interesting to note that these movements were conscious of one another; western

mized the agrarian frontier's penchant for "mobocracy" and the use of violence in the redress of grievances.[7] To historians, on the other hand, frontier uprisings embody what E. P. Thompson called "the moral economy of crowd action," a premodern form of political organization and resistance that New England's Calvinist farmers had carried over with them from medieval and early modern Britain. Acts of orchestrated violence against representatives of authority (in the American context, land surveyors, tax or quitrent collectors, courts and judges) permitted men with no regularized access to political processes their only opportunity to voice their outrages—and even to effect change.[8]

During the colonial era, distant eastern governments had accepted such uprisings as a frontier way of life. But Shays's Rebellion, occurring so soon after Independence, was seen as threatening the stability of the republican experiment. The Massachusetts General Court proclaimed the farmers to be in "open, unnatural, unprovoked, and wicked rebellion." Henry Knox fulminated that they were engaged in "a formidable rebellion against reason." Others denounced them as "Jacobites" and "political Jesuits." High Federalist Fisher Ames summed matters up by declaring the escalating political unrest to be the

---

Massachusetts's farmers, for example, selected the name "Regulators," first chosen by farmers along the Carolina frontier. This sharing of names also suggests that the farmers' anti-eastern identifications were even more powerful than their identifications as favoring or opposing the Revolution. The Carolina Regulators had opposed the Revolution motivated in large part by their opposition to the tidewater planters who supported it. Massachusetts's western farmers, in contrast, prided themselves on their Revolutionary valor. Shays's Rebellion was scarcely the last western uprising; only a few years later, frontier farmers in Pennsylvania staged the Whiskey Rebellion, which again sent federal troops scurrying into western hills. For discussions of western discontent, see Taylor, "Agrarian Independence," in Young, ed., *Beyond the American Revolution;* and James Roger Sharp, *American Politics in the Early Republic: The New Nation in Crisis* (New Haven, Conn., 1993).

7. James Logan, for example, was highly critical of western squatters as arrogant, destitute, and presumptuous, Benjamin Franklin of their "Outrages," "destroy[ing] Property, publick and private." See Ed White, *The Backcountry and the City: Colonization and Conflict in Early America* [Minneapolis, 2005], 44, 93).

8. E. P. Thompson, *Customs in Common: Studies in Traditional Popular Culture* (New York, 1993), 185–258. As Hoerder expressed it, frontier colonial America turned to the moral economy of crowd action when "cumbersome legal procedures seemed too slow, or the lawyers', clerks', and justices' fees too high; when institutional remedies had been exhausted or when no redress was to be expected from justices or representatives." Then the poor and the isolated felt justified in resorting to the moral economy of crowd violence *(Crowd Action,* 90). Philip J. Deloria points out that westerners often, ironically, dressed as Native Americans when protesting British or eastern speculators' incursions onto "their land" (Deloria, *Playing Indian* [New Haven, Conn., 1998], 10–11).

inevitable result of democracy, which, like "a volcano, . . . conceals the fiery materials of its own destruction."[9]

The volcano of frontier democracy erupted along a critical socioeconomic fault line, revealing the fragility of the economic, political, and cultural bonds that held the new Republic together. Upon this one point, western farmers and eastern commercial interests agreed. Both saw the Massachusetts uprising as a crucial event in an ongoing struggle between a largely precommercial agrarian West and an eastern commercial and fiscal elite for control of the state legislature, its courts and fiscal policies. Both sides also saw it as a battle that pitted paper money against hard currency, poll taxes against land taxes, tender laws against the sanctity of contracts, the right of the common citizen to self-governance against an economic elite's right to rule.[10] But both sides were equally convinced that even more was at stake: the very form political representation would take in the new Republic and the persona the new nation would present to the world—in short, Americans' new identity. In a battle that was simultaneously rhetorical, political, and military, westerners cast themselves as heroes in a classic republican melodrama. They were, they maintained, lovers of liberty who fought as bravely in 1786 against tyranny as they had in 1776.

The farmers had a valid claim to their revolutionary persona. From the initial protests against the Stamp Tax, westerners had played a critical role in colonial resistance. They had forced courts to close in Hampshire and Berkshire Counties until the Stamp Act was repealed, attacked the surveyor of the king's woods when he came to collect masts for the Royal Navy, boycotted tea, and, as early as 1772, formed extralegislative Committees of Safety and Correspondence. However, it was not until the Intolerable Acts in 1774 closed Boston's port, ended representative government in Massachusetts, and ordered the quartering of British soldiers throughout the colonies that western ire was thoroughly aroused. Denouncing Parliament, westerners called for active resistance. In the summer of 1774, 1,500 armed farmers descended on Pittsfield, closing royal courts and forcing loyalists to flee. Another 3,000 marched on

9. Knox, cited by Szatmary, *Shays' Rebellion*, 71; Fisher Ames, speech at the Massachusetts Convention, Jan. 15, 1788, in Jonathan Elliot, ed., *The Debates in the Several State Conventions on the Adoption of the Federal Constitution, as Recommended by the General Convention at Phila-delphia, in 1787 . . .* (Philadelphia, 1891), II, 10. "A Friend to Humanity and Good Government" called the contest one between "evil" and "good" while "Camillus"—that is, Fisher Ames— not only coined the volcano phrase but elsewhere called the farmers "emissaries of treason" (ibid., 164).

10. Szatmary, in his *Shays' Rebellion* (1980), and Richards, in his later *Shays's Rebellion* (2002), agree that these were the basic causes of the uprising.

Springfield. Then, on September 6, 5,000 men occupied the Worcester courthouse and town square. They proclaimed British rule tyrannical and the people of Massachusetts "to all intents and purposes reduced to a State of Nature." They then called on their representatives in the General Court "to exert yourselves . . . to raise from the dissolution of the old constitution . . . a new form wherein all officers shall be dependent on the suffrages of the people for their existence as such." From Worcester, the movement spread to Concord and Barnstable. The minutemen readied themselves. America's revolution had begun.[11]

From that September day in 1774 until the ratification of the Massachusetts constitution in 1780, the farmers of western Massachusetts governed themselves through extralegislative institutions—committees of correspondence, committees of safety, self-generated county conventions, and unauthorized town meetings. All these institutions were designed to encourage broad-based community participation. As a consequence, western farmers had time to develop a political vision and a political voice, time to internalize the radical principle that, when governments failed to govern for the benefit of all the people, the people had a right to rise up and establish a new, more popular and responsive government. They had time, as well, to make concrete a Revolutionary version of John Locke's social contract. Popular sovereignty was becoming very popular in western Massachusetts, and western farmers, very active political agents.[12]

It should not surprise us, though, that poor farmers—isolated within the hill towns of northwestern Massachusetts, their worldview colored by the dark hues of orthodox Calvinism—did not come upon the radical Enlightenment political vision on their own. Ironically, it was newspapers and pamphlets urging popular resistance to parliamentary legislation, written and disseminated by Boston's whig elite—James Otis, Samuel Adams, John Adams, John Hancock, James Warren—that first introduced them to that vision.[13] From the

11. Eighty percent of Worcester County's towns sent men to the Worcester demonstration in companies of 25 to 500 men. A total of 4,722 men stretched over a quarter of a mile around the center of Worcester. Each company elected an officer and a committee to confer with other companies. They then voted to close the courts and demanded that the judges appear before the people to be informed the courts were closed. They voted to reorganize militia and elected new officers. Finally, they authorized each town to elect its own officers, maintain order, and administer justice. British rule in western Massachusetts came to an end that day in Worcester (Hoerder, *Crowd Action*, 128–133, 280, 311–319, 326).

12. Richards, *Shays's Rebellion*, 19, 44–48, 53, 95–96, 111.

13. As early as 1765, Boston radicals had used the *Boston Gazette* to propound the radical

mid-1760s to the outbreak of revolution, the escalating pamphlet war by whig merchants, lawyers, and printers supplied the primers from which western farmers parsed their rights as free men and virtuous republicans. Of course, Boston's whig elite had not intended their writing to rouse European Americans to resist their own control of Massachusetts politics. Western farmers, however, proved unruly pupils, insisting on their own interpretations of key political principles. Significantly, they disagreed as violently town to town as they did with Boston's whig elite. And so it was that, during these unsettled years, divergent political discourses battled one another across the breadth of Massachusetts.[14]

From an eastern bourgeois whig perspective, it was, not an orderly Lockean state of nature that Hampshire and Berkshire farmers had enacted in September 1774, but a Hobbesean world, unrestrained by institutions, scornful of elite direction, threatening the sanctity of private property. Throughout the Revolution, bourgeois Boston fumed against western Massachusetts's "leveling spirit." Whig lawyers and merchants viewed the wartime closing of the courts in Springfield and Worcester with consternation (especially since it prevented eastern merchants from suing western farmers for debt). They further resented western insistence that Massachusetts's new state constitution be written by an elected constitutional convention rather than by a General Court controlled by the whig elite and that the new constitution be submitted to popular ratifica-

liberal doctrine that, if "those who are invested with Power and Authority to be employed for the publick Good, make use of it to injure and oppress their Brethren, in direct Opposition to the Design of their Appointment . . . then there always resides a power in the sacred Body of the People, sufficient to suspend and dissolve the powers they have given, or oblige those, who hold them to perform their Duty." Cited by Hoerder, *Crowd Action*, 116.

14. Certain western Massachusetts towns, especially in Worcester and Hampshire Counties— and often not those towns that supported the Regulator Movement—were especially susceptible to the liberal strains of Radical Whig rhetoric. Many in these towns, which were Baptist enclaves, had long railed against the established Congregational Church, resenting being tithed for a church they did not support. Baptists advocated the separation of church and state. Especially during the Revolutionary War years, they increasingly embraced a radical form of individualism, accepted diversity, and were often hotbeds of radical Universalist religious beliefs. They rejected the older communitarian assumptions of western Massachusetts's orthodox Congregationalist hill towns, where the Regulator Movement took root. As a consequence, they were, at best, lukewarm in their responses to the Regulator Movement, which they associated with their enemies, orthodox Congregationalists. Brooke depicts the hill towns of western Massachusetts as divided ideologically between the liberal individualism of Baptists and Universalists and the communitarianism of the orthodox Congregationalists, a communitarianism closely allied with a classic republican vision of community and state *(Heart of the Commonwealth,* 154–168).

tion.[15] John Adams captured much of the East's annoyance. "It is a Pity you should be obliged to lay it [the new constitution] before them [the voters]," he wrote the wealthy physician Joseph Warren, his friend and political ally; "it will divide and distract them." In the same spirit, Adams urged James Sullivan to write restrictive property qualifications for voting and officeholding into the new Massachusetts constitution. Without such qualifications, "new claims will arise . . . women will demand a vote, lads from twelve to twenty-one will think their rights not enough attended to, and every man who has not a farthing, will demand an equal voice with any other, in all acts of state."[16]

In the end, Adams, Warren, and Sullivan secured ratification of a conservative state constitution. Their victory, however, did little to mute the dissenting voices Adams had warned against. Deploying radicalized Revolutionary strictures, western town meetings reviled the new constitution.[17] It "Intirely Divests the good People of the State of many of the priviledges which God and Nature had given them," declared the residents of Greenwich, Massachusetts, in 1780. It gave "away that Power to a few Individuals, which ought forever to Remain with the people inviolate, who stile Themselves free and Independent."[18] When the newly convened General Court raised taxes (from £408,976 during the 1774–1778 period to £663,476 during the 1783–1786 period), placed them disproportionately on land rather than on movable goods (the richest ten shipping towns paid only 12 to 14 percent of the state's taxes), and replaced a Revo-

15. Indeed, the western committees and conventions forced four successive statewide elections before the new constitution was finally ratified in 1780. See Hoerder, *Crowd Action*, 378–381.

16. John Adams to James Warren, cited in Hoerder, *Crowd Action*, 333; Adams to Joseph Sullivan, cited in Ferguson, *American Enlightenment*, 155. The eastern elite, Hoerder tells us, debating the form the new state constitution should take, "brushed away any demands for increased participation of the people by declaring that . . . it was the voters' duty again to support, assist, and obey the appointed magistrates." "Disobedience and rioting, lumped together with debauchery and immorality, were to be punished"*(Crowd Action,* 378). Adams's opinion was shared by many among Massachusetts's eastern bourgeois. William Whiting commented in his pamphlet protesting the uprising in the Berkshires: "I can't but take notice, how shamefully that ancient maxim, vox populiest vox Dei . . . has been prostituted in this country" (Whiting, "An Address to the Inhabitants of Berkshire County, Mass.," cited by Ferguson, *American Enlightenment*, 119).

17. Westerners complained about the high property qualifications for voting that Adams and Sullivan had written into the constitution. They also objected to Boston's remaining the seat of government, since the high costs of sending representatives to the General Assembly meant that many western towns remained unrepresented in the new state government (Szatmary, *Shays' Rebellion*, 47).

18. Gregory H. Nobles, "Shays's Neighbors: The Context of Rebellion in Pelham, Massachusetts," in Gross, ed., *In Debt to Shays*, 185–203, esp. 200.

lutionary paper currency with specie, western farmers inundated the General Court with petitions to establish a land bank, reissue paper money, shift the tax burden from land to commerce, and reform the judicial system. The General Court—composed primarily of eastern merchants, commercial farmers, professionals, and, increasingly, fiscal innovators and speculators—rejected the western petitions as the disorderly rumblings of the democratic volcano. If republican virtue was to be maintained and private property protected, such rumblings must be contained.[19]

These differing political discourses reflected a larger discordance of experiences and worldviews. The ways of commerce and credit—a cash economy, compound interest, debts contracted and redeemed, the emergence of banks, corporate stocks and bonds, along with wild speculation in both commercial paper and western lands—characterized life along the eastern seaboard. This was a cosmopolitan and capitalist world, a world of economic modernity, social diversity, and religious heterodoxy.[20]

In contrast, the world of the orthodox Congregational communities that provided the backbone of Shays's Rebellion was community oriented. Village, church, and family formed a homogeneous and stable collective in which farmers planted to meet their families' needs and highly personalized barter and labor exchanges characterized commercial dealings. Not theirs, Franklin's

19. A severe credit crisis during the mid-1780s exacerbated a combative situation. British creditors called in American debts, specie fled Massachusetts—indeed, most of the eastern seaboard. Even in eastern towns such as Marlborough (situated halfway between Worcester and the ring of towns surrounding Boston), farmers, artisans, and merchants complained bitterly of hard times. Marlborough tax collector Peter Wood reported in 1785, "There was not then the money in possession or at command among the people in my quarter of the town, to discharge taxes." The state began to seize cattle and land to pay for arrears in taxes. "Great numbers of [the poor] have been constantly Striped of whatever Little Stocks they possessed, and those often Sold at public auxion for a meer Trifle," Common Pleas Judge William Whiting wrote from the more distant Berkshire County (Whiting, "Some Remarks on the Conduct of the Inhabitants of the Commonwealth of Massachusetts . . . ," in Stephen T. Riley, ed., "Doctor William Whiting and Shays' Rebellion," *Proceedings of the American Antiquarian Society*, LXVI [1956], 144). John L. Brooke modifies Szatmary's arguments, pointing out that it was not simply indebtedness that drove farmers to the extreme of armed resistance, for indebtedness was higher in the slightly more commercialized Baptist towns of Worcester County than in the more orthodox towns of the Berkshires. It was, he claims, the hard times, the insensitivity of the bourgeois elite and an older sense of communitarianism that the orthodox hill towns of the Berkshires shared (Brooke, "A Deacon's Orthodoxy: Religion, Class, and the Moral Economy of Shays's Rebellion," in Gross, ed., *In Debt to Shays*, 205–238; and Brooke, *Heart of the Commonwealth*).

20. For a discussion of the new Republic's urban culture, see Section 3, below.

vision of a countryside dotted with mills, artisan shops, and farms producing for burgeoning commercial markets. In Franklin's world, the farmers warned, agriculture would become the handmaiden, the feminized servant, of commercial and fiscal capitalism—perhaps even its enslaved handmaiden.[21]

The events of the mid-1780s confirmed western farmers' deep-seated fears. The sudden rise in state taxes to be paid in hard currency threatened those with little or no access to such currency. Suits against debtor farmers escalated in Worcester County and parts of Hampshire. Although many debtors did not join the Regulator Movement, the fear of foreclosures echoed across western

21. As Brooke tells us, "an almost ritual tradition of collective action" governed New England hill towns. Boston's cosmopolitanism, its economic and social diversity, its religious heterodoxy filled them with alarm ("A Deacon's Orthodoxy," in Gross, ed., *In Debt to Shays*, 227–228). Christopher Clark writes of Massachusetts between the 1780s and the 1820s, "Unlike the middle colonies and the tidewater South, interior New England had no staple export crop and was a relatively small market for imported manufactured goods. Labor was largely provided by family members, or swapped between households" (Clark, *The Roots of Rural Capitalism: Western Massachusetts, 1780–1860* [Ithaca, N.Y., 1990], 318). If any individuals exemplify J. G. A. Pocock's classic republicans, driven by nostalgia for a precommercial world, fearful of change, subject to paranoia, it was the self-sufficient farmers of Massachusetts's remote hill towns. Ironies complicate this association. Economically self-sufficient and hardworking, deeply devout Calvinists, politically radical and poorly spoken, western republican spokesmen could not have been more unlike England's Augustan gentry, yet it was the gentry's republican rhetoric that the farmers deployed to their own political and economic ends. Of course, "the West," that is, Massachusetts north and west of Worcester, was no more monolithic than Massachusetts east of Worcester. Economic diversity and disparities in wealth characterized many western towns. The "river barons," among Massachusetts's wealthiest landowners, merchants, and manufacturers, had ruled the Connecticut River valley for nearly a century. Throughout the valley, towns supported stores, taverns, and mills. Into the nineteenth century, a hierarchical social structure and politics of deference characterized these towns—as did religious diversity. Baptists and Methodists had made significant inroads into Calvinist orthodoxy. Deism and Masonry attracted the economic and social elite. Such economically and religiously diverse towns tended not to support agrarian protests—at least not enthusiastically (Brooke, *Heart of the Commonwealth*). See, as well, Nobles, "Shays's Neighbors," in Gross, ed., *In Debt to Shays*, 185–203. Social and economic historians have engaged in a long and bitter debate about the extent to which commercialization had reached into late-eighteenth-century American agricultural areas. Although most historians agree that market forces had reached far into agrarian America, they disagree as to whether farming families welcomed this invasion and as to what it meant for community and economic developments. For a more generalized view of agricultural self-sufficiency and the rejection of modernity in western communities, see James A. Henretta, "Families and Farms: *Mentalité* in Pre-industrial America," *WMQ*, 3d Ser., XXXV (1978), 3–32; Mary McKinney Schweitzer, "Elements of Political Economy in the Late Eighteenth Century: The Backcountry of Pennsylvania and the Shenandoah Valley of Virginia," paper presented at the Philadelphia Center for Early American Studies, Oct. 19, 1990.

Massachusetts. It was enough to witness one's neighbor's cattle driven off or farms in a neighboring village put on the auction block. Hill-town farmers valued their independence above life itself. To lose one's land was to lose one's independence and, hence, one's claim to virtuous republican citizenship. The town meeting in Conway captured these collective fears: *"Mortgage our farms—we cannot think of. . . . To be tenants to landlords, we know not who, and pay rents for lands, purchased with our money, and converted from howling wilderness, into fruitful fields, by the sweat of our brow, seems . . . truly shocking."* Common Pleas judge William Whiting, one of the few state judges sympathetic to the Regulator Movement, gave credence to Conway's alarm. "Great numbers of farmers," he wrote from Berkshire County, "have been constantly stripped of what ever little stocks they possessed, and those often sold at public auction for a mere trifling." All that the farmers had fought the Revolution to secure seemed about to be lost.[22]

Representing their bourgeois opponents as luxury-loving men of paper and place, hill farmers turned the fury of classic republican rhetoric against eastern merchants, speculators, and fiscal innovators. Such men, the farmers claimed, were nothing more than "two-penny shopkeepers, usurers, speculators," incapable of civic virtue. They belonged to the "class of men, that delight to fatten on the distresses of mankind," exclaimed "A New Hampshire Freeman." Escalating the rhetorical war, another "Freeman" lamented, "The virtuous yeomanry of Massachusetts, who disdained to stoop to foreign tyrants, now bow their necks to internal despots," whereas "A Countryman" condemned eastern merchants and creditors as "Tories and Enemies to America." A Hampshire County farmer drew the most explicit parallel between 1775 and 1786, pointing out that it had "cost them much to maintain the *Great Men* under George the 3rd, but vastly more under the Commonwealth and Congres. . . . *They were miserably deceived by Hutchinson's opposers* [Boston whigs], who were the men who brought all their burdens upon them which, they are told, they should have been ever free from . . . again."[23]

22. Gross, ed., *In Debt to Shays,* 7; Brooke, *Heart of the Commonwealth,* 42, 45, 140–141. The town meeting of Conway is cited in both Nobles, "Shays's Neighbors," in Gross, ed., *In Debt to Shays,* 194, and Szatmary, *Shays' Rebellion,* 33–34. For Whiting quotation, see ibid., 29, 33. For a lengthy discussion of Whiting's role in the Regulator Movement, see Richards, *Shays's Rebellion,* 14–15, 39–40.

23. Cited in Lienesch, "Reinterpreting Rebellion," in Gross, ed., *In Debt to Shays,* 161–182, esp. 163, 166, 170; Szatmary, *Shays' Rebellion,* 35. Note that "Freeman" and "Countryman" were popular classic republican pseudonyms going back to the gentry's attacks on London's capitalist elites.

Having used the radical implications of Revolutionary rhetoric to transform older, classic republican rhetoric, the hill-town farmers returned to the extra-legislative, extraconstitutional apparatuses that had served them so well during the Revolution. As early as 1782, they began to convene extraconstitutional county conventions to protest the hard times and restrictive economic legislation of the 1780s, sending their protests and memorials east to Boston. When the General Assembly remained intransigent, Massachusetts's western farmers resorted once again to the moral economy of crowd action. Almost to the day twelve years after they had led the revolt against British tyranny, farmers from hill towns in Worcester, Hampshire, and Berkshire Counties marched again—first on the court in Worcester and then to Springfield. Anxious that their republican experiment not deteriorate into a mobocracy, the Continental Congress dispatched the Continental army to Springfield, ordering them to rout the rebels, reopen the courts, and defend the sanctity of property and contracts. As the army moved west, the urban press readied its rhetorical cannons. The battle over how broadly the Revolutionary promises active citizenship would extend erupted that fall in western Massachusetts.

INSCRIBING THE CONFLICT

During the war years, Isaiah Thomas had transferred his newspaper, the *Massachusetts Spy*, famous for its ardent defense of the Revolution, from Boston to Worcester. Following the war, he transformed the *Spy* into a weekly publication and renamed it the *Worcester Magazine*.[24] Located at the geographic center of the struggle between West and East—in part still a newspaper responsible for reporting current events, in part a political magazine seeking to shape opinion—the *Worcester Magazine* became a critical stage upon which differences between agrarian and commercial visions of the new Republic were played out.

During the early stages of the agrarian protests, Thomas expressed sympathy for the western farmers, pointing to the absence of specie in the West and reprinting the resolutions adopted by the county conventions and their demands for redress. By the summer's end, however, Thomas had taken his stand with Boston's whigs. "There is in mankind a strange restlessness of temper," Thomas, the former revolutionary, remarked to a readership of eastern mer-

---

24. Its initial issue appeared the first week of April 1786. One principal reason for the move was a change in postal rates making the sending of newspapers by mail prohibitively expensive. Magazines, at that point, were not affected by the rate raise.

chants and lawyers only too ready to be convinced of westerners' irresponsibility and excitability. This, "together with their great credulity and proneness to believe every idle or malicious suggestion against their *rulers* . . . enables the crafty and ambitious to lead them on to the most wild and absurd conduct." The *Worcester Magazine* presented western protestors as "unwary" and "passionate," easily "seduced" by "desperadoes," "duped by the crafty and insidious schemes of desperate, designing men"—in short, exactly the poor and rowdy men British classic republicans knew were incapable of virtuous citizenship.[25]

As western farmers began to muster, the *Worcester Magazine's* condemnations escalated. The farmers' extralegislative conventions were "treasonous," Thomas declared, "unconstitutional from the very nature of such assemblies." The "professed object of them is to overawe the legislature in order to bring them into impolitick, iniquitous and partial acts, such as the issuing paper money, to gratify a few . . . *whose aim is to cheat and defraud.*" (We see here the *Worcester Magazine's* deployment of terms particularly meaningful to its commercial readers.) "Now is the time when men act before they reflect," argued a contributor choosing the classic republican pseudonym "Cassius"; "the passions are inflamed, the solid principles of reason and truth scarcely examined." "Nestor," another contributor, agreed, asking, How could it be otherwise when one was dealing with "wild beasts"? The *Worcester Magazine* went so far as to call those who attended the conventions *"traitor[s],"* "willing tools to the vile agents of a foreign tyrant." (The whig elite charged the "Rebels" with abetting Great Britain's efforts to divide and reconquer America.) "Rouse! rouse! ye freeborn sons of Massachusetts," the magazine cried, in much the same language as it had used ten years earlier to rally Massachusetts's residents against the British. "It is a moment of danger—it is a crisis big with the most interesting events."[26]

25. Initially, the *Worcester Magazine* presented both sides, endorsing western complaints that tax collectors were as "conspicuous for their success in obtaining money from the indigent part of mankind, as for any other qualification for the office they sustain" and noting that the state's judicial system "tends rather to the embarrassment, perplexity and expence of the people, than . . . [the] furtherance of their prosperity and happiness" (A Friend to Justice, letter to the *Worcester Magazine*, I [1786], 22; John Read, "To Mr. Thomas Clarke, Representative of the Town of Roxbury," ibid., 71). For Thomas's comments, see A Citizen [Thomas], "To the Citizens of Massachusetts: On Conventions," ibid., 262–263.

26. An Other Citizen [Isaiah Thomas], "To the Free and Independent Citizens of Massachusetts: On Conventions," ibid., 273–276; Cassius, "To the Publick," ibid., II (1787), 481–482; Nestor, "To the Publick," ibid., 484–486; "To the Inhabitants of Massachusetts," ibid., I (1786), 291. The rebels, another issue of the *Worcester Magazine* reported, were "without reputation, hardy and factious in their tempers, and eminent only for their vices and depravity." Earlier in

Like the western farmers, the eastern bourgeois press deployed classic republican rhetoric. Rather than invest it with radical possibilities, however, the bourgeois press reinscribed its insistence that only the propertied and well educated could govern virtuously, all others being dupes of demagogues. Ironically, the commercial press thus adapted a political discourse designed to attack Britain's commercial and fiscal capitalists in order to defend those very capitalists in America and attack their critics.

Out of these rhetorical inversions and conversions the urban magazines constituted their first political Other, western Massachusetts's rebellious farmers. Led by Isaiah Thomas, the bourgeois press engaged the enemy. But they had yet to conquer him. Not even military defeat silenced western insistence on republican citizens' right to self-rule. Continuing to assert the democratic principles they had learned to assert during the Revolution, westerners turned from the older moral economy of crowd action to a more modern form of political protest—electoral politics. Their success in reversing whig economic legislation was impressive. In the years following Shays's Rebellion, they successfully pressured Massachusetts's General Court to declare a moratorium on debts and cut direct taxes, shifting them from land and poll to indirect taxes. With state tax revenue no longer directed to paying interest on state notes (held primarily by speculators), payment on those notes fell into arrears, and they rapidly lost value. Indeed, western farmers were so successful in redirecting the state's fiscal policies that, in the eyes of eastern elites, they came to epitomize what many among the founders condemned as "majoritarian tyranny," or "democratic despotism": popular control of state legislatures resulting in legislation seen as inimical to capitalist interests.[27]

Eastern alarm increased. If popular sovereignty became truly popular—if, that is, the majority, those with little or no property, were permitted to exercise their political rights to the fullest—the economic rights of the minority, those

---

the same paragraph, the same essayist had remarked: "To men of this description, a time of confusion is the season for harvest; and the more frequent the revolutions in government, the greater is their chance of rising upon the ruin of others." "Far from being virtuous republicans," the magazine continued in another essay, the insurgents were "men of desperate fortunes, who have no resource but in publick disturbances" (A Citizen, "To the Citizens of Massachusetts," *Worcester Magazine*, I [1786], 262; An Other Citizen, "To the Free and Independent Citizens of Massachusetts," ibid., 274).

27. Cited by Hoerder, *Crowd Action*, 381; Richards, *Shays's Rebellion*, 119; Wood, *Creation of the American Republic*, 411. On the larger issue of the founders' fear of the political power the "propertyless" might be inclined to use, see Jennifer Nedelsky, *Private Property and the Limits of American Constitutionalism: The Madisonian Framework and Its Legacy* (Chicago, 1990).

with significant land and capital holdings, would be subject to the "tyranny of the majority." A political tract James Madison wrote two years after Shays's Rebellion spells out these concerns. "Wherever the real power in a Government lies, there is the danger of oppression. In our Governments the real power lies in the majority of the community, and the invasion of private rights is *chiefly* to be apprehended, not from acts of Government contrary to the sense of its constituents, but from acts in which the Government is the mere instrument of the major number of constituents." "In all the Governments," he continued, "which were considered as beacons to republican Patriots and lawgivers the rights of persons were subjected to those of property." Alarmingly, according to Madison, this was not the case in Rhode Island, Massachusetts, or Pennsylvania, states where agrarian groups had gained control of the legislatures and were thus in a position to oppress the minority of propertied men. For the bourgeois press, Shays's Rebellion and, even more, its successful legislative after-career epitomized, in Fisher Ames's words, the volcanic dangers democracy posed.[28]

In the months after the suppression of Shays's Rebellion and as demands for a new federal government escalated, Philadelphia and New York magazines picked up the tocsin Thomas had thrown down. Representations of Massachusetts's western farmers as disorderly, irresponsible, and debt-ridden became a central motif in the urban press's campaign to secure ratification of the new constitution. If the threat posed by "democratic despotism" was to be contained, a new federal government had to be constituted, one that would maintain social order and protect property rights against potentially demagogic states.

The urban press in this way began to orchestrate the new Republic's first "moral panic." A moral panic, Stuart Hall tells us, occurs when a society or a powerful subgroup within that society perceives a pattern of radiating social disorder and chooses an individual or group to embody the dangers that disorder threatens. The causes of their perception are varied: changing state structures; shifting ideological configurations; changing class relations or capitalist structures. The clergy, political leaders, and "other right-thinking people" man the "moral barricades." Predictions of threatening times, of disorder and danger escalate. Firm steps are called for. Moves are taken to intensify a culture of control. A radical disconnect between actual episodes and inflammatory repre-

28. James Madison, "Observations on the 'Draught of a Constitution for Virginia'" (1788), in Gaillard Hunt, ed., *The Writings of James Madison*, 9 vols. (New York, 1900–1910), V, 287; Wood, *Creation of the American Republic*, 410–411.

sentations emerges. "The depth of the crises," Hall says, "is to be seen . . . in the accumulation of [rhetorical] contradictions and breaks" in its mode of representation.[29]

The widening circle of press attacks upon Massachusetts's hill-town farmers, especially when read in the context of an ongoing, nationwide debate over the form republican government should take, exactly fit the picture Hall draws of moral panic and its pattern of ideological displacement. And what fits the pattern most is the violent excess of the press's representations. Depictions of wild-eyed western farmers not only garnered support for a new constitution; they worked, as well, to stabilize an image of the new American–as–virtuous bourgeois citizen.

But did they? Or did the press's rhetorical violence only further destabilize the new national identity that was slowly forming around that figure? "Violent excess" certainly describes the press's mounting attacks upon Massachusetts's "disorderly" farmers. "Pulled from plough-tail or dram-shop," "the fellow student and companion of . . . oxen," they were "the most ignorant and unthinking of our community," Camillus (Fisher Ames) railed in Philadelphia's prestigious *American Museum,* concluding, "[The] philosophic observer . . . the present confusion . . . will behold men who have been civilized, returning to barbarism, and threatening to become fiercer than the savage children of nature." What could be expected from such men? Their protests were but "the unmeaning din of vulgar clamour excited." They were "ragged banditti," "a public mad."[30] Camillus's fusillade was but the first strike in an ongoing rhetorical battle. As moral panic spread, the Philadelphia and New York presses became, if anything, harsher in their condemnations of the rebellious farmers than Isaiah Thomas had been.

Camillus's phrase "savage children of nature" is worth noting. It suggested two images to late-eighteenth-century urbane readers, neither of them figuring a propertied and respectable republican. The first was Victor, the Wild Boy of Aveyron, a child without language, understanding, or self-control. The other, far more familiar image was that of the savage Indian, the relentless enemy of God and white Americans. Since the earliest days of settlement, European Americans had portrayed the woodland tribes as vicious, uneducated, untrust-

29. Stuart Hall et al., *Policing the Crisis: Mugging, the State, and Law and Order* (London, 1978), 16, 218–219, 222, 229. Central to Hall's understanding of moral crises is the move to a more "coercive" form of social control "by the capitalist state" (218).

30. Camillus [Fisher Ames], "Observations on the Late Insurrection in Massachusetts . . . Letter I," *American Museum,* II (1787), 315–318, esp. 317, 318; Camillus, "Letter II," ibid., 318–320, esp. 319.

worthy, and certainly incapable of virtuous republican citizenship. The political magazines easily redeployed these images of savage Native Americans to represent those other brutes, the mutinous and ill-clothed frontier farmers. Frontier farmers and native savages inhabited the same woods, laid claim to the same lands, and engaged in similar forms of agriculture. Each violated the eastern elite's understanding of civility. As the *Worcester Magazine* presented this view, the rebellious farmers, by turning to armed resistance, had relinquished their birthright as white republicans and men of enlightened civility and culture to assume a "rank among the savages . . . somewhere below the Oneida Indians." The image of savages was particularly telling when reinscribed in Philadelphia magazines. From the onset of the Revolutionary War, Pennsylvanians had engaged in genocidal warfare against the native peoples of the Ohio Valley. With the end of the war with Great Britain (though not of the war with Native Americans), the Pennsylvania legislature exacerbated the situation by voting to pay its Revolutionary War debt with money raised by the sale of lands still claimed by the Native Americans. Bitter warfare continued into the 1790s as whites relentlessly appropriated native lands.[31]

But the press did not limit its comparisons of the farmers to the feral denizens of the woods. In bitter satirical doggerel, the *Columbian Magazine* described the rebellion's leaders as "still lurking." "So worn, so wasted, so despised a crew / As e'en Guy Carleton might with pity view." As patriotic readers knew only too well, Guy Carleton was the British general who, following the defeat of General Cornwallis, implemented the peace treaty and the evacuation of the last British troops from the newly independent states. Just as Isaiah Thomas had done earlier, Philadelphia's publishers associated Massachusetts's farmers not only with violent native savages but with an unjust, tyrannical—and defeated—Britain. In this way, the Philadelphia press re-formed and reinscribed Thomas's vision of western farmers as dupes of pro-British agitators.[32]

That the elite eastern press represented impoverished hill farmers as "dumb

31. Harlan Lane, *The Wild Boy of Aveyron* (Cambridge, Mass., 1976); Roger Shattuck, *The Forbidden Experiment: The Story of the Wild Boy of Aveyron* (New York, 1994). François Truffaut made an interesting film on this subject *(L'enfant sauvage* [1970]). For a discussion of European American representations of Native Americans, see Section 2, below. Throughout the eighteenth century, the eastern bourgeoisie had viewed western settlers as uncouth and illiterate. The press's attacks on Shays's rebels merely adapted this pattern to the specific Massachusetts situation. For a discussion of the more general pattern, see Chapter 4, below. Massachusetts newspaper comment cited in Szatmary, *Shays' Rebellion*, 73.

32. "Extract of a Letter from a Gentleman in Cumberland County . . . ," *Columbian Magazine*, I (1787), 731–732.

oxen" and "savage" democrats, indeed, even as pawns of the British, should not surprise us. They were, after all, appealing to America's bourgeoisie. What is startling, however, is that the same press depicted Massachusetts's stern, weather-worn farmers as sybaritic, degenerate, and effete—in short, as effeminate. Here we come to the final piece of the press's construction of the new American's first constituting Other. The *Worcester Magazine* began the rhetorical transformation of "dumb oxen" into effeminate sybarites early in the tumultuous summer of 1786. Contesting western claims that "the Times were hard," and therefore taxes should be lowered and paper money issued, "A Cobler" wrote to the *Worcester Magazine*. "I am a little man," he began, contrasting himself to the Great Men, a term Antifederalists used when condemning the eastern elite. "I have no learning, and do not know nor care anything about words; but will tell you my thoughts." The cobbler then blamed the farmers' hard times on their own extravagant tastes and purchases. "Some of you that are not worth a shilling, and perhaps owe fifty pounds," he continued, "must carry a watch, or ware ruffles, or two or three silk handkerchiefs whisking about, or a fine coat, or a beaver hat; . . . if your debts were paid . . . [you] would be as poor as Job's cat . . . yet you keep spending." The cobbler then switched his economic attack to one upon the farmers' manly self-identity: "We talk about women, but I think we are full as extravagant as they, and more so."[33]

In the years following the uprising, Philadelphia's and New York's press reiterated this argument. "The complaint of hard times . . . is all imaginary," a contributor to the *American Museum* assured Philadelphia's elite readers, adding, "Indolence and extravagance in dress are the source from which all the evils so bitterly complained of, flow." Benjamin Franklin added his voice to the rising clamor, insisting that indulgence in luxurious dress and imported trifles, not high taxes, had impoverished Massachusetts farmers. "Mr. Printer," he wrote, evoking his own artisan past and underscoring the role the print culture played in the Federalist political venture, "I saw a man . . . [bring] a lamb to market.—Lambs command cash and cash pays taxes—but the good country-

---

33. A Cobler, letter to the *Worcester Magazine*, I (1786), 23. The cobbler was probably referring to "book debts," a practice that permitted subsistence farmers to carry debts on shopkeepers' books from one harvest to the next—the sale of one year's harvest would pay off the debt of the preceding year and permit the farmer to borrow against the anticipated harvest of the following year. Farmers did not consider these to be debts but rather credit extended.

Other correspondents entered the lists: "Never *follow fashions*," one advised farmers dressed in homespun, and another attributed the cause of the rebellion to farmers' addictions to "foreign luxuries and superfluities" ("An Infallible Cure for Hard Times," *Worcester Magazine*, I [1786], 81; An Inhabitant of Worcester County, letter, ibid., 283–285, esp. 284).

man went to a store and bought a feather—5 shillings for a feather, mr. Printer." "Sugar, coffee, gauzes, silks, feathers, and the whole list of baubles and trinkets," he continued in another article, "what an enormous expense! . . . My countrymen are all grown very tasty!"[34] A number of other essayists reinscribed Franklin's satire of farmers who caused "hard times" and threatened eighteenth-century social order by dressing like urban(e) merchants and professional men. "For a few years past," one author complained, "farmers have, to appearance, been vieing with the merchants in dress. . . . By this means they have reduced themselves to poverty, and now loudly complain of the hardness of the times." Dressing inappropriately, the farmers impoverished themselves and appeared ridiculous in the eyes of the more sophisticated. "The other day," this writer continued, "I went to see some farmers who owed me a trifle. I found them in the field at work: one was clad in a velvet vest and breeches, and fine worsted stockings; the other in sattinet vest and breeches, stockings like his companion, and a fine holland shirt, with a ruffle at the bosom. I asked them for the money they owed me; and received payment in the solid coin of 'money is exceedingly scarce: the times are very hard: and it is an impossible thing to get money.'" "I mention this circumstance," he added, "to shew that the extravagance of people to decorate their bodies, is the origin of their poverty; and the hardness of the times arises from a foolish pride." Rather than present the decline in the use of homespun as evidence of the extension of a cash/consumer economy into rural America—an event essential to the commercialization of America and the prosperity of Philadelphia, New York, and Boston merchants and industrialists—this author represented it as an effeminate indulgence of the appetites and as an inappropriate aping of social superiors.[35]

In this way, charges of class and gender disorder fused. Clothing out of order signaled men out of order. Since eighteenth-century writers used clothing as a signifier for reason and civilization, as a sign of a man's elevation above brute (that is, unclothed) nature, the urban press seems to insist that only the bourgeoisie had a right to proclaim their reason and civility through their dress.

34. "On Hard Times," *American Museum*, I (1787), 536–538, esp. 536. See, as well, Amicus, "Essay on the Fatal Tendency of Prevailing Luxuries . . . ," ibid., II (1787), 216–220; An Industrious Man [Benjamin Franklin], "On Redress of Grievances," ibid., I (1787), 111–112. Franklin expressed similar sentiments in another essay: Tom Thoughtful [Franklin], "The Devil Is in You," ibid., 112–115. We should note that, with the exception of coffee, all these trifles Franklin complained of—gauzes, baubles, trinkets—were associated with the image of the extravagant woman of fashion.

35. "On Hard Times," ibid., 536–538, esp. 537–538.

Hardworking farmers, "companions of their oxen," must dress in an uncouth, even bestial manner. And, of course, the feminized man was the ultimate man out of order.

Sartorial attacks steadily multiplied. The author of "A Word of Consolation for America" concurred. "We have erred, greatly erred . . . by extravagant importations and consumption of foreign . . . gew-gaws and needless trumpery." Adopting traditional commercial republican rhetoric, the essay went on to contrast the waste of good money on such unmanly items to the investment of capital in business ventures. "This has taken away a good deal of our money, which we now want to carry on business." He ended by advising a good beating for those guilty of inappropriate dressing, such as one would impose on children, social underlings, or slaves. A similar spirit characterized a report by the Society for Political Enquiries, meeting at the house of Benjamin Franklin, then governor of Pennsylvania. Evoking the classic republican association of luxurious consumption with unsavory women, the report's authors complained, "Our money [is] absorbed by a *wanton* consumption of imported luxuries."[36]

What can we make of this refiguring of Massachusetts's rugged frontier farmers as "tasty," effeminate, and foppishly clothed? First, the spokesmen of America's commercial and fiscal revolutions used the urban magazines to displace classic republican representations of themselves as feminine creatures of an unreal world of corrupting desires and uncontrolled appetites onto the very men their nascent commercial revolution most threatened, men who had vigorously battled with them on literal as well as rhetorical battlefields. Second, and even more critically, these same spokesmen refused western hill farmers their hitherto unchallenged claims to virility, strength, and heroism. Bedecked as dandies, dripping with lace, tripping over their fashionable—and too-large—shoe buckles, or, alternatively, cowering in the wooded wastelands between the United States and Canada, their sad state commanding the pity of even the defeated British, the frontier farmers no longer embodied the republican subject's most critical attribute—his *virtu*, that fusion of civic virtue and virility. The rhetorical excesses of the urban press overwhelmed the western farmer, who emerges on their pages a fusion of destabilizing opposites: dandified

36. "A Word of Consolation for America . . . ," *American Museum*, I (1787), 187–190, esp. 188; T. C., Esq., "An Enquiry into the Principles on Which a Commercial System for the United States of America Should Be Founded; . . . Read before the Society for Political Enquiries, Convened at the House of His Excellency Benjamin Franklin . . . May 11, 1787," ibid., 496–514.

wastrel and dumb ox, savage native and hedonist. Denied a stable persona within his nation's press, how could the western farmer lay claim to the judgment and the manly self-control a virtuous republican citizen required?

But the magazines' ploy had an unintended and decentering effect. By questioning the farmers' manhood and virility, the magazines did more than rob western farmers of their self-image as virile republicans battling corruption and tyranny. They fractured the concept of masculinity itself by separating manliness from maleness. And they did so in a thoroughly counterintuitive fashion, by representing the refined, fashionably attired commercial elite as "manly" and those who plowed New England's rocky soil and hefted its bales of hay as effeminate. For the bourgeois press to have effected such a bold rhetorical displacement is stunning—and cautionary. True, the press had been able to exploit classic republican rhetoric to discountenance farmers' complaints of the selfishness of merchants and the hard times commercial adventures had brought on the country. But they had done so by significantly compromising their representation of the new American as a virile republican citizen. If the urban press had argued that Massachusetts farmers' manliness was of so exaggerated a form that it made them more animals than men and that they thus perverted republican *virtu* by pushing it to a bestial extreme, then manliness as a normative concept would have remained intact. But by representing farmers as "tasty" and womanish, the urban press disrupted the presumed natural connection between maleness and manliness. Disembodying the characteristics of gender, the press fractured the concept of masculinity itself. For if not all men are manly, if especially weathered western farmers are not manly, then masculinity is no longer a self-evident, "natural," physically grounded characteristic. It becomes performative, that is, artificial, calculated, something some men do well, others poorly, some not at all. As a result, which men "do" masculinity well and which do not is determined, not by the man himself, but by his audience's responses to his performance of manliness. And, for eighteenth-century readers, performance itself was tied to the theatrical, the unreal, indeed to counterfeiting, since an alternative word for "actor" was "counterfeit."

The urban press had rendered their new American dependent on, and thus subject to, his audience's approval. As a consequence, he could no longer lay claim to the independence, autonomy, and self-reliance republicanism demanded. This was a serious rhetorical move. By making manliness a performance dependent on audience approval, the press hollowed out the core of a virtuous republican identity. For an example of the way gender had begun to lose all meaning, let us look at another contribution to the *Worcester Magazine*.

In the midst of the rhetorical disputes leading to the Shays uprising, the *Worcester Magazine* published a satirical poem written by "four very smart and agreeable young ladies." The poem pointedly criticized European American men as effeminate. This time, however, the objects of the attack were, not western farmers, but young men of commerce and the city, "the young mercantile bucks of the present day," as the "ladies" put it, the very clerks and young lawyers who would later fly to arms to put down womanly rebellious farmers.[37]

The poem's satire calls for close examination. Certainly, it was critical of America's new men of fashion, men who dressed in the French mode and sought to impress others with their culture and refinement. (No true republicans, they.) Boston's young ladies wrote "T' expose those self admiring honies, / The puppy-beaux and macaronies, / Who ape our manners, lisp and sigh, / If frighten'd, faint—if troubled, die—, / Who dress in silk—paint—perfum'd are, / And beat us out in loads of hair." Finding the "puppy-beaux" more feminine than themselves, the "ladies" reversed roles, assuming the "manly" posture and role the "puppy-beaux" had abandoned. "Let us . . . With sword equip'd," they continued, "compose a band, / To wage continual war with all those, / Whose monkey tricks disgrace the small-clothes; / For all the world will call that plan good, / Which beats such reptiles back to manhood." We can only wonder who was left in the new Republic to play the role of virile citizen. The choice seemed to rest between western farmers in satin waistcoats, urbane "puppy-beaux and macaronies," or "four very smart and agreeable young ladies" who, armed with the pen of social satire, threatened to "beat" men into the appearance of proper masculinity. In the *Worcester Magazine,* manliness was becoming a floating signifier that, like pens and swords, anyone could pick up at will.[38]

But we have not yet plumbed this satire's destabilization of gender. On its very first line, we find a slang word, "honies." In the late eighteenth century, "honies" could have meant "a foolish good natured person." But it carried a second meaning: semen. Can the phrase "self admiring honies" be read as referring to masturbating young men who found sexual pleasure among themselves rather than with young women? In a few years, New England's press would become obsessed with social problems it associated with self-pleasure—the principal one being the alienation of young men from women and families. Is this the first sign of future concerns?[39]

---

37. "Effeminacy," *Worcester Magazine,* I (1786), 66.

38. Ibid.

39. For the meanings attached to "honey," see Harold Wentworth and Stuart Berg Flexner,

But pause a moment. It is unlikely that "agreeable young ladies" in eighteenth-century Boston would submit a social satire for publication, especially one that begins with a veiled reference to masturbation. Still other questions suggest themselves. Introducing the satire to his readers, Thomas mentions that it was written on "ass's-skin"—like the writing of satire itself, not a particularly ladylike choice. Is Thomas suggesting that "agreeable young ladies" might not have written this satire, that a male correspondent had—even that Thomas had? (We do know that Thomas published a pirated edition of *Fanny Hill,* one of the eighteenth century's best-known pornographic romances, again ostensibly written in a female voice.) But why would a male writer mask his identity behind a female authorial persona, especially in a satire disparaging the effeminate behavior of the Republic's urbane youth? This last question leaves us wondering who was more effeminate—"the puppy-beaux and macaronies" or a man who donned a female persona to criticize them? In the new urban press, gender had become very problematic.

THE VEXING NATURE OF REPRESENTATION

Rhetorical representation, so critical and so troubling a factor in the fabrication of a new national identity, did not stand alone—not in the urban magazines, not within eighteenth-century political practices. Two other forms of representation, triangulating with rhetorical representations and with one another, played as central a role in the construction of the new American. These other two were political and fiscal representation. Political representation defined relations between the citizen and his political representative, making the modern republic possible. Fiscal representation, as central to economic modernity as political representation was to political modernity, recognized commercial paper and paper money as legitimate representations of real wealth and value—that is, of real estates. What impact did these other two forms of representation have upon the new American's claims to manliness, especially manliness grounded on classic republicanism? Did they reaffirm the new American's virility and hence his claims to civic virtue, or did they further emasculate and effeminize him?

Political fictions and points of oppositional tension, political representation

---

Dictionary of American Slang, 2d ed. (New York, 1975). For a discussion of the "moral panic" over youthful male masturbation, see Carroll Smith-Rosenberg, "Sex as Symbol in Jacksonian America," in John Demos and Serane Babcock, eds., *Turning Points: Historical and Sociological Essays on the Family* (Chicago, 1978).

and popular sovereignty constitute the twin poles of the modern republican state. Popular sovereignty envisions empowered citizens, investing them with the inalienable right of self-governance. Political representation alienates that inalienable right, transferring the citizen's right of self-governance to the political representative. The relationship between the citizen/voter and the political representative is central to our understanding of the nature of citizenship and the structure of power within the republican state. Fictively, political representation signals "the marriage of true minds"—as well as a contractual relation between equals, that is, between the voter and the representative. But like so many other marriages, the fiction of political representation frequently cloaks a relationship of dominance and submission. The degree to which the relationship of representative and citizen is an interactive one will determine the degree to which the citizen's inalienable right to self-governance is preserved or alienated. In other words, it will determine which political fiction—that of popular sovereignty or of political representation—is more real.[40]

Rhetorical and political representation were not the only forms of representation to trouble the new nation. Their revolution fueled by classical republican rhetoric and its denunciation of the new ways of fiscal capitalism, late-eighteenth-century European Americans found paper money, bank notes, government bonds—all fictive representations of real wealth and real estates— deeply problematic. At the same time, as participants in the eighteenth century's commercial and fiscal revolutions, they found working with such fictions unavoidable. But it was not only fiscal representation's ability to accurately represent value that raised questions. Equally disturbing, the modern republic's growing involvement in and dependence upon credit and bonds significantly altered the nature of republican governance and the republic's relation with its citizens. The modern republic is Janus-faced. On the one hand, it is a sovereign political state dedicated to protecting the rights of its citizens and its own honor internationally. On the other, it is a fiscal capitalist institution

40. For a survey of the way political representation evolved in the Anglo-American world, see J. R. Pole, *Political Representation in England and the Origins of the American Republic* (New York, 1966). For a discussion of the difficulties of balancing popular and state sovereignty, see Samuel Hutchinson Beer, *To Make a Nation: The Rediscovery of American Federalism* (Cambridge, Mass., 1993). The relation of citizen to representative raises issues of the subordination of the individual citizen to state governance and to community cohesion that are critical to all classic republican theorists from Hobbes to Locke to Rousseau. For a particularly perceptive exploration of Rousseau's thoughts along these lines, see Elizabeth Wingrove, "Republican Romance," paper presented at the Center for the Study of Social Transformation, University of Michigan, October 1996.

whose credibility rests upon the opinions of its creditor-capitalist citizens. European Americans worried about the impact the new forms of fiscal representation would have upon the sovereign powers of their new republican state and the empowerment—or disempowerment—of its citizens. At times, these three modern forms of representation worked in tandem, reinforcing and stabilizing a new American national identity. At other times, they warred with one another, multiplying the new American's contradictory personas. Examining these interactions raises critical questions. What effect does the process of representation have upon that which is represented—be they events or individuals refigured through words, voters represented by their legislators, or material wealth abstracted as capital? What roles do these varied forms of representation play in the protean flow of power that characterizes the modern republic, and how is that flow engendered?

TAMING THE PEOPLE

Political representation was a seventeenth-century invention, created to legitimate the English Civil War and Parliament's beheading of Charles I. As Edmund Morgan somewhat cynically states the matter, members of Parliament "invented the sovereignty of the people in order to claim it for themselves. . . . In the name of *the* people [parliamentary representatives] became all-powerful in government, shedding as much as possible the local, subject character that made them representatives of a particular set of people." Morgan continues: "In this transformation, government . . . [became] something other, something external to the local community." So conceived, Morgan argues, political representation inscribes a world of make-believe. "Make believe that the people *have* a voice or make believe that the representatives of the people *are* the people. Make believe that governors are the servants of the people."[41]

Seventeenth- and eighteenth-century English political writers not only in-

41. Edmund S. Morgan, *Inventing the People: The Rise of Popular Sovereignty in England and America* (New York, 1988), 50, 53, 267 ("The sovereignty of the people had to be tamed. . . . It had to be given a close enough resemblance to fact to permit the willing suspension of disbelief, but it must not be interpreted so literally as to invite subversion either of the social order or of the accompanying political authority it was designed to support" [151]). As Puritan MP Richard Overton stated the argument, by voting for members of Parliament in 1646, the "Free-born People of England" had, in effect, told the MPs, "We possessed you with the same Power that was in our selves" (William Haller, ed., *Tracts on Liberty in the Puritan Revolution: 1638–1647,* III [New York, 1933], 353). Beer presents a very perceptive comparison of the concepts of virtual and actual representation *(To Make a Nation,* 64–66, 149–151).

vented "the People" and the political representative. As we have seen, they invented that other, potentially disruptive, player in the republican game—the virtuous republican. Passivity and deference to the opinion of others were anathema to this independent citizen who involved himself in governance and political issues. Seventeenth-century political radicals' calls for frequent parliamentary elections and rotation in office envisioned government built around the active citizen. We see here a conflict between two forms of political sovereignty—constituent sovereignty, evident in Parliament's invention of "the People" as the ultimate, but abstract, political authority, and governmental sovereignty, meaning the right of citizens to a direct voice in their own governance. In England, the power struggle between empowered republican citizens and parliamentary power was confined to the pages of political treatises. Transplanted to British North America, it burst those constraints. By the opening decades of the eighteenth century, New England town meetings began to instruct legislators. By the time revolution broke out, local constituents throughout the colonies had begun to instruct their representatives. Voters even in the conservative stronghold of South Carolina proclaimed the right to direct their legislators "the most invaluable privilege of a free people." To deny that right "will at one stroke transform us into *legal* SLAVES to our *lordly* SERVANTS."[42]

Of course, the urban elite viewed the practice of instructing representatives with horror. "The multitude . . . have not a sufficient stock of reason and knowledge to guide them," Alexander Hamilton commented acerbically. The

---

42. J. G. A. Pocock, *The Machiavellian Moment: Florentine Political Thought and the Atlantic Republican Tradition* (Princeton, N.J., 1975), chap. 7; Algernon Sidney, "Discourses concerning Government," cited in Beer, *To Make a Nation*, 165. See also J. Robertson, ed., *The Works of Algernon Sidney* (London, 1772), chaps. 1–3. During the Stamp Act crisis, James Otis introduced the radical new practice of announcing his position on key political issues when he stood for election. Representatives, he insisted, should be responsible to their electors, who had a right to know how their representative planned to vote on key political issues. See Otis, *The Rights of the British Colonies Asserted and Proved* (Boston, 1764). See, as well, Bernard Bailyn's "Introduction" to Bailyn, ed., *Pamphlets of the American Revolution, 1750–1776* (Cambridge, 1965). Otis, as part of Boston's whig elite, was far more concerned with establishing the fiction of the American people as a political authority equal to Parliament than in expanding popular political power (Beer, *To Make a Nation*, 169–171). See, as well, Gary B. Nash, *The Urban Crucible: Social Change, Political Consciousness, and the Origins of the American Revolution* (Cambridge, Mass., 1979), 192; Hoerder, *Crowd Action*, 91; Olton, *Artisans for Independence*, 43; Wood, *Creation of the American Republic*, 162–188. See also ibid., 193, and, more generally, 168–194. Popular insistence on the voters' right to instruct their representatives dovetailed with more radical extralegislative moves, especially in Massachusetts with the institutionalization of county conventions during and immediately after the Revolutionary War.

Republic must "look further than to the bulk of the people for the greatest wisdom, firmness, consistency, and perseverance," John Adams and other signers of the Essex Resolves insisted. "These qualities will most probably be found amongst men of education and fortune. From such men we are to expect genius cultivated by reading, and all the various advantages and assistances, which art, and a liberal education aided by wealth, can furnish."[43]

The new citizens, debating the ratification of the new constitution, faced a momentous decision. Which form of representation would prevail—that demanded by Revolutionary town meetings and extralegislative county conventions, rights informed by radical whig rhetoric, or that urged in the Essex Resolves, ones that reinscribed the right of the few to govern the many? The answer to this question would profoundly affect the empowerment of the citizen and the nature of representation in the new Republic.

Systematically challenging the further democratization of political representation, the urban magazines played a critical role in answering this question and in the process significantly affected the image of the new American as a republican citizen and his relation to political power. Insisting that the great mass of the People—whose potential for political unrest had just shaken the bourgeoisie to its core—must be kept at a safe remove from the exercise of political governance, urban writers and editors set about to reinscribe the political representative as an empowered and independent figure, the voter as a deferential subject. They did so in three distinct moves.

First, they began by impugning the competency of the average citizen to govern. Magazine essay after magazine essay insisted that the People lacked the ability to wisely govern either themselves or the Republic. "The opinion of the people at large, are often erroneous," the author of "Maxims for Republics" complained at the height of debates over the ratification of the Constitution. "Large collections of people are turbulent, tumultuous, led by clamorous demagogues," another added, not so obliquely referencing Shays's Rebellion. The

43. "The Essex Result, 1778," in Oscar Handlin and Mary Handlin, eds., *The Popular Sources of Political Authority: Documents on the Massachusetts Constitution of 1780* (Cambridge, Mass., 1966), 324–365, esp. 333–334; Harold C. Syrett, ed., *The Papers of Alexander Hamilton*, 15 vols. (New York, 1961–1987), I, 176–177. Thomas Doerflinger points out that Pennsylvania's Revolutionary state constitution of 1779 was no sooner adopted than the state's conservative whig elite began to organize for its repeal, an event they achieved in 1790 (Doerflinger, *Vigorous Spirit of Enterprise*, 254). Earlier, during the prewar struggles over nonimportation boycotts, similar merchants had expressed similar antipopulist opinions. See, for example, *To the Free and Patriotic Inhabitants of the City of Philadelphia and the Province of Pennsylvania* (Philadelphia, 1770). See, as well, Olton, *Artisans for Independence, 57.*

People were "not capable of that cool deliberation that is required in choosing legislators," much less in writing legislation. Ironically, Federalists, although advocating a strong national government, echoed Montesquieu's opinion that "the people collectively are extremely unfit . . . they ought to have no share in the government but for the choosing of representatives, which is within their reach."[44]

Denunciations of popular sovereignty multiplied in the aftermath of Shays's Rebellion. Fisher Ames condemned Massachusetts's electors as governed, not by reason, but by "the love of novelty, and the passion for the marvelous." "They have invited imposture, and drank down deception like water. They will remain as blind, as credulous, as irritable as ever." For men such as these to assert their right to a direct voice in governing or to instruct their representatives would threaten the very structure of government and society. "It is true that every man has the *right* of judging," another urban essayist argued, "but it is not true that every man has the *power*." "Without the *power*, what is the right but a dangerous weapon, that may wound the best of governments?" "There is a wide difference between power being derived from the people, and being seated in the people," yet another writer maintained. "The former proposition cannot be too often inculcated in a free country. Disorder and tyranny must ensue from all power being seated in the bulk of the people." Representative republics wisely distanced the average citizen from the direct exercise of governmental power.[45]

Having denigrated the average citizen and curtailed his right to participate in government, the urban press proceeded to idealize and empower his political representative. Again the Federalist press reinscribed elite whig valorizations of government by the virtuous few. The virtuous representative, essay after essay insisted, must be a man of education, blessed with breadth of vision and rational, considered judgment. Only by assiduously maintaining his independence from his constituents could the representative act his part as statesman. Judicious and wise, he would base his decisions "upon facts . . . after faction has ceased to distort, and enthusiasm to adorn them." "It is otherwise with the public," a

44. Sidney, "Maxims for Republics," *American Museum*, II (1787), 80–82, esp. 81; [Noah Webster], review of Isaiah Thomas, "Thoughts on the Political Situation of the United States, Etc.," ibid., I (1788), part 2, 804–806; Baron de Montesquieu, *Spirit of the Laws*, trans. Thomas Nugent (New York, 1949), book II, chap. 6, 154–155, cited by Beer, *To Make a Nation*, 227. See ibid., chap. 7 for an interesting discussion of Montesquieu.

45. Camillus, "Letter I," *American Museum*, II (1787), 316, and "Letter II," ibid., 318–320; "Of Politics . . . ," *Columbian Magazine*, I (1787), 819–822, esp. 821; "Maxims for Republics," *American Museum*, II (1787), 82.

Federalist writer commented with bitter irony. "Their judgment is formed . . . while the rage of party gives an acumen to their penetration."[46]

Governing, as represented on the pages of the urban press, had become too complex a task for the average voter. "A complicated science . . . [government] relates to that most complicated of all God's works, the mind of man," an essay addressed to the "Freemen of America" asserted. "It requires abilities and knowledge of a variety of other subjects, to understand it." The statesman and the legislator, an essay entitled "Of Politics" informed readers of Philadelphia's elegant *Columbian Magazine,* should be educated and talented, expert in the history of great empires and the classic forms of government. "If such knowledge and abilities are necessary to make political conversation rational and profitable, we may without breach of charity affirm, that the number of those who are qualified to censure the measures of government . . . is small indeed." Only a few months earlier, "The Improver," lecturing another group of urban readers about the people's "Ludicrous Thoughts on Money," criticized even such hardworking members of the urban middle class as small-scale merchants, tradesmen, mechanics, and farmers (all of whom had begun to exert their own political voice) for presuming to have opinions on political issues. Embracing an elite vision of political service reminiscent of tory defenses of royal government, he lamented that "the honest farmer, not content with cultivating the fruitful fields; the merchant, unwilling to be continually employed, in packing and unpacking goods, drawing out accounts, invoices, and bills of lading—and in short, almost all ranks of society, disdaining the mean, selfish principle of *minding their own business,* are generously interesting themselves in the affairs of the commonwealth."[47]

The rhetorical disempowerment of new American citizens, however, could not rest secure on such overtly elitist depictions of the political electors' inferiority and the political representatives' superiority. At least two pressing reasons prevented the new urban press from publicly espousing so bald an avowal of elitism and the politics of deference. First, popular assertions of the right of artisans, farmers, tradesmen, and lesser professionals to participate in

46. Camillus, "Letter I," *American Museum,* II (1787), 315, and "Letter II," ibid., 319; [Webster], review of Thomas, "Thoughts on the Political Situation," *American Magazine,* I (1788), 804–806.

47. Sidney, "Maxims for Republics," *American Museum,* II (1787), 81; "The Improver, No. LXX," *Columbian Magazine,* I (1787), 646–649, esp. 646; Harrington, "To the Freemen of America," *American Museum,* I (1787), 491–495, esp. 491; "Of Politics . . . ," *Columbian Magazine,* I (1787), 821; "On Public Faith," *American Museum,* I (1787), 405–408; "On Hard Times," ibid., 536–538.

the Revolutionary extraparliamentary committees and to instruct their political representatives were too fresh in the popular imagination, the empowerment of the average citizen still too intoxicating. Antifederalist critics could too easily link Federalists' arguments constraining the political voice of the average political subject to British insistence on virtual representation. The urban press had to couch their arguments in more nuanced ways.

Second, and perhaps even more important, Federalists were trapped by their own insistence on the sovereignty and independence of the newly proposed federal government. That government, they insisted, far from being the creature of, and thus subject to, the states, must be independent from and equal to those states. It must be strong and autonomous. But from where did the new federal state derive its sovereignty? Not from the states, or the new government would always be subject to them, as Congress was under the Articles of Confederation. Rather, as its preamble so boldly states, the new constitution derived its sovereign authority from "the People of the United States." James Madison, Morgan asserts, firmly believed the new government to be the creature of "an American people, a people who constituted a separate and superior entity, capable of conveying to a national government an authority that would necessarily impinge on the authority of the state governments." As the Long Parliament had done a century and a half earlier, so now Madison "invented the People." Although an avowed enemy of "democratic despotism," he knew the political benefits of enveloping the new government in the rhetoric of radical popular sovereignty. Thus he declared in Federalist no. 46: "The federal and State governments are in fact but different agents and trustees of the people. . . . The ultimate authority . . . resides in the people alone."[48]

The Federalists and their magazines, committed to an exclusionary vision of government exercised by the few for the general good, faced a serious dilemma. To simply assert the political representative's intellectual and social superiority to his political subjects was to undermine the principle of popular sovereignty that the new constitution claimed as its authorizing source—and that even the commercial elite had celebrated during the heady days of revolution. What other political authority than the People could whig patriots have brought to counter parliamentary authority?[49] Popular sovereignty and the authority of

48. Morgan, *Inventing the People,* 267; James Madison, no. 46, in Isaac Kramnick, ed., *The Federalist Papers* (London, 1987), 237. I am particularly indebted to Samuel Beer for underscoring the significance the concept of popular sovereignty played in constituting a powerful national government (Beer, *To Make a Nation,* 313–316, 339).

49. For a discussion of the importance of basing the new constitution and the new government it authorized on the generalized (and to a large extent fictional) voice of "the People" in

the average voter lay at the heart of that most powerful of Revolutionary chants—"No taxation without representation!" However, even, or perhaps especially, during those days of radical protest and revolution, there had been no consensus as to the extent to which people could actually exercise political authority. By the war's end, the elite had reembraced deferential political principles—without, however, explicitly rejecting the rhetoric of popular sovereignty or the influence of the People. How, then, were the urban magazines to deal with a problem that was both rhetorical and ideological?

Federalist publishers resorted to a third, far more complex, stratagem. To endow the political representative with governmental powers already bestowed in the popular imagination on the People, they had first to make the representative into the literal embodiment of the People. Positioned as indistinguishable from the citizens they represented, legislators could then claim to possess all the powers of the People, most especially the People's claim to governmental sovereignty. Once established as the sole possessors of governmental sovereignty, representatives could then assert their right to subject the People to their governance.[50]

To accomplish this transfer of power, urban publishers seized upon and inverted the very arguments that Radical Whigs, western farmers, and Antifederalists developed to establish the People's right to control their political representatives. Radical Whigs and Antifederalists had insisted that, to truly represent the wishes of their constituents, political representatives must be just like, and thus tied to, those constituents. "The representative is one who appears in behalf of, and acts for, others," New York Antifederalist leader Malancton Smith argued during those heated days of constitutional debate. "He ought, therefore, to be fully acquainted with the feelings, circumstances, and interests of the persons whom he represents."[51] Earlier, Thomas Paine had

---

elite discussions before the Constitutional Convention and during the convention itself, see Morgan, *Inventing the People,* chap. 11, esp. 260, 267.

50. Morgan, although not differing from me in the evidence he presents concerning the Founders' fear of truly popular government, presents the dilemma in somewhat different terms. He sees the "make-believe" of political representation and popular government as presenting a practical quandary to statesmen who sought to institutionalize a broad "continental" vision in the new Republic. State governments, dominated by average citizens during the 1780s, refused to see the larger national picture, Morgan explains, and therefore had to be circumvented by the new Federal constitution (*Inventing the People,* esp. chap. 10).

51. Morgan, *Inventing the People,* 272, 278. For a more elaborate analysis of Smith, see Saul Cornell, "Politics of the Middling Sort: The Bourgeois Radicalism of Abraham Yates, Melancton Smith, and the New York Antifederalists," in Paul A. Gilje and William Pencak, eds., *New York in the Age of the Constitution, 1775–1800* (Madison, N.J., 1992), 151–175; and, of course, the

expressed similar Radical Whig sentiments. The citizen and his political representative are but parts of the same body, Paine insisted. Political representatives "are supposed to have the same concerns at stake [as] those who appointed them, and . . . act in the same manner *as the whole body* would act were they present."[52]

This fusion of identities became increasingly central to the Federal press's efforts to rhetorically establish the political representative as his constituents' governor and master. Nowhere did this fusion assume a more sophistical form than on the pages of the *American Magazine*, published by Noah Webster, one of the most articulate of the new nation's new conservatives. Since these essays played a critical role in Federalists' rhetorical subjugation of the new political subject, let us examine them more closely, the better to map this process. "The Principle of Government and Commerce," written, significantly, under the pseudonym "An American," appeared in the premier issue of Webster's *American Magazine*. We can read it, therefore, as Webster's first word on the subject.[53]

"The Principle of Government and Commerce" opens with two statements that reiterate one another. (Was Webster simply trying to capture his readers' attention or did the message need doubly to be told?) Embracing the radical construction of "popular sovereignty," these reiterated statements appear at first to empower the political subject. Inscribing a politics of deference, they end by disempowering him. Let us examine this merging of what western farmers and Radical Whigs would see as opposites.

"ALL mankind are, by nature, free, and have a right to enjoy life, liberty and property. One person has no right to take from another . . . or lessen his freedom of thinking and acting," the essay began in a classic Lockean and politically empowering manner. Then, quickly repositioning the subject from the state of nature to the political state, Webster just as quickly asserted the state's need to subject the political citizen to governmental authority. "A collection of individuals forms a *society*," he said, "and every society must have a

---

classic study, Jackson Turner Main, *The Antifederalists: Critics of the Constitution, 1781–1788* (1961; rpt., Chapel Hill, N.C., 2004).

52. Thomas Paine, "Common Sense," in Phillip S. Foner, ed., *The Complete Writings of Thomas Paine*, 2 vols. (New York, [1945]), I, 43. Though political worlds apart, and representing a very different perspective, George Mason, debating at the Constitutional Convention, went even further, at least rhetorically: "The requisites in actual representation are that the Representatives should . . . think [as their constituents] think and feel as they feel." Mason, like Madison, was searching to establish a base for the new Federal government that was not the states. See argument above (Mason quoted by Morgan, *Inventing the People*, 272).

53. [Noah Webster], "American," *American Magazine*, I (1787), 9–12.

government, . . . to punish such as commit crimes. Every person's safety requires that he should submit to be governed. . . . It is necessary therefore that there should be laws to control every man."[54]

This argument is repeated in the next paragraph:

> The whole body of people in society is the sovereign power or state; which is called, the body politic. Every man forms a part of this state, and so has a share in the sovereignty; at the same time, as an individual, he is a subject of the state. . . . When a society is large, . . . the people . . . agree to appoint . . . representatives to act for them . . . [to] represent the whole state, and act as the sovereign power. The people resign their own authority to their representatives—the acts of these deputies are in effect the acts of the people —and the people have no right to refuse obedience.[55]

Sovereignty floats through this prose, passing from the free individual to "the body politic" (that was no body), to the government, to political representatives who "represent the whole state, and act as the sovereign power." (Indeed, we should note that, whereas in Paine's writing the trope of the political body empowers the citizen, in Webster's prose it virtually effaces the citizen. Put more simply, incorporating the citizen, Webster's body politic swallows him whole.)

The republican citizen, represented in the opening words as free in his thoughts and actions, his life and his estate, within but a few sentences loses his claim to governmental sovereignty and, hence, his control over his own deputies, becoming both the object of and subject to legislation instituted by those deputies. The citizen is then prevented from resisting or protecting himself from the acts his deputies take to regulate him because those acts are represented as his own, and man cannot protect himself from himself. (Indeed, Webster made this argument part of his resolute opposition to the adoption of a bill of rights.) By the paragraph's end, the European American political subject, having resigned his authority to his political representative, is left with "no right to refuse obedience." Although all republican political theory must ultimately secure the citizen's consent to be governed, what is significant about this argument is that it succeeds in replacing an empowered Radical Whig citizen with an Old Whig passive political subject, radical popular sovereignty with the politics of deference.

Month after month, Webster elaborated this argument. Take, for example,

54. Ibid., 9.
55. Ibid.

an essay he published in January 1788. "That a legislature should have unlimited power to do *right,* is unquestionable," the essay began; "but such a power they cannot have, unless they have all the power of the State." The essay insisted that "the liberty of a people does not rest on any reservation of power [for the people] . . . it rests singly on this principle, *a union of interests between the governors and the governed.*" Repositioning political representatives as the governors and European American citizens as "the governed," the essay then denied European American citizens the rights of political participation and thus political agency. Later that year, we find this argument reinscribed in satirical form. "What!" the *American Magazine* exclaimed, "have *servants* then the power of governing their *masters?* Of guarding public rights? Of legislating for their *superiors?* Do not the deputies of the people represent the full power of the people? . . . Their delegates then stand in their [the people's] place—possess all their powers." He concluded, "Representatives are therefore . . . masters of the people."[56]

The question is not simply how the essay reached this conclusion but how it made such a conclusion persuasive. The answer lies in Webster's complex interweaving of mimetic and metaphoric forms of representation. The essay begins by asserting that a mimetic relationship existed between the citizen and his representative, that is, that the representative/legislator precisely represented the individual political subject or voter in the legislative hall. Indeed, it insists that the representative represented his constituents absolutely, transparently. Bestowing a biological naturalness upon the closeness of the citizen/representative relationship, the essay proceeds, "The people will choose their Legislature *from their own body*—that Legislature will have an interest inseperable *[sic]* from that of the people." As another essay published in the *American Magazine* only a month earlier had stated, there was "a union of interests between the governors and the governed." But, whereas this argument, in Radical Whig hands, had affirmed the citizen's governmental as well as constituent sovereignty and hence his right to instruct his representatives how to vote, on the pages of the *American Magazine,* it rendered the citizen subject to his representative.[57]

56. Giles Hickory [Noah Webster], "Government," *American Magazine,* I (1788), 75–80, esp. 76. Having insisted that possessing all the power of the state gave legislators an unlimited power to do good, Webster also admitted in this same paragraph that it gave them "an unlimited power to do wrong." "Possess all their powers": [Webster], "Thoughts on the Political Situation . . . ," ibid., part 1, 744–747, esp. 745.

57. Hickory, "Government," ibid., 75, 142. W. J. T. Mitchell classifies "mimesis" as "imitation" as a form of "iconic" representation "that transcend[s] the differences between media" (Mitchell,

Indeed, it was precisely this mimetic transparency that authorized the political representative to act in the political subject's name, to assume the People's sovereign powers to legislate and to govern. It was precisely because no difference existed between the representative and the subject/voter that the latter was obligated to obey the laws his representative enacted in his name. As noted earlier, the *American Museum* had stated, "The acts of these deputies are in effect the acts of the people. The people have no right to refuse obedience."[58]

"The people have no right to refuse obedience." This phrase marks the point of logical slippage in the essay's argument as it does in the fiction of political representation. Out of mimetic representation, the essay constitutes a radical dissimilarity that both reflects and reproduces an unequal allocation of power. From being the lookalike of the individual citizen, the argument makes that representative other than—and emphatically more powerful than—the citizens he represents. Indeed, as we have seen, political representatives are now empowered to assert their right not only to govern for but, absolutely, to govern their constituents. In Webster's magazine, Radical Whig arguments constitute Old Whig subservience. Wiser, more virtuous than their constituents, the legislators, rather than representing the people to the state, now represent the state to the people. The people, no longer sovereign political subjects, become subject to the sovereign political power of the legislative assembly.

In this way, mimetic representation slides into metaphoric representation—a form of representation in which the representative (the signifier) is decidedly different from that which is represented (the signified). Yet, for a metaphor to work, the representation/representative must be made to appear to precisely mirror what it represents. The success of the fiction of political representation as originally formulated by the Long Parliament and reaffirmed by Federalist publicists such as Webster rests on being able to maintain the torturous coexistence of mimetic and metaphoric forms of representation, or, rather, on the ability of the mimetic to cover and obscure the underlying and empowering metaphoric form.[59]

"Representation," in Frank Lentricchia and Thomas McLaughlin, eds., *Critical Terms for Literary Study* [Chicago, 1990], 11–22, esp. 14).

58. [Webster], "American," *American Magazine*, I (1787), 9–12.

59. Roland Barthes discusses the relation of the signifier and signified at length in his early semiotic essay, "Myth Today." He does so in ways that greatly empower the signified in contrast to the ways twenty-first-century poststructuralist discussion of representation disempower that which is represented. But the fundamental point remains the difference that distinguishes the signifier/signified within metaphoric structures (Barthes, "Myth Today," in Barthes, *Mythologies*, trans. Annette Lavers [New York, 1972]).

Thus, although the *American Magazine* repeatedly asserts a mimetic relationship between political representatives and political subjects—a relation underscored by the fact that representatives and citizens alike are subject to the laws the representative passes—the magazine is equally insistent that political representatives are radically different from the citizens they represent. They are the citizen's superiors in education, wealth, breadth of vision, and political experience. "Permit me then to enquire," Webster asked his readers, echoing both the Old Whigs and Montesquieu, "whether the people of any district, county or town . . . are competent to judge of this *general good?*" "Little will it avail to say," he continued, perhaps with conscious irony, since his own *American Magazine* was not a financial success, "that the people acquire the necessary information by newspapers or other periodical publications: There are not more than two states in the thirteen, where one half the freemen read the public papers." "Our common people," he stated in still another essay, "are not sufficiently informed to govern themselves." As events in Massachusetts had so sadly proved, "they approach nearly to the nature of a mob, and a *mob* never reasons." (On the simplest level, this comment marks political magazines as elitist instruments with little influence among hardscrabble and frontier farmers or the urban laboring classes, none of whom could subscribe to those magazines even if they wished to—which, presumably, they did not.)[60]

Carefully, persistently, in a few short months, the *American Magazine* had redefined the critical republican concept of popular sovereignty. It had divested the citizen of his power to participate actively in the legislative process, power that Revolutionary Americans had repeatedly asserted. Within the *American Magazine*'s carefully crafted arguments, the sovereignty of the people was reduced to an abstract right to will a government into being—and the right to vote for representatives to whose governance they would then be subject. "The right of election," Webster insisted, "is . . . not merely *one*, but it is the *only* legislative or constitutional act, which the people at large can with propriety exercise." Once voters had chosen their representatives, they must submit to being governed by them. "Possess[ing] all their powers . . . political representatives are therefore . . . masters of the people." "As a Representative of a State," Webster explained, one "is invested with a share of the sovereign authority, and is so far a *Governor* of the people. In short, the collective body of Represen-

60. [Webster], review of Thomas, "Thoughts on the Political Situation," *American Magazine*, I (1788), 804–809; Hickory, "Government," ibid., 205. See, as well, [Webster], "Education: The Importance of Accommodating the Mode of Education to the Form of Government," ibid., 311–313, esp. 312.

tatives ... are ... *masters, rulers, governors.*" Voters must desist from all efforts to instruct their representatives, whose claim to civic virtue rested on their absolute independence from their constituents. "I have said 'that the people ought not to give binding instructions to Representatives.'—'That they cannot exercise any act of supremacy or legislation at all.'" Judicious and well informed, seeing beyond the special interests of their constituents, those representatives must guide and govern their political subjects as Locke suggests the paterfamilias governed his wife and children. The power and autonomy of the independent political representatives covered and effaced the power and autonomy of the virtuous republican subject, in late-eighteenth-century Federalist political theory, as in late-twentieth and early-twenty-first-century poststructuralist theories of language and representation. Despite the Revolution's radical promises, elective representatives, as the embodiment of the state, ruled that which they represented, "the People."[61]

It is noteworthy that, having banished women and the feminine from the political arena and the role of virtuous citizen, political representation combined mimetic and metaphoric forms of representation in the very way that the eighteenth-century Anglo-American marriage contract under coverture did—and to precisely the same end, to empower the representative in relation to the figure represented. In fact, striking parallels exist between political representation and marriage as established under the law of coverture. In marriage, the husband and wife "freely" contract to become one, and that one is the husband; in political elections, the citizen freely transfers his right of governmental sovereignty to his political representative, their voices become one, and that one is the representative's. As the wife, once married, loses her legal and economic subjectivity to her husband, so the political subject, after the election, relinquishes his political sovereignty and power to his representative. As the wife cannot resist the authority of the husband, who has the right to discipline her, so the political subject (especially as Webster defined the relationship) cannot resist the authority—and legislation—of the state. Husband and politi-

---

61. Hickory, "Government," *American Magazine,* I (1788), 75–76, 137, 204; [Webster], review of Thomas, "Thoughts on the Political Situation," ibid., part 1, 745. See, as well, Webster's "Education," ibid., 210–216, and his "Series of Original Letters from a Gentleman to His Friend: Letter 1," ibid., 303–304. See also Hickory, "On Bills of Rights," ibid., I (1787), 13–15; A Bostonian, "Letter II: On the Same Subject," ibid., 298–303. How to secure the citizen's consensual subjection to the state is a problem that lies at the heart of republican governance. Rousseau struggled with it. It arises out of the tension between two key political fictions— political representation and popular sovereignty.

cal representative were positioned as master and governor, the citizen and wife subject to their rule.[62]

Both the marriage and the election contract establish relations of subordination. But, because that subordination is the product of contractual agreements, as Carole Pateman argues, it masquerades as freedom. The masquerade is furthered by the fact that both contracts presume the consent of all the contractors and prescribe, and thus limit, the type of power that can be exercised and the degree of subordination imposed in terms of kind and time. The husband's powers end with the end of the marriage, the political representative's with the end of his term in office and the new election. Ironically, however, the woman is in fact positioned more powerfully than the elector is. If she does not remarry, as a widow, she regains her legal and economic subjectivities. But under the government as portrayed on the pages of the *American Magazine,* in the Constitutional Convention arguments of Madison, George Mason, Gouverneur Morris, and James Wilson, and inscribed in the Constitution, the elector will never regain his political sovereignty. He loses it with each new election— whether he chooses to vote (contract) or not. He can never become a political widow. Within the representative republic, as constructed by Federalist rhetoric, the republican citizen must always be governed—otherwise democracy and hence anarchy would ensue. The fragmentation of manliness and virtuous citizenship, which Federalist rhetorical representations of Massachusetts's rugged farmers after Shays's Rebellion had begun, Federalist constructions of political representation furthered. Given the extent of eighteenth-

62. John Locke, *First Treatise of Government,* in Locke, *Two Treatises of Government,* ed. Peter Laslett (Cambridge, 1965), 213. It is true that Locke insisted a husband's governance over his wife was social and not political. Nevertheless, as Carole Pateman points out in her critique of Locke, marriage, coupled to coverture, ended a woman's independence, her political and legal subjectivity. Domestic and dependent figures, married women were the antithesis of the freedom-loving and politically active citizen. Pateman goes on to argue that the preexisting "sexual contract" that underscores all Western social and political practices establishes women as men's social and economic subordinates. They cannot be equal parties to a marriage or any other contract. Modern debates over gay marriage indicate that the terms of the marriage contract itself are not open to negotiation among the contracting parties as the terms of true contracts are. Not only cannot women marry women, but—certainly in the eighteenth century and perhaps now—women and men cannot opt to exchange roles as they exchange vows, a woman assuming the rights and title of "husband," a man those of "wife." The marriage contract reinscribes the sexual contract that, Pateman insists, Locke used to legitimate women's exclusion from the liberal state—and that the founders incorporated into their new constitution (Pateman, *The Sexual Contract* [Stanford, Calif., 1988], esp. 39–76, 116–188).

century misogyny (which we will examine in Chapter 3), to position male citizens as women, to feminize them, was to disempower them.[63]

FOLLOW THE MONEY TRAIL:
FISCAL CAPITALISM AND REPUBLICAN AUTHORITY

As they made the republican citizen subject to his political representative, so bourgeois magazines subjected the new Republic to its capitalist investors. Just as it had challenged representations of the republican citizen as an empowered political agent, so Federalist rhetoric challenged republican understandings of political authority and of the power relations that ideally existed between the Republic and its citizens.

As discussed in Chapter 1, the classic republican citizen (and, to a large extent, the commercial republican citizen as well) was expected to devote himself to serving his republic, sacrificing his self-interest to the general good. Informed by liberal concepts of both the social and legal contracts, Federalist rhetoric transformed the classic republic into a modern liberal political state by modeling the Republic after its private citizens—and subject to those citizens' example. Federalist inversions of classical republicanism are explicit; phrases such as "for nations as for individuals," "honest nations, like honest men," "contracting nations . . . like individuals," and "contracts between nations like contracts between individuals" abounded in Federalist magazines. The result? "Nations" were repositioned "as . . . individuals." If "honest nations" were "like honest men," then the Federalist state must subject its behavior to the example of its subjects. As another author explained: "Societies, sir, become respectable on the same principles by which the character of individuals is maintained. Dishonesty in either is equally opposed to wisdom."[64]

As these quotations indicate, the Federalist political state was not only like and, consequently, subject to the example of its private citizens; it was subject to and modeled upon specific categories of citizens—men of commerce and fiscal management, its merchants, shopkeepers, and speculators in public credit, its

63. Pateman, *Sexual Contract,* 55–60. For a discussion of the ways this issue was argued at the convention, see Morgan, *Inventing the People,* 263–287.

64. "On Public Faith," *American Museum,* I (1787), 405–408; "Circular Letter Transmitted by the United States in Congress Assembled, to the Governors of the Respective States," ibid., 397–402; "On the Redemption of Public Securities," ibid., 417–419; "On Establishing a Sinking Fund in Pennsylvania . . . ," ibid., 487–491; "Thoughts on the Present Situation of Public Affairs," ibid., 306–310; "The Analogy between the Respective Forms of Government, and the Origins of the Several States of North America . . . ," *Columbian Magazine,* I (1787), 477–478.

fundholders and stockjobbers. These commercial and fiscal actors, depicted as suspect and potentially corrupting within classical republican discourses, emerged in the new urban press as idealized and empowered figures, their behavior held up as an example for the new federal government to follow. As merchants and men of business were bound by their private contracts, so the new Republic was bound by its public contracts—quite literally by its bonds. "The duty . . . and perhaps even the existence of a country, are involved in the performance of its contracts," a member of the Massachusetts General Court stated in an argument reprinted by the *American Museum*. The author of "Extract from the Late Address of the General Court of Massachusetts" made the demand that the state model itself on contracting subjects even more explicit. "In private life," he wrote, "the man who avails himself of artifice and fraud, will soon find his character blasted, and himself the object of contempt: while he who, encompassed with difficulties, maintains an honest course, may hope for the friendship of man, and the favour of heaven." "The same will be the case in states . . . so long as 'Righteousness exalteth a nation.'"[65]

Three radical and interrelated changes follow this initial inversion of the power relations republicans imagined existing between the virtuous Republic and its capitalist citizens. The first was to privilege the maintenance of public contracts to private investors above every other form of state responsibility, indeed, to write the sanctity of contract into the Constitution itself. The second was to reposition a particular class of economic subjects, merchants, and fiscal speculators as an abstraction: "the Public." The third positioned the political state as a private economic contractor. Let us look at each in its turn.[66]

"When a legislative body . . . makes *grants* or *contracts*," Webster, always willing to lecture his readers, explained in the midst of the New York ratification debates, it acts as [an equal] party, and cannot take back its grant, or change the nature of its contracts." "A state has no more right to neglect or

65. "Speech of a Member of the General Court of Massachusetts, on the Question whether the Public Securities Should Be Redeemed at Their Current Value," *American Museum*, I (1787), 412–417, esp. 412; "Extract from the Late Address of the General Court of Massachusetts, to Their Constituents," ibid., 419–420; Samuel Miles, "Address of the Board of Managers of the Pennsylvania Society for the Promotion of Manufactures and the Useful Arts," ibid., II (1787), 360–362, esp. 361. At times, this fusion of governmental and mercantile identity became absolute, as when the author of "Remarks and Facts relative to the American Paper-Money" anthropomorphized Holland as a responsible businessman. "Holland, which understands the value of cash . . . would never part with gold and silver for credit . . . if they did not think and find the credit a full equivalent."

66. The famous "contract clause" states: "No state shall . . . pass any law . . . impairing the obligation of contracts" (Constitution of the United States of America, article 1, section 10).

refuse to fulfill its engagements, than an individual," he added. "Bargains, conveyances, and voluntary grants, where two parties are concerned, are *sacred things*—they are the supports of social confidence and security—they ought not to be sported with . . .—they should be religiously observed." The state "cannot hesitate a moment about . . . [rendering] justice to the public creditors," a Massachusetts state legislator argued similarly about his own state's Revolutionary War debt.[67]

As this last quote makes explicit, Federalist rhetoric repositioned speculators (fundholders and stockjobbers) as public creditors, or, even more generally, as "the Public," whose faith the commercial state must constantly court. Another Federalist writer, voicing the implicit shift in power relations between the modern republic and its financial investors, denominated public creditors "the barometer, mr. Speaker, of modern power; . . . [they] explain the strength of a community beyond the calculations of arithmetic"—or, presumably, of individual political citizens, characterized, not as "the Public," but as "the People." "The Public" of private economic investors and speculators had come to replace the republican state and "the People" as the source of political and economic authority.[68]

As "the Public," speculators in government paper were creatures of "the public sphere," that complex space Jurgen Habermas associates with the rise of the bourgeoisie, their coffeehouses, clubs, and print culture. Within such bourgeois space, Habermas contends, men of reason, property, and education, informed by a proliferating print culture, positioned themselves as autonomous critics of the state—in much the same way as Federalist rhetoric positioned venture capitalists and speculators in government "paper" as independent critics of the state, associated with that new public institution, the bourse, or stock

---

67. [Webster], "American," *American Magazine*, I (1787), 10, 11; "Speech of a Member of the General Court," ibid., 414.

68. "Speech of a Member of the General Court," *American Museum*, I (1787), 413; Jurgen Habermas, *The Structural Transformation of the Public Sphere: An Inquiry into a Category of Bourgeois Society*, trans. Thomas Burger (Cambridge, Mass., 1989). Habermas's concept of the public sphere is one of the most transformative and hotly debated in contemporary cultural theory. For three suggestive collections of essays concerning this concept, see Craig Calhoun, ed., *Habermas and the Public Sphere* (Cambridge, Mass., 1992); Maurizio Passerin d'Entrèves and Seyla Benhabib, eds., *Habermas and the Unfinished Project of Modernity: Critical Essays on the Philosophical Discourse of Modernity* (Cambridge, Mass., 1997); Nick Crossley and John Michael Roberts, eds., *After Habermas: New Perspectives on the Public Sphere* (Malden, Mass., 2004). Feminists have been particularly critical of Habermas, who depicts eighteenth-century bourgeois society in exclusively masculine terms. See, in particular, Nancy Fraser, *Unruly Practices: Power, Discourse, and Gender in Contemporary Social Theory* (Minneapolis, 1989).

exchange. (Tellingly, America's first stock exchanges were housed in taverns and coffeehouses.) Here, the Republic's new speculators participated in one of the most inventive aspects of the urban print culture: the creation and circulation of commercial and government "paper."

Once private investors were repositioned as "the Public," indeed, as the very barometers of state credibility and creditability, it was easy for Federalist rhetoric to reposition the new republican state as a "private" contractor. From using rhetoric to empower the representative and the state in relation to the citizen, Federalists moved the political state into the realm of fiscal representation. As a result, the political state began to lose its clarity, its centeredness, its authority. Inscribed as a private commercial actor, committed to the performance of credibility, the modern republic, to classic republican eyes, began to appear as uncertain and theatrical as the credit-conscious merchants and businessmen it was to model itself upon. As a credit-conscious commercial state, that is, the modern republic had to solicit its private economic subjects to invest their venture capital in their government. Not patriotism, but their republic's creditability, coupled with their own desire for speculative profits, motivated the capitalist subjects' investments—the investments the modern republic depended upon.

The modern republic, in short, had become the object of the evaluating and appraising gaze of its private speculating citizens. As such, the Federalist state was positioned in much the same way as an eighteenth-century respectable woman and had, consciously or unconsciously, to mimic her traditional behavior. The commercial republic, like the respectable woman, had to represent itself to the Public (male capitalist) gaze as desirable and, yes, desiring of credit. The commercial republic had to represent itself as above Public (male) reproach, its virtue intact, its credit creditable. In both the commercial republic's and the respectable woman's complex juggling acts, everything—virtue, honor, credibility, and creditability—depended upon performance, appearance, and opinion.

Let us pause for a moment to examine the significance of the simple analogy "honest governments, like honest merchants." It marks a shift from political rhetoric to fiscal rhetoric—or, rather, it marks the fusion of systems of political representation and fiscal representation. Put another way, the uncertainties, the theatricality of fiscal representation (in which paper money and commercial paper stand for material goods or a man's signature stands for the money to pay for goods in the future) explode the would-be certainties of political representation. Federalist representations of the credit-conscious republic, dependent on its subjects' opinions and desires, fragmented and undid the power Federalist inscriptions of political representation had just invested in the political state and representative in relation to the citizen. In this way, authority shifted from the political to the financial sphere.

The identity of the credit-conscious political state now depended more upon the reception its public/private subjects gave it as a creditworthy object of their evaluating gaze than it depended upon intentions or even actions of its statesmen in the public weal or the independence and self-sacrifice of its virtuous republican citizens. The new nation's authority no longer rested purely on the electoral consent of its political subjects. As represented by the new magazines, it had come to depend upon its capitalist economic subjects' "repeated gesture of imagining the government as if it were an individual whose creditworthiness one were continually assessing"—assessing as eighteenth-century men continually assessed the credibility of the virtuous middle-class woman who had entered the marriage market, in the same way that woman's identity as virtuous depended upon appearances and the opinions those appearances inspired. This was, as Jean-Christophe Agnew so aptly reminds us, "the Age of the Spectator."[69]

Not only did Federalist rhetoric feminize the Republic by representing it as subject to and object of the evaluating gaze of its male economic subjects; it ensnared the Republic in an impenetrable web of theatrical representations and interlocking dependencies. This was a world in which speculation and the spectacular met in the gaze. So much that had been condemned by earlier republican discourses as corrupt and feminizing had become respectable, whereas those watchwords of earlier republican rhetoric—martial courage, manly independence, self-reliance, industry—appeared increasingly irrelevant and old-fashioned.[70]

69. Frances Ferguson, unpublished comments on an early draft of this essay, University of Pennsylvania Seminar on the Diversity of Language and the Structure of Power, December 1991; Jean-Christophe Agnew, *Worlds Apart: The Market and the Theater in Anglo-American Thought, 1550–1750* (Cambridge, 1986), esp. chap. 4. This invocation of the sexual and the feminine in analyzing Federalist repositioning of the male political subject is supported by the magazines' rhetoric. See, for example, the language one advocate used to couple the adoption of the Constitution with the redemption of the government's paper money: "When the promise is once plighted [paper money, bonds issued], government that moment descends to the rank of an individual, and all it has to do, is to fall on some effectual measures to fulfill its engagements" ("Speech of a Member of the General Court," *American Museum*, I [1787], 413).

70. For a nuanced discussion of the interface of speculation and the culture of the spectacular, see Agnew, *Worlds Apart*, esp. 161. For comments by merchants as recorded in letters and journals, see Toby L. Ditz's analysis of mercantile Philadelphia as a culture of risk and the theatrical, "Shipwrecked; or, Masculinity Imperiled: Mercantile Representations of Failure and

Paper in the form of money, stocks, bonds, and securities, the fiscal innovations of the long eighteenth century, was central to this theatrical world of speculation and the spectacular. Indeed, on the pages of the urban press, money became the ultimate form of representation as credit became its ultimate problematization. "Money is a mere representation of property," Webster had argued in the *American Magazine*. A form of representation, consequently, cannot be what it represents. It is not wealth, Webster continued, for "the *wealth* of a country is its *produce* . . . [and] its industrious inhabitants. . . . The laboring men are the support of a nation"—as they are the representative republic's source of political sovereignty. In this way, money's function within a system of fiscal representation parallels the legislator's function within a system of political representation. Both stand for actual subjects—the political citizen/subject and the industrious economic subject. But, as objects of representation within Federalist political and economic rhetoric, both the virtuous political subject and the industrious economic subject lose their subject status and agency. As objects, they easily slip into the role of feminized, negative Other. And so Federalist rhetoric represents both as lacking self-control, as passionate, self-interested, prone to extravagance and demagoguery. Both must be prevented from exercising undue influence upon their political or fiscal representatives.[71]

On the pages of Federalist urban magazines, popular efforts to secure state passage of paper money bills epitomized the threat the fused political citizen/laboring man posed to the orderly processes of metaphoric representation. We have seen Federalist rhetoric deny the citizen's right to influence his representative. So did Federalist rhetoric seek to restrain the industrious subject from uniting with his other self, the voter, to secure legislation that would regulate his fiscal representative, money. "Money will go where it is wanted," Webster argued. "Hence the mistaken policy of those people who attempt to increase the medium of trade by coinage or by a paper currency"—both legislative acts. "They can add to the quantity, . . . but not to the value" of money. Within Federalist discourse, money, like political sovereignty, floats above the power of those it represents.[72]

the Gendered Self in Eighteenth-Century Philadelphia," *JAH*, LXXXI (1994), 51–80.

71. [Webster], "American," *American Magazine*, I (1787), 11. Mathew Carey expressed similar opinions; see, for example, his essay "The True Interest of the United States and Particularly of Pennsylvania Considered," *American Museum*, II (1787), 23–34. For an examination of fiscal developments in late-eighteenth-century Philadelphia, especially of Robert Morris and the development of banks, see Doerflinger, *Vigorous Spirit of Enterprise*, 251–310.

72. [Webster], "American," *American Magazine*, I (1787), 11–12.

Federalist rhetoric represents a decentered world of sliding dependencies, of interchangeable and, hence, exchangeable genders and subjectivities. As commerce, paper, and print made value and property exchangeable and, hence, interchangeable, they made the Republic's honor and fiscal credibility interchangeable and, hence, exchangeable. As the Republic became a private contractor, its private economic actors became its Public, a public that played the role of independent and judgmental audience evaluating the credibility of their Republic's performances of creditability and political responsibility. As textual representation transformed rugged farmers into "tasty" items for urbane Federalist readers, political and fiscal representation positioned republican citizens —and the Republic itself—as bourgeois women were positioned in the marriage market. Civic virtue, that reservoir of martial vigor and manly independence, became dependent upon performance and display, opinion and reception—again, just as women were. Indeed, dependency, exchangeability, performativity, and display were all, within eighteenth-century discourses, marked as female.

The public and the private, the political and the economic, male and female, virtue and presentation, appearance and perception danced around one another, fused with and confused one another in a dazzling, theatrical performance. Indeed, as represented by the urban press, all the world had become a stage, citizens and their representatives, states and their creditors merely players, and all the old certainties but smoke and mirrors. To appropriate Gordon S. Wood's phrase, Federalist rhetoric represents the end of classical republican politics, of the virtuous Republic and the manly republican.[73]

Out of the cacophony of warring discourses that covered the pages of the urban magazines, a grotesque figure emerged, part zoon politikon, part self-interested fiscal speculator, part leisured, educated gentleman, part industrious, leather-aproned producer. Not only aesthetic but political confusion followed, for, as Peter Stallybrass and Allon White point out, "The logic of the grotesque . . . unsettle[s] 'given' social positions and interrogate[s] the rules of inclusion, exclusion and domination which structured the social ensemble." In his battle against his unsettling fusion of conflicting parts, the American grotesque's claim to coherence rested, in the end, on only one of his myriad parts— his masculinity. But, as we have seen, representation—iconic, ideological, polit-

73. Wood, *Creation of the American Republic*, 606.

ical, fiscal—obscured that very part. The urban press was left with an uncertain, a confused, indeed, a fragmented American republican subject. To rescue the manliness, the virility, his civic virtue and inner coherence depended upon, the press turned to women. Man's biological Other, his physical and emotional dependent—could woman's differences from men recuperate the rhetorical slippages that had so destabilized the bourgeois press's new American?[74]

74. For a pathbreaking analysis of the grotesque body and the politics of transgression, see Peter Stallybrass and Allon White, *The Politics and Poetics of Transgression* (Ithaca, N.Y., 1986), esp. 43. Stallybrass and White base their analysis on Mikhail Bakhtin's *Rabelais and His World*, trans. Hélène Iswolsky (Cambridge, Mass., 1968), esp. 465.

CHAPTER THREE

American Minervas

If perticular [sic] *care and attention is not paid to the Laidies, we are determined to foment a Rebelion, and will not hold ourselves bound by any Laws in which we have no voice, or Representation.* —ABIGAIL ADAMS

When we think of America's Revolutionary patriots, we think of farmers, muskets drawn, defending the road between Lexington and Concord, of Paul Revere's "midnight ride" and Patrick Henry's bold oratory. Male patriots, however, did not act alone. European American women were also children of the Enlightenment and the Revolution. Their ideals were borne aloft by the same intellectual winds that buoyed the image of the European American man as freedom-loving and endowed with inalienable rights. The tides of war that swept up struggling farmers and mechanics, leading them to assert their right to a political voice, ebbed and flowed around America's increasingly literate bourgeois and middling women, encouraging them to respond to radical times with radical appropriations and transformations of the discourses that precipitated the Revolution. From the initial protests against the Stamp Act to the production of a new, republican public sphere, European American women played active public and political roles. At the same time, the new magazines called on them to assume the critical role of Other to the virile and virtuous republican citizen. Inevitably, the public roles women chose to play and the symbolic roles the press chose for them clashed.[1]

1. See Abigail Adams to John Adams, Mar. 31, 1776, in *Adams Family Papers: An Electronic Archive,* Massachusetts Historical Society, http://www.masshist.org/digitaladams/aea/index.html. See, as well, William J. Bennett, ed., *Letters of John to Abigail Adams, 1762–1826* (New York, 2001).

In the turbulent years leading to and following the Revolution, European American women assumed ever more visible public roles, at times at men's insistence, at times at their own. Nonimportation agreements and consumer boycotts constituted European Americans' first collective response to Britain's changing imperial regulations. Patriots were certain that such agreements would send a powerful message, one that influential British merchants and manufacturers would respond to. To succeed, however, boycotts had to engage the hearts and hands of America's wives and daughters. European American women had to refuse to buy proscribed products; they had, as well, to produce alternative goods in order to preserve their families' comfort and well-being. Lastly, patriots insisted, America's wives and daughters had to sign nonimportation agreements in their own names, pledging their honor to uphold them. Signing any binding document, especially one that took the form of a political manifesto, and to do so in their own names, was a radical act for eighteenth-century women. Boycotts "were an occasion for instruction in collective political behavior," Linda K. Kerber explains, "formalized by the signing of petitions and manifestoes." Because wives as well as husbands were called upon to sign and cooperate with those petitions and manifestoes, consumer boycotts transformed women into public, political actors. As South Carolinian planter Christopher Gadsden remarked concerning the early boycott movement: "Without [our wives] . . . 'tis impossible to succeed."[2]

What a surprising admission! Indeed, Gadsden's remarks not only underscore women's centrality to the nonimportation movement; they disclose European American men's perception that their wives had come to exercise unusual domestic power and autonomy. On the pages of Gadsden's address "To the Planters, Mechanics, and Freeholders of the Province of South Carolina," whig efforts to secure the support of South Carolina's wives take on the appearance less of an exertion of patriarchal power than one of diplomatic nego-

2. Linda K. Kerber, *Toward an Intellectual History of Women: Essays* (Chapel Hill, N.C., 1997), discusses the political impact boycotts had on patriot women (76–77). See, as well, Kerber, *Women of the Republic: Intellect and Ideology in Revolutionary America* (Chapel Hill, N.C., 1980), esp. 36–42. For Christopher Gadsden's remark, see Gadsden, "To the Planters, Mechanics, and Freeholders of the Province of South Carolina, No Ways Concerned in the Importation of British Manufacturers," June 22, 1769, in Richard Walsh, ed., *The Writings of Christopher Gadsden, 1746–1805* (Columbia, S.C., 1966), 83–84. Kerber cites Gadsden's comments and underscores precisely this point *(Women of the Republic, 37)*. I am indebted to Kerber for drawing Gadsden's comments to my attention.

tiations between sovereign powers. The address unequivocally admits, "The greatest difficulty of all we have to encounter . . . is to persuade our wives to give us their assistance, without which 'tis impossible to succeed." It then continues:

> I allow of the impossibility of succeeding without their concurrence. . . . for 'tis well known, that none in the world are better œconomists. . . . Only let their husbands point out to the necessity of such a conduct; convince them, that it is the only thing that can save them and their children, from distresses, slavery and disgrace; their affections will soon be awakened, and co-operate with their reason.[3]

Gadsden's comments reinscribe a traditional vision of women. He represents them as wives and mothers, governed by "their affections" and far more interested in the welfare of their children and their families than in patriotic political concerns. At the same time, however, he describes them as empowered figures and excellent "œconomists." More important, they cannot be coerced to accede to their husbands' political desires. They must be "persuaded." Like male republican citizens within both republican and liberal discourses, women's consent has become critical to the virtuous republican cause. And that consent can be secured only if their reason can be convinced that to do so would be to act in their own self-interest. Contrast the verbs Gadsden uses when representing wives and their husbands. Wives "give," "save," "cooperate," "awaken," whereas husbands are left to "point out," "persuade," and attempt to "convince." In the end, winning their wives' consent, not persuading or intimidating Parliament and the king's councillors into repealing objectionable legislation, appears "the greatest difficulty of all we have to encounter." What a Lockean subject European American women had become.

As political agitation escalated in the wake of the Townshend Acts, some elite women turned from the power of the purse to the power of the pen. In words that presaged those of Isaiah Thomas's "four agreeable young ladies," Philadelphia salonnière Milcah Martha Moore, in her poem "The Female Patriot," chided men who, for reasons of "Party" and political favor (two of the principal forms of corruption within classic republican discourses), failed her test of patriotic fervor and love of liberty:

> *The Men from a Party, or fear of a Frown,*
> *Are kept by a Sugar-Plum, quietly down.*
> *Supinely asleep, and depriv'd of their Sight*
> *Are strip'd of their Freedom, and rob'd of their Right.*

3. Gadsden, "To the Planters," in Walsh, ed., *Writings of Christopher Gadsden*, 83.

Moore then goes on to demand that women take men's place as defenders of liberty:

> *If the Sons (so degenerate) the Blessing despise,*
> *Let the Daughters of Liberty, nobly arise,*
>
> · · · · · · · · · · · · · · · ·
>
> *Stand firmly resolved and bid Grenville to see*
> *That rather than Freedom, we'll part with our Tea*
>
> · · · · · · · · · · · · · · · ·
>
> *As American Patriots,—our Taste we deny.*

In contrast to Benjamin Franklin's "tasty" men, Moore's women willingly deny their taste for freedom's sake. Assuming the title of "Daughters of Liberty," deriding men as "degenerate" (an anathema to virtuous republicans and a marker of a corrupt aristocracy) and so pusillanimous as to be "strip'd" of their freedom while "supine" (if not rape, is some other form of sexual violation implied?) and without a struggle, Moore ends by proclaiming women's victory not only over Grenville but over degenerate sons.

> *We may Jostle a Grenville and puzzle his Schemes*
> *But a motive more worthy our patriot Pen,*
> *Thus acting—we point out their Duty to Men.*

It is women, not men, who resist Britain's theft of American liberty. It is daughters, not sons, who emerge as the virtuous defenders of liberty. That Moore was a prominent member of Philadelphia's Quaker elite (renowned for their pacifist and tory proclivities) makes this poem all the more remarkable.[4]

The historical record proves Moore an astute observer of the Revolutionary scene. Having signed pledges to support boycotts, women worked collectively to enforce them, harassing merchants and playing their part in incendiary street theater and parades. Once war commenced, women led one-third of the food riots reported between 1776 and 1779 and played an active role in nearly all the others. Women marched in phalanxes to country stores, ransacked them for hoarded goods, berated men who would not help them, and beat men who resisted. They rammed down distillery doors, seizing the mountains of sugar stored within. Once in possession of such goods, they gave the male mercantile

---

4. Catherine L. Blecki and Karin A. Wulf, eds., *Milcah Martha Moore's Book: A Commonplace Book from Revolutionary America* (University Park, Pa., 1997), 172–173. The poem is also cited in "Patriotic Poesy" (1768), *William and Mary Quarterly*, 3d Ser., XXXIV (1977), 307–308, and Kerber, *Women of the Republic*, 38.

community yet another lesson in republican virtue, selling the seized goods for the prices prescribed by the Continental Congress and contributing the profits to the patriot cause. In these ways, large numbers of ordinary women took up the role of active citizen.[5]

As the war stretched on and hardships increased, even respectable bourgeois matrons turned their fury against infamous price gougers and hoarders. Abigail Adams wrote John of witnessing a hundred Boston matrons besiege the home of socially prominent merchant Thomas Boylston, unceremoniously dump him into a waiting cart, seize the keys to his warehouse, and carry off his supply of hoarded coffee in carts they had had the foresight to provide. "A large concourse of Men," Abigail reported, "stood amazd silent Spectators." From the safe distance of Philadelphia, John could afford to display bemused disdain. "You have made me merry with the female Frolic," he wrote back, adding that he hoped that in the future the ladies would better control their passion for coffee (and, one wonders, political agency?).[6]

Of course, from the women's perspective, theirs was no frolic, motivated by their inability to restrain their passions. Their enforcement of nonimportation agreements, they insisted, was a rational and considered response to a crisis in the distribution of one of the nation's key wartime resources—food. Defending themselves, they insisted that, far from being driven by selfish, unpatriotic greed, like the targeted merchants and distillers, they had acted in the service of the general good—the care and feeding of the American people. Virtuous republicans, they worked to enforce price regulations enacted by the Continental Congress. Indeed, women often professed to be acting as agents of the Continental Congress, thus laying claim to a visible and legitimate place in the emerging republican agora.[7]

The war certainly encouraged women to do so. As British troops marched

5. Barbara Clark Smith, "Food Rioters and the American Revolution," *WMQ*, 3d Ser., LI (1994), 3–39, esp. 4–5, 7–8, 14, 22–24, 26–29. As Smith puts it: "When they modeled their actions on the activities of Revolutionary authorities, marched the streets as if in the army or enacted the rituals of male crowds, these women cast themselves as competent actors in a public context from which they had been largely excluded" (29).

6. Abigail Adams to John Adams, July 31, 1777, in L. H. Butterfield et al., eds., *Adams Family Correspondence*, 2d Ser. (Cambridge, Mass., 1963–), II, 295; John Adams to Abigail Adams, Aug. 11, 1777, ibid., 305. See also Fitch Edward Oliver, ed., *The Diary of William Pynchon of Salem: A Picture of Salem Life, Social and Political, a Century Ago* (Boston, 1890), 34; and Smith, "Food Rioters," *WMQ*, 3d Ser., LI (1994), 22, 26, 42–43. Kerber, *Women of the Republic*, also cites this incident (79).

7. Smith, "Food Rioters," *WMQ*, 3d Ser., LI (1994), 27–29.

through the American countryside and European American men enlisted in the Continental army, women took on men's roles—both economic and political. Anyone who has read Abigail Adams's letters to John during the long years of war that he spent in Philadelphia and she in Braintree knows what that entailed: supervising planting and harvesting, seeing that fields were drained, roofs repaired, children educated, the sick nursed, the dead buried and mourned—and, far from least, overseeing the collection of political and military news, which she evaluated and passed on. In Philadelphia, elite patriot women often remained after their husbands fled British occupiers—in hopes of preserving their estates. Many failed, forced to watch their homes burned to the ground in retaliation for their family's patriotism. Such was the fate of Polly Dickinson, wife of John Dickinson (author of *Letters from a Farmer in Pennsylvania* and a reluctant signer of the Declaration of Independence), and of Hannah Thomson, whose husband served as secretary of the Continental Congress. Other events propelled women even closer to the battlefield. The winter George Washington was encamped outside Philadelphia at Valley Forge, the Continental Congress asked Philadelphia matrons to raise money to supply soldiers with food, clothing, and blankets. Having produced and collected those supplies, the women then oversaw their battlefront distribution, making sure that the soldiers actually received the goods—and that they recognized that women, not Congress, had secured these necessities for them.[8]

Tory wives shouldered many of these same responsibilities. The arrest and imprisonment of that leading tory Quaker Henry Drinker not only forced Elizabeth Drinker to supervise an all-female household at a time when Phila-

8. Sarah E. Fatherly, "Gentlewomen and Learned Ladies: Gender and the Creation of an Urban Elite in Colonial Philadelphia" (Ph.D. diss., University of Wisconsin, Madison, 2000), 221, 229. For particularly telling letters describing Abigail's life at home in John's absence and the difficulties women faced in dealing with the exigencies of war and a wartime economy, illnesses and miscarriages, see, especially, Abigail Adams to John Adams, Jan. 26, Mar. 23, 26, Apr. 2, 17, 20, Aug. 5, 12, Sept. 10, 17, Oct. 6, 25, Nov. 16, 1777, all in *Adams Family Papers*, http://www .masshist.org/digitaladams/aea/index.html. Nor was Abigail alone. Most women had to scavenge for food, fuel, blankets, and clothing. The socially prominent Susanna Wright, concerned with providing for her own family, went on to wonder "how the poor in that City are able to Subsist . . . as it is said a loaf of Bread is not to be purchased under a Dollar and that of Silver too" (Wright to Hannah Thomson, Dec. 11, 1777, R. R. Logan Collection, box 13, folder 43, Historical Society of Pennsylvania, Philadelphia). For a general discussion of women during the Revolution, see Carol Berkin, *Revolutionary Mothers: Women in the Struggle for America's Independence* (New York, 2005), 26–91, 135–147. Kerber relates the Valley Forge efforts in some detail in *Women of the Republic*, 99–102.

delphia was governed by what she considered an enemy force of "American" patriots. It led her to assume the very public and political role of lobbying members of Pennsylvania's Revolutionary government and then appearing in person before the Continental Congress to petition for her husband's release.[9] Mary Pemberton faced similar dilemmas, finally going to Lancaster so she could appeal personally to Washington to get food to her arrested Quaker husband, imprisoned in Virginia. Tories Elizabeth Graeme Ferguson and Grace Galloway engaged in similar petition efforts to save their estates from confiscation. Graeme Ferguson, a member of Philadelphia's pre-Revolutionary social elite, turned personally to such leading patriot politicians as John Dickinson, George Clymer, and Thomas Mifflin, all of whom she had counted among her friends in more peaceful days. In the end, Ferguson succeeded. Galloway, her husband a British army officer, did not. In the process, these women formed deeply held political positions and expressed them in very public arenas.[10]

Although most women served at home, some went to war. In the eighteenth century, women not infrequently followed their husbands, lovers, or brothers to the battlefield. Martha Washington accompanied George throughout the war, as did the wives of other officers—and of enlisted men. Still other women made a business of war. Modern Mothers Courage drove their wagons from battlefield to battlefield, washing and cooking for the soldiers, nursing the wounded, and on occasion providing more intimate comforts. Eighteenth-century armies depended on their Molly Pitchers and Mothers Courage to function. Although George Washington associated women camp followers with social and sexual disorder, he admitted the necessity of including them in his military planning. An eighteenth-century rule of thumb appears to have been that the

9. Elaine Forman Crane, ed., *The Diary of Elizabeth Drinker: The Life Cycle of an Eighteenth-Century Woman*, entries for 1776–1778 (Boston, 1994), 57–78. Leaders of Pennsylvania's Revolutionary government ordered the summary arrest of the most prominent leaders of the Quaker community, most of whom did oppose the war and Independence. Some twenty men were deported, without trial, to an isolated Virginia village. See Peter Kafer, *Charles Brockden Brown's Revolution and the Birth of American Gothic* (Philadelphia, 2004), 2–10.

10. In all, the Pennsylvania Revolutionary State Government arrested eighteen wealthy Quaker Philadelphians, charging them as tory sympathizers and exiling them to a village along the Virgina frontier. Besides Mary Pemberton's husband, two of his brothers were also arrested, as were husbands, brothers, and sons from the Gilpin, Fisher, Wharton, and Pleasant families. Their wives were left to fight for their release and, in the meantime, to manage their estates and care for their families. This was heady business for women who had not played such public roles before. See Fatherly, "Gentlewomen and Learned Ladies," 222–227, and Berkin, *Revolutionary Mothers*, 92–106.

army needed at least one woman to support every fifteen soldiers. By the war's end, Linda Grant DePauw estimates that twenty thousand women had marched with the Revolutionary army.[11]

The urban press could not deny that, acting with bravery and resolution, women had helped bring the new Republic into being—and that, in working for political independence, they had learned to play public political roles. If Abigail Adams's famous letter to John is any indication, as Massachusetts's western farmers had, so European American women boldly appropriated the whig elite's political discourses. Robert A. Ferguson offers a telling analysis of Abigail and John's exchange, pointing out that, during the opening months of the Revolution, Abigail had positioned women in relation to their husbands as American patriots had positioned themselves in relation to England, anticipating the very logic and the phraseology of the Declaration of Independence. Asserting women's right to political agency, Abigail thus challenged the gendered nature of republican citizenship, civic virtue, and the Revolution. Of course, John's response is as telling as Abigail's assertions. "As to your extraordinary Code of Laws, I cannot but laugh," he wrote.

> We have been told that our Struggle has loosened the bands of Government every where. That Children and Apprentices were disobedient—that schools and Colledges were grown turbulent—that Indians slighted their Guardians and Negroes grew insolent to their Masters. But your Letter was the first Intimation that another Tribe more numerous and powerfull than all the rest were grown discontented.

And concluded: "We know better than to repeal our Masculine systems."[12]

BUT, ALTHOUGH CAREFULLY MAINTAINING their "masculine system" of power—coverture, the exclusion of women from electoral franchise, humorous denials of women's demands for political rights, satires of transgressive women —male patriots found themselves ceding significant public and political space to women. Following Independence, as the nation debated the form the new Republic should take, women were everywhere, elite bourgeois women especially, but middling women as well. Women participated in parades and

11. Linda Grant DePauw, *Fortunes of War: New Jersey Women and the American Revolution* (Trenton, N.J., 1975).

12. Robert A. Ferguson, *The American Enlightenment, 1750–1820* (Cambridge, Mass., 1997), 152–153; John Adams to Abigail Adams, Apr. 14, 1776, in Butterfield et al., eds., *Adams Family Correspondence*, 2d Ser., I, 382.

public celebrations as state after state ratified the Constitution. Following Washington's election, as his stately progress moved slowly north from Virginia to New York, matrons festooned ornamental arches, and their daughters, dressed in white, welcomed him with hymns of praise. During Washington's and Adams's administrations, women flocked to presidential inaugurations, congressional debates, and Supreme Court hearings.[13] But it was through the semiprivate yet intensely political "court" entertainments that encircled the official activities of the new government—Martha Washington's weekly levees, the exclusive musical evenings, cotillions, and dinners New York and Philadelphia merchant princes held for Washington, members of his Cabinet, and members of Congress—that elite bourgeois women established their centrality within the newly emerging republican polis. Self-consciously transposing French and British salons to a North American setting, deeply engaged in demonstrating their mastery of both republican virtue and the culture of politesse and wit, the wives and daughters of the bourgeois elite established their presence within the new Republic. Evenings at Elizabeth Powel's, Mary White Morris's, Lady Kitty Sterling Duer's, Sarah Livingston Jay's, and, most especially, Anne Willing Bingham's, where jewels sparkled and satin gleamed, attracted the leaders of European American society. Following the ladies came the men—presidents and vice presidents, senators and diplomats, New York patroons and, providing the capital that financed all, the merchant princes themselves—Robert Morris, William Duer, Thomas Bingham, Thomas Willing. Clever and informed in their conversations, elegant in their attire, the ladies charmed but also debated and lobbied. "Elite women capitalized on opportunities in the early republic to reconfigure their sites of power within the public domain," Fredrika J. Teute tells us. And they did so, Teute emphasizes, not as wives and mothers, but in their own right as educated and informed bearers of political opinions and wielders of political influence. As the Republic took form, elite women established themselves as producers of the new republican public sphere. But how artificial, how contrived, and thus unrepublican, this all was—the appropriation of an aristocratic institution (the salon) presided over by a Virginia planter (Washington) and attended by the wives and daughters of merchants and professionals engaged in the ostentatious dis-

13. Susan Branson, *These Fiery Frenchified Dames: Women and Political Culture in Early National Philadelphia* (Philadelphia, 2001), 30–31, 145; Simon P. Newman, *Parades and the Politics of the Street: Festive Culture in the Early American Republic* (Philadelphia, 1997), esp. 47–49, 66–68, 102–107; David Waldstreicher, *In the Midst of Perpetual Fetes: The Making of American Nationalism, 1776–1820* (Chapel Hill, N.C., 1997), esp. 82–84, 166–172.

play of wealth and courtly manners. Yet this was precisely how cross-sectional and at times cross-class alliances were cemented, with the grace and wit of "the ladies" bringing together merchants, professionals, and both northern and southern landed elites.[14]

Women's political agency was not limited to the display of wit at elite Federalist gatherings. As politics became increasingly partisan following the French Revolution, women ardently debated the nature of republican government and the virtue of revolution. Embracing the contesting sides, some donned Phrygian caps (named *fiches à la Marat)* and republican tricolor cockades; others, Federalist black cockades. Some Philadelphia women went even further. Intrigued by the French Revolution, Philadelphia's socially prominent Alexander sisters traveled to Paris, where they wrote of boldly rushing onto the streets to witness the return of the king after his thwarted escape to Versailles in 1791, attending sessions of the General Assembly, and attending Jacobin political meetings.[15]

Others remained home, deeply absorbed by Mary Wollstonecraft's newly published *Vindication of the Rights of Women.* The *Vindication* burst upon the American scene and into the libraries and minds of America's literate women. It was reprinted in Philadelphia within months of its initial British publication in 1792. Isaiah Thomas excerpted long sections for the opening issue of his *Massachusetts Magazine.* It quickly became the talk of fashionable sets

14. Fredrika J. Teute, "Roman Matron on the Banks of the Tiber Creek: Margaret Bayard Smith and the Politicization of Spheres in the Nation's Capital," in Donald R. Kennon, ed., *A Republic for the Ages: The United States Capitol and the Political Culture of the Early Republic* (Charlottesville, Va., 1999), 89–121, esp. 92, 96. See, as well, Fredrika J. Teute and David S. Shields, "Jefferson in Washington: Domesticating Manners in the Republican Court," paper presented at the Omohundro Institute of Early American History and Culture Third Annual Conference, Old Salem, N.C., June 7, 1997; Ethel Armes, comp. and ed., *Nancy Shippen, Her Journal Book: The International Romance of a Young Lady of Fashion of Colonial Philadelphia with Letters to Her and about Her* (Philadelphia, 1935), esp. 75–110; Jan Lewis, "Politics and the Ambivalence of the Private Sphere: Women in Early Washington, D.C.," in Kennon, ed., *Republic for the Ages,* 122–151. Teute differs from Lewis, who stresses women's self-image as republican wives. Teute, in contrast, sees them more as independent women playing at being sophisticated and cosmopolitan salonnières.

15. See, as well, Branson, *These Fiery Frenchified Dames,* 37–42; Lewis, "Politics and the Ambivalence of the Private Sphere," in Kennon, ed., *Republic for the Ages,* 126, 129, 133–140, 149; Newman, *Parades,* 154–156. Newman notes class divisions among women and their adoption of tricolor or black cockades. For the Alexander sisters, see Rush-Biddle-Williams Family Papers, Rosenbach Library, Philadelphia.

throughout the nation's capital. Elizabeth Drinker confessed that Wollstonecraft, "as some of our friends say, *speaks my mind.*"[16] Episcopalian Annis Boudinot Stockton, who, during the Revolutionary War, had presided over America's first republican salon while her uncle was president of the Continental Congress, shared Drinker's enthusiasm. Nor did reading William Godwin's memoir of Wollstonecraft, in which he revealed both her affair with him and her out-of-wedlock child, cause Stockton to change her mind. Indeed, Stockton wrote privately, Godwin's account only made Wollstonecraft seem the more human and attractive. She went on to chide her daughter, Julia Stockton Rush, for failing to share her impressions of the book with her. Another well-read Philadelphia lady, Margaret Murphey Craig, exclaimed after reading Wollstonecraft: "What a mind! How exquisitely sensible! And how extensive its powers," and a graduate of Philadelphia's Young Ladies' Academy in her baccalaureate address acclaimed Wollstonecraft the equal of Thomas Paine. Admiration for Wollstonecraft was certainly not limited to Philadelphia and Boston. Youthful intellectuals in New York City, who came together around meetings of the Friendly Club, embraced Wollstonecraft's ideas, along with those of her lover/husband, William Godwin. One, Margaret Bayard, reported that Wollstonecraft's death was "a deep wound to my hopes" and "an incalculable loss for intellect and truth."[17]

16. Crane, ed., *Diary of Elizabeth Drinker,* Apr. 22, 1796, 163. Actually, Drinker's comment continues, "In some others, I do not agree with her—I am not for quite so much independance [sic]." For an extended discussion of the *Vindication's* reception, see Branson, *These Fiery Frenchified Dames,* 35; Marion Rust, *Prodigal Daughters: Susanna Rowson's Early American Women* (Chapel Hill, N.C., 2008), 86. For a modern exploration of Wollstonecraft that places her and her work within a feminist perspective, see Barbara Taylor, *Mary Wollstonecraft and the Feminist Imagination* (Cambridge, 2003).

17. Margaret Murphey Craig to Marianne Williams, n.d., Rush-Biddle-Williams Papers, ser. 2, box 17; Branson, *These Fiery Frenchified Dames,* 37–42; Fredrika J. Teute, "Reading Men and Women in Late Eighteenth-Century New York," paper presented at the annual meeting of the American Society for Eighteenth-Century Studies, Charleston, S.C., Mar. 12, 1994, 12–13. See, as well, Teute, "A 'Republic of Intellect': Conversation and Criticism among the Sexes in 1790s New York," in Philip Barnard et al., eds., *Revising Charles Brockden Brown: Culture, Politics, and Sexuality in the Early Republic* (Knoxville, Tenn., 2004), 149–181. For discussions of women's involvement in the republican public sphere and, in particular, responses to Mary Wollstonecraft, see, among others, Chandos Michael Brown, "Mary Wollstonecraft; or, The Female Illuminati: The Campaign against Women and 'Modern Philosophy' in the Early Republic," *Journal of the Early Republic,* XV (1995), 389–424; Elaine Forman Crane, "Political Dialogue and the Spring of Abigail's Discontent," *WMQ,* 3d Ser., LVI (1999), 745–774; Philip Hicks, "Portia and Marcia: Female Political Identity and the Historical Imagination," *WMQ,* 3d. Ser. (2005), 265–294.

PLATE THREE *Annis Boudinot Stockton.* By John Wollaston, c. 1760. Oil on canvas. Stockton was an early American *salonnière* and Philadelphia socialite. Princeton University Art Museum. Bequest of Mrs. Alexander T. McGill. Photograph by Bruce M. White

While the Alexander sisters moved onto the streets and others engaged in heated discussions of the radical Wollstonecraft, still other early republican women themselves moved into print. The wealthy and outspoken Mercy Otis Warren published plays, the first history of the American Revolution *(The History of the Rise, Progress, and Termination of the American Revolution* [1805]), and a critically important Antifederalist attack on the proposed

PLATE FOUR *Mrs. James Warren (Mercy Otis)*. By John Singleton Copley, c. 1763. Oil on canvas. Museum of Fine Arts, Boston: Bequest of Winslow Warren, 31.212. Photograph © 2010, Museum of Fine Arts, Boston

Constitution.[18] In contrast to Warren, Judith Sargent Murray entered the public prints as a Federalist, collecting her essays, a play, and a novella into a single volume, *The Gleaner,* in 1798.[19] British émigré Susanna Rowson, author of the best-selling novel *Charlotte Temple,* had a number of her plays produced. In one, the very popular *Slaves in Algiers* (performed in the nation's capital in 1794), women characters literally enacted the role of heroic republicans. "A woman can face danger with as much spirit, and as little fear, as the bravest man amongst you," one character proudly proclaims. The prologue to another highly respected woman's play, Elizabeth Inchbald's *Everyone Has His Fault* (produced in New York, Baltimore, and Boston the same year *Slaves* played in Philadelphia), was even more outspoken in its assertion of women's rightful place within the public and political sphere. Referencing women's actions during the opening years of the French Revolution, the prologue might almost have been written by Wollstonecraft.

The Rights of women, says a female pen,
Are, to do every thing as well as Men,
To think, to argue, to decide, to write,
To talk, undoubtedly—perhaps to fight.
(For Females march to war, like brave Commanders,
Not in old Authors only—but in Flanders.)[20]

18. Otis Warren's plays include *The Adulateur: A Tragedy* and *The Blockheads; or, The Affrighted Officers: A Farce.* For recent scholarly studies of Mercy Otis Warren, see Pauline Schloesser, *The Fair Sex: White Women and Racial Patriarchy in the Early American Republic* (New York, 2002); Kate Davis, *Catherine Macauley and Mercy Otis Warren: The Revolutionary Atlantic and the Politics of Gender* (New York, 2006).

19. Murray is best known for her essays and fiction, at first published serially in *Massachusetts Magazine* in the 1790s under the name "Mentor" and then collected under the title *The Gleaner,* signed "Constantia" (Judith Sargent Murray, *The Gleaner: A Miscellaneous Production* [Boston, 1798]). *The Gleaner* was one of the most widely read of women's publications during the new national period. Seven hundred subscribers supported its publication in 1798, and excerpts were frequently parroted in newspapers and other magazines. It is reprinted in Sharon M. Harris, ed., *Selected Writings of Judith Sargent Murray* (New York, 1995). Susanna Rowson, writer, actress, and educator, was an equally popular writer during this period; see Cathy N. Davidson, *Revolution and the Word: The Rise of the Novel in America* (New York, 1986), esp. 129–130, and Julia A. Stern's provocative analysis in her *Plight of Feeling: Sympathy and Dissent in the Early American Novel* (Chicago, 1997), esp. 31–69. For an overarching discussion of women's post-Revolutionary political experiences, see Rosemarie Zagarri, *Revolutionary Backlash: Women and Politics in the Early American Republic* (Philadelphia, 2007).

20. Susanna Haswell Rowson, *Slaves in Algiers; or, A Struggle for Freedom,* an edition prepared by Jennifer Margulis and Karen M. Poremski (Acton, Mass., 2000), 52; [Elizabeth] Inchbald,

John Adams's worst fears "that another Tribe more numerous and powerfull than all the rest were grown discontented," or at least assertive, seemed to have come true. With the male bourgeoisie's "masculine systems" somewhat in disrepair, would the urban magazines be able to re-present this "numerous and powerfull" tribe in ways that would reaffirm the coherence of their new American–as–virile citizen? Could the press reharness the symbolic power of women as man's constituting, confirming, and comforting Other?

ALL THE KING'S HORSES AND ALL THE KING'S MEN

Fractious and contradictory, eighteenth-century political discourses had rendered the urban press's new American a divided and unstable figure. On one issue, however, they all agreed: women were the political citizen's unifying Other. Women's differences from men overshadowed the rhetorical and ideological confusions the press's representations of the new American had introduced. Eighteenth-century men were certain that, in contrast to women's physical, emotional, and intellectual weakness, man's natural claims to manliness, to classic republican *virtu,* and to Enlightenment reason was irrefutable. All shared John Adams's assurance—women must be excluded from the pure male polis. If allowed to penetrate the polis, women would endanger republican virtue and weaken the fraternity of liberty-loving men. Most seriously of all, women would unsettle already troubled gender distinctions.

The exclusion of women from the polis was a central tenet of classic republicanism.[21] Physically frail and sexually vulnerable, women, classic republicans

---

Everyone Has His Fault: A Comedy, in Five Acts, as It Is Performed at the Theatres Royal (London, 1822). The play was originally written and performed in England in 1793, meaning that, within a year of its publication, it was being performed in the new United States, demonstrating the speed with which cultural productions were disseminated around the Atlantic—and the great popular interest in women's plays. Branson, *These Fiery Frenchified Dames,* discusses the play's performance history (113).

21. This is a central argument in J. G. A. Pocock, *The Machiavellian Moment: Florentine Political Thought and the Atlantic Republican Tradition* (Princeton, N.J., 1975). Numerous feminist scholars concur. In contrast, Lewis argues that post-Revolutionary women were able to use republican discourses to establish a role for themselves as republican women within late-eighteenth- and early-nineteenth-century print culture. In doing so, she builds upon and modifies Kerber's well-known argument about republican mothers *(Women of the Republic).* I agree with both Kerber and Lewis that late-eighteenth- and early-nineteenth-century European American women used republican rhetoric to legitimate a role for themselves as rational subjects able to contribute to the new nation. At the same time, I maintain that, to do so, they had to significantly transform both

argued, lacked the physical strength and martial skills to defend their own and their nation's honor. Dependent on men, they could not assume the role of brave, independent zoon politikon. They lacked, as well, the maturity of judgment and cool reason the wise citizen/statesman must possess. They were childlike and flirtatious, beguiled by baubles, given to superstition and hysteria. Furthermore, as married women (and most eighteenth-century women married), their bodies, wills, and earthly goods were their husbands' properties. Far from being propertied citizens, they were a male citizen's property. Most alarmingly of all, women were corrupt and corrupting. They were driven by unrestrained appetites for the luxuries commerce introduced into Britain and the new United States, luxuries that, classic republican theorist Andrew Fletcher warned, would "sink Europe into an Abyss of Pleasures" and, by implication, effeminacy.[22] Women sought power over men, leading men down the thorny path of dangerous desires, lasciviousness, and loss of honor. References to Delilah, Salome, and Cleopatra, temptresses who had destroyed brave warriors and virtuous republics, were commonplace in classic republican texts.

Certainly, classic republicans scorned, women had nothing to contribute to the well-being of the state or to the general good. As Massachusetts attorney Theodore Sedgwick asked sarcastically in one of the first cases to address questions of women's citizenship, "Can any one believe it was the intention of the [Massachusetts] legislature to demand of *femes-covert* their *aid and assistance* in the support of their constitution of government?" A woman could not "deprive the government of the benefit of her personal services—she had none to render—none were exacted of her."[23] As Rogers M. Smith points out, "The revolutionaries' rhetoric

classic and commercial republican discourses and that those discourses, traditionally understood, barred women from the polis as dependent and corrupting. See Lewis, "Politics and the Ambivalence of the Private Sphere," in Kennon, ed., *Republic for the Ages*, 122–151.

22. Classical republican polemicist Andrew Fletcher elaborated that women's weakness for the luxuries of "the Orient"—silks, gauzes, brocades—would "sink Europe into an Abyss of Pleasures . . . rendered the more expensive by a perpetual Change of the Fashions in Clothes." All, Fletcher continued, would lead to "unspeakable Evils." After all, who more than women bedecked their bodies in Oriental luxuries and fashions, women whose very bodies were designated an "Abyss of Pleasures"? Classical republicans feared the "chaos of appetites," "dependence," and "loss of personal autonomy" all eighteenth-century men associated with women. In these ways, classical republican discourses denied women's right to full membership in a virtuous republican body politic (see Pocock, *Machiavellian Moment*, 430, 486).

23. Linda K. Kerber provides a powerful analysis of this important case in her "Paradox of Women's Citizenship in the Early Republic: The Case of Martin vs. Massachusetts, 1805," *American Historical Review* (1992), 349–378, rpt. in Kerber, *Toward an Intellectual History of Women*, 261–302, esp. 294, 289–290.

continually linked effeminacy with those ultimate republican evils, corruption and ignorance. It was hard for them to conceive that women might have the qualities that public-spirited, virtuous republican citizenship demanded."[24]

Commercial republicanism was equally determined in its insistence that women had no place in a virtuous republic, though, given the complex roles women played in the production of the bourgeoisie and middling ranks, commercial republican arguments were more strained and convoluted. The removal of their women from the world of economic productivity played a central role in bourgeois claims to elevated social status. This move, combined with common-law dictums that denied working married women the profits of their labor and their capital, rendered bourgeois and many middling women economic wards of their husbands or fathers. And this in the face of commercial republican insistence that republican virtue required economic independence and manly industry. Of course, as bourgeois men knew full well, women were industrious and productive, securing the comforts of the middling home and displaying the elegances of bourgeois establishments. Indeed, it could be argued that, by producing middling comforts and bourgeois elegance, women produced the middling classes and the bourgeoisie. On the economic level, this certainly was true. Women's desires in the form of domestic consumption drove much of America's import trade and enriched America's great merchants, small shopkeepers, and industrious artisans. On the symbolic level, women played an equally important role. Through their personal elegance, cultured manners, and leisured lifestyle, bourgeois women confirmed bourgeois men's social standing at home and to watchful eyes in Europe. Transposed to the middling classes, women's aspirations to culture and fashion similarly marked their families' social standing and ambitions for upward mobility.[25]

24. Rogers M. Smith, *Civic Ideals: Conflicting Visions of Citizenship in U.S. History* (New Haven, Conn., 1997), 111–112. Hostility toward any move by women to penetrate the pure male political sphere was common in Europe as well as England and North America. It informed the bitter and pornographic political satire aimed at Marie Antoinette in the years preceding the French Revolution and played an important role in her conviction and execution. See, for example, Lynn Hunt, ed., *Eroticism and the Body Politic* (Baltimore, 1991), and Hunt, *The Family Romance of the French Revolution* (Berkeley, Calif., 1992).

25. Kerber, *Women of the Republic*, esp. chap. 5. See, as well, Mary Beth Norton, *Liberty's Daughters: The Revolutionary Experience of American Women, 1750–1800* (Ithaca, N.Y., 1980), 242–250; Marylynn Salmon, "Women and Property in South Carolina: The Evidence from Marriage Settlements, 1730–1830," *WMQ*, 3d Ser., XXXIX (1982), 655–685; Salmon, *Women and the Law of Property in Early America* (Chapel Hill, N.C., 1986). For an exploration of the gendering of the British middle class, see Leonore Davidson and Catherine Hall's monumental *Family Fortunes: Men and Women of the English Middle Class, 1780–1850* (New York, 2002).

But bourgeois and middling demands that their women enact a life of leisure and social polish warred with commercial republicans' praise of productivity and frugality. Thus women found themselves placed in a double bind—and at the heart of an ideological conundrum. To claim class respectability, they had to be fashionably dressed and leisured. To claim republican virtue, they had to be frugal and industrious. Turn where they might, they would be found at fault. If frugal and industrious, they undermined their husbands' and fathers' claims to social refinement and political importance. If fashionable and leisured, they embodied the dangers commerce posed to the virtuous Republic. To keep the Republic pure, women must be confined within domestic space, subject to their husbands' governance. Then men could lament women's foolish extravagances within an exclusively male public sphere while privately luxuriating in the social status those extravagances signaled and the domestic pleasures they made possible. Thus both classic and commercial republicanism concurred. Women must be exluded from the republican body politic.

What, then, of political liberalism, "the emancipatory discourse par excellence," with its promise of equality and inalienable rights to all? Recall Nancy Leys Stepan's celebration of the liberal political subject as "disembod[ied] . . . unmarked by . . . [social or physical] specificities." Universal in its vision, Stepan continues, liberalism promises political subjectivity and active citizenship to all. Not wealth, education, gender, or race, but simple birth secured the individual's claim to inalienable political rights. Perhaps, in theory, this was true. As we have seen, however, the eighteenth-century liberal subject was anything but unmarked. "The great liberal revolutions," political theorist Anne Norton argues, far from liberating women, only "secured a more exclusive fraternity." "Women who had stormed the Tuilleries with the sans-culottes found themselves denied admission to Jacobin clubs"—just as European American women, having valiantly supported the Revolution, found that Independence secured them neither formal political or legal rights.[26]

How did liberal discourses exclude women from their promises of universal rights? They did so in several distinct ways. The first was grounded on the social contract. All eighteenth-century social contract theorists, Locke included, presumed that women, without exception, had entered a state of marriage while still in a state of nature, before the initial social contract was agreed to. No longer independent actors, women could not be signatures to the social

26. Anne Norton, "Engendering Another American Identity," paper presented at the Conference on Political Identity in American Thought, Yale University, New Haven, Conn., April 1991, 4.

contract and therefore could make not claims upon its promises of equality and political sovereignty. Thus, although Locke insisted that a husband's governance over his wife was not political but social, he was equally insistent that women, and married women in particular, be excluded from the polis.[27]

Thus women's differences from men eviscerated liberalism's commitment to universal inclusion. Within eighteenth-century liberal thought, French historian Genevieve Fraisse explains, the problem of "otherness had to be solved by exclusion." Because women were seen as radically unlike men, women could not be bona fide members of the body politic. Focusing on Rousseau's political theories, Fraisse continues, "It is woman's otherness [Rousseau] rejects. . . . Discussing the respective characteristics or merits of the two sexes is pointless. [Rousseau's] reasoning is based exclusively on . . . the idea of a . . . democratic system where every individual is reflected by the whole and belongs to a [single] totality." Women would destroy the cohesiveness of that totality.[28]

Nothing marked women as different more concretely than their bodies. "Hobbes, and Locke after him," Norton argues, "made the body fence and shelter for the mind. . . . Men with their bodies inviolable, protected from assault by other men, could think for themselves. The closed body sheltered the open mind." "The open body," in contrast, "was the body subjected." "The body that was open to the assaults of others held a mind occupied by fear, beliefs subject to coercion. . . . Opening the body closed the mind." Naturally open to penetration and pregnancy, women's bodies "could be properly closed only when they were coupled with men's, or confined in the fictive body of the household" as men's dependents—not as men's political equals.[29]

But here we see the greatest danger of all—at least from a continental liberal position. Women embodied not just vulnerability but connectedness. Connectedness presumes interdependency. Interdependency compromises the male liberal subject's autonomy and independence. If men became too closely connected to women, Rousseau argued in his *Discourse on Inequality,* the natural differences separating men and women would dissolve. Patterns of male bonding necessary to the ascetic and rational life of the Republic would be undermined. More ominously still, Rousseau, indeed, most Enlightenment theorists, worried that women's seductive charms would render men effeminate, thus trans-

27. Carole Pateman, *The Sexual Contract* (Stanford, Calif., 1988); Elizabeth S. Anderson, "Women and Contracts: No New Deal," *Michigan Law Review* (1990), 1799.

28. Genevieve Fraisse, *Reason's Muse: Sexual Difference and the Birth of Democracy,* trans. Jane Marie Todd (Chicago, 1994), 167–168. See, as well, Joan B. Landis, *Women and the Public Sphere in the Age of the French Revolution* (Ithaca, N.Y., 1988).

29. Norton, "Engendering Another American Identity," 6.

forming men into women. Only if women were excluded from the polis could the liberal republican state function as a virtuous fraternal order.[30]

The Founding Fathers and the male urban press were, it would appear, ideologically well positioned to rebuff women's efforts to enter the public sphere, influence politics, and establish an independent female political voice. So armed, the press should have easily reestablished women's absolute otherness from men, used that otherness to reconfirm manliness as an inherent characteristic of virtuous citizenship, and restored their new American as an internally coherent, virile role. The urban magazines are filled with examples of their valiant attempts to constrain women's social and political roles and, at the same time, to reassert manly difference. But rhetoric is a two-edged sword and gender "a sometime thing." Especially during periods of radical political, economic, and social change, words become slippery, their meanings easily transformed, and the boundaries between the self and its Others porous. Let us look at the ways men deployed the ideological tools at their disposal and then at women's redeployment of those same tools.

COULDN'T PUT HUMPTY DUMPTY TOGETHER AGAIN

Gathered in Philadelphia, the Founding Fathers were resolute. Women had no place in their new constitution or their new Republic.[31] But although absent from the pages of the Constitution, women filled the pages of the new urban

---

30. Jean-Jacques Rousseau, *Emile; or, On Education*, trans. Allan Bloom (New York, 1979), 358–359. For a discussion of Rousseau's attitude toward—and, most especially, his fear of—women, see Fraisse, *Reason's Muse*, trans. Todd, 14, 16–17, 32, 37, 119–120. For a female perspective on women's exclusion from the male fraternity, see Luce Irigaray, *Speculum of the Other Woman*, trans. Gillian C. Gill (Ithaca, N.Y., 1985); Irigaray, *This Sex Which Is Not One*, trans. Catherine Porter (Ithaca, N.Y., 1985); and Judith Benjamin, *Bonds of Love Psychoanalysis, Feminism, and the Problem of Domination* (New York, 1988), esp. chaps. 1, 5.

31. "The purpose of silence," Ferguson tells us, "is to minimize and control difference"—the difference the inclusion of women would make in conceptualizing the virtuous citizen and the nation's new body politic. "The fact that they [women] are not mentioned at all reflects . . . agreement . . . that women had no proper place in the public realm and only a subordinate one in the home" (Ferguson, *American Enlightenment*, 150); Rogers M. Smith agrees. That women had no legitimate place in the public, and especially the political, arena is one of the major points of his *Civic Ideals*. See, as well, Rogers M. Smith, "'One United People': Second-Class Female Citizenship and the American Quest for Community," *Yale Journal of Law and the Humanities*, I, no. 2 (May 1989), 229–293. It is highly significant that the only mention of women in the Constitution is of enslaved women, that is, women who doubly embodied difference and had no legal or political standing.

press. Women and their images were everywhere, in novels, plays, poems, and, in particular, on the pages of the new political magazines. Here they assumed multiple forms—those of the good wives, caring and loving women, but also of foolish and dependent women, luxury-loving, lascivious, and ambitious women, bold, outspoken women, ridiculous, ugly, and unmarried women. Indeed, they were as present on the pages of the political magazines as they were in the Republic's burgeoning commercial cities and in the formation of its urban culture. Were the new republican women, in fact, irrepressible, or did the magazine's inscriptions of their otherness repair the rhetorical damage wrought by representations of "tasty" western farmers and, more generally, by the impact of political representation?

The magazines worked hard to reinscribe the rule of patriarchal government and female subservience. The ideal European American woman they held up for their readers to admire—and enact—was beautiful and innocent, sensitive and selfless. Untouched by rank ambition, she was too wise to play "the female wit." Timid, vulnerable to attack, and in need of male protection, she was the tender wife and mother, the dutiful daughter, the devoted sister. Her physical and emotional weaknesses confirmed man's physical strength and military valor; her economic dependence, his economic independence and productivity; her natural fearfulness, his natural firmness and determination; her selfless devotion to others, his self-possession and ambition. Whereas the ideal European American man valued his independence above life itself and prided himself on his self-reliance, the ideal European American woman sought love and protection through the arts of pleasing and serving others.[32] In short, as one male contributor to Philadelphia's *American Museum* remarked, as "I look upon it . . . the elements are not only differently mixed in women from what they are in men, but that they are almost of different sorts." Another essayist reaffirmed this assessment: "Women, in themselves weak, timid, and defenseless, stand in the greatest need of [male] courage and bravery, to defend them from the assaults that may be made upon their persons, or advantages that may be gained over their minds."[33]

An essay published in the *Massachusetts Magazine* epitomizes the new Republic's ideal vision of male/female relations. "The good husband," the essay proclaimed,

32. Of course, these representations were all lightly touched with the brush strokes of romanticism and the sentiments.

33. "Comparison between the Sexes," *American Museum*, I (1787), 58–61; "On the Happy Influence of Female Society," ibid., 61–64.

treats his wife with delicacy as a woman . . . attributes her follies to her weakness, her imprudence to her inadvertency . . . and pardons them with indulgence; all his care and industry are employed for her welfare; all his strength and power are exerted for her support and protection: . . . the good husband . . . animate[s] her faith by his practice and enforce[s] the precepts of Christianity by his own example.[34]

The wife emerges from this homily as weak, imprudent, and totally dependent on her husband's support and protection. The husband, in contrast, "pardons," "executes," "supports," "protects," "animates," and "enforces." The home that appeared in the new nation's political magazines, deviating significantly from the pre-Revolutionary home Christopher Gadsden presented, but resembling that of Emile, was a training ground where men learned to govern wisely.

The urban press deemed women's subordination within the home essential to domestic happiness and national social order. Echoing both Locke and Rousseau, the magazines urged women to contest neither man's domestic nor his political power but to gracefully accept his protection and governance. Thus a poet signing himself "the good husband" advised his love to "despise the tricks of female art / And pride in nothing but a tender heart." If she did so, he promised, "Blest with her converse, joyful I'll blend / The tender husband with the faithful friend."[35]

But, as Rousseau noted, gender relations are not that simple. Even when polemically represented in the popular press as adoring and dependent, women repeatedly threatened men's autonomy and governance. It seemed that to be different (as in woman) was always to be dangerous and disruptive, and to be autonomous (as in man) was not to be free from dependencies. Using women's willing dependence to confirm men's autonomy, the urban press rendered men dependent on their dependent wives and thus threatened male claims to republican independence and virtue. Intentionally or not, this was the message of a "SENTIMENTAL and MORAL" essay Carey published in the *American Museum*. The essay began sternly enough, representing men as "enterprising and robust," women's providers and protectors. But, the essay continued, men as well as women had needs. Men needed "female softness." Without women, men were often "cruel," "rough," and "barbarous." Women refined men, taught men "to please and be agreeable," to submit to the wills of others. "In our sex," the

34. "Character of a Good Husband," *Massachusetts Magazine*, I (1789), 177.

35. "The Wish," supplement to *Pennsylvania Packet; and The General Advertiser*, February 3, 1772.

essayist admitted, "there is a kind of constitutional or masculine pride, which hinders us from yielding, in points of knowledge or honour, to each other; but we lay it entirely aside in our connections with women." From women, they learned "a submission, which . . . teaches us to obey, where we used to command." In this essay, at least, men who desired to acquire gentility and social polish submitted their "masculine pride" to women's guidance. As Rousseau had predicted, however, in learning to please women, men became like women —bending, obeying "where they used to command." Sexual difference, the central truth upon which republican liberal political logic rested, evaporated. As a result, women began to emerge on the pages of the urban press as dangerous, devious, difficult to control. The essay we are considering, while ostensibly praising women's power to refine men, ended by representing women as sexually and politically dangerous.

> In their forms lovely, in their manners soft and engaging, . . . [women] bend the haughty stubbornness of man . . . an insinuating word . . . even a smile . . . conquered Alexander, subdued Caesar, and decided the fate of empires and kingdoms.

Warning his readers of "the power of women to bend the stronger sex to their will," the author ended with the telling advice—"to enjoy any pleasure in perfection, we must never be saturated with it."[36]

Indeed, the political magazines were filled with essays warning husbands to beware their wives' wiles and deceptions. It was not enough to rhetorically banish women from the public sphere and confine them to domestic space. Women could appear subservient and dependent while they secretly worked to bind men to a state of dependency. Consciously or unconsciously, men experienced women's threats in political as well as domestic terms. As one magazine contributor cautioned, consciously or unconsciously deploying explicitly political, indeed military, rhetoric, it is by "exterior charms, that they [women] must establish their empire." "This is the weapon conferred on her by nature to compensate the weakness of her sex."[37]

Male readers must be warned. And women readers must be admonished.

36. "On the Happy Influence of Female Society," *American Museum,* I (1787), 61–64. The Founding Fathers might not have needed women's assistance to give birth to a new republic, but actual American men apparently needed women. This was especially true of men who desired to cloak themselves not only in the attributes of republican virtue but in the more tangible garb of bourgeois civility.

37. "Thoughts on the Dress of American Ladies," *Columbian Magazine,* I (1787), 638–639, esp. 638.

Women's desires for power and autonomy were dangerous. They would lead to madness, death, and the destruction of families, the diametrical opposite role to that women were supposed to play in society. This was the message of a short piece of didactic fiction that appeared in the *American Museum* entitled "History of Kitty Wells: A True Story." Interestingly, the story's title character, Kitty Wells, is not the dangerous woman in need of admonishing but that woman's innocent and demure daughter, a reassuringly vulnerable, dependent, and endangered figure. Soft, unthreatening, Kitty's name bespeaks her character. Not so, her mother. In sharp contrast to the gentle Kitty, her mother (who remains nameless throughout the story) is a proud and talented woman who leaves her husband, an obscure laborer, to take a well-paid position as head housekeeper in a grand manor house where she is responsible for the household economy and a large staff. The weight of her "manly" responsibilities, however, made her "eccentric," "disordered," and given to "whimsical excesses." She ultimately flees into the night, never to be heard of again. Left without parental protection, Kitty wanders to London where, penniless and alone, she is the prey of rapacious men—until she is rescued by an elderly male philanthropist and placed under her father's rightful guidance and protection. In this sentimental romance, the father's lack of command and ambition is not criticized, for, after all, he was but a poor laborer, supposed to depend upon the guidance of his betters. Here we see the grid of class overlapping and reinforcing the grid of gender, suggesting a deferential role the magazines wished Massachusetts's hill farmers had adopted.[38]

Fictively, independent women figured as awful examples of women out of social—that is, male—control. Actual independent women posed more immediate threats, especially when those women boldly entered the new Republic's public sphere. Philadelphia's leading republican editor, Mathew Carey, certainly thought so. Carey devoted a number of articles in his prestigious *American Museum* to exposing and denouncing the dangers he felt two such women posed—Mother Ann Lee, founder of the Shakers, and Jemimah Wilkinson, the Universal Friend. Particularly dangerous, Lee and Wilkinson threatened both domestic and divine order. The Age of Revolution was an age of religious as well as political unrest. Deism threatened orthodoxy. New sects

38. "History of Kitty Wells," *Columbian Magazine*, I (1787), 339–342, and II (1787), 381–389. Here we have yet another indication of the cultural influence Britain, as an imperial metropole, continued to exert over the newly independent United States. The *American Museum* undoubtedly copied this short piece from a British periodical. Certainly the story's setting moves back and forth between an English country estate and London, two important sites in the European American postcolonial imagination.

arose. Women and the poor raised their voices publicly to the Lord. But Lee and Wilkinson went further, claiming to be Christ returned in female form. Women enacting God, Carey thundered, signaled the breakdown of all distinction, all social and religious order.

Daring to call herself "the woman clothed with the sun" (Revelations), "holy—omniscient—and everywhere present, as God himself is; and as much to be revered, believed, and obeyed, as he," "the lamb's wife," Mother Ann Lee claimed, and Shakers believed, that "no blessing ever came down from heaven —nor shall any man ever ascend to that blessed state and world—but through her." Carey concluded that the Shakers were mad. Certainly, they were given to drunkenness, demented forms of body activity, and "obscenity." Although men could father republics, it appeared that women could not mother religions.[39]

Carey followed his attack on Mother Ann Lee with one attacking Jemimah Wilkinson, representing the Universal Friend as an even more radical offender against public decorum and gender norms. Wilkinson was, Carey roared, a "villainous impostor," "disfigured," "illiterate," and "very artful." Refusing to present herself as a woman, she appeared in public dressed in men's clothing. She wore her hair long and loose. Her neck cloth and outside garments resembled those of men. "Under [her outer robe]," the article continued in a rather titillating manner, "it is said, her apparel is very expensive: and the form of it conveys the same idea, as her external appearance, of her being neither man nor woman."[40]

Having undressed Wilkinson for his readers and thus rendered her the object of the dominant male gaze, Carey described his interview with Wilkinson, who, he complained, had addressed him in a "masculine, authoritative tone of voice." "The manner of her giving this exhortation was not in such a way as became a meek and good woman, but bespoke her very vain." "I saw instantly her design was to overawe me," he continued. Enraged by her appropriation of male authority, he counterattacked, berating her "on the impropriety of her dress and appearance; and told her it was so much like the dress and appearance of a man, that I conceived it to be very improper; that for any woman to appear as she did, was wrong; but . . . especially so in one coming to this city . . . in a religious character." As in attacks on protesting farmers, clothes out of order signaled persons out of order. Wilkinson's continued pres-

39. "Some Account of the Tenets and Practice of the Religious Society Called Shakers," *American Museum,* I (1787), 148–150.

40. "Account of Jemimah Wilkinson, Styled the Universal Friend, also of Her Doctrines and Followers," *American Museum,* I (1787), 150–154.

ence in Philadelphia (the nation's capital), Carey warned, would cause social disorder and encourage indecent behavior. Yet Wilkinson's was a presence Carey obsessively reinscribed on the pages of his Philadelphia magazine, devoting not one but four essays to attacking her. Disorderly women, like Tar Baby, proved a riveting object of attack—an object that came to obsess editors and contributors to the new urban press.[41]

Embedded in the midst of this lengthy portrayal lay what may have been the most telling condemnation of all. Wilkinson spoke in "the peculiar dialect of the most illiterate of the country people of New-England." So, presumably, did Massachusetts's angry farmers. Were these representations designed to show Jemimah Wilkinson as another example of the social and political anarchy the impoverished New England countryside was exporting to disrupt the peace of the new nation? Representing this bold, religious woman as an illiterate New England country woman, the *American Museum* again reinforced the urban fathers' gender grid with a class-based grid in a manner that both his bourgeois and middling readers—already alarmed by Shays's Rebellion and fearful of discontent among Pennsylvania's own urban and rural poor—would find particularly telling.[42]

The proliferation of essays representing gender as disordered and dangerous suggests that, as political and economic crises followed hard upon revolution and war, the nation's urban editors and their male contributors experienced gender relations, not as a source of reassurance, but one of added anxiety. If the new American—as—republican citizen could not govern his own home, his own church, and his own women, where and whom could he govern? The better to deny these fears, the magazines turned from condemnations of actual disorderly women to bitter satire and gross ridicule of fictive female figures.

The foolish woman was a time-honored butt of male humor. Contributors to the new magazines delighted in describing women's heads as crammed with foolish fancies, "airy vapour," and snuff. Unveiled on the pages of the new urban press, their charms were revealed to be but the composite of "cork rumps, false bums, false locks, elastic wigs . . . whitening for the neck, rouge for the cheek." Still other essays represented women as ludicrously promiscuous, sexually unrestrained, excessive in their amours and reproductive capacities. Some

41. "To the Printer," *American Museum*, I (1787), 333–338, esp. 338. For other essays on Wilkinson, see "To the Printer," ibid., 218–222; "Further Account of Jemimah Wilkinson," ibid., 462–467.

42. "Account of Jemimah Wilkinson," ibid., 150–154. For a contemporary exploration of radical religious women, see Susan Juster, *Doomsayers: Anglo-American Prophecy in the Age of Revolution* (Philadelphia, 2003).

women, one magazine reported in an amused tone, boasted of their power to produce children without the benefit of husband or state authorization, echoing and inverting men's claims to be able to "father" states without women's assistance and authority.[43]

But could humor really reassure when serious denunciations could not? Let us examine two of the urban press's more elaborate satirical attacks. The first was entitled "Speech of Miss Polly Baker, before the Court of Judicature, in Connecticut, Wherein She Was Prosecuted for the Fifth Time for Having Bastard Children." Not only is the name "Baker" a play on Polly's reproductive capacities; as the essay unfolds, we learn that Polly has a second name, Sarah Olitor. The *Oxford English Dictionary* has no entry for Olitor but tells us that "olitory" means "of or relating to pot-herbs or kitchen vegetables, or a kitchen garden. . . . 1696. . . . A world of vulgar plants and olitories." The satire and especially Polly's and Sally's surnames were designed to evoke peals of laughter from Carey's audience. Having introduced Baker/Olitor, the satire focused on her defense. "I have brought five fine children into the world, at the risque of my life," she began; "I have maintained them well by my own industry, without burdening the township. . . . Can it be a crime (in the nature of things, I mean) to add to the number of . . . subjects, in a new country that really wants people? I own it, I should think it a praiseworthy, rather than a punishable action." "The duty of the first great command of nature, and of nature's God—increase and multiply!" was "a duty from the steady performance of which, nothing has been able to deter me; but for its sake, I have hazarded the loss of the public esteem, and have frequently endured public disgrace; and therefore ought in my humble opinion, instead of a whipping, to have a statue erected to my memory." Polly further assumed the right to lecture the court on how to legislate: "I am no divine; but if you gentlemen, must be making laws, do not turn natural and useful actions into crimes, by your prohibitions."[44]

This is an old sore—lampooning promiscuous working-class women whose sexual and reproductive excesses "nothing has been able to deter." But by having Baker/Olitor present her actions as a productive contribution to the general welfare so soon after the Revolution, did Carey, consciously or unconsciously, seek to satirize actual women's wartime experiences, their bravery,

43. *Pennsylvania Packet, and Daily Advertiser,* May 13, 1788; Ardello, "To the Editor of the Columbian Magazine," *Columbian Magazine,* I (1786), 233–235; *Pennsylvania Packet, and Daily Advertiser,* May 13, 1788; "Account of a Buyer of Bargains," *American Museum,* I (1787), 345–348.

44. "Speech of Miss Polly Baker, before the Court of Judicature, in Connecticut, Wherein She Was Prosecuted for the Fifth Time for Having Bastard Children," *Philadelphia Monthly Magazine,* I (1798), 325–327.

their self-reliance? References to women's giving birth and raising children without male support must have evoked the courage and independence of so many patriotic women, their knitting the social fabric together while husbands and fathers were at war. Was this the male press's way of containing women's wartime social—and political—significance?

Female sexuality proved an endlessly fascinating subject for Carey and his *American Museum*. The portrayal of Baker/Olitor was followed with another satire entitled "Plan for the Establishment of a Fair of Fairs, or Market of Matrimony." This contribution initially assumed a serious tone, purporting to instruct men who would render social institutions more efficient and orderly to gather four times a year in an open market to examine women wishing to marry. "All ladies, desirous of disposing of their persons in wedlock, [would] have liberty to repair thither, and expose themselves for that purpose," the author explained. The fairgrounds would be divided into "wards . . . to denote the several *articles* to be disposed of therein . . . viz. No. 1. VIRGINS No. 2. WIDOWS No. 3. DEMIREPS No. 4. The COMMONALITY." Having reduced women's "liberty" to the right to expose themselves as "articles to be disposed of" (an interesting comment upon the marriage contract), the essay announced that two constables would be in charge of the women. Each would carry "a red staff, as a badge of his office, made after the manner described by Horace—*ruber porrectus ab inguine palus.*"[45]

Satirically refusing women's incorporation into the new American body politic, the essay plays on two aspects of the bourgeois public sphere—the political, with its reference to "wards," and the marketplace, where men as producers and capitalists gathered to buy and sell. The joke was twofold: first, that women had only themselves to sell and, secondly, that they could not constitute political "wards" as male republican citizens could. Rather, the satire herded women into wards as if they were farm animals to be examined and, if desirable, purchased for domestic consumption. All presumably was very funny. But the essay makes one rhetorical slip—its deployment of the word "commonality." Common words, as we know, have multiple meanings. Given the essay's tone, we might suppose the author to have meant "the state or quality of being in common with, or shared by, others," a popular mid-eighteenth-century meaning that, in the case of women, implied prostitutes. But the word "commonality" had a long history of political meanings as well. In Chaucer, it meant "a community, commonwealth." By the late seventeenth century, it had

---

45. "Plan for the Establishment of a Fair of Fairs, or Market of Matrimony," *American Museum* (1787), 140–142.

come to mean "a free or self-governing community." By the mid-eighteenth century, it commonly referred to the "Third Estate," as when David Hume wrote of "Three estates, the clergy, the nobility, and the commonality." Intending to denigrate women sexually, had our satirist constituted them as a new Third Estate, the very embodiment of a bourgeois republic, thus undercutting the explicit object of his satire?[46]

A still larger question demands our attention. Should we bother to take such political ridicule seriously? Yes, for it formed a powerful weapon in men's struggle to allay their sense of women's power and agency and to reassert their own. Male humor sought to contain women's threats to domestic and political tranquility in two ways. First, by representing women as an amalgam of cork and horsehair, powder, rouge and paint, as sexually excessive, multiplied through pregnancies, it constituted women corporeally multiple and grotesque. So depicted, women became the antithesis of the classical and closed body constituted by both civic humanism and Enlightenment liberalism. The classic body, M. M. Bakhtin had argued in his study of Rabelais, was elevated, static, monumental, without openings, disembodied. (Shades of Nancy Stepan.) Elaborating Bakhtin, Peter Stallybrass and Allon White see the classic body as "the radiant centre of a transcendent individualism . . . raised above the viewer and the commonality and anticipating passive admiration from below." But "the classical body was far more than an aesthetic standard. . . . [Associated with] the . . . 'high' discourses of philosophy, statecraft . . . and law. . . . the . . . protocols of the classical body came to mark out the identity of progressive rationalism itself." And, most pointedly, it marked the independent, empowered liberal body. The urban press endowed the new American–as–republican citizen with just such a classical, closed body. (We have only to think of the many portraits and statues of the stony-faced and somber Washington, father of his country—and similar ones of the statesman/philosopher Jefferson.) But not women, those amalgams of false parts, ungoverned sexuality, and vaporous thoughts, those threats to the pure male polis.[47]

Male humor worked on a second ideological and rhetorical level. Not only did satire denigrate and silence women (how could an eighteenth-century middle-class woman respond to the press's obscene reference to Horace?), it confirmed the very order it lampooned. The function of humor, Mary Douglas

---

46. *Oxford English Dictionary*, s.v. "commonality."

47. M. M. Bakhtin, *Rabelais and His World*, trans. Helene Iswolsky (Cambridge, Mass., 1968); Peter Stallybrass and Allon White, *The Politics and Poetics of Transgression* (Ithaca, N.Y., 1986), 21–22.

argues, is to explore order—not to challenge it. "The joke . . . affords opportunity for realising that an accepted pattern has no necessity. Its excitement lies in the suggestion that any particular ordering of experience may be arbitrary and subjective. It is frivolous in that it produces no real alternative, only an exhilarating sense of freedom . . . in general." These satirical essays permitted men to express their fear of women's power, their sense that the patriarchal order had "no necessity," that it was "arbitrary and subjective," without seriously endangering that order. For all knew that eighteenth-century political discourses produced no real alternative to marriage and common law's subjugation of women within marriage under coverture. These essays merely permitted men to laugh at their own fears—and to express, through humor, their deep-seated hostilities toward women.[48]

Deep-seated and apparently never fully assuaged, for the jokes obsessively continued, as did repeated references to women—references that, as we have seen, raised far more questions then they answer. For, as Rousseau had argued, once men allowed women into public, political discourses, women would reveal, not their dependence on men, but rather the reverse: men's dependence on women. Representing women in the new political magazines repeatedly exposed bourgeois and middling men's fears that women had the power to refuse male governance—indeed, to transform men into women.

Vicious though they were, satirical representations of vaporish and grotesque women, by themselves, were not enough to recuperate the American republican's manly stability and semblance of inner coherence. Urban editors resorted, therefore, to yet another tactic, one we already noted Mathew Carey experimenting with. Still within the satiric mode, editors and writers sought to fuse representations of the new republican's two constituting Others. Out of the confabulation, they hoped to constitute a figure whose doubled (duplicitous?) and grotesque characteristics would be sufficiently absurd and alien to dispel their fears. In this way, they hoped to finally repress the "eternal feminine" on the pages of the new political press and thus, at last, to succeed in constituting the American republican subject as virile and virtuous.

Let us return to that master of political rhetoric—Mathew Carey. In the March 1787 issue of his *American Museum*, Carey published several articles that, read sequentially, exemplify this satirical confabulation. At a time when western farmers associated the eastern elite and their newly proposed constitution with economic hard times and political repression, Carey's essays attacked

48. Mary Douglas, "The Social Control of Cognition: Some Factors in Joke Perception," *Man*, III (1968), 361–376, esp. 365, 368–369.

those objections—in a humorous vein—as the fears of silly, weak-nerved, and factious men. He then followed this attack with a piece of broad and brutal political satire entitled "On the Fear of Mad Dogs." This latter essay lampooned old women for spreading false alarms of dogs gone mad and consequently of disturbing the peace of "the capitol" (a word rent with multiple meanings: the seat of government and, with the slightest change of spelling, productive commercial wealth). It was not that dogs had gone mad or that the capitol (or capital) and the times had gone bad, Carey argued, but that hysterical women gossips had done both. Carey not only associated the rumors of hard times with devalued women; he constituted woman as an irrational and ridiculous Other to the sagacious middle class (and, by implication, white) male citizen, represented by the essay's narrator. "When epidemic terror is . . . excited, every morning comes loaded with some new disaster," the essay states. "A lady, for instance, in the country, of very weak nerves, has been frighted by the barking of a dog; the story spreads . . . grows more dismal . . . and, by the time it has arrived in town, the lady is described . . . running mad upon all fours, barking like a dog, biting her servants, and at last smothered between two beds"—of type, one wonders? As if this were not sufficient to convict women as illogical and politically dangerous, Carey's magazine repeated the story in only a slightly altered guise, now told to the male narrator, a sensible and bemused observer, by his landlady. "A mad dog . . . she assured me, had bit a farmer, who soon becoming mad . . . bit a fine brindled cow; the cow . . . began to foam at the mouth, . . . went about upon her hind legs, sometimes barking like a dog, and sometimes attempting to talk like the farmer."[49]

As already noted, twice-told tales hold many meanings. Carey's essay associates western farmers' serious economic and political complaints about the shortage of currency and the hard times that followed the Peace of Paris with the gossip of foolish and hysterical women. But, worse, he then associated those selfsame protesting farmers with dumb animals gone mad. How better to discredit political opponents (and politically contain women) than to link political protests to crazed animals and both to women whose political opinions, men of all stripes knew, could never be redeemed in the solid coin of reliable judgment and hard facts?

Silly women and mad farmers, fused through bitter satire, appeared momen-

---

49. "Evil Consequences of Party Spirit . . . ," *American Museum*, I (1787), 185–186; "Thoughts on Mobs . . . ," ibid., 186–187; "A Word of Consolation for America . . . ," ibid., 187–190; "On the Fear of Mad Dogs," ibid., 226–228.

tarily to recuperate the American republican's manly political stature, stabilizing his political identity, confirming his judicious civic *virtu*. But can satire, even the most caustic and grotesque, achieve lasting political and rhetorical stability? The joke and satire both self-consciously proclaim their frivolous nature. Inciting laughter, they are not intended to challenge the social order. But they do interrogate that order and reveal, in Mary Douglas's words, that it "has no necessity . . . [and is] arbitrary and subjective." Is the joke, then, like Pandora's box? Refusing closure, does it reveal more than it can recontain? As tellingly, if the republican subject's inner coherence depends on humor, is it, itself, a joke?

REBELLIOUS COQUETTES AND UNREQUITED DESIRES

The battles of the sexes over what place women should occupy in the new republican public sphere and whether women could claim any of the rights of citizenship continued unabated. In tracing struggles over disputed meanings and contested rights, it is critical to ask, Where did the struggles take place—in boudoirs and over teacups? In private correspondence and carefully guarded diaries? Or in the public prints? Were the Republic's educated women able to publicly engage their male leaders in a discussion about women's right to a political presence in the newly constituted nation?

On the surface, the answer is no. A few women, as we have noted, did intrude into public political debates. Judith Sargent Murray wrote for the Federalist cause. But she did so initially under a male pseudonym and, even when publishing *The Gleaner* as a collected work, deliberately obfuscated her gender. Her name certainly did not appear on the title page. Only Mercy Otis Warren engaged political matters in the public prints in her own name. But she positioned herself as the sister of a martyred Founding Father (James Otis), the wife of another Father (James Warren), and the friend and friendly opponent of a third (John Adams). Significantly, when she entered the political fray as an Antifederalist, she wrote anonymously. Most tellingly, Warren almost never addressed the issue of women as legitimate members of the new republican body politic in public print. Of course, as we know, some women playwrights did boldly proclaim women's rights. But we must remember that plays are designed to amuse, to take one's mind away from quotidian realities, and so, as Mary Douglas remarks, are "frivolous in that [they] produce no real alternative."[50]

50. Richard Henry Lee, *An Additional Number of Letters from the Federal Farmer to the Republican Leading to a Fair Examination of the System of Government, Proposed by the Late*

Late-eighteenth-century European American women, Robert Ferguson points out, faced a number of ideological and rhetorical obstacles in their efforts to politically authorize themselves. First and foremost, there was an "explicit contradiction between the right of assertion and the status of the lady—a contradiction that the eighteenth century assigns with special weight to polite circles of literary production." To be known as a "learned lady" or, worse, a learned lady who published, was to court scandal and public opprobrium. To be a learned lady who publicly demanded women's empowerment would garner attacks like those that so muddied Wollstonecraft's name. No matter how much they admired Wollstonecraft, few respectable women were ready to publicly walk in her footsteps.[51] Secondly, enlightenment rhetoric, with its emphasis on reason and progress, discouraged overt expressions of anger—especially from women's pens. "Nowhere is the cost . . . more evident," Ferguson continues, "than in the tonal controls placed on women's writing. The emotion most frequently denied the educated eighteenth-century woman . . . is anger in her own cause." It was, consequently, only with the greatest difficulty that eighteenth-century women developed a self-consciously female political voice. As Ferguson concluded, what women lacked was "the capacity to meet political conflict collectively in the public sphere as gentlemen of letters frequently do. . . . On politics, women write in isolation if at all." Furthermore, in attempting to assert a political presence, late-eighteenth-century European American women ran head-on into the disabling figure of the republican mother. As Kerber initially described it, this was a role men choreographed and women enacted. Its presumed players were educated and intelligent women, well versed in the political discourses of their times and conversant with their nation's history. Virtuous patriots, they sought always to serve the Republic—but never by seeking a public political role for themselves. Their duty, as they saw it, or rather were taught to see it, was to seclude themselves within the home, dedicating

Convention . . . (Chicago, 1962). Of course, men also wrote under political pseudonyms, but the absence of a name on the title page was far more significant in the case of a woman writer. Readers assumed that the writer of political tracts would be a man. For a discussion of Warren's place within the Antifederalist movement, see Saul Cornell, *The Other Founders: Anti-Federalism and the Dissenting Tradition in America, 1788–1828* (Chapel Hill, N.C., 1999), 55–59, 70–72.

51. Ferguson, *American Enlightenment,* 179, 181. A woman need not have liaisons outside of marriage. If she married, inappropriately, a man considerably younger than herself, as Catherine Macauley did, opprobrium would be heaped upon her for displaying what appeared to others as overt sexual desires. See Kerber, *Women of the Republic,* 226.

their lives to encouraging their husbands' patriotism and educating their sons to be the virtuous republican citizen they themselves could not be.[52]

During the very years that saw the creation of the republican mother, an alternative and rather spicier narrative attracted women—the novel of seduction. This was one of the eighteenth century's most popular genres and one women participated in both as authors and readers. Virtually every European American woman novelist between the 1790s and early 1800s wrote in this genre. Of course, all followed in the footsteps of Samuel Richardson, modeling their heroines upon Clarissa or Pamela. Moreover, all, like Richardson, addressed their novels to newly urbane bourgeois and increasingly middling women readers.[53]

Novels of seduction were sexual melodramas, depicting the tragic fate awaiting women who threw caution to the winds, defied parents and guardians, and insisted on the legitimacy of their independent judgment. Abandonment, dishonor, destitution, and death awaited them, lightened only slightly by their sincere repentance and self-abnegation. As Clarissa and her thousands of readers discovered to their sorrow, even the most virtuous woman could not survive outside the home—no matter how just her defiance of tyrannical authority. But before their preordained doom descended, women characters asserted their desires, challenged male authority, lived freely, had adventures, saw the world. The novel of seduction was most frequently an epistolary novel. Modeled on

52. Ferguson, *American Enlightenment*, 179, 181. The republican mother thus assumed a mediated political identity, living in the Republic through her husband and sons. "She had a responsibility to the political scene," Kerber explains, "though she was not active in it" *(Women of the Republic,* 211, 228). But it was not only as mothers that women served the new Republic. The influence wives exerted on husbands, Jan Lewis argues, constituted women's greatest exercise of political authority. As already noted, Teute takes this argument even further, arguing that women, especially bourgeois women, acted not only as wives and mothers but as intelligent, politically aware individuals deeply concerned with the well-being of their republic. (We will see this theme again in Ann Richman's bold declarations at the end of this chapter.) They also felt quite free to give voice to their own political opinions—not in the public prints, we must note, but only in private (though influential) social gatherings. See Lewis, "The Republican Wife: Virtue and Seduction in the Early Republic," *WMQ*, 3d Ser., XLIX (1981), 689–721; Teute, "Roman Matron," in Kennon, ed., *Republic for the Ages*, 89–121.

53. For two useful surveys of the early U.S. literature and especially of women novelists, see Davidson's older *Revolution and the Word* and Stern's *Plight of Feeling*. For an examination of the appeal of the novel of seduction to post-Revolutionary European American women across class lines, see Carroll Smith-Rosenberg, "Mis-prisioning *Pamela:* Representations of Gender and Class in Nineteenth-Century America," *Michigan Quarterly Review*, XXVI (1987), 9–28.

actual women's letters, epistolary novels gave women the opportunity to read stories written as if they came from their own desks.[54]

One of the stories these melodramas told was about anger—not (or at least not explicitly) about men's refusal to include women in the Declaration of Independence's promises of freedom and equality, but righteous anger over men's sexual exploitation and betrayal of women. Within these novels, the floodgates of women's resentment and rage opened. This, alone, would have made the seduction novel an attractive genre for women writers and readers. This and the fact that such novels made women—their loves, fears, and injustices, their willfulness and courage—the central focus. The dangers to women who indulged their desires lie at the heart of these melodramas.

But another aspect of the seduction novel might have been even more telling in its appeal to eighteenth-century women writers and readers—the opportunity, as we have seen rare indeed in the eighteenth century, to explore varied aspects of female desire. Indeed, the novel of seduction permits us, today, to ask a series of questions concerning the nature of eighteenth-century women's desires. Were these desires always, as men assumed, sexual and directed toward men? Was it possible, especially in the years following the Revolution, that women desired the very things that had spurred European American men to revolt against Great Britain—freedom, independence, self-determination, that is, the right to pursue happiness on their own terms? If women were driven solely by the desire for sexual pleasure or love, on the one hand, and luxurious consumer items, on the other, then, as all true republicans knew, women could never aspire to civic virtue and the role of active citizen. But, if women desired liberty and independence, if they were willing to sacrifice their comforts, security, their very lives to realize those desires, then despite their gender, they, too, present themselves as virtuous republicans.[55]

How ironic! Republican and liberal Enlightenment political discourses

54. Many middling women were what might be called new, that is, inexperienced, readers for whom scholarly tomes would have proved challenging. However, literate women were letter writers. They therefore found the epistolary novel a far more welcoming genre.

55. We must remember, as well, that many women's diaries and letters indicate that they had closer emotional relations with women than with their husbands. The heterosexual passions one finds in fiction, especially male fiction, might have been a projection of male desires. See, for example, Carroll Smith-Rosenberg, "The Female World of Love and Ritual: Relations between Women in Nineteenth-Century America," *Signs*, I (1975), 1–29. Stern, in *Plight of Feeling*, sees post-Revolutionary European American novels focused on the struggle between republican and liberal visions of the nation, civic virtue and the citizen.

thwarted women's open expression of their desires for a public political voice and identity at the very time that the discourses of sexuality, especially as represented in seduction novels, gave space for the expression of those desires. Of course, women's pleas for education also spoke to women's desires—and for their right to enter the public sphere of educational institutions and rational discourse. But seduction novels cathected those pleas. Indeed, they seized the very rhetorical tropes that men had so long and so effectively used to ridicule and silence women—their sexual passions—to express women's desires and women's right to pursue happiness. So transformed, the expression of female desire could become, to refer to Isaiah Thomas's "four very smart and agreeable young ladies," "a sword . . . to wage continued war."[56]

Certainly, novels of seduction focused on female characters who challenged male discourses. Contrast the "fallen woman," the central protagonist of these melodramas, to the idealized republican wife and mother of more canonical texts. The fallen woman appears the very antithesis of the republican wife and mother. The one was virtuous, the other, sinful; the one demure, secluded, and willing to act through others, the other, willful, driven by passion and desire, confident in her own judgment, no matter how wrong that judgment was. The trope of the republican wife and mother reinforced social norms; the seduced woman flung social conformity to the winds. Though she ended her life in misery, the fallen woman had tasted independence. Though ostracized, she could not be ignored. Rather, she captured the imagination of the new republic's women—and often male—readers. She represented a covert, transgressive refiguring of the idealized liberal republican subject. And when all was said and done, she was quite frequently a best seller.

This is a bold hypothesis, that late-eighteenth- and early-nineteenth-century women entered the republican public sphere by cloaking republican and liberal political discourses in the rhetoric of sexuality, the romance, and the melodrama. But this was true until at least the mid-nineteenth century. To explore this hypothesis, let us turn to one of the new republic's best-selling novels, Hannah Foster's *Coquette; or, The History of Elizabeth Wharton, a Novel Founded in Fact, by a Lady of Massachusetts* (1797). Rivaling Susanna Rowson's *Charlotte Temple* as early America's most popular novel, it was republished frequently throughout the nineteenth century. More than two hundred years

56. For a recent discussion of women's desires for education, see Mary Kelley, *Learning to Stand and Speak: Women, Education, and Public Life in America's Republic* (Chapel Hill, N.C., 2006).

after publication, it continues to attract the attention of feminist critics and historians—from the work of Cathy N. Davidson, Nancy Armstrong, and Kerber to later analyses by Julia A. Stern.[57]

"AN UNUSUAL SENSATION POSSESSES MY BREAST": THE RISK-TAKING FEMME FATALE

At first reading, *The Coquette* appears a melodramatic inscription of the values of commercial republicanism. The novel begins as Eliza Wharton, a young and virtuous woman, ventures into the eighteenth-century marriage market. She is the daughter of a respected, and recently deceased, minister who, living on a limited clerical salary, has left her without a dowry. Consequently, she is positioned within the marriage market as a venture capitalist is positioned within the commercial market, depending on her wit, her education, and her talents to compensate for her lack of capital. She confronts the same dilemmas a young merchant faced in the confusing markets of the late eighteenth century: how to transform talents into capital; how to credit financial and moral worth in a world of words and fancy, self-interest and deceit; whether to trust traditional community wisdom or, depending on her own judgment, to risk all for great gains. It is in the language of commercial metaphor that Foster has Eliza initially present herself and her chances in that market. "Fortune," Eliza tells her friend and confidante, Lucy Freeman, in one of the novel's opening letters, "has not been very liberal of her gifts to me; but I presume on a large stock in the bank of friendship, which, united with health and innocence, give me some pleasing anticipation of future felicity." Freeman responds in kind: "I shall be extremely anxious to hear the process and progress of this business" (9, 27).

---

57. I make this argument in more elaborate ways in Carroll Smith-Rosenberg, *Disorderly Conduct: Visions of Gender in Victorian America* (New York, 1987), and "Mis-prisioning *Pamela:* Representations of Gender and Class in Nineteenth-Century America," *Michigan Quarterly Review*, XXVI (1987), 9–28. For this analysis of *The Coquette*, I have used Cathy N. Davidson's edition (New York, 1986). Page citations are given parenthetically in the text. For a related but quite distinct reading of *The Coquette*, see Stern, *Plight of Feeling*, chap. 2. See, as well, Kerber, *Women of the Republic*, esp. chap. 8. See, as well, Nancy Armstrong and Leonard Tennenhouse, *The Imaginary Puritan: Literature, Intellectual Labor, and the Origins of Personal Life* (Berkeley, Calif., 1992). I first published on *The Coquette* in the late 1980s; see Carroll Smith-Rosenberg, "Domesticating 'Virtue': Coquettes and Revolutionaries in Young America," in Elaine Scarry, ed., *Literature and the Body: Essays on Populations and Persons* (Baltimore, 1988), 160–184.

The Coquette's plot revolves around the choice Eliza must make between two suitors. One, the Reverend Mr. Boyer, represents simultaneously the authoritative voice of social norms and the hardworking, honest, professional middling ranks. Offering Eliza a life of respectable dignity and service to the community, he is rational, honorable, and prudent—in short, a model commercial republican. Throughout the novel, his words harmonize with communal wisdom. The second suitor, Major Sanford, is a rake, corrupt and deceitful. He assumes the airs of the very wealthy and the distinction of a military title—the two equally suspect within both commercial and classic republican ideology.[58] Not only does Major Sanford pride himself on his past military standing (he seems otherwise unemployed); he has mortgaged his estate! An encumbered estate was an anathema to all forms of republicanism. A paper mortgage, masking the reality of an empty purse, proclaims the miscreant a false figure, pretending to an economic and social station he has no right to claim. Throughout the novel, Major Stanford refuses honest employment as beneath the dignity of a "gentleman and a man of pleasure." He prefers, instead, to prostitute himself to a marriage of convenience with a woman he neither loves nor respects. With double deceit, he holds out to Eliza the temptations of a gay life and marriage although he cannot afford the one and, because of her lack of capital, does not intend the other. He compounds his sins by encouraging her resistance to the constraints of domesticity and the advice of her family and friends. Asserting her independence, Eliza sets out on her own to evaluate the worth of these two men. Scornful of her family's advice, swayed by fancy and social ambition, Eliza judges wrongly and falls.

Read as a celebration of the values of commercial republicanism, this is just the novel we would expect to find in the New England of the 1790s—written in the aftermath of the dramatic burst of the nation's first great speculative bubble.[59] In this novel, as in the larger economy, speculation, social ambition, and the desire for a luxurious life that one cannot afford lead inevitably to moral

58. Jane Austen, *Pride and Prejudice*, ed. with an introduction by Harold Bloom (New York, 1987); Pocock, *Machiavellian Moment*, chap. 12. Commercial republicanism disdained the idle rich, in general, and sybaritic aristocrats in particular. Classic republicans had long warned of the corruptions a standing army would bring. Recall the suspicion with which Austen, that spokeswoman for Britain's landed gentry, viewed army officers in *Pride and Prejudice*.

59. William Duer's attempt to monopolize the market in Bank of the United States shares and bonds failed, plunging much of the East Coast into a major financial depression. See Thomas M. Doerflinger, *A Vigorous Spirit of Enterprise: Merchants and Economic Development in Revolutionary Philadelphia* (Chapel Hill, N.C., 1986), 310–314.

bankruptcy and financial ruin. Eliza Wharton's fall is a lesson in the link between morality and economics as perceived within a commercial republican frame.

It was also a lesson drawn from real life. *The Coquette* is not simply fiction but also a novelistic reprise of an earlier, male-authored historical text: the popular press's reporting of the scandalous death of Elizabeth Whitman (xi). Whitman, a respected daughter of New England's professional classes, a descendant of Jonathan Edwards, a cousin of Aaron Burr, the daughter of a highly respected Hartford minister, herself a frequently published poet and close associate of the Hartford Wits—and a relation of *The Coquette*'s author, Hannah Foster—died alone under an assumed name in a Massachusetts inn after giving birth to an illegitimate child. Newspapers and sermons thundered against her criminal sexuality at the same time as they voyeuristically speculated about the name of her seducer. Was it her cousin Aaron Burr, soon to be vice president of the United States? Or Hartford Wit and patriotic poet Joel Barlow? Perhaps New York State Senator James Watson? Ministers in their sermons and male commentators in the newspapers used Elizabeth Whitman's fate to emphasize women's social and sexual susceptibility—that woman's passion, uncontrollable when inflamed by novel and romance reading, easily overcame women's fragile hold on virtue (xi). Like Mary Wollstonecraft, Elizabeth Whitman, depending on her own judgment, had judged incorrectly. That Whitman, like Wollstonecraft, was both single and ambitious for literary renown only strengthened the connection in their eyes. (These newspaper harangues only echoed the often satiric condemnations of strong, independent women we have already read in the political magazines.)[60]

IN PURSUIT OF LIFE, LIBERTY, AND HAPPINESS

Hannah Foster's *Coquette*, adopting and transforming male renditions of Elizabeth Whitman's sexual fall, painstakingly complicates male texts of sexual seduction, corruption, and death. *The Coquette* presents Eliza Wharton's downfall not as the result of lust. Rather, Eliza's decline was driven by her desire for independence coupled with her wish to rise socially and enter a world of wit and refinement, a world in which her claims to intellectual equality would be honored. As such, Eliza represents those within the emergent middling ranks who, rejecting traditional norms, anxiously embody individualism while embracing risk and the new fiscal capitalism. But Eliza is a woman, not a business-

60. See Davidson, *Revolution and the Word*, 110–150, esp. 141–142.

man. To fully appreciate *The Coquette*, one must focus on the way it weaves gender into the political discourses of its time. Just as the long eighteenth century's commercial and fiscal revolutions problematized independence and virtue as understood within both commercial republican and liberal discourses, so *The Coquette* underscores the ways concepts of female independence and individualism further complicated the new Republic's political lexicon. Eliza can be read as taking the Declaration of Independence's promises of life, liberty, and the right to pursue happiness seriously—as made to women as well as men.

The book's opening sentence alerts the reader to the significance of these issues. "An unusual sensation possesses my breast," Eliza writes Lucy Freeman, "a sensation which I once thought could never pervade it on any occasion whatever. It is pleasure, pleasure, my dear Lucy, on leaving my paternal roof. Could you have believed that the darling child of an indulgent and dearly-beloved mother would feel a gleam of joy at leaving her? But it is so" (5). Two events, Eliza continues, have freed her: the death of her father and the death of the man her father had chosen as her husband, another minister, whom she did not love. While both patriarchal figures lived, Eliza had exhibited behavior appropriate to her class and gender. "Both nature and education had instilled into my mind an implicit obedience to the will and desires of my parents. To them, of course, I sacrificed my fancy in the affair, determined that my reason should concur with theirs, and on that to risk my future happiness" (5).

To read these statements in a political context, let us start by juxtaposing Eliza's comment "determined that my reason should concur with theirs, and on that to risk my future happiness" with one drawn from that primer of American liberal rhetoric, the Declaration of Independence. Here we find "certain unalienable rights . . . among these, life, liberty and the pursuit of happiness." *The Coquette* begins by telling us that the heroine, as a virtuous daughter, has resigned her liberty of choice and her pursuit of happiness in deference to parental wishes; she has agreed, that is, to link happiness to the sacrifice, not the assertion, of liberty—to submit her will to two patriarchal authority figures and beyond them to community wisdom. Her pious sacrifice is then contrasted to the pleasure she now reports experiencing at resuming her lost independence —"pleasure" being a word that she twice repeats and that Hannah Foster italicizes. Circumstances reversing her position, Eliza now associates liberty with pleasure—and with her ability to pursue happiness on her own, away from the governance of parents and the community in which she grew up.

The Declaration of Independence tells us that liberty and the pursuit of happiness are unalienable rights. Both republican and liberal texts warn Americans that to relinquish them will endanger virtue. But the Declaration also insists that a passion for liberty be balanced by prudence: "Prudence, indeed, will dictate that Governments long established should not be changed for light and transient causes." But Eliza's very first sentence signals a revolutionary resolve to defy prudence for the sake of freedom, a shift that challenges the traditional relation among pleasure, happiness, and prudence. Eliza has called pleasure an "unusual" emotion, especially when associated with independence and liberty. To most eighteenth-century republicans, it was both an unusual and a dangerous emotion. Popular versions of moral philosophy, especially those most common to Puritan New England, pitted pleasure against both happiness and prudence. For them, "happiness" signified contentment with one's place in life, "the attainment of what is considered good." It resulted from an individual's conquering desire.[61] It was subservient to, indeed rooted in, communal norms. "Pleasure," in contrast, implied delight in the sensations; it hinted at passion—an association reinforced when Eliza represents her pleasure in a physical, even sensual vocabulary. Pleasure, invoked by her newfound independence, she tells Freeman, "possesses my breast" (5). It illuminates her with "a gleam of joy." When independence is absent in this text, so are sensuality, pleasure, and happiness. In acquiescing to her parents' will, she had "sacrificed my fancy." "My heart" was not "engaged." "I never felt the passion of love" (6). Eliza, in short, has invested her female independence and liberty of choice with fancy, pleasure, and desire. She has also invested it with a second and, by implication, an equally dangerous emotion—individualism. Pleasure, especially in Eliza's usage, presumes individuals capable of fancying and privileging their own desires, of acting independent of society's approval in order to secure them. Eliza significantly ends her letter by underscoring this note of liberal individualism. "This letter," she confesses to Lucy, "is all an Egotism" (6).

Throughout the novel, Eliza Wharton will insist that pleasure can legitimately be wedded to a desire for independence and liberty, that marriage without such a "wedding" will destroy happiness. Her family and friends will tell her virtue and happiness are tied to prudence and a socially appropriate marriage. They will insist that pleasure and fancy will endanger both. Eliza will insist on her right as an independent woman to pursue happiness guided by her own rational standards.[62]

---

61. *OED*, s.v. "happiness"; Edward A. Bloom and Lillian D. Bloom, *Joseph Addison's Sociable Animal: In the Market Place, on the Hustings, in the Pulpit* (Providence, R.I., 1971), 43. See also, for example, Clyde A. Holbrook, *The Ethics of Jonathan Edwards: Morality and Aesthetics* (Ann Arbor, Mich., 1973). For British usage, see Bloom and Bloom, *Addison's Sociable Animal;* and see Julie K. Ellison's *Cato's Tears and the Making of Anglo-American Emotion* (Chicago, 1999).

62. The comments in the Declaration of Independence concerning the purpose of a just

The following exchange between Eliza and the proper and prosperously married Ann Richman schematically presents the conflict. Eliza, rejecting Richman's advice to cut short her newfound liberty and marry the minister, replies: "I hope my friends will never again interpose in my concerns of that nature. A melancholy event has lately extricated me from those shackles which parental authority had imposed on my mind. Let me, then, enjoy that freedom which I so highly prize. Let me have opportunity, unbiased by opinion, to gratify my natural disposition in a participation of those pleasures which youth and innocence afford" (13). Shackles are, of course, what slaves wear. Shackles are also what British trade restraints placed on European American commerce, and shackles are what European American patriots fought a revolution to remove. In 1797, "shackles" was a word fraught with political meanings. Eliza did not write it lightly. Her statement was self-assertive, indeed, aggressive— emotions respectable women were supposed to repress, even when among their closest female friends. But Eliza's statement went even further. Not only did it express her determination; it conflated her cause with her nation's, positioning Eliza as a representative of the new Republic. Within the shadow of the Revolution, Eliza tells Richman that she refuses to be enslaved by traditional wisdom—just as European American patriots had refused to be when declaring independence from Britain.

Ann Richman's response is equally portentous. Choosing her words carefully, she warns Eliza against conflating independence and pleasure, a conflation that Richman represents as linked to scenes of fashionable dissipation. "Of Such pleasures, no one, my dear, would wish to deprive you," Richman insists, "but beware, Eliza! Though strewed with flowers, when contemplated by your lively imagination, it is, after all, a slippery, thorny path" (13). A good classic republican committed to an aesthetic of simplicity and the morality of marriage and domesticity, Richman continues, "The round of fashionable dissipation is

government can also be read in relation to Eliza's concerns about the government of marriage and the family. The Declaration follows its initial sentence stating that life, liberty, and the pursuit of happiness are inalienable rights with its definition of a just government: "That to secure these rights, Governments are instituted among Men, deriving their just powers from the consent of the governed,—That whenever any Form of Government becomes destructive of these ends, it is the Right of the People to alter or to abolish it, and to institute new Government, laying its foundation on such principles and organizing its powers in such form, as to them shall seem most likely to effect their Safety and Happiness." Only then does the Declaration proceed to a discussion of prudence. A subversive reading of *The Coquette* (and of the Declaration) might suggest the question, If marriage and the family do not promote the liberty and happiness of women, do women have a right to alter or abolish them?

dangerous. A phantom is often pursued, which leaves its deluded votary the real form of wretchedness" (13). Far better to choose the mediated role of republican wife and mother, as Ann Richman, herself, had done. There, alone, lay female safety and respectability.[63]

Eliza's disruption of the easy relations between happiness and virtue through her desire for independence and pleasure underscores a second disjuncture that greatly troubled the eighteenth century: the one between perception and reality. Eighteenth-century republican texts praised mimesis and despaired of achieving it. They feared that fancy and passion, tied to individualism and to the twin paper revolutions of credit and printing, would disrupt the ability of words and the imagination to represent material reality. Especially with the emergence of fiscal capitalism, the reliability of representation began to appear more and more a chimera. In the dialogue just cited, Eliza insists that female independence is not only legitimate and pleasurable but a real option. The mature and experienced Richman dismisses Eliza's words as immaterial "phantoms" obscuring the material reality of "slippery, thorny paths" and the "real form of wretchedness." Eliza alarms rather than persuades her friends (and possibly her readers) by her willful and defiant response: "I despise those contracted ideas which confine virtue to a cell" (13).

Here, then, is the dilemma Foster presents. Independence endangers at the same time as it gives pleasure; domestic restraints destroy pleasure and liberty at the same time as they guarantee virtue and economic security. At all the key points in the novel, two critical disjunctures appear. The imagination and the passions threaten to distort perception; virtue and independence, liberty and happiness are divided against themselves. Eliza would like to unite all, as male patriots hoped their Revolution would do. Eliza's virtuous advisers tell her this is not possible for women. Take the correspondence between Eliza and Freeman in which Eliza contrasts social independence to marriage and public service. "My sanguine imagination paints, in alluring colors, the charms of youth and freedom, regulated by virtue and innocence," Eliza writes.

> Of these I wish to partake. . . . I recoil at the thought of immediately forming a connection which must confine me to the duties of domestic life, and make me dependent for happiness, perhaps, too, for subsistence, upon a class of

63. That Anne Richman is married to a Revolutionary general further elevates her as a republican spokeswoman. Indeed, Stern reads Richman as representing a high Federalist contempt for individualism and the new ways of urbanity that had entered the Republic in the post-Revolutionary days—a contempt grounded in classic republican principles (Stern, *Plight of Feeling*, 15, 72–74).

people [the minister's parishioners] who will claim the right to scrutinize every part of my conduct, and, by censuring those foibles which I am conscious of not having prudence to avoid, may render me completely miserable.

Eliza concludes her letter: "You must either quit the subject, or leave me to the exercise of my free will" (29–30).

Lucy Freeman, whose role in the novel is to express classic republican ideals fused with patriarchal community wisdom, snaps back. Eliza's fancy has obscured her own perceptions of reality. "You are indeed very tenacious of your freedom, as you call it but that is a play about words. A man of Mr. Boyer's honor and sense will never abridge any privileges which virtue can claim" (30–31). Indeed, liberty or "freedom" for women is so inconceivable to Freeman that it exists only "as a play about words." She replaces "freedom" with female virtue, which can only claim privileges from a posture of dependence. And privilege, other republican texts tell us, is dangerous, tied to corruption, as in the unearned privileges of birth, which commercial republicanism scorns.

Women's relation to liberty and freedom underscores the complexities, the uncertainties, the multiple shifting meanings those words assumed in the closing decades of the eighteenth century. Women's relation to economic independence does the same. *The Coquette* spells out the ways women's relation to independence limits their right to liberty—and predetermines the boundaries of their happiness. The same characters that tell Eliza that her independence/freedom is a play about words warn her that middle-class women lack the financial resources to support an independent social role (Eliza stretches the limits of her mother's income when visiting Freeman in Boston and must compromise her independence by accepting gifts of clothing so that she can appear at fashionable balls). Even more stridently, they warn her not to overstep her class in her ambition to make a fashionable show—a minister is just the right husband for her. "His situation in life," the prudent Freeman advises, "is . . . as elevated as you have a right to claim. Forgive my plainness, Eliza. . . . I know your ambition to make a distinguished figure in the first class of polished society, to shine in the gay circle of fashionable amusements, and to tear off the palm amidst the votaries of pleasure" (27).

It is Eliza's twin desires for the pleasures of intellectual independence and social eminence that attract her to the rake—and spell her doom. We see this most clearly in Boyer's final rejection of Eliza. It is not her loss of chastity that motivates him but her independence coupled with her extravagance in dress and her desire to rise above her father's social station. Significantly, it is at this point in the novel that Boyer enters into a debate about the contested meanings of the word "virtue," defining it as far more than sexual propriety, indeed, defining it in commercial republican terms. In a letter to his friend and colleague, the Reverend Mr. T. Selby, Boyer writes, "I would not be understood to impeach Miss Wharton's virtue; I mean her chastity. Virtue in the common acceptation of the term, as applied to the sex, is confined to that particular, you know. But in my view, this is of little importance, where all other virtues are wanting!" His letter then specifically refers to commercial republicanism's honored trio of "virtues"—frugality, prudence, temperance (78).

Boyer's denunciation of Eliza's assertion of social independence unsupported by economic independence is the turning point in the novel. Once the minister has rejected her as an appropriate wife for his class, no other man proposes. Eliza's passion for liberty has reached imprudent limits. It propels her into the classless state of the spinster, with only marginal rights to the economic resources of any man. In the end, her independence costs her what it at first promised: pleasure, happiness, free access to the world of wit and grace outside the middle-class home. As in the case of Mary Wollstonecraft, it costs her her sexual virtue as well. Although warned against the rake by friends and family, Eliza insists on judging him by her own criteria and falls.

THE DESIRE THAT DARES NOT SPEAK ITS NAME

Foster's telling of Eliza's story contains significant discontinuities and silences. Foster splits Eliza's decline into two almost unrelated events: her rejection by the Reverend Mr. Boyer and her affair with the rake. Years separate the two. The second, the sexual fall, comes unaccompanied by either sexual passion or pleasure. The requisite physical decay, in fact, rather than following her sexual seduction, precedes it by approximately a year. If anything, Eliza's seduction appears the formulaic conclusion demanded by the genre and the need to connect Eliza Wharton with Elizabeth Whitman, her real-life counterpart. We are drawn back to Cathy Davidson's suggestion that Foster deliberately wrote against an existing male narrative of sex and passion. Can the striking absence of sexual passion be explained by the fact that Foster's "coquette," like Henry James's Daisy Miller, died not from lust but from the imprudent desire to obtain an impossible social independence and to assert her right to control her own body?

Three letters that separate the two sections of the novel suggest an even more subversive reading—that Eliza's real seduction and fall occurred a year after Boyer's denunciation and long before her sexual fall with Sanford. At this point, realizing that no other man will propose, Eliza writes Boyer, acquiescing. He was right, she confesses; she had sinned. Indeed, his letter has led her to repent. She begs him to marry her. Boyer responds that he is pleased that she now accepts his reading of her character and behavior, but "Your letter came too late." He has chosen another, a "virtuous . . . amiable . . . accomplished" woman who will serve him better. The tone of his letter is authoritative, judgmental, and assured (101–104).

It is at this point that Eliza cries out to Freeman in language that fuses the lament of the "fallen women" with that of the bankrupt entrepreneur. Like an imprudent merchant, she confesses to having "been tossed upon the waves of folly, til I am shipwrecked on the shoals of despair." "Oh my friend, I am undone. . . . Oh that I had not written to Mr. Boyer!" She then reaffirms her submission to his text. "I blame not Mr. Boyer. He has acted nobly." From this submission comes, not inner peace, but inner torment and physical decline. For a second time in the book, Eliza appropriates language traditionally used to describe the sexual in order to discuss the social and economic. She writes Freeman: "I approve his conduct, though it operates my ruin!" "And what adds an insupportable poignancy to the reflection, is self-condemnation! From this inward torture where shall I flee? Where shall I seek that happiness which I have madly trifled away?" (105).

Eliza has finally accepted the rupture of virtue, independence, and happiness that eighteenth-century male discourses decreed for women. She has been seduced, not by the rake, but by the minister's text of female submission to social consensus. It is the relinquishing of her social and intellectual independence, not of her sexual virginity, that constitutes her true fall. It is this that she reports with all the anguish—and in the appropriate formulaic language—of a sexual fall. "My bloom is decreasing. My health is sensibly impaired" (105). Without the pleasures of independence and of "the exercise of my free will," Eliza's body wastes away.

And it is at this point that Freeman, heretofore always Boyer's advocate, reverses her position. She chides Eliza on her plunge from reason into sentimentality. To Eliza's lamentations, she sensibly responds: "Your truly romantic letter came safe to hand. Indeed, my dear, it would make a very pretty figure in a novel. A bleeding heart, slighted love, and all the etceteras of romance enter the composition" (107). Eliza has given her heart to two imprudent texts—the text of religious prudery (Boyer's) and the text of sentimentality and the romance. Freeman recalls her to the better text of independence, reason, and strength, the republican text that will lead her to happiness and virtue. "Where, O Eliza Wharton, . . . is that strength of mind, that independence of soul, that alacrity and sprightliness of deportment, which formerly raised you superior to every adverse Occurrence? Why have you resigned these valuable endowments and suffered yourself to become the sport of contending passions?" (107).

Ironically, then, Foster does in the end agree with the sermon and newspaper writers: reading romances led to Eliza's fall. Romances did so, however, not because they aroused women's sexual passion for men but because they taught women to renounce their own reason and independence. In this way, women lost their happiness. To cure Eliza from the excesses of male texts, Freeman tells her, a mutual friend, Julia—a sprightly, unmarried woman—will come to carry Eliza back to Boston, to her female friends and the rational company of witty women. Freeman, in other words, in virtually her last letter in the novel, denounces the texts middle-class men use to impose gendered restrictions on women and privileges, instead, the nontextual world of female friendship as a way back to the true text of republicanism.

But Julia comes too late. Eliza has already fallen victim, not to Sanford—he is secondary—but to the authoritative male discourses of her age. She has relinquished her quest to fuse independence and pleasure; she now accepts her community's definition of virtue as prudence. But such a definition, because it denies independence to women, brings neither happiness nor pleasure. "I frequent neither . . . the company [nor] the amusements of the town," she tells Julia. "Having incurred so much censure by the indulgence of a gay disposition, I am now trying what a recluse and solitary mode of life will produce. . . . I look around for happiness, and find it not. The world is to me a desart [sic]. And when I have recourse to books, . . . if novels, they exhibit scenes of pleasure which I have no prospect of realizing!" (135) Pallor, depression, an "emaciated form!" replace Eliza's gay independence (40). Only then, having lost independence, pleasure, and happiness, does Eliza relinquish her virtue as well, confirming the republican text that, without independence, virtue is impossible.

Cathy N. Davidson reads Hannah Foster's Eliza Wharton as the Everywoman, who, during years marked by political and economic revolution, lusted for independence. She sees *The Coquette* as a subversive novel that encourages the reader to applaud Eliza's desires and mourn her death. Yet there are additional layerings to this reading. Eliza Wharton is Everyman as well as Everywoman. Her career underscores the way economic change and emerging liberal discourses transformed the independence of classical republicanism, making independence both highly individualized and economically risky. Tied to liberty and economic change, independence no longer secures social order but rather exposes the individual to risk and endangers society. Foster dramatizes the new impotence of family and community against the autonomy of youth and the power of the individual that capitalism unleashed. In this novel, trustworthy familial and community spokesmen are no longer male ministers. They have become spokeswomen, the feminized Greek chorus of Richman, Freeman, and Eliza's widowed mother, who, at the end, can only mouth hollow platitudes as Eliza is seduced in her mother's parlor and then disappears into the night.[64]

Reading in this way, we see that Foster has radically rewritten woman's place within the male texts of nationalism and class. Bourgeois men had made bourgeois women their alter egos, bearers of criticisms the republican landed gentry had directed against bourgeois men and against the paper revolution of bank notes and speculative stocks. Doing so, they represented, not themselves, but bourgeois women as incapable of civic virtue. (This is certainly what Boyer does to Eliza.) Not only does Foster's text suggest that men, not women, are incapable of true virtue; she also makes Eliza the ego, not the alter ego, of the new nation and the new class. It is Eliza, not Boyer or Sanford, who takes on the challenges the new capitalism thrusts upon the new Americans. She lusts for independence, takes risks, boldly sacrifices all for freedom and social advancement. With steely nerves, she plays for high stakes. And it is Eliza, not Boyer or even Stanford, who assumes tragic proportions. It is in her language that the dilemmas of her age are debated. The principal question of *The Coquette* is the principal question of the new nation and the new class: how can independence and individual happiness be made compatible with social order? What behavior (economic and social) was appropriate in a new republic? Foster gives no firm answer. We are left to hypothesize that, in the late 1790s, European Americans had yet to resolve the fundamental inconsistencies between their new liberal capitalist and individualistic economy and the republican principles they had inherited from their Augustan ancestors and reaffirmed during the trying years of revolution and war.

Still, a notably subversive tone runs through *The Coquette*. Our sentiments

64. Stern sees Foster array Eliza against the conservative Federalist phalanx of Richman, Freeman, and Eliza's widowed mother, who constantly attack her desires for independence and intellectual engagement and seek to confine her within republican domesticity. Stern agrees with a much earlier analysis of *The Coquette* that I published in 1988. Where I continue to differ from Stern, as will become clearer below, relates to her renaming what I denominate "a Greek chorus" (Eliza's friends and mother) as a Federalist chorus. They might be seen as an example of New England Federalism, but they certainly differ from "the Republican Court" that represented the "ruling" Federalist cohort that collected around George Washington. What strikes me as most important is the way their advice changes by the novel's end.

are pulled toward the transgressive, especially toward Eliza's dream of self-fulfillment, independence, and wit. *The Coquette*'s subversive, transgressive theme suggests that the issues Abigail Adams raised in those heady days when Independence was first being discussed—that women have a right to partici-pate in their own political governance—remained a burning issue into the 1790s. It suggests as well that the founders'—and the urban press's—efforts to bar women from political discourse, to cast women as the new republican citizen's constituting Other, were hotly contested by women not only in private salons but in popular literature. Indeed, *The Coquette* makes a woman the exemplar of the dilemmas the new Republic faced.

REGIONAL DIS-EASE

Before leaving *The Coquette*, there is still one more layering to consider. *The Coquette*'s conservative spokeswomen and -men repeatedly condemned Eliza's desire for a life of fashionable independence, gaiety, and wit. Indeed, the novel revolves around the threats such a life poses for the virtuous daughters of New England. Why is *The Coquette* so obsessed, so fearful of social polish and refinement? What are the dangers *The Coquette* tries so valiantly to defend against?

The republican court was a world in which women shone as men's intellec-tual equals, indeed, not infrequently, as their superiors. Wit and their elite social standing, David S. Shields tells us, gave these women the liberty to display their intelligence and to assume the superiority and independence their talents justified. Here, within highly polished and mannered settings, women participated in intellectual conversations with foreign dignitaries, leading writ-ers, scientists, and statesmen. Political issues were never far from their tongues. Around tea tables and at musical evenings, the court's leading ladies—Martha Washington, Abigail Adams, Elizabeth Willing Powel, Anne Willing Bing-ham—cajoled and lobbied the new Republic's political leaders. They even commissioned prominent figures such as Benjamin Rush to write books ad-vocating improved women's education. Following Abigail Adams's warning, they made sure that the ladies were not forgotten. So when Thomas Jefferson, then Washington's secretary of state, criticized French salonnières for "med-dling" in politics, one of America's most famous salonnières, Anne Bingham, retorted hotly. Yes, it was true: "The Women of France interfere in the politics of the Country, and often give a decided Turn to the Fates of Empires." "Either by the gentle Arts of persuasion or by the commanding force of superior

Attractions and Address," she continued, "they have obtained that Rank and Consideration in society which the sex are entitled to and which they in vain contend for in other Countries."[65]

Jefferson was not the only one who worried about whether such a "court" and such ladies were appropriate in a new republic. As we have seen, many aspects of the republican court troubled bourgeois and middling male observers: the extravagance of its self-presentation (diamonds glittered on more than one head, ermine slid off more than one shoulder); its exclusivity, indeed, many said, snobbery and disdain for the "common man"; the newness of many of its leading economic figures and their involvement in highly questionable speculative ventures; and that which Jefferson, in particular, questioned, the public and quite political presence of women.[66] Did the republican court encourage civic virtue, or was it one of the first signs of the Republic's corruption and decay? Was this the threat that underlay *The Coquette*'s repeated condemnations of polished society and fashionable amusements—the nation's richest and most powerful citizens' embrace of European courtly behavior and, in particular, of France's women-centered salon culture? In condemning Eliza's desires, did *The Coquette* condemn the culture of the nation's capital?

The Coquette is filled with descriptions of fashionable amusements and elegant display, which it represents as scenes of potential, if not actual, danger and corruption. The pleasure Eliza reports on leaving her mother in her opening letter, for instance, is connected to a protracted visit she makes to her cousin Ann Richman, who, having married a rich man (as her name suggests), has entrée to the world Eliza desires to belong to. "The situation is delightful," Eliza tells Lucy on arriving. "I find my natural propensity for mixing in the busy scene and active pleasures of life returning" (7). In company with the Richmans, Eliza visits neighboring estates, sits down "to a table furnished with an elegant and sumptuous repast," and, after dinner, when "the gates of a

65. Anne Bingham to Thomas Jefferson, in Robert C. Alberts, *The Golden Voyage: The Life and Times of William Bingham, 1752–1804* (Boston, 1969), 463–465, esp. 464. For women and wit, see David S. Shields, *Civil Tongues and Polite Letters in British America* (Chapel Hill, N.C., 1997), 42–43; Branson, *These Fiery Frenchified Dames*, 133–140; and Teute and Shields, "Jefferson in Washington," 15–16.

66. Certainly, Antifederalists such as New York governor George Clinton and Boston bluestocking Mercy Otis Warren were highly critical, as was frequenter of the court Nabby Adams, Abigail and John's daughter. See Mark R. Patterson, *Authority, Autonomy, and Representation in American Literature, 1776–1865* (Princeton, N.J., 1988), 24; Branson, *These Fiery Frenchified Dames*, 134; Teute and Shields, "Jefferson in Washington," 1–10, 17.

spacious garden were thrown open," "mirth and hilarity prevailed, and the moments fled on downy wings; while we traced the beauties of art and nature so liberally displayed and so happily blended in this delightful retreat" (8–9).

Animated conversations lay at the center of this world, as a description of an evening at the Richmans' attests. On one particular night, politics dominate the discussion in which Ann Richman and Eliza take active parts. When one of the other ladies present suggests the inappropriateness of women's discussing politics, Mrs. Richman responds in much the same way as Anne Bingham. "We think ourselves interested in the welfare and prosperity of our country," Richman tells the offending woman in ringing classic republican tones;

> [we], consequently, claim the right of inquiring into these affairs, which may conduce to or interfere with the commonweal. . . . If the community flourish and enjoy health and freedom, shall we not share in the happy effects? If it be oppressed and disturbed, shall we not endure our proportion of the evil? Why then should the love of our country be a masculine passion only? Why should government, which involves the peace and order of the society, of which we are a part, be wholly excluded from our observation? (44)

Eliza burned with desire to enter this world, share in its social grace and intellectual intensity. An ambitious, risk-taking entrepreneur, Eliza felt her "accomplishments" and talents qualified her for admittance. Richman and Freeman repeatedly reminded Eliza that a girl from the middling social ranks, a girl without a dowry, could not gain admittance, no matter how impressive her "accomplishments." *The Coquette* frequently counterpoises Eliza's desires and her exclusion. Does this counterpoising capture the early Republic's deep ambivalence about its changing economy and the courtly aspirations of its would-be governing class? Can we read its twinned focus on Eliza's desires and its condemnation of those desires as a criticism of the republican court? If so, did this criticism emanate from the new Republic's middling ranks, critical of the airs the new bourgeois elite was assuming? Or is it more an expression of small-town New England's dis-ease with the growing cosmopolitanism of the new Republic's burgeoning entrepôts and their new culture of consumerism and politesse?

WHITE WOMAN / RED MAN:
TRIANGULATING FEAR AND DESIRE

What a tangled web the popular press wove when first constituting the new American as a manly republican citizen. Ideological conflicts and confusions opened the gates to contending claimants to the role: dirt-poor hill farmers suspicious of modernity; fashionable salonnières; poor and middling women, both those who defiantly attacked price-gouging merchants and those who timidly signed nonimportation agreements—along with those "chosen few," men of property and education. All this played out against the exigencies of war, which called on women to play manly roles and liberalism's radical insistence on unmarked citizenship. Ruefully, the political magazines turned to ill-tempered denunciations of transgressive claimants and ultimately to biting sarcasm and ribald humor. But the claimants would not be still. Not only did western farmers struggle to control state legislatures in Massachusetts, Pennsylvania, and New York, but women seized their pens to challenge men's exclusive claims to play the rights-bearing citizen. The gendered basis of a coherent national identity proved shaky at best, destabilizing the structure that rested upon it.

How could the urban magazines restore their new American's internal cohesion and the solidity, the consistency of their new national identity that he was designed to embody? Would race, as deployed in the urban magazines and elsewhere in republican popular culture, provide a more striking and consistent negative Other around which a new American identity could take form? The new American's most obvious contrasting Other was that *other* American, the Native American, whose land and name European Americans had seized. European/Native American, civilized/savage, cultured/primitive, clothed/naked, Christian/devil-worshiping, rational/superstitious—the oppositions go on. Would they be sufficient to cloak the contradictions and inconsistencies gender confusions and ideological conflicts rent in the new national fabric?

Dangerous Doubles

Masculinity and Masquerade

Selective memory requires public enactments of forgetting, either to blur the obvious
discontinuities, misalliances, and ruptures or, more desperately, to exaggerate them in order to
mystify a previous Golden Age. . . . In such dramas of sacrificial substitution, the derivation of
the word personality *from* mask *eerily doubles that of* tragedy *from* goat.—JOSEPH ROACH,
Cities of the Dead

O n July 21, 1790, with much fanfare—a flotilla of ships dotting New York
harbor, eminent citizens gathered, rounds of military salutes—a delegation of Creek warriors stepped ashore in New York City, then still the
nation's capital. They had been invited by President Washington to sign a
treaty of friendship with the new United States. Prominent among those greeting the Creek delegates were officers and members of New York City's Tammany Society. Carrying bows, arrows, and tomahawks and bedecked in "Indian" costumes, they proudly proclaimed themselves "sachems" and "braves."
So attired, they had marched from their "Great Wigwam" (as they called their
clubhouse in the old exchange building on Broad Street) to Coffee House Slip
to welcome the Creek delegation. From there, they escorted the Creek warriors
first to the home of the secretary of war and then to President Washington's
residence, where they were joined by the governor of New York, senators and
representatives from Georgia, and army and militia officers. The day ended
with a state dinner at Fraunces Tavern, attended by the secretary of war, the
governor, the Creek delegation, and the Tammany sachems. The historian of
the event reported that the Creek delegates were "very much pleased" to see
the Tammany members in full Indian costume.[1]

---

1. W. Harrison Bayles, *Old Taverns of New York* (New York, 1915), 353–355. To borrow a
metaphor from music, I think of this prologue as variations on themes by Joseph R. Roach

Two weeks later, the Tammany Society again honored the Creeks, this time with a formal dinner in their Great Wigwam. Secretary of State Thomas Jefferson attended, as did John Jay, chief justice of the United States, the secretary of war, the governor, the mayor of New York City, and the treaty's military negotiator, Colonel Marines Willett. Tammany members worked hard to mimic the reception the Creek Nation had given Colonel Willett on their lands in Georgia. A "richly ornamented Calumet of Peace" was passed. Toasts and speeches grew ever more numerous as night faded into dawn. George Washington was hailed as "the Beloved Chieftain of the Thirteen Fires," and the Creek title of "Toliva Mico"—"Chief of the White Town"—was bestowed on the grand sachem of the Tammany Society. The evening concluded with Tammany braves' singing patriotic songs and Creek warriors' performing a dance. Mirth, it was reported, marked the festivities. The Creek visit "gave to the Tammany Society an opportunity to make an impression on the public mind not often presented, and which could not be neglected."[2]

These were grand days for New York's Tammany Society. Founded but a year earlier, the society gathered its members, not from the city's economic and political elite, but from its middling classes. Its "braves" and "sachems" were ambitious but far-from-prominent merchants, small shopkeepers, and master craftsmen. A former tory upholsterer served as the society's president. Called on to perform before the Creek delegation, however, the society's members stepped center stage, standing shoulder to shoulder with the new Republic's political and social leaders—the president, senators, and Cabinet members.[3]

New York City's middling classes were not the first to declare themselves

---

(*Cities of the Dead: Circum-Atlantic Performance* [New York, 1996]) and Philip J. Deloria (*Playing Indian: Otherness and Authenticity in the Assumption of American Indian Identity* [New Haven, Conn., 1998]). Roach's *Cities of the Dead* has had a major influence on this book, helping me frame it in a circum-Atlantic perspective. Roach's explorations of the cultural significance of surrogacy and of sacrificial violence have been equally important, especially in this section of the book. In *Playing Indian*, Deloria offers a paradigm-breaking analysis of the multiple ways in which European Americans donned the mask of "Indianness," infusing that mask with borrowings from European popular and high culture. I am especially indebted to Phil for his critique of this section and the additions and explications he urged me to add. A draft of this prologue has been published as Carroll Smith-Rosenberg, "Surrogate Americans," *Proceedings of the Modern Language Association*, CXIX (2004), 1325–1335. I use the word "Indian" rather than "Native American" when racist stereotyping or denigration is involved.

2. Ibid., 355.

3. Edwin G. Burrows and Mike Wallace, *Gotham: A History of New York City to 1898* (New York, 1999), 315–316; David Waldstreicher, *In the Midst of Perpetual Fetes: The Making of American Nationalism, 1776–1820* (Chapel Hill, N.C., 1997), 70–71, 288, 297.

sons of Saint Tammany. They mimicked behavior initiated by members of an elite colonial Philadelphia social club, the Schuylkill Fishing Company of the Colony in Schuylkill.[4] The Fishing Company had been formed in 1732 by prominent merchants and professionals as part of an elaborate celebration marking Proprietor Thomas Penn's arrival in Philadelphia and designed to demonstrate the sophistication and erudition of the Fishing Company's members. America's colonial elite, as we shall see at some length in Section 3, ardently sought to emulate London's elite. On this occasion, they published a carefully composed court panegyric to honor Penn and celebrate themselves as the sons and heirs of the mythic Lenni-Lenape (Delaware) chief Tamanend. Fishing Company members then proclaimed Tamanend, anglicized as Tammany, the colony's patron saint and emblazoned his motto—"Kawania Che Keeteru" ("I am master wherever I am")—on the company arms. Of course, all was done in jest and with much laughter.[5]

An amusing occasion—but one rent with bitter ironies. Within two years of his arrival, Thomas Penn, along with his Indian agent, the celebrated colonial scholar James Logan, perpetrated a massive land fraud upon the Lenni-Lenapes. Through two fraudulent treaties, one the famed Walking Treaty, Penn and Logan forced the Lenni-Lenape nation to cede the entire western shore of the Delaware River as well as the lands between the forks of the Delaware, thus depriving the Lenni-Lenapes of virtually all their holdings in

4. Informed by Homi K. Bhabha's trope of colonial/postcolonial mimicry, I use the word "mimicry" with double irony. In his use of mimicry, Bhabha insists on the centrality of slippage, of the imitation's not being precise, of a dissonance between the original and the copy. Not only were these Tammany braves inaccurately mimicking the Native Americans, but they were also struggling to mimic their social betters, elite mid-eighteenth-century Philadelphians. Indeed, for these upwardly ambitious New York tradesmen, aping their betters might have been the real object of their play. See Bhabha, "Of Mimicry and Man: The Ambivalence of Colonial Discourse," in Bhabha, *The Location of Culture* (London, 1994), 121–131.

5. David S. Shields, *Civil Tongues and Polite Letters in British America* (Chapel Hill, N.C., 1997), 190–198, esp. 191. The Colony in Schuylkill was not the only elite Philadelphia club to incorporate a Native American identity. The Fort St. David's Fishing Company, founded in the 1750s, chose King Hendrick, a Mohawk chief famed for his heroism during the French and Indian War, as their patron figure. Fort St. David's members commissioned a portrait of King Hendrick for their clubhouse, hanging it next to one of George III. They then invited King Hendrick—unlike St. Tammany, still very much alive—to attend a feast in his honor. Shields reports, "Thereafter in the fort records, the interests of the fishing company were identified with those of the Mohawk federation; their enemies among the tribes became the fort's enemies" *(Civil Tongues*, 196–198, esp. 197). For a discussion of the panegyric, see Stephen Greenblatt, "Culture," in Frank Lentricchia and Thomas McLaughlin, eds., *Critical Terms for Literary Study* (Chicago, 1995), 225–233, esp. 226.

Pennsylvania and transforming them into a displaced and vengeful people exiled to the Upper Ohio Valley. Thomas Penn and his elite Philadelphia celebrants had indeed made themselves sons and heirs of St. Tammany, stealing the inheritance of his rightful sons as Jacob stole the inheritance of Esau (also known in the Bible as the "red man").[6]

Over the decades following Penn's arrival, the very decades during which the Lenni-Lenapes were driven from Pennsylvania, spring festivals honoring St. Tammany gained increasing social parlance among both the urban commercial elite and tidewater planters. By the century's end, Tammany Societies stretched from Charleston to New Jersey. Proclaiming May Day St. Tammany's Day, these societies adapted medieval British traditions to New World settings. Erecting imposing maypoles bestrewed with native American flowers, Tammany braves danced around them with tomahawks and feathers, laying claim both to a British medieval and an American indigenous world. Gala dinners, endless jovial toasts, and more "Indian dances" marked these celebrations, which ended with the ritualized burning of St. Tammany in effigy.[7]

New York City's Tammany Society built upon this earlier colonial pattern at the same time as they appropriated the tradition for the Republic's middling classes. Mimicking Native Americans, these new republicans played at being braves and sachems in public and often political settings. They did so at great affairs of state and on patriotic holidays. In full masquerade, Tammany Society braves assumed prominent roles in Fourth of July parades, celebrations of Washington's Birthday and Columbus Day. Indeed, within a few years, New York's Tammany Society anniversary parade became "the premier public event in the city." In these many ways, mock warriors and sachems positioned themselves as key players in the production of European Americans' emergent public sphere and the Republic's new national identity.[8]

Why would hardworking European American shopkeepers, artisans, and small-scale manufacturers, self-consciously determined to present themselves

6. The fraud involved in the Walking Treaty not only led to repeated acts of violence along the Pennsylvania and Ohio frontier, lasting till the end of the century. It haunted the European imaginary into the next century (see Chapters 4 and 5, below). For a discussion of the Walking Treaty, see Gregory Evans Dowd, *War under Heaven: Pontiac, the Indian Nations, and the British Empire* (Baltimore, 2002), 35–37; Daniel K. Richter, *The Ordeal of the Longhouse: The Peoples of the Iroquois League in the Era of European Colonization* (Chapel Hill, N.C., 1992), 274–275; and Daniel M. Friedenberg, *Life, Liberty, and the Pursuit of Land: The Plunder of Early America* (Buffalo, N.Y., 1992), 69. For more on the significance of Esau, see Chapter 5, below.

7. Deloria, *Playing Indian*, 27.

8. Burrows and Wallace, *Gotham*, 316.

as urbane and respectable citizens, parade down crowded streets in feathers and war paint? Most eighteenth-century European Americans shared Washington's belief that Native Americans were "beasts of prey." Time and again, captivity and frontier narratives and tales of Indian warfare (the new nation's first best sellers) presented Native Americans as heathen savages who murdered women, tortured children, and lacked any sense of God or, almost as telling, of private property. In grim tones, European Americans represented natives as their dark and dangerous mirror images, with Native American savagery contrasting sharply to European American civility, piety, and productivity.[9]

It is precisely these condemnations of Native Americans as savage and inhuman, their expulsion rhetorically and geographically from the American body politic, that makes the Tammany performances so puzzling. During the very years that the popular press circulated images of savage Indians dancing around the bodies of tortured women and children, elite and middling gentlemen, costumed as "Indian chiefs," laughingly danced around flower-bedecked maypoles or burned St. Tammany's effigy in a macabre displacement of European Americans' burning bodies. How can we begin to understand this pairing of horror and mirth, both intimately tied to the popular production of a new national identity? Why would elite and middling men play the surrogate, the counterfeit Indian? Why, at the very time that Washington's administration had launched an all-out military assault along the western frontier, would European Americans make such festive masquerades central to their new sense of national identity?[10]

9. Robert A. Ferguson, *The American Enlightenment, 1750–1820* (Cambridge, Mass., 1997), 169. For examples of such attacks on Native Americans, see a volume of captivity and frontier warfare narratives Mathew Carey published: *Affecting History of the Dreadful Distresses of Frederic Manheim's Family: To Which Are Added, The Sufferings of John Corbly's Family; An Encounter between a White Man and Two Savages; Extraordinary Bravery of a Woman; Adventures of Capt. Isaac Stewart; Deposition of Massey Herbeson; Adventures and Sufferings of Peter Wilkinson* [sic]; *Remarkable Adventures of Jackson Johonnot; Account of the Destruction of the Settlements at Wyoming* (Philadelphia, 1794), esp. 25. For an ongoing discussion of European American fear and denigration of Native Americans, see Richard Slotkin, *Regeneration through Violence: The Mythology of the American Frontier, 1600–1860* (Middletown, Conn., 1973).

10. European American policy on "Indian removal" was deeply ambivalent. The Northwest Ordinance (1787) promised to respect and protect native landownership. At the same time, Washington commissioned General "Mad" Anthony Wayne to train a western army that in 1794 would break Native American resistance along the Great Lakes and end Native American power within the Northwest Ordinance. See Anthony F. C. Wallace and Sheila C. Steen, *The Death and Rebirth of the Seneca* (New York, 1970), 164–166. For a more extended examination of Wayne's role, see Andrew R. L. Cayton, "'Noble Actors' upon 'the Theatre of Honour': Power

Answers to these questions may well lie in the nature of surrogacy itself. A surrogate, the *Oxford English Dictionary* tells us, stands for or replaces a lost or absent other. The term refers to an officially appointed successor or deputy, the person given authority to represent the absent one, act in his place, exercise his rights. In some of the new states, the term also referred to a court officer given "jurisdiction over . . . estates of deceased [or vanished] persons." European settlers repeatedly represented themselves as God's appointed successors to America's indigenous peoples with jurisdiction over their "estates," that is, the North American continent. Because European Americans would use native lands far more productively, native lands were rightly theirs. The name "American" was, in turn, rightly theirs. The new Federal constitution boldly held these truths to be self-evident: as "We, the People of the United States," European American men rightfully governed American lands, rightfully declared indigenous Americans "wards" of their new white state. But, to claim these rights, to exercise this authority, European Americans did not need to stick feathers in their hair or coat their faces with war paint. They acquired the rights to land, name, and authority through war and diplomacy, not charades and masquerades.[11]

Tammany performances were just that: charades, or, more accurately, masquerades, festive occasions involving "an assembly of people wearing masks and other disguises (often of a . . . fantastic kind) and diverting themselves with dancing and other amusements." Masquerades are performances. Performances assume audiences and convey social and political messages. Tammany's most obvious audience was, of course, the Creek delegation. One can only wonder what those powerful warriors thought of upholsterers and petty shopkeepers' parading around in bizarre Indian costumes and chanting garbled songs.[12] Tammany's intended message, however, was anything but obscure. In parodying native practices, the odd assortment of "braves" and "sachems" who welcomed the Creek delegation were declaring that European Americans had indeed replaced Native Americans as rulers of American lands. Manhattan was

---

and Civility in the Treaty of Greenville," in Cayton and Fredrika J. Teute, eds., *Contact Points: American Frontiers from the Mohawk Valley to the Mississippi, 1750–1830* (Chapel Hill, N.C., 1998), 235–269.

11. *Oxford English Dictionary*, s.v. "surrogate." I am far from denying the military threat Native Americans posed until the end of the nineteenth century. What I am interrogating are the ways mimicry and masquerade entered into the serious business of asserting sovereignty and authority.

12. *OED*, s.v. "masquerade." We should note, however, that the the Creek delegation had some familiarity with European American practices. The delegation's leader, Alexander McGillivary, was the son of a Scottish Tory father and had been educated in Charleston.

no longer an "Indian" island. "Dangerous savages" no longer prowled north of Wall Street. And, even more, Tammany braves' parodic mimicry proclaimed European Americans' power to misrepresent and recast those they claimed they were replacing in ways that served their own social and political needs.

Creek warriors were only one audience Tammany performed for. Their fellow new republicans constituted a second. And here issues of class enter the picture. Tammany artisans and shopkeepers were imitating earlier elite Philadelphians who, in their turn, had mimicked elite European aristocratic masques and masqueraders. As Philadelphia's colonial elite used masquerades to assert their cultural equality with the British elite (represented by Thomas Penn and his entourage), so New York City artisans used their masquerades both to establish a connection with this older colonial elite and to assert their right to participate in affairs of state alongside President Washington and his Cabinet.

But masquerades also carry meanings their players do not necessarily intend. They are designed to present a false outward show, to counterfeit the real. Tammany's mismatched costumes proclaimed their wearers counterfeit Native Americans. On one level, of course, that was precisely the intention. Tammany braves made no effort to resemble actual Native Americans. Unlike more scholarly European Americans (Jonathan Edwards, for example), they did not attempt to learn tribal languages or to reproduce actual tribal practices. Their costumes were little more than a hodgepodge of parts adopted from different tribes—and no known tribes. Thus European American performances functioned, not to obscure, but to draw the attention of fellow European Americans to differences between the surrogate Indians and those they mimed. Their carefully applied war paint accentuated the whiteness of the skin it only pretended to camouflage. But, as fraudulent Indians, were they consequently fraudulent Americans? The best that could be said of Tammany's braves was that they were a group of white men playing dress-up. An unlikely self-image for ambitious middle-rank men anxious to appear as virtuous citizens of a new republic!

But we have to consider still more complex aspects of surrogacy—especially its psychological dimensions, dimensions that weave the intensely serious into the whimsical and the parodic. As the act of standing in another's place, surrogacy requires an intense identification with that Other, the desire to be the Other. Sigmund Freud saw surrogacy as a critical component of the process through which individuals confront the loss of intensely cathected figures. When such loss occurs, one's "most obvious reaction is to identify oneself with [the lost figure], to replace it from within . . . by identification." Theater historian and performance theorist Joseph R. Roach focuses on surrogacy's broader cultural aspects. Societies, he argues, use surrogacy to imaginatively mediate their experiences of radical social change and loss. The sense of loss and confusion that follows the disappearance of critical members of the social fabric, even of those one considers one's enemies, Roach insists, must be masked, ameliorated. Imaginatively reenacting the vanished figures, surrogates weave the absent ones back into the social fabric, albeit not as they were but as those who remain choose to remember and represent them. "The process of surrogation" involves the enactment of cultural memory by substitution. "As actual or perceived vacancies occur in the network of relations that constitute the social fabric [of a culture, of a nation]," "survivors attempt to fit [in] satisfactory alternatives." In this way, surrogacy works to suture the open wounds change so violently gashes.[13]

European Americans sorely needed cultural instruments through which to articulate and ameliorate the radical social, demographic, and political transformations that had marked their own lives and the birth of the new Republic: their loss of a centuries-old British identity, their sense of being a solitary republic in a sea of monarchies, their fears of being isolated white settlements on the lip of a red continent. Few relations were more cathected and traumatic than those between European Americans and Native Americans. No matter how much they desired to, European Americans could not simply dismiss Native Americans as "beasts of prey," destined to vanish without critically distorting the new nation's history and its sense of self. Native Americans and European settlers had shed too much blood, committed too many atrocities for European Americans to simply drop Native Americans from their consciousness. The horror, rage, and guilt Native Americans inspired in European American minds and psyches had to be pacified. The figures of both the savage, terrifying Native American and the savage, terrifying European American who had relentlessly battled him had to be domesticated, incorporated into the ongoing civil and orderly world European Americans worked to create. Chanting make-believe Indian songs might have helped mitigate the terror that Native American war whoops echoing through the night had imprinted in European America's cultural memory. Painting their own faces gave Europeans some way of recuperating the fear Native American warriors had inspired

13. James Strachey, ed. and trans., *The Standard Edition of the Complete Psychological Works of Sigmund Freud*, 24 vols. (London, 1953–1974), vol. XXIII, *New Introductory Lectures on Psychoanalysis and Other Works*, 193, quoted in Diana Fuss, *Identification Papers* (New York, 1995), 1; Roach, *Cities of the Dead*, 1–2, 4–7.

since Powhatan had attacked Jamestown and King Philip had attacked Plymouth Colony. In stitching beads and feathers onto their costumes, middling New York shopkeepers and tidewater planters stitched carefully re-formed and tamed memories of their nation's past, including their own often savage behavior, into the ongoing psychic and cultural fabric of their new Republic. They did so, however, not in ways that denied change or obliterated absences. As we have seen, difference, not sameness, lies at the heart of surrogacy.

European Americans' mimicking of Native American practices was not simply a determined assertion of European American power. It was also an anxious admission of need. European Americans, Philip J. Deloria reminds us, needed to feel connected to the American continent and to America's indigenous peoples. How else could they affirm their innate Americanness? They had to assert that residence in the New World had rendered them different from Europe—and potentially far more powerful. The American continent spread out before eighteenth-century European American settlers, vast, open, a superabundance of promised riches as well as of real terrors. This vastness, these riches, they sought to take into themselves. The rousing chorus in Rodgers and Hammerstein's *Oklahoma!*—"We know we belong to the land / And the land we belong to is grand!"—captures the intensity of European Americans' ongoing identification with their continent.[14]

But so does Freud's concept of introjection. Originally developed to describe an infant's desire, indeed lust, for the mother's breast, the term "introjection"

14. D. H. Lawrence, Deloria reminds us, was struck by the desire European Americans expressed to be connected to America, to "the spirit of the [American] continent" *(Playing Indian,* 3). We can see this pride in the power of the American continent informing Timothy Dwight's "Valedictory Address to the Young Gentlemen, Who Commenced Bachelors of Arts, at Yale College, July 25th, 1776," *American Magazine,* I (1787), 42–47. In the dark days of 1776, he called it "the greatest empire the hand of time ever raised up to view" and stated, "All that the wish of an epicure, the pride of a beauty, or the curious mind of a naturalist can ask to variegate the table of luxury, to encrease the shine of splendor, or delight the endless thirst of knowledge, is showered in profusion on this, the favorite land of heaven" (43, 44). We see this, as well, in Thomas Jefferson's *Notes on the State of Virginia* (Philadelphia, 1788), in John Filson's *Discovery, Settlement, and Present State of Kentucke* . . . (Wilmington, Del., 1784), and in Filson's later *Adventures of Colonel Daniel Boon: One of the First Settlers at Kentucke* . . . (Norwich, Conn., 1786). See Richard Slotkin, *Regeneration through Violence: The Mythology of the American Frontier, 1600–1860* (Middletown, Conn., 1973), esp. chaps. 9, 10; Carroll Smith-Rosenberg, "Discovering the Subject of the 'Great Constitutional Discussion,' 1786–1789," *Journal of American History,* LXXIX (1992), 841–873. Roach proposes an interesting connection between superabundance and violence, especially in *Cities of the Dead,* 40–41. In regard to Rodgers and Hammerstein, there is a further irony that we must note. Although *Oklahoma!* effaces Native Americans, it was based on a play by Cherokee writer Lynn Riggs.

suggests passionate desire tied to a possessiveness that borders on the sadistic. The infant seeks to take the mother's breast into himself, to possess and control it absolutely. This desire can appear insatiable and relentless—much as America's "town destroyers'" (a common Seneca expression for European Americans) desires for native lands must have appeared to Seneca women and children. European Americans lusted after native lands, suffered untold miseries to stake claims upon them, saw them as the source of America's greatness, wealth, and unique identity. Their desire to incorporate the superabundance, the plenitude, the power of the continent—coexisting with a nationalistic need to differentiate themselves from Europe—possessed all of "introjection's" emotional excessiveness and insatiability.[15]

Nor were European Americans' needs and desires limited to Native American lands. Playing surrogate Indians brought European Americans a step closer to internalizing and thus possessing the strength and power they believed Native Americans had gained from their long connection to the land. Although European Americans generally represented Native Americans as inhuman predators, enemies of civilization and religion, they also thought of them as powerful warriors, resourceful hunters, intrepid denizens of America's woodlands. European settlers believed that Native Americans garnered true nobility from their association with the land: the love of freedom that only the land's vast expanses could give; a sense of honor, uncorrupted by the niceties of refined culture; and, above all, a fierce, wild courage in defense of liberty and honor. Imagined in this Romantic light, Native Americans were the embodiment of freedom.[16]

15. Jean Laplanche and J.-B Pontalis, *The Language of Psycho-analysis*, trans. Donald Nicholson-Smith (New York, 1973), 229–231. The phrase "town destroyers" is taken from a speech the Seneca chief Kiontwagky (Cornplanter) presented to the president and Congress in the 1790s, just a few months after Tammany braves met the Creek delegation. Speaking temperately but bitterly, he told George Washington,

> When your army entered the country of the Six Nations, we called you *Caunotaucarius*, the Town Destroyer; and to this day when that name is heard, our women look behind them and turn pale, and our children cling to the knees of their mothers. . . . When you gave us peace, we called you father, because you promised to secure us in possession of our lands. Do this, and so long as the lands shall remain, the beloved name will remain in the heart of every Seneca.

(Ferguson, *American Enlightenment*, 165).

16. This theme, Slotkin claims, was central to John Filson's presentation of the education of Daniel Boone. Before moving to Kentucky, immersing himself in its forests and living closely with Native Americans, Boone had been naive and inept. Life in the forests made him a man,

Modern scholarship underscores the importance of these qualities to the eighteenth-century imagination. Hunting in Europe was an aristocratic right; poaching, a capital crime. Native Americans ranging across the American landscape, hunting where and what they pleased, challenged European class presumptions. At the same time, their freedom of movement, combined with their skills as hunters, transformed them into emblems of a uniquely American form of empowered manhood, their status, independence, courage in battle, fortitude, and Spartan simplicity, not inherited, as in Europe, but dependent on their prowess and courage. To quote the Baron de Lahonton: "Among them the true Qualifications of a Man are, to run well, to hunt, to bend the Bow, to understand War, . . . [and] to be able to travel an hundred Leagues in a wood without any Guide, or other Provision than his bow and Arrows." So romanticized, Native Americans embodied all that was believed to be specifically American.[17]

This freedom, these skills, European Americans were sure, would make them not only true Americans but virtuous republicans. European settlers, as we know, had cut their political eyeteeth on the crusty tenets of classic republicanism, and those tenets could not have been clearer. Courage, self-reliance, and love of liberty were essential for the practice of civic virtue. Modernity—commerce, consumerism, and the niceties of fashionable life—would corrupt aspiring republicans and plunge their republics into tyranny. Yet it was the modernizing world of commerce, consumerism, and fashion that America's urban classes seemed bent on embracing. Incorporating the noble Indian warrior's masculine traits would help urban and would-be urbane European Americans recuperate their claims to manly civic virtue. Put another way, as European Americans romantically imagined Native Americans' merging with the land, so they romantically imagined themselves merging with Native Ameri-

---

indeed, a great man. This became a popular theme among readers in France, where Filson's biography of Boone was widely read (Slotkin, *Regeneration through Violence*, 268–312, esp. 290). For additional examples of Native Americans idealized as nature's noblemen, see James Fenimore Cooper's *Leather Stocking Tales* and Lydia Maria Child's *Hobomok: An American Tale of Early Times*. For discussions of this fiction, see, among others, Renée L. Bergland, *The National Uncanny: Indian Ghosts and American Subjects* (Hanover, N.H., 2000); and Jared Gardner, *Master Plots: Race and the Founding of American Literature, 1787–1845* (Baltimore, 1998).

17. Gordon M. Sayre, *Les Sauvages Américains: Representations of Native Americans in French and English Colonial Literature* (Chapel Hill, N.C., 1997), 33–34. The Baron de Lahonton is a somewhat questionable source for anything other than his own romantic vision of nature's noblemen.

cans, shedding their Europeanness, becoming virile, freedom-loving American republicans.[18]

Essential to the production of an American national identity, surrogacy must be seen as a form of colonization as exploitative as the seizure of actual Native American lands. Identifying with the Other, internalizing the Other, personifying the Other, the surrogate incorporates the Other, drains the Other of his most desired characteristics. "Read psychoanalytically," Diana Fuss explains, "identification operates on one level as an endless process of violent negation, a process of killing off the other in fantasy in order to usurp the other's place, the place where the subject desires to be." Identification, she continues, "is itself an imperial process, a form of violent appropriation in which the Other is deposed and assimilated into the lordly domain of Self." "Through a psychical process of colonization, the imperial subject builds an Empire of the Same and installs at its center a tyrannical dictator, 'His Majesty the Ego.'" To borrow Frantz Fanon's telling phrase, surrogacy can reduce the Other to "crushing objecthood." The colonized Other, denied the basic characteristics of subjectivity, not only gives up his essence to the colonizer; he is transformed into a dark mirror that reflects and affirms the colonizer's power. Hence the importance of playing Indian in the presence of actual Native Americans. It was important that the Creeks acknowledge European Americans' right to masquerade, that they declare themselves "very much pleased." By appearing to acquiesce to Tammany's parody of themselves, they appeared to acquiesce to European Americans' appropriation not only of their lands but of their very identity.[19]

Playing the colonizers, however, European Americans assumed the role Europeans had long played in North America. Nor was this the only way European Americans, in playing Indian, ironically played the European. Incorporating the noble savages, European Americans incorporated a European literary trope: the image of the idealized native warrior was the imaginary product of Enlightenment salonnières and philosophes. It drew upon Michel de Montaigne's sixteenth-century image of a Golden People in a Golden Land and later Romantic representations of Native Americans. These images were born of European reformers' desires to use an idealized, imaginary Other

18. J. G. A. Pocock, *The Machiavellian Moment: Florentine Political Thought and the Atlantic Republican Tradition* (Princeton, N.J., 1975); Richard L. Bushman, *The Refinement of America: Persons, Houses, Cities* (New York, 1992); Paul Staiti, "Accounting for Copley," in Carrie Rebora and Staiti, eds., *John Singleton Copley in America* (New York, 1995), 25–51, esp. 30–35.

19. Fuss, *Identification Papers*, 9, 145; Frantz Fanon, *Black Skin, White Masks*, trans. Charles Lam Markmann (New York, 1967), 109–112, esp. 110.

to critique the corrupt practices of early modern and Enlightenment Europe. Certainly, Puritan New Englanders never represented Native Americans in those terms, nor did Scotch-Irish settlers along the Pennsylvania and Carolina frontiers. Actual European American settlers were far more likely to revile Native Americans as "hell-hounds" prowling a harsh wilderness, as "devils" seeking to drive godly saints from the chosen land. How ironic: the figure of the Native American as scripted by elite European philosophes and performed by European Americans for elite audiences—this was how the whitening of America's national identity was staged, and this was how the European American's virility, his republican virtue, was recuperated. Desiring Europeans' noble savage, European Americans positioned themselves as Europeans had done.[20]

Of course, in many ways, European Americans desired just that: to position themselves as Europeans were positioned—heirs of the Enlightenment, bearers of civilization, polished gentlemen. European Americans certainly did not wish to be seen as savages in a savage land. Thus, although needing to perform the virile American, they felt an equally strong need to perform the enlightened and cultured (European) gentleman. For them, both roles were deeply, emotionally entwined. It was as if the new Republic's national identity were played out on a revolving stage. At times, the erudite gentleman claimed the spotlight; at other times, the noble warrior did. At times they fused, for European Americans could not disentangle these two roles. The urban gentleman without the noble warrior would have appeared too effete, too European, to build an American national identity around. The noble savage without the urban gentleman would have seemed too brutal for eighteenth-century audiences. Combined, they strengthened European Americans' self-presentation. But they also confused that presentation, revealing the European American to be a deeply divided and contradictory figure. Part gentleman, part savage, his claims to Americanness depended upon his successful enactment of European fan-

20. See, for example, the Indian captivity narrative of Puritan matron Mary White Rowlandson, *The Soveraignty and Goodness of God, together, with the Faithfulness of His Promises Displayed; Being a Narrative of the Captivity and Restauration of Mrs. Mary Rowlandson, Commended by Her, to All That Desires to Know the Lords Doings to, and Dealings with Her, Especially to Her Dear Children and Relations* (Cambridge, 1682), rpt. in Richard Slotkin and James K. Folsom, eds., *So Dreadfull a Judgment: Puritan Responses to King Philip's War, 1676–1677* (Middletown, Conn., 1978), esp. 341, 351, 353. For an extended discussion of European American settlers' vision of Native Americans, see Chapter 5, below. For the European construction of Native Americans as noble savages, see Michel de Montaigne, "Of Cannibals," in *Essays*, trans. M. A. Screech (Harmondsworth, 1994).

tasies. Above all, his fusion and confusion of roles revealed the European American to be a man of many, perhaps too many, parts, an actor without a center playing a role with no internal coherence.[21]

Nevertheless, in terms of constructing a new national identity, the processes we have discussed—European Americans' seizure of native land, their idealization and introjection of the Native American as a marker of the European settler's Americanness, their distancing from that idealization through parodic performances—was logical, if counterintuitive. All, however, depended on Native Americans' absence. That, after all, is what surrogacy is all about—the replacement/displacement of one figure with another, the surrogate for the dead or absent one. Certainly, absence is central to both Freud's and Roach's understanding of surrogacy. However, in the 1790s, Native Americans were anything but absent from the North American continent. For decades to come, they would inhabit most of that vast area. Time and again, they would score devastating military victories; they would remain a military force to be reckoned with far into the nineteenth century. To understand Tammany performances—and, more generally, European Americans' repetitive acts of playing Indian—we must see them as part of a complex psychological engagement in which desired absence was entwined with feared presence. If Native Americans had been what Benjamin Franklin, Thomas Jefferson, and others wished they were—a vanishing race—then the need to reenact their replacement would not have been so pressing. Behind Tammany's playful performances lay a deadly fear and even more deadly threats. European Americans had to replace Native Americans and displace their villages and cultures until all that remained was the parodic performance of Native American absence.

But it was not only Native Americans' real presence that complicated relations. It was their desired presence. As noted, European Americans not only desired Native Americans' land and name. They desired the Native American's idealized self. The desire to displace versus the desire to possess, absence versus presence, difference versus sameness, circulated through European American rhetorical self-presentations in blinding confusion. Differences became muddled: American and European, erudite gentleman and noble savage, self and Other. "Cultural order," Rene Girard argues, "is nothing more than a regulated system of distinctions in which the differences among individuals are used to establish their 'identity' and their mutual relationships." This was especially true of the new United States, in which a rigid hierarchy of social and even more

21. Shields, *Civil Tongues*.

fundamental racial distinctions established identities and social order. Desiring the Native American, introjecting his most salient characteristics, European Americans had woven the Other into their very beings. They thus threatened the most fundamental distinctions structuring their nation and violated the eighteenth century's insistence on categorical distinctions between civil and savage, Christian and heathen, white and red. By destroying these key differences, the European American, as surrogate American, threatened to confirm Europe's worst suspicion—that the settler in America had degenerated, become no different than the savage men and animals with whom he shared the continent. "Crises of distinctions" are "crises effecting the social order," Girard continues. They lead relentlessly to sacrificial crises. But if the Native American were really sacrificed, really effaced from the European American imaginary landscape, the settlers would themselves cease to exist. Furthermore, the true transgressor was the European American himself, or, more specifically, the part of him that desired rather than despised the Native American. But neither could the European American sacrifice himself, most especially his desiring, transgressive self, and maintain his claims to his Americanness.[22]

And so European Americans proclaimed playing Indian a joke, a carnival performance. The true objective of Tammany's feathers and painted faces, they insisted, was to underscore the differences that separated them from natives, not to assert similarities. But if that were true, then European American claims to belong to the land, their claims to native courage and virility, their native love of liberty, all, too, were jokes. Without his beads, feathers, and tomahawks, the European American would stand forth merely as a displaced European, perched at the far edge of the known world.

Faced with an insoluble dilemma, occupying a no-man's-land between Europe and America, the European American turned upon the Native American with rage, literally and rhetorically. As genocidal warfare raged along the frontier, the new national press represented the Native American as a deadly Other, as savage as the animals he prowled among—as savage as the rage he inspired in European American hearts.

And so we see that all who threatened the new American's delicate psychological and ideological balance—effeminate men, transgressive women, Native Americans—became objects of rage and violence. But violence is no more successful in stabilizing national identities than jokes are. Both only further undermine the new American and his national identity. In this section, we will

22. Rene Girard, *Violence and the Sacred,* trans. Patrick Gregory (Baltimore, 1977), 49.

turn first to the real world in which Native and European Americans met in friendship and in fear. We will then move on to an examination of the transgressive intersections of desire, dread, and disdain that haunted the European American imaginaire, asking how these transgressions affected the new Republic's emerging sense of a national self.

CHAPTER FOUR

Seeing Red

For this world, which seems
To lie before us like a land of dreams,
So various, so beautiful, so new,
Hath really neither joy, nor love, nor light.

—MATTHEW ARNOLD, Dover Beach

T he western frontier has long played a central role both in the construction of the United States as a modern nation-state and in the formation of a mythic American national identity. On the most practical level, without the West, the thirteen states would have remained just that: thirteen small, semiautonomous states crammed between the Atlantic and the Appalachian Mountains. The United States' control of the West opened a vast continent to European American settlement, foreclosed other empires' claims to that continent, and secured access to an abundant reservoir of natural resources. Management of western lands created administrative challenges and a unifying goal for the new federal government. Sale of western lands helped finance the new government. Romantically envisioned, the West captured the imagination of both those who lived within its wide spaces and those who had never set foot west of the Appalachians. Its "purple mountains majesty," "its amber waves of grain" confirmed Timothy Dwight's vision of the United States as "the greatest empire the hand of time ever raised up to view." It helped European Americans, so often troubled and acrimonious, to see themselves as a unique, powerful, and virtuous people—a "we," united by collective ownership of the land. But, by grounding their national identity on their collective possession of the West, European Americans embraced a thoroughly racialized sense of self, born of centuries of savage frontier warfare and compounded by the systematic exclusion of Native Americans' claims to the rights and privileges of American citizenship. A source of a racialized unity, the frontier, at the same time, embodied many of the contradictions and contestations that destabilized the new nation and its identity. Throughout the eighteenth century, easterners viewed western settlers as little better than the savages they lived among, whereas westerners denigrated easterners as effete, corrupt, and tyrannical. East/West violence, as we have seen, was a frequent occurrence as western squatters battled eastern surveyors and tax collectors, the Paxton Boys threatened to burn Philadelphia to the ground, and George Washington and Alexander Hamilton led Federal troops west to suppress the Whiskey Rebellion. Far into the nineteenth century, the West continued to divide the nation it helped create. Whether the West would be a free white man's country or an extension of the South's plantation slave economy drove northerners and southerners to fratricide. National expansion south and west to the Rio Grande and the Pacific opened the Republic to a host of new residents drawn from Mexico, China, Japan, and the Pacific Islands. Geographic expansion thus complicated ethnic and cultural patterns, breeding paranoid fears of penetrated borders and enemies within at the same time as it bred hybridity and transgressively amalgamated social practices and identities. In short, from the very beginning of European settlement, the western frontier was a borderland of cultural crossings and contested loyalties, of rupture and danger. Repeatedly, it challenged any simple, cohesive sense of being American.[1]

Certainly, throughout the eighteenth century, the frontier was a place of shifting populations, demographic heterogeneity, cultural diversity, and accommodation. It was, as well, a site of bitter, ongoing conflict.[2] From one

1. "America's empire of liberty," Eric Hinderaker argues, was "voluntarily constituted, racially defined, indefinitely expansive, and democratically governed. Within the Republic's embrace, citizens enjoyed extraordinary liberties; beyond it, the systematic exploitation of nonwhite peoples was extended and deepened" (Hinderaker, *Elusive Empires: Constructing Colonialism in the Ohio Valley, 1673–1800* [Cambridge, 1997], 267–277, esp. 267). For discussions of crossroads and borderlands as sites of hybridity and transgression, see Peter Stallybrass and Allon White, *The Politics and Poetics of Transgression* (Ithaca, N.Y., 1986), especially chap. 1; and Jean-Christophe Agnew, *Worlds Apart: The Market and the Theater in Anglo-American Thought, 1550–1750* (Cambridge, 1987), 34–36.

2. On the mixed and shifting nature of western populations and imperial alliances, see, for example, Andrew R. L. Cayton and Fredrika J. Teute, eds., *Contact Points: American Frontiers from the Mohawk Valley to the Mississippi, 1750–1830* (Chapel Hill, N.C., 1996), esp. James H. Merrell, "Shamokin, 'The Very Seat of the Prince of Darkness': Unsettling the Early American Frontier," 16–59, Jane T. Merritt, "Metaphor, Meaning, and Misunderstanding: Language and Power on the Pennsylvania Frontier," 60–87, and Elizabeth A. Perkins, "Distinctions and Partitions amongst Us: Identity and Interaction in the Revolutionary Ohio Valley," 205–234. See, as

perspective, it could be said that the American West belonged to the world. Here, rival European empires (the Spanish, French, and British) met—and met their match in the newly emergent United States empire. Here powerful and warring indigenous peoples, the Iroquois, Ottawas, Cherokees, and Creeks, at times collaborated, at times locked in bloody warfare. Here, too, the world's dispossessed battled for land and new beginnings: Calvinist farming families fleeing New England's rocky hillsides, Delawares and Mohicans from the Delaware Valley, Scotch-Irish Presbyterians and Moravian Pietists, Canoys and Nanticokes from Maryland, French Acadians and Huguenots, Tuttelos and Tuscaroras from the Carolinas, Indian traders of who knew what racial heritage. The West also attracted the established and enterprising: British, continental, and East Coast speculators, or at least the surveyors they sent west to map their claims. Many of these speculators were new venture capitalists seeking a quick kill. But their number also included British and French aristocrats, Virginia planters, and careful Quaker merchants. Differing among themselves, speculators united on only one point: the rage and disdain they felt for poor, uneducated squatters who seized their lands and, from their perspective, hindered the orderly development of a commercialized West.[3] Adding appreciably to the confusion, different colonies (and later states) contested claims to lands that their founding charters had promised stretched as far as "the western sea." Connecticut, Pennsylvania, and Virginia battled over the Wyoming Valley in western Pennsylvania, the Erie triangle along the southern shore of Lake Erie, and rights to the Ohio Valley and Kentucky. In these multiple, contentious ways, a world of different peoples and cultures took form along the western frontier's "darkling plain."[4]

---

well, Gregory Evans Dowd, *War under Heaven: Pontiac, the Indian Nations, and the British Empire* (Baltimore, 2002); Alan Taylor, *William Cooper's Town: Power and Persuasion on the Frontier of the Early American Republic* (New York, 1995); Taylor, *The Divided Ground: Indians, Settlers, and the Northern Borderland of the American Revolution* (New York, 2006); Gregory H. Nobles, *American Frontiers: Cultural Encounters and Continental Conquest* (New York, 1997); Richard White, *The Middle Ground: Indians, Empires, and Republics in the Great Lakes Region, 1660–1818* (Cambridge, 1991).

3. For discussions of eastern speculators' and bureaucrats' hostility toward western squatters, see, among others, Nobles, *American Frontiers,* 50–51, 106–109; David L. Preston, "Squatters, Indians, Proprietary Government, and Land in the Susquehanna Valley," in William A. Pencak and Daniel K. Richter, eds., *Friends and Enemies in Penn's Woods: Indians, Colonists, and the Racial Construction of Pennsylvania* (University Park, Pa., 2004), 180–200, esp. 182–184, 194; Taylor, *William Cooper's Town,* 45–47.

4. Nobles, *American Frontiers,* 78, 82, 95. For other discussions of divisions among European Americans, see esp. Preston, "Squatters, Indians, Proprietary Government, and Land,"

They met here because America's great eastern rivers, the Delaware, Susquehanna, Ohio, Maume, and Miami, provided complex highways through the wilderness, facilitating trade and encouraging the intermingling of cultures. The villages that dotted their banks, historians agree, were "dynamic multicultural environment[s] . . . cockpit[s] of competing international interests," "the passing scene . . . a carnival of peoples and cultures." On a single day in a western Pennsylvania village, one might meet native warriors, their faces fierce with red and black paint or tattooed with coiled snakes, searching for strayed cattle and conversing in fluent English; Moravian-converted Indians visiting from Bethlehem; European American squatters; enslaved Africans assisting Virginia surveyors; Métis fur traders heading to Philadelphia; or Quaker traders trekking west.[5]

Often multiethnic composites of many dispossessed native groups, native villages furthered their multiplicity by allowing European artisans to settle in their midst. European American gun- and plowsmiths, millers, and sutlers offered useful skills. Moravian missionaries sought residence there, as well, though they also established separate villages for their native converts. In addition, poorer European American settlers, seeking to avoid the high land prices eastern speculators charged, arranged long-term leases with Native Americans for land adjacent to these heterogeneous villages. Native and European architectural forms nestled side by side, until it became difficult to tell whether a Native or a European American family resided in a rough log cabin or a carefully constructed brick house with stone cellar and chimney.[6]

Out of these interactions and cohabitations, a mixed frontier economy emerged. In eighteenth-century Europe, hunting was an aristocratic sport; poaching by those of lesser rank, a capital offense, with felons hung or trans-

in Pencak and Richter, eds., *Friends and Enemies in Penn's Woods*, 182–184, 194; Taylor, *William Cooper's Town*, 45–47, 52; and Merrell, "Shamokin," in Cayton and Teute, eds., *Contact Points*, 35.

5. Perkins, "Distinctions and Partitions amongst Us," 206, Merrell, "Shamokin," 17–18, 24, and Stephen Aron, "Pigs and Hunters: 'Rights in the Woods' on the Trans-Appalachian Frontier," 175–204, esp. 186, all in Cayton and Teute, eds., *Contact Points*.

6. At times, one might find upward of twenty European American shopkeepers and artisans in one of the larger native villages. See Hinderaker, *Elusive Empires*, 176–183; Aron, "Pigs and Hunters," in Cayton and Teute, eds., *Contact Points*, 170; Preston, "Squatters, Indians, Proprietary Government, and Land," in Pencak and Richter, eds., *Friends and Enemies in Penn's Woods*, 188–189; Taylor, *William Cooper's Town*, 35–36; Patrick Griffin, "Reconsidering the Ideological Origins of Indian Removal: The Case of the Big Bottom 'Massacre,'" in Andrew R. L. Cayton and Stuart D. Hobbs, eds., *The Center of a Great Empire: The Ohio Country in the Early American Republic* (Athens, Ohio, 2005), 11–35.

ported. On the American frontier, hunting was an essential way of life. Without hunting, settlers new to the frontier could not feed their families during the difficult years of clearing and planting fields. At all times, the sale of pelts provided a valuable supplement to a farmer's income. Since European Americans did not bring hunting skills with them, they had to learn its mysteries from their Native American neighbors: how to track and decoy game, how to live off the land while stalking their prey. In return, European Americans provided guns and shot and helped repair the long rifles so necessary to Native and European American survival. European Americans also learned the ways of frontier agriculture from native cultivators—the clearing of fields, the planting of corn and squash in virgin lands. But, as game grew scarce in increasingly populated river valleys, Native Americans turned to European Americans to learn the skills of cattle raising and herding and of market-oriented agriculture. In this world, neighbors repaired each other's equipment, celebrated together, aided one another during the difficulties of birth and death. Throughout the first half of the eighteenth century, David Preston reports, "Peaceful dealings with their neighbors were a necessity on a frontier that was still an Indian world and one increasingly threatened by French imperial power." By the 1760s, Europeans touring the Ohio Valley commented on Native American skill in the production of butter and cheese and the excellence of their cattle. Iroquois farms in the Finger Lake district of New York were similarly praised for their well-cultivated and extensive orchards. Thus, by midcentury, a market-driven economy in which both Native and European Americans participated had emerged in the West. On a native chief's or a successful European American farmer's or trader's table, one might find western game and tea from China, Caribbean sugar along with squash and corn cooked with spices from the Indies, all set out on a tablecloth woven in the Lancaster mills.[7]

The West was a place of linguistic as well as cultural hybridity. Living side by side with the Other, learning from the Other, required an increasing mastery of the Other's languages. Of course, European Americans captured and raised by Native American families mastered their adopted language. Moravian converts read the Bible. On a more secular plane, diplomats (both native and European), military commanders, and warriors needed to be intelligible in one another's languages. Responding to the pressures of commerce, Pennsylvania

7. Preston, "Squatters, Indians, Proprietary Government, and Land," in Pencak and Richter, eds., *Friends and Enemies in Penn's Woods*, 181, 185; Aron, "Pigs and Hunters," in Cayton and Teute, eds., *Contact Points*, 175–176, 180–182, 190; Taylor, *William Cooper's Town*, 35–37; Hinderaker, *Elusive Empires*, 177–182.

and Ohio Valley traders and settlers of all stripes developed a pidgin form of Delaware through which to conduct their business. Yet, as we know, language is a slippery medium. Metaphors and analogies translate uncertainly. Misunderstandings abound. Nevertheless, from the mid-seventeenth to the mid-eighteenth century, Native and European Americans managed to communicate with one another, lived in one another's villages, traded with one another, drank, ate, and prayed with one another, farmed in similar ways, wore much the same clothing, indeed, were often indistinguishable from one another in terms of personal appearance, language, and dwellings.[8]

Social and linguistic commingling and appropriation might have led to a fusion of cultures and identities; from cohabitation might have emerged a shared American West; from the contingency of social relations might have come racial hybridity and a creolization of western culture. But no such synthesis occurred. Rather, the blurring of clear defining markers gave birth to fears of disorder and danger, to a "widespread sense of being adrift on a turbulent, forbidding sea."[9]

GUARDING THE BORDERS OF IDENTITY

Native and European Americans alike experienced the erosion of differences as chaotic, "bewildering," and deeply threatening. What each was sure they knew—that Delawares, Shawnees, or Ottawas, no matter how many languages they spoke, how they dressed, or to what god they prayed, were not whites, and that European Americans, no matter how coarse their clothing or speech, were still (to quote James Fenimore Cooper's Natty Bumppo) men "without a cross" —was central to both Native and European American identities. Without the Other's remaining other, how could either European Americans or Native Americans know who they were within the western frontier's multiple confusions? All agreed, the stronger the similarities that bound frontier residents together, the more ethnic difference and distinctions mattered. As Stephen Aron argues, "That the worlds of Indians and pioneers could not easily be separated did not mean their ways had become indistinguishable. . . . The convergence of subsistence systems and property regimes . . . was no basis for

8. Merritt, "Metaphor, Meaning, and Misunderstanding," 63–67, 70, and Merrell, "Shamokin," 16–59, both in Cayton and Teute, eds., *Contact Points;* Preston, "Squatters, Indians, Proprietary Government, and Land," in Pencak and Richter, eds., *Friends and Enemies in Penn's Woods,* 188–189.

9. Merrell, "Shamokin," in Cayton and Teute, eds., *Contact Points,* 22.

peaceful coexistence. What made Indians and pioneers similar did not make them the same." Similarity and the need to distinguish self from Other went hand in hand.[10]

As the eighteenth century progressed, the need to maintain fundamental distinctions and hence fundamental identities grew ever more pressing, fusion and cultural appropriations ever more worrying. Native prophets urged their followers to eschew European culture, warning that European ways would turn strong warriors into women. Only a return to the purity and authenticity of their grandfathers' ways would bring a return of the deer, good hunting, and attunement with nature. Native villages began to expel white settlers just as European Americans began to express similar fears of fusion. The ability to see through similarities to detect true differences, European Americans were certain, was key to survival in the West. The failure to do so could be fatal, as when settlers or militia killed European American scouts and traders, mistaking them for Native Americans because they were "dressed fine in ind[ia]n dress" or, alternatively, when European American children ran into the arms of Native American kidnappers, believing them to be white men come to protect them. European American villages began to exclude Native Americans from their midst. Formerly heteroglot trading posts confined Native Americans to their peripheries, though always within range of the posts' cannons.[11]

More critical still was the need to map differences onto systems of racial hierarchy. Given the animosities that divided European Americans along the frontier—outbreaks of vigilante violence among Pennsylvania, Virginia, and Connecticut settlers in western Pennsylvania as well as between speculators and squatters throughout the Ohio Valley; deeply ingrained religious and cultural differences separating French Catholics, Scotch-Irish Presbyterians, Moravian Pietists, New England Baptists, and elite eastern Quakers—whiteness itself was in danger of losing its coherence. Except, that is, when whiteness was contrasted to redness. Increasingly, from the mid-eighteenth century on, western settlers' "property interest in whiteness," sutured to an insistence on Native Americans' innate inferiority, was the message frontier parents inculcated among their children. Native Americans, European American settlers were certain, were ignorant, lazy, drunken, superstitious, deceitful, cruel to the point

10. Ibid., 21, 22, 37; Aron, "Pigs and Hunters," 176, 194. See, as well, Perkins, "Distinctions and Partitions amongst Us," 219.

11. Perkins, "Distinctions and Partitions amongst Us," 215, 219; Merritt, "Metaphor, Meaning, and Misunderstanding," 63, 70–71, both in Cayton and Teute, eds., *Contact Points*.

of sadism—in short, no different from the "beasts of prey" they lived among. Even Moravian missionaries who lived among Native Americans, helped birth their babies and nurse their sick, reviled Native Americans as "very Fierce and Bloody" "children of Satan." Only if Native Americans converted and became exactly like whites could they be trusted—but, of course, they could never become exactly like whites. (What an excellent example of the colonial pattern Homi K. Bhabha has designated "not quite/not white!") In this way, frontier settlers maintained a hierarchical vision of racialized difference.[12]

A hierarchical vision that the eastern elite refused—and in refusing fractured representations of whiteness, just as the urban magazines, when representing rebellious Shaysites, had fractured representations of manliness. Easterners were horrified by frontier squatters' poverty, lack of literacy, homespun cloth-ing, sexual lapses—and, most especially, by their seizure of land owned by others (eastern speculators). Such behavior, in conjunction with the absence of roads, churches, schools, and other accoutrements of civility, marked the fron-tier as a wild and disorderly land, its inhabitants no different from the savages they fought. Violating the rhetorical moderation expected of a gentleman, Anglican missionary Charles Woodmason, touring the Ohio Valley, vilified westerners as "the Skum of the Earth and Refuse of Mankind." "Profligate, audacious vagabonds" living a "low, lazy, sluttish, heathenish, hellish life," they could claim no brotherhood with respectable Anglican congregants. Rather, they were "lewd, impudent, abandon'd Prostitutes Gamblers Gamesters of all Sorts—Horse Thieves Cattle Stealers, Hog Stealers." Tellingly, he concluded, they went about "Naked as Indians." J. Hector St. John de Crèvecoeur agreed. Frontiersmen bore a far greater resemblance to Native Americans than they did to Crèvecoeur's churchgoing, commercially successful farming neighbors in New York's Hudson Valley, whom Crèvecoeur praised as God's chosen people, purified by their connection to the earth. Living more in a Hobbesian than a Habermasian world, frontiersmen brutally assaulted one another, gouging out eyes, biting off noses and ears. They were, in short, "no better than carnivorous animals." Their children would "grow up a mongrel breed, half civilized, half

---

12. Cheryl I. Harris, "Whiteness as Property," *Harvard Law Review*, CVI (1993), 1707–1791; Merrell, "Shamokin," in Cayton and Teute, eds., *Contact Points*, 17–18, 48–49; Homi K. Bhabha, "Of Mimicry and Man: The Ambivalence of Colonial Discourse," in Bhabha, ed., *The Location of Culture* (London, 1994), 121–131. Henry Clarke Wright recalls that no child was "allowed to grow up in that region, without imbibing more or less hatred and horror of the Indians" (Wright, *Human Life: Illustrated in My Individual Experience as a Child, a Youth, and a Man* [Boston, 1849]), 112.

savage." Predictably, Philadelphia's Quakers joined the verbal assault. Elder George Churchman (a relative of Charles Brockden Brown) condemned frontiersmen as "a banditti of cruel unmerciful men . . . a Company of Rioters," while another Quaker recorded a dream in which frontiersmen appeared as a "Herd of the most feirce [sic] and savage Beasts."[13]

Class, obviously, played a critical role in these diatribes. But ethnicity and religion did, as well. Frontier squatters tended to be Scotch-Irish Presbyterians, detested equally by the East's Anglican and Quaker elites. New England Baptists, another religious minority found along the frontier, were viewed with almost equal disdain. Even more significant was the ideological threat dirt-poor squatters posed. European Americans supported their claims to western land on the Lockean ground that European American settlers cultivated the soil, making the "howling wilderness" bloom, by which they meant that settlers quickly engaged in commercial agriculture, sending goods to both domestic and foreign markets. Such commercially oriented settlers would construct orderly towns, roads, and mills along with churches and schools. Native Americans, in contrast, were hunters and gatherers who added nothing to the natural land. By Lockean logic, they must be displaced by productive settlers. But frontiersmen, especially as represented by the eastern elite, were a "mongrel breed" and "mutinous spirits." Without roads or mills, they did not engage in commercial agriculture but rather "cut and mangle[d] the best parts of the

13. Richard J. Hooker, ed., *The Carolina Backcountry on the Eve of the Revolution: The Journal and Other Writings of Charles Woodmason, Anglican Itinerant* (Chapel Hill, N.C., 1953); Nobles, *American Frontiers*, 104–105, 114. It is important to note that British and eastern elites did not simply equate western settlers and "savage Indians" rhetorically. Administratively and militarily they treated them as equals and thus refused to acknowledge the settlers' insistence on their racial difference from and superiority to Native Americans. Washington's actions as commander in chief during and after the Revolution certainly mark squatters and Native Americans as equivalents. During the war, Washington ordered the Continental army to burn Native American villages and crops. After the war, as president, he commanded Federal troops to burn squatters' cabins and crops. Even more telling were the implications of Britain's Proclamation Line of 1763. The proclamation not only divided the West into Native and European American territories; by setting limits on European Americans' migration west with the object of protecting Native American settlements and preventing further frontier warfare, the Proclamation Line declared European and Native Americans to be equal parts of a diverse and multiethnic empire—the one having no greater rights or privileges than the other. Whitehall thus denied western settlers their most fundamental sense of self: that they were British with special claims to British citizenship that no Native American (or French Canadian, for that matter) could make. On the Quakers' comments, see Peter Kafer, *Charles Brockden Brown's Revolution and the Birth of American Gothic* (Philadelphia, 2004), 178–179.

country." They thus threatened European Americans' Lockean claims to legitimate possession of the land.[14]

In these ways, eastern diatribes denied what frontier settlers prided themselves upon—their whiteness and hence the legitimacy of their claims to acceptance as civilized and Christian men and heirs to all the rights and privileges of Englishmen. If, as Rene Girard contends, "cultural order is nothing more than a regulated system of distinctions in which differences among individuals are used to establish their 'identity,'" if, as well, crises of distinctions lead to the sacrifice of those who threaten such distinctions, then the western frontier was a tinderbox about to ignite.[15]

A DARK AND BLOODY LAND

And ignite it did! Between the 1750s and the century's end, neighbors turned fiercely on neighbors. Violence bred violence, fear of sameness bred sameness, until brutal warfare obliterated all distinction between savage and civil, red and white. From the onset of the Seven Years' War in 1754 until the United States' victory forty-one years later at the Battle of Fallen Timbers, atrocity and retaliation turned the West into a "dark and bloody land," from the Mohawk Valley to the Carolinas, from the Great Lakes to Kentucky. White settlers and native warriors burned fields and villages to the ground, scalped women and children, attacked the peaceful and neutral as well as the militant and armed. The causes of nearly half a century of bloody warfare were many and diverse: imperial conflicts between France and Great Britain; conflicting claims to western land by rival colonies and states; related rivalries among contesting land speculators and western squatters; and, overriding all, European Americans' unquenchable desire for native lands. But the repeated collapse of the differences upon which Native and European Americans alike constituted their sense of order, authenticity, and psychological cohesion added an emo-

---

14. Preston, "Squatters, Indians, Proprietary Government, and Land," in Pencak and Richter, eds., *Friends and Enemies in Penn's Woods*, 182. We should note, however, that frontier squatters used a similar Lockean argument to challenge eastern speculators' claims to western lands, pointing out that speculators did nothing to develop the land and that, rather, squatters took unoccupied land and did develop it. See Nobles, *American Frontiers*, 106–107.

15. Rene Girard, *Violence and the Sacred,* trans. Patrick Gregory (Baltimore, 1977), 49. It is important to remember that the East's emerging bourgeoisie was as afraid of being associated with western squatters and illiterate farmers as those farmers and squatters were of being associated with Native Americans. A sliding and very fragile system of differences was in play in late-eighteenth-century North America.

tional intensity that quickly evolved into fratricidal rage. By the century's end, the earlier patterns of hybridity, cultural cohabitation, and exchange had been replaced by entrenched racial divisions and clear-cut lines between "American land" and Indian reserves.[16]

It all began with the Seven Years' War, the last of the great imperial wars France and Great Britain fought that affected the American West. With this war, control of the West was no longer a peripheral issue, haphazardly drawn into European-centered conflicts. Control of the West had become *the* point of conflict between Europe's two great imperial powers.[17] Attacks led to counterattacks, setting western settlements ablaze from the Lehigh Valley to the Great Lakes and from New Jersey to the western Carolinas. The bloated bodies of men and animals polluted rivers and wells. Delawares and Shawnees descended on villages within the infamous Walking Treaty, decimating Moravian settlements at Nazareth, Bethlehem, Easton, and Gnadenhütten. The Ottawas, allied with France, ravaged the Great Lakes region. British and European American troops responded with equal, perhaps greater, savagery. Initiating a "take no prisoners" policy, they hunted Native Americans down with bloodhounds and beaver traps and distributed smallpox blankets, hoping the disease would spread through entire tribes.[18]

Peace, not surprisingly, brought no peace. The wounds of one war bled into the next. Even before the Treaty of Paris confirmed Britain's victory, a confederacy of western tribes, led by the Ottawa warrior Pontiac, declared war against Great Britain, seizing all but one of the western forts Britain had just gained from France. In response, white vigilante violence inflamed the Pennsylvania frontier. Significantly, the Native Americans most frequently targeted were those most successful in adopting European ways—praying Indians, native traders, leaders known for their accommodation policies. Racist rhetoric escalated. Even the usually moderate *Pennsylvania Gazette,* the newspaper

16. Hinderaker, *Elusive Empires,* 260–270; Pencak and Richter, eds., *Friends and Enemies in Penn's Woods,* xvi–xvii; Nobles, *American Frontiers,* 260–270. See, as well, Aron, "Pigs and Hunters," in Cayton and Teute, eds., *Contact Points,* 188; Preston, "Squatters, Indians, Proprietary Government, and Land," 185, 188, and Steven C. Harper, "Delawares and Pennsylvanians after the Walking Purchase," 167–179, esp. 167–170, both in Pencak and Richter, eds., *Friends and Enemies in Penn's Woods,* 185, 188; Nobles, *American Frontiers,* 78–82.

17. See Nobles, *American Frontiers,* 78, for a discussion of this point.

18. Preston, "Squatters, Indians, Proprietary Government, and Land," in Pencak and Richter, eds., *Friends and Enemies in Penn's Woods,* 171, 175–180; Dowd, *War under Heaven,* 41–53; Merritt, "Metaphor, Meaning, and Misunderstanding," in Cayton and Teute, eds., *Contact Points,* 71, 80, 82, 86–87; Harper, "Delawares and Pennsylvanians after the Walking Purchase," in Pencak and Richter, eds., *Friends and Enemies in Penn's Woods,* 170–178.

of record for Philadelphia's Quaker elite, called loudly for "Revenge for the Butcheries committed by Barbarians." It was within this climate that settlers from the central Pennsylvania towns of Paxtong (Paxton), Donegal, and Hempfield turned upon a mixed community of Conestoga, Seneca, Delaware, and Susquehanna farmers who, for fifty years, had leased farming land from the Penn Proprietors and lived peacefully among their white neighbors. Calling the Conestogas "the Progeny of Ham," a mob of European American settlers descended on the community, systematically slaughtering women and children. When the survivors fled for safety to the Easton workhouse, the mob killed all within and left "the mangled bodies helter-skelter about the yard." Having assassinated as many of the community as they could lay their hands on, the mob then proceeded toward Philadelphia, threatening to burn the city if the General Assembly did not vote for military support for the western settlers and offer bounties for Native American scalps, with the highest bounties going for the scalps of women and children.[19]

Native American communities as far away as the Finger Lakes retaliated. Atrocities mounted, spurred on by conflicts among Virginia, Pennsylvania, and Connecticut land speculators and the relentless press of settlers. By the early 1770s, a steady of flow of white settlers had spread beyond the Ohio to what was to become Kentucky and from there to the Great Lakes. The western woodland tribes continued to resist. A bloodbath of attack and counterattack ensued. Virginia militia and squatters provoked war with the Shawnees and Ottawas. Carolina squatters burned Cherokee villages to the ground. Mohawks descended on white settlements in the Wyoming and Cherry Valleys, and Delawares and Ottawas sought to drive squatters out of Tennessee.

Lord Dunmore's War, the polite name given these mutual atrocities, seeped into the Revolutionary War, perhaps the most brutal of all European/Native American wars. Shawnees, Delawares, and Mohawks burned white settlements. Washington ordered General John Sullivan to destroy native villages, crops, women, and children. Relentlessly, Continental army troops hunted their prey, bayoneting even the children they found hiding in cornfields.[20]

19. This is a paraphrase of Nobles, *American Frontiers,* 78. For a detailed examination of Pontiac's Rebellion and key events in the Ottawas' history leading up to it, see Dowd, *War under Heaven.* Dowd points out that the vicious military policies the British army first adopted during the Seven Years' War continued during Pontiac's Rebellion (175–177). For Dowd's discussions of white vigilante attacks on native communities, see 191–209, esp. 191–192.

20. Violence was more than reciprocal. General Sullivan destroyed forty Iroquois villages in the Finger Lake/Genesee Valley region alone, burning cornfields, cutting down orchards. Two thousand Native American children were left without fathers. To the west, militias engaged in

In the face of this violence, settlers along the Ohio, from Fort Pitt into Kentucky, retreated into hastily constructed forts that quickly became sites of entrapment. Those who left their protective walls exposed themselves to native attack. Yet to remain within the forts was equally intolerable. Overcrowding, polluted water, insufficient food supplies, rampant dysentery, and high infant mortality rates transformed the forts from military outposts into pesthouses. Yet many western settlers spent the war years trapped inside their palisades. The vulnerability of their situation, their close confinement, their intense sense of helplessness were seared into the settlers' psyche. It became, Eric Hinderaker tells us, "a defining experience that challenged western settlers to interpret their persistence in the landscape in transcendent terms." "Memories and tales drawn from the years of Indian fighting, of danger, uncertainty, and triumph, undergirded a broadly shared regional identity." A return to the accommodations and cohabitation of the prewar years became unthinkable.[21]

Especially since violence between European and Native Americans continued unabated. European American settlers scorned eastern efforts to work peacefully with the western tribes at the same time that the passage of the Northwest Ordinance, which proclaimed the West the white man's country, elicited armed resistance along the northern Ohio. In November 1791, a confederacy of the western tribes descended upon a mixed force of regular United States troops and militia led by General Arthur St. Clair. One thousand out of twelve hundred European American soldiers died that day, the worst defeat the U.S. ever experienced at Native American hands. This was a defeat the new government could not tolerate. The Northwest territories had to be opened to orderly white settlement. The honor of the new nation demanded it. The treasury of the new nation required it. For the next two years, General Anthony Wayne built up a strong force and, at the Battle of Fallen Timbers in 1794, finally defeated the western confederacy. Peace came at last to the trans-Appalachian region—but it was peace accompanied by searing memories and a bitter insistence on excluding Native Americans from American land and an American national identity. The West had been thoroughly racialized. Could this racialization play a critical role in solidifying a coherent national identity? Could the regional solidarity born of inhuman atrocities be transformed into a unifying national identity?

---

ruthless pillaging. Taylor tells us: "Brutal and Bloody, divisive and destructive, the war wreaked a havoc underestimated by historians who describe the American Revolution as orderly and consensual" (Taylor, *Divided Ground,* 84–100). See, as well, Nobles, *American Frontiers,* 88, and Hinderaker, *Elusive Empires,* 189–197.

21. Hinderaker, *Elusive Empires,* 258–259.

*The gradual extension of our Settlements will as
certainly cause the Savage as the Wolf to retire;
both being beasts of prey tho' they differ in shape.*
—GEORGE WASHINGTON

As we have seen, from an eastern bourgeois perspective, the West was indeed multiple, wild, and excessive. A land of almost inordinate beauty and riches, it was also a dark and brutal wilderness, as bitterly divided by class and religion as by race. Hobbesean squatters, Shays and Whiskey rebels, fiery Baptist and Methodist preachers, claim jumpers and eye-gougers threatened the orderly settlement of the West as much as or more than its native inhabitants. At the same time, as we know, European Americans superimposed multiple conflicting images on Native Americans, seeing them not only as skulking butchers but as noble savages, the romantic remnants of a vanished people. Would the eastern press be able to override these multiple disruptive images and constitute the Native American as a stabilizing Other to the imagined new American citizen? Or would the fractious frontier, its wild white settlers and its multiply perceived Native Americans, continually destabilize the new America and the new American? Could the line between national self and excluded Other ever be unambivalently drawn?[22]

In pondering these questions, one must recall that the actual carnage that characterized the American frontier—the slaughter of the Conestoga community, the Paxton Boys' assault on Philadelphia, the burned villages, red and white, the frontier forts where so many languished through the Revolution's hard years—were not remote abstractions for Carey's readers or for Noah Webster's or Isaiah Thomas's. Philadelphia, New York, and Massachusetts newspapers kept urban readers well informed of western atrocities and suffering. Trade further connected East and West, as urban merchants sent wagonloads of goods west for European and Native American consumers alike and so gained firsthand information. Of course, eastern speculators were fully informed of western events, not infrequently playing a role in the West's escalating violence. At the same time, Quaker and Moravian communities publicly commemorated the praying Indians who had fallen victim to frontier savagery. When reading the popular press for these years, we must carefully note the moments when actual events surfaced through the multiple layers of

---

22. See George Washington, quoted in Robert A. Ferguson, *The American Enlightenment, 1750–1820* (Cambridge, Mass., 1997), 169.

PLATE FIVE *Joseph Brant*. By Gilbert Stuart, 1786. Oil on canvas. Brant was the leader of Mohawks allied with the British during the Revolutionary War. Collection of the Duke of Northumberland, Syon House. Photograph: Photographic Survey, The Courtauld Institute of Art

conflicting representations, intrusive pentimentos disturbing the never quite finished ideological surface.

By the end of the eighteenth century, a mixed genre of captivity narratives, descriptions of frontier warfare, tales of Indian atrocities, and descriptions of western exploration and settlement (along with romances that appropriated themes from all the rest) captured the new nation's imagination. In the years following Independence, older colonial captivity narratives were republished, often rewritten in stridently nationalist ways. Descriptions of western explorations and settlements proliferated: John Filson's several biographies of Daniel Boone; Robert Rogers's *Reminiscences of the French War;* Franklin's *Narrative of the Late Massacres, in Lancaster County.* Descriptions of frontier warfare—the hardships western settlers suffered at the hands of marauding Indians, the tortures young girls endured at the hands of sadistic savages, the sufferings of prisoners whom Indians sold as slaves to French Catholics in Canada—all presented in ways calculated to arouse bourgeois horror and sympathy—were actively marketed in the 1780s and 1790s, creating a pantheon of European American martyrs and heroes. Indeed, this fusion of captivity/frontier war narratives remained a popular genre well into the nineteenth century. All justified the relentless removal of Native Americans so that industrious, God-fearing European American farming families could occupy their land and their villages. All worked to unite literate eastern readers with hardscrabble frontier families. Would racialized horror and rage form the core of the new national identity? "The great and continuing popularity of these narratives," Richard Slotkin tells us, "the uses to which they were put, and the nature of the symbolism employed in them are evidence that the[y] . . . constitute the first coherent myth-literature developed in America for American audiences."[23]

23. [John Filson], *The Adventures of Colonel Daniel Boon, One of the First Settlers at Kentucke . . .* (Norwich, Conn., 1786); Robert Rogers, *Reminiscences of the French War: Containing Rogers' Expeditions with the New-England Rangers under His Command, as Published in London in 1765 . . .* (Concord, N.H., 1831); Rogers, *Ponteach; or, The Savages of America, a Tragedy* (London, 1766); Benjamin Franklin, *A Narrative of the Late Massacres, in Lancaster County, of a Number of Indians, Friends of This Province, by Persons Unknown, with Observations on the Same* (Philadelphia, 1764); Richard Slotkin, *Regeneration through Violence: The Mythology of the American Frontier, 1600–1860* (Middletown, Conn., 1973), 95. Slotkin was one of the first scholars to subject this literature to thorough exploration. His work remains the benchmark for the field. Many have followed Slotkin, though their emphasis has been more on captivity narratives than on frontier warfare. See, for example, June Namias, *White Captives: Gender and Ethnicity on the American Frontier* (Chapel Hill, N.C., 1993); Michelle Murnham, *Captivity and Sentiment: Cultural Exchange in American Literature, 1682–1861* (Hanover, N.H., 1997); Gary L. Ebersole, *Captured by Texts: Puritan to Postmodern Images of Indian Captivity* (Charlottes-

Certainly, the entrepreneurial Mathew Carey early sought to profit from the popularity of such narratives. In 1794, he published a collection of eight Indian warfare and captivity narratives, *Affecting History of the Dreadful Distresses of Frederic Manheim's Family: To Which Are Added, the Sufferings of John Corbly's Family; An Encounter between a White Man and Two Savages; Extraordinary Bravery of a Woman* (1794). Most of these stories also appeared as excerpts in Carey's and other political magazines. All dealt with savage encounters in the western regions of Pennsylvania and New York during the Seven Years' War or the American Revolution. Even earlier, a number of other, similar accounts had been published in Philadelphia—all focusing on the violence that ripped across the Pennsylvania frontier, such as *Narrative of the Adventures of Capt. Isaac Stuart: Taken from His Own Mouth, in March, 1782, A Narrative of the Captivity and Sufferings of Benjamin Gilbert and His Family Who Were Surprised by the Indians, and Taken from Their Farms, on the Frontiers of Pennsylvania in the Spring, 1780* and David Humphreys's *Life of Major-General Israel Putnam.* In this way, images of savage Indians, their tomahawks and scalping knives stained with the blood of white innocents, became deeply imprinted in the bourgeois imagination. Let us see whether this genre helped solidify a new national identity.[24]

---

ville, Va., 1995). For a useful exploration of women's experiences of frontier violence, and more specifically of European American representations of women's experiences, see Kathryn Zabelle Derounian-Stodola, ed., *Women's Indian Captivity Narratives* (New York, 1998). See, as well, Derounian-Stodola and James Levernier, *The Indian Captivity Narrative, 1550–1900* (Toronto, 1993). Jill Lepore takes her analysis back to the beginning of captivity narratives in British North America in her *In the Name of War: King Philip's War and the Origins of American Identity* (New York, 1998). Linda Colley's *Captives: Britain, Empire, and the World, 1600–1850* (New York, 2002) places American captivity narratives in a larger British imperial frame contrasting narratives of capture by Algerian "pirates" in India and Afghanistan. For a discussion of Mary Rowlandson's ur-captivity narrative, see Chapter 5, below.

24. *Affecting History of the Dreadful Distresses of Frederic Manheim's Family: To Which Are Added, The Sufferings of John Corbly's Family; An Encounter between a White Man and Two Savages; Extraordinary Bravery of a Woman; Adventures of Capt. Isaac Stewart; Deposition of Massey Herbeson; Adventures and Sufferings of Peter Wilkinson* [sic]; *Remarkable Adventures of Jackson Johonnot; Account of the Destruction of the Settlements at Wyoming* (Philadelphia, 1794); "A True and Faithful Narrative of the Surprizing Captivity and Remarkable Deliverance of Capt. Isaac Stewart," in *A True and Wonderful Narrative of the Surprising Captivity and Remarkable Deliverance of Mrs. Frances Scott* . . . (Boston, 1786), 19–24 (additional editions of Stewart's captivity narrative appeared in 1799, 1800, and 1811); *A Narrative of the Captivity and Sufferings of Benjamin Gilbert and His Family Who Were Surprised by the Indians, and Taken from Their Farms, on the Frontiers of Pennsylvania, in the Spring, 1780* (Philadelphia, 1784); as well as David Humphreys's *Life of Major-General Israel Putnam: Presented to the Society of the Cincinnati and*

War cries rend the night air. Muskets echo through the dark. A rain of burning arrows sets fields and houses aflame. Wielding muskets and toma-hawks, dark forms burst through barricaded doors and windows. Resistance is bitter but brief. Shrieks replace war cries as the weak and infirm are murdered, their loved ones watching, helpless to stay the massacre. Young mothers, their infants at their breasts, are scalped, the babes' brains bashed out, hatchets buried in the heads of watching children. Gore and blood mark the sites. Those not killed are carried off along with the farm's livestock and grain. With no time to mourn or bury their dead, captives are force-marched through woods and swirling streams. Complaints and tears are met with torture and death. A young boy, weeping uncontrollably after seeing his three-year-old brother's head bashed against a wall, is tomahawked and scalped. A man too weak to bear the heavy burdens the savages heap upon his back is summarily executed. Those who seek to escape face deaths even more terrifying. Some have their bellies ripped open and their entrails burned before their eyes. Others are tor-tured, red-hot irons cutting, piercing, and tearing the flesh from their breasts, hands, arms, and legs. Still others are thrown into roaring fires and held down with pitchforks or buried up to their heads, around which fires are built until their brains literally boil.[25]

This was how European American descriptions of frontier warfare, fused with the earlier genre of captivity narratives, depicted Native Americans' heart-less slaughter of innocent white settlers. "To be cast into the Power of Savages,

---

Then Published for the General Public (Hartford, Conn., 1788). It is worth noting that David Humphreys printed Carey's collection of frontier narratives and that Noah Webster reprinted an excerpt of Humphreys's *Essay on the Life of the Honorable Major General Israel Putnam* that dealt specifically with the case of a European American woman sold by Native Americans to French Canadian Catholics as a slave. See "Review of New Publications: Essay on the Life of the Honorable Major General Israel Putnam. . . ," *American Magazine*, I (1788), 799–809, esp. 801–804. For other captivity narratives that circulated in Philadelphia in the 1780s and 1790s, see Mary Lewis Kinnan, *True Narrative of the Sufferings of Mary Kinnan, Who Was Taken Prisoner by the Shawnee Nation of Indians . . .* (Elizabethtown, N.J., 1795); and [Susannah Willard], *The Captive American; or, A Narrative of the Sufferings of Mrs. Johnson, during Four Years Captivity, with the Indians and French . . .* (Carlisle, Pa., [1797]). Ebersole, *Captured by Texts,* discusses a number of these captivity narratives. His readings differ somewhat from mine.

25. See, for example, "Affecting History, Etc.," 5–6, esp. 6, "Sufferings of Peter Williamson, One of the Settlers in the Back Parts of Pennsylvania . . . ," 19–31, esp. 21, 26, "Remarkable Adventures of Jackson Johonnot, a Soldier," 31–42, and "Account of the Dreadful Devastation of the Wyoming Settlements, in July 1778," 42–48, all in Carey, ed., *Affecting History*.

who, from Infancy, are taught a Hardness of Heart, which deprives them of the common Feelings of Humanity, is enough to intimidate the firmest Mind," one narrative begins; "But when we hear of helpless Women and Children torn from their Homes, and dragged into the Wilderness, we shudder at the Thought, and are bound to acknowledge our infinite Obligations to the Almighty, that we are so much more enlightened than these unhappy Wretches of the Desert." "Terrible and shocking to human nature were the barbarities daily committed by these savages!" another narrative reported. "Scarce did a day pass but some unhappy family or other fell victims to savage cruelty. Terrible, indeed, it proved." In one family, marauding Indians "without the least remorse" scalped the parents and their five children. "Nor could the tears, the shrieks, or cries of poor innocent children, prevent their horrid massacre." Another narrative reported an attack upon the farmstead of an elderly man, during which the marauders were reported to have slaughtered his four small children and scalped his wife before his eyes. But, "inhuman and horrid as this was, it did not satisfy them; for when they had murdered the poor woman, they acted with her in such a brutal manner, as decency will not permit me to mention." At still another cabin, having killed a farmer, his wife, and their seven children, the raiders cut the bodies into pieces and fed them to the farmer's hogs.[26]

As bloodthirsty sadists, the murderers of nursing mothers and babies, Native Americans would appear incapable of sinking any lower. But they could. Since Columbus's initial reports to the Spanish Crown, Native Americans had been accused of cannibalism, accusations that were then used to justify Europe's brutal wars of conquest. What Columbus started, North American captivity and frontier warfare narratives continued. Rapt readers were entertained with tales of unspeakable acts—such as those of a band of Indian warriors, who, having killed a woman and her nine children and scalped her husband, began to

---

26. *Narrative of the Captivity and Sufferings of Benjamin Gilbert,* [iv]; "Sufferings of Peter Williamson," 20–25, "Account of the Sufferings of Massy Herbeson, and Her Family . . . ," 15–18, esp. 16, both in Carey, ed., *Affecting History.* See, as well, examples of "horrid barbarity" in the "Narrative of the Adventures of Capt. Isaac Stewart" (ibid., 12–14, esp. 12) or of butchery and the scattering of body parts in "Account of the Dreadful Devastation of the Wyoming Settlements," 42–48, esp. 47. Elsewhere in the Gilbert narrative, the narrator complains of what it called "the customary cruelty [Indians] exercised upon Captives on entering their Towns." "The Indians, Men Women, and Children," the narrative explained, "collect together, bringing Clubs and Stones, in order to beat them, which they usually do with great Severity, by Way of Revenge for their Relations who have been slain . . . until . . . wearied with the cruel Sport" *(Narrative of Benjamin Gilbert,* 24).

roast him before he had died and "then, like cannibals, for want of other food, eat [sic] his whole body, and of his head made, what they called, an Indian pudding." The ultimate European taboo, cannibalism emerged as the fundamental mark of Native American otherness.[27]

And still tales of brutalities multiplied, proving that Native American cruelty knew no bounds. Take one of the narratives Mathew Carey published in the mid-1790s—complete with a graphic illustration. Two innocent young girls, left alone while their industrious father tended his fields and their mother and younger sisters visited a neighbor, were seized by two Conestoga braves, who, disagreeing as to which sister belonged to which brave, took their dispute to the tribal council. The council resolved that, having brought dissention into the tribe, the girls should be killed, "agreeably," Carey added, "to the abominable usage of the savages." Carey then presented the inhuman scene:

> These furies assisted by their comrades, stripped the forlorn girls, already convulsed with apprehensions, and tied each to a sapling, with their hands as high extended above their heads as possible; and then pitched them from their knees to their shoulders, with upwards of six hundred of the sharpened splinters [dipped, we are told, in mulled turpentine] . . . which, at every puncture, were attended with screams of distress, that echoed and re-echoed through the wilderness. And then to complete the infernal tragedy, the splinters, all standing erect on the bleeding victims, were every one set fire, and exhibited a scene of monstrous misery, beyond the power of speech to describe, or even the imagination to conceive. It was not until near three hours had elapsed from the commencement of their torments, and that they had lost almost every resemblance of the human form, that these helpless virgins sunk in the arms of their deliverer, Death.[28]

27. "Sufferings of Peter Williamson," in Carey, ed., *Affecting History,* 25. Peter Hulme discusses the invention of the word "cannibal" based on myths and fears of the Caribs whom Columbus encountered on his first voyage and the significance of its supplanting the earlier Greek anthropology (Hulme, *Colonial Encounters: Europe and the Native Caribbean, 1492–1797* [London, 1986], chap. 1). Interestingly, by the mid-nineteenth century, comic almanacs, published primarily for a youthful lower- and lower-middle-class urban male audience, began to joke about cannibalism, associating the eating of Indians with that mythic folk hero, Davy Crockett. See Carroll Smith-Rosenberg, "Davy Crockett as Trickster: Pornography, Liminality, and Symbolic Inversion in Victorian America," *Journal of Contemporary History,* XVII (1971), 325–350, rpt. in Smith-Rosenberg, *Disorderly Conduct: Images of Gender in Victorian America* (New York, 1985), 90–108.

28. "Affecting History, Etc.," 5–6, in Carey, ed., *Affecting History;* "Cruelty of Savages," *American Museum,* I (1787), 329–332.

But, as Carey's Philadelphia readers knew all too well, by the 1790s, the Conestogas had long been driven from their lands in eastern Pennsylvania. The few Conestoga communities that remained lived peacefully among their white neighbors, tenants of the Penn family. Far from being perpetrators, it was Conestogas who were the victims of European American vigilante violence, for it was a peaceful Conestoga farming community that the Paxton Boys descended upon in the 1760s, massacring the inhabitants and then marching on to Philadelphia with their threats of arson and mayhem. Carey's narrative reverses the flow of violence, making perpetrators into victims and justifying white fear of red Others.

How can we characterize these frontier narratives through which effaced memories resurface? "Chiaroscuro" is a term that comes to mind. Flashes of sudden brightness—a woman's nursing breast, the face of a sleeping babe, of a terrified young girl, dramatically lit by the flames of burning buildings or, more horribly, by fires consuming bound victims. All these figures stand out in stark contrast to a dark and bloody background—charred remains of torched buildings and human bodies, pools of red blood staining well-scrubbed kitchen floors, black war paint smeared across savage red faces. On the narratives' pages, one finds no nuanced shading, no subtle coloring, only the stark contrasts of white and black and red. Native Americans are represented as the antithesis of the pious and civilized European American, blood-red mirror images of the enlightened white man. No native nobility shines forth, no savage love of liberty or honorable courage, no sign of mercy or benevolence. Native American husbandry, commodious native villages surrounded by carefully cultivated fields, their fine cheeses and well-bred livestock are never acknowledged—nor are Iroquois and Cherokee constitution-building skills. Rather, Native Americans are presented as creatures of the night, creeping through the wilderness. Their howls and shrieks resound through the dark, striking terror into settlers.[29]

Food, cooked or raw, marks the presence or absence of civilization. It does not surprise us, then, that white captives find Native American food inedible—raw, filthy, and revolting. At one point, readers are told, "their Provisions, notwithstanding it was a Season of great Plenty, was often Deer Guts, dried with the Dung, and all boiled together, which they consider strong and wholesome Food." Proclaimed savages by their food, they were proclaimed savages as

29. "Account of the Wyoming Settlements," 42, 46, "Remarkable Adventures of Jackson Johonnot," 37, "Sufferings of Peter Williamson," 21–24, all in Carey, ed., *Affecting History*.

well by their lack of civilized speech. Their conversations are repeatedly declared "unintelligible," a "Jargon of Words." In these and many other ways, European American frontier narratives deny Native Americans' claim to a shared humanity. Never do European Americans express sympathy for Native Americans, although pathos and sentimentality dominate their narratives. Never do they admit that Native Americans might feel sorrow for the loss of home and kinsmen, although desolated fields and dead Native American bodies are frequently noted. Throughout the eighteenth century, the ability both to feel sorrow and to extend sympathy characterized persons of refinement, civility, and a native nobility. They signified sameness, connection within the eighteenth century's increasingly complex world. They were the glue that purportedly held the civilized, Christian world together. But they were seldom, if ever, extended to Native Americans, those sadistic "barbarians," those savage animals. No civilized person could sympathize with them![30]

When examples of Native Americans' extending sympathy to their captives occasionally break through to the surface of the texts, they are unacknowledged or explained away. When a chief gives his horse to a weary woman captive, it is seen only as another example of Indian cruelty because the horse is "dangerous to ride" and frightens the woman. When a Native American family dresses their adopted white daughter in native finery, including a hat with gold trim, the clothes are condemned for making the child appear savage. The many Native American villages destroyed by General Sullivan in his slash-and-burn campaign in western Pennsylvania and New York during the Revolution are noted only to indicate the "natural" desolation of Native American lands. That fields, now abandoned because of war, had been carefully cultivated or that a native family could produce seventy-five bushels of corn in one summer—far beyond the skills of European American farmers—are mentioned only to indicate that this land would make good settlements for white farmers.[31]

In contrast, narratives constantly stress the industry of European American

---

30. *Narrative of Benjamin Gilbert*, 46, 61, 76. At another time, the Gilbert family narrator remarked, "They caught some Fish and made Soup of them, but Rebecca could eat none of it, as it was dressed without Salt, and with all the Carelessness of Indians" (62). See, as well, "Adventures of Jackson Johonnot," in Carey, ed., *Affecting History*, 40. Claude Lévi-Strauss places great emphasis on cooked food as a symbol and central characteristic of civilization, raw food of savagery (Strauss, *The Raw and the Cooked*, trans. John Weightman and Doreen Weightman (New York, 1975).

31. *Narrative of Benjamin Gilbert*, 14–15, 61.

farmers. How young men, come to America as indentured servants, have become the owners of rich farms and full barns through their hard work and resourcefulness is a repeated theme. Thus frontier narratives not only darken Native Americans; they enlighten western settlers—those dirt-poor farmers the elite eastern press elsewhere vilified with such fervor. Gone from the pages of captivity narratives are any references to lazy, illiterate, and drunken squatters, to "Horse Thieves Cattle Stealers, Hog Stealers" and their "mongrel children." Rather, we find European American settlers presented as industrious and pious churchgoers, their daughters, not prostitutes, as Charles Woodmason charged, but "helpless virgins." Being victims of Native American savagery rendered frontier families honorable members of the American body politic, deserving government protection and the sympathy of genteel urban readers. Offering readers a constituting Other, these narratives sought to unite European Americans across regional and class divides, solidifying their self-image and national identity as white Christians—if only on their pages and only momentarily.[32]

Late-eighteenth-century captivity narratives carried two clear messages. First, Native Americans are European Americans' absolute, contrasting Others. Racial hierarchies structure the western world, securing social order and reinforcing European Americans' fundamental sense of themselves as civilized bearers of white, Christian culture. Second, Native Americans must be driven beyond human settlement, barred forever from the new republican body politic. As one narrative declared, "May the remembrance of my sufferings, escapes, perseverance through divine support, and repeated mercies received, kindle a flame of heroism in the breast of many an American youth, and induce him . . . to exert himself to defend the worthy inhabitants on the frontiers from the depredations of savages; whose horrid mode of war is a scene to be deprecated by civilized nature, whose tender mercies are cruelties and whose faith is by no means to be depended on, though pledged in the most solemn treaties." In this way, eastern publishers adopted the rhetoric and goals of western set-

---

32. "Remarkable Adventures of Jackson Johonnot," 31–32, "Affecting History, Etc.," 5, "Remarkable Encounter of a White Man with Two Indians . . . ," 9–11, esp. 10, "Sufferings of Peter Williamson," 23, all in Carey, ed., *Affecting History*. This new image of frontier settlers reversed Benjamin Franklin's admonitions against driving productive farming families west by failing to support manufacturing (see Chapter 1, above). It also reverses eastern elite condemnations of frontiersmen as a "mongrel race" no better than savage natives. On the other hand, the encouragement of western settlements was essential if the land speculations so many of the eastern elite engaged in were to prove profitable.

tlers. It would seem that representations of the savage Indian Other had unified white men, East and West.[33]

ENGENDERING RACIAL DISORDER

But had they? Did they reinforce Revolutionary visions of the new American as brave, virile, and heroic or liberal ones of him as a self-reliant entrepreneur and bearer of Enlightenment culture, thus helping to solidify a coherent new national identity?

No. Presenting the new nation locked in a bloody battle between violent savages and defenseless, suffering women and children, the captivity narratives had the unintended effect of marginalizing and disempowering European American men and of presenting European American women as capable of the very savage behavior they suffered from. Finally, the America these narratives represented was neither productive nor urbane but rather a treacherous and uncivilized land, filled with dark woods, barren fields, howling demons, and weeping victims. This was not the national image the urban classes wished to internalize—or to present to Europe's judging eyes.

To explore these points further, let us return to the captivity and frontier narratives. European American men rarely appear in these narratives. Indeed, of the nine narratives Carey published in 1794, five focus on women and children. Only one focuses on a heroic soldier (Jackson Johonnot). When European American men appear, they are almost always represented as fearful, infirm, and ineffective. Those who do attempt to defend their wives and children are invariably vanquished. We see them lying dead in their own gore, their families murdered, their homes and barns in flames. Others surrender or, even more shamefully, flee, abandoning homes and families.

This latter was the case of the Reverend John Corbly, a Baptist minister in western Pennsylvania whose narrative appeared both in Carey's captivity volume and his *American Museum*. As Corbly reported in a letter to a brother minister in Philadelphia, while on his way to conduct services accompanied by his wife and children, he was surprised by a band of "savages." Terrified, Corbly fled into the woods, where he watched the Indians shoot his wife, murder and scalp the "little infant" at her breast, and sink the hatchet into the brains of the six-year-old son at her side. "A daughter, besides the infant," he reported, "they also killed and scalped." Two other daughters were also scalped, though both "miraculously" survived. When the Indians left the scene, Corbly rushed to his

33. "Remarkable Adventures of Jackson Johonnot," 41–42, ibid.

family's side, but finding them covered in gore, "I instantly fainted away, and was borne off by a friend." (One wonders where the friend was during this scene of carnage—like Corbly, hiding in a tree?)[34]

At no time does Corbly report remorse for failing to defend his family. Rather, he expresses sorrow for himself ("Oh the anguish of my soul!"), the inconvenience of having to care for the two scalped daughters who survived ("As you must think, I have had, and still have, a great deal of trouble and expense with them"), and a fatalistic resignation to God's will ("The government of the world and of the church is in his [Jehovah's] hands.—May it be taught the important lesson of acquiescing in all his dispensations"). These are not the responses one would expect from a heroic republican citizen. Indeed, if anyone plays a heroic role in this narrative, it is Corbly's wife, who, even as a native warrior is about to tomahawk her, shouts to her husband to flee into the woods, thus saving his life. Underscoring this feminization of Corbly, his narrative takes the classic feminine form of an epistolary romance. Entitled "*Sufferings* of the Rev. John Corbly and Family" and presented as a letter Corbly wrote to a "brother" minister, it is filled with tears and pathos designed to play on its readers' sympathies.[35]

If Corbly fails the test of republican *virtu*, so, too, does Peter Williamson, another victim of Native American brutality whose story was also widely reprinted. Terrified when a war band surrounds his farm, Williamson surrenders without a struggle, only to watch in shock as Native Americans burn his home and barns to the ground. The savages then force Williamson to become a beast of burden. Carrying the loot the band stole from his own and his neighbors' farms, he continues to watch as the war band goes from one of his neighbor's farms to another, torturing and murdering, by Williamson's count, dozens of women, children, and infirm men. One old man they had captured was repeatedly stripped naked, his body painted with obscenities, his hair pulled from his head. "In vain were all his tears," Williamson continued, "for daily did they tire themselves with the various means they tried to torment him; sometimes tying him to a tree, and whipping him; at other times, scorching his furrowed cheeks with red-hot coals, and burning his legs quite to the knees." Williamson's only response to all these horrors is to weep and wait for God's deliverance. Wrapping himself in pathos, he writes, "I suffered their brutalities, without being

34. "Sufferings of the Rev. John Corbly and Family from the Indians . . . ," in Carey, ed., *Affecting History*, 7–8. Carey also reprinted the Corbly story with the title "Cruelty of Savages" (*American Museum*, I [1787], 329–332).

35. "Sufferings of the Rev. John Corbly and Family," in Carey, ed., *Affecting History*, 8 (emphasis added).

allowed to vent my anguish otherwise, than by shedding silent tears. . . . How I underwent these tortures has been a matter of wonder to me, but God enabled me to wait with more than common patience for the deliverance I daily prayed for."[36]

Ironically, women were virtually the only European Americans to heroically resist "Indian savagery." Indeed, Elizabeth Bozarth, a farm woman from western Pennsylvania, accomplished what no man seems to have in these narratives —she organized community resistance, gathering her neighbors together in her stone farmhouse for defense. When the attack came, every male defender fell. Unfazed by the bodies and blood surrounding her, Bozarth responded quickly: she seized her ax and met the invaders at her door. Driving the blade through the skulls of two Indians and the belly of a third, which scattered his entrails around her room, she chased the "savages" from her home. Significantly, whereas captivity narratives about men are entitled "Affecting History of Dreadful Distresses" or "Sufferings of," Elizabeth Bozarth's tale is called "Signal Prowess of a Woman."[37]

Massey Herbeson, the wife of a Continental soldier away at war, fared less well than Elizabeth Bozarth but nevertheless displayed far greater courage and resourcefulness than the men represented in the captivity narratives. Herbeson and her three children were captured during one of the engagements that reduced the Ohio Valley to a bloody battlefield for nearly thirty years. Her two sons, weeping hysterically, were immediately killed. Massey and her daughter were then forced to march across Pennsylvania's mountains. Rather than crying and praying like Williamson, Herbeson plotted revenge. Unable to steal either a rifle or tomahawk to kill her abductors, she finally slipped the ropes that bound her and escaped—leaving her daughter behind.[38]

Depictions of Elizabeth Bozarth, bloody ax in hand, Massey Herbeson, plotting murder and abandoning her remaining infant in order to secure her own escape, were scarcely the picture of a Christian and civilized America that the bourgeois press wished to project to a watching Europe. Nor was the picture of Maria and Christina Manheim, tortured until "they had lost almost every resemblance of the human form." Such images only confirmed Europeans' worst suspicions. America was a crude and violent land. Far from ennobling its inhabitants, the New World rendered its white men fainting cow-

36. "Sufferings of Peter Williamson," ibid., 21–25.

37. "Signal Prowess of a Woman, in Combat with Some Indians . . . ," in Carey, ed., *Affecting History*, 11–12.

38. "Account of the Sufferings of Massey Herbeson," in Carey, ed., *Affecting History*, 15–18.

ards and its white women ruthless slayers. At the Revolutionary War's end, George Washington called on the Republic's new citizens to assume the role of "lords and proprietors of a vast tract of continent . . . actors on the most conspicuous theater . . . designed for the display of human greatness." The frontiersmen represented in the captivity narratives failed to assume that role. They failed, as well, in their second, equally important role, to underscore the differences that rendered Native Americans the absolute, defining Other. On the pages of frontier narratives, differences evaporated into sameness. We see this at the end of Peter Williamson's narrative, when Williamson, finally managing to escape, returns home. On seeing him emerge from the woods, his wife flees in horror, thinking him an Indian, so savage has his appearance become. Was the captivity narratives' underlying message exactly the one it was designed to refute—that the distinction between Native and European Americans was merely a matter of clothing and surface appearance, that the frontier turned all men into savages?

THE NOBLE SAVAGE—EUROPE'S IDEALIZED AMERICAN

Alternative representations of Native Americans that appeared in the eastern press further confused and destabilized both Native and European American identities. Horror and fear were not European Americans' only response to natives. Heirs of the European Enlightenment, literate European Americans were heirs to the romantic European vision of Native Americans as "Nature's Noblemen." To maintain their claims to Enlightenment culture, European Americans could not completely reject that vision. Otherwise the distance polished easterners wished to maintain between themselves and ax-wielding frontierswomen was in danger of evaporating. Critical European observers might begin to think all Americans were heartless beasts. Moreover, as already argued, many educated European Americans genuinely admired Native American knowledge of the continent and its resources. To extend their rule westward, a number of magazine contributors insisted, European Americans needed to work with Native Americans rather than against them.

Ironically, given the captivity and frontier narratives' presentation of Native Americans as a guttural and illiterate people, the magazines made learning native languages key to the acquisition of native knowledge and also to establishing European Americans' independence from Europe, their connection to the American continent, and their cultural uniqueness. European Americans, magazine after magazine insisted, must turn their backs on the dead languages of Europe. To become truly American—to learn the secrets of America's woods, how to navigate its rivers, hunt, or plant in virgin land—they must study native languages and benefit from Native Americans' willingness to share their knowledge.[39] A *Columbian Magazine* essay, possibly written by Francis Hopkinson, called on patriotic readers to master "the tongues of the Six Nations, Chickasaws, Cherokees, etc." instead of the dead ones in vogue in Europe and Great Britain. From Native Americans steeped in the lore of America's forests, European Americans would learn how to use native herbs to cure their diseases. Knowledge of Native American languages would help them explore, settle, and develop American land and natural resources. "Among these tribes of savages," Hopkinson assured Massachusetts readers, "there is more useful knowledge of our country . . . than in Europe, Asia and Africa." In much the same spirit, Noah Webster (with Hopkinson, long an advocate of dispensing with Greek and Latin and learning native languages) praised Jonathan Edwards for mastering a number of New England languages and for preparing an English-Muhhekaneew dictionary. Indeed, Webster's praise of Edwards's linguistic skills echoes his celebration of the British linguist Sir William Jones, a renowned master of Sanskrit and other Indian languages. If Englishmen strove to master the languages of old India, should not European Americans master "new" American Indian languages? How different these images of Native Americans, possessed of valuable knowledge and generously sharing it with white explorers, were from those that haunted the bloody pages of the captivity and frontier narratives.[40]

39. See, for example, "American Natural History," *Massachusetts Magazine,* I (1789), 67–70, 136. Of course, European Americans had been doing just this since John Rolfe had married Pocahontas and the Pilgrims landed on Cape Cod. It seems odd that late-eighteenth-century magazines would act as if these were novel suggestions. On the other hand, it was just this borrowing of native practices that the eastern elite used to denigrate frontiersmen and -women as little better than the savages they lived among. And so, once again in the political magazines, confusion followed contradiction.

40. "Review of New Publications: Observations on the Language of the Muhhekaneew or Mohegan Indians, by Jonathan Edwards . . . ," *American Magazine,* I (1788), 587–590; "An Account of the Life and Writings of Sir William Jones, Knt.: A Celebrated Literary Character . . . ," *American Magazine,* I (1787), 36–38 (for a longer discussion of this essay, see Chapter 7). For Hopkinson's comments, see Doctor Plainsense, "To the Editor of the Columbian Magazine," *Columbian Magazine,* I (1787), 805–806, esp. 806. In this vein, another magazine contributor reported that being able to speak with the Assinipolis, the Naudowessies, and the Chippewas had helped him explore the northern reaches of the Great Plains and discover the source of America's four great rivers—the St. Lawrence, the Mississippi, and what he called the Bourbon and the Oregon. "It is an instance not to be paralleled on the other three quarters of the globe," he wrote, "that four rivers of such magnitude should take their rise together, and each

Other European Americans accepted the Romantic European belief that, as children of the new Eden, Native Americans had garnered true nobility and moral sensitivity from their surroundings. Magazine contributors frequently praised indigenous Americans' "native" honesty, integrity, and dignity, urging European Americans to emulate "native" virtues. (We should not forget that charges of duplicity and chicanery were commonplace among urban merchants and shopkeepers and that classic republican texts continued to denounce the new ways of fiscal capitalism and bourgeois display.) Noah Webster, whose *American Magazine* contained by far the most essays on Native Americans, regaled his readers with stories of native integrity and generosity. In one, he described the fate of a young boy who had been carried off by Native Americans and, years later, returned the very model of youthful republican virtue. While a captive, Webster explained, the boy had developed a natural sense of dignity, had become honest and transparent in all his dealings, lost any inclination to lie or steal, and indeed was always surprised to find a person saying one thing and meaning another. In short, "he knew not any thing but honesty and undistinguished frankness and integrity." Despite frequent representations of Native Americans as liars and thieves, including essays he had himself published, Webster insisted, "Moral principles seem to be as perfect in them as in more enlightened nations." Referencing Locke's defense of private property, he continued: "The savages have as correct ideas of *meum* and *tuum,* of theft, trespass, etc. and are as careful to guard private property from invasion, by laws and penalties, as any civilized people." Indeed, he concluded, "Among those tribes which have had no intercourse with civilized nations, and which have not been deceived by the tricks of traders, the common arts of cheating, by which millions of enlightened people get a living or a fortune, are wholly unknown." If European Americans were to become the "new men" that Crèvecoeur envisioned, Webster's essay implied, they must eschew the deceitfulness and chicanery they had learned in Europe and become like these noble savages.[41]

Isaiah Thomas agreed. Although, like Webster and Carey, Thomas had published terrifying captivity narratives, he also published tales of native nobility—and pathos. One of Thomas's stories described the fate of a young British soldier taken captive during the Seven Years' War, at a time when British and European American soldiers were brothers-in-arms. About to be tomahawked

after running seperate courses, discharge their waters into different oceans at the distance of two thousand miles from their sources." See Carver, "Sources of the St. Lawrence, Mississippi, Bourbon, and Oregon, the Four Capital Rivers of North America," *Massachusetts Magazine,* I (1789), 113–114, esp. 114.

41. "Morality," *American Magazine,* I (1788), 526–530, esp. 526–528.

by two savage warriors, the young officer was saved by an aged chief because of his likeness to the chief's dead son. Adopting the young Englishman, the chief tended his wounds, instructed him in native customs and skills, and gradually transformed him into a noble inhabitant of the American forests. In perhaps the most striking inversion of the captivity trope, Thomas permits the chief to speak, presenting Boston readers with the spectacle of a Native American instructing the young officer not only in forest lore but in generosity and morality. "What wast thou when I took thee to my hut?" the chief asks. "Thy hands were those of an infant; they were fit neither to procure thee sustenance nor safety. Thy soul was in utter darkness; thou wast ignorant of every thing; and thou owest all things to me." Wise in the ways of the forest, Thomas's chief is even wiser in matters of the heart. On learning that the British soldier's father is old and infirm and that the young man longs to see him before he dies, the chief frees the young man to return home. "Dost thou know that I have been a father?" the aging chief asks, adding, "I am a father no more—I saw my son fall in battle—he fought at my side—I saw him expire; but he died like a man—He was covered with wounds when he fell dead at my feet. . . . Go, return back, that thy father may still have pleasure when he sees the sun rise in the morning, and the trees blossom in the spring." Distinctions between Native and European Americans fall away in this story. Native Americans love their sons as European Americans do. They are touched by sympathy, can act with grace and nobility—even to one of the nation that killed their chief's son.[42]

Yet, although it ennobles the Native American, the essay suggests a tragic end. Invoking the trope of the vanishing race, it looks forward to the destruction of Native American people and ways. "Wilt thou then go over to thy nation, and take up the hatchet against us?" the chief asks on parting with the soldier. "The officer replied, 'that he would rather lose his own life than take away that of his deliverer.'" Yet Thomas's readers knew perfectly well that, as Britain's heirs to the new world, European Americans would take up the hatchet and drive the chief and his tribe from the land. The European American as a white "infant" would grow up to become a "town destroyer." Thomas thus transformed the fear-invoking image of the savage Native American warrior into a subject of pathos, a tragic specter at the feast of European Ameri-

42. "A Remarkable Story of an Indian Warrior and a Young British Officer," *Massachusetts Magazine,* I (1789), 281–283. Note the staged, archaic language of the European pastoral. Of course, Thomas might have pirated this "American" story from a British publication, though the archaic language might also have underscored European Americans' vision of Native Americans as archaic/primitive figures, doomed to pass from the American scene. Certainly, that is the overall message of Thomas's story.

can greatness. But, in doing so, Thomas rendered both the Native and the European American subject multiple, contradictory, and remarkably like one another—savage predator/generous deliverer, grateful infant/future town destroyer. One is left to wonder, Who was the most savage, the most dangerous predator?[43]

None exemplified the noble savage–as–tragic figure more poignantly than Logan, a wise and generous Mingo chief bent low by the murder of his wife and children. Logan's story is simple. He had long befriended European American settlers, working to keep the peace between his tribe and them. One day, however, Colonel Cresap, a renegade frontiersman "infamous for the many murders he had committed," fired on the canoe carrying Logan's wife and children. All were killed. In his final speech, Logan cried out, "I appeal to any white man to say, if ever he entered Logan's cabin hungry, and he gave him not meat. If ever he came cold and naked, and he clothed him not." Logan led his tribe against those he had so long befriended—and was defeated. Rather than continue a futile war, Logan acknowledged European American military supremacy and wisely urged his young braves to make peace. But, riven by the loss of his family, Logan could not join in the treaty signing. He disappeared, withdrawing from all human contact. "Col. Cresap . . . in cold blood and unprovoked, murdered all the relations of Logan, not sparing even my women and children. There runs not a drop of my blood in the veins of any living creature. . . . Who is there to mourn for Logan? Not one."[44]

Logan's oration captured European American imaginations. Jefferson featured it prominently in his *Notes on Virginia,* using it to prove that America's indigenous people were as capable of eloquent oratory as any European. It was endlessly reprinted in *McGuffey's Readers,* memorized and performed by generations of European American children in elocution classes, and printed in numerous magazines and newspapers, Webster's *American Magazine's* 1788 republication being perhaps the first. Defeated in battle, deprived of heirs, a disembodied spirit haunting America's woods, Logan could safely haunt the pages of the new urban press.[45]

Logan's speech both mimics and inverts European American captivity narratives. Frontiersmen become "infamous murderers" despised by pious, law-

43. Ibid.; and see Ferguson's citation of Kiontwagky's (Cornplanter) speech in *American Enlightenment,* 165.

44. Philip J. Deloria, *Playing Indian* (New Haven, Conn., 1998), 64–65. Logan's speech, Deloria tells us, was "the founding statement of the . . . vanishing Indian" trope.

45. "Eloquence of the Natives of This Country, from Mr. Jefferson's *Notes on Virginia,*" *American Magazine,* I (1788), 106–108.

abiding eastern readers. Native American women and children become their innocent victims. The European American reader is led to identify with Logan, share his sense of outrage, pity his loneliness. "Pity" is the key word. Logan emerges as a character in a romance—brave and swift in his demand for revenge but, when revenge is denied, draped in pathos. Webster's comments (following his excerpt from Jefferson's *Notes on Virginia*) go even further in capturing the spirit of European American identification with Logan. "The instantaneous transition from undaunted courage, to unaffected sorrow . . . is inconceivably beautiful," Webster notes, cultivating a sympathetic response that will prove his readers as noble and refined as Logan—or, more to the point, as refined as British readers well-versed in enacting sympathy. "A Hero, that in battle *never knows* fear, is feelingly alive to parental grief . . . he is softened into the *man*, the *hopeless parent*." "We cannot read this address of Logan," Webster continues, "without feeling the most generous emotions—We love him for his hospitality, peaceable disposition and unshaken attachment to the whites—We detest the murder of his family, and can hardly withhold a sympathetic tear for his loss . . . his manly grief and heroic bravery extort from us the highest respect and admiration."[46]

THE NOBLE SAVAGE/VANISHING Indian trope serves European Americans in many ways. It presents an ennobled vision of America and its primeval inhabitants: independent, resourceful, wise, and generous. In manners and rhetoric, they are masters of an American oratory that is clear, unadorned, yet elegant and moving—in Jefferson's words, "little inferior to the sublimest passages of the Caledonian Bard [Ossian]." The trope figures European Americans as the adopted sons and heirs of these archaic figures, tutored by them in the ways of nature, inspired by them to scorn the corruptions and excessive refinement of European culture. At the same time, it presents the Native American as a powerless victim. Defeated, he will pass into history, mourned not by young warriors but by European American schoolchildren mouthing words whose full significance they cannot comprehend. In this way, European Americans could confess sorrow at the demise of these noble people without directly admitting their complicity in that demise. It was only "natural" that Native Americans would vanish in the presence of a superior, far more modern people. As Supreme Court Justice Joseph Story expressed in an 1828 decision:

46. Noah Webster, remarks, "Eloquence of the Natives of This Country," *American Magazine*, I (1788), 107–108.

"By a law of nature, they [Native Americans] seem destined to a slow, but sure extinction. Everywhere, at the approach of the white man they fade away."[47]

But Logan's story was actually far more interesting than either Jefferson's or Webster's retelling would lead one to surmise. The late 1760s and early 1770s saw Virginia and Pennsylvania engaged in a vicious internecine war over control of western Pennsylvania. Both sent surveyors into the area. Land speculators quickly followed and, after them, a relentless surge of settlers. Hundreds of thousands of acres were at stake. Border violence broke out. Shawnee and Mingo leaders strove to keep the peace, but, as Gregory Nobles points out, "frontiersmen's preparations for war took on a momentum of their own." Professing fear of native attacks, frontier settlers attacked peaceful native villages. Lord Dunmore's War commenced and, as already noted, bled into the American Revolution. It was during these struggles that Logan's family was killed. And it was at this time, as well, Nobles continues, that a racialized American identity emerged along the frontier. The Revolution, with all of its atrocities, established the earliest and most salient context for the invention of a collective European American identity. At the center of that shared identity was a commitment to rapid western expansion, racial separation and removal, and, when it seemed necessary, the extirpation of Native American peoples. Collective Indian rights and identities lost their force in American law, and the foundation was laid, first, for decades of racial conflict and, second, for the dispossession of Native Americans from their place in the American landscape.[48]

Telling Logan's story as Jefferson, Webster, and *McGuffey's Readers* told it—

47. Ibid., 108; Deloria, *Playing Indian*, 64. Indeed, Noah Webster, despite the pathos he expresses for Logan's loss, puts the blame ultimately on Native American savagery. The affair began, Webster's excerpt told his New York readers, when two members of the Shawnee nation robbed and murdered a European American family. So provoked, it was only natural that frontiersmen "according to their custom, undertook to punish this outrage in a summary way." We must note two things here. First, Webster's excerpt represents the robbing and killing of a European American family, not their squatting on native land, as the "outrage." Second, it uses the pronoun "they" to distance New York readers from frontiersmen's "summary" behavior. Indeed, from the excerpt's perspective, an Indian always remains an Indian. Despite the deep sympathies Native American sufferings inspired in cultivated European American breasts, as presented in this excerpt, Native Americans remained savages, governed by their violent and uncontrollable instincts. "A savage," it explains, "rarely violates the laws of hospitality, till he has been injured; but after an injury, his passion for vengeance is uncontrollable. . . . Such injuries awakened all his feelings to vengeance, and like an untutored savage, he triumphs in revenge" (107).

48. Nobles, *American Frontiers*, 180–187, esp. 186.

that is, as a highly individualized tragedy perpetrated by an unnamed "infamous murderer" whom all right-feeling people condemned—effaced European Americans' rapacious desire for native lands and the racial violence from which both the murders and the new American nation emerged. Telling it as a story saturated in pathos served European Americans in yet other ways. It permitted them to simultaneously demonstrate their mastery of cultivated European sympathies, their claims to Native American eloquence (Logan's legacy to all Americans), and, finally, their military dominance (although the forces of the Ohio Confederacy were spreading terror along the frontier). In contradistinction to those frightening warriors, Jefferson and Webster's Logan emerged a mourning and far from threatening father. As Logan himself said so eloquently, "Who is there to mourn for Logan? Not one."

TROUBLING AMALGAMATIONS

Pairing the figure of the Native American—as—nurturing, grieving father, the magazines called forth another figure from America's mythic past: a nurturing mother, the female progenitor of the new race of European Americans—Pocahontas. As she emerged in popular imagination, Pocahontas, far more than Logan, embodied both cultural fusion and sexual "amalgamation." Certainly, as myths would have it, she had repeatedly risked her life to save John Smith's and those of Smith's struggling colonists. She had brought them food during the "starving time" and had even crept through the woods to warn them of Powhatan's approaching warriors. The "king's" favorite daughter, time and again she had appealed for these invaders' lives and for cooperation with them. Amenable to cultural exchange, when captured and held for ransom by the very men whose safety she had pleaded for, she piously converted to Christianity and married one of her captors. She was, indeed, a figure of fusion and amalgamation. As Noah Webster, appropriating Smith's seventeenth-century text to his eighteenth-century purposes, explained to his New York readers, she was "the first Christian ever of that nation, the first Virginian ever spake English, or had a child *in marriage* by an Englishman." This child, a son, raised in England as a gentleman, returned to Virginia in the 1640s to take his place as a wealthy planter. To this day, many Virginians proudly trace their heritage back to Pocahontas through her son and his daughter.[49]

49. "A Letter from Captain John Smith to the Queen," *American Magazine*, I (1788), 776–778. "Amalgamation" was the standard eighteenth- and early-nineteenth-century term of racial mixing. The word "miscegenation" was a neologism of the Civil War and Reconstruction.

As both a literal mother and an imagined "Indian Princess," Pocahontas served as the political progenitrix of Virginia. Her marriage to John Rolfe was viewed by Smith and other colonists as legitimating their settlement of Virginia. As Smith responded to James I's complaint about an Englishman's marrying "a savage," "This kingdom may rightly have a kingdom by her means." Of course, Powhatan's "kingdom" was not England. Pocahontas could not bequeath her father's kingdom to John Rolfe or their son, as Jamestown's settlers painfully discovered in 1622. Nevertheless, British settlers, imposing their understanding of hereditary monarchies onto Powhatan's chiefdom (with Webster following in their train), asserted that claim.[50]

It also led them to represent Pocahontas as their own European American princess, in fact, as America's only true princess. After all, Webster boasted, she had been presented at the Court of St. James's, where Queen Anne had formally acknowledged her, James I danced with her, and courtiers flocked to her side. And she had done all with unique grace and dignity. The shadow Pocahontas cast, stretching from Virginia's wild woods to the highest circles of British society, gave depth and legitimacy to European American claims to European gentility and refinement. Pocahontas did indeed fuse European and American cultures. Occupying a place of pride within European American mythology, she crowns the Capitol dome in Washington in statue form.

But Pocahontas, or rather her son and his descendants, fused not only cultures but blood. They literally embody miscegenation. Miscegenation can be seen positively as a celebration of connection, a fusing of Native and European American identities, the creation of a hybrid people with all the dynamic power hybridity can bring. But it also signaled the negation of critical categories of difference and of the social order grounded on those differences.

Rolfe and Smith were not the only European Americans to espouse marriage between white men and Native American women. A century later, a fellow Virginian, William Byrd, made a similar suggestion, though in a very different context. While surveying the western boundaries of Virginia and the Carolinas in the late 1730s, Byrd had extended contact with both European and Native American frontiersmen—and their women. Byrd suggested that the solution to repeated and costly frontier wars might lie in formal marriages between frontiersmen and Native American women. Those families and their descendants could then form a perpetual borderland between the two warring peoples—a point through which trade would pass, a buffer that would preserve peace between antagonistic cultures. It would become a true "middle ground."

50. Ibid.

Byrd had made his suggestion while unsuccessfully wooing an aristocratic British heiress. He certainly did not think of an interracial marriage for himself or for any in his social class. But, for the lower-class frontiersmen (squatters, Indian traders), the formal recognition of their sexual relations with Native American women might well promote the general good.[51]

An early-eighteenth-century gentleman like Byrd could play with such ideas (with Byrd, "play" may well be the appropriate term), but, in the more democratic times that followed the American Revolution and, later, during the Era of the Common Man, suggestions of lower-class marriage with Native Americans were angrily denounced. The children of such marriages would never be considered white; they would always be "half-breeds," more animal than human in their social standing. And this was just the charge the colonial eastern elite—Charles Woodmason, for example, or Crèvecoeur—had leveled at frontiersmen, insisting that their close relations with Native Americans marked them as equally uncivilized. The frontier refused amalgamation. Natty Bumppo said it all when he insisted time and again that, in spite of his leather stockings and lack of education and, in the face of his unexcelled knowledge of the forest, he was "a man without a cross." Difference implemented by exclusion lay at the heart of European Americans' sense of themselves, indeed, of their claims to the very name "American."[52]

Still, the late-eighteenth-century bourgeoisie did strongly identify with Pocahontas, at times using her as a displacement figure through which to discuss their relations with Great Britain. Webster, for example, ends his account of Pocahontas by describing a moment of confrontation between her, representing a virtuous, young America, and John Smith, an emblem of im-

51. William Byrd, *Histories of the Dividing Line between Virginia and North Carolina*, ed. William K. Boyd (New York, 1967), 114–116. Richard Slotkin discusses Byrd's sexual adventures along the Virginia/Carolina border and his suggestions about sexual liaisons between frontiersmen and Native Americans in *Regeneration through Violence*, 220–221. Fellow planter/aristocrat Robert Beverley agreed with Byrd. If British settlers had adopted Rolfe's model, he wrote in 1705, "the Colony, instead of all these Losses of Men on both sides, would have been increasing in Children to its Advantage." See Beverley, *The History and Present State of Virginia* (1705; Chapel Hill, N.C., 1947).

52. James Fenimore Cooper, *The Last of the Mohicans* (New York, 1981), 117. For a useful discussion of the phrase "without a cross" and issues of racial purity in Cooper, see Richard Hancuff, "Without a Cross: Writing the Nation in *The Last of the Mohicans*," in Hugh C. MacDougall, ed., *James Fenimore Cooper: His Country and His Art* (Oneonta, N.Y., 1999), 56–59. The Davy Crockett almanacs, published in the 1830s through the 1850s, illustrate (quite literally) the racism endemic in Jacksonian America (Smith-Rosenberg, "Davy Crockett as Trickster," *Journal of Contemporary History*, XVII [1971], 325–350).

perial Britain. Pocahontas, Webster explained, was deeply hurt when Smith failed to recognize her as his "daughter" when she arrived in London. The term "daughter" had great diplomatic significance to both Native Americans and British courtier/adventurers: it signified a deep-seated connection of one people with another. Meeting Smith at court, Pocahontas, with a "well set countenance," publicly turned her back on Smith and then, in an angry voice, demanded that he reaffirm the relationship of connection and interchangeability that she and Powhatan felt Smith had promised them while in Virginia. "You did promise, Powhatan, what was yours should be his, and he the like to you," she rebuked him; "you called him father being in his land a stranger, and by the same reason so must I do you . . . [but] fear you here I should call you father; I tell you then I will, and you shall call me child, and so I will be for ever and ever your countryman." Webster followed this description with a second scene of confrontation, in which Uttamatomakkin, Powhatan's ambassador to James I, confronted Smith with similar charges. "You gave Powhatan a white dog, which Powhatan fed as himself, but your king gave me nothing," Uttamatomakkin reminded Smith, adding simply, "I am better than your white dog." Webster comments, "How ought Christians to blush to be charged with *lying* and *ingratitude* by savages!" Logan's theme returns, the voice of the noble savage—honorable, generous, and betrayed—embodied in the voices of Powhatan, Pocahontas, and Uttamatomakkin. But, most specifically and significantly, Webster presents them as betrayed, not in their requests for goods ("your king gave me nothing"), but in their demand to be treated as the equals of Britain—in Pocahontas's case, as British, the equivalent of John Smith; in Powhatan's, as the equivalent of Britain's king. Indeed, Pocahontas's determined cry "I will be for ever and ever your countryman" insists on a sameness, an interchangeability born both of diplomatic negotiations ("you did promise Powhatan") and her marriage to John Rolfe.[53]

What was at stake in this exchange may seem a bit obscure to modern readers. I suspect it was quite clear to Webster and his readers. I read it as a displacement onto Pocahontas of European Americans' resentment of Britain's refusal, in the years following the Seven Years' War, to continue to consider European Americans as full British subjects, equals and thus interchangeable in all ways to British subjects resident in Great Britain ("I will be for ever and ever your countryman" said the "Virginian" to the British courtier). The issue is one of equivalency, sameness. The scene between Pocahontas and Smith, as reinscribed by Webster, can be read as the reenactment of European Americans' resentment of

53. "A Letter from Captain John Smith to the Queen," *American Magazine*, I (1788), 778.

two particular actions taken by the British government. These were the Proclamation Lines of 1763 and 1770, which limited European American settlement west of the lines as a way of preventing conflicts with Native Americans, and the Quebec Act of 1774, which granted religious toleration and civil rights to French Catholics and extended Canada's boundaries to the Ohio River. In the face of European Americans' (both frontier settlers and eastern speculators) assumption that the western territories were theirs by right of habitation and charter, the British government allocated those lands to Native Americans and placed their governance under the (French) Canadians. The passage of these acts led residents of the thirteen colonies to two disturbing realizations: that, on the one hand, the acts established a fundamental distinction between British subjects resident in Britain (who had the right to allocate American land to Native Americans if they so chose) and European Americans, who did not have an automatic right to those lands; and that, on the other hand, the British had established a fundamental equivalency between Europeans, Native Americans, and French Canadian Catholics. All were seen in Britain as equally subjects of (and to) the British Crown. By the 1770s, Alan Taylor explains, British administrators had begun to think of their empire as a compilation of multiple, divergent peoples whose interests the administrators had to balance as they governed for the well-being of the homeland and the greater good of the empire. They no longer privileged European American frontiersmen as British subjects who happened to reside along the Ohio rather than in England. Rather, they saw European Americans and Native Americans as disruptive members of a complex empire. Native/European Americans, European American Protestants/French Canadian Catholics—all had become interchangeable in the big imperial picture. European Americans could not tolerate this. "Rejected as full partners in the British Empire," Taylor notes, "the Patriots sought their own 'empire of liberty' premised on the majority's rights to hold private property (including slaves) and to make new property by dispossessing Indians." How ironic, then, that Webster displaced expressions of such European American resentment onto the figures of Pocahontas and Uttamatomakkin. What a redoubling of the fusion of European and Native American identities! No matter how the urban press struggled to establish Native Americans as European Americans' constituting Others, the boundary between self and Other repeatedly disappeared, and differences repeatedly collapsed into sameness.[54]

54. Taylor, *Divided Ground,* 80–81. See, as well, Colley, *Captives,* and Edward Countryman, "Indians, the Colonial Order, and the Social Significance of the American Revolution," *William and Mary Quarterly,* 3d Ser., LIII (1996), 342–362.

How was the urban press to recuperate both its embrace of the Native American–as–noble savage and nature's nobleman and its rhetorical fusion of European and Native Americans? To the rescue came the new discourses of scientific racism, which assured urban readers that European and Native Americans were incontestably different, indeed, that European Americans were superior in every way to Native Americans. Science offered European Americans a way to sidestep moral responsibility for the destruction of America's indigenous peoples: Native Americans were a dying race. Unable to compete with European Americans' superior culture and technology, they would simply fade away, like Logan. As Timothy Dwight insisted, in a few years, only one kind of American would remain—the European American.

Racially oriented ethnography was one of the first forms scientific racist discourses assumed. It permitted European and European American observers to map difference and inferiority onto the natives of Africa, the Americas, and the Pacific Islands. Eagerly, the political magazines seized upon this new "scientific" genre, publishing a number of accounts of Native American customs representing Native Americans as "superstitious," engaged in "devil worship," lacking written languages, without technological or engineering skills, incapable of developing or maintaining complex social or material structures.[55]

Ironically, Noah Webster assumed the position of spokesman for the new scientific representations of Native Americans as inferior. Webster did so during a lengthy debate with Yale president Ezra Stiles over the origins of Indian fortifications that explorers had discovered along the banks of the Mississippi and that present archaeologists associate with the Tennessee civilization. (Always the self-publicist, Webster published the debate in his *American Museum* at the very time he and his readers engaged in heated debates over New York State's ratification of the new constitution.) Despite the evidence Styles presented of the monumental architectural remains of Incan and Aztec civiliza-

---

55. See "American Occurrences," *New Jersey Magazine,* I (1786), 67–68; Noah Webster, "History: Smith's History of Virginia," *American Magazine,* I (1788), 156–158; "An Account of the Discovery of Vineland or America, by the Icelanders, in the Eleventh Century . . . ," *American Magazine* (1788), 4–5; "An Historical Account of the First Settlement of the Swedes in America," *Columbian Magazine,* II (1788), 28–30; "The Origin of Quebec," *American Magazine,* I (1787), 717–718; "Narrative of the Death of Capt. James Cook," *New Jersey Magazine,* I (1786), 7–11; "An Account of the Indians Inhabiting the Country on the West of Hudson's Bay, Extracted from Elliott's Relation of Voyage for Discovering a North-West Passage," ibid., 11–14; "American Occurrences," ibid. (1786), 67–68.

tions, Webster insisted that Native Americans lacked the intellectual and technological ability to build even relatively simple fortifications. "That the natives of the country did sometimes throw up breast works of earth is a fact," Webster somewhat grudgingly admitted. "Such remains are discovered in every part of America, but in none of them do we find such traces of immense labor and proficiency in the art of fortification, as in the works of Muskingum." Webster's assertions, however, contradicted eyewitness reports of discovering elaborately fortified Native American towns. William Cooper, for example (the founder of Cooperstown and father of James Fenimore Cooper), described a series of "vast fortresses or entrenched camps, surrounded by ditches and guarded by pit-falls artfully conceived" not far from Cooperstown. To Stiles's mix of amusement and annoyance (and possibly to Cooper's, if he happened to read the *American Magazine)*, Webster insisted that these fortifications had been constructed by Fernando de Soto and his small expeditionary force (of whom, Stiles pointed out, half died fairly early in their explorations from disease and Native American assaults). Webster concluded his argument by asserting that Native Americans were so lacking in intelligence and talent that they would do well to study the dams of America's natural engineers—beavers. Compared to beaver constructions, Indian villages were filthy and wretchedly disorganized. It is hard to balance Webster's denigrations of Native Americans as "filthy" and "disorganized" with his sympathetic portrayals of Logan and Uttamatomakkin or with an earlier essay he had published celebrating Native Americans for their building and artistic skills.[56]

Even more telling than Webster's disparagement of Native American engineering skills was an essay Benjamin Rush published in the *Columbian Magazine*—more telling because its tone of intolerance is quite unexpected in a man who embraced so many liberal causes. Rush began his essay by attacking European Enlightenment celebrations of the noble savage as a poorly disguised assault on European Americans, indeed, on Christianity itself. "It has become fashionable of late years," Rush wrote, "for the philosophers of Europe to

56. Noah Webster, "Antiquity: Copy of a Letter from Mr. Webster, to the Rev. Dr. Stiles, President of Yale College, dated Philadelphia, October 22, 1787," *American Magazine,* I (1787), 15–19; Webster, "Antiquity, Letter II . . . Containing a Particular Account of the Famous Expedition of Fernando De Soto, into Florida," ibid., I (1788), 87–93; "Antiquity, Letter III: From Mr. N. Webster to the Rev. Dr. Stiles . . . ," ibid., 146–156, esp. 148; Ezra Stiles, "A Letter from the Rev. Ezra Stiles, S.T.D. President of Yale College, to the Editor," ibid., 291–294; "The Force of Instinct Exemplified in the Natural History of the Beaver," ibid., 653–657, esp. 653, 655. For Cooper's quotation, see Taylor, *William Cooper's Town,* 34.

celebrate the virtues of the savages of America—Whether the design of their encomiums was to expose christianity, and depreciate the advantages of civilization, I know not; but," he added, "they have evidently had those effects upon the minds of weak people." Seeking to counteract these effects, Rush announced that he "shall briefly add an account of some of their vices, in order to complete their *natural history*." Almost all the vices Rush listed foregrounded Native American bodies and sexuality. Significantly, Rush's list began with two words most commonly used to connote female sexual impurity: "UNCLEANNESS" (which he used in this case to represent bestiality) and "NASTINESS" (the *Oxford English Dictionary* offers a late-eighteenth-century definition as "foulness of person . . . moral foulness or impurity . . . obscenity"). Having implicitly conflated Native Americans' and women's sexual impurities, Rush then concluded, "The infamy of the Indian character is completed by the low rank to which they degrade their women." Completely misreading Native American gender parity, Rush, like a number of other European American writers, translated Native American women's ownership of land and control of the means of agricultural production as a sign, not of their economic and social power, but of their debasement and exploitation.[57]

> *And we are here as on a darkling plain*
> *Swept with confused alarms of struggle and flight,*
> *Where ignorant armies clash by night.*
> —MATTHEW ARNOLD, Dover Beach

Multiple conflicting Native American figures march across the pages of the new magazines—violent warriors whose bestial war cries shatter the night; sadistic cannibals; vanishing noble savages; nurturing fathers caring for "infant" European American "sons." Manly in their savagery, they were feminine in their pathos and powerlessness. Their villages were represented as collections of filthy hovels, yet their elaborate burial mounds dotted the American countryside. And not only did the same magazines publish discordant and conflicting visions of Native Americans; the same editors and writers did—Noah Webster and Mathew Carey, to mention only two. But the destabilization of identities did not stop there. An equally contradictory medley of imagined European Americans march across those same pages—"hapless" victims and ax-wielding women, productive frontier farmers and "infamous" rene-

---

57. [Benjamin Rush], "An Account of the Vices Peculiar to the Savages of N. America," *Columbian Magazine*, I (1786), 9–11; *Oxford English Dictionary*, s.v. "nastiness."

gades. Subjectivities multiplied and fractured, differences evaporated—as did any hope of finding a stable center, a cohesive sense of self in the midst of these overlapping images.

An Indian warfare narrative Mathew Carey published may best capture the fusion and confusions that characterized the press's representation of the European/Native American divide. Carey's story began as an elderly white farmer, fearful of marauding Indians like so many other farmers along the Ohio frontier, moved his family to the protection of a local fort. One day, however, with no warriors in sight, the farmer sent his children out to his farm and later went to join them. No sooner had the farmer come to his fields than he spied two Native Americans. Assuming the worst, the farmer began to run, the Native Americans to chase him. Finding flight impossible, the farmer turned, shot one of the Native Americans and grappled with the other, gouged out his eye, bit off his ear, and drove a knife deep into his stomach. The farmer then ran for help. Neighboring farmers, alerted by his cries, found the injured Native American hiding in a tree. "How do do, broder, how do do, broder?" the Native American called down to them, appealing, presumably, for human sympathy. "Alas! poor savage," Carey's essay reported, "their brotherhood to him extended only to tomahawking, scalping, and, to gratify some peculiar feelings of their own, skinning them both; and they have made drum heads of their skins."[58]

Sex and gender color this narrative. The elderly farmer appears at first more like the feminized victim of one of Carey's captivity narratives than an archetypal forceful and daring republican hero. Like a woman, the farmer hides himself in the enclosed space of the fort, sending his children out as proxies. Upon seeing two Native Americans, he runs, not to protect his children, but to evade the native warriors. Only when the warriors are about to catch him does the farmer turn and, in so doing, reverse gendered behavior. At that moment, the farmer becomes brave and phallic, penetrating the Native American as if the other were a woman. Then, in a final conflation of identities, European American farmers, rejecting the Native American's pleas for brotherhood, enact their own savage brotherhood, behaving just the way captivity narratives traditionally represent "American savages," skinning their victims and using the hides for drumheads. What were frontiersmen doing with drums? Playing Indian? And where does Carey, the eastern sophisticated political commentator and publisher, fit into this picture? Is he celebrating the frontier farmers for

58. "Remarkable Encounter of a White Man with Two Indians," in Carey, ed., *Affecting History*, 9–11.

defending their farms and killing their savage attackers, or is it his intention to hold those farmers up to the censure of his bourgeois readers? The phrase "to gratify some peculiar feelings of their own" effectively distances Carey and his readers from the scene he depicts.

Looking in the mirror of rhetoric and ideology, European Americans saw only grotesque confabulations of themselves, amalgamations of the European and the native, figures that doubled one another and in the doubling divided and fractured, shattering any hope of stabilizing difference and therefore self.

Male magazine publishers were not the only European Americans to focus their literary attentions on Native/European American relations. Women also addressed these issues. Let us turn to two women writers to see how they envisioned the new American nation, the American West, and European/Native American relations—and authorized themselves as authentic participants in the emerging European American public sphere.

CHAPTER FIVE

Subject Female Authorizing an American Identity

Women were nowhere and they were everywhere.

—JAN LEWIS, "Politics and the Ambivalence of the Private Sphere"

The myth of coherence . . . requires a constantly visible yet constantly receding perimeter of difference. . . . Its mythic and potentially bloody frontiers must be continuously negotiated and reinvented, even as its most alarmist defenders panic before the specter of its permeability.

—JOSEPH ROACH, Cities of the Dead

Euiropean American women played a complex role in the construction of the Native Americans as savage and inhuman and of European Americans as men of reason and heirs of the Enlightenment. In so doing, these women both constructed a national and political identity for themselves and participated in the process by which Native American women in nations as distinct and widespread as the Wampanoags and Narragansetts, the Iroquois, Creeks, and Cherokees, lost their rights to landownership, their control of agricultural production, their right to a significant political and religious voice in tribal affairs. The process that Gayatri Chakravorty Spivak referred to in her reading of *Jane Eyre* as a colonialist text—that to contest with white men for a liberal humanist subjectivity, nineteenth-century white women joined with men in espousing Europe's imperial venture and thus denied subjectivity to women of color—began decades before Charlotte Brontë put pen to paper. It began, in fact, in the seventeenth century, in Puritan North America.[1]

1. Earlier versions of this chapter appeared as Carroll Smith-Rosenberg, "Subject Female: Authorizing an American Identity," *American Literary History*, V (1993), 481–511, and Smith-Rosenberg, "Captive Colonizers: Ambivalence and an Emerging 'American' Identity," *Gender and History*, V (1993), 177–195. For Spivak's commentary, see Gayatri Chakravorty Spivak, "Three Women's Texts and a Critique of Imperialism," *Critical Inquiry*, XII, no. 1 (Autumn

European American women helped construct European Americans as true Americans and Native Americans as savages in three distinct moves: by assuming the role of innocent victims of barbarity; by assuming the role of authoritative writers; and by authorizing themselves as an alternative white icon for the new European American Republic. Appropriating the right to write and to represent a white America, European American women appropriated the dominant male discourses of imperialism and patriarchal Christianity. But, since language works in complex ways and ideology is never simple, by the late eighteenth century, European American women writers had also acquired the agency to resist and subvert the very discourses they had helped to construct— to an extent, and far from completely.

In exploring women writers' role in representing both Native/European American relations and the new Republic they helped form, we must return to the paradigmatic captivity narrative from which all other such narratives—and fiction—derived: Mary Rowlandson's *Soveraignty and Goodness of God*. First published in Boston in 1682, then republished in both New England and England, revived during the American Revolution in five new editions, and repeatedly republished in the nineteenth century, Rowlandson's captivity narrative quickly became a best seller on both sides of the Atlantic.[2] But *The*

1985), 243–261. For a suggestive theoretical analysis of women's positioning inside and outside of ideology and of women's power to resist hegemonical discourses, see Teresa de Lauretis, *Technologies of Gender: Essays on Theory, Film, and Fiction* (Bloomington, Ind., 1987), 1–30.

2. Mary White Rowlandson, *The Soveraignty and Goodness of God, together, with the Faithfulness of His Promises Displayed; Being a Narrative of the Captivity and Restauration of Mrs. Mary Rowlandson, Commended by Her, to All That Desires to Know the Lords Doings to, and Dealings with Her, Especially to Her Dear Children and Relations* (Cambridge, 1682), rpt. in Richard Slotkin and James K. Folsom, eds., *So Dreadfull a Judgment: Puritan Responses to King Philip's War, 1676–1677* (Middletown, Conn., 1978) (hereafter cited as Rowlandson, *Soveraignty*). Slotkin and Folsom introduce the narrative with a useful summary and a biographical sketch of Rowlandson. Alden T. Vaughan and Edward W. Clark also reprint Rowlandson's narrative in their *Puritans among the Indians: Accounts of Captivity and Redemption, 1676–1724* (Cambridge, Mass., 1981), 29–76. For information concerning the publication and dissemination of the narrative, see Slotkin, *Regeneration through Violence: The Mythology of the American Frontier, 1600–1860* (Middletown, Conn., 1973), 95–96; and Kathryn Zabelle Derounian, "The Publication, Promotion, and Distribution of Mary White Rowlandson's Captivity Narrative in the Seventeenth Century," *Early American Literature,* XXIII (1988), 239–261. See, as well, David L. Minter, "By Dens of Lions: Notes on Stylization in Early Puritan Captivity Narratives," *American Literature,* XLV (1973), 335–347. Slotkin and Folsom consider Rowlandson's narrative "the starting point of a cultural myth affecting America as a whole." "Gradually, 'the captivity' became part of the basic vocabulary of American writers and historians, offering a symbolic key to the drama of American history: a white woman, symbolizing the values of Christianity and

Soveraignty and Goodness of God was not simply the template for all subsequent captivity narratives. It was resurrected and restructured in the late eighteenth century, its original Puritan teleology softened into sentimentality, its initial identification as a British text (it was widely read in Britain; indeed, it was published there in the same year it appeared in the Massachusetts Bay Colony) transformed into a patriotic attack on British tyranny and a defense of European American liberties. It was republished seven times during the 1770s, its new title page modeled upon Paul Revere's engraving of the Boston Massacre. *The Soveraignty and Goodness of God* thus takes its place as one of the Revolutionary period's premier patriotic texts. Certainly, it can be read as one of the primary texts of European American racism and imperialism.[3] At the same time, it is seen as the prototype of the sentimental novel and thus the genesis of the sentimentalized captivity fiction that proliferated during the 1790s and early 1800s.[4] Born of King Philip's War and crises within late-seventeenth-century

---

American civilization, is captured and threatened by a racial enemy and must be rescued by the grace of God (or, after the Puritan times, by an American hero)" *(So Dreadfull a Judgment,* 302). The literature on Rowlandson's narrative is extensive. Far from exhaustive, the following brief list is intended to be merely suggestive: Slotkin, *Regeneration through Violence,* esp. 95–114; Mitchell R. Breitwieser, *American Puritanism and the Defense of Mourning: Religion, Grief, and Ethnology in Mary White Rowlandson's Captivity Narrative* (Madison, Wis., 1990); Susan Howe, "The Captivity and Restoration of Mrs. Mary Rowlandson," *Tremblor,* II (1985), 115; David Downing, " 'Streams of Scripture Comfort': Mary Rowlandson's Typological Use of the Bible," *Early American Literature,* XV (1980), 252–259; Derounian, "Puritan Orthodoxy and the 'Survivor Syndrome' in Mary White Rowlandson's Indian Captivity Narrative," *Early American Literature,* XXII (1987), 82–93.

3. On the Revolutionary period's reviving of Rowlandson's narrative, see Captain Greg Sieminski, "The Puritan Captivity Narrative and the Politics of the American Revolution," *American Quarterly,* XLII (1990), 35–56; Michelle Burnham, *Captivity and Sentiment: Cultural Exchange in American Literature, 1682–1861* (Hanover, N.H., 1997), 63–65. Some scholars have questioned whether we can talk of racism before scientific racism developed in the mid- and late eighteenth century. Barbara J. Fields, analyzing the rhetoric surrounding the origins of the African slave trade, argues that a white European racist discourse developed side by side with the development of the African slave trade in the sixteenth and seventeenth centuries (Fields, "Race and Ideology in American History," in J. Morgan Kousser and James M. McPherson, eds., *Region, Race, and Reconstruction* [New York, 1982]). A similar assumption informs Hortense J. Spillers's generative essay "Mama's Baby, Papa's Maybe: An American Grammar Book," *Diacritics,* XVII, no. 2 (Summer 1987), 65–81.

4. Nancy Armstrong and Leonard Tennenhouse make this argument in both their "American Origins of the Engilsh Novel," *American Literary History,* IV (1992), 386–410, and *The Imaginary Puritan: Literature, Intellectual Labor, and the Origins of Personal Life* (Berkeley, Calif., 1992). Burnham stresses the ties between Rowlandson's *Soveraignty and Goodness of God* and late-eighteenth-century fictionalized captivity narratives (see, for example, Rene Michel Hil-

New England Puritanism, *The Soveraignty and Goodness of God* was vitally alive a hundred years later as the descendants of those Puritans created an independent new Republic. Once we have explored key themes in Rowlandson's narrative, beginning with its original publication and the surrounding events, we will then turn to two late-eighteenth-century appropriations of that narrative. Such a comparison will permit us to examine the ways republican writers, appropriating themes central to Rowlandson's vision, expressed the concerns and experiences of their times. It will also permit us to explore the ways at least one woman novelist read and transformed Rowlandson's narrative while maintaining Rowlandson's choice of women as the emblematic representation of a people and her authorization of women's public voice. Since the questions will arise—What is unique to women writers? What is more general to the times?—this chapter will contrast a novel by a best-selling woman novelist and playwright, Susanna Rowson's *Reuben and Rachel,* to one by the "father" of American literature, Charles Brockden Brown's *Edgar Huntley.*[5] Our fundamental questions remain the same: how is the construction of the Native American—as–Other engendered? What deep ambivalences lie within this engendering? Can fiction succeed where captivity narratives and political magazines failed in using representations of Native Americans to stabilize the United States' national identity?

THE BLACK DEVILS OF PURITANISM

The Soveraignty and Goodness of God represents the experiences and sufferings of Mary White Rowlandson. Born in England, Rowlandson migrated as a child with her parents to Lancaster, a town in western Massachusetts. In the mid-seventeenth century, Lancaster lay on the border between Native Ameri-

---

liard d'Auberteuil's *Miss McCrea: A Novel of the American Revolution* [1784; Gainesville, Fla., 1958]) in her *Captivity and Sentiment,* 75–79.

5. Julia A. Stern critiques this appellation routinely given to Charles Brockden Brown, claiming that it figures in a literary critique that values Brown's gothic style while it denigrates women writers' deployment of the sympathies. "In acknowledging the seriousness of the female writers' emphasis on feeling as a literary subject," Stern writes, "I reverse prevailing scholarly procedure which particularly privileges the 'complex' art of Charles Brockden Brown over the critically debased works of his 'sensational and popular' female cohort. Certainly to suggest that American novelists working in the 1790's are even remotely confederated on intellectual, artistic, or affective grounds, much less to propose the unlikely existence of a fiction-making community in which Brown figures as (feminized) inheritor rather than as (masculine) progenitor, is to counter the intuitions of the tradition's finest recent critics" (Stern, *The Plight of Feeling: Sympathy and Dissent in the Early American Novel* [Chicago, 1997], 3).

can and Puritan lands, a crossroads, a point simultaneously of connection and demarcation. Here her father, John White, laid out his extensive landholdings, marking him as one of the colony's wealthiest settlers. Here, Mary White married Joseph Rowlandson, a highly respected and well-connected minister, confirming her position within the colony's social and intellectual elite. And here, surrounded by sisters, cousins, nieces, and nephews, she raised a family and sank her roots deep into American soil.

King Philip's War, one of the most brutal of Native–European American wars, violently disrupted the border world of Whites and Rowlandsons, demonstrating its vulnerability, a vulnerability Rowlandson fully experienced as she and her three children were captured and carried deep into Indian territory. What her narrative does not mention but what Puritan settlers and Native Americans knew full well, was that Metacom (or King Philip, as the Puritans called him) had organized a confederacy of five woodland nations in response to aggressive Puritan land takeovers that encroached significantly on Narragansett and Wampanoag ancestral lands—lands they needed to maintain their tribal integrity and economic viability. The igniting moment came when the Massachusetts Colony executed two members of the Wampanoag nation who had been accused of killing an English settler. Wampanoag outrage opened the door to military contestations. The pattern of land seizure, retaliation, and counter-retaliation, a pattern we saw time and again in the Ohio Valley, began at least a century earlier along the New England frontier.[6]

The Soveraignty and Goodness of God begins with Rowlandson's seizure: the town of Lancaster burning around her, her own home in flames, her sister, nephew, and many of her neighbors and friends brutally killed before her eyes. The classic opening of a captivity narrative was born. "It is a solemn sight to see so many Christians lying in their blood. . . . All of them stripped naked by a company of hell-hounds, roaring, singing, ranting and insulting, as if they would have torn our very hearts out," Rowlandson begins, then continues, "Thus were we butchered by those merciless heathen, standing amazed, with the blood running down to our heels." Of the thirty-seven residents of

6. For discussions of King Philip's War and its impact on New England society along with a telling analysis of how it was represented textually, see Jill Lepore, *The Name of War: King Philip's War and the Origins of American Identity* (New York, 1997); Slotkin and Folsom, eds., *So Dreadfull a Judgment*, 3–35; Slotkin, *Regeneration through Violence*, 57–94; Francis Jennings, *The Invasion of America: Indians, Colonialism, and the Cant of Conquest* (New York, 1975); and Stephen Saunders Webb, *1676: The End of American Independence* (Cambridge, Mass., 1985); Alden T. Vaughan, *New England Frontier: Puritans and Indians, 1620–1675*, 3d ed. (Norman, Okla., 1995).

her extended family, Rowlandson tells her readers, thirty-six were either killed or captured.[7]

In representing the horrors of her personal narrative, Rowlandson represented the horrors of the larger war, which saw the frontier in flames, forty Puritan towns destroyed, thousands of Puritans killed or carried into captivity, and the Confederacy army advance to within a day's march of Boston. A far higher percentage of European Americans died in King Philip's War than in any subsequent American war. Philip's Confederacy came close to terminating the Puritan "errand in the wilderness." A hundred years would pass before New England's economy would recover. At the same time, Native American homelands were destroyed and large numbers of women, children, and old men either were killed in open warfare or died from the widespread starvation that resulted from the war. Those who were captured, including Philip's wife and only son, were sent as slaves to the Caribbean. Following Philip's defeat and death, the Confederacy nations were forced from their ancient lands up into the New Hampshire hills, thus beginning an ongoing pattern of British/European American imperial advances and native displacements.[8]

The war did not stand alone as a moment of horror and disorder. It cut a bloody swath through settlements already agonized over a sharply declining male church membership and beset with a pervading sense of spiritual failure—a sense intensified by the increasing numbers of New Englanders who, in the years following the English Civil War, renounced Puritan orthodoxy to join Baptist congregations and Quaker meetings. Political crises mirrored spiritual failures. Puritan New England's autonomy crumbled before the Stuart kings' resolution to revoke the colony's original charter. King Philip's forces burst upon New England's frontier communities at a time when the Puritan elite's mandate to rule in God's name was under bitter attack at home and abroad.[9]

Their leadership seriously undermined, the ministerial elite seized on the war as a sign and portent—both of God's anger with his chosen people for their waywardness and disobedience, as evinced in waning church membership, and, when the tides of war turned, of his reaffirmation of his covenant with them. This elite, led by Increase Mather, chose Mary Rowlandson's narrative as one of the principal texts to represent God's mercy and continued

7. Rowlandson, *Soveraignty,* 325.

8. For a chronology of the war, see Lepore, *Name of War,* xxv–xxviii. For a discussion of the effects on Native Americans in New England, see 173–190.

9. Perry Miller, *The New England Mind: The Seventeenth Century* (Cambridge, Mass., 1954); David D. Hall, *The Faithful Shepherd: A History of the New England Ministry in the Seventeenth Century* (Chapel Hill, N.C., 1972).

commitment to their errand in the wilderness. Increase Mather arranged for its publication in both New England and England and wrote its introduction. He and Cotton Mather featured it in their histories of New England and of King Philip's War. It echoed and reechoed through countless Puritan sermons until, though a woman's text, it entered the canon of Puritan New England history and literature.[10]

Writing to praise God's goodness and mercy, Rowlandson composed a bitter, violent text that reaffirmed Puritans as God's chosen people, expelled Native Americans from the human race, and confirmed America as the Puritans' promised land. There are no good Native Americans in Rowlandson's narrative, not John Eliot's praying Indians, not John the Printer, who set the type for the narrative's Cambridge edition. Condemning Native Americans' "savageness" and "brutality," Rowlandson depicts them as "ravenous beasts," "wolves," and "barbarous creatures." "Yelping" and howling, they mourn their dead "like dogs . . . which have lost their ears." Like wild beasts, they eat "old bones . . . full of worms and maggots . . . yea, the very bark of trees," "filthy trash" that repulses Rowlandson's civilized palate. Worse than animals, they are cannibals. Her exclamation—"as if they would have torn our very hearts out"— evokes an image of Aztec cannibalistic rituals well known to seventeenth-century English readers. Rowlandson builds upon this image, depicting Native Americans with necklaces of human fingers rattling around their necks, boasting of having roasted and eaten Puritan children. Their humanity doubly denied, they emerge on Rowlandson's pages as satanic, roaming the howling wilderness, seizing and tormenting God's chosen people. "Hell-hounds," they "roar and dance," giving their camp the "lively resemblance of hell."[11]

Representing the Native American–as–negative Other to the Puritan-as–civil Christian, Rowlandson's text similarly constitutes them as Other to the

---

10. Derounian, "Publication, Promotion, and Distribution," *Early American Literature,* XXIII (1988), 239–261. Increase and Cotton Mather themselves both wrote extensively about King Philip's War, seeing it as a time of chastisement and of reaffirmation. See Increase Mather's *Brief History of the War with the Indians in New-England . . .* (London, 1676) and his *Relation of the Troubles Which Have Hapned in New-England by Reason of the Indians There, from the Year 1614 to the Year 1675 . . .* (Boston, 1677). For a discussion of these war narratives, see Slotkin, *Regeneration through Violence,* 83–87, 113–115.

11. For examples of Rowlandson's castigations of praying Indians, see Rowlandson, *Sovereignty,* 329, 341, 343, 349. For examples of her disparaging remarks on Indians, see 325–327, 330, 333, 335, 337, 343, 344, 346, 352, 354, 359. Slotkin and Folsom see Rowlandson's narrative as a key text marking Puritans' increasingly bitter attitude toward the American Indians. They describe her narrative as filled "with a hatred almost unimaginable" (304). On dismemberment and roasting, see 325, 342, 353; for satanic descriptions, see 325, 326, 344, 352–354, 360.

Puritan-as–productive cultivator of America's lands. Her narrative counterposes the orderly and productive world of British houses and "English fields" to the rough camps in which the war bands live and the barren fields in which they scavenge for food. The welcome sight of an "English path," which she notices in one of her many wearying removes, makes more dismal the morass of swamps and impenetrable forests, the "vast and desolate wilderness" through which Native Americans prowl, in rhetoric that suggests a moral as well as a physical wilderness. Rowlandson thus sets the tone for all captivity narratives to come.[12]

But, ultimately, it is the pious Puritan family that constitutes Native Americans absolute negative Others to God's chosen Puritans. At a time in New England history when Puritan tribalism, institutionalized by the Mathers in the Half-Way Covenant, made the family central to the Puritan church and state, Rowlandson's narrative counterpoises Puritans' devotion to their families to brutal Native American attacks upon those families. Her story opens by vividly depicting the slaughter of her own kin: "Oh the doleful sight that now was to behold at this house! . . . To see our dear . . . relations lie bleeding out their heart's blood upon the ground." Passage after passage represents her anguish over her infant daughter's sufferings, her ceaseless search for her remaining children. Only when her family is reunited does her narrative—which began with her family's dispersal—end. And then, it is the reunion of parents and children, not Rowlandson's individual ransoming, that signs God's reaffirmation of his covenant with New England and brings closure to her narrative.[13]

Portraying herself as a caring parent and devoted family member, Rowlandson refuses Native Americans a similar representation. Never does she describe them as loving husbands and wives comforting one another in the midst of war or tenderly caring for their own children—not even when she reports specific

12. As we have seen, British and European American imperialist arguments frequently cited American Indian failure to cultivate the land in the British manner as a sign that God intended to replace them with British settlers as the rightful possessors of America's land. Such a representation of American Indians exists in sharp contrast to early settlers' dependence on tribal food supplies for help in surviving their "starving times." "Vast and desolate wilderness," "English fields": Rowlandson, *Sovraignty*, 326, 334–335. Here, Rowlandson employs standard Renaissance symbols for post-lapsarian fallen nature.

13. Rowlandson, *Sovraignty*, 325, 339, 344–345, 350, 355, 361–364. I am indebted to Ann Little's excellent analysis of Rowlandson's narrative for drawing my attention to the significance of the family in that text. For discussions of Puritan tribalism, see Miller, *New England Mind;* Robert G. Pope, *The Half-Way Covenant: Church Membership in Puritan New England* (Princeton, N.J., 1969); Robert Middlekauff, *The Mathers: Three Generations of Puritan Intellectuals, 1576–1728* (New York, 1971).

incidents that testify to just such behavior, such as warriors offering her food or a knife if she will knit stockings for their babies, or King Philip, locked in a life-or-death struggle with the Puritans, pausing to ask her to make a shirt for his baby son. Seeing them as ravening beasts and devils, Rowlandson refuses to represent them as having families like her own. Never does she express any form of human sympathy for them, not when their children die, not when, as a people, they face starvation and the loss of their ancestral homelands, not even when, motivated by human compassion, they forego the comfort of a dry bed and warm food so that she may have them. As already noted, sympathy is born of identification with the Other. Captivity narratives, from Rowlandson's on, refuse the possibility of identifying with and hence feeling sympathy for Native Americans.[14]

Indeed, Rowlandson refuses them that most basic form of humanity—agency and will. Native Americans do not act in Rowlandson's narrative. God acts through them. They exist only as tools God uses to chastise and reaffirm his chosen people. Never does Rowlandson's narrative present Native Americans as thoughtful military strategists, never as members of a complex culture in which women as well as men possess political authority and personal wealth. Represented in fragmented, disconnected episodes, madly scrambling through the wilderness murdering Christians, they are but shadow figures in God's great drama of redemption.[15]

By representing Native Americans as inhuman devils, Rowlandson's narrative reaffirmed the Puritans as the legitimate possessors of America's land. Representing Native Americans as passive conduits of God's justice, Rowlandson constituted herself the representative of the Puritan state in New England. Her captivity and redemption not only confirmed her own sanctity; they reaffirmed New England Puritans as God's people. Her many removes into the hellish wilderness and dismal swamps, her myriad sufferings and humiliations,

---

14. Rowlandson, *Soveraignty*, 337–338, 344. On Rowlandson's lack of sympathy for Indians, see, for example, her response to the deaths of two American Indian infants. The first infant she found dying at the side of a Puritan boy, John Gilbert; both were lying on the cold ground outside a wigwam. "They had turned him [John] out of the wigwam, and with him an Indian papoose, almost dead (whose parents had been killed). . . . There they lay quivering in the cold . . . the papoose stretched out, with his eyes and nose and mouth full of dirt, and yet alive, and groaning. I advised John to go and get some fire." Or again, on the death of her mistress's baby: "My mistress's papoose was sick, and it died that night, and there was one benefit in it, that there was more room. I went to a wigwam, and they gave me a skin to lie upon" (344–346; see also 340).

15. Ibid., 328–330, 354–356, 360, 364.

her final return to God's church—all allegorically represented the Puritans' own errand into the New England wilderness. Rowlandson emerges, in her own narrative, in Increase Mather's introduction to her narrative, and in numerous sermons, as the embodiment of the Puritan church, its representative to God and the world (or, at the very least, to the British reading public). As Mather argued in his introduction, Rowlandson's capture/redemption "was a dispensation of public note, and of universal concernment." "Methinks this dispensation doth bear some resemblance to those of Joseph, David and Daniel; yea, and of the three children [in the fiery furnace] too, the stories whereof do represent us with the excellent textures of divine providence." His remarks reproduced an already existing construction of Rowlandson-as—representative Puritan. To mark her safe return, the General Court had declared a colonywide day of fasting and thanksgiving. Numerous sermons publicly, ritualistically celebrated this sign of her—and their—redemption. Rowlandson's narrative did more than authorize her own political subjectivity, however; by constituting her a political subject, it feminized the symbolic representation of the New England state. (But more on this point later.)[16]

Authorize her *self* is exactly what Rowlandson did. It is her name, not Increase Mather's, that appears on the title pages of the various editions. (Mather's validating preface is unattributed, signed only "*Ter Amicam*.") Her authorship is then immediately reaffirmed, again on the title page, with the words "Written by Her Own Hand." A forceful, authoritative "I" resounds throughout the narrative as Rowlandson writes not only in the voice of one of God's chosen but in the voices of his greatest male prophets, warriors, and kings— Isaiah, Job, Samson, and Lot. In the words of the Patriarch, Jacob, she laments her children: "Me (as he said) have ye bereaved of my children, Joseph is not, and Simeon is not, and ye will take Benjamin also." In those of King Hezekiah, she urges God to "Remember now O Lord . . . how I have walked before thee in truth." The psalms of King David dot her pages. Appropriating male texts and images, she clothes herself in male theocratic and political authority and so authorizes herself symbol and allegory for Puritan New England.[17]

Typology was central to the Puritan worldview. It involved what Eric Auerbach called "figural interpretation," or the substituting for a biblical person or event an earthly person or event "in such a way that the first [the biblical]

---

16. Ter Amicam [Increase Mather], "The Preface to the Reader," ibid., 320–321.

17. Rowlandson, *Soveraignty*, esp. 328–329, 331–332, 334, 336, 343, 345–346, 348–349. True, we are also told on the same title page that her text was originally written "for Her Private Use," but Increase Mather said the same thing about his 1676 *Brief History of the War with the Indians in New-England.*

signifies not only itself but also the second [earthly figure], while the second involves and fulfills the first." Chronology, causation do not matter within figural interpretations. What matters, Auerbach insists, is the "oneness" of the biblical and the earthly figure. By invoking the psalms of David or the prophecies of Isaiah, Rowlandson saw herself—as did her Puritan readers—as one with David or Isaiah, as their spiritual reincarnation in New England which, itself, was the spiritual reincarnation of the biblical "promised land."[18]

We should not underestimate the importance of this act of figuration/authorization. It came at a significant moment not only in the history of the Massachusetts Bay Colony but in the history of white women within that colony. Rowlandson wrote at the nadir of women's public authority in Massachusetts. Her narrative was published roughly forty years after the silencing of Anne Hutchinson and at a time when Puritan women, although a majority of those claiming a conversion experience, were no longer permitted to publicly give witness to their own experiences of salvation at church services. Rather, male ministers read their statements to the congregation. Like their voices, their names were also effaced as church records increasingly subsumed women's Christian names under their husbands' patronymics. Discursively repressed within church records, Puritan women were materially oppressed and trivialized in church disciplinary actions. Although serious theological charges against women decreased following the Hutchinson trial, church actions against women for minor domestic matters, for being scolds, disobedient, etc., increased significantly. At the same time, English common law and Puritan inheritance practices kept most women landless and hence economically dependent. In light of this disempowerment, it is especially significant that the emblematic text celebrating God's mercies and redemption at the end of King Philip's War was a woman's text and that the representative body that was chosen to be scourged, tested, and redeemed for the chosen people was a woman's body. Although Rowlandson's texts and thus her voice were frequently male, her body is always emphatically, unmistakably female. It is, indeed, a mother's body. Pieta-like, she bears her dying child in her arms; like Niobe, she

18. Burnham includes a succinct and helpful discussion of typology, Auerbach's position, and their relevance to reading Rowlandson's narrative in *Captivity and Sentiment*, 16–17. See, as well, Eric Auerbach, *Mimesis: The Representation of Reality in Western Literature* (New York, 1985). It is interesting to think of Auerbach's understanding of "figural interpretations" and mimesis generally in relation to Joseph R. Roach's use of "surrogacy" to discuss the ways American cultural performances figure remembering and forgetting the "American holocaust" (slavery and genocide of Native Americans). See Roach, *Cities of the Dead: Circum-Atlantic Performance* (New York, 1996), chap. 1.

weeps for her children and will not be comforted; like Lot's wife, she longs to look back on a world consumed by God's wrathful fires.[19]

How did Rowlandson succeed in so authorizing herself? She did so, in part, at least, by writing within the existing male discourses of Puritan typological exegesis and British imperialism. Rowlandson exploited the social status of her husband and father (not an insignificant factor in her authorization) and demonstrated her mastery of the biblical scholarship and rhetoric so highly valued in Puritan New England, which their status made possible. Skillfully, she uses biblical citations to show how the events of her own life, and hence of Puritan New England, are prefigured in the Old Testament and tied to the Book of Revelation. Puritan publishers in New and old England bound her narrative together with her husband's last sermon. But this linkage proved redundant. Rowlandson's narrative was itself a sermon, one of the most forceful in the Puritan's long tradition of jeremiads, designed to be read both as a private spiritual meditation and as a prod to greater spiritual dedication among God's saints at large. A generation after Anne Hutchinson and her women followers were told to learn in silence from their husbands, a book published by a Puritan matron under her own name boldly interpreted the texts central to Puritan exegesis. Quoting the Psalms, Rowlandson laments, "Oh, that my people had harkened to me, and Israel had walked in my ways, I should soon had subdued their enemies and turned my hand against their adversaries." And like Isaiah, she encourages, "For a small moment have I forsaken thee, but with great mercies will I gather thee."[20]

19. Rowlandson, *Soveraignty*, 326–330, 334. See also Mary Maples Dunn, "Women of Light," in Carol Ruth Berkin and Mary Beth Norton, eds., *Women of America: A History* (Boston, 1979), 114–138; Lyle Kohler, "The Case of the American Jezebels: Anne Hutchinson and Female Agitation during the Years of Antinomian Turmoil, 1636–1640," *William and Mary Quarterly*, 3d Ser., XXXI (1974), 55–78; David D. Hall, *The Faithful Shepherd: A History of the New England Ministry in the Seventeenth Century* (Chapel Hill, N.C., 1972); Larzer Ziff, *The Career of John Cotton: Puritanism and the American Experience* (Princeton, N.J., 1962); Carol F. Karlsen, *The Devil in the Shape of a Woman* (New York, 1987); Philip J. Greven, Jr., *Four Generations: Population, Land, and Family in Colonial Andover, Massachusetts* (Ithaca, N.Y., 1970); Lawrence Stone, *The Crisis of the Aristocracy, 1558–1641* (New York, 1967); Laurel Thatcher Ulrich, *Good Wives: Image and Reality in the Lives of Women in Northern New England, 1650–1780* (New York, 1982); Carole Pateman, *The Sexual Contract* (Stanford, Calif., 1988).

20. Rowlandson, *Soveraignty*, 334, 335, 345. Interestingly, the captivity narrative, in both Rowlandson's day and in the late eighteenth century, was more a compilation of different Puritan genres than the replication of any one type. It was simultaneously a sermon, a jeremiad, a spiritual autobiography, a conversion testimony—and, scholars now believe, a protonovel. And containing something of each genre, it was far more than the total of its varied parts. See

So authorized, Rowlandson is emboldened to move from familial to military, from religious to political matters. Having begun by chastising Puritans' spiritual coldness, she ends by castigating their political and military failures. Self-consciously interrupting her narrative of personal sufferings to comment on "a few remarkable passages of providence, which I took special notice of in my afflicted time," she sets off her comments typographically:

1. Of the fair opportunity lost in the long march, a little after the fort fight, when our English army was so numerous, and in pursuit of the enemy, and so near as to take and destroy them. . . .

2. . . . the slowness, and dullness of the English army. . . .

3. . . . that [the Baquag] river should be impassable to the English . . . [but] the heathen [along with foot-sore Mary Rowlandson] . . . could go in great numbers over. . . .

As John Winthrop had warned, having asserted her religious authority, the outspoken woman would waste no time in asserting her political authority.[21]

Rowlandson was familiar not only with biblical exegesis and military campaigns but with British texts of exploration and colonization. Her description of Native Americans as animals, as devil worshippers, as devils, and her claim that the Puritans were the rightful possessors of Massachusetts land because they cultivated it in God's name, all existed within sixteenth- and early-seventeenth-century accounts of British explorations, in John Smith's *History of Virginia*, in earlier Puritan writings about God's settling the Puritans on Massachusetts's fruitful land. Her description of the Wampanoags' feast celebrating the destruction of Lancaster closely follows Smith's description of Algonquian "Powwows" in Virginia. Although her extreme views of Native Americans and her assurance that God had unequivocally promised New England to the Puritans more closely reflect the writings of Mather and other New England clergy than earlier, British-based writers (and thus bespeaks a British-American more than a cosmopolitan British vision), her narrative worked within and worked to reproduce an existing British racism and imperialism.[22]

Burnham, *Captivity and Sentiment*, 34–38, 49. See, as well, Armstrong and Tennenhouse, *Imaginary Puritan*.

21. Rowlandson, *Soveraignty*, 358–359.

22. John Smith, *The Generall History of Virginia, New-England and the Summer Isles, with the Names of the Adventurers, Planters, and Governours from Their First Beginning . . .* (London, 1624); John Underhill, "Newes from America; or, A New and Experimentall Discoverie of New England" (1638), Massachusetts Historical Society, *Collections*, 3d Ser., VI (1837), 1–28; P[hilip] Vincent, "A True Relation of the Late Battell Fought in New-England between the English and

Reworking British imperial discourses, Rowlandson rewrote them. A commentary on a bloody and near-disastrous war, written near the edge of North America's frontier settlements, Rowlandson's narrative rejects the ambivalence of early European texts—John Smith's grudging respect for Powhatan, John Eliot's millennial insistence upon the conversion of Native Americans. Instead, we find her bitter refusal of humanity and redemption to Native Americans—a refusal that echoes not only Increase Mather's representation of the Wampanoags as "atheistical, proud, wild, cruel, barbarous, brutish (in one word) diabolical . . . the worst of heathen" but Dominican Tomaso Ortiz's description of the Aztecs: "They eat human flesh. They are more given to sodomy than any other nation. . . . They are brutal. . . .They eat fleas, spiders and worms raw. . . . They exercise none of the human arts or industries." By the late seventeenth century, a self-conscious European American voice had begun to develop along the margins of Britain's empire, the voice of Europeans committed to life on the American continent and engaged in ongoing confrontations with Native Americans for control of American land and natural resources. This is the same voice that would sound forth decades later among both Scotch-Irish and New England frontiersmen along the Pennsylvania and Ohio frontiers and, in the end, would seek to justify the Paxton Boys' homicidal rampage through the Easton workhouse.[23]

---

the Pequet Salvages," ibid., 29–44. I am indebted to Richard Slotkin for references to these sources (*Regeneration through Violence*, 70–78). Among the numerous essays Noah Webster printed about Smith, one features Smith's depiction of wild native rituals of "devil worship" very suggestive of the type of dancing Rowlandson describes. See "Curiosities," *American Magazine*, I (1787), 49–52. Current scholars of racism insist that early modern racial categories did not focus on figure phenotype and skin color but rather on "habit." "Habit" was used to refer to internal dispositions and modes of behavior. Christian piety, industry and productivity, clothing, the encouragement of science and the arts all comprised habit and marked a people or social group superior to those whose habit involved nakedness, sloth, heathen practices, and the failure to develop the accoutrements of civilization. Rowlandson's narrative reinscribes and reinforces this system of categorization. See Roxanne Wheeler, *Complexion of Race: Categories of Difference in Eighteenth-Century British Culture* (Philadelphia, 2000), 1–48; and Valerie Traub, "Mapping the Global Body," in Peter Erickson and Clark Hulse, eds., *Early Modern Visual Culture: Representation, Race, and Empire in Renaissance England* (Philadelphia, 2000), 44–97.

23. Ortiz cited by Tzevetan Todorov, *The Conquest of America*, trans. Richard Howard (New York, 1984), 150–151. Rowlandson, Mather, and Ortiz wrote as creoles committed to life on the American continent, not as cosmopolitans focused on matters European—European wars, for example, or the fur trade with Native Americans. Their rhetoric bespeaks the vision of Europeans whose commitment to life on the American continent made them actively competitive with the indigenous population for control of American land. So pervasive and pressing was this vision that it transcended the most bitter of European ideological divisions, that between

But Rowlandson's narrative alters the discourses of British imperialism in a second, even more striking manner. It reverses the traditional engendering of the British imperial body, making that body female. Until Rowlandson's narrative, the European imperial body had been an aggressive, penetrating male body, the feminine body it penetrated, none other than the American continent itself, iconically represented by the alluring body of a naked Indian woman. We can see this in Jan Van der Straet's widely circulated engraving of Amerigo Vespucci naming the New World, in Sir Walter Ralegh's *Discoverie of Guiana,* in Hakluyt's and Purchas's descriptions of sixteenth-century voyages of discovery. We can see this especially in the self-representation of that ultimate spokesman for early modern British imperialism, John Smith.[24] In his writing and Court persona, Smith represented himself—and was repeatedly represented throughout the seventeenth and eighteenth centuries—as a forceful soldier, an adventurer, a master of seraglios and of languages, a Trickster, cunning and wily. Had he not seduced Pocahontas, penetrated Virginia, and planted the seeds of his colony there?[25]

Catholics and Protestants. Bartolomé de Las Casas's *Devastation of the Indies,* for example, circulated widely in England, fomenting hostility toward Catholic Spain and sympathy for Native Americans, sympathy Rowlandson rejected as she echoed Ortiz's Catholic sentiments. I am aware of and deliberately wish to deploy the double meaning of the word "creole," which can mean either a European resident in the Americas or a person of mixed European and African descent. This double meaning underscores the multiple/decentered subjectivity of European colonials in America. America gets "under their skin" ever more relentlessly, setting them off from speakers at the cosmopolitan/imperial center.

24. Walter Raleigh, *The Discoverie of the Large, Rich, and Beautifull Empire of Guiana, with a Relation of the Great and Golden Citie of Manoa . . .* , rpt. in Richard Hakluyt, *The Principal Navigations, Voiages, Traffiques, and Discoveries of the English Nation . . .* , 2d ed., 3 vols. (London, 1598–1600); Smith, *Generall History of Virginia;* Smith, *A Map of Virginia: With a Description of the Country, the Commodities, People, Government, and Religion . . .* (Oxford, 1612). For secondary analyses, see Peter Hulme's highly suggestive analysis, "Polytropic Man: Tropes of Sexuality and Mobility in Early Colonial Discourse," in Francis Barker et al., eds., *Europe and Its Others: Proceedings of the Essex Conference on the Sociology of Literature, July 1989,* 2 vols. (Colchester, 1985); Bernadotte Bucher, *Icon and Conquest: A Structural Analysis of the Illustrations of de Bry's Great Voyages,* trans. Basia Miller Gulati (Chicago, 1975); Hugh Honour, *The New Golden Land: European Images of America from the Discoveries to the Present Time* (New York, 1975).

25. See Karen Ordahl Kupperman, "Introduction," in John Smith, *A Selected Edition of His Writings,* ed. Karen Ordahl Kupperman (Chapel Hill, N.C., 1988), 1–23. As we have seen, Noah Webster's *American Magazine* was filled with excerpts from Smith's *History of Virginia.* My reading of Smith's encounter with Pocahontas is strongly influenced by Hulme's excellent essay, "Polytropic Man," in Barker et al., eds., *Europe and Its Others.* One could argue, of course, that

But unlike Smith and Ralegh, Rowlandson purifies the British imperial body. Indeed, she emphatically desexualizes it. Her body is starved, beaten, and frozen. But, she insists, during the four months she spends at the mercy of hellhounds and beasts, it is never sexually threatened. Wounded, she returns pure. It is in this context that she most directly associates her body with Daniel's. Both are rescued by God from threatening beasts. "I have been in the midst of those roaring lions, and savage bears, that feared neither God, nor man, nor the devil," she tells her readers, "sleeping all sorts together, and yet not one of them ever offered me the least abuse of unchastity. . . . God's power is as great now, and as sufficient to save, as when he preserved Daniel in the lions' den." And it is precisely her sexual purity that permits Rowlandson to substitute her body for Smith's as the emblem of British imperialism and thus establish herself as a political subject. To do so, Rowlandson's body must be asexual, for within British political discourse, the sexualized female body always connotes political corruption.[26]

Yet, at the same time, Rowlandson also represents her body as maternal—that of a suffering mother, infant in arms—thus insistently fusing maternity and asexuality. Indeed, her narrative continuously conflates opposing subjectivities. She is simultaneously the asexual embodiment of British imperial

---

Smith as Trickster and "polytropic man" transcended gender distinctions, conflating in himself male and female sexualities. Thus he could be both the seducer, that is, feminine, and the planter of seeds, that is, masculine. Slotkin comments upon the engendering and sexualization of the British imperial body, pointing to Ben Jonson's *Eastward Hoe*, a satirical play written in 1605 and produced in both London and Jamestown. *Eastward Hoe* quite explicitly represents Virginia (America) as a desiring and available American Indian woman, a willing concubine for the British adventurer. As one character, Seagull, states: "Come, boyes, Virginia longs till we share the rest of her maidenhead. . . . A whole country of the English is there man, bred of those that were left [at Roanoke]; they have married with the Indians, and make them bring forth as beautifull faces as any we have in England; and therefore the Indians are so in love with 'hem that all the treasure they have they lay at their feet" (*Regeneration through Violence*, 192).

26. Rowlandson, *Soveraignty*, 360–361. Indeed, here we see Rowlandson not only making American Indians ravenous beasts but transforming their respect for her sexual autonomy into a divine miracle. We should note that later captivity narratives made similar assertions. It was not until the *Affecting History of the Dreadful Distresses of Frederic Manheim's Family*'s description of two young girls stripped naked and tortured that sexual violence enters the captivity narrative, and even then it is rarely suggested. Certainly, Massey Herbeson and the Gilbert women suffered no sexual affront. Virtually the only examples of sexual threat suggested in late-eighteenth-century narratives involve French Catholics in Canada, and these undoubtedly play off centuries-old Protestant suspicions of Catholics. Regarding asexuality: I am indebted to Nancy Armstrong's analysis of *Pamela* for suggesting such a reading of Rowlandson's narrative (personal communication).

penetration, a weeping mother who speaks the words of Samson and David, a Protestant Pieta fluent in Algonquian. Rowlandson's self-representation refuses dyadic oppositions—even, or most especially, the one her text works so hard to constitute, that of God-chosen British subject and demonic Algonkian Other. Like her savage captors, she wanders a nomad through spiritual swamps and literal wilderness. Like them, she is a mere agent of God's will, a helpless sinner in his hand. Like them, she gorges on uncooked food till the blood runs out of her mouth.[27]

As we saw in later captivity and frontier narratives, food is central to the destabilization of subjectivities we find in Rowlandson's narrative. For Rowlandson, food rivals religion as a sign of Native American otherness. She uses bear meat and raw horse liver, horses' hooves and fetal deer, ground nuts and roots to underscore the bestial, other nature of Native American customs. Yet all become "savory to me that one would think was enough to turn the stomach of a brute creature." Taught by hunger, like her captors, she sucks the sweetness out of horses' hooves. Avidly, she dips her cup into their pots, broils her food on their fires.[28]

Destabilizing the difference it originally signed, food leads Rowlandson to deny another critical demarcator of racial difference and superiority her narrative seeks to construct—the Puritans' devotion to family and children. Toward the end of her sojourn in the wilderness, Rowlandson finds a captive Puritan infant helplessly sucking on the grizzle of a horse's hoof. Far from nurturing him, she unashamedly seizes his food for herself—Leaving him to die? the reader wonders. Equally unashamedly, she invokes God's blessing upon her act: "I took it of the child, and ate it myself, and savory it was to my taste. . . . Thus the Lord made that pleasant refreshing, which another time would have been an abomination." (Which was the abomination—the food or the taking of it from an infant?)[29]

Her face smeared with Native American food stolen from a starving Puritan infant, Rowlandson can no longer unequivocally constitute Native Americans (who gave the child food) savage child murderers and herself, as representative Puritan, civil and (re)productive. Indeed, what boundaries do Rowlandson and her narrative not transgress? She is a British American, a highly educated

27. Rowlandson, *Soveraignty,* 335, 339, 347–348, 351. Her narrative details the complex material exchanges the productive Rowlandson engaged in, trading her sewing and knitting for food, knives, and other Wampanoag goods. Exchanging goods, she seems also to have exchanged subject positions. For examples of her trading activities, see 345, 351, 354.

28. Ibid., 350.

29. Ibid.

frontierswoman who speaks in the voice of David and Hezekiah but is also fluent in Algonkian, an asexual mother who savages starving children! Seduced by the food of the underworld, Rowlandson, like Persephone, no longer demarcates the clear line between the world of darkness and of light. She stands for the permeability of worldly boundaries, for the decentered instability of subjectivity itself. Yet this is the paradigmatic captivity narrative, the template for distinguishing European and Native Americans.

But, although Rowlandson's self-proclaimed identity as the representative of both the Puritan "Errand in the Wilderness" and Britain's North American empire fractures and becomes self-contradictory, it never disappears. All through the eighteenth century, European Americans read, misread, and rewrote Rowlandson's captivity narrative. As a consequence, they wove the figure of the white female subject into the previously exclusively male narratives of European exploration and settlement. Often a minor character within the male texts that re-formed the sixteenth-century British explorer/warrior figure into the eighteenth-century European American hunter/settler (turning John Smith into Daniel Boone), she nevertheless is almost always there. Often, she is invoked simply to underscore Native Americans' inhumanity. But, even then, her very helplessness made vivid the twinned helplessness of the men who could not save her—the husbands who hide in trees while she is tomahawked, the fathers forced to watch her torture. Whenever the white woman assumed a more central role within the captivity narrative, however, her subjectivity grew more complex. Re-fusing conventional dyadic oppositions, the white female victim problematized both the Native Americans' savage otherness and the frontiersman's manliness and virility. And so, just as we saw in *The Coquette*, for example, or in the case of Elizabeth Bozart—ax in hand, splitting the skulls of attacking warriors while European men lay dying at her feet—women repeatedly disturbed the clear demarcations the new Republic needed to proclaim its unity, its coherence.[30]

---

30. Ibid.; Slotkin, *Regeneration through Violence*, 268–394; [John Filson], *The Adventures of Colonel Daniel Boon, One of the First Settlers at Kentucke* . . . (Norwich, Conn., 1786). Captivity narratives were an extremely popular literary genre in late-eighteenth- and early-nineteenth-century America. For one particularly popular collection, see *Affecting History of the Dreadful Distresses of Frederic Manheim's Family: To Which Are Added, The Sufferings of John Corbly's Family; An Encounter between a White Man and Two Savages; Extraordinary Bravery of a Woman; Adventures of Capt. Isaac Stewart; Deposition of Massey Herbeson* . . . (Philadelphia, 1794). Hannah Dustin did not write her own narrative. Cotton Mather included it in his *Humiliations Follow'd with Deliverances: A Brief Discourse on the Matter and Method, of That Humiliation Which Would Be an Hopeful Symptom of Our Deliverance from Calamity; Accompanied*

To further explore the role gender plays in narratives of imperial expansion, let us turn now to two late-eighteenth-century novels that focused on European/Native American conflicts in western Pennsylvania and the Ohio Valley. These novels also permit us to examine the insights fiction, as a genre, offers on the tense interplay of self and Other that marks the complex processes of national identity formation. Both novels are concerned with establishing a European American identity. Both express tensions that, in the late eighteenth century, accompanied the production of that identity. Both were written by authors who identified with the emergent European American middling classes and their popular print culture—albeit they occupied quite different places within the middling classes and their culture. Charles Brockden Brown, a leading light in the new nation's intellectual and literary elite, was the nephew of one of Philadelphia's most prosperous and respected Quaker merchants— although Brown's father was a failed merchant whose questionable business ethics had led to his expulsion from the Quaker meeting. British-born Susanna Rowson was an even less conventional representative of the emergent middling classes. Before becoming the proprietor of a respectable girls' school outside Boston, Rowson had been a well-known actress in England and then a best-selling novelist and playwright, first in England and then in America.[31]

Despite his Quaker upbringing, Brown's novel, *Edgar Huntly*, maintains Rowlandson's vision of the Native American as savage Other. Brown, how-

---

and Accomodated with a Narrative, of a Notable Deliverance Lately Received by Some English Captives, from the Hands of Cruel Indians; and Some Improvement of That Narrative (Boston, 1697). See also Slotkin, *Regeneration*, 100–101, 112–114.

31. William Dunlap, *The Life of Charles Brockden Brown* . . . , 2 vols. (Philadelphia, 1815); Cathy N. Davidson, "Introduction," in Susanna Rowson, *Charlotte Temple* (New York, 1986), xix–xxviii. Most social historians concur with Stuart M. Blumin, *The Emergence of the Middle Class: Social Experience in the American City, 1760–1900* (New York, 1989), rooting American class identity in socioeconomic experiences and dating its emergence to the Middle Period. Although I think of class as tied to material practices, I also see it as discursively constituted. We must search for the origins of America's class identities not only in economic changes but, as well, in the discourses America inherited from eighteenth-century England. I see late-eighteenth- and early-nineteenth-century discourses of class as anticipating and informing much of the behavior that Blumin associates with the 1830s. As Gareth Stedman Jones argues, class is a "congested point of intersection between many competing, overlapping or simply differing forms of discourse" (Jones, *Languages of Class: Studies in English Working-Class History, 1832–1982* [Cambridge, 1983], 2). In support of my perception of middle-class identity as in process of formation as early as the 1780s and 1790s, see Raymond Williams's observation that the first "modern" use of the concept of "class" in America appears in *The Federalist Papers* (Williams, *Keywords: A Vocabulary of Culture and Society* [New York, 1976], 52).

ever, replaces Rowlandson's conflation of religion and imperialism with his own conflation of class and imperialism. At the same time, Brown transforms Rowlandson's mature female narrator into a young man, appropriately named Huntly. Marginalizing and sexualizing the figure of the white woman victim, Brown constitutes the European American subject male (though, in the end, a problematic male figure). The other novel, Susanna Rowson's *Reuben and Rachel*, also transforms Rowlandson's captivity narrative, but in ways that differ radically from Brown's. Representing Native Americans as nature's noblemen and the Puritans as instruments of evil, Rowson replaces Rowlandson's religious focus with her own late-eighteenth-century European American Enlightenment vision and her concern with severing European Americans' cultural and economic dependency on Great Britain. In spite of these dramatic inversions, Rowson never fails to reaffirm Rowlandson's politicization and empowerment of the female subject.[32]

BLOODY FRONTIERS ALARMINGLY PERMEABLE

That *Edgar Huntly* is a complex and contradictory novel, at times as wild and undisciplined as its subject matter (frontier violence), is a truism in American literary criticism. *Edgar Huntly* has been described by Leslie Fiedler as an examination of the Freudian unconscious; by Stephen Shapiro as an exploration of suppressed same-sex desires; by Peter Kafer as an articulation of elite Quaker fear and hatred of Scotch-Irish frontier culture; by Paul Downes as a meditation on Revolutionary violence and the uncertainties of democratic governance; by Renée Bergland as inscribing European American male racism; and by others as a critique of that racism. One could go on and conclude that all these themes are present in a novel that fascinates by its convolutions.[33]

32. Charles Brockden Brown, *Edgar Huntly; or, Memoirs of a Sleep-Walker*, ed. Sydney J. D. Krause and S. W. Reid (Kent, Ohio, 1984); Susanna Rowson, *Reuben and Rachel; or, Tales of Old Times: A Novel* (Boston, 1798).

33. Paul Downes, "Sleep-Walking out of the Revolution: Brockden Brown's *Edgar Huntly*," *Eighteenth-Century Studies*, XXIX (1996), 413–443; Renée L. Bergland, *The National Uncanny: Indian Ghosts and American Subjects* (Hanover, N.H., 2000); Leslie A. Fiedler, *Love and Death in the American Novel*, rev. ed. (New York, 1966), 126–161, esp. 160–161; Roland Hagenbüchle, "American Literature and the Nineteenth-Century Crisis in Epistemology: The Example of Charles Brockden Brown," *Early American Literature*, XXIII (1988), 121–151; Beverly R. Voloshin, "*Edgar Huntly* and the Coherence of the Self," *Early American Literature*, XXIII (1988), 262–280; Michael P. Sullivan, "Reconciliation and Subversion in Edgar Huntley [*sic*]," *American Transcendental Quarterly* (1989), 5–22; Norman S. Grabo, *The Coincidental Art of Charles Brockden Brown* (Chapel Hill, N.C., 1981); David Stineback, introduction, in Charles Brockden Brown,

In many ways, *Edgar Huntly* is, not one, but two, perhaps three novels. It could be described as a series of novels within novels, though which ones frame and which ones are framed remains uncertain. Plot and characters repeatedly double one another, multiply and fragment as the novel moves from a former site of British imperialism, Pennsylvania, to ongoing sites of British imperialism, Ireland and Bengal, and back again; from the struggle of a landless Pennsylvania youth to find a secure niche within the middle classes to the struggle of a landless Irish boy to find the same security, to the story of an Anglo-Irish heiress seeking to secure her own autonomy and at the same time find domestic happiness. The stories they tell refract one another, (re)fusing both the racialized European American identity Rowlandson's narrative constituted and the American middle-class subjectivity that was hesitantly emerging during the closing years of the late eighteenth century.

Questions of land connect the stories the two young men tell to the story of the American frontier and its simultaneous fusion and disruption of cultures and identities. Like everything else within the novel, the issue of land itself fragments, doubling into twinned questions of class and imperialism. How can penniless and unconnected young men gain land and thus middle-class status and economic security in the throes of a capitalist revolution where claims to land divide along racial and imperial lines (red/white; Irish/Anglo-Irish; indigenous/imperial)? Who are the rightful owners of the land? In the case of Pennsylvania, is it the Delawares, its original farmers and hunters, or, representing the infant American empire, is it European American yeoman farming families (Huntly's, for instance) who promise to bring the land to greater fruition? In Ireland, is it indigenous Irish peasants or, representing the British Empire, the Anglo-Irish gentry, who also claim to develop the land for commercial agriculture? Without land, can either the European American or the young Irishman ever marry and assume a middle-class identity? Mirroring one another, the European American story interrogates the legitimacy of imperial expansion against a shadowy backdrop of uncertain class identities while the Irish story plays class tensions against the dark issues of colonial domination. And all meet in the wild abysses and subterranean caverns of western Pennsylvania.

Edgar Huntly; or, Memoirs of a Sleepwalker, ed. Stineback (Schenectady, N.Y., 1973). For two recent analyses of Brown and his fiction, see Peter Kafer, *Charles Brockden Brown's Revolution and the Birth of American Gothic* (Philadelphia, 2004), esp. 167–185; and Philip Barnard, Mark Kamrath, and Stephen Shapiro, eds., *Revising Charles Brockden Brown: Culture, Politics, and Sexuality in the Early Republic* (Knoxville, Tenn., 2004), esp. 216–251. For a more historical analysis, see Slotkin, *Regeneration through Violence,* 382–390.

Edgar Huntly starts with a doubled mystery. The body of a young frontiersman has been found murdered on the edge of his farm in western Pennsylvania. A poor Irish émigré is discovered sleepwalking and, in that state, weeping and frantically digging in the ground near where the young man's body was found. Why is he weeping? What is he digging for? The character Edgar Huntly discovers the sleepwalker when he, too, returns to the grave site at night. He is driven, he writes the dead man's sister (and Edgar's own fiancée), by the need to discover the murderer and to secure justice. "To forbear inquiry or withhold punishment was to violate my duty." Edgar Huntly thus assumes the role of judge and punisher that God played in Mary Rowlandson's narrative. At the same time, we know how ethically fraught ascertaining the guilt of a murderer along the Pennsylvania frontier could be. By what right is Waldegrave, the murdered farmer, there in the first place? Who was Edgar Huntly, a highly educated, if penniless, youthful European American to judge the case?[34]

From the scene of the mysterious Irish sleepwalker, we segue to a second mysterious sleepwalking scene, one that brings Edgar into a dark and bloody struggle with a band of Native American warriors who Huntly believes have just murdered his sisters. (It is important to note that this sleepwalking event follows immediately upon Huntly's discovery that his fiancée, on whose inheritance he depended, is as penniless as he is.) Huntly awakes from his sleepwalk to find that he has fallen into a cave deep under the mountains that run along the upper Delaware River. The cave, Huntly tells us, lies at the heart of a confusing and tortuous landscape marked by "openings and ascents . . . which seem to promise you access to the interior region, but always terminate . . . in insuperable difficulties, at the verge of a precipice, or the bottom of a steep." It is hard not to read the cave as America's womb. It is dark, reached by convoluted paths, and lies deep in the belly of the earth. Deep within this mysterious cave, blinded by the dark, naked, thirsty, and hungry, Huntly appears like a newborn infant. He cries out his terror in words that echo Mary Rowlandson's reference to Job: "Naked came I out of my mother's womb, and naked shall I return."[35]

With whom does Huntly share America's womb? Within its dark recesses, he encounters two indigenous inhabitants whom he must hunt and kill in order

34. Brown, *Edgar Huntly*, ed. Krause and Reid, 8.

35. Ibid., 97, 158–240; Rowlandson, *Soveraignty*, 336. Steven Watts remarks that Huntly's sleepwalking incident, fall, and subsequent adventures "can only be described as a journey into the unconscious" in Watts, "Masks, Morals, and the Market: American Literature and Early Capitalist Culture, 1790–1820," *Journal of the Early Republic*, VI (1986), 127–149, esp. 147–148.

to gain access to American land outside the cave and return to civilization: a savage Native American "panther" (a misnomer that actually refers to black leopards and evokes images of India that Brown will later build upon) and the panther's alter ego, savage Native Americans. Painstakingly justifying each killing, Huntly explains that panthers, members of a "ferocious and untameable . . . detested race," kill livestock and endanger the cultivators of America's land—"These I thought no breach of duty to exterminate whenever they could be found." Crossing the boundary between civil and savage, however, Huntly does not simply shoot the panther; he kills it "Indian style," that is, with a tomahawk thrown in the dark. Inexplicably ravaged with hunger (since presumably it is but a few hours since he ate and drank), Huntly then consumes the animal, literally incorporating it, gorging himself on its raw flesh and drinking its blood. The scene not only commingles Native (animal) and European American blood; it reminds us of Rowlandson's dependency on, indeed craving for, raw and bloody Native American meat and her simultaneous revulsion with such food. Echoing Rowlandson's shock at her own admixture of desire and repugnance, Huntly writes, "I review this scene with loathing and horror. Now that it is past I look back upon it as on some hideous dream."[36]

The second inhabitants of America's depths are armed Native American warriors. Again echoing Rowlandson and later captivity and frontier narratives (Carey's, for instance, remembering that these were printed not far from where *Edgar Huntly* was also printed—and from where Brown had grown up), Huntly describes their "disfigured limbs" and their grotesquely decorated, "strange and uncouth" bodies and "terrific visage," bearing "every token of enmity and bloodshed." Huntly's narrative, like those of Rowlandson and Carey, also obscures the line between Native Americans and animals. Huntly's Native Americans "moved upon all fours," "reared [themselves] above the bushes," were easily mistaken for wolves or panthers, and, like panthers, roamed the wilderness killing livestock and the innocent, productive "cultivators." (Not surprisingly, Huntly finds himself unable to distinguish Native Americans from "panthers" in the night.)[37]

Face to face for a second time with natives of America's woods, Huntly again agonizes. Is killing moral? Yes, he decides. If he does not, these warriors, like the "panther," will "commit . . . the most horrid and irreparable devastation" on

36. Brown, *Edgar Huntly*, ed. Krause and Reid, 124, 167. At the same time, in an American context, the word "panther" could refer to a subspecies of cougar found in Florida. So, as with almost all aspects of this novel, confusion and doubling dominate.

37. Ibid., 171–173, 191, 199–200.

the peaceful, white inhabitants of the district. Indeed, he concludes, if he does not shoot the "Indians" who besiege him, they will continue "to drink the blood and exalt in the laments of . . . unhappy foes," as they have done before. Huntly then tells us a story that explicitly references the beginning of Rowlandson's narrative—and the history of western Pennsylvania for fifty years before *Huntly* was published. A few years earlier, he explains, a band of "assassins" similar to the one he now finds at the mouth of the cave had "pillaged, and then burnt [Huntly's own home] to the ground." "My parents and an infant child were murdered in their beds" by "this savage band." Their brutality rendered Huntly both parentless and landless, dependent, along with his sisters, upon an elderly uncle whose death, in its turn, will leave them penniless, unable to marry or establish their economic subjectivity within the new European American middle class. Discovering his parents' bodies and one of their savage assailants dead nearby "produce[d] lasting and terrific images in my fancy." "I never looked upon . . . the image of a savage without shuddering." On discovering the present band, he wonders whether they could be the very savages that had earlier murdered his parents. In these ways, Huntly reports the very feelings that countless frontiersmen expressed during the endless warfare that marked white penetration west and Native American resistance.[38]

Inexplicably, Huntly still hesitates to attack—until he discovers a white woman in the cave, "bound hand and foot" and, he imagines, "reserved for torment or servitude." Only then, feeling himself doubly justified, does Huntly kill—wildly, viciously, with tomahawk and rifle, killings, he insists as much to himself as to his reader, that "may surely be deemed an indispensable necessity." Following this attack, Huntly wanders through a "wilderness" of Native American lands in a series of removes not unlike those described a century earlier by Rowlandson. These wanderings do not end until he buries his bayonet deep within the last Native American body. Then, "prompted by some freak of

---

38. Ibid., 173, 174, 200. What Pennsylvania reader would not have applauded Huntly's bloody desire "to kill the whole number of my foes" (ibid., 188)? The very years during which Brown wrote *Edgar Huntly,* the Pennsylvania frontier was in flames. Driven by the need to open western lands promised to Revolutionary War veterans in lieu of payment for service, the new state and national governments engaged in genocidal warfare against the Senecas, the Delawares, and the Pawnees, the outcome of which remained uncertain into the late 1790s. Indeed, this warfare had commenced with the opening shots of the American Revolution. And so it was that in Pennsylvania, as in *Edgar Huntly,* racial and national identities, infused with economic tensions, constituted a world of deadly, irreversible oppositions—just, indeed, as they had done a hundred years earlier in Rowlandson's Puritan New England and in her narrative. Among other sources, see Anthony Wallace, *The Death and Rebirth of the Seneca* (New York, 1970).

fancy, I stuck his musquet in the ground, and left it standing upright in the middle of the road." (One cannot help but notice that two phalli represent this bloody battle. Would they help the popular press resolve tensions concerning European American manliness, recuperate the magazines' denigration of western farmers as "tasty"?) It is only after repeatedly penetrating and thus marking his sexual dominance over the Delaware warrior that Huntly can regain access to cultivated European American land and European America's civil society.[39]

Being literally bathed in the blood of Delaware warriors and rescuing a European American woman, and thus performing the role of frontier hero, however, do not regain for Huntly his father's land or the wife he desires. No true European American identity emerges from his rebirth and baptism in blood, no morally unambivalent entitlement to land (any more than similar actions by frontier squatters would have gained them unambivalent entitlement to land, at least from the perspective of eastern speculators and government officials). Not only does the novel end with Huntly as impoverished and marginalized as he was at the novel's beginning; in the midst of it, we learn that his father's farm was part of a tract of land gained by Pennsylvania as a result of the infamous Walking Treaty—gained, that is, by fraud and deception, land that the Delawares never acknowledged alienating. Where did truth and justice (Huntly's declared objectives) lie in Huntly's revenge killings? Who, within the Walking Treaty territory, is the savage assassin, who the innocent victims?[40]

In *Edgar Huntly*, as in Rowlandson's narrative, self and Other refract and fragment one another: the hunter becomes the hunted; the white man, a savage; the man, an animal. Fusion leads to confusion; clearly drawn categories and systems of inclusion and exclusion crumble as Huntly, Delaware warriors, and panthers scramble through a dark and chaotic wilderness and convoluted, womb-like caves. With his "spirit vengeful, unrelenting, and ferocious," "satiated and gorged with slaughter," reddened by his own blood and that of Native

39. Brown, *Edgar Huntly*, ed. Krause and Reid, 175–180, 191, 200–203. This scene of phallic penetration returns one to the argument Stephen Shapiro makes in his essay "'Man to Man I Needed Not to Dread His Encounter': *Edgar Huntly's* End of Erotic Pessimism," in Barnard, Kamrath, and Shapiro, eds., *Revising Charles Brockden Brown*, 216–251. Shapiro focuses on the erotic tensions connecting Huntly's relation with his deadly double, Clithero Edny. Where would he place this act of deadly penetration? Does it suggest European American desire to erotically penetrate Native American warriors?

40. Brown, *Edgar Huntly*, ed. Krause and Reid, 207–209; Krause, "Historical Essay," ibid., 379–390.

Americans and panthers, by the end of the novel's central episode, Huntly has become indistinguishable from those he hunts. No wonder a band of white farmers, seeking to rescue him, end by hunting him—almost to death or, when finding him fainted from his wounds, leave him with the "other" dead native bodies that are strewn over the battlefield. (This fusion/confusion reminds us of the ending of Peter Williamson's narrative, when Williamson's wife flees from him in terror, believing him to be an "Indian"—or of the frequency with which European American frontiersmen mistook one another for savage natives.) In this way, collapsing white into red, civil into savage, illegitimate land titles into legitimate ones, *Edgar Huntly* (con)fuses the legitimacy of European American settlers' claims both to America's land and to a coherent, stable American identity.[41]

The introduction of the Irish native, Clithero, as Huntly's destabilizing twin—indeed, as his mad and dangerous double—constitutes the text's ultimate destabilizing move. Clithero stands at the center of *Edgar Huntly*'s representation of America as a world of fragmenting and refracting identities. It is Clithero's narrative that doubles and mirrors Huntly's narrative and Clithero who doubles Huntly as problematized native, rebel against British imperial authority, and emblematic middle-class subject. The novel introduces us to Clithero in a midnight scene at the graveside of the murdered frontiersman, Edgar's friend and intended brother-in-law, where Clithero, sleepwalking, is madly digging. Let us unpack some of these confusions.

The son of poor Irish peasants, without land or opportunity, Clithero was adopted by a member of the Anglo-Irish gentry, Mrs. Lorimer. She educated him with her son, appointed him steward of her estates, in short, made him a member of the salaried professional middle class. "My station was a servile one," Clithero explains to Huntly, revealing the status anxieties of the eighteenth-century middling classes. However, Clithero continues in a more positive tone,

> My personal ease and independence were less infringed than that of . . . the freest members of society. I derived a sort of authority and dignity from the receipt and disbursement of money. . . . My lady's . . . servants were my inferiors and menials. My leisure was considerable, and my emoluments large enough to supply me with every valuable instrument of improvement or pleasure.

41. Ibid., 192, 199, 219–222.

Clithero's career reaches its height when Mrs. Lorimer offers him her illegitimate niece/adopted daughter in marriage.[42]

In these varied ways, Clithero epitomizes the position of the Atlantic world's emerging middle classes. His roots lie in the peasantry; he is the son-*in-law* (or should we say *in-the-professions*) of the landed gentry. His social status depends on education, talent, responsibility—and his salary. Yet, detached from real property, his position is unstable, illegitimate (reflecting the status of his proposed bride), and vulnerable to change. And change it does. In a series of bizarre events, Clithero kills Mrs. Lorimer's twin brother and, driven by madness, attempts to kill Mrs. Lorimer and his fiancée, Clarice. "I came to murder you," he tells Mrs. Lorimer, his knife raised in homicidal fury. "Your brother has perished by my hands. Fresh from the commission of this deed, I have hastened hither, to perpetrate the same crime upon you." Murdering and attempting to murder three members of the Anglo-Irish elite, Clithero enacts the threat the middle class posed to the aristocracy throughout Europe, made frighteningly explicit during the French and Haitian revolutions. *Edgar Huntly,* we must remember, was written in the aftermath of both reigns of terror, indeed, in the very midst of the Haitian Revolution. It was also written in the shadow of Ireland's own 1790s nationalist uprisings, during which mobs of Irish peasants stormed estates just like those of Mrs. Lorimer, threatening murder and mayhem in retaliation for the seizure of native lands and the destruction of native culture.[43]

But Clithero is not only the representative of the new middle class. He is, at the same time, a savage and irrational native Irishman. His murderous attack echoes Native American attacks on oppressive and land-hungry European American settlers. Indeed, his attack by night and by stealth upon the sleeping Mrs. Lorimer and Clarice, his dagger held high over their sleeping bodies, replicates almost exactly Huntly's description of the Delawares' murder of his parents and infant sibling, Clithero's dagger replacing the tomahawk. In this way, Clithero fuses the persona of educated and ambitious professional, the threat the middle classes posed to the landed gentry, and the figure of savage native in arms against his imperial oppressors.

But these fusions by no means exhaust the complexities Clithero brings to the novel. In many ways, the failed Irish revolution of the 1790s constitutes a dark mirror image of the successful American Revolution of the 1770s and 1780s. During both revolutions, patriotic leaders turned to France for crucial

42. Ibid., 40–44, 50–57.
43. Ibid., 70–87, esp. 86.

financial and military support. In the case of the United States, France delivered its promised support, turning the tide and securing Independence. In the case of Ireland, France's promised support never appeared, and the Irish uprising failed. One would think that the Irish rebellion would have touched a deep cord of European American sympathy. But, by the 1790s, France itself had become a revolutionary state. Ireland had reached out to a French Republic viewed by many in the United States as a bloody, irrational, and dangerous republic, America's own contested dangerous double in a sea of doubling revolutions. Seen from this perspective, the mad, knife-wielding Clithero fused the savage native with the sans-culottes, the savage revolutionaries of the Terror (and of the Haitian Revolution, Haiti's Afro-Haitian revolutionaries being for the most part barely clothed). As such, the multiply layered Clithero had no claim on European American sympathy, at least not that of the eastern bourgeois elite.

Still, the fusions mount. An Irishman along the frontier in eighteenth-century America would not have been a radical Irish émigré but a Scotch-Irish frontiersman. Clithero is thus doubly Irish—and doubly dangerous. We must not forget that it was Scotch-Irish frontiersmen from Paxton who attacked the peaceful Conestogas and then terrified Philadelphians by threatening to invade their city and burn it to the ground. Certainly, Philadelphia's bourgeois elite, Anglican and Quaker, never forgot the incident. They viewed Scotch-Irish frontiersmen as illiterate, violent Presbyterians, the murderers of innocent praying Indians, threats to peaceful, orderly government, the very savages who killed Logan's wife and children. The Irish Clithero, like the European American Edgar Huntly, thus fuses two totally contradictory identities—the savage, blood-covered native and the determined hunter and killer of those natives.[44]

Edgar Huntly's mad doubling of red and white, savage and middle-class professional, native and imperial agent is redoubled yet again in a third enigmatic figure, the improbable Sarsefield, the Oedipal father figure whose narrative bridges Clithero's and Huntly's. Like them, Sarsefield began life a poor boy in a colonized land (Ireland). Like them, he seeks economic security and respectability through marriage to an Anglo-Irish heiress (none other than Mrs. Lorimer). When Mrs. Lorimer's parents reject his suit and drive him

---

44. Kafer traces Brown's family's deep involvement in the Paxton and other incidents of frontier violence to the influence of Brown's cousin, George Churchman, a prominent Quaker figure who received visions urging the Quakers to work with Native Americans to remove the guilt involved in the Walking Treaty, the very land that Brown uses as the site of his novel. Churchman was a leading Quaker voice urging negotiation with the western nations, not war (Kafer, *Brown's Revolution*, 167–186, 230–231).

from Ireland, he removes to another site of British colonialism, India, where he joins the British army in Bengal and acquires a rifle. Sarsefield then brings that Indian ("Bengali") rifle with him to the third imperial site that he occupies, Pennsylvania, and gives it to Edgar Huntly. It is with Sarsefield's Indian rifle that Huntly fights and kills the Delaware warriors—thus linking Huntly's European American imperial thrusts to Sarsefield's Anglo-India/Anglo-Irish imperial ventures. The rifle, as a symbol of British imperialism, is then doubled in its turn as Sarsefield proffers Huntly a second gift, the hand of the Anglo-Irish, but illegitimate, heiress, Clarice (who had earlier been Clithero's fiancée). Marriage to Clarice will enrich Huntly, endow him with landed estates, secure the fortunes of his sisters—and cement the ties between British and European American colonial ventures. All Huntly must do to gain this favor is to give up his obsessive involvement with Clithero, that is, accept Sarsefield's representation of Clithero as a mad savage.[45]

But Huntly cannot relinquish Clithero, his mirror image; to lose Clithero would be to lose himself. European/Native American, self/Other, as we have so clearly seen, are inseparable. Consequently, Huntly pursues Clithero through the wilderness, then tenderly nurses him back to health. When Clithero again disappears, Huntly again relentlessly retraces him, despite Sarsefield's warnings. Huntly at last finds Clithero in the hut of "Queen Mab," the last leader of the Pennsylvania Delawares and the person responsible for the death of Waldegrave, Edgar's friend and the young Pennsylvania farmer whose murder begins the novel. And it is here, in the heart of Walking Treaty territory, that Huntly betrays Sarsefield to Clithero—a betrayal that results in the death of Sarsefield's child, in Sarsefield's withdrawal of his offer of marriage, and in his final rejection of Huntly. Sarsefield's bitter "farewell" constitutes the novel's final word—and the end of Huntly's dream of a secure middle-class identity in the tumultuous economic world of the emerging Republic.[46]

What lies behind Huntly's dark devotion to Clithero, his obsessive bonding with the crazed, homicidal Irishman? Critics have frequently turned to psychoanalytic models to decipher their, perhaps incestuous, twinning.[47] Let us

45. Brown, *Edgar Huntly,* ed. Krause and Reid, 185–188.

46. Ibid., 269–290, 293.

47. Huntly's behavior has long puzzled Brown's readers. Self-destructive, it seems the product of a fractured, unstable subjectivity, prompting one to wonder whether Huntly doubles Clithero as insane subject as well. See, for example, George Toles, "Charting the Hidden Landscape: *Edgar Huntly,*" *Early American Literature,* XVI (1981), 133–153; William L. Hedges, "Charles Brockden Brown and the Culture of Contradictions," *Early American Literature,* IX (1974), 107–142. Certainly, much in *Edgar Huntly* problematizes reason. Refusing Lockean psychology,

consider an alternative reading, one that focuses on Clithero's and Huntly's conflation of colonized and colonizing subjects. As we know, in the years immediately following the American Revolution, the new Republic saw itself as both the first postcolonial nation, victorious against British imperialism, and as the legitimate heir of British imperialism in the West. Focusing on this doubled national vision, can we read Huntly's refusal of Sarsefield's protection—Sarsefield, the one male figure who makes peace with and profits from British imperialism—as echoing European Americans' need to sever their ties with Great Britain? Does his obsessive fusion with Clithero echo European Americans' cathected fusion with Native Americans? Although desiring the respectability confirmed by connection to Europe and its enlightened culture (figured by Mrs. Lorimer), the European American, Brown's novel seems to say, could never completely abandon his connection with the Native American (figured by Clithero). As mentioned above, Stephen Shapiro suggests that *Edgar Huntly* is a novel about repressed homosexual desire. Fusing Shapiro's interpretation with my own raises an interesting question. Can we read Clithero's and possibly Huntly's desire for the most forbidden of connections as itself doubled: the desire for a forbidden male/male connection fused with the desire for an equally forbidden connection between savage and civilized, red and white? Is *Edgar Huntly* telling us that a European American identity is always transgressive, fraught with uncertainty—divided? Brown's dark gothic and the Tammany Society's parodic vision double one another. European/Native American identities are inseparable. European/Native Americans are one another's dangerous doubles.

But what about gender, the question with which we began this chapter? Refusing a new European American subject as a product of forbidden male bonding, *Edgar Huntly* refuses Rowlandson's regendering of that subject female. The novel's narrator is a youthful male hunter, not a suffering mother. Within his narrative, unlike Rowlandson's, white women do not speak. Denied the authoritative voice Rowlandson constructed in her narrative, their minds are easily swayed by corrupting men. "Unable to talk coherently," they appear

---

Huntly questions the ability of the subject to reason correctly from perception. Huntly cannot detect the murderer of his friend (and double), Waldegrave. Indeed, is the somnambulist, Huntly, the murderer? Huntly never fully perceives Clithero's insanity. The experienced and world-traveled Sarsefield cannot find Huntly's whereabouts. A good republican, Huntly repeatedly claims to love his fellow men and to be devoted to the general welfare, yet death, destruction, and disorder follow always in his wake. So troubled is his judgment, we are led finally to ask, Has he even judged the Native Americans correctly? Were they really "on the warpath" or, like the Conestogas, simply hunting?

incapable of rational discourse. Most often nameless, they double and refract into an endless chain of decentered and unstable subjects: Huntly's unnamed fiancée (and Waldegrave's sister) doubles Weymouth's unnamed wife; Huntly's fiancée also doubles Clarice (the young woman Sarsefield offers him as a wife), and both of these young women double Huntly's unnamed sisters; Mrs. Lorimer, the Anglo-Irish landed aristocrat, doubles "Queen Mab," the landless Delaware matriarch; and Mrs. Lorimer and "Queen Mab" double Huntly's and Clithero's own colonizer/colonized twinning. One could go on. *Edgar Huntly's* representation of Huntly's fiancée suggests a telling comparison with Rowlandson's representation of herself. Whereas Rowlandson uses her mastery of Puritan typology to authorize her self, Huntly's unnamed fiancée's reason and religious sentiments are so weak, so suggestible, that Huntly refuses to let her see her own brother's letters for fear that their forceful (and male) espousal of atheism will pollute her innocent and tender (female) faith.[48]

The matriarchal Mrs. Lorimer appears at first an exception to the novel's representation of women as inarticulate and irrational, powerless victims. But Mrs. Lorimer suffers from an idée fixe that, if her twin brother should die, so would she (an obsession that proves to be Clithero's and her unborn child's undoing).[49] Moreover, it is only when she is a widow that Mrs. Lorimer can claim an autonomous and powerful subjectivity. Remarried to Sarsefield, Mrs. Lorimer loses her voice, her commanding presence, and her self-control.

EPIC NOBILITY/DOMESTIC EXCLUSIVITY

But actress, playwright, and novelist Susanna Rowson did not. A year before *Edgar Huntly* appeared, Rowson published a complex female reconstruction of Rowlandson's narrative. Her novel *Reuben and Rachel* constitutes a matriarchal origin myth in which America is repeatedly represented as female and America's women as authoritative figures. Rather than pitting European Americans against Native Americans and men against women, and then fracturing and

---

48. Brown, *Edgar Huntly*, ed. Krause and Reid, 173, 182, 190, 195. Brown has Huntly write to his nameless and wordless fiancée words that, as the author of *Alcuin*, he might have scorned: "Thou, like others of thy sex, art unaccustomed to metaphysical refinements. Thy religion is the growth of sensibility and not of argument. Thou art not fortified and prepossessed against the subtleties, with which the being and attributes of the deity have been assailed." Obliquely raising the theme of incest, which runs throughout the novel, Huntly continues, "Would it be just to expose thee to pollution and depravity from this source? To make thy brother . . . the author of thy fall?" (133)

49. Ibid., 76.

destabilizing the resultant subjects, as Brown does in *Huntly*, Rowson represents an American subject constituted through fusion but not confusion—as Rowson may have felt her own subjectivity had been constructed. Brought up in Boston by British parents, the adolescent Rowson returned with her parents to England at the outbreak of the American Revolution. There she married, entered the British theater, and, with the publication of *Charlotte Temple*, became a best-selling British novelist. The 1790s, however, found her back in Boston, where she established herself this time as an American novelist, playwright, and educator. Rowson's authorial voice, like Rowson's life, represents a fusion of British and European American voices. Her initial expressions of hatred against Spain along with her respect for America's noble savages reflect her roots in British and European thought as she reinscribes the Black Legend of Spanish genocide. Her final effacement of Native Americans as legitimate authorizing subjects, then, can be read as her assumption of an emerging European American identity.[50]

With these varied voices in mind, let us briefly trace Rowson's rewritings of Rowlandson. *Reuben and Rachel* revolves around two quite distinct stories. Both feature the child and grandchildren of an American Indian "princess" and a European "discoverer"/adventurer. A briefer episode, an inverted retelling of Rowlandson's captivity narrative and King Philip's War, bridges these two main stories. The novel is actually divided into two volumes: the first story and the inverted captivity narrative constitute volume 1, and the second story, which shifts our focus to the new U.S. Republic and the settlement of European Americans on Native American land along the Pennsylvania frontier, constitutes volume 2.

Throughout volume 1, Rowson assumes a European epic voice that presents women as authoritative political subjects. Early in the novel, we meet Queen Isabella of Spain and Mary and Elizabeth Tudor, who, taken together, represent European imperialism and emerging nation-states. The New World is represented by a regal and virtuous Princess Orrabella, the daughter and heir of the "King of Peru." Later, we meet Oberea, the brave daughter of an Algonquian sachem. All these women are imperial, courageous, and virtuous.

The young Columbia, central protagonist of the novel's first story, is the granddaughter of Orrabella (heir to the Incan fortunes) and Columbus's son,

50. Rowson, *Reuben and Rachel*. For discussions of Rowson's life, see Marion Rust, *Prodigal Daughters: Susanna Rowson's Early American Women* (Chapel Hill, N.C., 2008); "Introduction: Toward a History of Texts," in Cathy N. Davidson, *Revolution and the Word: The Rise of the Novel in America* (New York, 1985), 3–14; and Patricia L. Parker, *Susanna Rowson* (Boston, 1986).

Ferdinando (heir of European imperialism). Columbia possesses the ideal characteristics of the young American nation. She is blessed with "an understanding naturally good" and "virtues, which nature with a liberal hand had implanted in her heart." She is "remarkably lovely in her person" and possesses "valuable qualities of good sense, good nature, and benevolence" and "unbounded vivacity." And, throughout her youth, she is nursed by a noble Native American who is her moral guide.[51]

Using the trope of the family as an allegory for the nation, through marriage and births, Rowson depicts Columbia's progeny as accruing the basic characteristics of Rowson's America. Puritans, Quakers, colonial adventurers, and the Algonquian princess are added to the original Spanish/Incan stock. Virtuous civic Europeans and Americans love, marry, and reproduce genetically hybrid European American children until, in the penultimate generation, Reuben—the son of the Algonquian Oberea and a Puritan farm boy (captured in King Philip's War, as Rowlandson's son was captured)—turns merchant, marries a Quaker, and goes to Pennsylvania to establish an estate for his twin children, Reuben and Rachel, the new Americans (the focus of volume 2). At the novel's end, these twinned European Americans, each happily married and comfortably established on land along the Delaware (the dark and bloody land of the American frontier; the twisted, violent land of Edgar Huntly), emphatically reject further British connections and refuse titles and land left them by a distant British relative. "Our sons are true-born Americans," they state, "and while they strive to make that title respectable, we wish them to possess no other. . . . Of the immense property of which we are become possessors, we shall retain no more than will set our sons forward in business, and give our daughters moderate portions."[52]

The contrast between the ways *Edgar Huntly* and *Reuben and Rachel* reconstruct Rowlandson's original narrative is underscored by the different ways Brown and Rowson use the eighteenth-century literary device of doubling. Where Brown's doubling fractures and problematizes, Rowson's augments and unites subjects that seem at first in opposition. Take the similarity Rowson constructs between the names of two queens, Isabella of Castile and Orrabella of Peru, and between the novel's two matriarchs—Orrabella, Columbia's Incan grandmother, and Arrabella, Reuben and Rachel's Puritan grandmother. South and North America are presented by two parallel princesses, Orrabella and Oberea. Reuben, the son of a European American colonizer and warrior and an

51. Rowson, *Reuben and Rachel*, 3, 47, 79–81.
52. Ibid., 363.

Indian princess, doubles the original Columbia, the great-granddaughter of Columbus and the last Incan "king," and their doubling is redoubled by Reuben's twin children, the final European Americans, male and female, Reuben and Rachel.

Edgar Huntly and *Reuben and Rachel* differ most dramatically in their representations of Native Americans. *Huntly* preserves Rowlandson's (and other captivity narratives') insistence on racial antagonisms and racist hierarchies. *Reuben and Rachel,* in contrast, inverts, reverses, and undoes this racism. Deploying the European Enlightenment's use of the noble savage trope to critique European savagery and an even older British critique of Spanish barbarism in the New World, *Reuben and Rachel* represents Native Americans as nature's noblemen, European men as savage barbarians who rape, murder, and destroy families, indeed, whole cultures. The Spaniards, the British-American Rowson insists, are avaricious, deceitful, and corrupt, licentious, degenerate, and tyrannical. They seize the riches that belong to native peoples and despoil the land. In short, *Reuben and Rachel* reinscribes the Black Legend. Only, in *Reuben and Rachel,* the authoritative voice that denounces ravenous Europeans and asserts the innate nobility of the Native American is not that of a Spanish canon lawyer (Bartolomé de Las Casas) but the female voice—and, in the first instance, a Native American female voice. Listen to the regal Orrabella denouncing a degenerate Spanish courtier, the murderer of the Incan king, her father: "Insolent Spaniard, the king, my father, though you term him a savage, was your superior in every virtue! What though unpolished, he had but nature for his guide [and] that nature taught him humanity, honour, patience, fortitude, and Orrozombo would have died rather than deceive a friend, or insult a fallen foe. . . . Tell me, barbarian, . . . do you hold the lawful king of this territory in bondage, whilst you usurp his rights, and riot in the spoils of his devoted subjects?"[53]

Reuben and Rachel then proceeds to quite self-consciously invert Rowlandson's narrative of King Philip's War, insisting that Puritan colonizers had transgressed Native American lands and rights. Compare Rowson's discussion of the origins of King Philip's War with Rowlandson's.

The new settlers made daily encroachments on the native inhabitants, drove them from their lands, robbed them of their wives, and made their children prisoners. Was it in human nature to bear these injuries tamely? No; they resented them. . . . War was declared on both sides, and pursued with unremitting fury.

53. Ibid., 25–32, 43–45, 142.

Indeed, she transforms Rowlandson's captivity narrative into a love story and depicts Native Americans as noble, brave, and resourceful and Puritans as deceitful and weak. One of Orrabella/Columbia's New World descendants, raised by Narragansetts, marries the daughter of their sachem and succeeds his father-in-law as tribal leader. In the end, he is murdered in a treacherous Puritan attack. Thus throughout volume 1, Native Americans are represented as honorable and just figures, Europeans as corrupt and tyrannical.[54]

However, the novel's last retelling of this story is in volume 2, which effects a radical break with volume 1, in its turn inverting Rowson's inversion of Rowlandson. Native Americans reemerge as savages, wreaking havoc on Pennsylvania frontier farmers who are no longer figured as ruthless colonizers but as virtuous and productive agriculturalists. Radical alterations of voice and authorizing discourses accompany Rowson's volte-face. Gone is the epic voice of volume 1 with its evocation of classic republican rhetoric and values. Gone are the noble heroes who struggled for liberty and honor, the corrupt courtiers and the rapacious arrivistes who opposed them. Gone, as well, is the grand stage of continents conquered and empires founded. Volume 2, representing the resettling of a British gentry family in Pennsylvania, is a middle-class romance, its scenes domestic, its concerns bourgeois. It asks how merchants can discern whom they can trust in trade and how they can secure their children's inheritance, thus social and economic standing. It presents the dilemmas a young woman faces in choosing a good husband and shows how youths, cut loose from the protection of parents and family, can establish themselves as self-reliant and autonomous subjects in a new economic and geographic world.

But the world that emerges in Rowson's second volume seems to value neither Native Americans nor female political subjects. In this world of the young American Republic, Reuben, the descendant of Incan kings, the great-grandson of a North American sachem, fuses the identity of white male hunter and merchant. Moving to Philadelphia, Reuben renounces Quaker pacifism that he had acquired from British ancestors, joins the Pennsylvania militia, attacks and kills Delawares. In a scene that echoes John Smith's tale about Pocahontas, Reuben is captured by Delaware warriors and then rescued by the chief's daughter (a half-French and half-Delaware young woman) who has fallen in love with him. Having helped him escape, she follows him to Philadelphia in hopes of marrying him. Unlike his grandfather, William Dudley,

54. Ibid., 142–168, esp. 160.

this second Reuben refuses to marry the Indian princess and instead marries an Englishwoman of independent means. The princess, whom he then employs as a domestic servant on his estate outside of Philadelphia, drowns herself in the Delaware River—the same river that Huntly prowled along. In the new world of bourgeois Philadelphia (a world Huntly could never gain access to), the American hero's Native American ancestry must remain safely in the past. His future must be pure, white, and (agri)cultured. In the new world of middling America, Rowson, too, must change her European authorial and forceful female voice for that of a modest republican mother, concerned with educating daughters—and legitimating claims to American land.

The biblical associations that Reuben's name evokes foreshadow this sudden shift. Indeed, they suggest that a deep-seated racial ambivalence is woven into the structure of the novel. The biblical Reuben's mother is Leah, Jacob's unloved and rejected wife, forced on Jacob through trickery. We can read Oberea, Reuben's Indian princess mother in the novel, as representing Leah, the sound of the Native American name mimicking the biblical name. The biblical Reuben's father, Jacob, deceived his own father, Isaac, and stole the rightful inheritance of his first-born brother, Esau. The biblical Reuben, in his turn, jealous of his brother Joseph, throws Joseph into a pit, leading to Joseph's unjust enslavement by the Ishmaelites. Rowson's text underscores these biblical associations when the father of the novel's first two Reubens explains his choice of his son's name. "I have been a bondman and a servant unto my wife's father, and this my first born shall pay my ransom." Rowson's choice of Reuben as the doubled name of her heroes evokes a history of brothers' deceiving and enslaving brothers, a heritage of praise and curses. The Bible captures these ambivalences when Jacob, dying, first praises and then curses his son Reuben. "Reuben, you are my first-born, my strength and the first fruit of my vigor, excelling in pride, excelling in might, turbulent as the flood; you shall not excel; because you climbed into your father's bed; then you defiled his concubine's couch" (Gen. 49:3–4). Rowson has constructed a strange, bitter heritage for Columbia's ultimate scion, for the happy Reuben settled on land along the Delaware.[55]

And what of Rachel? Implications proliferate in dizzy profusion. In the Bible, Rachel was, not Reuben's sister, but his aunt, the desired, the beautiful wife Jacob preferred to Reuben's mother, Leah. What incestuous convolutions does Rowson suggest in so twinning Reuben and Rachel as the exemplars of

55. Ibid., 158.

the new America? Or is Rowson simply suggesting that the female half of her androgynous embodiment of the new America is the more desirable, less ambivalent half?

More desirable, perhaps, but not as political. At the novel's end, a devoted wife and mother, Rachel cannot claim to represent the new Republic as her grandmother Oberea and her ancestor Orrabella represented the New World or as Mary Rowlandson represented the new British imperialism. Subject to American common law, the married Rachel cannot own land in America. Subject to the American constitution, she has neither a legal nor a political subjectivity. Rather, she recedes within the domestic space the new American nation and the new republican and liberal discourses have allotted to her as a subject female. Indeed, she occupies the constrained space Thomas Jefferson imagined for women within his idealized vision of a virtuous, agrarian Republic. And so it is that Susannah Rowson reconstitutes and transforms Mary Rowlandson's narrative of female captivity and confinement within the new American Republic: neither the European American bourgeois romance and discourses nor European American bourgeois society can constitute women as authoritative political subjects.

So it seems. Or has Rowson, in reality, reconstituted Rowlandson's selfsame narrative, in which white, middle-class women can authorize themselves as writers by espousing white male discourses of racism and imperialism? Although Rowson played momentarily with European Enlightenment tropes of the noble savage to reverse Rowlandson's racism (volume 1), in the end (volume 2), she reinscribes that racism and so authorizes herself as a professional writer and representative of the new European American middle classes—though, significantly, not of the new republican state.

Still, like a half-solved mystery, this explanation leaves one serious loose end unaccounted for—Rowson's volume 1, in which women assume political subjectivity and noble Native American heroic stature. Novels, as political vehicles, have certain advantages that political essays, legal documents, and court decisions lack. They can play with the forbidden and momentarily indulge in the fantastic. For one brief volume, Rowson presented to her readers politically powerful female subjects and a world in which racism did not govern and distort, a world of empowered fusion and hybridity. Adopting the discourses of the bourgeoisie in order to represent bourgeois America, Rowson then repudiated that vision. But not before it had danced before her readers' eyes.

Novels do not always achieve closure. Their transgressive possibilities and contradictions may live on in the imaginations of their readers long after and despite their prescribed bourgeois endings. Although it could be argued that bourgeois discourses, for the most part, functioned to contain dissent and resistance, the multiple ideological contradictions within the republican and bourgeois discourses of that time might well have informed and authorized resistance and change. Almost immediately following *Reuben and Rachel*'s publication, bourgeois women in Philadelphia and Boston, seeking to ameliorate slavery, began to join colonizing societies. Within a few decades, they were actively protesting the Federal government's program of American Indian removal. They organized abolition societies and publicly denounced the worst forms of American racism. In all these ways, working within the space that the romance and bourgeois ideological inconsistencies made possible, they asserted their own political subjectivity. But that subjectivity never successfully fused with that of those they sought to represent. Throughout the nineteenth century, the discourses of the sympathies retained the racist, exclusionary tones we find in Rowson's volume 2. Language constructs—and constrains—its writers and readers. Bourgeois discourses inscribe both sexism and racism. But language and discourses, like women, are "a sometimes thing"—confining when they promise to empower and empowering when they seem most to confine. Containing resistance, they also produce it.

The New American–as–Bourgeois Gentleman

The Ball

Shall we dance?
On a bright cloud of music
Shall we fly?

—RICHARD RODGERS AND OSCAR HAMMERSTEIN II, The King and I

On July 15, 1782, patriot and physician Benjamin Rush described an elaborate state ball given by Anne-César, Chevalier de La Luzerne, minister of France to the United States, in the new national capital, Philadelphia. The chevalier's proclaimed purpose was to simultaneously celebrate the birthday of the dauphin and the birth of the new American Republic. The chevalier's ball was one of the first public recognitions of Independence. (The date, July 15, is significant: formal peace talks had just begun in Paris.) The excitement with which the new Americans embraced the ball was, consequently, intense. A sense of wonder and spectacle, of theater and display, resonates through Rush's letter, suggesting the ball's psychological and political significance for the new citizens' sense of themselves as independent Americans.[1]

For Rush and his fellow Philadelphians, the chevalier's ball provided a stage upon which to perform the fusion of civility and the civil state they saw as

---

1. Benjamin Rush, "The French Fête in Philadelphia in Honor of the Dauphin's Birthday, 1782," *Pennsylvania Magazine of History and Biography*, XXI (1897), 257–262. David S. Shields cites a lengthy excerpt from Rush's letter. See Shields, *Civil Tongues and Polite Letters in British America* (Chapel Hill, N.C., 1997), 1–5. As will become clear in this prologue and in Chapter 6, below, Shields's work has greatly influenced my vision of eighteenth-century European American culture and society. See introduction, esp. xiv, xix, and chap. 1, esp. 6–7. Less concerned with the private world of belles lettres and sociability and more with the public, political production of an idealized new American and the national identity he embodied, I read Rush's letter for its highly self-conscious presentation of political spectacle.

central to their production of a new nation and a new national identity. Class played a major role in the festivities, from the day the first invitations were written until the last candle was extinguished. So did a highly self-conscious theatricality—from the erecting of the ballroom through the composition of Rush's letter. Let us begin with a few excepts from Rush's letter, written to a woman, presumably an urbane and fashionable one:

> Dear Madame:—For some weeks past our city has been amused with the expectation of a most splendid entertainment to be given by the minister of France, to celebrate the birthday of the Dauphin of France. . . . Hundreds crowded daily to see a large frame building which he had erected for a dancing room on one side of his house. This building, which was sixty feet in front and forty feet deep, was supported by large painted pillars, and was open all round. . . . The garden contiguous to this shed was cut into beautiful walks, and divided with cedar and pine branches into artificial groves. . . . We were told that the minister had borrowed thirty cooks from the French army, to assist in providing an entertainment suited to the size and dignity of the company. . . . For ten days before the entertainment, nothing else was talked of in our city. The shops were crowded with customers. Hair dressers were retained; tailors, milliners and mantua-makers were to be seen, covered with sweat and out of breath, in every street.

With a carefully choreographed sense of drama, Rush then led his reader through the events of the much-anticipated day. As night turned into dawn, expectations fused with agitation. Hairdressers elbowed night watchmen as they rushed through the city's dark streets, many ladies being "obliged to have their heads dressed between four and six o'clock in the morning so great was the demand and so numerous the engagements this day of gentlemen of the comb." The city's environs had long been scoured for available rental carriages. As the day progressed, all Philadelphia, it seemed, was gathering to watch the festivities. "The doors and windows of the streets which led to the minister's were lined with people, and near the minister's house was a collection of all the curious and idle men, women and children in the city, who were not invited to the entertainment, amounting, probably, to ten thousand people." The chevalier, aware that this audience must be served, erected "a neat palisado fence" through which the masses could watch—at the same time as they were kept at a distance.[2]

2. Rush, "French Fête in Philadelphia, 1782," *PMHB*, XXI (1897), 258.

And now to the heart of Rush's letter—his and his family's arrival at the ball. On entering, Rush found that

> the scene now almost exceeds description. The numerous lights distributed through the garden, the splendor of the room we were approaching, the size of the company which was now collected and which consisted of about 700 persons: the brilliancy and variety of their dresses, and the band of music which had just begun to play, formed a scene which resembled enchantment. Sukey Stockton said "her mind was carried beyond and out of itself."

Presenting himself as a spectator at a patriotic performance of national unity, Rush continued, meticulously noting the rank and social standing of the other guests,

> We entered the room together, and here we saw the world in miniature. All the ranks, parties and professions in the city, and all the officers of government were fully represented in this assembly. Here were ladies and gentlemen of the most ancient as well as modern families. Here were lawyers, doctors and ministers of the gospel. Here were the learned faculty of the college, and . . . many who knew not whether Horace was a Roman or a Scotchman. . . . Here were merchants and gentlemen of independent fortunes, as well as many respectable and opulent tradesmen. Here were Whigs and . . . Tories. . . . the president and members of congress, governors of states and generals of armies, ministers of finance and war, and foreign affairs; judges of superior and inferior courts, with all their respective suites and assistants, secretaries and clerks. In a word, the assembly was truly republican. The company was mixed, it is true, but the mixture formed the harmony of the evening. Everybody seemed pleased . . . and the whole assembly behaved to each other as if they had been members of the same family.[3]

Rush's letter bestowed a patriotic glow over the scene. "The appearance and characters," he noted, "suggested the idea of Elysium given by the ancient poets."

3. Ibid., 258–259. Rush's description of the "world in miniature" recalls Timothy Dwight's remark : "Innumerable must be the Actors in so vast a plot, and infinitely various the parts they act" ([Dwight], "A Valedictory Address to the Young Gentlemen, Who Commenced Bachelors of Arts, at Yale College, July 25th, 1776," *American Magazine*, I [1787], 42–47, and I [1788], 99–103, esp. 99). Rush's sister-in-law Sukey Stockton's awe is telling, since her mother, Annis Boudinot Stockton, was one of eighteenth-century North America's most polished salonnières, and no stranger to politesse.

Here were to be seen heroes and patriots in close conversation. . . . Washington and Dickinson held several dialogues together. . . . Dickinson and Morris frequently reclined together against the same pillar. Here were to be seen statesmen and warriors, from the opposite ends of the continent, talking of the history of the war in their respective states. . . . Here were to be seen men who had opposed each other in the councils and parties of their country, forgetting all former resentments and exchanging civilities with each other. . . . Here were to be seen men of various countries and languages, such as Americans and Frenchmen, Englishmen and Scotchmen, Germans and Irishmen, conversing with each other like children of one father. And lastly, here were to be seen the extremes of the civilized and savage life. An Indian chief in his savage habits, and the count Rochambeau in his splendid and expensive uniform, talked with each other as if they had been the subjects of the same government, generals in the same army, and partakers of the same blessings of civilized life.

Ablaze with lights, the evening nevertheless possessed secrets and shadowy figures. "Under the orchestra, there was a private room where several Quaker ladies, whose dress would not permit them to join the assembly, were indulged with a sight of the company through a gauze curtain."[4]

And what sights lay before their eyes! The heavens shone, tables glistened, and poise reigned supreme. Rush went on, a bit breathlessly,

At nine o'clock were exhibited a number of rockets from a stage erected in a large open lot before the minister's house. They were uncommonly beautiful and gave universal satisfaction. At twelve o'clock the company was called to supper. . . . Intemperance did not show its head; levity composed its countenance, and even humour itself forgot for a few moments its usual haunts; and the simple jest, no less than the loud laugh, was unheard at any of the tables. . . . In a word, good breeding was acknowledged, by universal consent, to be mistress of the evening, and the conduct of the votaries at supper formed the conclusion of her triumph. . . . About one o'clock the company began to disperse. . . . Before three o'clock the whole company parted, every candle was extinguished, and midnight enjoyed her dark and solitary reign in every part of the minister's house and garden.

The curtain descended. Players and audience withdrew to their beds.[5]

4. Rush, "French Fête in Philadelphia, 1782," *PMHB*, XXI (1897), 260–261.
5. Ibid., 261–262.

Of course, the ball was an ephemeral performance, a moment of enchanted impermanence, its transience underscored by the chevalier's temporary shed and artificial bowers. What remains of the evening is Rush's epistolary performance of what he believed the new nation should be. Rush's letter was designed to present a picture of national harmony enhanced by cosmopolitan politesse (though we know that, at the very moment the nation's elite danced quadrilles in Philadelphia, Native American warriors danced very different dances along the frontier, and western farmers were readying to revolt).

Certainly, Rush reveled in the fact that republican harmony and patriotic unity governed the evening. Faction, he boasted, hid her face; political disputants publicly embraced. "Warriors, from the opposite ends of the continent," represented the new Republic's heroism and military accomplishments; patriot statesmen, members of the Continental Congress, state governors and judges affirmed the Republic's claim to orderly governance. The new nation's ability to cement the peace and build the future was demonstrated as tories and patriots, as well as men from different regions and ethnicities, embraced. As a final example of national unity, Rush presented the picture of a "savage" Indian chief, the only authentic American present, and the Count Rochambeau, representative of aristocratic Europe, conversing "as if they had been . . . partakers of the same blessings of civilized life."[6]

To this political mix, Rush quickly added the nation's bourgeois elite—and just possibly a few from its middling ranks. If numbers count, and they tend to in bourgeois republics, then the bourgeois elite played a major role in the evening's spectacle. Its representatives, brilliant in their dresses and jewels, outshone the political figures. Capturing the complex nature of America's bourgeoisie, Rush reported a "mixed" assembly that included "ladies and gentlemen of the most ancient as well as modern families," "gentlemen of independent fortune," merchants, members of the professions, judges and their clerks, scholars and those "who knew not whether Cicero plead in Latin or in Greek." Critical for Rush was that the assembly presented a cross section of the bourgeoisie (with a modest admixture of middling sorts) and that its disparate members mingled amicably. It was the harmonious fusion of these differing groups that Rush proclaimed to be "truly republican."[7]

Republican, but certainly not democratic. No artisans, mechanics, petty shop- or tavernkeepers, no marketwomen or laborers made their appearance in

6. Ibid., 260. So Miranda exclaimed on her first sight of young Prince Ferdinand (William Shakespeare, *The Tempest*, V, i, 183).

7. Rush, "French Fête in Philadelphia, 1782," *PMHB*, XXI (1897), 259.

Rush's letter—nor, it would appear, did any of the nation's new manufacturers. Absent, as well, not surprisingly, were spokesmen for the agrarian West, its hardscrabble farmers and frontier squatters. In short, all who might mar the grace and polish of the evening and of the bourgeoisie's understanding of a genteel America were excluded, presumably from the ball and most certainly from Rush's letter. Excluded, as well, from the letter were the many working-class men and women who made the evening possible, producing, preparing, and serving the food or obsequiously attending the guests. The chevalier and Rush seemed to agree—only the fashionable bourgeoisie could enter their "Elysium," there to be transfigured by Rush's belles lettres style as "enchanted," "carried beyond and out of itself." Of course, Rush was fully aware that this was not the real world Philadelphians inhabited; yet this was the world that mattered to Rush, to his fellow guests, and, they were sure, to the ruling elites of Europe.

To be complete, this performance of national harmony and respectability required an audience. The chevalier provided four. The first was "the curious and idle" gathered outside the minister's residence. To transform this motley crowd into an audience, the chevalier not only replaced a solid board with a palisado fence; he constructed his temporary ballroom without walls, ensuring that performers and their performances could be easily viewed. And viewed they were, as Rush tells us, by ten thousand citizens not invited to the ball. The simultaneous presence and exclusion of such a multitude, Rush was well aware, formed one of the most critical components of the event. If the virtuous Republic was a bourgeois republic, then "the curious and idle," its artisans, shop-keepers, marketwomen, and laborers, must be excluded. At the same time, they must be present. So soon after the conflicts of war, conflicts not only military but class-based and political, it was critical that "the People" re-gather to watch pacifically as many of these same gentlemen performed their proper roles as republican statesmen and national leaders. If only for that one evening, the guests could read the crowd's passivity—or possibly simple curiosity—as acceptance of the legitimacy of their representation of the new nation and of their modeling of a new American.[8]

8. Gregory T. Knouff, *The Soldiers' Revolution: Pennsylvanians in Arms and the Forging of Early American Identity* (University Park, Pa., 2004), 80, 84. See, as well, Eric Foner, *Tom Paine and Revolutionary America* (New York, 1976), 174–178. Only a few years had passed since the Private's Committee of the Pennsylvania State Militia threatened to mutiny if gentlemen officers were appointed to govern them without their consent, and since other members of the Pennsylvania Militia turned their rage and muskets against some of the city's leading merchants and political leaders, Robert Morris and James Wilson, for example, for price-gouging.

The second audience was equally critical—the elite cadre of Quaker ladies who watched demurely from their gauze-draped retreat. For nearly a century, a Quaker elite had governed Pennsylvania, politically, economically, and socially. During the war, however, most Quakers had either sided with England or, clinging to their pacifism, refused to support the patriots militarily. Some had been arrested; some had their estates attacked.[9] The evening's first and second audiences thus stood in stark contrast—the masses of the propertyless supporters of the Revolution on one side, a discrete propertied tory elite on the other; the one in possession of the streets, the other hidden from view; the one largely male, the other, in this instance, at least, female; the one asserting the power of numbers (and the potential tyranny of the majority of the propertyless), the other, significant financial resources and mercantile expertise. If the nation was to present a cohesive face to the world, it would have to draw the latter from behind their veil of silence, incorporate former tories in a new national coalition, make them part of "We, the People."[10]

Women could play a critical role in the process of incorporation. Within colonial (and British) elite circles, women had long circulated as vectors connecting different members of the ruling class through marriages and family lines. In the postwar years, European American bourgeois women eagerly assumed this task. Through their marriages, their self-consciously politicized

9. Frederick B. Tolles, *Meeting House and Counting House: The Quaker Merchants of Colonial Philadelphia, 1682–1873* (Chapel Hill, N.C., 1948); Thomas M. Doerflinger, *A Vigorous Spirit of Enterprise: Merchants and Economic Development in Revolutionary Philadelphia* (Chapel Hill, N.C., 1986), 218–223; Wallace Brown, *The Good Americans: The Loyalists in the American Revolution* (New York, 1969), 233–234; Anne M. Ousterhout, *A State Divided: Opposition in Pennsylvania to the American Revolution* (New York, 1987). Perhaps Rush felt as if he were watching an enactment of James Madison's dream of the majority of the propertyless (those outside the fence) accepting the leadership of the propertied (the seven hundred invited guests) as their representatives. For Madison on the relation of the propertyless and the propertied in an orderly republic, see Jennifer Nedelsky, *Private Property and the Limits of American Constitutionalism: The Madisonian Framework and Its Legacy* (Chicago, 1990), esp. 203–211.

10. Knouff, *Soldiers' Revolution*, 201–203, refers to patriot attacks on Quakers but relates the hostilities less to Quakers' active support of the British cause than to their general pacifism and their refusal to either serve in the militia or pay for a substitute to do so. Elizabeth Drinker, in her *Diary,* expresses hostility bordering on rage toward the patriots and considered their governance of Philadelphia illegitimate. As already noted (see Chapter 3, above), her husband was one of the Quaker merchants arrested and imprisoned by the patriots (Elaine Forman Crane, ed., *The Diary of Elizabeth Drinker: The Life Cycle of an Eighteenth-Century Woman* [Boston, 1994], 59–82). See, as well, Peter Kafer's description of Quaker reaction to patriot attacks in Kafer, *Charles Brockden Brown's Revolution and the Birth of American Gothic* (Philadelphia, 2004), 1–14.

social engagements, and their salons, they worked to solidify a nationalist elite. Was that one of the elements drawing Quaker matrons to the chevalier's ball—a desire on the part of Quakers and non-Quakers to discreetly insert such a female Quaker presence into one of the first social expressions of the new nation's political solidarity?[11]

The third audience was, of course, the French. Rush and his fellow invitees were well aware that their performances were carefully observed by members of France's and, through them, Europe's, highly judgmental ruling classes. Those classes viewed republics with abhorrence and colonials with disdain. Their opinion of their own bourgeoisie was not much elevated. One of the key questions of the evening was, Would European Americans' performances mitigate some of this disdain and prove the new Republic worthy of membership in the convention of civilized nations? This is, of course, the classic concern of the newly independent colonial subject: how would he be perceived by the metropole?

It is the fourth audience, however, that, from the perspective of national identity formation, might well have been the most critical audience of all. I refer to the bourgeois performers themselves—the generals and the judges, the merchants and the professors—and their ladies. If these players could not convince themselves that they formed a ruling class worthy of leading the new nation, they would not be able to convince the other audiences and, if they did not, class would have failed, as gender and race had, to provide a stable basis for a coherent new national identity. Carefully watching others perform as they

11. Fredrika J. Teute, "Roman Matron on the Banks of the Tiber Creek: Margaret Bayard Smith and the Politicization of Spheres in the Nation's Capital," in Donald R. Kennon, ed., *A Republic for the Ages: The United States Capitol and the Political Culture of the Early Republic* (Charlottesville, Va., 1999), 89–121, esp. 92, 96. See, as well, Teute and David S. Shields, "Jefferson in Washington: Domesticating Manners in the Republican Court," paper presented at the Omohundro Institute of Early American History and Culture Third Annual Conference, Old Salem, N.C., June 7, 1997; Sarah E. Fatherly, "Gentlewomen and Learned Ladies: Gender and the Creation of an Urban Elite in Colonial Philadelphia" (Ph.D. diss., University of Wisconsin, Madison, 2000), 230.

The feminine nature of the Quaker presence that night suggests that, with the war scarcely over, patriotic republicans might not have wished to mix socially with men whom, only a few years before, they had summarily arrested as suspected spies and traitors and incarcerated without trial in frontier settlements hundreds of miles away from family and friends. A veiled feminine presence might have symbolized both Quaker and patriot ambivalence, the one about the legitimacy of the new Republic, the other about the legitimacy of Quaker inclusion in the new nation.

themselves were observed and commented upon, they collectively and self-consciously sought to create the evening's vision of republican harmony and civility.[12] And, if they could enact that vision to Rush's and the chevalier's taxing standards, would their performances help bring a harmonious and civil new national identity into being? Clearly this was Rush's desire, a desire very much on his mind as he composed his letter reinscribing those performances.

STEPPING ONTO THE WORLD'S STAGE

Traditionally, the state ball was considered the most elegant and elaborate setting for the public display of national greatness fused with gentility. Celebrating moments of national and political importance—the birthday of a monarch, great military victories—state balls infused the civil with civility. (We must note as well that, in the process, they invoked a feminine presence to embellish the pure male political state.) The urban colonial press had frequently described such balls when they were held in European capitals. Now European Americans participated in one of their own, held in their own capital, so recently disrupted by war—a ball that, to the participants, appeared in no way inferior to those of the European aristocracy. And, the participants were also certain, they had performed the roles they had been called to play with gentility and social polish. Representatives of the new nation, brave and virtuous republicans, these new Americans had proved themselves graceful partners of an elegant and ambitious French imperial state. "Good breeding was acknowledged, *by universal consent*, to be mistress of the evening," Rush boasted; "the conduct of the *votaries* at supper formed the conclusion of her triumph."[13]

Perhaps, however, good breeding's triumph was too complete. One has the sense that secretly Rush might have worried that his fellow diners seemed a bit too nervous as they carefully observed the proprieties, betraying that stiffness, those small awkwardnesses and insecurities that characterize provincials not quite used to cosmopolitan ways. "So great and universal was the decorum," Rush admitted elsewhere in his letter, "that several gentlemen remarked that the 'company looked and behaved more as if they were worshipping than eating.'" The culture of gentility required its devotees to display lightness,

12. See, for example, Shields, *Civil Tongues*, 26–28.

13. Ibid., 145–158; Rush, "French Fête in Philadelphia, 1782," *PMHB*, XXI (1897), 262 (emphasis added).

grace, and wit. Certainly it required that gentility appear natural, at ease. Had Rush's fellow dancers failed after all in their emulation of French politesse?[14]

Eighteenth-century European gentility was the prized monopoly of gentlemen of distinguished families, landed wealth, classical education, good connections, and, above all, leisure. Gentility was the birthright of men like the Chevalier de La Luzerne and Count Rochambeau. But for how many of the European Americans gathered at the chevalier's ball was gentility second nature? Was it for Benjamin Rush, whose mother, when widowed, opened a small shop in which she sold liquor, groceries, and tableware?[15] Was it for Benjamin Franklin, the printer's runaway apprentice, who had taught himself literary style by closely studying issues of the *Spectator*? For Robert Morris, who began his mercantile career as a sweating supercargo in the Caribbean?[16] Even the

14. Ibid., 262. Lawrence E. Klein, *Shaftesbury and the Culture of Politeness: Moral Discourse and Cultural Politics in Early Eighteenth-Century England* (Cambridge, 1994); Joel Weinsheimer, "Shaftesbury in Our Time: The Politics of Wit and Humour," *Eighteenth Century Theory and Interpretation*, XXXVI (1995), 178–188; Shields, *Civil Tongues*, 26–28. The suggestion has been made that, given the strength of Rush's religious beliefs, he might have been pointing out an area of European American superiority to Europeans—the sincerity and intensity of European Americans' religious faith. This is very interesting, especially if we recall Rush's attack on European philosophes' celebration of Native Americans and nature's noblemen, which Rush read as an attack on European American religious beliefs. However, I do not see this as a theme in this letter, at least not an overt one. I read Rush's comment more as an expression of his own concern that he and his other celebrants had lacked the wit, the lightness believed "natural" to a natural aristocracy.

15. Norbert Elias, *The Civilizing Process*, trans. Edmund Jephcott (Oxford, 1994); Klein, *Shaftesbury*; J. G. A. Pocock, "Virtue, Rights, and Manners: A Model for Historians of Political Thought," in Pocock, *Virtue, Commerce, and History: Essays on Political Thought and History, Chiefly in the Eighteenth Century* (Cambridge, 1985); Richard L. Bushman, *The Refinement of America: Persons, Houses, Cities* (New York, 1992); Marc L. Harris, "What Politeness Demanded: Ethnic Omissions in Franklin's Autobiography," *Pennsylvania History*, LXI (1994), 288–317; Shields, *Civil Tongues*, 12–13, 37–40. Rush's mother opened a shop "Under the sign of the Blazing Star" on Second Street, selling groceries, liquor, and, later, chinaware (David Freeman Hawke, *Benjamin Rush: Revolutionary Gadfly* [Indianapolis, 1971], 11–12). See, as well, Ethel Stephens Arnett, *Mrs. James Madison: The Incomparable Dolley* (Greensboro, N.C., 1972), 47–48.

16. Benjamin Franklin, *Autobiography and Other Writings*, ed. Kenneth Silverman (New York, 1986), 16–17; Clarence Lester Ver Steeg, *Robert Morris, Revolutionary Financier: With an Analysis of His Earlier Career* (New York, 1976), 3–4. Even George Washington had felt the need to pore painstakingly over the translation of a Renaissance courtesy book until he had learned by heart the one hundred ten rules for genteel behavior he found there. Only then did he feel prepared to enter Virginia's polite society. See Kenneth A. Lockridge, "Colonial Self-Fashioning: Paradoxes and Pathologies in the Construction of Genteel Identity in Eighteenth-Century

wealthiest and most polished of America's planter elite, those who circulated covert manuscripts among a small coterie of friends, composed cantatas and never stepped within a countinghouse, were considered parvenus by British and continental standards. Thus the Chevalier de La Luzerne's aide-de-camp, the Comte de Mosloy, felt it his privilege—indeed, his duty—to chide the daughter of one of Philadelphia's oldest merchant families for her social naïveté and unwitting sexual faux pas.[17]

If such men and women could be found wanting, what, then, of the tradesmen, no matter how opulent, their clerks, no matter how ambitious, or those who "knew not whether Horace was a Roman or a Scotsman"? Did any of the guests at the ball wonder with secret anxiety whether the Count Rochambeau considered them only a bit less savage than the Indian chief with whom he engaged in such animated conversation? That evening, European Americans did not act like jaded courtiers attending one more ball. Rush's letter presents them as transfixed provincials, starstruck by the elegance and novelty of their surroundings. They performed their roles studiously—and hence perhaps with just a little less of the ease that they had been told came so naturally to the true gentry. Despite Rush's effort to affect a witty, slightly detached epistolary style (as in his reference to Horace as a Scotchman), did he worry that this was equally true of his letter?

Other aspects of Rush's letter underscore the bourgeois composition of the evening. David S. Shields points to Rush's attention to the production aspects

America," in Ronald Hoffman, Mechal Sobel, and Fredrika J. Teute, eds., *Through a Glass Darkly: Reflections on Personal Identity in Early America* (Chapel Hill, N.C., 1997), 274–339, esp. 333; Richard L. Bushman, *The Refinement of America: Persons, Houses, Cities* (New York, 1992), 31, 39.

17. Milady Old-Fashion [Louis Guillaume Otto, Comte de Mosloy] to Miss Inconstant [Nancy Shippen], Nov. 13, 1780, in Ethel Armes, ed., *Nancy Shippen, Her Journal Book: The International Romance of a Young Lady of Fashion of Colonial Philadelphia with Letters to Her and about Her* (Philadelphia, 1935), 96–97. William Byrd II, one of Virginia's elite planters and a longtime resident of London, was continually frustrated by his inability to be accepted in London society as a high-standing gentleman. He was especially pained that his offers of marriage were repeatedly rejected by members of the British gentry, culminating in the rejection of his 1722 marriage proposal to "Charmante." Byrd, Kenneth A. Lockridge and his fellow editors note, experienced these rejections both as comments on his "Americanness," that is, creoleness, and his sexual prowess. Can we read this as an early example of colonized and postcolonial men experiencing themselves as feminized and excluded by the metropole? (Lockridge, "The Commonplace Book of a Colonial Gentleman in Crisis: An Essay," in Kevin Berland, Jan Kirsten Gilliam, and Kenneth A. Lockridge, eds., *The Commonplace Book of William Byrd II of Westover* [Chapel Hill, N.C., 2001], 90–115, esp. 106).

of the ball. A physician who spent his days hurrying from patient to patient, Rush was well positioned to note those other hardworking Philadelphians who shared the streets with him that hot summer—the sweating tailors, milliners, and mantua makers, "the corps of hair dressers" that rose before dawn to prepare the nervous participants (few evidently rich enough to employ skilled hairdressers and maids of their own), the hundreds who daily watched the construction of the chevalier's temporary "shed." But perhaps most telling of all bourgeois compositions was Rush's letter itself. Proudly representing himself, in a polished and witty style, as one of the few chosen to attend the ball, Rush doubly inscribed his own self-consciously practiced gentility along with the significance of gentility to the bourgeoisie's imagined American identity.[18]

It was evident that Rush, republican patriot, noted friend of Philadelphia's struggling and impoverished African American community, and supporter of that other radical cause, women's education, wanted his fellow European Americans to perform the refined American as well as they enacted the virtuous republican. He cared deeply that they should infuse the civic with civility and perform up to Europe's most demanding social codes. But, as we have already noted, anxiety lurked behind Rush's polished phrases, leading one to ask: Why did the hardworking doctor place such importance on the success of his own and his fellow citizens' genteel performances? Why was it so important that the new Republic's would-be ruling elite of successful merchants, their professional allies and political spokesmen, prove themselves the equals of French noblemen and military officers in the performance of politesse? Why was it so important to perform beneath the scrutiny of European gentlemen and, especially, that those gentlemen, like the Creek warriors a decade later, express themselves as "very much pleased" by the performance?[19]

POSTCOLONIAL UNCERTAINTIES

The answers to the questions raised in Rush's letter lie, in part, in the new Republic's geopolitical positioning—a narrow band of white settlements on the edge of a largely unmapped and savage continent. Cut off by their own revolutionary acts from one of the world's great empires and cosmopolitan cultures,

18. Shields, *Civil Tongues*, 8–9.

19. For a discussion of Rush's protofeminism, see Linda K. Kerber, *Women of the Republic: Intellect and Ideology in Revolutionary America* (Chapel Hill, N.C., 1980), 210–213. See, as well, Charles Brockden Brown's fictionalized depiction of Rush in Brown, *Alcuin: A Dialogue* (New York, 1798). For a discussion of Rush's vigorous public acclamation of antislavery, see Hawke, *Benjamin Rush*, 104–107.

European Americans might well have suffered from a postcolonial sense of inferiority and isolation, what we might call postcolonial panic. (We must never forget that the United States was the first modern postcolonial republic to emerge in the West, a republic struggling for recognition in a world of empires.) By metropolitan standards, their bustling ports were little more than clapboard villages; their great estates, but clearings in the wilderness; their merchant princes, hardworking tradesmen. The sharp distinction between the chavalier's hastily constructed dancing shed and garden paths and the ballrooms at Versailles or the Court of St. James underscores the material disparity between European American and European claims to gentility. Nevertheless, European Americans continued to hope that carefully cultivated manners, a familiarity with both classic and modern literature, and clothes cut in the latest London or Paris fashions would help them prove to skeptical European eyes that migration to North America did not automatically turn civilized men into savages any more than the Revolution would open the door to mobocracy or invite the masses outside the palisade fence into America's Elysium. It was the bourgeoisie's responsibility to prove by their manners and wit that educated and judicious men governed the new Republic and that civility refined their civic world. They had to convince each of their audiences that the bourgeois elite were indeed capable of wisely representing the new nation, that an almost magical fusion of sameness and difference qualified them to stand for all European Americans, much as political representatives stood for their constituents (as in Noah Webster's elite Federalist imagination). In this way, they worked hard to represent themselves as the embodiment of their new nation—and hoped others would see them in that light as well.

Playing the gentleman helped European Americans hold another postcolonial specter at bay—fearful visions that they were little better than barbaric and often sadistic Native Americans. European Americans felt they needed to convince Europeans—and, perhaps more important, themselves—that residence in America had not reduced them to savagery, that they were far more like "the Count Rochambeau in his splendid and expensive uniform" than the Native American "chief in his savage habits."[20]

As hinted already, the performance of refinement also addresses the critical

20. For a detailed exploration of European Americans' complex psychological interdependency on Native Americans, see Section 3 and especially Prologue 3. See, as well, Carol F. Karlsen, "The Savagizing Process and the Practice of Race in Western New York, 1770–1850," paper presented at "Possible Pasts: Critical Encounters in Early America," cosponsored by the McNeil Center for Early American Studies and the Omohundro Institute of Early American History and Culture, Philadelphia, June 1994.

issue of how a coherent and stable national identity was to take form on the pages of the urban press. Could the appearance of yet another imagined new American—the European American—as—republican gentleman—help constitute a coherent American national identity when representations of gender and race had failed, a national identity built around the United States' mannered equality with the empires of Europe? Seen from this perspective, Rush's concern with his fellow celebrants' performances, a concern that unwittingly surfaces through his own painstaking display of belletristic style, assumes additional significance. Civility was not only a class-defining social grace. Upholding the new nation's claim to international respectability had become the bourgeoisie's civil responsibility.[21]

The urban press worked hard to produce their readers as republican gentlemen, representing them to themselves as urbane gentlemen. The new American, they insisted, was famed not only for his love of liberty but for his intelligence and civility. In culture and manners, he was the equal of the British gentleman; in love of liberty, his superior.[22]

But class is never a simple matter, especially in times of radical economic and political transformations. How precisely to categorize European American merchants, shopkeepers, entrepreneurs, manufacturers, and professionals puzzled eighteenth-century observers, as it continues to puzzle twenty-first-century historians. These uncertainties can be formed into three broad-reaching questions.

The first is a classic late-eighteenth-century question—one found creeping in at the edges of Rush's polished missive. Who could claim the status of a cultured gentleman? As the British gentry were quick to point out, wealth was not enough. What, then, was required? Did one have to have been born in the metropole? Have connections to the British gentry? Be educated in Edinburgh or Paris? Correspond with Enlightenment intellectuals? These last queries suggest a far more fundamental one. Was it possible for any man born or long resident in America, even if he could claim impeccable white European origins, to ever fully claim the title "gentleman" to the satisfaction of European

---

21. For examples of eighteenth-century European Americans' desire to appear genteel and respectable, see Bushman, *Refinement of America,* along with the work of T. H. Breen: "Baubles of Britain: The American and Consumer Revolutions of the Eighteenth Century," *Past and Present,* CXIX (1988), 73–104; "An Empire of Goods: The Anglicization of Colonial America, 1690–1776," *Journal of British Studies,* XXV (1986), 467–499; and *The Marketplace of Revolution: How Consumer Politics Shaped American Independence* (New York, 2004). For a further discussion of this pattern, see Chapter 5, above.

22. For a thorough discussion of this literature, see Chapter 6, below.

gentlemen? Could the European gentleman, that is, ever acknowledge those born in the colonies—in that sense, creoles—as true gentlemen, his equals in civility and civilization? (We must remember that, in the eighteenth century, the term "creole" carried a dual and deeply vexed meaning, referring both to a person born in the Americas and a person of mixed race.) Or, in the eyes of Europeans (and hence of themselves), would the American creole remain forever an amalgamation, part savage, part white, and thus never quite white or European enough?[23]

If creole European Americans insisted that they were the equal of Europeans in reason, talent, virtue, and social polish, as insist they must, then new questions emerge. Just how much fortune and education did the European American need to be considered a gentleman? Was the status of gentleman reserved for men of landed wealth whose families had belonged to the colonial ruling elite, men who had been carefully trained in the niceties of British gentility—William Byrd II, for example, or Thomas Jefferson? Or did the political and economic changes accompanying the Revolution open the door to some (though not all) new men? Did the door open wide enough to admit the new nation's commercial and financial elite, from a classic republican perspective, men whose wealth floated upon tempestuous seas, and from the perspective of commercial London, men with far from enough wealth? Would social interaction or, better, intermarriage with the landed elite (tidewater planters, New York patroons) carry such men into the Elysian Fields of gen-

23. I am playing with Homi K. Bhabha's telling phrase, "not quite/not white" (Bhabha, "Of Mimicry and Man: The Ambivalence of Colonial Discourse," in Bhabha, *The Location of Culture* [London, 1994], 121–131). The *Oxford English Dictionary* stresses the racial ambivalence that lay at the core of the word "creole": "According to some 18 c. writers originally applied by S. American negroes to their own children born in America as distinguished from negroes freshly imported from Africa; but D'Acosta, 1590, applies it to Spaniards born in the W. Indies. . . . In the West Indies and other parts of America . . . *orig.* A person born and naturalized in the country, but of European (usually Spanish or French) or of African Negro race." A similar understanding was common in French eighteenth-century texts. See Doris Lorraine Garraway, *The Libertine Colony: Creolization in the Early French Caribbean* (Durham, N.C., 2005). Perhaps more to the point was the reaction of Britons to European Americans' or British Caribbeans' claims to an unqualified British identity. William Byrd II was not the only European American to feel the harsh disdain of those born and living in the British Isles. These attitudes can be seen in two highly influential late-eighteenth-century studies of the British Caribbean. See, for example, Edward Long, *The History of Jamaica; or, General Survey of the Antient and Modern State of That Island* . . . , 3 vols. (London, 1774); and Bryan Edwards, *The History, Civil and Commercial, of the British Colonies in the West Indies* (Charleston, S.C., 1810). Both writers insisted that life in the Americas reduced Englishmen, and more especially Englishwomen, to a state of barbaric incivility, making their behavior little different from that of their slaves.

tlemanly status? If they could gain admission to that Elysium, what about American-educated doctors and lawyers, ambitious, middling merchants, or upwardly mobile manufacturers who embraced the Protestant ethic of hard work and frugality? If they could enter, could printers and publishers, the very men whose hands, stained with printers' ink, inscribed a new national culture of gentility? In short, how flexible, how changing were the new commercial world's social categories? If the appearance of gentility had become a marker of republican virtue and national belonging (as Rush's letter suggests), then a man's claim to a legitimate political voice, to civic virtue, to inclusion in the new European American body politic rested on the answers to these questions. Can we wonder, then, that members of America's new bourgeoisie were as desperate to be applauded for their social performances as for their economic successes, republican bravery, or statesman-like qualities?

Social and political historians raise our second key question. How do we categorize this European American—as—republican gentleman? Was he the last representative of a dying colonial elite, his head turned nostalgically toward Britain, even after his glorious struggle for independence?[24] Or was he, as new as his new nation and his new government, a figure of modernity, a force for economic transformation, an emergent capitalist, a fiscal innovator?[25] Alternatively still, was he a Janus-faced, hybrid figure, an innovative capitalist desperately mimicking Europe's culture of gentility? Hybrids, Peter Stallybrass and Allon White remind us, are socially threatening. Internally unstable, they underscore the instability of established categories.[26]

Our last question is the cultural historian's. Did the image of the European American as a republican gentleman, a man of property, propriety, and possibly fashion—the image Rush so desperately attempted to depict—stabilize the European American's divided republican political identity and thus help to redress the damage gender and racial uncertainties had wrought? More con-

24. A number of social historians insist that a world of clearly demarcated social and economic hierarchies marked by patterns of social deference continued to be the norm long after Independence. See, for example, Richard R. Beeman, "Deference, Republicanism, and the Emergence of Popular Politics in Eighteenth-Century America," *William and Mary Quarterly*, 3d Ser., XLIX (1992), 401–430; and Christopher Clark, *The Roots of Rural Capitalism: Western Massachusetts, 1780–1860* (Ithaca, N.Y., 1990).

25. Other historians see the new commercial and fiscal capitalists who arose during and following the Revolutionary War, Robert Morris and his Philadelphia associates, for example, or William Duer in New York, as representing a radical new economic force within the new nation. See, especially, Doerflinger, *Vigorous Spirit of Enterprise*, chap. 7, esp. 296–310.

26. Peter Stallybrass and Allon White, *The Politics and Poetics of Transgression* (Ithaca, N.Y., 1986), 39–41, 65, 78–79.

cretely, would the discourses of bourgeois respectability and the aesthetics of gentility and politesse be able to anchor the political discourses of republicanism and the imperial ones of whiteness? Or would these political and social, discursive and aesthetic systems war with one another, further destabilizing the European American's uncertain sense of self?

We cannot begin to answer these questions without some understanding of the ways the concept of the eighteenth-century gentleman evolved, first in Britain and then in North America. Consequently, we must shift our attention momentarily away from an analysis of the textual representations and discursive conflicts that dotted the new urban press and explore the social context of those conflicts. What did it mean to be a gentleman in the eighteenth-century Atlantic world? What happened when the concept of "gentleman" moved from Britain's system of landed estates to North America, a land with few traditions, no landed gentry—and where raw ambitious commercial capitalism reigned? In the following chapters, we will explore these issues, seeking a material and social context in which to place Rush's letter and the fears and desires it reveals.

CHAPTER SIX

Choreographing Class / Performing Gentility

But this is Circe's island; marriage to this enchantress means that we must live in a world of magic and transformation; and the price to be paid is admission that we are governed by our fantasies and passions.—J. G. A. POCOCK, Machiavellian Moment

W as the image of the European American–as–republican gentleman, a man of wealth, education, and politesse, stable enough to ground the identity of the emerging new Republic? Or did the inherent theatricality of the role render it precisely that—a role, learned in the act of its performance? The shifting winds of fashion spun its meanings like a weather vane in a storm, while the disparate desires of its multiple players—elite planters like George Washington, ambitious but illegitimate West Indian boys like Alexander Hamilton, the equally ambitious poor farming boys seeking a niche within the new urban middle classes—rendered this image a poor anchor in the stormy process of building a new Republic and a new republican identity.

Certainly, the role of gentleman was anything but static. From the Renaissance on, the rules governing a gentleman's behavior were extensively choreographed. Instructions appeared everywhere: in literature, portraits, legal codes, and, most especially, courtesy books. Courtesy books first appeared in the fifteenth century, initially designed for the education of Italian princes and courtiers. Discussing the nature of statecraft and the histories of great empires, they circulated widely through the city-states. On their pages, the sons of noblemen learned the wisdom of Cicero and the fate of Rome, the intricacies of polished conversation, and the rituals of the table and the court mask.[1]

1. See J. G. A. Pocock, *The Machiavellian Moment: Florentine Political Thought and the Atlantic Republican Tradition* (Princeton, N.J., 1975), 471. Baldassare Castiglione's *Il Libro de cortegiano* . . . (Venice, 1528) exemplifies the ideal courtesy book (Castiglione, *The Book of the Courtier: The Singleton Translation*, trans. Daniel Javitch [New York, 2002]). To this day, Ital-

As the Renaissance—and commerce—moved north, so did courtesy books. Within decades, Italian courtesy books were being translated for French and Tudor sovereigns and their courtiers. Propelled by the ripple effect of emulation, these books soon found their way into Jacobean manor houses. Nor did emulation stop there. By the early eighteenth century, courtesy books had become the prized reading matter of Britain's emerging bourgeoisie. In this way, rules and manners initially designed for princes and courtiers were first transposed by the landed gentry into a culture of gentility and politesse and, ultimately, by the bourgeoisie into a code of respectability. During these latter years, courtesy books' influence not only reached down the social ladder; it crossed the Atlantic, where American-born sons of planters and merchants assiduously studied their prescribed rules and manners. "The adoption of gentility could not be accomplished without effort," Richard L. Bushman explains. "The colonials had to attend to every aspect of life to achieve even a pale facsimile of English gentility. Manners had to be studied and formed with great diligence." All was so elaborately designed, all so performative. It was these manners that European Americans genteel enough to be invited to the chevalier's ball struggled to perform. And so the question remains: What impact did these movements across classes and oceans have upon the role and upon its civil and civic significance?[2]

WHAT ARE GENTLEMEN MADE OF?

Of what did the culture of gentility consist? How was the Italian prince–turned-British-or-creole-gentleman to carry himself and conduct his conversation? How were his bodily movements and social gestures choreographed?[3]

---

ians call it *Il Libro d'oro*. Renaissance portraits graphically represented the advice given in courtesy books, picturing the young man, elegantly but simply clad, in his library holding a book or pen, a globe or astrolabe. Early modern theater foregrounded the actions of noble, heroic characters, a focus Renaissance odes reinscribed. See Richard L. Bushman, *The Refinement of America: Persons, Houses, Cities* (New York, 1992), 31–35.

2. Bushman, *Refinement of America*, 30; Norbert Elias, *The Civilizing Process*, trans. Edmund Jephcott (Oxford, 1994); Lawrence E. Klein, *Shaftesbury and the Culture of Politeness: Moral Discourse and Cultural Politics in Early Eighteenth-Century England* (Cambridge, 1994); Michael McKeon, "Politics of Discourses and the Rise of the Aesthetic in Seventeenth-Century England," in Kevin Sharpe and Steven N. Zwicker, eds., *Politics of Discourse: The Literature and History of Seventeenth-Century England* (Berkeley, Calif., 1987), 35–51.

3. And choreographed they were—quite literally. Dancing masters and fencing instructors were central to the refashioning of the genteel body. See F. Nivelon, *The Rudiments of Genteel Behaviour* . . . ([London], 1737); and see Amanda Vickery, *The Gentleman's Daughter: Women's*

As we have seen, the traditional British gentleman was, first and foremost, a man of landed wealth. His standing in society and his political authority rested upon his family's possession of landed estates. Through the seventeenth century and into the early decades of the eighteenth, the landed gentleman most likely was a classic republican concerned with the preservation of British liberties and the well-being of his shire. Suspicious of commerce and change, deeply committed to the maintenance of tradition, social order, and social cohesion, he rarely allowed his vision to stray beyond his shire's hedgerows and village green. The simple country life contented him. Henry Fielding idealized him as Squire Allworthy.[4]

As the seventeenth century edged into the eighteenth, and imperial wars, commerce, and prosperity brought a cosmopolitan air to Britain, a new figure, the fashionable gentleman, stepped upon the British stage. Antique republican heroes did not stir *his* imagination. Rather, he cast his eyes toward London and the Continent. Though land and economic independence remained essential markers of gentility, politesse and manners became equally important. The political passions and straightforward manners celebrated by classic republicans now appeared crude. Pleasure, enjoyment, and sociability were celebrated.[5] Complaisance—the art of accommodating and pleasing others—became the

---

Lives in Georgian England (New Haven, Conn., 1998), 198–199, plates 38, 39. See, as well, Anna Bryson, "The Rhetoric of Status: Gesture, Demeanor, and the Image of the Gentleman in Sixteenth and Seventeenth-Century England," in Lucy Gent and Nigel Llewellyn, *Renaissance Bodies: The Human Figure in English Culture, 1540–1660* (London, 1990). For the metaphoric usefulness of the term "choreography" when discussing the performance and internalization of social roles, see Susan Leigh Foster, "Choreographies of Gender," *Signs*, XXIV (1998), 1–34.

4. Linda Gregerson, *The Reformation of the Subject: Spenser, Milton, and the English Protestant Epic* (Cambridge, 1995); Pocock, *Machiavellian Moment*, chaps. 13, 14; Henry Fielding, *The History of Tom Jones* (London, 1749).

5. J. G. A. Pocock, "Clergy and Commerce: The Conservative Enlightenment in England," paper presented at the Western Society for Eighteenth-Century Studies, San Marino, Calif., Feb. 18, 1984, 19–21. Gentility, David S. Shields tells us, had been "displaced . . . from person . . . [to] manners and things" and now lay in "the assumption of a style of conduct and thought" (Shields, *Civil Tongues and Polite Letters in British America* [Chapel Hill, N.C., 1997], 37). Shields also notes that reason, graced by wit, distinguished the new eighteenth-century gentleman's conversation and correspondence. Shunning pedantry, his speech must be, by turns, gay and touched by sentiment, his phrasing elegant and never argumentative. He learned to frame his remarks to suit the occasion and increase the pleasure of his social circle (22–23, 35). As Shields points out, the new manners were also aversely inculcated. Foppishness and false pretensions rarely escaped vicious lampooning. For an example, see *The Humours, and Conversations of the Town, Expos'd in Two Dialogues: The First, of the Men; The Second, of the Women* (London, 1693).

gentleman's governing virtue. Far from being a zoon politikon, the fashionable gentleman avoided political and sectarian disputes. Any mention of trade was, of course, de trop, the culture of gentility being explicitly designed to insulate its practitioners from the quotidian world of commerce and the street. Key to all was taste, defined in the eighteenth century as an instinctive sense of the appropriate, a sensitivity to beauty, and a desire and ability to heighten pleasure. Instinctive, but not quite natural, taste had to be refined within the confines of what the Earl of Shaftesbury denominated the *sensus communis*, or the community of the sensitive and tasteful.[6]

And so we see that taste was no more natural than performing the gentleman was. Like identities in general, taste had to be carefully taught and tirelessly practiced. John Locke laid out the regimen in his *Thoughts concerning Education*. "To form a young Gentleman, as he should be," Locke began, "'tis fit his *Governor* should himself be well-red, understand the Ways of Carriage, and Measures of Civility in all the Variety of Persons, Times and Places, and keep his Pupil as much as his age requires, constantly to the Observation of them." "Breeding," he continued, "is that, which sets a Gloss upon all his other good qualities, and renders them useful to him, in procuring him the Esteem and Good Will of all that comes near." Those who would proclaim their gentility must master an intricate pattern of behavior. Rules dictated how one entered and exited, sat and stood, bowed and gestured. The gentleman had become an elaborately staged role. Dancing masters, fencing teachers, music teachers, hairdressers, and tailors all became essential components in his production.[7]

Ideally a sensus communis, the world of the gentry in reality was intensely materialistic. As an orgy of spending engulfed eighteenth-century British society, "gentility," Amanda Vickery astutely observes, "found its richest expression in objects. Indubitably mahogany, silver, porcelain and silk all announced the wealth and taste of the privileged." No object in this litany was more critical than dress. "You will not easily believe how much we consider your dress as

6. Shields, *Civil Tongues*, 22–23, 32–37, 39; Anthony Ashley Cooper, Third Earl of Shaftesbury, *Sensus Communis: An Essay on the Freedom of Wit and Humour* . . . (London, 1709). See, as well, Joel Weinsheimer, "Shaftesbury in Our Time: The Politics of Wit and Humour," *Eighteenth Century Theory and Interpretation*, XXXVI (1995), 178–188; Julie K. Ellison, *Cato's Tears and the Making of Anglo-American Emotion* (Chicago, 1999), esp. 16, 25–27, 46. Mr. Darcy, in *Pride and Prejudice*, is justly castigated for his sullen and superior behavior at a country dance. He has not acted with complaisance (Jane Austen, *Pride and Prejudice* [London, 1813]).

7. John Locke, *Directions concerning Education: Being the First Draft of His Thoughts concerning Education* (Oxford, 1933), 94.

expressive of your character," one eighteenth-century British father wrote his daughter. "An elegant simplicity is an equal proof of taste and delicacy." "Elegant simplicity," then as now, was a costly item. The soft fall of silk, muslin, or Flanders lace, the subtle drape of cashmere, the shine of silk stockings did not come cheap. Nor easily. Taste required a self-conscious attention to the latest fashions. The length of a vest, the size of a shoe buckle, whether prints or stripes were in vogue were subjects of constant debate and anxiety for gentlemen and their ladies. And, as we shall see shortly, taste had become the subject of calculated commercial manipulation by merchants in London and manufacturers in Lancaster—all in quest of ever-greater profits.[8]

The performance of gentility required not only precisely correct costumes but an elegant stage and carefully arranged sets. The gentleman's home no longer offered the country republican a virtuous retreat from the seductive glitter of the court or the fiscal snares of the city. It had been refigured as a stage for the performance of the elaborate culture of gentility and politesse.[9] Newly

8. Vickery, *Gentleman's Daughter,* chap. 2, 161; Neil McKendrick, "The Consumer Revolution of Eighteenth-Century England," 10, and "The Commercialization of Fashion," 34–98, both in McKendrick, John Brewer, and J. H. Plum, eds., *The Birth of a Consumer Economy: The Commercialization of Eighteenth-Century England* (Bloomington, Ind., 1982); Shields, *Civil Tongues,* 31; Sarah E. Fatherly, "Gentlewomen and Learned Ladies: Gender and the Creation of an Urban Elite in Colonial Philadelphia" (Ph.D. diss., University of Wisconsin, Madison, 2000), 115–116, 126. Bernard L. Herman, referring to both Great Britain and North America, states the situation most succinctly: "Social identity depended on [the] material world for its expression" (Herman, *Town House: Architecture and Material Life in the Early American City, 1780–1830* [Chapel Hill, N.C., 2005], 38).

9. Not only private homes but entire cities (or at least their fashionable centers) were transfigured. The commercial prosperity that enriched late-seventeenth- and eighteenth-century England encouraged a renaissance in urban planning and domestic architecture. Post-Fire London, Edinburgh, and Bath, among many other cities, were gradually transformed into Georgian cities, graced with residential circuses, parks, and promenades. Sir Christopher Wren and other fashionable architects adapted plans, originally intended for aristocratic manor houses, to the needs of the country gentry and, eventually, the rising bourgeoisie. They designed these homes to signal the gentleman's social status, secure wealth, and refined taste (Peter Borsay, *The English Urban Renaissance: Culture and Society in the Provincial Town, 1660–1770* [Oxford, 1989]). As already noted, the culture and practice of gentility moved quickly from the aristocracy to the gentry to the merchant prince and from thence to the colonies until, by the mid-eighteenth century, one could talk of a circum-Atlantic culture of politesse expressed in common material forms. And nothing was more central to this culture than the house. Concerning the North American mercantile elite, Herman writes: "The merchant family's town house, the most visible outward expression of its status and identity, had to function successfully in multiple

constructed grand entrance halls and wide, curving stairwells were designed to permit hosts and guests to display the rituals of arriving and receiving. Imported crystal chandeliers and gilt-framed mirrors reflected a series of formalized social performances. Within the drawing room, attention focused on the tea table, with its complement of fashionable accoutrements. Around it, ladies gathered to gossip, display the latest London fashion, discuss novels, exchange poems, patronize famous writers, even discuss women's rights. And they did more. By their presence and wit, they maintained an air of moderation and civility that was not always found within the masculine surrounds of the eighteenth-century coffeehouse. Reinscribing in fantastical dimensions the gracious scenes playing out beneath them, family portraits looked down majestically.[10]

Within these settings, every movement, every word of host, guest, and servant was observed and evaluated. To enter these rooms was to fashion oneself simultaneously as spectacle and spectator. "Gentility heightened self-consciousness . . . in the common meaning of becoming aware of how one looked in the eyes of others," Bushman tells us. Especially as the eighteenth century progressed, "life became a continuous performance, perpetually subject to criticism." "Everyone and virtually everything could be brought to judgment before the bar of refinement and beauty." Nor was the performance of others the eighteenth-century gentleman's only concern. With self-conscious

---

overlapping situations. The exterior of the structure, its scale, construction, and ornament, reinforced local distinctions. . . . The interior of the house, through its room uses, decorative appointments, and fashionable furnishings, engaged social relationships that transcended place and were defined in the competitive culture of Atlantic cosmopolitanism" (*Town House,* 39). Homes were critical, but so were the gardens that surrounded them. Especially with the Romantic era, the layout of a garden revealed the gentleman's soul. Elizabeth in *Pride and Prejudice* finally admits that she loves Darcy when she sees his garden and understands suddenly the inner worth of a man who could have designed such a garden. Darcy's naturally superior character contrasts sharply with that of the foolish and cuckolded husband in *Mansfield Park* (1814), who doesn't have a clue how to lay out a garden, and indeed, it is in his ill-conceived garden that the rake seduces his future wife.

10. Borsay, *English Urban Renaissance.* The tea table was one of the most expensive items in any genteel house and a principal site for the performance of gentility and refinement (Vickery, *Gentleman's Daughter,* 206–208). The coffeehouse, with its mix of classes and its embrace of equality, was a site of modernity that pointed to a number of ideological contradictions and social confusions that emerged as the culture of gentility moved from the court and aristocracy to the country gentry and ultimately to the bourgeoisie of merchants, manufacturers, and professional men. For a discussion of eighteenth-century coffeehouses in America, see Shields, *Civil Tongues,* 55–98.

intensity, he observed his own behavior. Performance and self-scrutiny, Bushman adds, were "unrelenting"—as they had been in Benjamin Rush's carefully constructed letter.[11]

Elaborate codes of dress, speech, and behavior, along with stately homes and rich accoutrements, existed to distinguish the man of landed estates and leisure from all who worked but most pressingly from England's economically powerful and socially ambitious merchants and manufacturers. Yet, ironically, the culture of gentility was, in large part, the creation of the very men it was designed to exclude. The markers of gentility, the silks and muslin, cashmere and porcelain that announced the man of landed estates and leisure were all imported by the great and small merchants of London, Bristol, Liverpool, and Glasgow or manufactured by the new entrepreneurs of Lancaster and Manchester. And these men produced not only the goods but the dictates of fashion. Seventeenth-century fashion had percolated down from the French to the British court and from there to the aristocracy, the gentry, and, finally, to the bourgeoisie. In the early eighteenth century, suddenly the chain of command reversed directions, moving from London counting rooms and Lancaster mills to London's bon ton and from thence to the court at Westminster. The "pseudo gentry," as the top echelon of great merchants and manufacturers came to be called, now set the codes that all who would be fashionable and therefore of good character must follow. Nor did the confusions end there. While elevating merchants and manufacturers to the role of fashion arbiters, the consumer revolution turned Britain's aristocracy into men of commerce as manufacturers solicited the endorsements of the nobility for luxury items they hoped to sell. (Josiah Wedgwood's relation to the Duchess of Devonshire, who displayed his porcelains, or John Foster's to the Countess of Bective, who endorsed his carpets, are only two examples of a growing trend.)[12]

11. Bushman, *Refinement of America,* 14.

12. McKendrick, "Consumer Revolution," 28, and "Josiah Wedgwood and the Commercialization of the Potteries," 99–144, esp. 104, both in McKendrick, Brewer, and Plum, eds., *Birth of a Consumer Economy.* As McKendrik points out: "All those tiny London satellites to the Lancashire cotton mills—the tailors, dressmakers, milliners and mantuamakers—would produce enough minor variations on the prevailing fashions to satisfy the market, keep its interest alive and allow the factories to churn out stripes or muslins or whatever was required . . . until the next major change was introduced—if possible, carefully stage managed and timed to suit the needs of commerce." The ebb and flow of fashions were easily disseminated through London's proliferating fashion magazines and the "English fashion doll," a paper doll that was issued each year with six complete changes of clothes for "the season." These dolls were sold very cheaply and distributed very widely (ibid., 21).

Taste, that marker of "natural" superiority and social exclusion, was for sale. Indeed, taste had to be purchased.[13] And, if taste was purchasable, then anyone with money could purchase it—and did. The economic and political changes that marked first post-Restoration and then Georgian Britain precipitated a rapid expansion in the wealth and power of London, Bristol, and Liverpool merchants and only a bit later of the new manufacturers of Lancaster and Manchester. By the 1720s and 1730s, possessing wealth that beggared the imaginations of many country gentlemen, these new men could easily afford the accoutrements of gentility. They were, moreover, cosmopolitan in their experiences, intelligent, and often well educated. By the mid-eighteenth century, they, too, could boast of magnificent country estates, "improved" gardens, extensive art collections, elegant tea tables, and well-bred ladies to officiate at them. They, too, had studied the latest courtesy books. Why, then, were they not gentlemen?[14]

Of course, there were breaks in the armor of class—especially on the level of the parish gentry, especially in geographically marginal and industrialized regions in the north of England, and most especially as the long eighteenth century came to an end within the shadow of recurrent revolution. Studying the rural parishes in the north of England, Vickery discovered a pattern of social interaction between what she calls the "parish gentry" (families of modest landed wealth) and an increasingly prosperous bourgeoisie of professionals, manufacturers, and tradesmen, social interactions that spanned the broad spec-

13. T. H. Breen, "Ideology and Nationalism," in Jack P. Greene and J. R. Pole, eds., *Colonial British America: Essays in the New History of the Early Modern Era* (Baltimore, 1984), 15–18; and Breen, "An Empire of Goods: The Anglicization of Colonial America, 1690–1776," *Journal of British Studies*, XXV (1986), 467–499; Shields, *Civil Tongues*, 24; McKendrick, "Introduction," in McKendrick, Brewer, and Plum, eds., *Birth of a Consumer Economy*, 1; Kathleen Wilson, *The Sense of the People: Politics, Culture, and Imperialism in England, 1715–1785* (Cambridge, 1995), 57–59. Not only was taste for sale; sales were incessant and ongoing. Novelty was in the air, and fashion changed with the season—to the profit of merchants and mill owners. "Where once a fashion might last a lifetime," McKendrick tells us, "now it might barely last a year" (1). This shift is exemplified by a contrast between the rapid and cheap dissemination of the English fashion paper doll and the earlier, stately progress of the French fashion doll. The French fashion doll had not been a paper cutout but a life-size manikin sent each year from the French court to the British court, from whence it passed down the social scale from nobility to gentry. It had stimulated fashions but had not, itself, been an object of sale and profit (43–45).

14. For a description of the country estates, equipage, and art collections of a group of successful provincial merchants, see David Hancock, *Citizens of the World: London Merchants and the Integration of the British Atlantic Community, 1735–1785* (Cambridge, 1995), 279–381. The merchants Hancock studied, he carefully notes, were far from being the richest or the best connected of Britain's elite.

trum from invitations to tea to marriage. But most historians are convinced that an "oppositional culture" of the greater gentry and the middle classes pervaded England, discursively and, in many ways, actually. The landed gentry continued to view merchants and manufacturers as uncultured and narrowly self-interested.[15] No matter how great their fortunes, how elegant their equipage, in the minds of the gentry, London merchants and Lancaster manufacturers were irrevocably associated with countinghouses, wharves, and factories with sweating slave- and wage laborers. Throughout the long eighteenth century, land and trade, tradition and innovation, real estates and speculative fortunes constituted binaries around which the landed gentry sought to ground meaning, value, and identities.[16]

But, resist as they might, England's gentry were no more able to control the tides of change than King Connaught had been able to command the seas. As the eighteenth century progressed, imperial wars and commerce not only increased the wealth of Britain's great merchants and manufacturers; it greatly expanded the numbers of provincial shopkeepers, bankers, brokers, insurance agents, attorneys, and appraisers—its middling ranks—and the capital they had to purchase the markers of gentility and taste.[17] Given the unstable and com-

15. Vickery, *Gentleman's Daughter,* 13–37. Horace Walpole, Hancock notes, was shocked that a merchant would ever be mistaken as gentleman *(Citizens of the World,* 281). With growing fervor, the "greater" gentry fought back against the incursions of the merchants and manufacturers. Embracing a self-image designed to exclude, they presented themselves as guarantors of "British-ness," their ancestral lands securing not only wealth and social status but an association with English history and long-standing service to the state. Scornfully, they emphasized the differences between themselves and the new men of commerce and industry. The new men's conversations, they scoffed, were filled with pat phrases conned from courtesy books or fashion magazines, riddled with ridiculous neoclassical references and usages, devoid of wit, grace, or taste. Even more significantly, their wealth, though vast, was ephemeral, tied to ships on distant seas, speculation in fluctuating stocks and bonds, credit received and given. Dealing in the far-flung markets of Africa, China, India, and the Caribbean, these "pseudogentlemen" reeked of work—and, worst of all, the foreign.

16. Pocock takes a somewhat different view, seeing men of land and trade as meeting in a middle space—that of genteel, clubby London. "The invention of gentility," he says, "did more to unify the ruling elites and the upwardly mobile than it did to divide them. The Town was the capital of gentility, its ideology was politeness." And it was here that these traditionally distinct groups interacted with increasing regularity (Pocock, "Clergy and Commerce," 12). Even the most casual reading of *The Spectator* confirms Pocock's observation.

17. Their efforts were greatly facilitated by the ready availability of British manufactures. Wedgwood creamware, far less expensive than Chinese import-ware, became just as fashionable. Silver plate from Birmingham mimicked the aristocracy's heirlooms. Eighteenth-century Britain had a "compressed class structure," McKendrick explains. The ascent between ranks—

petitive nature of eighteenth-century Britain's class structure, characterized, as N. Forster described it in 1767, by "the perpetual restless ambition in each of the inferior ranks to raise themselves to the level of those immediately above them," the desire for "fashionable luxury . . . spread through it like a contagion." That astute observer of English social practices Henry Fielding captured the spirit of the age. "While the Nobleman will emulate the Grandeur of a Prince and the Gentleman will aspire to the proper state of a Nobleman," he remarked archly, "the Tradesman steps from behind his Counter into the vacant place of the Gentleman. Nor doth the confusion end there: It reaches the very Dregs of the People[,] who aspire still to a degree beyond that which belongs to them."[18] And so the world of British gentility shifted from one centered around land, leisure, and authenticity to one of fashion, novelty, and performance. The "Century of the Spectator" became a century of masquerade and imposture. All who could—and dared—played the role of those above them. The role of the British gentleman became increasingly unstable, indeed, quite literally "up for grabs." The cultural meaning of gentility became multiple, contradictory. Skim milk masqueraded as cream. The gentry fretted (as any reader of Jane Austen knows) but could not stem the tide.[19]

STEPPING OUT IN THE "NEW WORLD":
THE CREOLE AS FAUX GENTLEMAN

What happened when manners and behaviors choreographed to represent the world of landed gentlemen were transplanted to a world with few, if any, such gentlemen, a world perched on the edge of a savage continent? European Americans not only faced the troubled distinctions between gentry, "pseudo

---

from petty shopkeepers and manufacturers to larger shopkeepers and professionals and from thence to great merchants and manufacturers (the pseudogentry), to the landed gentry, and then to the aristocracy—went by easy and gradual steps ("Consumer Revolution," in McKendrick, Brewer, and Plum, eds., *Birth of a Consumer Economy*, 10–11, 20, 23). For a discussion of the close relations provincial gentry maintained with established merchants in their communities, see Vickery, *Gentleman's Daughter*, 168–175. For a slightly later period, see Leonore Davidoff and Catherine Hall, *Family Fortunes: Men and Women of the English Middle Class, 1780–1850* (New York, 2002).

18. Fielding, *Works*, II, 783, and Nathaniel Forster, *An Enquiry into the Causes of the Present High Price of Provisions* (London, 1767), 41, both cited by McKendrick, "Consumer Revolution," in McKendrick, Brewer, and Plum, eds., *Birth of a Consumer Economy*, 11, 22, 25.

19. For a revealing discussion of spectacle and spectatorship, money and representation in eighteenth-century Great Britain, see Jean-Christophe Agnew, *Worlds Apart: The Market and the Theater in Anglo-American Thought, 1550–1750* (Cambridge, 1986), especially chap. 4.

gentry," and bourgeoisie; they faced British contempt for things colonial. From a refined British perspective, European Americans' association with slavery and savagery along with their merchants' relatively modest capital resources placed them "beyond the pale." Facing these multiple handicaps, could the class status and gentility of an emerging American bourgeoisie solidify the new national identity?[20]

Throughout the colonial period, the ruling classes in Britain's North American colonies were multi-tiered. Representing the political and military authority of the Crown and the prestige of elite British culture, royal officeholders, especially governors and military officers, stood at its apex. Below them, in the North as well as in the plantation South, were the great American-born landholding families, proud of their superior wealth and social standing—the tidewater planters of Virginia and the Carolinas (Byrds and Randolphs, Pinckneys and Manigaults), the Hudson Valley's great landholders (De Lanceys and Phillipses, Van Rensellears and Livingstons). These two groups, British officeholders and European American landed families, unquestionably constituted the colonial ruling class. They took the "grand tour" and frequented fashionable British spas (Tunbridge Wells was a particular favorite among planters). Their Georgian homes dotted the American countryside, self-consciously named after famous British estates.[21]

Below them in status, affluent merchants and their professional allies were ardent pupils of the colonial ruling elite. With impressive speed, they, too, mastered the intricate and changing choreography of Anglo-American gentility. America's growing commercial prosperity facilitated such emulation—as did the expanding print culture of newspapers, magazines, and novels that ardently disseminated the latest fashions and rules of etiquette. By the closing years of British colonial rule, art historian Paul Staiti tells us, European American merchants and professionals "were becoming more self-consciously British than ever before, and they were willing to spend money as their transatlantic cousins did, especially on objects that expressed their Englishness." Their "inflated sense of self-worth encouraged them to ape English aristo-

20. I have deliberately chosen an exclusionary phrase from that other British colony, Ireland, to express British residents' feelings about those not born or resident on their island.

21. Richard L. Bushman, "American High-Style and Vernacular Cultures," in Greene and Pole, eds., *Colonial British America*, 345–383, 350–351. See, as well, Bushman, *Refinement of America*; and Philip L. White, *The Beekmans of New York in Politics and Commerce, 1647–1877* (New York, 1956). For a discussion of spas, see Shields, *Civil Tongues*, 41. For a discussion of grand tours, see Kenneth A. Lockridge, *The Diary, and Life, of William Byrd II of Virginia, 1674–1744* (Chapel Hill, N.C., 1987).

crats at the same time that insecurity about their provinciality intensified cravings for culturally identifying forms that validated their transatlantic status." "Elites," Staiti concludes, "were using luxury consumer goods to define themselves."[22] To appreciate the importance the colonial bourgeoisie placed on the elegance and showiness of their possessions, we have only to read comments John Adams, that ambitious lawyer and farmer's son who was gradually edging up Massachusetts's social ladder, made on visiting the residence of Nicholas Boylston, one of Boston's premier merchants. "Dined at Mr. Nick Boylstones *[sic]*," Adams wrote.

> An elegant Dinner indeed! Went over the House to view the Furniture, which alone cost a thousand Pounds sterling. A Seat it is for a noble Man, a Prince. The Turkey Carpets, the painted Hangings, the Marble Tables, the rich Beds with crimson Damask Curtains and Counterpins, the beautiful Chimny Clock, the Spacious Garden, are the most magnificent of any Thing I have ever seen.[23]

22. Paul Staiti, "Accounting for Copley," in Carrie Rebora and Staiti, eds., *John Singleton Copley in America* (New York, 1995), 25–51, esp. 32, 33, 35. See, as well, T. H. Breen, "The Meaning of 'Likeness': American Portrait Painting in Eighteenth-Century Consumer Society," *Word and Image*, VI (1990), 325–350; Bushman, "American High-Style," in Greene and Pole, eds., *Colonial British America*, 366. Margaretta M. Lovell, in her *Art in a Season of Revolution: Painters, Artisans, and Patrons in Early America* (Philadelphia, 2005), takes issue with both Staiti and Breen. She does agree that European Americans both before and after the Revolution saw portraiture as a critical way of demonstrating their gentility. In doing so, Lovell contends, they merely reflected eighteenth-century attitudes toward gentility, attitudes they shared with the metropole. They were not particularly envious of Britain. Nor did their desire to appear genteel indicate class insecurity (18, 53). On the other hand, Lovell cites William Hazlitt's statement that the European American mercantile elite "wish[ed] to be represented as complete abstractions of persons and property" (P. P. Howe, ed., *The Complete Works of William Hazlitt*, 21 vols. [London, 1933], XVIII, 108–109, cited in Lovell, *Art in a Season of Revolution*, 46).

23. Staiti, "Accounting for Copley," in Rebora and Staiti, eds., *Copley in America*, 54. Herman views the merchant prince's home as both a site and a metaphor for power relations in commercial North America. "Larger social continuities suggested by the furnishing strategies echo in the town houses" of merchant princes, Herman tells us. "Dining room and parlor offered an important venue for face-to-face negotiations, where the competitive culture of trade coincided with hospitality." "The . . . dining room table," Herman continues, "established an arena for one aspect of these competitive exchanges; the tabletop could function metaphorically as a representation of the city itself." "The rituals of the dinner table mirrored the negotiation of the world of trade. . . . As two elements in an embedded landscape, the architecture and actions of trade and table informed and reinforced each other" *(Town House*, 71, 73). For a fascinating diagram of the dining table as the scene of commercial advancement, see 72.

Boston, however, could not equal Philadelphia for its commercial success and the Georgian elegance its merchants were able to display.[24] The Palladian estates Philadelphia merchants built during the mid-eighteenth century were unrivaled in North America for their display of elegance and taste. None succeeded as well as John Cadwalader, the scion of one of Philadelphia's richest mercantile families. Returning from three years abroad on the grand tour, Cadwalader married a Maryland plantation heiress (a common marriage pattern among Philadelphia's non-Quaker merchant elites), Elizabeth Wye. The Cadwaladers' town house was surrounded by elaborate gardens, orchards, stables, and, of course, slave quarters. The glamour of the building's interior decorations mirrored that of its exteriors. Gilded neoclassical moldings surmounted marble fireplaces and adorned walls and ceilings. Imported furniture graced the rooms. Tea services from Japan and Dresden and enameled chocolate cups and saucers adorned their table. An elaborate portrait of John and Elizabeth Cadwalader and their daughter Anne, painted in 1772 by Charles Willson Peale, hung on their wall. But the pièce de résistance was the "great bed" that dominated the Cadwaladers' bedroom. "The appearance of John Cadwalader's great bed must have been truly majestic," Philadelphia historian Nicholas Wainwright notes, "swathed as it was in many yards of colorful materials, betasseled and crowned with a cornice of carved wood on which were mounted plumes." It was "a spectacle of almost barbaric splendor." (All in all, the Cadwaladers spent more than £9,000 on their home, a sum made possible by Betsy Wye Cadwalader's ample dowry that included a Maryland plantation and its slaves.)[25]

24. Bushman, "American High-Style," in Greene and Pole, eds., *Colonial British America*, 350; Fatherly, "Gentlewomen and Learned Ladies," 50–72, 143–144. Architectural historians Roger W. Moss and Tom Crane note that these houses were all carefully modeled upon British manor houses. Guides to the production of Georgian material culture circulated widely in colonial North America, and Philadelphia merchants were major consumers. Architectural books such as Abraham Swan's widely used *Collection of Designs in Architecture*, horticultural guides such as John Worlidge's *Systema Horticulturae; or, The Art of Gardening in Three Books* (London, 1677), Jan Kip and Leonard Knyff's *Britannia Illustrata* (London, 1707), even catalogues of fashionable hardware—wrought-iron fences and balustrades, door handles and drawer pulls, fireplace tools and door locks—found their way from London to Philadelphia, New York, Boston—and beyond. See Moss and Crane, *Historic Houses of Philadelphia: A Tour of the Region's Museum Homes* (Philadelphia, 1998), 96.

25. For a copy of Peale's portrait of John and Elizabeth Cadwalader, see Lovell, *Art in a Season of Revolution*, 157, fig. 63. For a detailed description of the Cadwalader home, see Nicholas B.

By all accounts, the result was worth the effort. The Cadwaladers' home, Wainwright reports, "furnished a brilliant setting for the social and financial elite of the city, and in its parlors were discussed some of the most advanced ideas of the day." Violin music graced their dinners. Majesty, if just a bit "barbaric," reigned. Gatherings at Samuel Powel's home next door, where balls were frequent in the upstairs drawing room, were equally grand, both before the war and after, when Philadelphia became the capital of the new nation and President Washington resided next door in the town house that had been colonial proprietor Thomas Penn's.[26]

In North America, as in Great Britain, the choreographies of gentility revolved around the tea table. Of course, men complained. Women's tea rituals were expensive. In Boston in the 1720s, a mahogany tea table with its fashionable settings cost more than £250. Regular participation, moreover, encouraged indulgence in fashionable expenditures, especially clothes. Worst of all, the tea table constituted a domain where women ruled—and men came to court (in both senses of that word). Gathered there, women could assess men's performances of civility, compliment accomplished players, correct others. Tea-table gossip established and enforced the rules that governed polite society. A creole bourgeoisie desiring to assert its cultural equality with England could not do without the tea table and its ladies.[27]

Wainwright, *Colonial Grandeur in Philadelphia: The House and Furniture of General John Cadwalader* (Philadelphia, 1964), 43. It is important to remember that the public, even "barbaric" display of sexuality was not de trop in the eighteenth century as it would become in the nineteenth.

26. Wainwright, *Colonial Grandeur*, 60. John Powel, if anything, had married even better than Cadwalader, though not into the landed classes. His wife, Elizabeth Willing Powel, came from one of Philadelphia's richest merchant families. Her sister, Mary, married William Byrd III, and all resided near one another in Philadelphia's "aristocratic quarter." Elizabeth would become one of the stars of Martha Washington's "republican court." For photographs of the Powels' dining room and music room, see Moss and Crane, *Historic Houses*, 36–39. See, as well, Bushman, "American High-Style," in Greene and Pole, eds., *Colonial British America*, 35–52; Ethel Armes, comp. and ed., *Nancy Shippen, Her Journal Book: The International Romance of a Young Lady of Fashion of Colonial Philadelphia with Letters to Her and about Her* (Philadelphia, 1935), 55–59.

27. For a photograph of an eighteenth-century creole tea table ensemble and a description of carefully choreographed tea rituals, see Herman, *Town House*, 73–76. For other detailed descriptions of creole ladies, their tea tables, and their salons, see Shields, *Civil Tongues*, 99–140; and Fatherly, "Gentlewomen and Learned Ladies," 119–123. In the post-Revolutionary period, elite women assumed important additional tasks, principally encouraging national unity and smoothing over political disputes among the new Republic's political leaders. But whatever their specific social and political tasks, the practice of gentility around the tea table and through the salons that grew around them remained critical. See Fredrika J. Teute, "Roman Matron on

Nor could it do without the elegant salons that grew up around those tables. By the mid-eighteenth century, emulation was in the air, bon mots on the tongue, and belles lettres on the writing desks of the fashionable. By the 1760s, Philadelphia boasted a number of stylish ladies' salons, where the colonial intelligentsia gathered. Courtship and socially appropriate marriages were critical salon agendas, but so was the practice of wit, gentility, and sensibility. In neoclassical cadences, the salons' members wrote to each other of platonic friendships, the beauties of nature, and the dangers of love. They then read these poems to one another over tea, criticizing and admiring wit and elegance. With the presence of the ladies elevating discussion far above that common to men's coffeehouses, these salons provided a place where late-eighteenth-century educated and talented women from both the landed and the mercantile elite developed a sense of their own intellectual powers—and the voice to express those powers—at the same time as they demonstrated their ability to perform gentility with the best at Bath or Tunbridge Wells. (Indeed, ladies' tea tables and salons were two principal places where landed and mercantile elites met, married, and formed political and economic alliances.)[28]

"Smart" tea tables and salons required educated women. From the mid-eighteenth century on, America's merchant families exhibited an increasing interest in educating their daughters. Between the 1720s and the 1770s, some fifty schools for girls advertised in Charleston newspapers alone. More flourished in and around Philadelphia, New York, and Boston. Mrs. Rogers's School for Young Ladies in Trenton, New Jersey, was one of the most fashionable, attracting the daughters of New York merchant James Beekman and the socially

---

the Banks of the Tiber Creek: Margaret Bayard Smith and the Politicization of Spheres in the Nation's Capital," in Donald R. Kennon, ed., *A Republic for the Ages: The United States Capitol and the Political Culture of the Early Republic* (Charlottesville, Va., 1999), 89–121.

28. Shields, *Civil Tongues*, 119–140, esp. 120–128, 136–137; Karin A. Wulf, *Not All Wives: Women of Colonial Philadelphia* (Ithaca, N.Y., 2000); Teute, "Roman Matron," in Kennon, ed., *Republic for the Ages*, 151. Moss and Crane, *Historic Houses*, 184–187, presents photographs of Graeme Hall and of Rebecca's upstairs bedroom in which the salon took place. Although far from plain, Rebecca's bedroom laid no claim to "barbaric" splendor. Around Milcah Moore's tea table, genteel Quaker ladies gathered to exchange and read poetry that Moore then recorded in her commonplace book, providing literary and social historians with a record of one of America's first literary salons and of some of America's first women poets. Following the Revolution, Moore published a collection of these poems for use in Quaker academies. She devoted the proceeds of her earnings to the school for "indigent girls" she had founded near her rural retreat in Montgomery, Pennsylvania (Karin A. Wulf, "Preface" and "Introduction," in Catherine L. Blecki and Wulf, eds., *Milcah Martha Moore's Book: A Commonplace Book from Revolutionary America* (University Park, Pa., 1997), xi–xviii, esp. xiv–xviii, and 1–57, esp. 22–37).

PLATE SIX Ballroom, second floor of Powel House, 244 South Third Street, Philadelphia, 1765. Tom Crane Photography, Inc., Bryn Mawr, Pa.

connected Philadelphia physician William Shippen II (scion of an elite Philadelphia mercantile and professional family and senior medical officer of the Continental army). These schools taught reading and writing, French and arithmetic. But, from the perspective of at least some of the parents, the social "finishing" of the daughters of the colonial bourgeoisie—instructions in posture, deportment, needlework, music, and dancing—was the principal goal.[29]

Certainly the letters William and Alice Lee Shippen sent their daughter Nancy while she was enrolled at Mrs. Rogers's School demonstrates the importance parents placed on the finishing of their daughters in the manner of

29. For an insightful discussion of women's education in the late eighteenth and early nineteenth centuries, see Mary C. Kelley, *Learning to Stand and Speak: Women, Education, and Public Life in America's Republic* (Chapel Hill, N.C., 2006). See, as well, White, *Beekmans of New York*, 482–483. It is important to note that, although James Beekman's daughters attended Mrs. Rogers's School and his sons Princeton, Beekman himself had not attended college but like so many other European American merchants had gone early into trade, serving as a supercargo for his father in Barbados (ibid., 338–339). Quakers had always taken a major interest in the education of their daughters; consider the early founding of Westover Academy outside of Philadelphia.

PLATE SEVEN Bedroom, Graeme Park, 859 County Line Road, Horsham, Pa. Elizabeth Graeme Ferguson's bedroom, pictured here, was the meeting place of one of the most celebrated eighteenth-century American salons. Library of Congress, Prints and Photographs Division, HABS PA, 46–HORM, 1–29

the British gentry (though that gentry was far more likely to employ its own tutors). The letters that remain were written during the most dismal years of the Revolutionary War: while Philadelphia was occupied, the British army freely roamed the Jersey countryside, the Continental army suffered defeat after defeat, and Dr. Shippen's family, in flight from the advancing British, was scattered up and down the coast. Nevertheless, the Continental army's chief medical officer took the time to discuss his daughter's proficiency in French and English spelling. "My dear Nancy," he wrote, "[I] was pleased with your french letter which was much better spelt than your english one, in which I was sorry to see four of five words wrong. Take care my dear girl of your spelling and your teeth. . . . Your loving Father."[30]

Alice Lee Shippen's letters to her daughter during the same months were, not surprisingly, more detailed. At a time when capture or death faced her every day, her daughter's training in the niceties of genteel ceremony, deference, and theatrical self-presentation were still a concern. Indeed, as William's letters indicate, it was a family concern. Marrying their daughters well was a Shippen

30. Armes, comp. and ed., *Nancy Shippen*, 36, 62.

PLATE EIGHT Writing desk, American. Attributed to William Sinclair, c. 1801–1805. This lady's writing desk was crafted from mahogany, satinwood, ivory, and inlaid woods, with mirrors. Philadelphia Museum of Art: Bequest of Miss Fanny Norris in memory of Louis Marie Clapier, 1940–46–2

family practice, and a good marriage without proper finishing was unthinkable. And so, in August 1777, Alice Lee Shippen took the time to write, "Your Papa has not time to write and I am scarcely able but I am pleased with your letter. . . . Ask Mrs Roger where she supplys herself with materials for Japaning, Crowning, Painting and if they can be got you shall have them for I would willingly do anything in my power that would assist in your improvement. Much depends on your being improved. Neglect nothing that will make you agreeable." A month later, Alice Shippen asked Nancy,

> Tell me how you have improved in holding your head and shoulders, in making a curtsy, in going out or coming into a room, in giving and receiving, holding your knife and fork, walking and seting. These things contribute so much to a good appearance that they are of great consequence.

She then added hastily:

> There is an alarm here the enemy are said to be coming this way, tis lucky you are not with me. Your Uncle F. Lee and his Lady and Mr and Mrs Haywood are with me in the same house. They set out today for Lancaster and I for Maryland. I believe I will write to you as soon as I get settled. Farewell my dear. Be good and you will surely be happy.[31]

Ladies had their tea tables, salons, and japanning. Gentlemen had their clubs. Among the most famous and fashionable of the latter were the Tuesday Club of Annapolis, Philadelphia's Schuylkill Fishing Clubs, and the Societies of the Sons of Saint Tammany. None, however, outstripped the Scottish Rite Masonic Lodges for the theatrical display of genteel status. Pennsylvania's elite—James Hamilton, lieutenant governor of Pennsylvania, William Allen, his student and Pennsylvania chief justice, Robert Hunter Morris, governor of Pennsylvania and chief justice of New Jersey, and Benjamin Franklin—all served as grand master of the Philadelphia Lodge. William Smith, provost of the College of Philadelphia (later the University of Pennsylvania), served as grand chaplain. "Colonial leaders saw the fraternity as a means to build elite solidarity and to emphasize their elevation above the common people," Steven C. Bullock informs us. "Masonry's public processions and orations portrayed colonial elites as they wished to be seen, secure in their dignity and open in their sympathies."

31. Ibid., 39–41. The Shippens were connected not only to Philadelphia's leading mercantile families but to leading tidewater planter families. Alice Lee Shippen, a Virginia Lee, was the sister of Revolutionary War hero Light Horse Harry Lee and the diplomat Arthur Lee. As noted, William Shippen's sister, Mary, was married to William Byrd III (ibid., 54–55, 59).

"Seen" is the key word. Each summer, Philadelphia's Masonic elite paraded through the streets, led by musicians and Lodge officers bedecked in ceremonial jewels and bearing drawn swords and white staffs of office.[32]

Seen and known. Club membership facilitated the forming of political and economic alliances and provided routes whereby men new to wealth and polite society could make connections. They provided a modern formula for structuring the relation of patron and dependent, training talented new men in the ways of social and political leadership and authority. Benjamin Franklin's access to the patronage of William Allen and James Hamilton was built through membership in Philadelphia's Masonic Lodge, where Franklin served as Deputy to Grand Masters Hamilton and Allen. (It is also important to note that Franklin was not invited to join Philadelphia's Masonic Lodge until he had retired from trade. He could not put on the Mason's white lambskin apron, that is, until he had taken off the artisan's brown leather one.) Thus it was at club meetings and fishing parties that talented men from the middling ranks (Franklin for instance) began their climb into the Elysium Fields of social and political power and that the culture of politesse reached down to the middling ranks.[33]

Elegant mansions, well-performed curtsies, and Masonic white aprons provided visual confirmation of the merchant's social preeminence—if not in Britain, at least in the colonies. Formal portraits provided another form of graphic self-presentation. Well aware of the importance the British gentry placed on family portraits, European American merchants did the same. Portraits by rising colonial artists such as John Singleton Copley, Charles Willson Peale, and Gilbert Stuart graphically proclaimed their sitters' wealth and elegant possessions and thus reaffirmed these sitters' cultural ties to England and England's landed gentry. The consumption of art, Paul Staiti tells us, constituted a critical form of "social capital." "The actual possession of works of art . . . was of immeasurable social value. . . . And that value, the ability of the object to calibrate status, was amplified if the picture was filled with coveted consumer objects—furniture, silks, pearls, rugs, columns, and the like."[34]

32. Shields, *Civil Tongues*, chap. 6; Steven C. Bullock, *Revolutionary Brotherhood: Freemasonry and the Transformation of the American Social Order, 1730–1840* (Chapel Hill, N.C., 1996), 51, 53, 58. See also Alexander Hamilton's *History of the Ancient and Honourable Tuesday Club*, ed. Robert Micklus, 3 vols. (Chapel Hill, N.C., 1990).

33. Ibid., 78–79.

34. White, *Beekmans of New York*, 403. Although detailed representations of possessions filled these canvases, the eighteenth-century portrait was not intended to realistically portray objects

Equally critical to the subjects' self-image and the portraits' success, the artists self-consciously copied fashionable British paintings, positioning North American merchants and their wives as British paintings positioned British nobility and gentry. Indeed, European American artists copied the very dresses, hairpieces, and postures found in eighteenth-century aristocratic portraits, often so precisely that it seemed they merely substituted a European American head for a British one.[35] Of course, American patrons loved the results. Here, at last, they could, in their own and the artist's imagination, if nowhere else, graphically assume the place of an English gentleman or lady.[36] Fundamentally, what their portraits showed was a genealogy connecting the creole subject to the metropolitan subject, creole culture to metropolitan culture, a link America's

---

the sitter literally owned. Rather, it functioned as a semiotic node in the production of the new American self. Thus Copley, Peale, and Stuart filled their portraits with masses of fabric—billowing silks, yards of velvet, and brocades—far beyond the ability of anyone in North America, even John Cadwalader or Nicholas Boylston, to actually possess. Grecian urns and columns, Roman statues, aristocratic parks and prospects, never actually seen in Boston, New York, or Philadelphia, added classical authority to the portraits of men and women who might never have left their provincial port towns but who knew, through their careful perusal of fashionable magazines and travel accounts, the social capital of those classical urns and prospects. These portraits presented their elite sitters with "persuasive fictions" of themselves and made the sitters, like the portraits, products of the artist's brush, the "subject" of the portrait, in a double meaning of that term (Staiti, "Accounting for Copley," 31–35, and "Character and Class," 53, both in Rebora and Staiti, eds., *Copley in America*).

35. Ibid., 33–35. As already noted, Lovell chides both Staiti and Breen for the harshness of their criticism of Copley and his sitters for what I have called "postcolonial mimicry." According to Lovell, the eighteenth century was all about performance: "Our model of eighteenth-century personhood (as well as our admiration for period entrepreneurial spirit) needs to take into account the acceptability of these reproductive processes and practices with regard to personal identity." Lovell refers to the miming of British aristocratic portraiture that we find in Copley's paintings more neutrally as "visual quotation." As part of her discussion, Lovell offers an elaborate analysis of three portraits of the women in three New England mercantile families. All of these portraits are almost exact copies of Faber's 1746 portrait of Mary Finch, Viscountess Andover—except that the viscountess is painting and Mrs. Hubbard is embroidering, an interesting shift from an aristocratic to a bourgeois woman's "prop." See Lovell, *Art in a Season of Revolution*, 77, and chap. 3.

36. Lovell does admit that the performance of gentility was a central component of Copley's work. "Instructing and orchestrating the exhibition of . . . deportment, artistic 'accomplishments,' and costume," she writes, "Copley . . . assisted in the realization and demonstration of gentle birth and civil behavior. If birth was a primary (but in America not necessary) ingredient of gentility, performance was its absolute (and necessary) essence. Therefore enactment, including costume (and such records of enactment as portraits), were essential social markers" (Lovell, *Art in a Season of Revolution*, 91).

PLATE NINE *Mrs. Daniel Hubbard (Mary Green).* By John Singleton Copley, 1764. Oil on canvas. The most ambitious European American artists routinely copied the clothes and poses found in the portraits of British aristocrats when painting European American clients. For example, see the ways this portrait of Mary Greene was patterned on John Faber's portrait of Mary, Viscountess Andover (plate 10). © The Art Institute of Chicago, Purchase Fund, 1947.28

PLATE TEN *Mary (Finch), Viscountess Andover*. By John Faber, Jr., after Thomas Hudson, 1746. Mezzotint. National Portrait Gallery, London

bourgeoisie desperately desired. Upon such legitimacy, European Americans rested their claims to inclusion in the larger culture of Enlightenment Europe and their new Republic's right to be included among the civilized countries of the world. A great deal rested on the performance of that genealogy.[37]

37. As Fredrika J. Teute and David S. Shields explain, it would be "[m]anners not laws or institutions [that would] entitle the United States to be numbered among the most civilized

Yankee Doodle went to town
A-riding on a pony
Stuck a feather in his cap
And called it macaroni.[38]

This British doggerel captured the situation perfectly. If the commercial and fiscal revolutions and the resultant fetishization of fashionable consumerism destabilized the role of gentleman in eighteenth-century Britain, the state of destabilization was far more extreme in colonial America. Not only did European Americans bear the stigma of being colonials; eighteenth-century North America could claim few, if any, leisured gentlemen. Indeed, even those who thought of themselves as European American aristocrats—the great tidewater planters, for all their slaves and overseers—were a very hardworking group, spending their mornings supervising the laying out of manure, their afternoons counting the number of tobacco seedlings planted, and their evenings at their counting books.[39] Those who turned their energies from planting to politics and statecraft soon found themselves in financial straits. A southern gentle-

nations." But the British manners and institutions European Americans so assiduously emulated had a long genealogy, patina, and provenance. Those that European Americans sought to establish were but decades old. See Teute and Shields, "Jefferson in Washington: Domesticating Manners in the Republican Court," paper presented at the Omohundro Institute of Early American History and Culture Third Annual Conference, Old Salem, N.C., June 7, 1997, 5–6.

38. The song was originally sung by British military officers to mock the disheveled, unorganized colonial "Yankees" with whom they served in the Seven Years' War. At the time, the most common meaning of the word "doodle" was "simpleton," or "fool." It is important to focus not only on the word "doodle" but on the word "macaroni." Clearly, the song was not referring to pasta. The word "macaroni" was used to refer to "an exquisite of a class which arose in England about 1760 and consisted of young men who had travelled and affected the tastes and fashions prevalent in continental society. . . . A fop, dandy" *(Oxford English Dictionary,* s.v. "macaroni").

39. Homi K. Bhabha, "Of Mimicry and Man: The Ambivalence of Colonial Discourse," in Bhabha, *The Location of Culture* (London, 1994), 121–131. On the hardworking planters, see, for example, Rhys Isaac, *Landon Carter's Uneasy Kingdom: Revolution and Rebellion on a Virginia Plantation* (Oxford, 2004), esp. 59–84, in which Isaac examines Carter's work schedule as laid out in his diary. Eliza Lucas Pinckney's letterbook presents a similar picture of hard work, scientific experimentation, and hands-on plantation management, especially when, as a young girl, she managed her father's Carolina plantation while he served in the Royal Navy in the Caribbean. See Elise Pinckney, ed., *The Letterbook of Eliza Lucas Pinckney, 1739–1762* (Chapel Hill, N.C., 1972). For an excellent example, see her letter to Mrs. Boddicott, May 2, [1740], 6–8.

man planter (or lady) was a very different character from a British gentleman planter, who managed his Caribbean estates in absentia and looked down on all—white as well as black—who resided in the tropics.[40]

What was true of the tidewater South was even truer of the commercial North. Scrutinized, the merchant elite of Pennsylvania, New York, and New England were solidly bourgeois. Stripped of their carefully crafted veneers, they stepped forth as industrious tradesmen. The sailing ships and business ledgers that Copley and other American-born painters included in their portraits proclaimed their subjects' roots in trade—at the same time that images of Chippendale furniture and shimmering silks worked to obscure those roots. Of course, no one was fooled. Everyone knew that trade filled his or her pockets and confirmed his or her social standing.

From the British gentry's perspective, even the North's great landholding families had compromisingly close ties to the world of commerce and manufacturing. The founders of New York patroon families were not transplanted members of the British gentry. All had arrived as ambitious but struggling merchants. Robert Livingston and Stephanus van Cortlandt were initially involved in the provision trade to Barbados. Despite Adolph Philips's ostentatious self-nomination as Lord of Philipsburgh Manor, he, too, had begun his American career as a commission merchant, sending his financial backers in the Netherlands shipments of fur, lumber, and slaves. Many of the founders of the great patroon families had engaged in piracy. Philips supplied Martinique pirates with clothing, liquor, guns, and ammunition. Livingston engaged in a lively trade with French buccaneers at Hispaniola. Nicholas Bayard, Stephen De Lancey, Philips, and van Cortlandt used profits garnered from piracy to invest in city and Westchester County real estate, wharf space, and ships. Almost all were involved in the slave trade.[41]

Even after they had acquired great landed estates, these families did not cut

---

40. The average southern planter could not play Sir Thomas Bertram of Mansfield Park—as William Byrd II discovered when he went to England in search of an heiress to marry. See Lockridge, *Diary, and Life, of William Byrd II;* and Lockridge, "Colonial Self-Fashioning: Paradoxes and Pathologies in the Construction of Genteel Identity in Eighteenth-Century America," in Ronald Hoffman, Mechal Sobel, and Fredrika J. Teute, eds., *Through a Glass Darkly: Reflections on Personal Identity in Early America* (Chapel Hill, N.C., 1997), 274–339. See also Austen, *Mansfield Park.* For another example of British metropolitan attitudes toward British colonial subjects, see Maria Nugent and Philip Wright, eds., *Lady Nugent's Journal: Of Her Residence in Jamaica from 1801–1805* (Kingston, 1966).

41. Cathy D. Matson, *Merchants and Empire: Trading in Colonial New York* (Baltimore, 1998), 58–64.

PLATE ELEVEN *Isaac Royall*. By John Singleton Copley, 1769. Oil on canvas. A wealthy Boston merchant explicitly points at his ledger book. Museum of Fine Arts, Boston: The M. and M. Karolik Collection of Eighteenth-Century American Arts, 39–247. Photograph © 2010, Museum of Fine Arts, Boston

their ties to trade and manufacturing. James De Lancey did not spend his days composing billets-doux or riding to hounds but rather trading in bricks and sassafras roots, negotiating the price of peas to be sent to Saint Kitts and of whale fins and coconuts bound for London. Walter Livingston, whose lands stretched along the Hudson River, remained an active and, many said, highly unethical merchant and fiscal speculator into the 1790s (as we will discuss later in this chapter). Others among colonial New York's great families ran sugar refineries, rum distilleries, or snuff factories.[42]

The same was true of Pennsylvania's merchant princes. Thomas Lloyd, whom William Penn had appointed Pennsylvania's first governor, before migrating to Philadelphia had been a Welsh merchant, not a member of the landed gentry. James Logan's fortune came less from William Penn's largesse of extensive land grants than from his control of the lucrative Indian trade.[43] Being married to one of Thomas Lloyd's granddaughters did not prevent Richard Hill from having to flee his Philadelphia creditors and start his mercantile career over in Madeira. Financial failure, which was not uncommon even among well-married and -connected merchants, meant an immediate loss of social status. "We were shund and neglected on every side when needy . . . for Poverty and contempt . . . go hand in hand," Deborah Hill wrote her cousin Hannah Moore. Not even those at the apex of Philadelphia society escaped "the taint" of trade. George Washington might have danced in Samuel Powel's elegant second-floor music salon, but the ground-floor front room of Powel's home served as his counting room and office. Its floor and windows were bare, as befitted a provincial merchant's office.[44]

42. Rhinelanders, Bayards, and Alexanders were sugar merchants; Beekmans and Lispenards were rum distillers. Nicholas Bayard, Peter Livingston, and Henry Cuyler operated highly successful sugar refineries, as did Nicholas Roosevelt and John van Cortlandt. Nicholas Bayard also manufactured snuff (Matson, *Merchants,* chap. 5, 7; White, *Beekmans of New York,* 361–364).

43. Isaac Norris's father was a carpenter in England who removed the family to Jamaica. It was here that the youthful Isaac met the Lloyds and courted their daughter, Mary. The Lloyds then helped establish Norris as one of Philadelphia's upwardly mobile merchants. Both James Logan and Isaac Norris brought up their sons to be merchants. Only on their own deaths did their sons close their countinghouses in Philadelphia and take over the Stenton and Fairhill estates. Fatherly points to the newness and uncertainty of wealth among Philadelphia's Quaker elite. "By the 1720s and 1730s," she writes, "Philadelphia's merchant families had . . . substantial wealth thanks to a combination of trade, manufactures, and landholding and they had a firm hold on the city's and colony's political offices. . . . [Yet] even as they achieved economic dominance . . . there were some hints that their positions of power and privilege lacked permanence. In addition to memories of earlier days of hardship, they faced two new challenges to their authority and power from increased non-British immigration and the rising success of petty merchants" (Fatherly, "Gentlewomen and Learned Ladies," 16–20, esp. 21).

44. Deborah Hill to Hannah Moore, June 6, 1750, Guilielma M. Howland Papers, box 4, fol. 2, Quaker and Special Collections, Magill Library, Haverford College, Haverford, Pa., cited in Fatherly, "Gentlewomen and Learned Ladies," 25; Moss and Crane, *Historic Houses,* 36–37. Pennsylvania was always, at heart, a commercial settlement. Merchants and other men of trade remained the economy's driving force and social leaders (ibid., 14–16, 20–21). See also

The picture became ever clearer and, to British eyes, quite predictable. Provincial tradesmen and professionals were not gentlemen by British or continental standards. At best, they were what Moll Flanders called her second husband: "This amphibious creature, this land-water thing . . . a gentleman tradesman." Her metaphor suggests the ways those who were born of the sea, that is, of trade and commerce, became unnatural "things," freaks of nature, when they attempted to raise their rank by claiming the status due to men of landed wealth.[45]

As Moll's comment suggests, British eighteenth-century discourses treated work and gentility as an oxymoron. And few worked harder than America's merchants. Like the industrious artisans Noah Webster disparaged, they were tied, if not to their lasts, then certainly to their counting rooms and desks. The dust of the harbor settled on their broadcloth coats and powered wigs; mud crusted their shoes. The late afternoon might find them in the noisy and smoke-filled coffeehouses that nestled along the crowded streets leading in from the harbor. They came, not to trade in bon mots or observe the latest fashions, as London's bon ton did, but to collect their mail, study foreign papers for news of blighted harvests, wars declared or ended, disasters at sea. Here, too, they traded commercial paper, dealt in bills of exchange, and, most critical of all, carefully observed their rival merchants. The topic of their conversations at home and abroad was most often that which Britain's gentlemen most disdained—trade.[46]

The layout of eighteenth-century cities tells all. Despite their fanciful summer villas and their desire to play the gentleman, America's merchants built their homes along the narrow streets that twisted in from bustling harbors. They did so because, for men of uncertain fortunes and hard, hands-on work, easy proximity to ships and news was essential to economic survival. One of New York's great merchants, William Beekman, established his home on congested Hanover Square, within two blocks of the East River piers. Even that apogee of elegant neighborhoods, Philadelphia's "aristocratic square," home to Powels, Cadwaladers, Dickinsons, Shippens—and President Washington—

Thomas M. Doerflinger, *A Vigorous Spirit of Enterprise: Merchants and Economic Development in Revolutionary Philadelphia* (Chapel Hill, N.C., 1986), esp. chap. 1. For an exploration of the career of John Nicholson, see Robert D. Arbuckle, *Pennsylvania Speculator and Patriot: The Entrepreneurial John Nicholson, 1757–1800* (University Park, Pa., 1975).

45. Daniel Defoe, *The Fortunes and Misfortunes of the Famous Moll Flanders* (New York, 1989), 41.

46. Doerflinger, *Vigorous Spirit of Enterprise*, 44; Elizabeth Blackmar, *Manhattan for Rent, 1785–1850* (Ithaca, N.Y., 1989), 78–79; Herman, *Town House*, 71–76.

PLATE TWELVE Office, ground floor of Powel House, 244 South Third Street, Philadelphia, 1765. Depicted here is the highly functional office of Samuel Powel, Philadelphia merchant and society leader. Tom Crane Photography, Inc., Bryn Mawr, Pa.

abutted the cattle market and was near the poorhouse. Henry Drinker, husband of the erudite Elizabeth Drinker and one of Philadelphia's richest merchants, built his home immediately adjacent to the pier and warehouse he owned, one block from the crowded and polluted Delaware River. There he spent most summers, in spite of yellow fever alarms and the pleas of his wife to flee to their Germantown retreat. John Ross, another of Philadelphia's merchant princes, built his grandiose house immediately adjacent to the new city market, infamous for its noise, filth, and odors.[47]

All these locations were notoriously unpleasant. Wagons lumbered past noisily, spewing up dust in dry weather, splattering mud in wet. Stevedores sweated and cursed, sailors swaggered, artisans and tradesmen went to and fro because even the richest merchants dealt directly with millers, grain and livestock dealers, coopers, and sailmakers. Farmers' carts and livestock from

47. White, *Beekmans of New York*, 329–335, esp. 337; Doerflinger, *Vigorous Spirit of Enterprise*, 23, 34–35, 39; Elaine Forman Crane, ed., *The Diary of Elizabeth Drinker: The Life Cycle of an Eighteenth-Century Woman* (Boston, 1994), 21 n. 1.

the countryside added to the babble and confusion. In front of even the most fashionable townhouses, garbage piled up—spoiled goods discharged from ships, rotting produce and carcasses from city markets. Manure was everywhere.[48]

What was true of merchants and entrepreneurs was true as well of their professional allies. Benjamin and Julia Stockton Rush were leading lights in post-Independence Philadelphia, but their home was also home to a number of Rush's medical students, to his examining rooms, and even to some of his patients. William Shippen entertained General Washington and members of the Continental Congress along with his brothers-in-law, Arthur and Richard Henry Lee, in his elegant drawing room. Members of the French legation courted his daughter while he conspired to force her to marry the great New York landowner Henry Livingston. Nevertheless, his surgery was attached to the back of his Georgian townhouse, and his daughter's diary routinely noted his early leavings and late returns as well as the long, hot summers he spent in the city. In short, he spent far more time purging yellow fever victims than dining with Samuel Powel or driving out with George Washington.[49]

Nor could the wealth of American merchants, even of the socially prominent ones, compare to that of their British counterparts. At the height of his financial successes, James Beekman's estate was estimated at approximately £25,000. Betsy Lloyd Cadwalader brought her husband a dowry of £10,000, a prince's ransom by American standards. But consider the estate of London merchant James Fludyer, estimated at £900,000. Indeed, compared to their London or Bristol correspondents, European American merchants were chronically undercapitalized. A young man could enter the coastal or provision trade with as little as £500. Only the wealthiest firms began with a capital of £4,000— again, by British standards, shockingly paltry. European American merchants in the dry goods trade worked primarily on credit, liberally advanced during boom years by London and Manchester suppliers. But, when times grew

48. Dirt, noise, and disorder were endemic in eighteenth-century cities. As Herman points out, "Visitors and residents alike assayed the chaotic aspect of cities through the world of the senses: the viscous, clinging muck of muddy streets, the searing stench of rot and sewage, the clattering din of tavern and market, and awkward-looking town houses reflecting shoddy and often flammable construction" *(Town House,* 5). A decade or so later, John Pintard continued to complain to his daughter Eliza, resident in New Orleans, about the filth that regularly accumulated on New York City streets and the failure of the city to address the problem. See John Pintard and Dorothy C. Barck, eds., *Letters from John Pintard to His Daughter, Eliza Noel Pintard Davidson, 1816–1833* (New York, 1940).

49. Armes, comp. and ed., *Nancy Shippen,* 53–54, 195, 197.

hard, as they frequently did, bankruptcies were common (even among "merchant princes," as we saw with Richard Hill). No respecters of practiced politesse, commercial uncertainties and financial insecurities haunted not only the cramped parlors of middling merchants but the music and drawing rooms of merchant princes.[50]

NEW PIPERS AND NEW DANCES

Revolution and war burst rudely into this expanding but uncertain world of colonial emulation. Nonimportation agreements constrained fashionable purchases. Classic republican virtues—celebrations of Spartan asceticism, the valorization of virility and military prowess, the sacrifice of self for the common good—assumed ideological ascendancy. Britain, no longer the apogee of civility and culture, stepped forth upon the stage of European American history as a corrupt tyrant, threatening to enslave freedom-loving men and betray the Magna Charta. European American families divided. Those who favored the patriot cause were attainted traitors in Britain while revolutionary governments seized the homes and goods of declared tories. European Americans' seamless identity as Englishmen in America was rent. For the first time, they had to choose between knowing themselves as British subjects or as American citizens.[51]

Did the dogged emulation of British gentility survive the war and Independence? As the letters of Alice Lee Shippen and Benjamin Rush demonstrate, it did. At the same time, the war brought with it radical changes in economic structures, class composition, and possibilities for acquiring the markers of refinement. The role of gentleman, always, at best, shifting and contested, underwent even greater alterations. Beginning with the political protests of the 1760s, merchants gained ever-greater political visibility and authority. Disputes over British taxes, nonimportation agreements, the Intolerable Acts, and, ultimately, Independence drew them more and more deeply into politics. They dominated committees of correspondence, county conventions, and the Continental Congress, gaining control of key government institutions and of

50. White, *Beekmans of New York,* 361; Doerflinger, *Vigorous Spirit of Enterprise,* 18, 26, 48, 53–54, 140–146. On the insecurities experienced by European American men of commerce, see Toby L. Ditz, "Shipwrecked; or, Masculinity Imperiled: Mercantile Representations of Failure and Gendered Self in Eighteenth-Century Philadelphia," *Journal of American History,* LXXXI (1994), 52–90.

51. This was what so agitated European Americans, East as well as West, about the Proclamation Line and the Quebec Act. See Chapter 4, above.

the press. As the war further convulsed the economy, still newer men—those recently arrived from the Caribbean (Alexander Hamilton from Nevis, for example, or William Duer from Antigua) along with those formerly on the margins of the commercial establishment—elbowed their way into the Republic's new governing coalitions and onto the dance floor of respectability. And after them came mechanics and artisans. During the rapidly changing war and postwar years, new men and established merchants alike hungrily sought to advance themselves politically, economically, and socially. Though intensely self-interested, all were also motivated by a postcolonial determination to prove the new Americans as refined as their former British "overlords." Let us first examine the ways the Republic's new ruling class choreographed their performance of gentility. We will then examine the performers themselves, where they came from and how these turbulent years affected them. Our fundamental question remains—could these men's performances of gentility augment troubled representations of gender and race and so produce a coherent "American" identity?[52]

"OH MY DEAR SUCH A SWARM OF FRENCH BEAUX"

The war had brought a soupçon of Gallic gaiety and élan to the new Republic's port cities. As French ships, guns, and money rescued the new Republic militarily and won it critical diplomatic and financial support, gallant French officers and diplomats brought a new spirit of flirtation and urbanity to North American society. Settling into Philadelphia, the Republic's capital, French officers and diplomats invited the city's patriot bourgeoisie to weekly balls, concerts, and other musical events. The Chevalier de La Luzerne and his secretaries enjoyed the company and accolades of the deeply impressed European American ladies. Martha Dangerfield Bland, one of the Virginia planter class to marry into Philadelphia's commercial families, fondly remembered "the Balls at the french minister and particularizing a petit maître—oh my dear such a swarm of french beaux, Counts, Viscounts, Barons and Chevaliers." Of the Chevalier de La Luzerne, she wrote, "He is one of the most amiable, the politest, *easiest* behav'd Men I ever knew."[53]

52. Dirk Hoerder, *Crowd Action in Revolutionary Massachusetts, 1765–1780* (New York, 1977); Bernard Friedman, "The Shaping of the Radical Consciousness in Provincial New York," *JAH*, LVI (1970), 781–801; Jesse Lemisch, "Jack Tar in the Streets: Merchant Seamen in the Politics of Revolutionary America," *William and Mary Quarterly*, XXV, 3d Ser. (1968), 371–407.

53. Armes, comp. and ed., *Nancy Shippen*, 78, 93. The presence of polished French diplomats and military officers permitted the European American bourgeoisie to continue emulating

Philadelphia merchants and professionals strove to follow the French lead. The Marquis de Chastellux described an evening held at Dr. Shippen's house, where Nancy, now fifteen, presided under her mother's careful eye. "This was the first time since my arrival in America," the marquis wrote,

> that I had seen music introduced into society, and mix with its amusements. *Miss Rutledge* played on the harpsichord. . . . Miss Shippen sung with timidity, but with a pretty voice. Mr. Ottaw [Otto], Secretary to M. de la Luzerne [and one of Nancy's suitors], sent for his harp, he accompanied Miss Shippen, and played several pieces. Music naturally leads to dancing: the Vicomte de Noailles took down a violin, which was mounted with harp strings, and he made the young ladies dance, whilst their mothers and other grave personages chattered in another room.

The marquis then added an interesting note, suggesting both the educational role the visiting French saw themselves playing and a compliment to their bourgeois American pupils. "When music, and the fine arts come to prosper at Philadelphia," he predicted, "when society once becomes easy and gay there, and they learn to accept of pleasure when it presents itself, without a formal invitation, then may foreigners enjoy all the advantages peculiar to their manners and government, without envying any thing in Europe." This was what the new national bourgeoisie most desired to be told—that European Americans would become equals of Europeans in manners and gaiety, civility, and charm.[54]

As the French dazzled Philadelphia's merchant princes, so Philadelphia's merchant princes dazzled other European Americans. John Adams commented with gusto about the dinners Samuel Powel served during the war to members of the Continental Congress: "A most sinful feast again!" he wrote Abigail, who, at the time, was much oppressed by the difficulty of surviving in war-torn Boston with its shortages of food and threats of deadly epidemics. "Everything which could delight the Eye, or allure the Taste, Curds and Creams, Jellies, Sweetmeats of various sorts, 20 sorts of Tarts, fools, Trifles, floating Islands, whipped Sillabubs, etc., etc.—Parmesan Cheeses, Punch, Wine, Porter, Beer."[55]

The exigencies of war dispersed members of the new would-be ruling class to

---

European civility while leaving them free to heap tirades upon Britain for its own corrupt and tyrannical ruling elites. The French presence, that is, permitted them to maintain their delicate balance between their identity as Americans and their claim to European Enlightenment culture.

54. Ibid., 94.

55. Cited, Moss and Crane, *Historic Houses,* 36.

PLATE THIRTEEN "Wallpaper Depicting Captain John Cook after His Rediscovery of the Sandwich or Hawaiian Islands." By Jean Gabriel Charvet, c. 1806. Block print on paper. This French wallpaper demonstrates the new elites' embrace of French imperial visions even in their ostentatious home furnishings. Philadelphia Museum of Art: Gift of Dr. Anne Mitchell McAllister in memory of William Young McAllister, 1921

Europe as diplomats and merchants, in search of diplomatic recognition and supplies for the Continental army. These men and their ladies returned home far more cosmopolitan than they had left. Inspired by new pleasures, emboldened by new desires, they introduced their fellow citizens to the latest continental fashions in architecture and furniture, clothes and wine. Thomas Jefferson returned from Paris with 145 rolls of hand-painted wallpaper. Anne Willing Bingham returned to Philadelphia with gowns designed by Marie Antoinette's dressmaker—along with black umbrellas, the latest Parisian fashion.[56]

The "Federal Court" that Martha Washington presided over as First Lady,

56. Marquis de Chastellux, *Travels in North America in the Years 1780, 1781, and 1782*, trans. Howard C. Rice, Jr., 2 vols. (Chapel Hill, N.C., 1963), I, 234; Susan Branson, *These Fiery Frenchified Dames: Women and Political Culture in Early National Philadelphia* (Philadelphia, 2001), 134; Edward G. Burrows and Mike Wallace, *Gotham: A History of New York City to 1898* (Oxford, 1999), 301.

first in New York City and then in Philadelphia, constituted the ultimate stage upon which the nation's emerging elite of merchants-cum-statesmen sought to enact their equality to the courts of the Old World. Here, at musical evenings, balls, and stately dinners, new political and economic leaders mingled with an older social elite of planters, patroons, and established merchant princes. Nor was emulating Britain the only object of these carefully choreographed evenings. The new political and economic leaders sought as well to solidify the ties that bound the new nation together and, at the same time, to establish their own economic and political legitimacy as the Republic's official ruling class. The revolution had been won and a new republic born, but "courts" still met and courtly behavior still mattered.[57]

Not all new Americans took delight in these courtly ways. Especially as political disputes flared following the French Revolution, those critical of Federal politics turned their ire against the republican court. Governor George Clinton of New York (initially an Antifederalist, later a Jeffersonian, and at all times known for his own extremely simple lifestyle) acerbically accused the court of setting itself above—and against—the people. "The language and manners of this court," he complained, "will be what distinguishes them from the rest of the community, not what assimilates them to it; and in being remarked for a behavior that shows they are not meanly born, and in adulation to the people of fortune and power." Another of the country's Antifederalists, Mercy Otis Warren (who, it is important to note, had earlier posed for a particularly "courtly" portrait from John Singleton Copley) also criticized the republican court's potential for "immediate aristocracy tyranny." By the 1790s, a young, new generation of intellectuals (Charles Brockden Brown, James Kent, Elihu Hubbard Smith) denigrated the culture of politesse as, at best, artificial and performative and, at worst, duplicitous, aristocratic, and authoritarian. Clearly Federalists and Antifederalists (joined on this particular issue by those Fredrika J. Teute calls "Enlightenment radicals") viewed republican society— and hence the nation—in radically different ways. The Federalists, Mark Patterson tells us, envisioned a hierarchical society of distinct, theatrically defined

57. When performed in New York, the "court" featured the Misses Jay, Hamilton, Clinton, Duane, Livingston (wife of the chancellor), Livingston (of Clermont Manor), Smith (daughter of the vice president), and, far from least, Duer and her mother, Lady Sterling (Burrows and Wallace, *Gotham,* 301; Teute and Shields, "Jefferson in Washington," 2, 13–14). When staged in Philadelphia, "the court" starred members of the older colonial elite and representatives of the new economic risk takers. Powels, Shippens, Dickinsons, Cadwaladers, Stedmans, Lees, and Byrds mingled easily with the new capitalist elite—Morris, Willings, and William and Anne Bingham (Branson, *These Fiery Frenchified Dames,* 142).

classes led by a social elite; the Antifederalists, an antiaristocratic society mirroring the desires of the quasi-democratic constituency.[58]

As in those two other elite societies, Britain and France, women played critical roles in the court and the social vision it was designed to produce and maintain. Certainly, the French were acutely conscious of the new European American *citoyennes'* charms. The Marquis de Chastellux praised Elizabeth Willing Powel, Samuel Powel's wife, for being "well read and intelligent," adding, "what distinguished her most is her taste for conversation, and the truly European use that she knows how to make her understanding and information." Joshua Fisher celebrated Mrs. Gabriel Manigault, whose family combined trade with Carolina sugar plantations. Her "taste for literature," he wrote, "made her house the centre of all the educated men and women of her time." But none received more accolades than Anne Willing Bingham. Her dress, manner, beauty, and gaiety won the attention of all. "She blaz'd upon a large party at Mr. [Robert] Morris's in a dress which eclips'd any that has yet been seen," reported Molly Tilghman, one of Philadelphia's more conservative social leaders. "Her Head ornamented with Diamond Sprigs interspers'd with artificial flowers, above all, wav'd a towering plume of snow white feathers." The experienced diplomat Arthur Lee was smitten, as a letter to his niece Nancy Shippen indicates: "Do not forget to lay me at Mrs Bingham's feet," he wrote. "Ask her by what means she escaped from France after robbing the ladies there of all their graces and attractions. It was no petty Larceny; and had she been arraigned, she must have been convicted, as the stolen goods would have been found upon her." That the Binghams had just commissioned a London architect to construct a town house modeled after the Duke of Manchester's home in Manchester Square—to be called "Mansion House" and surrounded by iron gates, a carriage drive, landscaped gardens, a conservatory, and greenhouses—as a stage for Anne's conquests escaped no one's attention,

58. Fredrika J. Teute, "A 'Republic of Intellect': Conversation and Criticism among the Sexes in 1790s New York," in Philip Barnard, Mark L. Kamrath, and Stephen Shapiro, eds., *Revising Charles Brockden Brown: Culture, Politics, and Sexuality in the Early Republic* (Knoxville, Tenn., 2004), 149–181, esp. 151, 157; Mark R. Patterson, *Authority, Autonomy, and Representation in American Literature, 1776–1865* (Princeton, N.J., 1988), 14, 23–25. Saul Cornell agrees that the most critical difference between Federalists and Antifederalists might well have been their warring visions of the ideal republican society. Certainly, Cornell sees fear of the Federalists' aristocratic pretensions as central to Antifederalist critiques of the would-be new ruling elite and their constitution (Cornell, *The Other Founders: Anti-Federalism and the Dissenting Tradition in America, 1788–1828* [Chapel Hill, N.C., 1999], 26–34). See, as well, Cornell, "Aristocracy Assailed: The Ideology of Backcountry Anti-Federalism," *JAH,* LXXVI (1990), 1148–1172; Gordon S. Wood, *The Creation of the American Republic, 1776–1787* (New York, 1972), 513–514.

not in Philadelphia or even Boston, where the architect Charles Bulfinch emulated it when building a number of mansions for wealthy Bostonians. Nor was Bulfinch the only enthusiast. Even the Antifederalist senator from Pennsylvania William Maclay was unstinting in his praise: "I cannot say barely that he [William Bingham] affects to entertain in a Stile beyond every thing in this place, or perhaps in America. He really does so. There is a propriety a neatness a Cleanliness that adds to the Splendor of his costly furniture, and elegant Apartments."[59]

Clearly, the republican court circled around these dazzling women as moths to a flame. Clearly, as well, the women were fully aware of their power and of the responsibilities that came with it in a new republic. Whereas others saw them as constituting a decidedly antidemocratic and a potentially tyrannical social vision, they thought of themselves as bringing social harmony to the new Republic and strengthening a new national identity built upon the Federalist vision of a hierarchical and theatrically defined society. However, not only did that vision divide the new nation as much as it united the new governing groups; we can never forget that the gentility and politesse the ladies made the centerpiece of their new national identity were, as Arthur Lee so artfully stated, stolen from aristocratic Europe and most especially from the new Republic's tyrannical enemy, Great Britain. Was this the solid ground upon which a cohesive national identity would grow?[60]

NEW MORRIS DANCES:
MERCHANT PRINCES AND THE ARROGANCE OF DESIRE

Who were the men who, accompanied by their ladies, made respectful bows at Martha Washington's levees, attended Betsy and John Powel's musical evenings, and formed part of Anne Bingham's coterie? Some had been members of

59. Fisher cited by Beatrice B. Garvan, *Federal Philadelphia, 1785–1825: The Athens of the Western World* (Philadelphia, 1987), 23–25; Doerflinger, *Vigorous Spirit of Enterprise*, 42, 44; Armes, comp. and ed., *Nancy Shippen*, 253; Shields, *Civil Tongues*, 311; Branson, *These Fiery Frenchified Dames*, 136, 137. See, as well, Teute and Shields, "Jefferson in Washington," 11–12. It is interesting to note that, despite his praise of Bingham, Maclay was listed as an antiadministration senator, indicating the allure of the court even among Antifederalists. For further information about William Maclay and his political position, see Edgar Stanton Maclay, ed., *Journal of William Maclay, United States Senator from Pennsylvania, 1789–1791* (New York, 1890).

60. Fredrika J. Teute, "Reading Men and Women in Late Eighteenth-Century New York," paper presented at the annual meeting of the American Society for Eighteenth-Century Studies, Charleston, S.C., Mar. 12, 1994, 4, 9–10, 24.

PLATE FOURTEEN *Anne Willing Bingham*. Engraved portrait by an unknown artist after a painting by Sir Joshua Reynolds. Bingham dazzled the society of the new nation's capital. Putnam Collection, Broome County Historical Society. Courtesy of the Broome County Historical Society

the colonial ruling elite. No longer admiring subjects of the British monarchy, they now formed the core of a new national elite, determined to secure their new Republic's place on the stage of world power. We think, of course, of the Virginia triumvirate, Washington, Jefferson, and Madison, but also of elite New Yorkers Gouverneur Morris, Philip Schuyler, and Robert Livingston and of the ambitious young men who married into leading families—Hamilton, married to Elizabeth Schuyler, or John Jay, married to Sarah Livingston. Slightly lower on the social scale, we find Massachusetts's powerful Essex Junto, John Adams, James Warren, and Eldridge Gerry. All of these men dreamed of creating a powerful and respected nation, one they believed only possible if they could create an equally powerful and respected national government born of the newly proposed Federal constitution.

But there were others—new men who gained prominence by the practice of new measures during the war's tumultuous years—and whose wealth had been significantly augmented during the conflict. These included Silas Deane, James Wilson, and William Bingham of Philadelphia, William Duer of New York, Henry Knox of Massachusetts—and, above all, Robert Morris, "Financier of the Revolution." Caught up in the turmoil and challenges of revolution and war, this cadre of merchants and speculators proved themselves masters of fiscal improvisation and expert at games of risk and chance. They were equally determined to succeed in the twin worlds of politics and politesse, no one more so than Robert Morris. Before the war, Morris had been the junior partner of Thomas Willing, a well-connected merchant. With the commencement of the war, Morris had been elected to the Continental Congress and then moved quickly into the inner circles of power, gaining control of congressional finances and assuming responsibility for supplying the army. Working through a loose network of Philadelphia merchants positioned at key points around the Atlantic—Silas Deane and John Ross in France, William Bingham in Martinique, George Meade, J. M. Nesbit, and John Wilcocks in Philadelphia—Morris arranged to have desperately needed European manufactured goods and munitions shipped to Philadelphia via Hamburg, Amsterdam, and Nantes. He kept trade open with the West Indies, while gerrymandering inland transportation routes to supply the army at Valley Forge. To pay for these shipments, Morris sent American grain, rice, indigo, and tobacco to France, most frequently through William Bingham at Martinique; bought ships and backed privateers; and speculated in American bonds, in American and European currencies, and in British stocks.[61]

61. Doerflinger, *Vigorous Spirit of Enterprise*, 198, 212–213, 237, 259, 288–289.

At times, Morris acted as an agent for Congress; at other times, for himself and his business associates. Increasingly, the line between the public official and the private capitalist blurred, as classic republican texts predicted it would. Indeed, time and again, Morris insisted that no conflict existed between self-interest and public interest, between service to the state and private gain. As he declared in a letter to his close associate Silas Deane, "I shall continue to discharge my duty faithfully to the Public and pursue my Private Fortune by all such honorable and fair means as the times will admit of, and I dare say you will do the same." His letter urging William Bingham to miss no opportunity to profit personally from his wartime trading was even more direct: "Where cargoes arrive . . . the profits are now so great it is well worth risking largely." Members of the older elite looked askew at Morris's blatant enactment of self-interest. Popular elements—the Philadelphia militia, stressed housewives—accused Morris and his associates of price-gouging and corruption. But the troubled times and wartime crises overshadowed their protests.[62]

Risk largely, Morris and his coterie did. And, for a while, at least, they profited largely as well. Even while the war still raged, they acquired impressive fortunes. As the Marquis de Chastellux commented to a correspondent in France, "It will scarcely be believed that amid the disasters of America, Mr. Morris, the inhabitant of a town barely freed from the hands of the English, should possess a fortune of eight million livres [£300,000–400,000]. It is, however, in the most critical times that great fortunes are acquired and increased." Of Morris and his nationalist cadre, Thomas M. Doerflinger tells us,

> The spirit of 1776 was not what drove them. Centralized power disturbed them far less than the licentiousness of the people and the shortsighted localism of state legislatures. These acquisitive men of affairs hoped that a vigorous government and an enterprising citizenry would turn the United States into a state of "power, consequence, and grandeur."[63]

62. Ibid., 237. Morris, Doerflinger tells us, scoffed at those who, using tried and true republican rhetoric, charged that "private gain is more our pursuit than Public Good" (cited 239–240).

63. Chastellux, *Travels in North America*, trans. Rice, I, 125–136; Doerflinger, *Vigorous Spirit of Enterprise*, 239, 259; E. James Ferguson, *The Power of the Purse: A History of American Public Finance, 1776–1790* (Chapel Hill, N.C., 1961), 120. The Morris circle benefited from innovative genius, the willingness to work incessantly—and the significant competitive advantage their position as government insiders gave them over other merchants. Certainly Morris's position on the secret committees of correspondence and of trade gave them ready access to insider information, and they benefited as well from the transatlantic network of merchants the war opened to them. They had access to the largest and fastest ships, profited personally from the huge sales they made directly to Congress, and, most significantly of all, could use public funds to establish

New York boasted a similar group of merchant entrepreneur-cum-nation-alists who shared Morris's Mandevillian fusion of private and state interests.[64] Some were forward-looking members of the older landed elite such as Philip Schuyler, former wartime governor of New York, or Walter Livingston, Schuyler's political and financial associate. Fusing established wealth to new political power, these established patroon families had each married a daughter to one of the leading Federalist statesmen. Others were new men—William Duer, for example, a recent émigré from Antigua. Like Morris and Bingham, these New Yorkers often walked a fine line between public service and political corruption. During some of the hardest days of the Revolutionary War, Livingston was accused of making profits of 500 percent when selling pork to the New York militia through the auspices of his sometime partner and then–New York governor, Philip Schuyler. During those same years, Schuyler and Livingston were both accused of speculating in supplies and of fraud and cowardice leading to the failure of the Continental army's Canadian campaign. Duer, working closely with them and with Silas Deane (accused by Arthur Lee of Virginia of using government funds to personally profit from speculation on the London exchange), formed a junta to supply the Spanish navy with timber and masts—this, at a time when the American navy was in dire need of such

---

their own credit throughout Europe. Of course, they also provided invaluable services, not only in the opening days of war but in its closing days as well. When things looked darkest in the 1780s, with the Continental dollar worthless, troops starving, and the Pennsylvania militia threatening mutiny, Morris lent Congress large sums from his personal resources and devised a plan to secure government credit and hold the loyalty of the commercial community. The line distinguishing Robert Morris and the government of the newly independent United States at times appeared invisible.

64. Bernard Mandeville, author of *The Fable of the Bees; or, Private Vices and Publick Benefits* (1714), took a moral and political position diametrically opposed to that of classic republicanism. Self-interest, pleasure in a luxurious lifestyle and ostentatious display, far from corrupting society, enriched the economy, employed thousands of artisans and mechanics, and strengthened the state. Mandeville, Pocock tells us, "argued that the mainspring of social behavior was not self-love—based on knowledge of one's self as one was . . . but what he called self-liking . . . based on the figure one cut in one's own eyes and those of others. . . . At bottom he was saying that the real world of economy and polity rested on a myriad fantasy worlds maintained by private egos" *(Machiavellian Moment, 465)*. See, as well, Pocock, "Modes of Political and Historical Time in Early Eighteenth-Century England," 91–102, and "The Mobility of Property and the Rise of Eighteenth-Century Sociology," 103–124, both in Pocock, ed., *Virtue, Commerce, and History: Essays on Political Thought and History, Chiefly in the Eighteenth Century* (Cambridge, 1985); and Malcolm Jack, *The Social and Political Thought of Bernard Mandeville* (New York, 1978).

supplies. Spain, however, could afford to pay higher prices. Duer might have gone even further than his associates. Not only was he accused of selling munitions manufactured in his New Jersey factory to the British in New York City; at the height of the war, he established business relations with the British superintendent of the Port of New York, Andrew Elliot. At the war's end, Elliott remained in New York, where he later became a top officer in the Bank of New York, in whose notes Duer recklessly speculated. Windfall profits proved irresistible to patriots of easy virtue. Economic historian Cathy Matson claims Duer was "only one among many to pursue these opportunities; false clearances, forged bonds, collaboration with customs officials at foreign ports, and 'a little greasing of the palm for favor' were familiar techniques."[65]

Driven by ambition, global in their perspectives, and fiscally inventive, at the war's end, this cadre of nationalist entrepreneurs moved quickly to gain control of the new nation's economy. Using the fortunes they had amassed during the war, along with the contacts and influence they had garnered in Europe and America, they worked aggressively to re-form the new national economy, push that economy in modernizing directions—and profit handsomely in the process. The circle's most innovative and daring venture was founding the Bank of North America, modeled, of course, on the Bank of England. This was the United States' first commercial bank, a venture Doerflinger considers "the furthest-reaching economic innovation of the 1780s." It revolutionized European American mercantile and fiscal practices. Substituting bank notes for book debts, expanding the flow of credit, providing a stable, if privately controlled, currency, it made fluid what had been illiquid, accelerated mercantile growth and stimulated the economy. The bank's viability depended on venture capital that resulted from the great profits Morris and his group accumulated during the Revolution. With the war's end, the Philadelphia experiment was quickly emulated by William Duer, who helped found the Bank of New York City. As one of Hamilton's undersecretaries of the Treasury, Duer would also become deeply involved in the First Bank of the United States.[66]

65. Cathy D. Matson, "Public Vices, Private Benefit: William Duer and His Circle, 1776–1792," in William Pencak and Conrad Edick Wright, eds., *New York and the Rise of American Capitalism: Economic Development and the Social and Political History of an American State, 1780–1870* (New York, 1989), 72–123, esp. 84.

66. Burrows and Wallace, *Gotham*, 276; Doerflinger, *Vigorous Spirit of Enterprise*, 278, 296–297. For Doerflinger's detailed analysis of the bank, see 296–310. The central role a few leading venture capitalists played in jump-starting the new nation's economy cannot be overestimated, in Doerflinger's opinion. "The economic resurgence of the 1780s and early 1790s was led by a few major fortune builders, notably Robert Morris, William Bingham, Joseph Ball, Charles Pettit,

No one symbolized this new age with greater fidelity or profited from it more aggressively than Robert Morris. Morris emerged from his wartime services the new nation's acknowledged new "Colossus."[67] His personal wealth seemed almost beyond calculation—and he used it aggressively. Not only did he mastermind the founding of the Bank of North America; he backed America's first commercial voyage to China. Increasingly, however, it was large-scale speculation that captured his imagination and absorbed his interests. In the mid-1780s, Morris cornered the Chesapeake tobacco market and then plotted to sell at a huge profit to France—having erased all competitors. When this failed because of political opposition in France, Morris's losses were enormous. But so was his determination to recoup. Turning to land speculation, he quickly purchased five million acres of land in New York State (land still claimed by the Iroquois Federation), largely on credit, and as quickly sold 1 million of those acres to William Pultney, one of Britain's greatest land capitalists, and another 2.8 million to Dutch investors. In these efforts, Morris led a pack of other "opulent adventurers," men who delighted in opulent display, were of easy fiscal virtue and given to "risky" investment strategies. They had no interest in developing western lands and selling them to actual settlers. (Some investors did; Quaker Henry Drinker, for example.) They traded in land as they traded in bonds and stock because other men did, and, if they acted quickly enough, they could make a killing on another's gullibility and move on to other speculations. A crazy spiral ensued. "Transfixed by the excitement of the land market and out of touch with underlying economic reality," Doerflinger tells us, "they bought land simply because it was expected to go up in price. . . . By the mid-1790s these land jobbers had been sucked into a sordid whirlpool of land-grabbing." Nor was land the only object of their speculations. Bank stock, especially that issued by Hamilton's new federal bank and by the Bank of New York, captured speculators' imaginations.[68]

Some of Morris's associates, though almost as wealthy, were more cautious. William Bingham, who boasted a fortune of more than £600,000 (compare

---

Jeremiah Wadsworth of Connecticut, and William Duer of New York." All had played key roles in Robert Morris's creative schemes to finance the war and remained close financial collaborators after the war (284–285).

67. Kings have their courts. Morris's court of commercial associates included John Nicholson, Thomas Willing, and Willing's new son-in-law, William Bingham, along with former tory Tench Coxe, whose advocacy of the new constitution we will recall below.

68. Doerflinger, *Vigorous Spirit of Enterprise*, 163, 278, 310–326, esp. 323–324. For Doerflinger's discussion of Drinker's real estate investments and how they differed from those of Morris et al., see 321–322.

this to James Beekman's prewar capital of £25,000!), had quickly bailed out of the Morris land speculation endeavors and focused more conservatively on trade. Morris's old partner, Thomas Willing, now the manager of the Bank of North America, similarly engaged in more traditional pursuits. But others followed Morris down the speculative path—the buoyant Tench Coxe (that harsh critic of Shays's Rebellion and Antifederalists, a staunch Federalist about to become a Jeffersonian Republican) and, most especially, Morris's New York associate William Duer. Indeed, of them all, Duer nearly equaled Morris in daring, innovation, and brashness.[69]

Innately political, these men wedded financial innovation to political ambition. Morris and his cohort dominated Pennsylvania's seven-member delegation to the Constitutional Convention.[70] They played a critical role in writing the new Federal constitution and advocating its ratification, in repealing Pennsylvania's radical Revolutionary constitution in 1790 and securing the adoption of a far more conservative one. Morris served as one of Pennsylvania's first U.S. senators. Six years later, Bingham succeeded Morris in the Senate. Their nationalist compatriots in New York exercised similar power. Philip Schuyler, Walter Livingston, John Jay, Gouverneur Morris, and William Duer constituted a political phalanx not surprisingly called the "Aristocratic Faction," a faction that played a critical role in securing New York's ratification of the new Federal constitution, a faction that maintained its preeminence through Washington's two administrations. (As already noted, it was the wives of these two groups, Morris's in Philadelphia and the Aristocratic Faction in New York, who dominated the republican court during Washington's and Adams's administrations.)

Quite literally, these men had constituted the new nation, financing its war for Independence, writing its constitution and the political treatises (John Jay and Alexander Hamilton were two of *The Federalist Papers'* three authors) that remain the principal source of the founders' "original intentions." They dazzled their fellow citizens with their wealth, their mercantile daring, their political power. Jefferson supporter Philip Freneau reported, "When I walk the streets of this city [Philadelphia], I can instantly tell who are people in authority, simply by the assumed significant superiority of countenance displayed on these occasions by the great men." To many of their contemporaries in both

69. Ibid., 310–333; Burrows and Wallace, *Gotham*, 270–271.

70. The Pennsylvania delegation included Morris, James Wilson, George Clymer, Thomas Fitzsimons, and Thomas Mifflin. Max Farrand, *The Records of the Federal Constitution of 1787*, 3 vols. (New Haven, 1911), lists the delegates to the Constitutional Convention of 1787 in an appendix in vol. III.

Europe and America, they represented the new American. But not everyone enjoyed being so dazzled. Middling merchant William Pollard complained bitterly to a friend about William Bingham's disdainful manner, reporting that he "has treated me with greater hauteur than I ever was treated by my Master during my youthfull apprenticeship."[71]

They were rich, haughty, and polished. But were they gentlemen? Many had attended the chevalier's ball. Thousands had watched them lean gracefully against the chevalier's gaily painted pillars, engaging in animated conversation. Their wealth and financial practices impressed the diplomatic corps and banking houses of Europe. They were at ease with the latest fashions and had the wealth to flaunt them. Even worse, from a classic republican perspective, they were men of paper and speculation, fancy and appearance. On one day, they might amass huge paper profits, but on the next day, they might as surely lose them. Yet, if the status of Morris, Bingham, Duer, and Willing was not secure, then who within the new Republic could be? As we have seen, much was at stake in the answers to this question: the new Republic's claim to the respect of European nations, the new commercial and professional elite's claim to social status and respectability, bourgeois citizens' claims to civic virtue and political authority, and the new nation's hopes for economic stability.

AFTER THE BALL IS OVER

Economic, political, and social disruptions made these issues particularly pressing. Revolution and war had not only destabilized the elites that had governed in the late colonial period; they occasioned massive cultural transformations—transformations that simultaneously benefited and frightened America's new men. The Republic's bourgeois elite did not want to turn the social or political worlds upside down. They simply wished to assume the authority, power, and claims to deference that the older colonial elite had exercised. Although in commercial and fiscal matters they initiated a radically new economy, in social matters, nostalgia colored their vision along with a colonial—and postcolonial—deference toward the culture of the imperial metropole. They assumed, indeed, they desired a society little changed from the one they had grown up in, characterized by clearly defined social and political hierarchical structures across which a few new and unusually talented men could move. The upward mobility of the talented had always defined British North America and

71. Freneau, quoted in Patterson, *Authority, Autonomy, and Representation*, 25; Doerflinger, *Vigorous Spirit of Enterprise*, 36.

had done little to destabilize the politics of deference and social distinction. "Movement must necessarily exist in a republic, if talent alone were to dominate. . . . But such inevitable movement must be into and out of clearly discernible ranks," Gordon S. Wood explains, summarizing the attitude of the new would-be "natural aristocracy." "Those who rose in a republic . . . must first acquire the attributes of social superiority—wealth, education, experience, and connections—before they could be considered eligible for political leadership." All the more reason, then, that the new would-be governing elite would work so hard to establish its claims to gentility. All the more reason (as we saw in the case of Noah Webster) that they would attempt to limit claims to political leadership to gentlemen, as they defined the term.[72]

In these twin efforts, none excelled Robert Morris. Certainly no one assumed the attributes of the fashionable gentleman with greater aplomb—not even his dear friend George Washington. Philadelphia buzzed with the news that Morris had imported three cooks from Paris, in addition to a dancing master and a hairdresser for his wife. Of course, the city's gossips added, his china and Mrs. Morris's millinery were all imported as well. His carriage and horses, all agreed, outshone even Washington's. His country estate, the Hill, overlooking the Schuylkill, was famous for its extensive greenhouses and wine cellar. But it was through the new town house that Morris commissioned in the early 1790s that he made his most dramatic bid for social preeminence. As the nation's capital returned to Philadelphia, Morris began its construction at Chestnut and Ninth Streets, far removed from the noise and congestion of Philadelphia's wharves and the press of daily business affairs. He chose Pierre Charles L'Enfant for his architect, Washington having employed L'Enfant to remodel New York's city hall for the nation's first capitol. His eye always upon Europe's elite, Morris had L'Enfant model his republican dwelling on a Louis XVI *hôtel*, the Paris fashion in the 1770s. Philadelphians gossiped animatedly about the design, the expense, the social and political statements Morris sought to make. But at least one observer, Benjamin Latrobe, Jefferson's preferred architect (and the architect of Philadelphia's monument to Greek Revival style, the First Bank of the United States), was horrified. "All the proportions are bad, all the horizontal and perpendicular lines broken to pieces," Latrobe reported to Jefferson. "The angle porches are irresistibly laughable things, and violently ugly."[73]

Latrobe's contempt reflected more than a budding political rivalry between

72. Wood, *Creation of the American Republic*, 479–480.
73. Garvan, *Federal Philadelphia*, 58.

urban Federalists and the future leaders of the Republican Party. It pointed to the Achilles' heel of the new merchant class's performance of gentility. Latrobe stated boldly what many Philadelphians were afraid to say—that, although America's economic emperor had many clothes—too many clothes, in fact—he had no taste. For all his fabled wealth and political power, Robert Morris lacked the grace, wit, and moderation considered "natural" to a true gentleman. If architectural detail and tasteful gardens proclaimed the gentleman, as the British gentry insisted, then Morris had failed. Not only was his collapse of self and state interests suspect by both classic republican and gentry standards; in the end, Robert Morris failed to perform gentility in a convincing manner. His home declared him a parvenu, an arriviste, a talented merchant, a creative financier who had socially overreached himself. (Contrast Latrobe's scorn to the praise Jefferson's architectural innovations received—established tidewater planter versus northern, hardworking merchant.)

And, it shortly turned out, he had financially overreached himself, as well. Morris would never complete his regal mansion. The grand schemes he had embraced at the war's end failed, one after another, as did his bold effort to recoup all through desperate land speculations. In February 1798, Morris declared bankruptcy. "My money is gone, my furniture is to be sold," he wrote; "I am to go to prison and my family to starve, good night." Shortly thereafter, Robert Morris rode past the unfinished walls and glassless windows on his grand mansion on his way to Philadelphia's Prune Street debtors' prison. Philadelphians came to call the house "Morris's Folly." In the eyes of many, it stood a synecdoche for Morris's economic, social, and political ambitions.[74]

Morris's career exemplifies the trajectory of the new nation's first generation of mercantile adventurers and financial innovators. They were, without question, men of great talent and ambition. They had successfully ridden on the crest of three revolutions—the commercial and consumer revolutions that swept across America during the last third of the eighteenth century and the political revolution that gave birth to the new Republic. But no matter how elegant their town houses and suburban villas, unlike the real British gentry, they could not turn to entailed estates and family histories to secure their social status and political authority. As we have just seen, for them, land was something one speculated in—not preserved through entail and primogeniture. They were men on the make, their eyes always on the main prize. Each

74. Doerflinger, *Vigorous Spirit of Enterprise*, 310–339, esp. 326; Norman B. Wilkinson, "Land Policy and Speculation in Pennsylvania, 1779–1800" (Ph.D. diss., University of Pennsylvania), 195, 243, 299.

PLATE FIFTEEN *An Unfinished House in Chestnut Street, Philadelphia.* Printed by William Birch and Son. The home Robert Morris hoped would cement his social status at home and abroad became known as "Morris's Folly" when it became clear that he lacked the funds to complete it. The Library Company of Philadelphia

windfall profit only increased their ambition, egging them on to greater adventures. "Gambling was in the blood of these men," Doerflinger observes; "when luck ran against them [as it often did in the uncertain economic world of the late eighteenth century], they were tempted to play double-or-nothing in order to mend their fortunes with a single spectacular deal." "Mired in financial difficulty, they concocted grandiose projects in order to stay afloat, and when their calculations proved mistaken, they drowned."[75]

75. Doerflinger, *Vigorous Spirit of Enterprise,* 162–163. Doerflinger points out that Morris was far from alone in these wild speculations. Henry Knox, soon to be Washington's secretary of war, joined with Morris's associates William Duer and William Bingham to purchase three million acres of worthless land in Maine. That ardent advocate for a Federalist vision, Tench Coxe, facing bankruptcy when the dry goods bubble of the mid-1780s burst, also turned to land speculation. "I have ascertained to a certainty purchases in Virginia, Penn. and New York to the amount of 1,100,000 Acres in the present and last Week," he reported hopefully (ibid., 325). Yet it was not his quick killings in the high-risk land market but his family's wealth that rescued him from debtors' prison. "Transfixed by the excitement of the land market and out of touch with underlying economic reality," Doerflinger observes, "these land jobbers had been sucked into a

Drown they did, especially the high fliers. Robert Morris was far from alone. His close associate, John Nicholson, from 1782 to 1794 comptroller general of Pennsylvania and involved in the same land speculation schemes as Morris, fell when Morris fell. Dying in the debtors' prison that confined Morris, he left his widow with $4,000,000 in debts. William Duer's crash in New York was even more dazzling. Wildly trying to corner the market in the bonds of both the Bank of New York and Hamilton's First Bank of the United States, he embezzled funds from Hamilton's other project, the Society to Encourage Manufacturing. Falling, he pulled thousands into the vortex of his own bankruptcy. New York's economy collapsed. Enraged crowds gathered outside New York City's debtors' prison. Had the city's mayor not called out the militia, they would have burned the prison to the ground and lynched Duer.[76]

In the wake of these bankruptcies, the élan of the first republican court dimmed. The first great American ball was over. With the dawn of the new century, the glitter of lights and diamonds that had dazzled so many of America's new bourgeoisie—and the watching crowd—the night of the chevalier's ball and, subsequently, at Martha Washington's receptions and Anne Bingham's fetes, faded. The dancers were revealed as performers, tricksters, gentlemen manqués. Lady Kitty Sterling, Duer's wife, ended her life running a boardinghouse in the city she had reigned over socially. As Thomas Jefferson entered the White House, the ladies of the republican court exited. The era of the elegant public and political woman had ended along with the world she had helped bring into being and strove to symbolize.[77]

Eighteenth-century European American merchant princes and financiers were figures of change and modernity—and of disorder and illusion. Liminal creatures, they balanced precariously between an older, land-based culture of gentility—a world of ascribed status, carefully choreographed ceremonies of deference, a world that valued stability and order above all—and the new

sordid whirlpool of land-grabbing that eventually filled the Prune Street debtors' prison with some of the greatest businessmen of the Revolutionary era" (323–326).

76. Matson, "Public Vices, Private Benefit," in Pencak and Wright, eds., *New York and the Rise of American Capitalism*, 72–123, esp. 106. For another discussion of Duer and debtors' prison, see Bruce H. Mann, "Tales from the Crypt: Prison, Legal Authority, and the Debtors' Constitution in the Early Republic," *WMQ*, 3d Ser., LI (1994), 183–202.

77. Daniel Defoe, *The Review: Reproduced from the Original Editions*, VI (New York, 1938), 523. Of course, women continued to play a key role in private social events, which had significant political under- and overtones. However, with Jefferson's election, their sphere was confined to domestic, not public, spaces. See Teute and Shields, "Jefferson in Washington," and Teute, "Roman Matron," in Kennon, ed., *Republic for the Ages*, 89–121.

capitalist world they, quite literally, were creating, an economically individualistic democratic and uncertain world, a world of accumulation, risk, and ruthless competition. Looking nostalgically back to a world they had never belonged to, boldly forging the future into being, they beckoned others to follow them, to cross the threshold between the old and the new, the known and the unknown. For their own and future generations, they modeled a classic American type—the confidence man, the hustler, the trickster. While successful, the confidence man intrigues his fellow citizens. He promises them that the ordinary could rise to greatness, that to the clever belong the race. But when the confidence man or hustler fails, those same citizens turn on him with scorn—and often rage. His failure reveals the fraud at the heart of the dream: that, although a hardworking and well-connected merchant such as Nicholas Boylston might become a republican prince, the sweating supercargo-cum-speculator was no true emperor.

"AN AGE OF PLOT AND DECEIT, OF CONTRADICTION AND PARADOX"

We have explored two of the three questions Benjamin Rush's letter raised: Could the creole play the gentleman? and, Was the new American gentleman of the postwar years a figure of nostalgia or modernity? But what of our third question: Did the introduction of the concept of the republican gentleman add stability and inner cohesion to the divided republican political identity that hesitantly emerged on the pages of the political magazines? Could the concept of the republican gentleman help stabilize a national identity that representations of masculinity, savagery, and civilization had so seriously compromised? An initial problem lay, of course, in the shifting meanings of the term "gentleman." With the term's carrying so many contradictory meanings—zoon politikon, hardworking merchant or manufacturer, fashionable gentleman, pseudogentry, or aristocrat manqué—how was the reader of the new urban magazines to know which steps to follow in the new Republic's complex choreography of class and national identity?

Additional difficulties present themselves. The most obvious relates to the ideological confusions that existed between the concept of the fashionable gentleman and the aesthetics and principles of both classic and commercial republicanism. Certainly no two figures could have been more dissimilar than classic republicanism's zoon politikon and the eighteenth-century fashionable gentleman. Of course, there were some similarities. Both disdained manual and wage labor. Both were presumed to be men of landed estates and independent wealth, well educated, widely read in the classics and the histories of great republics and empires. But there the similarities end. The classic republican gentleman emerged from the political writings of Henry, Lord Bolingbroke, the fashionable gentleman from the polite letters of the third Earl of Shaftesbury, and even, perhaps, of Lord Chesterfield. A chasm separated these men's worldviews. The zoon politikon's aesthetics, as we know, were Spartan. Military valor, hardiness, and simplicity bordering on roughness were his values. He was suspicious of commerce, disdainful of urbanity, fashion, and material display. The aesthetics of gentility stood in sharp contrast. Pleasure, beauty, grace, and the sentiments held center stage—as did the gentlewoman.

Indeed, the most telling difference between the classic republican world and the world of eighteenth-century gentility might well have been the place women held in each. Whereas eighteenth-century classic republicanism banished women from the political and the civil as threats to civic virtue, discourses of gentility and politesse made women central players in a world of civility, culture, and even politics.[78] Rather than corrupt the eighteenth-century gentleman, gentlewomen refined and improved him. Performing for women's accolades made both merchants and politicians gentlemen. The rules of gentility and politesse were clear. As ladies were graceful, so must the gentleman be. As ladies were concerned with fashions, so must the gentleman be. By the late eighteenth century, it was clear that the gentleman, far from being an independent aesthete, at war with cities and modernity, had become the creature of commerce, the devotee of fashion, the self-conscious object of the gaze of others and, mirroring theirs, of his own. Women not only refined the man; eighteenth-century advocates of gentility and politesse were certain they refined the political arena itself. Polished ladies (Martha Washington, Elizabeth Jay, Anne Bingham) prided themselves on bringing political animosities and ideological conflicts under the reign of compliance and politesse as they made their tea tables and fetes de rigueur for those who would succeed on the new nation's political stage.

Not surprisingly, classic republicans viewed the man of fashionable gentility and politesse with contempt. They saw him as an unproductive, private, and

78. See, for example, Vickery, *Gentleman's Daughter;* Hannah Barker and Elaine Chalus, eds., *Gender in Eighteenth-Century England: Roles, Representations, and Responsibilities* (London, 1997); and Robert W. Uphaus and Gretchen M. Foster, eds., *The "Other" Eighteenth Century: English Women of Letters, 1660–1800* (East Lansing, Mich., 1991). For the situation in France, see Dena Goodman, *The Republic of Letters: A Cultural History of the French Enlightenment* (Ithaca, N.Y., 1994), esp. "The Enlightenment Salonnière," 73–89, and "Governing the Republic of Letters: Salonnières and the Rule(s) of Polite Conversation," 90–135.

domesticated man—indeed, as effeminate. To refer back to John Adams's acerbic comment at the war's beginning, a man of "Taste and Politeness. . . . Elegance in Dress. . . . Musick and Dancing" was the model monarchical subject, not the ideal republican citizen. Such a man contributed little to the state or the general good. Most dangerously of all, courting the gaze of others, he was dependent on their opinion. He could lay no claim to the manly, rugged independence virtuous citizenship required. Within the classic republican script, the new eighteenth-century gentleman not only played to corrupt and corrupting women; he played the part of a corrupt woman.

In no way did the classic republican and the man of gentility differ more radically, J. G. A. Pocock tells us, than in the basis of their self-knowledge, their understanding of themselves. New capitalist ways and values had altered the basis of the citizen's self-knowledge. The classic republican "knew himself to be a citizen and knew how to play his role and take decisions within the *politeia* or *modo di vivere* of a republic." He "knew and loved [him]self in [his] relation to a *patria, res publica* or common good." The classical republican's self-esteem (his *amour de soi-même)* was based on the firmness of this knowledge. The man of gentility, consumerism, and display, in contrast, was governed by *amour-propre,* that is, by a self-love that depended "on the figure one cut in one's own eyes and those of others." Within the eighteenth century's world of capitalism and consumerism, a man's worth was no longer measured in hectometers planted or rents received in solid specie. It rested, rather, on his projecting an appearance of credibility, respectability, and polish. Surety about oneself and others disappeared. The new gentleman, the classic republican insisted, was "activated by nonrational forces." Yet, ironically, it was the classic republican, the man "who knew himself to be a citizen and . . . how . . . to take decisions within the *politeia,* "who was the man of nostalgia, his face turned always to the past. The fashionable gentleman, the man of desires, turned his face toward the future. Tied to commerce and manufacturing, he embraced technology, change, and innovation. Defoe was right. It was an age of contradiction, paradox, and performance—as was modernity itself.[79]

But, of course, classic republicanism was not the only republican discourse to inform political and economic subjectivities in the new nation. Throughout the eighteenth century, many European Americans, especially those in trade, embraced commercial republicanism and its Protestant work ethic of industry, frugality, and delayed satisfaction. Civic virtue, they argued, lay in productivity and hard work. The hardworking middling merchant-cum-commercial re-

79. Pocock, *Machiavellian Moment,* 464–466, 486.

publican would never have modeled his town house after the Duke of Manchester's Regency establishment or imported Parisian hairdressers and dancing masters. At the same time, William Allen would never have asked him to join Philadelphia's exclusive Masonic Lodge, nor would his wife have been invited to one of Eliza Powel's musical evenings.[80]

The gentleman of fashion devoted to the cult of gentility and politesse violated the core principles of both classic and commercial republicanism, revealing the term "republican gentleman" to be an oxymoron. The efforts of the new nation's mercantile elite to model themselves upon him only intensified the ideological confusions already destabilizing the new American. Certainly, the figure of the republican gentleman did nothing to reaffirm the new American's virility or reestablish the connection between maleness and manliness, nor did he gain any credence along the frontier or help heal the fissure between East and West.

Psychological confusions followed upon ideological conflicts, further disturbing the republican gentleman as a model for the virtuous new American. Whether a merchant prince or a struggling entrepreneur, the trading man lived in a highly competitive and deceitful world. Secrecy was a mercantile way of life; trust was seen, at best, as foolhardy. As one Quaker merchant warned a colleague, "Keep thy business to thy self, and don't let it be known, who thou dost Business for, or what Sorts of goods thou Ships of. Some will want to know . . . with a Design to Circumvent thee." In the undercapitalized world of American commerce, no merchant ever knew whether he would be the next to fail. But all merchants could be certain that their competitors waited like sharks to pick the bones of the fallen.[81]

80. Indeed, it was hardworking middling men who, revolting against the elitism of eighteenth-century Scottish Rite lodges such as Philadelphia's, formed an opposing Masonic order, the Ancient Masonic lodges, that proliferated during the late eighteenth and early nineteenth centuries, attracting their members from an emerging middle class of shopkeepers, successful artisans, and American-educated professionals. For a discussion of the Ancient Masonic orders, see Bullock, *Revolutionary Brotherhood,* chap. 3. For discussions of black Masonic orders, see Joe William Trotter, "African American Fraternal Associations in American History: An Introduction," *Social Science History,* XXVIII (2004), 355–366. For an older analysis, see Charles H. Wesley, *Prince Hall: Life and Legacy* (Washington, D.C., 1977). See, as well, Bullock, *Revolutionary Brotherhood,* 158–162.

81. "On Fraud and Retaliation," *Columbian Magazine,* II (1788), 213–215. Another merchant conveyed a commonplace warning to a friend who had just arrived in America hoping to set up in trade: "Most of our trading people here are complaisant sharpers: and the maxim in trade, to think every man a knave until the contrary evidence appears, would do well to be observed" (cited by Toby L. Ditz, "Secret Selves, Credible Personas: The Problematics of Trust and Public

But an intricate pattern of connection and dependency also lay at the heart of the commercial world. Commercial ventures required cooperation, trust, and reliability. Merchants depended on the honesty and sagacity of their super-cargoes and factors (the merchants or middlemen who represented them in foreign ports) and on the trustworthiness of a growing network of bank directors, insurance brokers, and underwriters. Merchants daily met one another in taverns and coffeehouses, on street corners and wharves to exchange information about markets, cargoes just arrived, or vessels about to leave, to exchange revealing gossip, to suggest cooperative ventures, to form partnerships. And to watch, carefully, intensely. In short, the nature of commerce forced merchants to be independent, trusting, and honorable in a world that required dependency, refused trust, and rewarded duplicity. They had at all times to mask their weaknesses, deny crises, outface rumor-driven doubts. Performers in the repertory theater of eighteenth-century commerce, they had to play as numerous and diverse characters as did the would-be fashionable gentleman.[82]

To meet these challenges, cultural historian Toby L. Ditz argues, eighteenth-century merchants divided themselves into inner and outer selves. They enveloped their inner self, their frightened and vulnerable self, within a public self constructed to both shield the true inner self from and represent him to the combative, risk-filled world of commerce and the other many players in that world. Efficient, well-defended, ever observant—when necessary, deceptive, even avaricious—this public figure represented the interests of the inner man at the same time as he constituted a protective cordon sanitaire around the inner self. As paper money purported to represent real value, so this representative figure purported to represent a real person. A counterfeit, a theatrical double, he aimed, above all, to appear lifelike. In doing so, he played always to two audiences, his inner self and an outer world of other merchants, creditors, social equals and inferiors whom he sought to trick into suspending disbelief. Flawless on the surface, painstakingly orchestrated, solipsistically self-reflective, these outer figures, or characters, seemed only too natural in a world representation, appearance, and opinion had already structured. The merchant and the

<hr />

Display in the Writing of Eighteenth-Century Philadelphia Merchants," in Robert Blair St. George, ed., *Possible Pasts: Becoming Colonial in Early America* [Ithaca, N.Y., 2000]). See, as well, Doerflinger, *Vigorous Spirit of Enterprise*, 19.

82. The late-eighteenth-century credit-driven U.S. economy was built far more around personalities and personal connections than around any formal structures. See Doerflinger, *Vigorous Spirit of Enterprise*, 18–19; Ditz, "Secret Selves," in St. George, ed., *Possible Pasts*, 220–222, 226–228. See, as well, Ditz, "Shipwrecked," *JAH*, LXXXI (1994), 52–90.

gentleman, as actor/counterfeiter, did in the end become one. But was that one a stable, coherent subject? Knowing that he was but one player in a series of masquerades, how could the merchant/gentleman ever rest secure in his sense of self? More pressingly still, could that multiple, divided, and theatrical subject ever successfully model a virtuous republican citizen?[83]

A final conundrum remains. The chevalier invited seven hundred guests to his ball. Doerflinger estimates that, in the 1780s, great merchant princes constituted but one-tenth of Philadelphians engaged in overseas trading, that is, fifty out of five hundred merchants. In addition, the chevalier invited members of the Continental Congress (approximately another fifty, if all attended), at least some members of the Pennsylvania legislature (one presumes not the radical agrarianists from the western counties), army officers, judges and their staff, foreign dignitaries, clergymen, scholars associated with the College of Philadelphia, and one Native American chief. Even assuming that each invitee brought two additional guests (as Rush did), that would still leave a number of the seven hundred unaccounted for. Clearly, the chevalier extended invitations to some among the new Republic's middling ranks. Rush admits, "All the ranks, parties and professions in the city . . . were fully represented," including both "ancient as well as modern families." How did these middling European Americans fit into the image of a republican gentleman? As readers, they desired—and needed—instruction in the quotidian ways of social and economic survival in the new cities and the new capitalist economy. The magazines' printer/publishers and their more elite contributors were only too happy to offer these middling men instruction in the choreography of gentility. How, otherwise, would they learn to appreciate and admire the bourgeois elite's mastery of that choreography? Even more critically, if not impressed with the complexity and importance of that performance, would they willingly defer to the bourgeoisie's self-proclaimed right to govern them as their political representatives? The magazines thus became a venue through which the bourgeoisie reached out to form social and political alliances with their middling urban neighbors.[84]

One final point remains. Subjects, as we know, need constituting Others to give them the appearance of internal coherence. The more unstable and uncer-

83. Ditz, "Secret Selves," in St. George, ed., *Possible Pasts,* 219–242.

84. Doerflinger, *Vigorous Spirit of Enterprise,* 20; Benjamin Rush, "The French Fête in Philadelphia in Honor of the Dauphin's Birthday, 1782," *Pennsylvania Magazine of History and Biography,* XXI (1897), 257–262, esp. 259.

tain the identity, the greater the need for constituting Others. In a deeply counterintuitive manner, two such figures emerged—the bourgeois woman herself and the enslaved African American. How could these two figures bring coherence to the urban fathers' imagined new American? Let us turn to the pages of their newspapers to find the answer.

CHAPTER SEVEN

Polished Gentlemen, Troublesome Women, and Dancing Slaves

Interest at the level of the consciousness of each individual who goes to make up the population, and interest considered as the interest of the population regardless of what the particular interests and aspirations may be of the individuals who compose it, this is the new target and the fundamental instrument of the government of population: the birth of a new art, or at any rate of a range of absolutely new tactics and techniques.
—MICHEL FOUCAULT, "Governmentality"

Thy life to mend
This Book attend

—New England Primer (1819)

ELEGANT STEPS FOR ELEGANT DANCERS

Self-consciously emulating London's fashionable *Gentleman's Magazine* and *Critical Review*, the editors and publishers of America's new magazines announced that their publications were designed to appeal to the "discerning publick," to "men of ability," "men of genius, and erudition"—in short, to gentlemen. To attract this discerning audience, publishers announced that their periodicals would be "fertile in literary productions . . . weighty in matter, pure in sentiment, elegant in style, and entertaining to the fancy." On their pages, "the philosopher may . . . communicate the result of his researches, the moralist lay down rules of ethics and discipline—the satirist lash the vices and follies of the time . . . the poet invoke the muses." Seeking the well-read and scholarly reader, editors promised that their magazines would "reward studious application—increase an acquaintance with natural and civil history, with arts . . . law, physick and divinity . . . [and stimulate] literary emulation and effort." Aiming to assuage the concerns of decorous ladies, they promised, as well, to reject all that "would give uneasiness to a respectable body of people" or might be "too indelicate for the female eye." They strove, that is, both to appeal to those who could already claim to be refined gentlemen and ladies and to transform their other readers (those able to pay their subscription rates though they lacked a classical education) into such elevated figures. The goal: to make both elite and middling readers the cultural equals of London magazine readers. Noah Webster expressed the broad-reaching ambitions of all the editor/publishers while underscoring their class focus:

> It is the Editor's wish to gratify every class of readers—the Divine, the Philosopher, the Historian, the Statesman, the Moralist, the Poet, the Merchant and the Laborer—and his *fair readers* may be assured that no inconsiderable pains will be taken to furnish *them* with entertainment.[1]

As the new nation took form, the political magazines played a critical role in disseminating an Enlightenment culture of gentility and belles lettres. In North America, David S. Shields explains, "where populations had little experience of the metropolis . . . imported books and periodicals portrayed the beau monde's glories so compellingly that a cadre of writers dedicated themselves to creating similar worlds in . . . Boston . . . New York . . . Philadelphia . . . Charleston, [and] Savannah." In this way, print culture "enabled the transmission of a secularized, cosmopolitan, genteel culture into North America . . . [and] adopted the forms and symbols of belles lettres, fashioning from them the republic of letters and the 'public sphere.'" In other words, the popular press "offered a middling readership the opportunity to participate imaginatively in a discursive analogue of genteel company."[2]

Positioning themselves as conduits for the transfer of genteel culture to the new Republic, the magazines solicited original poetry, reviewed the latest novels, reprinted American and British fiction, published essays on philosophy

---

1. "On the Utility of Well Regulated Magazines," *Massachusetts Magazine,* I (1789), 7–9; General Observer, "For the Massachusetts Magazine: The General Observer, No. I," ibid., 9–10; "Introduction," *Columbian Magazine,* I (1786), n.p.; "Introduction," *American Magazine,* I (1787), 3–4.

2. David S. Shields, *Civil Tongues and Polite Letters in British America* (Chapel Hill, N.C., 1997), 12. I have taken Shields's comments somewhat out of context, since he was writing about early- and mid-eighteenth-century genteel culture as it took form largely in manuscript circulation. On the other hand, he would agree that newspapers and magazines played their role in translating that elite culture for the reading public. And the magazines themselves testify to their role.

and history. Webster's *American Magazine* featured extracts from Joel Barlow's *Vision of Columbus*, along with contributions from other Hartford Wits. Charles Brockden Brown's first essay on literary criticism appeared in Mathew Carey's *American Museum*. As already noted, the *Massachusetts Magazine* included excerpts of Wollstonecraft's *Vindication of the Rights of Women* in its opening issue.[3] Indeed, publishing many of America's early novelists, Isaiah Thomas became known as an important patron of European American letters. Reflecting genteel British literary taste, the magazines celebrated belles lettres. As the *Massachusetts Magazine* explained to its readers, "All that relates to beauty, harmony, grandeur, and elegance, all that can soothe the mind, gratify the fancy, or move the affections, belongs to their province." Belles lettres, it promised, would "embellish [the] mind" and render the reader "a being endowed with . . . taste and imagination."[4]

But, for a readership engrossed with hard work and the practical concerns of commerce, magazine editors were equally assiduous in recruiting essays that addressed economic and scientific issues. Essays on developments in scientific agriculture and chemical advances were commonplace. Benjamin Franklin and Benjamin Rush were frequent contributors to the *American Museum*, which also carried notices on the activities of the American Philosophical Society. Webster's *American Magazine* reprinted lengthy sections from Jefferson's *Notes on Virginia*.[5]

3. See, for example, "Reflections on the English Drama: Tragedy," *American Magazine*, I (1788), 641–646; Francis Walsh, Jr., "A Gothic Story," ibid., 779–782. The *Columbian Magazine* began publishing poetry and literary reviews in its June 1790 issue. The *American Museum* concluded each issue with fifteen to twenty pages of poetry. Frank Luther Mott surveys the magazines' literary forays in his *History of American Magazines, 1741–1930*, 5 vols. (Cambridge, Mass., 1957–1968), I, 54, 57, 60–64, 104–107.

4. "Beneficial Effects of a Taste for the Belles Lettres," *Massachusetts Magazine*, I (1789), 105–106; "Letter IX," "Letter X: Frederick to Felicia," *American Magazine*, I (1788), 709–711. For a general discussion of the cultural and literary significance of belles lettres, see David S. Shields, "British American Belles-Lettres," in Sacvan Bercovitch, ed., *Cambridge History of American Literature*, I, *1590–1820* (Cambridge, 1994), 307–343.

5. See, for example, Noah Webster, "Antiquity: Copy of a Letter from Mr. Webster, to the Rev. Dr. Stiles, President of Yale College, Dated Philadelphia, October 22, 1787," *American Magazine*, I (1787), 15–19; "Eloquence of the Natives of This Country, from Mr. Jefferson's *Notes on Virginia*," ibid., I (1788), 106–108. See, as well, "The Contemplative Philosopher: Reflections on Vegetation," ibid., 664–669; "On the Preservation of the Health of Persons Employed in Agriculture," ibid., 30–36. Webster was not the only editor to include scientific articles in his magazine. The *American Museum* and the *Columbian Magazine* also interspersed scientific essays among their other offerings. The *Columbian Magazine* routinely featured sketches of scientific and agricultural devices and inventions.

Clearly, education was central to the republican gentleman's production and self-presentation, and in almost every issue magazine editors and contributors urged its importance. Carey used his *American Museum* to celebrate the activities of the College of Philadelphia, reprinted Benjamin Rush's call for a Federal university, and, more radically, advocated women's education. All the new magazines insisted that education would establish European Americans' cultural equality with Europe. It was a national priority.[6]

Just as education signaled European America's cultural equality with Europe, within America, it marked class distinctions. We see this quite clearly in the Philanthropist's letter on education, which appeared in the *Massachusetts Magazine* and counterpoised education to vulgarity and refinement to savagery. "The advantages of education," the Philanthropist proclaimed, "[create] as great a difference between the *refined* and the *savage* mind, as reason does between the savage and the brute." In the late 1780s, the phrase "the savage and the brute" suggested the "savages" along the frontier (and we know that, from an elite eastern perspective, these included white as well as red savages), the "savage" farmers of western Massachusetts, and the "savages" in "darkest Africa." The race and class prejudices that colored the Philanthropist's worldview are even more pronounced in an earlier letter on education.

> Human nature . . . affords but a melancholy spectacle. In every part of the globe it wears the evident marks of imbecility, corruption and degeneracy. . . . The unnumbered tribes of ignorant and stupid animals in the shape of men, who inhabit the known and unknown territories of Asia, Africa, and Europe, as well as America, are humiliating proofs to what depths of abasement *poor human nature* may sink.[7]

6. *American Museum*, IV (1788), 443; "On the Invention of Letters," ibid., I (1788), 712–713. Timothy Dwight, in his baccalaureate address, celebrated learning and the establishment of schools: "Our Ancestors, inspired with the same generous attachment to science, as to freedom, have, by that *wisest of all political establishments*, THE INSTITUTION OF SCHOOLS, diffused light and knowledge through every part of their settlements" ([Timothy Dwight], "A Valedictory Address to the Young Gentlemen, Who Commenced Bachelors of Arts, at Yale College, July 25th, 1776," *American Magazine*, I [1787], 42–47, esp. 46, and I [1788], 99–103). In much the same vein, fellow Yale graduate Noah Webster stated: "If you wish for happiness at home, or safety to the state,—EDUCATE YOUR CHILDREN" (Belzebub [Webster], "Letter III," *American Magazine*, I [1788], 161–163, esp. 161).

7. [Philanthropist], "For the Massachusetts Magazine: The Philanthropist, No. III, Addressed to Students at Colleges and Universities," *Massachusetts Magazine*, I (1789), 137–141, esp. 137, and "The Philanthropist, No. I," ibid., 10–11, esp. 10. On the various "savages," recall Fisher Ames's attacks on Shays's rebels (Camillus [Fisher Ames], "Observations on the Late Insurrec-

Complimenting Thomas's elite readers on their superiority to "the unnumbered tribes of [the] ignorant and stupid," these two letters contained a not-so-subtle warning. Inhabiting a middle ground between the British gentry, on the one hand, and the uneducated inhabitants of America's western lands and southern plantations, on the other, European Americans could not afford to deviate even slightly from British standards of civility and education. If they did, they could be included among the essayist's "unnumbered tribes." The magazines saw their task as one of simultaneously educating their readers and of projecting the image of an educated, cultured America both at home and overseas.

And how better to do so than by appropriating that most genteel of eighteenth-century literary forms, the pastoral romance? This genre, especially as deployed by the new Republic's print culture, had two principal objectives. The first was to please—and educate—new urban readers anxious to polish their social and literary skills. The second was to refigure rural America as a neoclassical and highly cultured Eden. The pastoral romance's stylized and courtly rhetoric was originally designed to celebrate the purity and virtue of rural life in contrast to the corruptions of the fashionable world. (Americans tended to present themselves as exemplars of rural purity and Europeans as the embodiment of urban corruption.) At the same time, pastorals worked to distance would-be urbane readers from any of the realities of the rural world—in North America, mob violence, illiteracy, and sexual irregularities. This was precisely what "Letter from Maria to Eliza," appearing in the *Massachusetts Magazine*, sought to accomplish. Though ostensibly set in rural Massachusetts, the content and language of this pastoral romance suggest that Thomas might well have copied it, with very few modifications, from a British publication—either that, or its New England author had very self-consciously set out to reproduce the rhetoric of a British sentimental romance, itself a significant example of postcolonial emulation. True to genre, the story begins as Maria, a young woman of wealth and education, chides her friend Eliza for urging her to leave bucolic western Massachusetts and return to the "balls, concerts and assemblies" of Boston, where she would meet with corrupting "dissipation and the buz *[sic]* of flattery from an hundred fops." (Recall the "four very smart and agreeable young ladies'" criticism of Boston fops that Thomas had printed in the *Worcester Magazine*. Recall, as well, Eliza Wharton's corruption while in fashionable Boston.)[8]

---

tion in Massachusetts . . . Letter I," *American Museum*, II [1787], 315–318, esp. 316). Recall, as well, eastern attacks on frontier squatters, detailed in Chapter 4, above.

8. "Letter from Maria to Eliza," *Massachusetts Magazine*, I (1789), 309–310. Raymond Wil-

A recent experience has transformed her, Maria's letter continues. Taking a late afternoon walk,

> when Sol, tired with his journey, was about to repose himself on his watery bed—the warbling of the feather'd songster was no longer heard . . . I . . . lost in the maze of thought . . . [was] roused by the voice of distress, which proceeded from a neighboring hut. . . . I hastened to [the] cot to afford relief.

Within the "cot," Maria finds a young girl in tears. Her mother is dying, and her father, a farmer, has died in debtors' prison, unable to pay his debts after being deceived by a cunning neighbor into mortgaging his farm. The mother soon passes, leaving their daughter defenseless, starving, and alone.[9]

Save for the contrived rhetoric, this tale bears a striking resemblance to the stories poor western farmers told immediately before and after Shays's Rebellion. Complaining of being led into debt by neighboring storekeepers and pressed by relentless tax collectors, they feared that their farms would be seized for debt and their economic, and hence their political, independence destroyed. Few men were more familiar than Isaiah Thomas with the events that led to Shays's Rebellion. (We will recall that his *Worcester Magazine* reprinted the farmers' angry petitions and documented the shortage of specie and high taxes that oppressed the western farmers.) But listen to how the story of rural poverty sounds when, three years later, with his magazine transplanted to Boston, Thomas reinscribed it in belletristic style crafted to please the taste of genteel Boston ladies. In this second telling, the indebted western farmer, far from resisting eastern tyranny, dies of grief and shame. His orphaned daughter (romantically christened Laura—after Petrarch's Laura, one wonders?), facing a life worse than death, is saved, not by farmers' armed resistance to Boston capitalists—now the *Massachusetts Magazine*'s subscribers—but by Maria, the refined, tender-hearted, and tearful upper-class philanthropist (Thomas's idealized new reader?). Maria's elegantly composed letter to Eliza continues:

> After the [mother's] funeral obsequies were performed, I took Laura (for that was the name of the rustick fair one) home, where she might eat of my bread, and drink of my cup. . . . Could you, Eliza, but see this lovely girl

---

liams, *The Country and the City* (New York, 1973), positions the British pastoral in an interesting social and economic context. Thomas's "Eliza," presumably male literary conceit, differs greatly from Hannah Foster's far more troubled—and interesting—Eliza. See Chapters 2 and 3, above.

9. "Letter from Maria to Eliza," *Massachusetts Magazine*, I (1789), 309–310; "Correspondence between Maria and Eliza: Maria to Eliza, Letter II, Containing the History of Laura:—A Pathetic Tale," ibid., 422–425, esp. 423–424.

[elsewhere described as a "lovely young creature. . . . Thoughtless of beauty, she was beauty's self"], I'm sure . . . your generous heart would heave one sigh, to think of the danger she would have been exposed to.[10]

On the pages of the *Massachusetts Magazine*, the hard economic realities and unresolved political conflicts that covered the pages of the *Worcester Magazine* were sexualized, sentimentalized, and feminized. Riotous farmers were recast as "rustic fair ones" whose sexual purity, not political authority, was endangered. (Of course, "fair ones" do not have any political authority to be endangered. They are daughters, vulnerable and dependent, not hardworking and rights-bearing republican citizens.) The Massachusetts Militia led by General Knox was replaced by two genteel young women, resolved to perform "our duty to rescue virtue and innocence from distress" and in this way to secure social justice and harmony. Conflating classic republicanism's social elitism and liberalism's praise of private philanthropy, Maria's letter produces a romanticized vision of class conflict and conflict resolution. And more, it accomplishes the ultimate feminization of Massachusetts's rugged and riotous farmers.[11]

The *Massachusetts Magazine* was far from alone in presenting an idealized society structured around sentiments of pity, benevolence, and humility. The *Columbian Magazine* and the *American Museum* carried a number of stories about gentlemen, tears of sympathy shining in their eyes, giving shillings and sovereigns to impoverished urban dwellers (often crippled war veterans), all of whom received the pittances with deferential gratitude.[12]

But Thomas's romance demands closer reading. Bankruptcy and debtors' prison did not only threaten hardscrabble families. They were far more likely to ensnare America's ambitious merchants, risk-taking entrepreneurs and artisan/manufacturers. Given the erratic postwar market, financial solvency was a sometime thing. For Thomas's new subscribers, the world the *Massachusetts Magazine* used Maria and Eliza to invoke was a postcolonial fantasy. The world that most of Thomas's new subscribers knew was one of rough-and-tumble commerce, specie and credit crises, long days and nights spent balanc-

---

10. "Letter from Maria to Eliza," *Massachusetts Magazine*, I (1789), 310; and see Chapter 2, above.

11. Maria's letter also calls to mind the story of Charles Churchill, the kindhearted rake who rescued a beggar girl and her starving family from life on the streets ([Charles Johnstone], "Affecting Anecdote, of the Late Charles Churchill: Written by the Author of 'The Adventures of a Guinea,'" *American Magazine*, I [1788], 109–113).

12. See, for example, "The Worthy Soldier," *Columbian Magazine*, I (1786), 188–191.

ing books and collecting debts. It was a world haunted by fears of bankruptcy and the reality of debtors' prison.[13]

Read in this way, the "rustic fair one's" dilemmas might well have spoken with greater immediacy to Thomas's Boston readers than to Berkshire farmers—had Berkshire farmers ever had the desire or the two dollars and fifty cents to subscribe to the *Massachusetts Magazine*. One further aspect of the story strongly reaffirms this suggestion: Laura's father had mortgaged his farm not simply because of the hard times but because a neighbor had lured him into a career of gambling! Gambling was not a common practice among the self-sufficient and orthodox Calvinist farmers of western Massachusetts. But it was among urban dwellers—especially fashionable young men. More generally, gambling was a commonly invoked metaphor for commerce and especially for the speculation mania that ruined so many of the nation's new elite and the middling figures in the 1790s. Maria's story only seems a pastoral fantasy. It actually spoke intensely to urban readers and contributors.[14]

FROM THE BON TON TO THE COUNTINGHOUSE: ENTER THE MAN OF COMMERCE AND HARD WORK

Pastoral romances had their charms, but, if the contents of the new magazines tell us anything, they tell us that magazines' subscribers—even the richest and most socially prominent among them—were practical men of business, tied to their wharves and account books, their stores and workshops. Isaiah Thomas was the first to admit that the majority of his subscribers and contributors were not persons of leisure and inherited wealth given to writing letters about "feather'd songster[s]." "Engaged in the business and active scenes of life," they might well "not hav[e] many leisure moments [and] . . . will be more likely to read a short essay . . . than to set down and peruse . . . a lengthy dissertation." Consequently, the *Massachusetts Magazine*, along with the other political magazines, filled its pages with articles of interest to overseas merchants: fact-filled descriptions of trade patterns in Portugal, Malta, Nova Scotia, the west coast of Africa, and Japan; reports on Dutch commercial settlements at the Cape of Good Hope and Java; accounts of Captain Cook's

13. For an example of such concerns expressed in the urban magazines, see "On Fraud and Retaliation," *Columbian Magazine*, II (1788), 213–215. See, as well, Toby L. Ditz, "Secret Selves, Credible Personas: The Problematics of Trust and Public Display in the Writing of Eighteenth-Century Philadelphia Merchants," in Robert Blair St. George, ed., *Possible Pasts: Becoming Colonial in Early America* (Ithaca, N.Y., 2000), 219–242.

14. "Maria to Eliza, Letter II," *Massachusetts Magazine*, I (1789), 423–424.

explorations of the Pacific. Commercial news from the Caribbean was commonplace. On the reverse of each month's table of contents, the *Massachusetts Magazine* listed the "Current Prices of Public Securities."[15]

Serving commercial and fiscal interests, the political magazines pronounced commerce the lifeblood of the Republic. It was a spur to industry, encouraged agriculture, rewarded talent, and refined manners. The magazines also heaped similar praise on domestic manufactures. Phrasing their acclaim in patriotic rhetoric, they urged European Americans to break free of their "enslavement" to British fashions and goods. Tench Coxe (one of his city's most fashionably dressed gentlemen yet one who had heavily invested in manufacturing enterprises) excoriated Philadelphia readers for their "extravagant and wasteful use of foreign manufactures," insisting that they "consider our untimely passion for European luxuries as a malignant and alarming symptom, threatening convulsions and dissolution to the political body."[16] Strong words, indeed—fashionable consumption, the emulation of polite British society, suddenly presented as "malignant" disorders that threatened the body politic with epidemics, "convulsions," and "dissolution." Eighteenth-century Philadelphians took the threat of epidemics very seriously. Summer after summer, yellow fever

15. "Letter from Maria to Eliza," ibid., 309; General Observer, "For the Massachusetts Magazine, No. I," ibid., 9–10; American, "Essay on the Advantages of Trade and Commerce," *American Museum*, II (1787), 328–332; William Barton, Esq., "On the Propriety of Investing Congress with Power to Regulate the Trade of the United States," ibid., I, 13–16; A Bostonian, "A View of the Federal Government of America: Its Defects, and a Proposed Remedy, Letter I," ibid., 294–298; "On Public Faith," ibid., 405–408; "A Word of Consolation for America," ibid., 187–190; "On the Origin of Commerce," *American Magazine*, I (1788), 713–714. For examples of urban magazines' focus on the Pacific (as Robert Morris was preparing to send the first European American ship to China), see "An Account of the Pelew Islands, Lately Situated in the Western Part of the Pacifick Ocean," which appeared in four issues of the *Massachusetts Magazine:* "New Discovered Islands in the Pacifick Ocean," *Massachusetts Magazine*, I (1789), 38–44, 89–93, 142–146, 201–205; and "Narrative of the Death of Capt. James Cook," *New Jersey Magazine*, I (1786), 7–11.

16. Tench Coxe, "An Address to an Assembly of the Friends of American Manufactures . . . ," *American Museum*, II (1787), 248–255, esp. 253; Coxe, "Thoughts on the Present Situation of the United States," ibid., IV (1788), 401–404. See, as well, Amicus, "Essay on the Fatal Tendency of the Prevailing Luxuries . . . ," ibid., II (1787), 216–220. Coxe's comments fit in with his decision to invest heavily in domestic manufacturing. Referring to Coxe as "the Defoe of America," Thomas M. Doerflinger tells us that, through a series of pamphlets and other publications, "Coxe introduced the Industrial Revolution into the American imagination." He was an active investor in a number of early industrial projects in the new Republic (Doerflinger, *A Vigorous Spirit of Enterprise: Merchants and Economic Development in Revolutionary Philadelphia* [Chapel Hill, N.C., 1986], 45, 275, 285, 330–332).

brought literal dissolution to citizens, throwing the city's economy and government into convulsions. Coxe's attack might well have reflected his own heavy investments in domestic manufacturing. From our perspective, however, what is especially interesting is that the new nation's would-be elite magazines saw no contradiction between praising gentility and politesse in one essay and, in another, condemning fashionable consumption as "malignant." Subject to the pressures of nationalism, the magazines celebrated the emulation of European culture and manners as a sign of European American equality with Europe at the same time as they celebrated economic independence from Europe as a sign of republican virtue.

Merchant princes and daring speculators were scarcely the magazines' only readers. The magazines worked actively to attract their cities' ambitious shopkeepers and prosperous mechanic/entrepreneurs.[17] Many of these men were new to cities, commerce, and consumerism. The riches they saw displayed in shops, through the windows of private homes, and on the persons of the elite bourgeoisie dazzled them. They were also confused by the noise and density of the new urban landscape and even more by the complexity and uncertainties of the new market economy.[18] Of course, these latter confusions did not only affect country families. City-born artisans, mechanics, and putting-out merchants, ambitious to expand and prosper, were equally in danger of losing their way—socially and economically. In the new nation's bustling entrepôts, everything was so uncertain—business practices, social status, identity itself.

17. In the world of eighteenth-century publishing, numbers were as telling as social status. As we know, the new nation's social elite was small, even if we number manufacturers and actively engaged merchants among them. Nor was it easy for publishers to turn to a regional market, as sometime–magazine editor Charles Brockden Brown explained to readers of his *Monthly Magazine*. "The thin population of the United States renders it impossible to procure sufficient support from any one city," he reported, "and the dispersed situation of readers, the embarrassments attending the diffusion of copies over a wide extent of country, and the obstacles to a prompt collection of small sums" made larger markets impractical. Publishers felt they needed five hundred subscribers to keep their magazines afloat. Certainly they needed that many to support their pressing political agenda—to gain popular urban support for the ratification of the new constitution (Brown, "Preface," Jan. 1, 1801, in monograph edition of *Monthly Magazine*, III (1800). As Noah Webster commented, "The expectation of *failure* is connected with the very name of a Magazine" (Webster, editor's note, *American Magazine*, I [1788], 130). For a recent study of nineteenth-century periodicals, see Kenneth M. Price and Susan Belasco Smith, eds., *Periodical Literature in Nineteenth-Century America* (Charlottesville, Va., 1995).

18. For a telling representation of the young man new to the city filled with wonder, desire, and fear, see Charles Brockden Brown, *Arthur Mervyn; or, Memoirs of the Year 1793, First and Second Parts* (Kent, Ohio, 1980), which we will examine at length in Chapter 8, below.

With these middling readers' situations in mind, the magazines filled their pages with economic and social advice. Heedless of having just celebrated the leisured opulence of their richer readers, they proceeded to celebrate the Protestant work ethic, especially its calls for industry, frugality, and self-reliance. "All the train of virtues which should adorn the human character, require activity," the *Massachusetts Magazine* advised middling shopkeepers and ambitious artisans, adding, "indolence in society is the mildew, the rust, the canker, which corrupts and destroys the social virtues." In bitter, misogynous terms, Thomas's General Observer continued, "From the *bosom of indolence, that filthy quagmire of corruption and debauchery,* proceed those deadly exhalations which pollute the morals and manners of society: From hence spring all the mean and sordid vices which debase humanity." Threatening social exposure and ridicule, the Observer then drove home his point.

Can the liveliest fancy of man paint a more odious monster than a scurvy lazy lubber, sauntering about, or lying at a grog shop, breathing invectives against the virtuous sons of honest industry? I would teach the boys in the streets to hiss at the ragged dirty drone, and tell them that indolence was the source of his disgrace.[19]

Creating a negative Other whose laziness made a virtue of northern industry, General Observer's comments helped create a sense of shared values and experiences uniting the bourgeois elite and the middling ranks. What, though a host of differences, separated Philip Schuyler and Tench Coxe from a struggling retail tradesman or an ambitious sailmaker? Their mutual difference from "scurvy lubbers" would unite them. Of course, the term "scurvy lubber" was far from politically innocent; it was a term commonly used to denigrate sailors and their compatriots along the waterfront (stevedores and other day laborers) who were seen as disorderly and politically dangerous—although, only a few years earlier, they had been invaluable actors in the political street theater leading up to the Revolution. How interesting that, in the post-Revolution political climate, the magazines routinely represented the Revolution's radical political actors—sailors, day laborers, Massachusetts's western farmers—as indolent, drunken, or effeminate, thus proclaiming them "monstrous" members of the republican body politic.

Next to industry, the magazines ranked frugality as the virtue most appropriate for their middling readers. Surrounded by the riches of the world, editors

---

19. General Observer, "For the Massachusetts Magazine: The General Observer, No. III, *Massachusetts Magazine,* I (1789), 162–164 (emphasis added).

thundered, men ambitious to succeed must restrain their passions and defer their desires. "Frugality is so necessary to the happiness of the world—so beneficial, in its various forms, to every rank of men, from the highest of human potentates, to the lowest labourer or artificer—and the miseries which the neglect of it produces, are so numerous and so grievous—that it cannot be too often or too forcibly recommended," Benjamin Franklin insisted. Especially for the middling ranks, frugality—and prudence—were essential virtues.[20]

For those new to cities or to affluence, "another precept . . . is yet necessary to be distinctly impressed upon the warm, the fanciful and the brave," Franklin continued. "Let no man anticipate uncertain profits. Let no man presume to spend upon hopes . . . to give loose to his present desires, and leave the reckoning to fortune." (Of course, America's most flamboyant entrepreneurs, Robert Morris, William Duer, and Tench Coxe, did just that, repeatedly.) Similar advice abounded on the pages of other urban magazines. One writer noted that men new to trade were often led into debt by the advice or urging of those they supposed their friends (like the "rustic fair one's" indebted father). These remarks underscore the financial insecurity experienced by most small players in the new national economy. Magazine editors and contributors repeatedly addressed these readers, trying to incorporate them into the bourgeoisie's vision of a new national identity.[21]

Young men were special objects of concern. Philadelphia's fashionable *Columbian Magazine* advised the youthful clerks many of its subscribers undoubtedly employed to work diligently and behave deferentially toward their superiors.

> Observe the most strict integrity, truth, sincerity and honour, in every thing you say or do. Be punctual, diligent and attentive. . . . Employ as much of your time as you can spare, in reading, and acquiring useful knowledge, especially such as more immediately relates to the profession which you have chosen. . . . Be civil, obliging, and polite to every body; but most attentively so to those under whose direction you will be placed.[22]

But honesty, frugality, and deferential behavior were not the only lessons the editors sought to inculcate among young readers. Recognizing that many en-

20. [Benjamin Franklin], "On Frugality," *American Museum,* I (1787), 67–68.

21. Ibid., 68. See, as well, Franklin, "Consolation for America . . . ," *American Museum,* I (1787), 5–8; [Franklin], "Causes of a Country's Growing Rich," ibid., 13; Q. S., "Harriot; or, The Domestick Reconcilliation, Sketched from the Life," *Massachusetts Magazine,* I (1789), 3–7; "Bathmendi: A Persian Tale," *Columbian Magazine,* I (1787), 240–243, 289–292.

22. Y. Z., "To the Editor of the Columbian Magazine," *Columbian Magazine,* I (1786), 11–12.

tertained social as well as economic ambitions, they published articles advising young men on ways to refine their conversation and polish their writing style. Grace and wit were essential; otherwise, they would appear as country bumpkins. Affectation, "the swelled, bombastic style [that] obtains with the lower (by far the most numerous) class of readers," must be avoided.[23] Advice about sartorial style followed. Again, excess was condemned as essayists satirized arrivistes for their displays of "Self-Conceit and Vanity," one writer remarking, "The strut of the turkey cock is but a faint symbol of [the would-be beaux's] majesty." Could taste not be purchased after all?[24]

SYNTHESIZING DIFFERENCE

The American dance floor was becoming far more crowded than Benjamin Rush's letter had suggested. Rather than the regulated number of dancers characteristic of painstakingly choreographed state and assembly balls, a motley collection of disparate figures crowded onto the new national floor. Some, like Nancy Shippen or her uncle Arthur Lee, had been carefully instructed on the rituals of the ball. Others—middling merchants, country shopkeepers newly come to the city, ship captains who would be merchants, mechanics who would be manufacturers, and, of course, their wives and daughters—seemed far more at home with the fast movements of a jig and the rough notes of a country fiddle. While all assayed the dance of republican gentility, each moved to a slightly different tune. It was this ill-assorted conflation of bourgeois elite, arriviste adventurers, solid, hardworking merchants, and ambitious mechanics and shopkeepers that constituted the new magazines' targeted audience. The challenge the magazines faced was how to draw harmony out of cacophony, reaffirm the vision of elegance Rush's letter so elaborately inscribed. The press's ability to do so depended on the efficacy of its representations of two constitut-

23. Dr. Ladd, "Critical Remarks on the Late Dr. Johnson," *American Museum*, II (1787), 92–94. In a similar vein, the *Columbian Magazine* warned young clerks to avoid the extremes of "pedantry" "run mad" and the "hyperbolic." See Ardelio, "For the Columbian Magazine," *Columbian Magazine*, I (1787), 233–235; Doctor Plainsense, "To the Editor of the Columbian Magazine," ibid., 805–806.

24. Jack Flash, "To the Editor of the Columbian Magazine," *Columbian Magazine*, I (1787), 748–750. For another example of satiric attacks on young men's fondness for foppish dress, see Ardelio, "For the Columbian Magazine," ibid., I (1786), 233–235. See, as well, Philanthropist, "For the Massachusetts Magazine, No. III," *Massachusetts Magazine*, I (1789), 137–141. Sexually aggressive behavior on the part of youth also attracted the magazines' ire. See "On the Virtues of a Billiard Table," *American Museum*, II (1787), 90–92.

ing Others, one of whom we have already met, one of whom is new: white bourgeois and middling women and enslaved African Americans. Apparently as unlike the republican gentleman as they were unlike one another, would their differences from the male dancers obscure those differences that divided the bourgeois and middling classes—or would deep-seated contradictions continue to fragment the new national identity?

TROUBLING GENDER

The American woman stood at the center of the contradictions swirling around the new American–as–republican gentleman, threatening to destabilize his and his nation's identity. Classic republicans knew that the man who would be a virtuous citizen had to disdain women and the feminine. Yet if that same citizen desired to be a gentleman, then he had to court women and embrace their ways. Here lay the republican gentleman's dilemma. Republican discourses castigated women as weak, seductive, and dangerous, especially women who were witty, outspoken, and powerful. And these were just the women whom the discourses of gentility celebrated. Like an invitation to a ball, such women established a gentleman's civility, his social standing. And more, deployed by the new nation's political leaders and literati, she confirmed the young Republic's cultural equality with the monarchies of Europe.

Nor were elite men the only ones to face this gendered dilemma. The tradesman who would be a gentleman needed the polished lady as much as the merchant elite did. A middle-class wife's or daughter's education, refinement, and social skills proclaimed her husband's or father's cultural equality with elite gentlemen—and his superiority to those who labored solely with their hands. The middle-class woman's sexual purity, in its turn, confirmed the middling shopkeeper/entrepreneur's moral superiority to both the elite and laboring classes, each of whom middling spokesmen (doctors and clergymen in particular) delighted in portraying as depraved and licentious. Finally, the middle-class woman's frugality and finely honed housewifely skills were critical to her husband's economic well-being and sense of social order and thus to the commercial republican trinity of civic virtues: productivity, self-reliance, and rational self-control.[25]

But, although frugality was one of middling women's principal duties, con-

---

25. We must remember that the sexual reputation of the new nation's political elite—Alexander Hamilton, Aaron Burr, and Thomas Jefferson—was subject to ribald attacks in the press of the 1790s.

sumption was another. Women's purchases drove America's commercial economy and consumer culture. Farming women's desires for "a yard and a Quarter of Lase for a Cap" and some "smole trifles" sparked the ambition of farming families to produce in excess of their immediate needs. At the opposite end of the social spectrum, Anne Willing Bingham's and Hannah Nicholson's desires to mimic the elegance displayed by British and French belles led their husbands to maximize every commercial opportunity, spurring America's fiscal revolution. The standards these grand ladies set stirred the imaginations and desires of sensible housewives up and down the new Republic's social landscape. We find evidence of these desires in the rapid increase in the number of dry goods merchants operating in America's entrepôts, the fashionable consumer goods that filled their shops, the rapid growth of the entrepôts themselves. We see it, as well, in the bills of lading kept by hundreds of middling merchants and country shopkeepers who provided their neighbors with a few pieces of Wedgwood creamwear, some ribbons, or a few yards of imported silk. Benjamin Franklin and Tench Coxe could rail against extravagant purchases in the public prints, the Observer could associate the moral "deformities" and the "filthy quagmire of corruption" that emerged from (women's?) bosoms, but America's economy depended on women's desires.[26]

As did America's editor/publishers. Urban periodicals had to appeal to "the ladies." How otherwise could they affirm the legitimacy of their claims to gentility and refinement and expand their readership and hence their list of subscribers, upon which their financial stability rested? The new magazines' publisher/entrepreneurs solicited women readers and women contributors. They promised women entertaining essays designed to appeal to their sensitivities. They published women authors and defended them from the attacks of men who found women's appearance in the public prints offensive.[27] They filled their pages with pleas for improvements in women's education, calls for

26. The two farm women are quoted in T. H. Breen, "An Empire of Goods: The Anglicization of Colonial America, 1690–1776," *Journal of British Studies*, XXV (1986), 467–499, esp. 467. Breen has long argued that the material markers of gentility penetrated far down the European American class structure. For his most recent work on this theme, see his *Marketplace of Revolution: How Consumer Politics Shaped American Independence* (New York, 2004), esp. part 1, "An Empire of Goods." See, as well, Richard L. Bushman, "American High-Style and Vernacular Cultures," in Jack P. Greene and J. R. Pole, eds., *Colonial British America: Essays in the New History of the Early Modern Era* (Baltimore, 1984), 345–383; and Bushman, *The Refinement of America: Persons, Houses, Cities* (New York, 1992).

27. See, for example, "To Our Correspondents," *Massachusetts Magazine*, I (1789), 130; "To Our Patrons," ibid., 66; Q. S., "On the Antiquity and Dignity of Riddles: To the Editors of the Massachusetts Magazine," ibid., 107–108.

the reform of coverture laws, satirical jibes at self-important husbands whose amateurish scientific experiments threatened to burn women's homes to the ground. Poems written by women, poems dedicated to women, along with advice to women, dotted their pages, as did romances and essays celebrating women's benevolence, refinement, and wit.[28] In the new Republic's political magazines, the culture of virtuous gentility and refinement emerged as woman-centered and woman-dependent—in sharp contrast to the Constitution's effacement of women from its pages.

In its efforts to contain the threat women posed to male ideological coherence and cultural preeminence, the urban press's most powerful rhetorical move was to project the criticisms classic republicanism directed against men of trade onto elite and middling women and girls. Did the leisured and fashionable gentleman seem indolent and foppish to readers brought up on classic republicanism's ascetic strictures? Did the hardworking tradesman seem petty and driven by self-interest? Male-authored essay after essay insisted that, if commerce and gentility violated the norms of classic republicanism, it was neither refined gentlemen nor hardworking merchants who were responsible but their luxury-loving and willfull wives and daughters.

Such displacement proved a powerful rhetorical tool. It permitted the press to reaffirm both elite and middling men's claims to the manly republican virtues their desire for refinement called into question. Reasserting the gentleman/tradesman's manliness, it then permitted the urban magazines to reassert his differences from—indeed, his superiority to—women. Bonding "man to man," editors and contributors called on their manly readers to reclaim their mastery over women. If women's will and fancies could be controlled, civic virtue and the Republic would be safe. By displacing all that republican discourses found "unmanly" and corrupt in commerce and consumerism onto women, the urban press sought to create so powerful a negative Other that the shadow she cast would obscure the differences that distinguished the gentleman from the tradesman/mechanic and rendered them both problematic republicans.

28. See, for example, "A Tract on the Unreasonableness of the Laws of England, in regard to Wives," *Columbian Magazine*, II (1788), 22–27, 61–65, 126–129; Lady's Magazine [London], "The Duelist and Libertine Reclaimed," *Massachusetts Magazine*, I (1789), 205–208; Mrs. Catherine Macaulay, "A Quaker Sermon," ibid., 44–45; A Female Enquirer, "For the Massachusetts Magazine: On the Government of the Passions," ibid., 179–180; S. E., "To the Editor of the Columbian Magazine," *Columbian Magazine*, I (1787), 642–646; "On Trifles," *American Museum*, I (1787), 444–450; Q. S., "Harriot," *Massachusetts Magazine*, I (1789), 3–7; "To the Editors of the Massachusetts Magazine . . . Beauties of 'The "Power of Sympathy,"'" ibid., 50–53; "For the Massachusetts Magazine: The Dreamer, No. II," ibid., 101–104.

The fears women's beauty, power, and wit generated came to the fore in a fairy tale Noah Webster featured in the opening issue of his *American Magazine*. The author was none other than the canonical British literary figure Samuel Johnson. Since this is an odd piece to reprint in the opening issue of a political journal founded to celebrate the new Republic's independence from Great Britain and to secure the ratification of a strong Federal constitution, it behooves us to read the story carefully.[29]

Four powerful women play central roles in this tale: a powerful fairy queen; Floretta, a virtuous, at times naïve, young woman; her materialistic mother; and a foolish, disobedient fairy. The fairy tale begins as Floretta courageously rescues a small bird from the talons of a hawk. Urged by her mother to cage the beautiful creature, Floretta, in true republican fashion, explains that she has not saved its life only to enslave it. Suddenly, a beautiful fairy steps forth. The fairy queen had turned the fairy into a bird to punish her disobedience. She was to be released only when a virtuous person rescued her. To celebrate Floretta's bravery and generosity, the fairy queen offers to grant Floretta's every wish. Even more important, Floretta will be allowed to return wishes that make her unhappy. Immediately, Floretta, like most young women, wishes for beauty, but she quickly finds that beauty generates envy among women and unwanted sexual attentions from men. Returning beauty, Floretta asks for "spirit" and the right to govern herself free from her mother's dictates. Again, disaster follows, for, as Johnson explains, "The vehemence of mind which to a man may sometimes procure awe and obedience, produce to a woman nothing but detestation." Learning a hard lesson, Floretta "quitted her spirit and her own way," again subjecting herself to her mother's authority. She next wishes for wealth—and again finds she has wished unwisely. Made ambitious by Floretta's newfound fortune, her mother plans to force Floretta to marry an elderly man Floretta detests. Only by renouncing her wealth can Floretta rid herself of her suitor. Finally, Floretta requests wit, realizing that "wit was sweeter than riches, spirit, or beauty." But wit renders her critical and unpleasant. "Wherever she went," Johnson reports, "she breathed nothing but censure and reformation. . . . Her conversation was generally thought uncivil." Bright young women were warned to curb their tongues or they would become bluestockings like Floretta. All avoided her. Floretta prepared to return wit—but did not, realizing that

29. "The Fountains: A Fairy Tale," *American Magazine*, I (1787), 27–36. This is an odd pairing—Johnson, the author of the most famous eighteenth-century dictionary designed to establish an elevated and universal "English" language, while Webster wrote explicitly to challenge Johnson's transatlantic authority, self-consciously striving to create an oppositional American "English."

wit would forever remind her how foolish it was for a woman to desire wealth and power.[30]

One could read this British fairy tale as a political homily—even as an attack on American colonists' desire for "spirit" and independence from the governance of England. But it is unlikely that Webster intended such a reading. Nor is there anything in the fairy tale to suggest that Webster used it to evoke images of unruly farmers demanding political authority inappropriate to their class. We are left, therefore, with a gendered reading. With the exception of the fairy queen (Johnson, though not Webster, was, after all, a monarchist), the story's powerful women are represented as dangerous.[31] The willful fairy causes floods and havoc. Floretta's mother arranges unwise marriages and wishes to curtail freedom (both Floretta's and the bird's). Female power in the form of beauty and wealth brings only misery. In the end, Floretta has the wit to refuse inappropriate powers and resume her traditional role of obedient, dependent daughter. Was Webster admonishing America's republican wives and daughters to refuse the powers the political and consumer revolutions gave them, and return happily to their traditional subservience within patriarchal social and political structures?

But as Floretta's tale demonstrates, it was not so easy to dispense with middle-class women's growing power. Three aspects of the story underscore these difficulties. Firstly, it is a woman, Floretta, who embodies republican bravery and virtue. Secondly, Floretta provides a poor blueprint for female submission. Never asking for advice, she makes every decision on her own. Lastly, lurking behind (or within?) Floretta, we catch sight of another, more ominous female figure. Brimming over with desires, one wish cascading after another, Floretta emerges as an eighteenth-century Pandora, repeatedly entertaining subversive desires that will not be quieted. Could the urban press be sure their homilies would permanently close the lid on women's desire for power and wit?

Satire offered a powerful outlet for male frustration. Betraying a playful indebtedness to Bernard Mandeville's *Fable of the Bees,* Titus Blunt offered Webster's readers an amusing account of women's fashions. "It is perfectly right, in manufacturing countries," Blunt began, "for Ladies to draw fifty or a hundred thousand yards of silk upon the ground; for the destruction of it is a

30. Ibid., esp. 32.

31. This character, of course, can be read as referring back to Spenser's famous celebration of Elizabeth I, *The Faerie Queene.*

public benefit."[32] "But," he added, knowing best how to wound a woman's pride, "it betrays a total *want of taste and elegance in dress;* and when the American Ladies adopted the fashion, they paid fifteen or twenty thousand pounds to foreign nations, for the *trouble* of being *very inelegantly dressed.*" Note Blunt's nationalist and commercial republican theme. Fashionable ladies weakened their country's economy and disgraced themselves by submitting their persons to the authority of British fashions. "Americans could hardly run into absurdities of these kinds, were they to consult their own taste or interest," Blunt continued. "It is the authority of foreign manners which keeps us in subjection, and gives a kind of sanction to follies, which are pardonable in Europe, but inexcusable in America." In this way, responsibility for the problems European American emulation of British culture posed to virtuous classic and commercial republicans—not to mention the economic hard times of the late 1780s—was displaced onto the billowing skirts of fashionable ladies.[33]

Other satires scorned women for exactly the opposite behavior, for being too frugal. Neither elite nor middling women, it would seem, could escape male censure. One such story began with a long-suffering husband's lament: "I am the husband of a buyer of bargains." "My wife has somewhere heard," he

32. Titus Blunt, "To the Editor of the American Magazine," *American Magazine,* I (1787), 39. "Yards of silk": This was, of course, a reference to Bernard Mandeville's brazen defense of fashionable extravagance, *The Fable of the Bees.* As already noted, J. G. A. Pocock discusses Mandeville at some length in his *Machiavellian Moment: Florentine Political Thought and the Atlantic Republican Tradition* (Princeton, N.J., 1975), chap. 14. We must remember that fashionable portraitists prided themselves on filling their canvases with images of just such billowing "yards of silk." Here again we see the conflict between republican values and the demands of fashion in self-doubting postcolonial nations.

33. Blunt, "To the Editor," *American Magazine,* I (1787), 39. Betraying his fellow citizens' anxieties, another Philadelphia writer warned against the fashionable belle whose social authority threatened to invert the natural hierarchy of male dominance. "When I see pride, or scorn forever peeping out of her eyes and folly speaking out of her mouth; when every motion . . . tend[s] . . . to inspire love, that she may exercise tyranny, when every action is tinged with self-love, and want of regard for every one else," this author concluded, "I cannot help being concerned, that beauty should act so unnatural a part." The author also warns women against the dangers of "unbecoming desires." Likening "a fine lady's" reputation for sexual propriety to "a vessel of penciled china," one pre-Revolutionary writer pointedly asked: "Is not her reputation as frail? Can you solder up the flaws of either of the one or the other so completely as not to be pried into and commented upon?" (Renaldo, "To the Editor of the Columbian Magazine," *Columbian Magazine,* I [1787], 640–641, esp. 641). See also "Meditations on a Tea Pot: A Moral Tale," *Pennsylvania Packet; or, The General Advertiser,* May 13, 1788. Other attacks on women's appearances are discussed in Chapter 3, above.

continued, "that a good housewife never had any thing to purchase, when it was wanted. This maxim is often in her mouth, and always in her head." To begin with, we must note that his wife does not read or study this "truth but garners it from women's gossip" (and we will recall republican denigrations of gossiping women). However, it is not only the power his wife derives from household management that excites this husband's ire but her assumption of the role of "œconomist." (How different his remarks from those of William Gadsden when he appealed to America's wifely "œconomists" to lend their support to their husbands' nonimportation movements.) With national independence secured and the consumer revolution and women's consuming power far more advanced, this husband, rather than patriotically appeal to his wife's common sense, could only rail. "She is not one of those philosophical talkers that speculate without practice, and learn sentences of wisdom only to repeat them," he notes.

> Whatever she thinks cheap, she holds it the duty of an œconomist to purchase; in consequence . . . my house has the appearance of a ship stored for a voyage across the Atlantic. . . . She knows before any of her neighbours, when the stock of any man, leaving off trade, is to be sold *cheap for ready money*. Such intelligence is to my *dear* one, the siren's song. No engagement, no duty, no interest, can with-hold her from a sale, from which she always returns congratulating herself upon her dexterity at a bargain.

The very qualities that made it possible for small businessmen to survive and prosper—their ceaseless energy, their ability to get the jump on their competitors and to bargain with "dexterity," characteristics both classic republicanism and the discourses of gentility disparage—are projected onto the hardworking "œconomist" wife, where they can be safely lampooned. Perhaps even more tellingly, she outstrips tradesmen at their own game, forcing bargains out of failing merchants and shopkeepers faced with bankruptcy. What tradesman would not share this husband's annoyance?[34]

Another essay, "Consequences of Extravagance," expressed, only a little less satirically, the economic anxieties of shopkeepers newly come to Philadelphia and seeking to excel in the new commercial economy. The author tells us he is a young man recently come to Philadelphia from the country with four hundred pounds' capital (enough, Thomas M. Doerflinger has told us, to set up as an overseas trader; see Chapter 6, above). "Frugality, and strict attention to a little

---

34. "Humour: Account of a Buyer of Bargains," *American Museum*, I (1787), 345–347; and see Chapter 2, above.

shop, in which I did business to advantage, made me a happy man." But now his display of prosperity has begun to conflict with that happiness which was wedded to contentment. It was women, of course, who introduced temptation and extravagance into the young shopkeeper's frugal eden. "As soon as our neighbours found we were thriving, [women] visitors crowded from all the houses in the square, to pay their respects to my wife. This gave me great satisfaction at first; but was afterwards the occasion of much disquiet to me." This "club" of women neighbors, the term the tradesman uses to describe them, turned his wife—until their visits, a contented and productive helpmeet—into an increasingly willful matron ambitious to display her husband's new-earned claims to genteel status. She urged her husband to engage in ever more ambitious commercial ventures and refused any longer to stand behind his counter and serve his customers. Continually badgered by his wife—and daughter—the tradesman "commenced merchant extensively; was concerned in ships; wrote at offices, without fear, every risque that offered." He rented a large house, hired a fashionable complement of servants, and purchased a carriage. His expenses grew astronomically; the chambermaid tried to seduce him; bankruptcy loomed—until his wife suddenly freed herself from the unnatural influence of the "club" of fashionable women who had misled her. She dismissed the unnecessary servants and "determined to live happy with her family as usual."[35]

Undoubtedly intended as a pointed lesson for the *American Museum*'s middling male as well as female readers, this essay expressed men's sense of powerlessness in a rapidly expanding and uncertain economy. Interestingly, the author and the publisher represented (and perhaps experienced) that economy as driven by the desires of strong, autonomous women who, gathered in clubs (or around tea tables), constituted an alternative form of social organization. Yet the message of the essay was highly ambivalent. Admonitions and titillation jostled for ascendancy as the essayist, by detailing his fashionable purchases and extravagant social arrangements, warned his readers of the dangers threatening small shopkeepers when they attempted to imitate the luxurious lifestyle Philadelphia's richest merchants adopted; aroused those shopkeepers' desires by detailing his fashionable purchases; and instructed them on the makeup of an upper-middle-class household (what furnishings were essential, what constituted a fashionable complement of servants, what exceeded rational self-interest).

Casting his net a bit wider to include country shopkeepers and commercial farmers, Benjamin Franklin presented Philadelphia's readers with a similar tale that condemned wives and daughters for propelling husbands and fathers into

35. "Consequences of Extravagance," *American Museum*, I (1787), 547–550.

the maelstrom of consumerism and debt. It should not surprise us that Franklin's tale took the form of an explanation of the "Cause of, and Cure for, Hard Times," by "A Farmer." (Talking of masks and masquerades, no one assumed more of the former or played more with the latter than Pennsylvania's much-celebrated publicist/scientist/governor.) In this particular essay, Franklin again chose the persona of a prosperous farmer to espouse commercial republican principles of civic virtue—and to voice pointed social criticism. Living well within his means, the "farmer" reported, he had been industrious, reinvested his profits to expand his productivity, and depended on the unpaid labor of his wife and daughters. His life, he reports, was idyllic.

> At this time, my farm gave me and my whole family a good living on the produce of it; and it left me, one year with another, one hundred and fifty silver dollars: for I never spent more than ten dollars a year, which was for salt, nails, and the like. Nothing to wear, eat, or drink, was purchased, as my farm provided all. With this saving, I put money to interest, bought cattle, fatted and sold them, and made great profit.[36]

Like King Lear, this farmer has three daughters. His first daughter married young and simply. But, by the time his second daughter was ready to marry, his wife's social ambitions had expanded. "Come, you are now rich," the farmer reports his wife as saying. "You know Molly had nothing but what she spun—and no other clothing has ever come into our house for any of us. Sarah must be fitted out a little. She ought to fare as well as neighbour N——'s Betty. I must have some money, and go to town." The husband responded: "Well, wife, it shall be as you think best. I have never been stingy; but it seems to me that what we spin at home would do." His wife and daughter purchased prudently. "They cost but little—I did not feel it—and I confess I was pleased to see them. Sarah was as well fitted off as any girl in the parish." But once women started down the path to fashion, as once the American economy started down the path to consumer and fiscal capitalism, the *American Museum* warned its urban readers, little could stop them. Again, Franklin as Farmer:

> In three years more my third daughter had a spark—and wedding being concluded upon, wife comes again for the purse: but when she returned, what did I see! a silken gown, silk for a cloak, a looking-glass, chine tea-geer, and a hundred other things, with the empty purse. But this is not the worst of it, mr. Printer. Some time before the marriage of this last daughter, and

36. A Farmer [Benjamin Franklin], "Cause of, and Cure for, Hard Times," ibid., 11–13.

ever since, this charge increased in my family, besides all sorts of household furniture unknown to us before. Clothing of every sort is bought—and the wheel goes only for the purpose of exchanging [that is, selling] our substantial cloth of flax and wool, for gauze, ribands, silk, tea, sugar, etc. My butter, which used to go to market, and brought money, is now expended at the tea-table. . . . so that, instead of laying up one hundred and fifty dollars every year, I find now all my loose money is gone—and, being straitened, I cannot carry on my farm to so good advantage as formerly.[37]

The pleasure his wife derived from ostentatious display had brought the honest producer close to bankruptcy. The time had come for him to assert mastery over his home and family and so to return to true commercial republican (and patriarchal) values. "I am still master in *my own* house," the farmer informed his Philadelphia readers. "I am determined to alter my way of living to what it was twenty years ago." We cannot help noting, in this particular instance, that Franklin's masterful capitalist looked back twenty years (before America's political and consumer revolutions) for his utopian vision.[38]

What un-Franklinesque sentiments! Franklin was always the first to insist that America's commercial and consumer revolution must not be turned back. Time and again, Franklin urged the new Republic to aggressively expand her consumer markets and build up her manufactures. Farmers must produce ever-larger export crops. Wives and daughters must leave their wheels, go to town and purchase domestically produced consumer items—if not baubles and gauze. If they did not, manufactures would decline, national prosperity would wither, and European Americans would sink to a state as savage as that of the native savages and savage frontiersmen. Deep contradictions ran through Franklin's contributions to Carey's *American Museum*. What made them appear consistent was his repeated displacement of the desires that drove late-eighteenth-century European American consumerism—male and female, rural and urban alike—onto women (and effeminized hardscrabble farmers). In this way, Franklin was able to displace the multiple contradictions that so distressed European Americans' republican discourses—those between republican principles and the ways of commerce, between the fashionable gentleman and the frugal tradesman. Cloaked in the rhetoric of misogyny, European American men's anxieties and contradictions could be externalized, satirized, and comfortably laughed at.

But how nervous was that laugh? Could the magazines' readers ever distance

37. Ibid., 12.
38. Ibid. (emphasis added).

themselves completely from the desires of consuming women who provided them with markets for their goods? To appear credit-able in a market that still rode on the wings of credit and appearance—as well as to make valuable financial connections—an upwardly mobile man needed a fashionable wife. Furthermore, European Americans, be they mechanics, artisans, or merchants, were caught in the financial vortex of the consumer revolution and thus were subject to women's whims and desires. Gone were the classic republican's manly independence, rugged self-reliance, and stern aesthetics. Gone, as well, was much of the commercial republican's frugality. As the independence of the European American−as−republican gentleman was compromised by women's grace and fashion, so the independence of middling shopkeepers and entrepreneurs was compromised by women's fancy and desires. To shore up the image of a virile, independent new American−as−republican gentleman, the urban press had to constitute a second negative Other. Figuring the contrast of free to slave labor, the independent entrepreneur to the bound chattel, the political magazines called forth the enslaved African American. But even he would prove a contradictory and destabilizing Other for the freedom-loving European American.[39]

FREEDOM'S DARK SHADOW

On the surface, what contrast could have been starker—or more reaffirming—than that between the white republican and the black slave? The one was a virtuous, independent, rights-bearing citizen, the other, a debased, dependent, disenfranchised bondsman. The one was a free worker, the other an enslaved laborer. The one was rational, the other ignorant; the one refined, the other brutish; the one educated, the other illiterate; the one talented, the other

39. Race combined with enslavement was apparently such a strong demarcator of otherness and inferiority that gender appears to play virtually no role in these early discussions of African Americans, either by those critical of slavery or those in favor of it. The following quote underscores the insignificance of gender when trumped by race in these descriptions: "Two or three negroes and a white woman were killed" (W. M., "Letter from Dr. M. to Dr. Franklin . . . ," *American Museum,* II [1787], 79). This quote brings to mind the effacement of enslaved women in Aristotle's social categories: men, women, and slaves. Black feminist legal theorists focus on this effacement of women of color within contemporary American legal practice. See, for example, the collection of essays in Adrien Katherine Wing, ed., *Critical Race Feminism: A Reader,* 2d ed. (New York, 2003), including those by Kim Crenshaw and Angela P. Harris. Literary critic Hortense Spillers presents a sophisticated analysis of why gender was so insignificant in eighteenth-century white male representations of African Americans; see Spillers, "Mama's Baby, Papa's Maybe: An American Grammar Book," *Diacritics,* XVII, no. 2 (Summer 1987), 65–81.

unskilled; the one an independent producer, driven by ambition and determination, the other a will-less drudge, driven by the lash. The enslaved African American emerges from this comparison unfree, uncultured, uneducated, unskilled, unwilling, an un-being—the northern freedom-loving citizen's deviant and defining Other.[40] So configured, the figure of the enslaved African American was informed by and reinforced the rhetorical contrast between the free and the slave that republican discourses had made central to the practice of civic virtue and virtuous citizenship. The African-as-slave served as a dark mirror in which the white American–as-citizen could study his refined and enlightened self.[41]

On the surface, this was how the new urban magazines represented Africans and African Americans. Recall the Philanthropist's deployment of race as signifying difference and inferiority, his "Letters" in Isaiah Thomas's *Massachusetts Magazine* positioning refined Europeans and European Americans at the apex of human advancement, the "unnumbered tribes of ignorant and Stupid animals in the shape of men, who inhabit . . . Asia, Africa, . . . America" as their antithesis. Nor was the Philanthropist alone. Time and again, the magazines presented Africans and African Americans as stabilizing counterpoints to their self-presentations as freedom-loving, cultured Americans.

Northerners' day-to-day experiences of slavery reinforced this contrast. (John Wood Sweet points out that, on his famous midnight ride to rouse resistance to a tyrannical king, Paul Revere passed the body of an executed slave that had hung for some twenty years on the side of the main road between Boston and Lexington as a warning to any other slave conspiring to murder his master.) Throughout the colonial period, slavery had been a well-entrenched social and economic institution in the North as well as the South. On the eve of the Revolution, it remained an economically viable institution in maritime Rhode Island, Boston, and other Massachusetts port towns. Half the farming households in Connecticut owned slaves, as did half of all Connecticut ministers and public officials and one-third of the colony's physicians. Philadelphia

40. The Constitution itself reinforced the rhetorical contrast between free and slave, so central to republican discourses, by constituting slaves only part men (the Three-Fifths Compromise) and by requiring all citizens to assist in the capture and return of escaped slaves (the Fugitive Slave Clause).

41. Joanne Pope Melish agrees that the contrast of slave and free, African and European American, was central to the new Republic's sense of social and political order and the new citizens' understanding of themselves as men endowed with inalienable rights (Melish, *Disowning Slavery: Gradual Emancipation and 'Race' in New England, 1780–1860* (Ithaca, N.Y., 1998), 1–2.

possessed a large African American population, which, around midcentury, had been augmented by a wave of slaves imported directly from Africa. Although, following the Revolution, northern states began to adopt complex systems of gradual emancipation (Pennsylvania was the first in 1780), slavery remained entrenched well into the nineteenth century. Connecticut did not formally abolish slavery until 1848, the year of the Seneca Falls Convention.[42]

For years after the Declaration of Independence was proclaimed and the Liberty Bell rung, liveried slaves marked the elite's social standing in New York and Philadelphia. John and Betsy Cadwalader staffed their Philadelphia town house with slaves and held hundreds more on their Maryland plantations. New York's governor George Clinton owned eight enslaved African Americans; Aaron Burr, five; John Jay, the president of the New York Manumission Society, another five. Even Benjamin Rush, that ardent spokesman for Philadelphia's free African American community, delayed freeing a slave he had bought in the early 1770s until he felt that the man's labor had fully compensated him for the original purchase price, with the result that ten years elapsed between the Pennsylvania legislature's adoption of gradual emancipation and Rush's emancipation of his own enslaved African American servant.[43]

Such prominent members of the new republican elite were far from alone. In 1790, five years after the New York legislature had adopted a gradual emancipation program modeled on similar legislation in Pennsylvania, Shane White reports, two-thirds of New York City's merchants still owned slaves. Nor was northern slavery an exclusively elite practice. In 1790, a third of all New York City shopkeepers continued to own slaves, as did an eighth of New York City's artisans and 40 percent of householders in the surrounding agricultural areas (Queens and Kings Counties, Staten Island, and the northern reaches of Manhattan—all commercial farming communities). Indeed, between 1790 and 1800, the number of slaves in New York City increased 22 percent and the

---

42. John Wood Sweet, *Bodies Politic: Negotiating Race in the American North, 1730–1830* (Baltimore, 2003), 147; Melish, *Disowning Slavery,* 7–17, 55–56.

43. For recent discussions of slavery in the North during the colonial and early national periods, see, among others, Sweet, *Bodies Politic,* chaps. 4–7 (chapters 6 and 7 focus specifically on the processes of gradual emancipation); and Melish, *Disowning Slavery.* See, as well, Thelma Wills Foote, *Black and White Manhattan: The History of Racial Formation in Colonial New York City* (Oxford, 2004). Although Foote focuses on the seventeenth and eighteenth centuries, her final chapters explore emancipation following the Revolutionary War. See also Jill Lepore, *New York Burning: Liberty, Slavery, and Conspiracy in Eighteenth-Century Manhattan* (New York, 2005), for discussions of the famous slave uprising in 1741. Gary B. Nash's *Forging Freedom: The Formation of Philadelphia's Black Community, 1720–1840* (Cambridge, Mass., 1988) has long been one of the principal texts exploring northern slavery and emancipation.

number of slaveholders, 33 percent. Many of these new slaveholders were themselves new men on the rise. Forty-six percent of men holding stock in the Bank of New York in 1791 owned slaves, as did the majority of stockholders in the New York Manufacturing Society. Forty percent of merchants holding slaves in 1800 had been small retailers ten years earlier and risen socially and economically during the speculative boom days of the 1790s. As White states: "What is important . . . is that those involved in . . . the 'entrepreneurial efflorescence' of the early national period were increasingly turning to slavery."[44]

Northerners not only owned, bought, and sold slaves; their economic prosperity depended on slavery. Slaves were everywhere. They played a central role in large-scale northern agriculture from New York to Narragansett Bay. They worked as skilled artisans, milliners, stevedores, mariners, cooks, and housekeepers. They were, Joanne Pope Melish reports, "vitally important to the operation of the household performing virtually all its services and its productive activities." Most significant, the entire northern economy depended on the profits garnered from the provision trade to the West Indies. Northern farmers raised wheat, livestock, and vegetables to feed Caribbean slaves, dried and salted meat for those slaves, spent their winters making crude (and undoubtedly uncomfortable) shoes for them. New England fishermen shipped tons of salt cod to the islands every year. Carpenters, sailmakers, and stevedores built ships for the Caribbean trade. New York sugar refiners, rum distillers, and candy manufacturers—and their employees—depended on slave-produced Caribbean sugar for their livelihoods. Even desperately poor northern seamstresses depended on the provision trade to the Caribbean, their pitiful income pieced together sewing pantaloons and shirts for Caribbean (and southern) field hands. Without the profits from the provision trade, the North would not have been able to trade with Great Britain or have had the cash to pay for exotic luxuries imported from India and China. Indeed, without Caribbean markets, most northerners would have been driven back into self-sufficient agriculture. The North's prosperity, spiraling population, and displays of cultured refinement, along with the pleasures northerners derived from the possession of luxury goods—none would have been possible without slavery. In short, freedom-loving European Americans depended upon plantation slavery for

44. Shane White, *Somewhat More Independent: The End of Slavery in New York City, 1770–1810* (Athens, Ga., 1991), 35, and chap. 1. White points out that four of every ten merchants owning slaves in 1800, when traced back to the 1790 census, were found to have been retail shopkeepers. Northern slaveholding was far from being an elite economic practice.

their economic prosperity, prized possessions, and, most centrally, their very sense of self as prosperous and cultured heirs of the Enlightenment.[45]

Yet, as the eighteenth century came to an end, criticisms of slavery mounted. Having cried, "Give me liberty or give me death!" railed against British efforts to "enslave" them, and declared all men equal and endowed with the inalienable right to liberty, at least some European Americans began to have second thoughts about the naturalness of slavery.[46] During the opening days of the Revolution, British émigré Thomas Paine, watching the buying and selling of slaves from the room in which he wrote *Common Sense*, angrily asked about his fellow European Americans "with what consistency, or decency they complain so loudly of attempts to enslave them, while they hold so many hundred thousands in slavery?" Paine was a self-declared radical. Slaveholding Arthur Lee was not, yet even Lee had raised this same question ten years earlier when writing in a Virginia newspaper—adding that God's punishment must descend upon so hypocritical a people. We know that Thomas Jefferson privately shared Lee's concerns. Benjamin Rush did so publicly—in his 1773 pamphlet attacking slavery and ten years later in the 1780s as a principal founder of the Pennsylvania Abolition Society. (Yet, just as Rush delayed freeing his own slave, so Lee, when a Virginia delegate to the Constitutional Convention, did not speak against the Three-Fifths Compromise.) Revolutionary logic could not dispel European American ambivalence.[47]

Revolutionary concerns coincided with religious-based calls for the end of both slavery and the slave trade. As early as the 1680s, the Germantown, Pennsylvania, Quaker Meeting had raised questions about the sinfulness of owning slaves, concerns that steadily grew as the eighteenth century progressed. In the years immediately preceding the Revolution, Quaker meetings throughout the North actively pressed members to manumit those they held in bondage and recompense them for their years of unpaid labor. Other denominations joined forces with the Quakers on this issue. Benjamin Coleman, Congregational minister in Newbury, Massachusetts, denounced slavery

45. Melish, *Disowning Slavery*, 15.

46. See, for example: Harrington, "To the Freemen of America," *American Museum*, I (1787), 491–495, or "On Trifles," ibid., 440–450; St. George Tucker, "Reflections on the Policy and Necessity of Encouraging the Commerce of the Citizens of the United States of America . . . ," ibid., II (1787), 263–274; and Sylvius, "Letter VI: Further Remarks on an Excise . . . ," ibid., 20–24; "Address to the Heart, on the Subject of American Slavery," ibid., 538–544, esp. 541.

47. Daniel Edwin Wheeler, ed., *Life and Writings of Thomas Paine . . .* , II (New York, 1908), 110; Benjamin Rush, *An Address to the Inhabitants of the British Settlements, on the Slavery of the Negroes in America . . .* (Philadelphia, 1773).

as a "God-provoking and wrath-procuring sin," and the "Pope of New England Calvinists," Samuel Hopkins, called slavery a "sin of crimson die, which is most particularly pointed out by the public calamities which have come upon us."[48]

Political and religious criticism of slavery coalesced in the Revolutionary moment. The telling event was the Declaration of Independence. Calling a new, independent nation into being, the Declaration created the two most salient markers of political modernity—the political republic and republican citizenship. But it did far more. By declaring all men free and equal, it opened rights-bearing citizenship to the entire world. In doing so, it threw the eighteenth century's elaborate categorization of difference (class, racial, gendered) into question. Universal equality meant universal sameness. All men were equal; therefore, all men were the same. Theoretically, differences among men were insignificant, at least in terms of their claims to equal rights. As a result, the importance of social categories, privileges based on class, race, and place of origin, were effaced. The liberal body, we will recall, was a body unmarked by race, class, or gender. Yet, throughout all the eighteenth century's multiple transformations, the one thing European Americans felt they could be certain of was that freedom was the natural condition of the white European, slavery of the black African. All that European Americans thought they knew and thought they were had therefore been rendered uncertain. If the enslaved could be, by right and nature, free, if they could claim that ultimate sign of political modernity, rights-bearing citizenship, then what distinguished them from European Americans as rights-bearing citizens? If they were indistinguishable from European Americans, were they quite simply Americans? And if Americans could be of African descent, what effect would that have on European Americans' sense of themselves as heirs of the European Enlightenment and the equals of any polished European gentleman? At a time of relentless transformations, a principal anchor around which European Americans had sought to structure a coherent vision of their world and of themselves—the clear, uncontested contrast between free and slave, white and black, Enlightened European and African heathen—had become uncertain. Indeed, it became worse than uncertain. In Samuel Hopkins's ringing words, it had became an offense against the Almighty, the cause of God's wrath toward a sinful people.[49]

48. Melish, *Disowning Slavery*, 50–61.

49. Melish claims that the closing years of the eighteenth century found European Americans displaying "a great nervousness about the stability of social identity, nervousness produced by the coincidence of post-Revolutionary social change and emancipation." "The emancipation

Not surprisingly, these confusions found their way into the political magazines. Contesting their readers' ability to live easily with slavery, bitter attacks on slavery and on European Americans as hypocrites dotted magazine pages. "Humanus," the author of one such essay (possibly Benjamin Rush?), confessed himself "distressed to see our printers continue to advertise negro slaves for sale in their newspapers," a common practice through the 1790s. "I think it holds out to the world that we are an inconsistent people," Humanus chided Philadelphia readers. "In reading such an advertisement (if habits of cruelty had not blinded our eyes or hardened our hearts) we should naturally ask—what has this man done to subject himself to be *sold* for life?" Humanus's question refers his readers back to John Locke's assertion that under certain circumstances—conviction for theft, for example—a sentence of life enslavement was an acceptable alternative to the imposition of capital punishment. In the case of an escaped African American slave, Humanus asks what he had done—and answers, "the advertisement says [only]—he is sold—for *no fault!!!!*" Refusing the Philanthropist's racial markers of difference and the naturalness of slavery for Africans, Humanus insisted on applying the same standards and laws to enslaved African Americans as European Americans applied to themselves. If a white man could not be enslaved for "no fault," then neither could a black man.[50]

That same year, Mathew Carey made an even more radical editorial move, reprinting in its entirety a petition presented to the Massachusetts legislature by Belinda, a former slave. Belinda did not petition for her freedom (she had already secured that during the Revolution). Far more radically, she demanded reparations for the uncompensated labor she had performed for more than fifty

---

process," Melish continues, "took place during a post-Revolutionary period of social and economic uncertainty that interrogated the stability of social identity and the meaning of citizenship for whites as well as people of color. In this context, emancipation raised questions about the nature of difference and citizenship which affected the social identities of whites as well as people of color" (ibid., 1, 2). Laura Doyle traces Englishmen's claims to liberty back to the emergence of a racialized Anglo-Saxon discourse as part of seventeenth-century resistance to Stuart absolutism. True Englishmen, Anglo-Saxon discourse asserted, had always struggled against foreign (Norman, Stuart) efforts to suppress their heritage of liberty and self-governance. Doyle specifically connects the emergence of Anglo-Saxonism with the first British Empire and British involvement in the slave trade and slave economies. To be white and British was to be free. See Doyle, *Freedom's Empire: Race and the Rise of the Novel in Atlantic Modernity, 1640–1940* (Durham, N.C., 2008).

50. Humanus, "On Slavery," *American Museum*, I (1787), 471; John Locke, *Second Treatise of Government*, in Locke, *Two Treatises of Government*, ed. Peter Laslett (Cambridge, 1965), chap. 3, sect. 17–18.

years as an enslaved person in Medford, Massachusetts. Belinda's petition was part of a widespread movement among enslaved and formerly enslaved residents of Massachusetts for compensation for their time and labor. Belinda's claims rested on the Lockean principle that individuals had the right of ownership in themselves, their labor, and the fruit of that labor. The petition thus positioned Belinda as a hardworking and productive Lockean subject, no different from other hardworking Massachusetts citizens, except that the laws that transformed persons of African descent into European Americans' private property had deprived her of her Lockean rights.[51] As her petition stated: "The laws rendered her incapable of receiving property and though she was a free moral agent, accountable for her own actions, yet never had she a moment at her own disposal! Fifty years her faithful hands have been compelled to ignoble servitude for the benefit of an Isaac Royall." The petition continued, "She, by the laws of the land, is denied the enjoyment of one morsel of that immense wealth, a part whereof hath been accumulated by her own industry, and the whole augmented by her servitude." Echoing American arguments against parliamentary efforts to tax the colonies during the 1760s and 1770s, Belinda's petition ends with the argument that slavery violated "the just returns of honest industry."[52]

Belinda did not act alone. Coinciding with European American protests against the Stamp Act, African Americans in Massachusetts had begun to

51. Furthermore, slavery also violated American mercantilist sentiments, the purchase of slaves necessitating the export of bullion from the United States to Great Britain. See, for example, "Political Economy: Part of Judge Pendleton's Charge to the Grand Jurors of Gagetown . . . ," *American Museum*, I (1787), 483–487, esp. 485; and Black Beard, "Ludicrous Plan for the Benefit of Rhode Island," ibid., II (1787), 66–67, esp. 66. For a discussion of earlier British benevolent and mercantilist opposition to slavery, see John E. Crowley, *This Sheba, Self: The Conceptualization of Economic Life in Eighteenth-Century America* (Baltimore, 1974), 32–33.

52. Belinda, "Petition of an African Slave, to the Legislature of Massachusetts," *American Museum*, I (1787), 536–538. Belinda's brief argued that her continued enslavement violated article 1 of the Massachusetts Declaration of Rights, adopted in June 1780, which declared, "All men are born free and equal and have certain natural, essential, and unalienable rights; among which may be reckoned the right of enjoying and defending their lives and liberties; that of acquiring, possessing, and protecting property; in fine, that of seeking and obtaining their safety and happiness" (Massachusetts Constitution of 1780). See Oscar Handlin and Mary Handlin, eds., *The Popular Sources of Political Authority: Documents on the Massachusetts Constitution of 1780* (Cambridge, Mass., 1966), 441–472, esp. 442. *(Popular Sources* also includes the Revolutionary Constitution of 1778 and instructions to the representatives by various towns.) Not only did slavery deprive her of her personal "liberty," the *American Museum* essay argued and Belinda and her supporters claimed; it violated her right to "acquire, possess, and protect property," both in herself and resulting from her labors. Slavery thus violated her rights as a commercial republican.

PLATE SIXTEEN *Mary and Elizabeth Royall*. By John Singleton Copley, c. 1758. Oil on canvas. Note not only the elegant clothing of the two young girls but the exotic tropical bird the older girl (left) holds in the palm of her hand. Museum of Fine Arts, Boston: Julia Knight Fox Fund, 25.49. Photograph © 2010, Museum of Fine Arts, Boston

initiate freedom suits against their owners, deploying the same natural-rights rhetoric as European American patriots. By the end of the Revolution, eighteen freedom suits had been registered. In 1783, they bore fruit as the Massachusetts Supreme Court, in *Commonwealth v. Jennison*, declared that slavery violated the equality clause in the Massachusetts State Constitution and freed former slave Quock Walker. But, like Belinda, Boston's free and enslaved

African Americans moved in an even more radical direction. Claiming to have been inspired by America's revolution and "the Lawdable Example of the Good People of these States," they petitioned and sued for economic reparations. At times, they succeeded. In 1773, for example, Caesar Henrick of Newburyport, having sued his owner, Richard Greenleaf, for "unlawfully detaining him in bondage," was awarded his freedom and eighteen pounds. Ten years later, Anthony Vassall of Cambridge won a similar suit in his and his wife's name. Vassall's legal suit and Belinda's legislative petition might have succeeded in part because their owners were notorious tories who had fled to England at the war's commencement.[53] But there was, as well, radical white support for their claims. James Swan, British émigré, patriot pamphleteer, and Son of Liberty, turned to Deuteronomy 15 to justify reparations—"Thou shalt not let [the slave] go away empty."[54]

Carey was not the only magazine editor to represent African Americans as empowered economic subjects. That same summer, Philadelphia's *Columbian Magazine* published an article attacking the Atlantic slave trade as a violation of human rights and constituting Africans as active commercial subjects, the equals of European and European American merchants. This essay began by refuting a long-standing defense of slavery—that prisoners captured in "just wars" could be enslaved. There was nothing just about slave wars in Africa, the essay insisted. Europeans had induced Africans to engage in these wars "for no other motive, than to furnish slaves for the Europeans." European slave traders sup-

53. Roy E. Finkenbine, "Belinda's Petition: Reparations for Slavery in Revolutionary Massachusetts," *William and Mary Quarterly*, 3d Ser., LXIV (2007), 95–105, esp. 100–101. Copley's portrait of Isaac Royall pictures him as a portly gentleman, elegantly dressed, seated in his countinghouse, his finger pointing to his ledger books, the model of the hardworking and successful merchant. Royall commissioned a second Copley portrait, one of his young daughters that portrayed them as the embodiments of elegant refinement. In that painting, the young girls float toward us swathed in lustrous satin and delicate laces. A hummingbird, like Belinda one of Royall's West Indian imports, sits on his oldest daughter's finger—somewhat more comfortably, one surmises, than Belinda sat in Royall's kitchen. See Carrie Rebora and Paul Staiti, eds., *John Singleton Copley in America* (New York, 1996), fig. 166 (182), catalogue item no. 10 (183).

54. Finkenbine, "Belinda's Petition," *WMQ*, 3d Ser., LXIV (2007), 100. For further discussion on the movement among African American residents of Massachusetts for both emancipation and financial compensation for their enslavement, see T. H. Breen, "Making History: The Force of Public Opinion and the Last Years of Slavery in Massachusetts," in Ronald Hoffman, Mechal Sobel, and Fredrika J. Teute, eds., *Through a Glass Darkly: Reflections on Personal Identity in Early America* (Chapel Hill, N.C., 1997), 67–95; Emily Blanck, "Seventeen Eighty-Three: The Turning Point in the Law of Slavery and Freedom in Massachusetts," *New England Quarterly*, LXXV (2002), 24–51; Melish, *Disowning Slavery*, 64.

plied African slavers with arms and ammunition and "frequently bribed [them] for the purpose." Far more radically, the essay continued, it was not only that slave wars were cruel and unjust; they were economically unsound. They impeded a far more lucrative form of trade—that between European Americans and Africans. The trade in enslaved Africans "is replete with misery and destruction to the human race, and is beneficial to a few individuals." Trade with Africans, in contrast, would enrich the world. Africa produced a host of valuable products: "cotton, indigo, tobacco, rice, coffee, spices, drugs, mahogany, dying woods, wax, and ambergris, honey, ivory, gold, etc." The trade with Africans in these goods "would be of national advantage, as . . . [Africa is] the cheapest market for raw materials. . . . [It would] open a new and extensive market for our manufacturers . . . and be attended with public benefits." Representing Africans as valuable trading partners for the new Republic, producers of rare raw materials and potential consumers of manufactured goods, the essay tied Africans and European Americans to one another by the bonds of legitimate commerce, establishing a fundamental sameness and thus equality of one trading/consuming people with another. The sameness of European American and African trader/consumers was reinforced by the essay's reference to commercial contracts. Commerce revolves around contracts, and contracts, as we know, presume equal parties. The *Columbian Magazine*'s essay thus refused the sharp dyad of white/black, free/slave, contracting individual/chattel that had been designed to racially stabilize the European American's uncertain identity.[55]

55. "A Summary View of the Slave Trade . . . ," *Columbian Magazine*, I (1787), 870–872. Olaudah Equiano makes a similar plea for trade with Africa rather than trade in Africans in his widely circulated and influential autobiography (see Robert J. Allison, ed., *The Interesting Narrative of the Life of Olaudah Equiano, Written by Himself* [Boston, 1995], 193–194). The original date of publication was 1788, or the year after the *Columbian Magazine* article. This argument was in the air in abolitionist circles. We should note that Britain's trade relations with African nations had long provided a lucrative market for British manufactured goods. The *Columbian Magazine* was thus attempting to position the United States as an effective commercial competitor with Great Britain.

Until at least the American Civil War, the North and the South competed vigorously for political and cultural supremacy. Throughout this period, northerners fretted over the South's political domination of the Federal presidency, noting that, during the Republic's first half century, only three presidents came from the North—John Adams, John Quincy Adams, and Martin Van Buren. As early as the summer of 1787, this struggle had acquired racial overtones, after southern delegates to the Constitutional Convention had blocked any effort on the part of northern delegates to ban slavery from the new Republic. Philadelphia Quakers and other antislavery advocates were concerned. Presumably, Carey, who not only had reprinted Belinda's petition but was a member of Philadelphia's Colonization Society, was concerned as well.

The new Republic's appearance abroad always played a significant role in European American visions of their relation with African Americans. At times, however, the introduction of African Americans into the European/European American dyad confused and destabilized rather than clarified European Americans' new identity. We see this quite forcefully in another issue of the *American Museum*, one obsessed with the need to refute assertions of European American cultural inferiority. The issue began with an excerpt from Jefferson's *Notes on Virginia* that focused on Jefferson's refutation of the Count de Buffon's charge that the New World, lacking the maturity of the Old, was inferior and underdeveloped. Not so, Jefferson (and Carey) insisted. American landscapes were as noble as any in Europe. American bison were mightier than European mammoths. America's indigenous peoples were more eloquent than Europe's peasantry (Jefferson gave the example of Logan's final speech). A second essay boasted that European Americans received high prices for their paintings in London, one of them even hanging in the City of London's Guild Hall. A third essay shifted focus somewhat, though its object remained the same. The essay was actually an excerpt from the Marquis de Chastellux's popular *Travels in America,* entitled "Manner of Living of the Inhabitants of Virginia." It is a deeply ambivalent comment on southern slavery and, simultaneously, a defense against European criticisms of European Americans by displacing those criticisms onto European Americans other than the *Museum*'s Philadelphia readers—that is, onto the "inhabitants of Virginia." As such, it participated in an ongoing struggle between northern and southern elites for political and cultural dominance in the new Republic.[56]

The "Manner of Living of the Inhabitants of Virginia" stressed the different, exotic nature of the American South. In all likelihood, many of the marquis's French metropole readers did find Virginia an exotic land (though, of course, not planters in the Francophone Antilles or Louisiana). It is highly unlikely, however, that Carey's subscribers would have found Virginia exotic. George Washington, Alice Lee Shippen, and William Byrd III, along with numerous southern delegates to the Constitutional Convention and later to the new Federal Congress, called it home. On the pages of Carey's *American Museum,* however, Virginia appeared in much the way that Mary Louise Pratt claims "darkest Africa" appeared when represented in European travel narratives—

---

56. "Thoughts on American Genius," 206–209, and "Manner of Living of the Inhabitants of Virginia," 214–216, both in *American Museum,* I (1787). Both the *Columbian Magazine* and the *Massachusetts Magazine* also published excerpts from the Marquis de Chastellux's *Travels* that focused on the savagery of slavery.

different, exotic, and decidedly not a land for civilized men. Virginia's climate was extreme, the marquis explained. Its heat was oppressive. Its "pernicious insects, the musketoes," made life a living hell.[57]

The essay proceeded to represent Virginia's white inhabitants as utter strangers to northern (white) ways. In contrast to Philadelphia's hardworking merchants, professionals, and artisans, who were on the streets often by the first rays of dawn, the southern planter did not rise until nine o'clock. Spending his days in languid ease, he rarely exerted himself more vigorously than "to walk as far as his stables . . . which are seldom more than fifty yards from his house." Using language that evoked eighteenth- and nineteenth-century pornographic art (Manet's painting of Olympia comes to mind), the essay pictured the planter lying "on a pallat . . . in the coolest room . . . in his shirt and trowsers only, with a negro at his head, and another at his feet, to fan him, and keep off the flies." (In this portrait, the white male planter played Olympia.) Below the planter in the Virginia social hierarchy, readers were told they would find middling farmers, men who worked harder than planters but were given to strong drink. The marquis also noted, tellingly, that their wives "very seldom drink tea," bringing to mind elite eastern representations of savage frontier farmers from western Virginia and the Carolina frontier.[58]

In contrast to these white nonproducers, the essay continued, "the poor Negro slaves alone work hard, and fare still harder. It is astonishing and unaccountable . . . what an amazing degree of fatigue these poor . . . wretches undergo." Virtually everything produced in the South was produced by them. In this way, America's premier political magazine used images of productive blacks to prove the southern white degenerate and unproductive. It then went on to use planter mistreatment of enslaved African Americans to prove the southern slaveowner tyrannical and brutish. Inhuman enemies of liberty, slaveholders and their overseers mutilated slaves who sought simply to protect their lives and human dignity. So oppressive were Virginia's slave codes that "the law

---

57. "Manner of Living," *American Museum*, I (1787), 215; Mary Louise Pratt, *Imperial Eyes: Travel Writing and Transculturation* (London, 1992); and Pratt, "Scratches on the Face of the Country," in Henry Louis Gates, ed., *"Race," Writing, and Difference* (Chicago, 1986), 138–162.

58. "Manner of Living," *American Museum*, I (1787), 214. See also Charles Bernheimer, "The Uncanny Lure of Manet's *Olympia*," in Dianne Hunter, ed., *Seduction and Theory: Readings of Gender, Representation, and Rhetoric* (Urbana, Ill., 1989), 13–28; Bernheimer, Charles T. Jefferson Kline, and Naomi Schor, eds., *Decadent Subjects: The Idea of Decadence in Art, Literature, Philosophy, and Culture of the Fin de Siècle in Europe* (Baltimore, 2002); and Sander L. Gilman, *Difference and Pathology: Stereotypes of Sexuality, Race, and Madness* (Ithaca, N.Y., 1985), esp. chap. 3.

directs a negro's arm to be struck off, who raises it against a white person, should it be only in his own defence, against the most wanton and wicked barbarity and outrage." Evoking language only recently directed toward British oppressors, Philadelphia's popular press condemned Virginia's white overseers as the "unfeeling sons of barbarity . . . who are permitted to exercise an unlimited dominion over" the slaves. Philadelphian readers could rest assured, compared to barbarous and degenerate southern planters, they were indeed the very models of freedom-loving, cultured gentlemen.[59]

Nevertheless, a dangerous slippage accompanied this deployment of African American slaves to constitute southern whites Other to the northern white readers. This essay, especially when read alongside Carey's reprinting of Belinda's brief and the *Columbian Magazine*'s call for trade with, not in, Africans, suggested that northern European Americans and enslaved African Americans were equally productive and freedom loving—the enslaved African American being unjustly deprived of his freedom and compensation for his labor by effete aristocratic southern planters. The fundamental distinction between free labor and slave labor, European and African, that constituted a stable core of European Americans' identity was in danger of collapsing into a threatening sameness and equality. The remainder of the excerpt quickly retreated from this dangerous erosion of racial difference by re-emphasizing the slave's innate racial nature. Economically oppressed, deprived of every political freedom, the marquis went on, if the slave were really like the northern white republican (or the enlightened Frenchman), he would have railed at his chains and struggled against his fate. Instead, slaves were unnaturally happy. "Notwithstanding [their] . . . degrading situation and rigid severity to which fate has subjected this wretched race, they are certainly devoid of care, and actually appear jovial, contented, and happy. Fortunate it is indeed for them, that they are blessed with this easy, satisfied disposition of mind; else human nature, unequal to the weight, must sink under the pressure of such complicated misery and wretchedness." In the end, it appeared that African Americans did not, after all, share the same "human" nature with northern white free producers. Equally industrious, the black slave was not equally freedom loving or emotionally sensitive. Certainly, the marquis continued, enslaved Africans and African Americans did not have the same physical constitution as white men had. In contrast to the white man, the slave possessed unnatural vigor and took an animalistic pleasure in dancing. At the end of a day of killing labor, did he sink to the ground as the white man would? Quite the contrary, "instead of retiring to rest,

59. "Manner of Living," *American Museum*, I (1787), 215, 216.

as it might *naturally* be concluded he would be glad to do," he walked six or seven miles to "a negro dance," where "he performs with astonishing agility." A crude contrast, indeed, to the ball the Chevalier de La Luzerne had given in Philadelphia.[60]

EMBODYING DIFFERENCE

Other articles appearing in the new urban press were far more explicit in insisting on fundamental differences between black and white, African and European American—and in grounding their arguments in the body. In doing so, these essays exemplified the rising importance of the new discourses of scientific racism. The Declaration of Independence was wrong. All men were not created equal. Sameness did not threaten to unhinge social order. Roxanne Wheeler sees the late eighteenth century as a borderland between social structures based on systems of deference and ones based on rigidly maintained racial hierarchies. No one better illustrated the new discourses of scientific racism than Jamaican writer Edward Long. Long's *History of Jamaica* is famous for its bitter racism and, in particular, for its advocacy of polygenesis, the insistence that Africans were so inferior to Europeans as to be the product of a separate creation. It is significant, therefore, that the same year Carey excerpted the marquis's travel account the *Columbian Magazine* printed an extensive excerpt from Long's *History*.[61]

Long's basic message was simple and encapsulated the central argument of scientific racism. By their bodies, you would know them.

The particulars wherein Negroes differ most essentially from the whites, are, first, in respect to their bodies, viz. the dark membrane which communicates

60. Ibid. (emphasis added) True, the essay was written by the marquis, but Carey did reprint a lengthy excerpt; nor can we forget that late-eighteenth-century France was every bit as invested in defending slavery as U.S. southerners, the slave colonies of the Antilles (Saint-Domingue, Martinique, Guadeloupe) being a major source of French wealth far into the nineteenth century. Certainly Napoleon invested a fortune and tens of thousands of French lives trying to recapture Saint-Domingue (Haiti) and restore slavery to the island. The marquis's ambivalence about slavery and African "nature" paralleled U.S. ambivalence.

61. [Edward Long], "Observations on the Gradation in the Scale of Being between the Human and Brute Creation: Including Some Curious Particulars respecting Negroes (From a Late History of Jamaica), *Columbian Magazine*, II (1788), 14–22. This excerpt was taken from Edward Long, *The History of Jamaica; or, General Survey of the Antient and Modern State of That Island with Reflections on Its Situation, Settlements, Inhabitants, Climate, Products, Commerce, Laws, and Government* (London, 1774).

that black colour to their skins, which does not alter by transportation into other climates. . . . Secondly, A covering of wool, like the bestial fleece, instead of hair. Thirdly . . . tumid nostrils, flat noses, invariable thick lips, and general large size of the female nipples. . . . Fourthly, the black colour of the lice which infest their bodies. . . . Fifthly, their bestial or fætid smell.

Degenerate in appearance, Africans were equally degenerate in intellect. "They are void of genius, and seem almost incapable of making any progress in civility or science," Long insisted, adding that they were "a brutish, ignorant, idle, crafty, treacherous, bloody, thievish, mistrustful and superstitious people . . . incestuous, savage, . . . devourers of human flesh, and quaffers of human blood." Cannibals, they had no moral conscience. Lacking self-control, they embraced idleness, eschewed beauty, and reveled in "women; gormandizing, and drinking to excess." So unlike the elevated European, there was little to distinguish them from the animals with whom they shared the African continent. (How similar to frontier attacks on Native Americans.) "When we reflect on the nature of these men, and their dissimilarity to the rest of mankind," Long continued, "must we not conclude, that they are a different species?"[62]

The implications of the *Columbian Magazine*'s decision to entitle its excerpt "Observations on the Gradation in the Scale of Being between the Human and Brute Creation" are clear. Africans inhabited a no-man's-land between human and brute. Underscoring Africans' physical otherness, the *Columbian Magazine* sexualized and engendered that otherness, reprinting Long's contention that orangutans not infrequently carried off Hottentot women and "mated" with them. This was not as unnatural as it might at first seem, Long hastened to add. The orangutan was a noble animal, humanlike, in contrast to the African, who was far more bestial than human. "The oran-outang," Long insisted, bears "the strongest similitude to mankind, in countenance, figure, stature, organs, erect posture, actions or movements, food, temper, and manner of living." "Their females suckle their young in the same manner [as humans]. . . . They seem to have a sense of shame, and a share of sensibility. . . . Nor must we omit the expression of their grief by shedding tears, and other passions, by modes entirely resembling the human." One suspects that Long's object (and by implication that of the *Columbian Magazine*'s editors, as well) was less to elevate the orangutan then to depress the African. "Ludicrous as the opinion may seem, I do not think that an oran-outang husband would be any dishonour to an Hottentot female; for what are these Hottentots?—They are, say the most

62. [Long], "Observations," *Columbian Magazine*, II (1788), 14–15.

credible writers . . . more like beasts than men." Thus Philadelphia's urban magazines moved easily from celebrating Belinda's rights to reprinting Edward Long's racist insistence of Africans' absolute otherness, an otherness grounded in bodily differences.[63]

But we should pause a moment. The excerpt the *Columbian Magazine* reprinted is significant for still another reason. Long, onetime lieutenant governor of Jamaica, insisted that Europeans born or long resident in the Americas were inferior to Europeans resident in Europe. The unnatural heat of tropical summers, along with their close association with enslaved Africans, caused white creoles to no longer resemble Enlightenment Europeans but rather behave like African Caribbeans, meaning they were no longer fit for self-government. The decision to reprint parts of Long's *History*, despite Long's denigration of white creoles and their right to self-government, exemplifies the growing appeal scientific racist arguments held for European American readers, North as well as South.[64]

An essay published in the *Massachusetts Magazine* continued this disparagement of the Hottentots—though this time the comparison group was not orangutans but Dutch settlers at the Cape of Good Hope. Represented in the magazine, the Dutch were everything good settlers should be. They were industrious, educated, religious, well clothed, successful at trade—in short, just what Thomas's Boston readers wished to be. The contrast between the Dutch and the Hottentots with whom the Dutch shared the Cape could not have been drawn in more dramatic tones. The Hottentots were "an excessively dirty people, covered with filth, and clothed in the untanned hides of animals." "Does it not seem astonishing, notwithstanding their long intercourse with the

63. Ibid., 15, 17, 21–22. But the chain does not end there. A few months after publishing Long's account of orangutan rape of Hottentot women, it published a refutation of Long ("An Answer to a Circumstance on Which Some Writers, in Defence of the Slave-Trade, Have Founded Much of Its Legality," ibid., II [1788], 266–268). On the other hand, Noah Webster also entered the fray, on the side of enslaving Africans, publishing an essay by M. Chenier that argued Africans were naturally slaves (Chenier, "An Account of the Character, Manners, and Customs of the Moors," *American Magazine*, I [September 1788], 716–722). The urban fathers' ambivalence concerning race matched their general ideological inconsistencies.

64. Long's position has strong ironic overtones. While a royal official, Long was also one of Jamaica's richest planters. Indeed, the Long family had been among the first British families to settle in Jamaica after capturing it from the Spanish in the seventeenth century. Long and his family were themselves longtime residents of the tropics; consequently, what Long wrote about whites in the West Indies had to apply to his own family. His attacks were explicitly directed toward British long resident in the West Indies. Their implication even for northern residents of the United States would not have been lost on Carey and his readers.

Dutch," the *Magazine* continued, echoing Long's assertion that Africans were "incapable of progress," "there never has been a single instance of their relinquishing their dress, manners or customs, for those of their polished neighbours?" "But still prefer the skin of an animal to the richest clothes; and his entrails to the most sumptuous fare."[65]

The new Republic's community of enlightened readers could rest assured. Humanus's was a misguided and idealistic vision. Africans and African Americans were not their "fellow creatures." They could lay no legitimate claim to membership in the American body politic. The *Columbian Magazine* settled the matter. Reprinting another excerpt from the Marquis de Chastellux's *Travels in America,* harsher by far than the one Carey reprinted, the magazine concluded, "It is not only the slave who is beneath his master, it is the negro who is beneath the white man. No act of enfranchisement can efface this unfortunate distinction." Scientific racism was the language of modernity and the Enlightenment. It claimed its proofs were irrefutable.[66]

But not everyone was persuaded. Indeed, the magazines, refusing any claim to consistency, published a number of other essays overtly challenging the contentions of scientific racism—especially the claim that Hottentots and orang-utans cohabited sexually. The author of "An Answer to . . . the Slave Trade" insisted that, if such charges were true, Africans would be sterile, as mules were. Asserting the Africans' kinship, if not absolute equality, with Europeans, the author continued, "The negro of Africa is a branch of the same stock with the European, whether English or French, a Spaniard or a Portuguese; the difference in the colour of his skin, perhaps, is the effect of climate; the poorness of his intellectual faculties may arise from the same cause; but still he is as much a human creature as the most refined European."[67]

ROMANCING RACE

Increasingly, however, those insisting on Africans' humanity turned away from the discourses of liberalism and commercial republicanism that had characterized Belinda's petition and the call for trade with Africans. They chose, instead, the radically different discourse of the sympathies. The northern magazine's editors and contributors appear to have found in sentimental rhetoric

65. M., "For the Massachusetts Magazine: Sketches of the Cape of Good Hope," *Massachusetts Magazine,* I (1789), 366–370.

66. "The State of Slavery in Virginia and Other Parts of the Continent, from the Marquis de Chastellux's Travels in America," *Columbian Magazine,* I (1787), 479–480, esp. 480.

67. "An Answer," ibid., II (1788), 267.

and the pastoral romance a more emotionally compelling language in which to criticize slavery. Fusing sympathy with an insistence on fundamental racial and class differences, these discourses captured and reproduced the deep ambivalence European Americans felt toward the African Americans they found in their midst.

Take, for example, an essay in the *American Museum* that described the injustices of slavery and the cruelty of slavers in the very highly romanticized rhetoric that the *Massachusetts Magazine* had used when depicting rural poverty (Maria's letter to Eliza). The remnants of a political discourse were still present—rights and property were mentioned—but they played second fiddle to noble white emotions.

> Ye who repose under the delightful shades of peace—ye whose rights and property fear no invasion—ye whose nights of soft slumber are undisturbed, whose days are spent in conjugal love, and whose children are ripening in age, under the kind indulgences of parental affection, forget, for a moment, the voluptuous couch, the luxurious table, the splendid equipage, the sumptuous robe, the enchanting scenes . . . that surround you; and consider that many of your poor brethren are harrassed with . . . heavy labour . . . and [are] considered only as beasts of burden. They have children as yourselves, and are subject to the same feelings.[68]

Here we find romantic rhetoric trumping Edward Long's scientific racism—at least for the moment. Difference fades before the empathy of sameness. Enslaved Africans were as much God's creatures as well-to-do Philadelphians were. They were not a "different species." They were not lower than orangutans. Africans loved their children just as deeply as Thomas's Boston readers did. They were "subject to the same feelings." They are even given names and personal histories. Most significant of all, they speak in as eloquent and as refined a manner as an elite Philadelphian. By implication, this essay repeated Humanus's question: "What has this man done to subject himself to be *sold* for life?"

The essay continues by describing Morni, an enslaved African now an old man, and his memories of his bucolic home in Africa—before, that is, slave traders burst into his valley and rent his life asunder. Moving his listeners to tears, Morni described a day, years earlier, when, a young husband and father, his children playing by his side, he reclined happily under a tree his own father had planted. A feast was in process. Young men and women danced and sang.

68. "Address to the Heart," *American Museum*, I (1787), 540–541.

(Here the reference to dancing in Africa was clearly intended to encourage identification, not to set the African apart, as it had been in the Marquis de Chastellux's representation of slavery.) Suddenly, slave traders burst into this edenic scene. "The shrieks of the dying victims are now the only music of the groves!" Morni tells his spellbound listerners, then asks: "Can the bleating of the lamb raise the pity of the wolf? No: nor the cry of the babe stay the hand of the barbarous ruffian! The afflicted mother is torn from her child, for the protecting hand of the father is laid low in the dust. . . . The groans of men are heard with the clanking of chains! . . . The valley of Morni is now become the valley of death! The sacred groves are become the shades of misery!" (Parallels between Morni's and Logan's stories suggest themselves. The wronged are presented as objects of pity, powerless victims, not feared actors intent on violent retribution.)[69]

The northern press used the rhetoric of the sympathies to establish a senti-mental bond between the European American and the slave. At the same time, the northern magazines also used it to reaffirm the slaveholder as the European American's inhuman Other in ways that echoed the Marquis de Chastellux's description of Virginia as a strange and exotic land. In Morni's tale, the slave trader appears a "barbarous ruffian," a pitiless "wolf." A poem, "The Slave," dedicated to James Oglethorpe, leader of the British movement to end the Atlantic slave trade, similarly represented slave traders and -owners as in-human. Deploying romantic rhetoric of such extravagance that it verged on the gothic, the poem began by banishing both the slave trader and the slave-owner from the human race. They, not the African, belonged to an inferior, "blacken'd," indeed, damned, species.

Who was the fiend,
(for such his deeds proclaim
His real kind, tho' clad in human frame)
Who by the rev'rend form of man not aw'd

. . . .

While total hell inspir'd his blacken'd mind,
Of heav'n's best gift . . .
And dar'd the name of slave, and all the woes
Of servile bond on the good impose?

Answering its own question, the poem invoked God's curse on Cain:

69. Ibid.

Scarce match'd in guilt, by him who earliest smote
A brother's breast, and acts of murder taught.
While virtue lives on earth, immortal shame
Shall blast the outcast of the human name.[70]

While striving to appear apolitical, romantic imagery, as we have already seen, carries significant political implications. Almost all the northern press's sentimental representations of the plight of the slave were set in Africa and focused on the violence involved in the original act of enslavement. They did not examine slavery as it was practiced in the American South—or, more tellingly, in Philadelphia, Boston, or New York. While seeking to arouse passionate sympathy for the oppressed slave, these pleas, in fact, precluded actual identification with the enslaved African by distancing him from the reality of America's cities. We should note that, in the essay on Morni, the name of the slave and the valley he comes from are the same. Slave and Africa became one. Such moves made it increasingly difficult to think of Morni or other enslaved Africans as Americans, as taking their place side by side with other productive and liberty-loving Philadelphians, New Yorkers, or New Englanders as legitimate members of the republican body politic. We should also note that Carey was an active member of the American Colonization Society, whose solution to slavery was to return freed slaves to Africa, leaving America a white Republic.[71]

The shift to sentimental rhetoric had a second effect. Transposing the discussion of slavery from one of rights (Belinda's rights to profit from her labors) and economics (trading *with* Africans versus trading Africans), it represented the enslaved African as a pathetic and powerless victim—the subject of compassion, not rights. We find this even in Carey's reprinting of Belinda's petition. On the one hand, the petition presents Belinda as a Lockean individual with rights not only to life and liberty but to property. It urges that her freedom and her property in herself should be returned to her. But it then embeds Belinda's claims to equal rights within a romantic fantasy of her childhood in Africa. Belinda grew up, according to Carey's reprinting of the original peti-

70. Theophilus Rowe, "The Slave: Inscribed to James Oglethorpe, Esquire," in W. R., "The Columbian Parnassiad," *Columbian Magazine*, I (1787), 293–294.

71. As we shall see in the following chapter, Carey appears to have been ill at ease with including African Americans among Philadelphia's virtuous republican citizens. At least that is one way to read his vitriolic attack on African Americans' response to Philadelphia's yellow fever epidemic of 1792.

tion, in a beautiful, pastoral Africa surrounded by "the mountains, covered with spicy forests—the vallies, loaded with the richest fruits, spontaneously produced." Her childhood would have been marked by "the most complete felicity, had not her mind received early impressions of the cruelty of men, whose faces were like the moon, and whose bows and arrows were like the thunder and the lightning of the clouds." Like Morni's, Belinda's experiences exceeded her worst fears.

> An armed band of white men, driving many of her countrymen in chains, rushed into [her valley's] hallowed shades! Could the tears, the sighs, and supplications, bursted from the tortured parental affection, have blunted the keen edge of avarice, she might have been rescued from agony. . . . She was ravished from the . . . arms of her friends . . . cruelly separated . . . from her [parents] for ever.

This part of the petition transposed Belinda's narrative from the New England law court and political arena to the world of the belletristic pastoral or perhaps the gothic melodrama. The object, presumably, was to make it more appealing and less threatening to Massachusetts legislators and Philadelphia readers. As an innocent child, a pathetic victim, an African, Belinda appears a far different figure then she did when presenting herself as an industrious Bostonian deserving the protection the Massachusetts constitution offered its citizens. Then she appeared the abused equal of patriotic European Americans who had fought British economic and political tyranny to preserve their rights. But, when Belinda was presented as a tearful child brutally torn from her African home, the obvious solution to Belinda's dilemma—and to European Americans', as well—was to send her and other enslaved African Americans back to Africa.[72]

An essay published in the *Columbian Magazine* proposed just such a solution. The author described a dream he had of America fifty years later, a prosperous, united America from which all African Americans had been benevolently removed. Transplanting African Americans would attest to European Americans' philanthropic instincts. It would also reaffirm Americans' unalloyed whiteness. It would make the American South like the American North, transforming the southern planter into a hardworking and independent producer, just like the virtuous and industrious northerner. It would thus affirm

---

72. Belinda, "Petition of an African Slave, to the Legislature of Massachusetts," *American Museum* I (1787), 540.

the northern bourgeois subject as the true new American, the model for all other European Americans. And, tellingly, it would make the reintroduction of equal political and economic rights for African Americans increasingly difficult —rhetorically and politically.[73]

But still northern whites could not quite relinquish their connections with African Americans. Let us return to the excerpt from the Marquis de Chastellux's *Travels* in the *Columbian Magazine:* "It appears . . . that there is no other method of abolishing slavery, than by getting rid of the negroes." But the marquis (and presumably the editors) then went on to modify this stand in significant ways. Commenting first that deporting African Americans was "a measure which must be very gradually adopted," it proceeded in ways that simultaneously objectified and sexualized all African Americans. "The best expedient would be to *export* a great number of [African American] *males*, and to encourage the marriage of white men with the *females*. For this purpose the law must be abrogated which transmits slavery by the side of the mother." The deep ambivalence that runs through European American reflections on African Americans rises as pentimento through these comments. On the elegant pages of the *Columbian Magazine,* enslaved African American women are referred to as "females," not as "women"; negroes must be *exported* like cattle or grain. At the same time, African American women are to be kept in the United States to be married to white men, and their children are to be born free. The new American will be a fusion of European and African peoples. Difference will be erased, though confusions abound.[74]

Gender, infusing race, plays a critical role in these fantasies. It is European American men who will cross racial and sexual barriers, erasing racial, if not class, differences. African American men, on the other hand, will be "exported." Within this system, European American men will maintain their control over all women, European and African American, just as they did under slavery. African American men will lose all rights to women, as they did under slavery. Nevertheless, this essay does propose that African American "females" take their place alongside European American women as republican mothers.

73. "For the Columbian Magazine," *Columbian Magazine,* I (1786), 5–6.

74. "The State of Slavery in Virginia and Other Parts of the Continent," *Columbian Magazine,* I (1787), 479–480 (emphasis added). We will recall William Byrd II's similar suggestion that half-savage frontiersmen marry savage Native American women in order to establish a borderland that would protect affluent eastern planters. The aristocratic marquis thus echoed the earlier remarks of a home-grown American "aristocrat."

Oh, what a tangled web magazines' editors and contributors wove when first presenting themselves and their readers as republican gentlemen! The urban magazines constituted a crazy quilt of subjects and Others. Dyadic oppositions piled one on top of the other, creating a destabilized and contradictory layering of multiple selves and confusing Others. The genteel European American woman was designed to confirm the European American man as a gentleman at the same time as she threatened his standing as a virtuous republican. The industrious and frugal housewife confirmed the commercial republican's virtue as an industrious producer, yet her very frugality and industry earned the republican gentleman's and his lady's disdain and, at the same time, made her like the enslaved African in terms of her productivity and lack of political and legal subjectivity. Slave and free producer alike worked hard, yet they were linked in dyadic opposition, the slave's bondage defining the citizens' freedom and rights. Southern planters dominated much of the new Republic's social and political life. In graceful step with Philadelphia and New York elites, they moved effortlessly through carefully choreographed quadrilles; their voices blended harmoniously during musical evenings at John Powel's or Robert Morris's. Yet the political magazines represented them as the liberty-loving and productive northerners' constituting Other. Northern free white producer, southern free white slaveholder, and enslaved African American came together and separated in a convoluted and confused dance of identification and difference. In still another layering, the republican gentleman, the fashion-driven European American woman, and the enslaved African American fused and then refused the shared identity. Complications proliferated, threatening to rupture the distinctions ideological surety demanded. European American discourses could not represent two more dissimilar figures than the delicate white woman, leisured and refined, and the ignorant slave, more brute than human, the appropriate "mate" of an orangutan. Yet the *Columbian Magazine*'s Morni was as sensitive and as romantic a subject as the most refined lady, while African American "females" stepped forth as mothers of future republicans, shadowing such figures as Abigail Adams and Anne Bingham (as perhaps Sally Hemmings did on Philadelphia and Washington streets). Indeed, from the perspective of commercial republicanism, the hardworking slave had a greater claim to civic virtue than the leisured lady dedicated to ostentatious display. How could an internally coherent national identity emerge from this swirling mix of bodies?

The refined dances of republican citizens threatened to reel out of control. The new American–as–republican gentleman was no more coherent a subject than the new American–as–republican citizen or -as–white American. As the lights dimmed on the first American ball, America's new national identity appeared a patchwork of discordant images.

A critical, though rarely achieved, objective of the political press is to obscure ideological inconsistencies and discursive contradictions. As we have seen, popular fiction thrives on those very inconsistencies and ambivalences. Let us turn now to two early republican novels to explore the ways they presented the intermix of sameness and difference, class, race, and gender during the opening days of the new Republic, when radical economic and political change intersected.

CHAPTER EIGHT

Black Gothic

Blackness, the blackness of night and of dungeons; secrets, masked and festering; duplicity and the spectral—all lie at the heart of the gothic novel, a genre that emerged in England in the mid-eighteenth century and, crossing the Atlantic, remained popular through much of the nineteenth.[1] No language, no vision could be more unlike republican discourses. The celebration of virtue, civil and individual, constitutes the heart of republican discourses, as do the valorization of reason and the transparency of language and intention. Republicanism is the discourse of the agora. Fused with liberalism, it celebrates an enlightened public sphere and a future governed by reason, law, and science. In sharp contrast, the gothic looks back to a decadent and aristocratic world darkened by horror, superstition, and the unnatural. It is obsessed with the irrational twists and turns of depraved and perverse psyches.

Charles Brockden Brown is considered the father of the American novel.[2] He was the preeminent literary spokesman for the nascent American Republic, as committed as Benjamin Franklin and Thomas Jefferson to projecting his new nation, its civic virtues, and its republican culture onto the grand stage of

1. An early version of this chapter was initially presented at the international conference "Possible Pasts: Critical Encounters in Early America," co-sponsored by the McNeil Center for Early American Studies and the Omohundro Institute of Early American History and Culture, Philadelphia, June 1994. An enlarged version was then published as Carroll Smith-Rosenberg, "Black Gothic: The Shadowy Origins of the American Bourgeoisie," in Robert Blair St. George, ed., *Possible Pasts: Becoming Colonial in Early America* (Ithaca, N.Y., 2000), 243–269. A later version was presented as part of the conference "The Common Wind: Conversations in African American and Atlantic Histories," University of Michigan, Ann Arbor, Nov. 14–15, 2008. For a discussion of the gothic, see Peter Kafer, *Charles Brockden Brown's Revolution and the Birth of American Gothic* (Philadelphia, 2004), xii–xxi.

2. We will recall Julia A. Stern's demurring, noting that that statement effaces numerous women writers in the new Republic (Stern, *The Plight of Feeling: Sympathy and Dissent in the Early American Novel* [Chicago, 1997]); see Chapters 3 and 5, above.

world recognition. The duty of the American republican writer, Brown proclaimed, was to present the "new views" America offered the "moral painter," views "growing out of the condition of our country." Yet, time and again, Brown, as the Republic's self-proclaimed "moral painter," selected the gothic novel as his preferred venue, publishing four between 1798 and 1800. Why did Brown choose the gothic, with its focus on blackness and the dark ways of the human heart, to present a moral painting of the new Republic? What secrets, what duplicities did Brown discover behind the gleaming white façade of reason, virtue, and law the new Republic sought to present to the world— especially through its two key political documents, the Declaration of Independence and the Federal constitution?[3]

For more than two hundred years, citizens of the United States have followed Timothy Dwight in proclaiming their nation "the favorite land of Heaven," a place of "peace, purity and felicity." The rolling cadences of the Declaration of Independence, we insist, proclaim us a land of liberty and equality, our Constitution, a government of law and justice. But, shadowing the image the founders sought to project as wise and disinterested statesmen, observers caught sight of the hidden figures of speculators, price gougers, embezzlers, deceivers, and rogues. The economically and politically discontented—Daniel Shays's hardscrabble farmers, the Whiskey rebels of western Pennsylvania, Antifederalist critics—were not the only ones to see the new nation's mercantile and political elite in this light. Many European Americans across the economic and regional spectrum continued to hold dear the civic ideals of classic republicanism: its fears of credit and speculation, its commitment to disinterested heroism and Spartan discipline. Others espoused the commercial republican celebration of industry and frugality. Both groups watched with mounting ill ease as the national elite grew increasingly at home with the new ways of fiscal capitalism, their embrace of spectacles and the spectacular, of risk and, yes, deception.

Philadelphia, the new Republic's political and financial capital, became the emblem of both the promise and the fears the new Republic represented. On the surface, the gleaming façade of Benjamin Latrobe's First Bank of the United States, its regular columns referencing the republican virtue of Athens and Rome, spoke of the strength and transparency of the new Republic. It

3. Charles Brockden Brown, *Edgar Huntly; or, Memoirs of a Sleepwalker*, ed. David Stineback (Schenectady, N.Y., 1973), 29. Brown published *Weiland* in 1798, *Ormond* in 1799, *Arthur Mervyn*, part I, in 1799, part II in 1800, and *Edgar Huntly* in 1799. In addition, he published an early feminist tract, *Alcuin* (1798), edited three literary magazines, and later published two romances very different in tone and focus from the five gothic novels.

proclaimed that even the new ways of fiscal capitalism could shine forth honestly and responsibly. But, as we know, Latrobe's bank was only one architectural representation of the new capital. The merchant princes' new mansions and fantastical reproductions of aristocratic European forms were seen by many as representing the dark side of the new Republic, its reckless greed for ever-greater profits and for ever-more-dramatic self-representation and display, its fascination with the corruptions of Europe.

Certainly, deception, embezzlement, and fraud marked the careers of such republican spokesmen as William Duer, Philip Schuyler, and Walter Livingston. Sexual corruption shadowed even those who rose above fiscal corruption. Alexander Hamilton publicly confessed to a lurid affair at the same time as he accused Aaron Burr (soon to be Jefferson's vice president) of incest with his own daughter, and the popular press sneered at Jefferson's liaison with Sally Hemmings. Evidently, fashionable balls and receptions were not the only things the new elite indulged in in the darkness of the night. Hardworking members of the middling ranks, small-scale merchants, American-educated professionals, commercial farmers, and mechanics seeking to rise suspected the Republic's flamboyant merchant princes of irresponsible gambling with the nation's economic well-being, of speculative enthusiasm that drove up prices of land and corporate paper only to see those prices crash in the cool light of day. "Trust no one," conservative Quakers warned one another. One's closest associates might well "Design to Circumvent thee." To return to Daniel Defoe, this seemed to many "An Age of Plot and Deceit, of Contradiction and Paradox." Under the republican gentleman/financier's multiple masks, who could "see the true countenance of a man?"[4]

A second question troubled middling European Americans. How were new men—talented youths from the countryside, shopkeepers, and mechanics ambitious to rise socially and economically—to find their way through the new economic maze, to read the man behind the mask, to trust the economy? Republican virtue depended in large part on the openness of social and economic structures to men of talent, determination, and ambition. If deceit, insider knowledge, and corruption made upward mobility difficult, if not impossible, for them, what did that say about the new Republic?

Hovering over all was the dark cloud of slavery. Philadelphia, the new

4. Quaker merchant quotations are cited by Toby L. Ditz, "Secret Selves, Credible Personas: The Problematics of Trust and Public Display in the Writing of Eighteenth-Century Philadelphia Merchants," in St. George, ed., *Possible Pasts,* 228; Daniel Defoe, *The Review: Reproduced from the Original Editions,* VI (New York, 1938), 523.

national capital, was home to the Liberty Bell. Here Jefferson and Adams had collaborated to secure the Republic's Declaration of Independence, with its ringing commitment to universal brotherhood and its vision of freedom and equality as the inalienable right of every man. But Philadelphia was also the birthplace of the Constitution, with its moral and legal acquiescence to slavery inscribed in its Three-Fifths Compromise and Fugitive Slave Clause. We have witnessed European Americans' deep ambivalence on the issue of racial equality, an ambivalence revealed in the gradual emancipation programs adopted by every northern state except Vermont. In the summer and fall of 1793, some Philadelphians began to wonder whether the ominous cloud of slavery had begun to rain pestilence and death in the form of a yellow fever epidemic most believed had been carried by white planters fleeing the Haitian Revolution, many accompanied by their still-enslaved Africans and Afro-Caribbeans.

Charles Brockden Brown called *Arthur Mervyn* his Philadelphia novel. On its convoluted pages, Brown probes the dark side of the new capitalism and the seductive nature of the new consumerism. Leading us into the bedrooms of great merchants, it lays bare the fears haunting the new nation's youthful exuberance. In the process, it pulls out from the shadows two of the new nation's most destabilizing Others—the Revolution's newly vociferous bourgeois women and still-enslaved African Americans.

Of course, Brown was not alone in discovering secret fears lurking behind the new nation's projection of republican virtue. Bourgeois women and free blacks were even more aware than Brown of discrepancies between the nation's public face and the horror that unsettled its secluded spaces. The dark secrets their writings reveal both paralleled and differed from those that drove Brown's gothic. To grasp their perspectives, we will turn to a second, equally complex novel, Leonora Sansay's *Zelica, the Creole*, published in 1820 but based on an earlier semifictional work by Sansay, *Secret History; or, The Horrors of St. Domingo*, published in 1808.[5]

But still this will not be enough. A chapter on dark secrets cannot depend alone on the writings of white Americans. African American writers addressed many of the same issues. For them, however, these concerns lay not in the realm of fiction but in the very real world of politics and social commentary. Leaders of Philadelphia's African American community entered the public prints in the

5. Charles Brockden Brown, *Arthur Mervyn; or, Memoirs of the Year 1793* (Kent, Ohio, 1980), 51 (all citations from this edition); An American [Leonora Sansay], *Zelica, the Creole: A Novel in Three Volumes* (London, 1820); Sansay, *Secret History; or, The Horrors of St. Domingo, in a Series of Letters, Written by a Lady at Cape Francois* (Philadelphia, 1808).

1790s to defend their community against aspersions Mathew Carey had leveled against their honesty and humanity in the aftermath of the great yellow fever epidemic of 1793. In the small world that was late-eighteenth-century literate, urban America, these varied publications did not exist in isolation. Rather, they can be read as engaged in an intense dialogue in which urban Americans debated the moral trajectory of their new economy and the nature of republican citizenship. Did their dialogic exchanges hold out the promise of an emerging coherent national identity—or did they underscore the ways repressed secrets relentlessly destabilized that identity?

THE DARK LABYRINTH OF COMMERCE

A classic novel of initiation, *Arthur Mervyn* used the figure of a youthful naïf to explore the emergence of a capitalist urban and urbane America and the confusions and dangers innocent farm boys faced as they sought to establish themselves within that world. The passage of its title character from innocence to maturity parallels the new Republic's transformation from a largely agrarian culture to the world of commercial and fiscal capitalism. Charles Brockden Brown could have written this story as a rags-to-riches romance, as Benjamin Franklin did in his *Autobiography* and as countless uplift books have since. Instead, Brown wrote a gothic melodrama. Three dark secrets lie at the heart of *Arthur Mervyn,* secrets it repeatedly uncovers and yet seeks to mask. The first involves the corruption Brown, a resistant member of a troubled Philadelphia mercantile family, discovered lying at the heart of American capitalism. Lies, theft, fraud, and the heartless drive for self-advancement, Brown tells his readers, formed the core of the new American economy and its business practices. The second is slavery. Set during the yellow fever epidemic of 1793, *Arthur Mervyn* points to the economic ties that connected the new white republican North—its farming families, hardworking artisans, and bustling ports—to the horrors and guilt of plantation slavery. Third, *Arthur Mervyn* demonstrates how porous the new nation's borders were. America did not arise new and pure at its Atlantic shore but was deeply tied to the Caribbean and Africa— economically and morally. The story *Arthur Mervyn* tells did not begin in Philadelphia but in Guadeloupe and, even before Guadeloupe, in Africa. It ends with its virtuous European American hero setting sail for England to begin life anew with his wife, a wealthy and exotic Sephardic Jew. Where did the new Republic begin, *Arthur Mervyn* pointedly asks—and where will it end?

One of Brown's most contradictory works, *Arthur Mervyn* offers a bitter, somber critique of late-eighteenth-century capitalism. At the same time,

Arthur Mervyn constitutes its title character—and, through their identification with him, its readers—subject to and of that capitalist culture.[6] Concern for the general good, ethical business practices, morality, and honesty had no place within the world of commerce as Brown portrayed that world on the pages of *Arthur Mervyn*. Fraud and deception characterize every commercial venture. In the darkness of night, merchants plot to defraud one another; fraudulent bills of exchange are presented as real—or perhaps real ones are represented as forgeries (one never truly knows). Heiresses are seduced and abandoned, fortunes stolen, friendships betrayed, murders committed, bodies buried in crypts under imposing Philadelphia mansions. Self-interest reigns supreme. Hedonistic delight in opulent display drives all before it at the same time as insecurity haunts countinghouses and parlors.

Arthur Mervyn's initial view of Philadelphia tells all. Penniless and friendless, he has left his family's farm to seek his fortune in Philadelphia, confident that his inner moral rectitude, extensive reading, and fine penmanship will help him succeed. Arriving in the city at night, he is mesmerized by the glimmer of lights in the windows of the great town houses, by the lamps illuminating the great market on High Street, by the play of light and shadow that permits him to imagine what he cannot see. It seems that a fairyland has opened before him. "Night had fallen," he tells Dr. Stevens, his virtuous mentor and guide through the city's labyrinths,

> and a triple row of lamps presented a spectacle enchanting and new. My personal cares [his homelessness, his poverty] were . . . lost in the tumultuous sensations with which I was now engrossed. . . . I for a moment conceived myself transported to the hall "pendent with many a row of starry lamps and blazing crescents fed by naphtha and asphaltos." (27–28)

To his eyes, the city "wore the aspect of miracle or magic" (28). Its houses "were of gigantic loftiness" (34). Spacious gardens stretched behind them. The contrast between rural and urban life came quickly to his mind. "My father's dwelling" (a farmer who lived but a day's walk from Philadelphia), "did not equal the height of one story" of these mansions "and might be easily comprised in one fourth of those buildings which here were designed to accommodate the menials" (47). Mervyn soon discovered that magnificent appointments complemented exterior elegance. Misled by a false friend on his

---

6. Kafer, *Brown's Revolution*, 19, 28–32, discusses the religious and financial tribulations that marked and marred the career of Charles Brockden Brown's father, the failed Quaker merchant Elijah Brown.

first night in Philadelphia, he stumbled through a darkened home, finding what seemed to his rural eyes a treasure trove of glistening furniture and "brilliant hangings." "Curtains of a rich texture and glossy hues" encircled windows and beds. "Opulence" was everywhere (35). (Mervyn's description recalls John and Betsy Cadwalader's home with its extensive accommodations for slaves, carefully laid-out gardens, magnificent interiors, and "barbaric" bed hangings.)

But, where Mervyn discovered opulence, he also discovered fraud and villainy. Every contact Mervyn had with the world of commerce was riddled with deceit and ended in theft—be it of money, goods, or honor. On his very first morning away from his father's farm, he was cheated by a country innkeeper, who, laughing at Mervyn's bumpkin appearance, took his last penny for an unappetizing meal. Once in the city, Mervyn trusts an urbane young clerk, who then for sport deceives and abandons him to shame and possible imprisonment. He becomes the protégé of a great "nabob," whose vast fortune and luxurious lifestyle incited the envy of all and established his social preeminence but was initially stolen and then embellished through false impressions. In the darkness of night, Mervyn discovers that well-established merchants plot one another's financial ruin, never scrupling at the means or menials they employ to do so. Indeed, nothing was as it seemed. Wealth spoke not of industry but of deceit and embezzlement. Elegantly clothed ladies were revealed as prostitutes, great merchant princes as villainous rakes. How appropriate that the description Mervyn used when depicting his first impression of Philadelphia—his reference to a great hall "pendent with many a row of starry lamps and blazing crescents fed by naphtha and asphaltos"—was taken from John Milton's description of Satan's palace in Pandæmonium. Evil, the novel insists, lurks behind every scene in this modern Pandæmonium. How can the young develop a sense of self in a world so filled with deception and secrecy? How can one detect reality beneath the layered masks of masterful representation? *Arthur Mervyn* raises the very questions that bedeviled Philadelphia merchants and tradesmen on a daily basis—then adds a political one: Can republican virtue flourish in such a world?[7]

Underscoring the corruption and danger Mervyn describes as characterizing

7. John Milton, *Paradise Lost,* lines 726–729. As Fredrika J. Teute points out, Brown was early influenced by the radical philosophy of William Godwin, who stressed the importance of honesty and the evil that lurked within artificiality (Teute, "A 'Republic of Intellect': Conversation and Criticism among the Sexes in 1790s New York," in Philip Barnard, Mark L. Kamrath, and Stephen Shapiro, eds., *Revising Charles Brockden Brown: Culture, Politics, and Sexuality in the Early Republic* [Knoxville, 2004], 149–181).

commercial Philadelphia, Brown set his story during the 1793 yellow fever outbreak, possibly the most fatal epidemic to beset an eighteenth-century American city. Pestilence, like villainy, penetrated every section and stratum of the city. Twenty-five hundred died. Stores, churches, and schools closed as thousands upon thousands fled the capital. President Washington, Vice President Adams, and Secretary of State Jefferson retreated to the countryside, along with the rest of the Cabinet and all of Congress. Pennsylvania's governor, state legislature, and most municipal officials departed. The new Republic's capital was left ungoverned. Social and political order collapsed. The sick lay uncared for. Orphans were abandoned. Corpses, unburied, festered. The stench reached into every home and assaulted every nostril. But those who fled fared not much better than those who remained: many perished by the roadsides, as country dwellers barred their doors against those contaminated by their association with Philadelphia. A Hobbesean war of all-against-all replaced the optimism premised on John Locke's vision of the social contract. Courage and selfless devotion to the common good, those central republican virtues, evaporated. Brown uses the horrors of the yellow fever epidemic as an apt metaphor for the corruption self-interested capitalism brought to the new Republic. Such horrors frame our descent into this dark morass until, at the novel's darkest point, we come upon the specter of race.[8]

Commerce and yellow fever wove in and out of one another in the American imagination, choreographing a macabre dance of death with slaves serving as the spectral musicians. Popular wisdom saw yellow fever as but one more crop produced on the slave plantations of the Carolinas, Louisiana, and, especially, the Caribbean. Every summer and fall, America's cities waited to hear whether fever had again broken out in Kingston, Le Cap, New Orleans, or Charleston. If so, had it already stowed away in the holds of the ships that carried sugar, coffee, and rice north? Popular wisdom insisted that the fever bred at the doors of slave cabins and infested the crops slaves raised. The educated and elite, especially those most closely connected to the world of commerce, denounced this vision as the product of popular prejudice and ignorant superstition, none more forcefully than Benjamin Rush. But the mass of urban Americans believed that the fever was born on the wings of southern commerce. Whatever Brown's personal opinion, this is the vision that dominates his novel. It swirls

8. J. H. Powell, *Bring out Your Dead: The Great Plague of Yellow Fever in Philadelphia in 1793* (Philadelphia, 1993) offers the classic history and analysis of the epidemic. See also J. Worth Estes and Billy G. Smith, eds., *A Melancholy Scene of Devastation: The Public Response to the 1793 Philadelphia Yellow Fever Epidemic* (Philadelphia, 1997).

through key scenes of revelation and denouncement, suggesting that neither Mervyn nor the world he traversed could be understood without dealing with slavery's impact upon the new Republic. But we get ahead of our tale. To better understand the role race played in Brown's gothic vision of the new Republic, let us focus our analysis on the development of his central protagonist, the youthful Arthur Mervyn, long considered by literary critics the archetypal white American Adam.

In Brown's novel, Arthur Mervyn twice studies his reflection in a mirror. The first time occurs toward the beginning, shortly after Arthur, a barefoot and impoverished farm boy, is hired as an amanuensis by the merchant manqué and archtrickster Thomas Welbeck. Welbeck installs the bedazzled farm boy in his opulent mansion (one of the buildings that so impressed the gawky boy on his first arrival in Philadelphia) and dresses him in the latest European fashion, clothes Mervyn sees as magical, as transforming him into a new being.[9] Mervyn muses while staring at his reflection:

> Appearances are wonderfully influenced by dress. Check shirt, buttoned at the neck, an awkward fustian coat, check trowsers, and bare feet were now supplanted by linen and muslin, nankeen coat, striped with green, a white silk waistcoat, elegantly needle-wrought, casimer pantaloons, stockings of variegated silk, and shoes that in their softness, pliancy, and polished surface vied with sattin [sic]. I could scarcely forbear looking back to see whether the image in the glass, so well proportioned, so galant, and so graceful, did not belong to another. . . . Twenty minutes ago, . . . I was traversing that path a barefoot beggar; now I am thus. . . . Some magic that disdains the cumbrousness of nature's progress, has wrought this change. (51)

Introducing classic gothic tropes, Arthur continues,

> I have read of palaces and deserts which were subject to the dominions of spells. . . . Heaths vexed by a midnight storm may be changed into an hall of choral nymphs and regal banqueting; forest glades may give sudden place to colonnades and carnivals. . . . These miracles are contemptible when compared with that which placed me under this roof. (53–54)

9. We will later discover that these clothes had been stolen from the son of a Guadeloupe planter dying of yellow fever, part of the plunder Welbeck used to establish himself as a Philadelphia merchant prince. Sean X. Goudie calls them West Indian fashions (Goudie, "On the Origins of American Species: The West Indies, Classification, and the Emergence of Supremacist Consciousness in *Arthur Mervyn*," in Barnard, Kamrath, and Shapiro, eds., *Revising Charles Brockden Brown*, 60–87, esp. 69).

A knock on the door ends Arthur's entrancement with his new self. "I was roused from these doubts by a summons to breakfast, obsequiously delivered by a black servant" (51).

The second mirror scene occurs many chapters later, when a far less naive Arthur Mervyn, representing himself as a heroic exemplar of disinterested republican benevolence, returns to a Philadelphia now ravaged by yellow fever. His return, Mervyn tells his virtuous mentor Dr. Stevens, is motivated solely by altruism; he comes to rescue a young clerk he fears has been struck down by fever.[10] While moving through now-darkened mansions reeking of pestilence, Arthur discovers, stretched out upon a once-magnificently curtained bed, the hideous remains of a yellow fever victim. The corpse's face is "ghastly and livid"; "a vapour, noisome and contagious, hovered over him" (147). Horrified, Arthur turns away to discover the room filled with "traces of pillage," most particularly a cabinet broken open and ransacked. He suspects "some casual or mercenary attendant, had not only contributed to hasten the death of the patient, but had rifled his property and fled." At that moment, a sudden movement in a mirror catches Mervyn's eye. Behind his own white figure, he glimpses a lurking black form.

> One eye, a scar upon his cheek, a tawny skin, a form grotesquely mispropor-
> tioned, brawny as Hercules, and habited in livery, composed, as it were, the
> parts of one view. *To perceive, to fear, and to confront this apparition were
> blended into one sentiment.* I turned towards him with the swiftness of light-
> ening, but my speed was useless to my safety. A blow upon my temple was
> succeeded by an utter oblivion of thought and feeling. (148)

One can view these two mirror scenes as fictive pier glasses in which not only Arthur but Philadelphia's new urban male readers could see themselves transformed as the new gentlemen of fashion and respectability.[11] Certainly, the

10. Approximately 15 percent of Philadelphia's 45,000 inhabitants died from yellow fever between mid-August and the beginning of November. As the epidemic gathered force, another 20,000 fled the city. Anarchy reigned for some weeks until a voluntary group of merchants and doctors reestablished some degree of medical, social, and political order. For details, see Powell, *Bring out Your Dead,* and Martin S. Pernick, "Politics, Parties, and Pestilence: Epidemic Yellow Fever in Philadelphia and the Rise of the First Party System," *William and Mary Quarterly,* 3d Ser., XXIX (1972), 559–586.

11. The novel does offer numerous representations of genteel women's fashion, which presumably would have interested both women and men readers. Shortly after this first mirror scene, for example, the novel presents a vivid representation of the dress of an elegant urban lady, in the person of Welbeck's mistress, Clemenza Lodi. It also has Mervyn describe the appointments of

scenes evoke the Lacanian trope of the mirror as a key moment in the emergence of the individual as subject to language and ideology, a time when the infant, until then experiencing himself only as a series of disconnected body parts, looks into a mirror and first perceives himself as a unified figure.[12]

Arthur Mervyn's initial mirror scene invites the new urban reader first to vicariously participate with Arthur in his meticulously detailed dressing and then to gaze, as he gazes, self-absorbed, in the mirror. Some years earlier in America's economic development, the same reader might have seen himself as a fragmented part of an embryonic middle-class body (a leather-aproned artisan, an awkward farmer newly come to the city, a petty tradesman, a provincial merchant). Now, subject to and constituted by the new urban print culture, he could see himself re-formed in Arthur's transformation, like Arthur a well-proportioned, gallant, and graceful gentleman. Desire abetted this reformative process, desire for the luxurious goods in which Arthur Mervyn is garbed, the importation and marketing of which played a critical part in Philadelphia's expanding market economy. Sensual pleasure is there, too, in imagining the feel of silk and cashmere upon the body and in the fantasy of their possession. But so is the aura of unreality and of the magical, for it is with these that Brown repeatedly invests the scene. Might this sense of unreality be related to the speed with which America's urban economy and culture had been transformed? A decade earlier, many of Brown's readers might well have been struggling artisans, small-town tradesmen, or their wives and daughters. The capitalist ventures war and Independence made possible transformed many such men and women almost as suddenly as Welbeck's largesse had transformed Arthur. How many, then, like Mervyn, "could scarcely recognize any lineaments of my

---

Welbeck's house in elaborate detail: crystal decanters, Turkish carpets, velvet draperies, mahogany tables, etc.—quite enough to whet the imagination and desires of any number of male and female middle-class readers. It is equally important to remember, however, that only the most elite of Philadelphia's bourgeoisie could have afforded the clothing and appointments that Brown describes. These descriptions were teases, invitations into a fantasy world that Brown's readers knew they could never enter in fact.

12. See Jacques Lacan, *The Four Fundamental Concepts of Psycho-analysis*, ed. Jacques-Alain Miller, trans. Alan Sheridan, International Psycho-analytical Library, no. 106 (New York, 1977). "He" is the correct pronoun to use in summarizing Lacan's argument, since Lacan's theories deny subjectivity to women. Of course, Lacan is not without his critics. Stuart Hall points out that Lacan conceived of an isolated individual when he wrote of the mirror scene. But the child would not have been alone. A mother, nurse, or caretaker would have led the child to the mirror, interpreted the scene for him. The self, in short, is never without its defining Others (Stuart Hall, "Introduction: Who Needs 'Identity'?" in Hall and Paul Du Gay, eds., *Questions of Cultural Identity* [London, 1996]).

own" (51) in their newly acquired image as republican gentlemen? Examining the scene from yet another perspective, did Arthur's sense of his sudden affluence as unreal and unnatural mirror the new urban economy and culture's celebration of speculation and the spectacular?[13]

Recasting this Lacanian scene in Althusserian terms, one might say that, through such scenes, the city's popular print culture interpellated, constituted, its new readers as gentlemen, instructing them in correct manners, dress, virtues, and desires, setting them off and complementing them by the introduction of the shadowy figure of the obsequious black servant announcing breakfast. White waistcoat, black servant—here, indeed, we see a scene resplendent with a self-congratulatory sense of tranquility and social order. When the white man is in his waistcoat, all's right with the world.[14]

What a contrast the second mirror scene presents! Desire is replaced by danger, a young man's pleasurable fantasies by fears of pestilence and death, the morning sun by darkness and night. The novel's invocation of the "malignant pestilence" of yellow fever, its representation of a grotesque corpse and the merchant's ransacked cabinet, suggest that commerce brings not only linen and muslin to America's political and economic capital but pestilence, corruption, and death.

Strikingly different though they seem, these twinned mirror scenes, read together, reaffirm the new urban reader as a genteel, white bourgeois subject. In a true Bakhtinian manner, they counterpoise the classic male body of European philosophical thought and the grotesque body of the servant or peasant classes. The classic body, alluringly represented by the young Arthur, is free and in-

13. For a sophisticated description of America's late-eighteenth-century print culture, see Michael Warner, *The Letters of the Republic: Publications and the Public Sphere in Eighteenth-Century America* (Cambridge, Mass., 1990). See, as well, Thomas M. Doerflinger, *A Vigorous Spirit of Enterprise: Merchants and Economic Development in Revolutionary Philadelphia* (Chapel Hill, N.C., 1986).

14. For a discussion of the term "interpellate," see Louis Althusser, "Ideology and Ideological State Apparatuses," in Althusser, ed., *Essays on Ideology* (New York, 1976). "Tranquility" is the term Mervyn uses when thinking back to his feelings on that day. His memory is ironic, since he quickly loses the sense of tranquility Welbeck's wealthy lifestyle first inspired in him. One cannot help but note at this point that, as Arthur himself tells us, appearances render man a composite of his clothes, a rendering the rest of the novel will problematize but, in the end, with Arthur's marriage to a rich and urbane widow, reaffirm.

In late-eighteenth-century America, only the richest city houses boasted mirrors. For Arthur Mervyn to gaze at himself in a mirror meant that, in entering Welbeck's mansion, he had entered the self-referential, magical looking-glass world of genteel identity formation, a world in which reality and representation, endlessly refracting, seemed indistinguishable.

dependent, self-possessed, a unified, coherent whole, harmoniously propor-
tioned, graceful, white as marble, the forehead a very "temple" to reason and
romantic rhetoric. The figure of the servant, caught at the mirror's edge, is
"grotesquely misproportioned," its body crude and peasantlike, its face deformed. Far from appearing a well-proportioned, unified whole, it is "composed . . . of parts." The servile status of this dangerous figure is denoted by
his livery, which, in eighteenth-century Europe, signals a servant—but, in
eighteenth-century urban America, most commonly signifies a slave, an indication his "tawny" color affirms. Contrasting the white gallant to the servile
black, virtue to violence, benevolence to thievery, tranquillity to disease, and
social order to disorder, these two scenes work in tandem to confirm the new
white middle-class subject as the virtuous new American and the black man as
his hideous and threatening Other.[15]

AMERICAN SHADOWS

Toni Morrison argues, in her critical volume *Playing in the Dark,* that "the
literature of the United States has taken as its concern the architecture of a *new
white man.*" "The process of organizing American coherence through a distancing Africanism became the operative mode of a new cultural hegemony."
She continues, "Africanism [i.e., white figurations of African Americans and of
blackness] has become both a way of talking about and a way of policing
matters of class, . . . formations and exercises of power, . . . meditations on
ethics and accountability. Through the simple expedient of demonizing and
reifying the range of color on a palette, American Africanism makes it possible
to say and not say, to inscribe and erase, to escape and engage, to act out and act
on, to historicize and render timeless. It provides a way of contemplating chaos
and civilization, desire and fear, and a mechanism for testing the problems and
blessings of freedom."[16]

Read in this way, Brown's inscription of the tawny and grotesque apparition
in livery—and his association of that figure with violence, irresponsibility, and
crime—provided eighteenth-century northerners with "a way of talking about

15. M. M. Bakhtin, *Rabelais and His World,* trans. Helen Iswolsky (Cambridge, Mass., 1968).
See also Peter Stallybrass and Allon White, *The Politics and Poetics of Transgression* (Ithaca,
N.Y., 1986), esp. introduction, chap. 1. Recall discussions of gradual emancipation that characterized all the northern states, including Pennsylvania, in Chapter 7, above. Slavery was alive
and very evident in Philadelphia in the 1790s.

16. Toni Morrison, *Playing in the Dark: Whiteness and the Literary Imagination* (Cambridge,
Mass., 1992), 7–8, 14.

and a way of policing matters of class . . . power . . . ethics and accountability," a way to "inscribe and erase" the dark underbelly of Philadelphia's commercial and agricultural economy. The North's prosperity—although intimately tied to British and European markets and increasingly benefiting from trade expansion into southern Europe and the Mediterranean—continued, as we know, in the 1780s and 1790s to rest squarely upon its Caribbean trade. Philadelphia's provision merchants gathered the produce of Pennsylvania's farms and forests, shipped it on Philadelphia-made ships to the Caribbean, and brought back sugar and rum for quick profits plus badly needed specie and often questionable bills of exchange. Philadelphia's urbane merchants and bankers, her sturdy Quaker and German farmers, and her industrious artisan-manufacturers all served and benefited from one of the world's richest slave economies. What was true of Philadelphia and Pennsylvania was equally true of New York City and the agricultural areas tied to it—the family farms of New Jersey, Long Island, the Hudson Valley, and Connecticut. New England's prosperity was equally dependent on the plantation/slave economies of the Caribbean. Her fishermen supplied dried fish, her coopers, barrels, and her farmers, salted meats, along with cheaply manufactured shoes and textiles to clothe the slaves.[17]

We have seen, as well, how the eighteenth-century northern print culture constituted Benjamin Franklin, artisan-turned-statesman, as the virtuous white American—in the process valorizing free trade and free labor. Still, dark, servile figures shadow its urban white American, color its efforts to distance him from connections to and crimes against enslaved Africans. In this, eighteenth-century urban print culture was hardly unique. As Morrison reminds us, "The fabrication of an Africanist persona [by white America] is . . . an extraordinary meditation on the [white] self . . . an astonishing revelation of [white] longing, of terror, of perplexity, of shame, of magnanimity." "It requires hard work *not* to see this."[18]

Let us spend a few minutes working hard to see the role black figures and figurations of blackness played in making the new white middle-class American a contradictory and inherently unstable subject, first in our two mirror scenes and then, more generally, in Brown's complex novel. At first glance, these two scenes constitute an idealized bourgeois subject, invoking obsequious, dependent, grotesque, and dangerous blacks to reaffirm the new white American's coherence and virtue—along with the coherence of a social order based on

17. Doerflinger, *Vigorous Spirit of Enterprise,* 100–108.
18. Morrison, *Playing in the Dark,* 17.

a racist hierarchy. In the first scene, we see Arthur Mervyn, as the elegant young man of fashion, summoned to breakfast by a black servant, the juxtaposition of white master and black servant inscribing a racially based social order of tranquillity and peace. In the second, the selfless and brave white Arthur is struck down by the murderous black ruffian, a figure who, when coupled with the black pestilence, symbolizes social order endangered and in disarray.

If we reexamine these mirror scenes, however, we will find that race erases as well as inscribes social order, that black figures fuse with and thus multiply and fracture the hegemonically constructed white subject. The submissive black servant in the first scene suggests closure. He is not, however, the principal negative Other against which the new urbane Arthur takes form. Rather, new Arthur's true negative Other is the old Arthur, the impoverished, ill-clothed, and uncouth farm boy.[19] Embodying anything but the noble agrarian ideal, Arthur, as farm boy, is a barefoot beggar, dirty, hungry, and penniless. We also discover that he is the son of a Jukes-like rural family whose moral standing is widely questioned. The old Arthur's positioning in the first mirror scene closely parallels the positioning of the servant/slave in the second mirror scene. The one is "awkward," the other "misproportioned." Both are poor; both are unskilled. Both are economically dependent, Arthur on his master Thomas Welbeck's benevolence, the servant/slave, in his turn, on his own master's wealth. Nor do the parallels end there. Both Arthur and the black figure, by stealth and by night, take what does not belong to them. Just as Arthur discovers the slave ransacking the contents of his master's chest, so does he confess to Dr. Stevens that he also secretly entered Welbeck's home at night, took a fortune in bank notes, and then stole away through the city's darkened and diseased streets.[20] At another time, Mervyn admits, he helped Welbeck bury an innocent man Welbeck had just murdered, just as the monstrous black in the second mirror scene almost murdered Mervyn. Is *Arthur Mervyn* pointing to the sameness connecting black and white figures, not their differences? Thus we see a complex triangulation connecting the poor white farm boy, the tawny servant/slave, and the resplendent republican gentleman. The figures of the poor white farm boy and the liveried servant become twin pawns in a discursive dialectic that establishes the white bourgeois subject as the virtuous, true American.

19. If the new Arthur is the American Adam, dare we call the old Arthur the old Adam?

20. We should note that both houses in question are rented by transients, underscoring the instability of Philadelphia's commercial community—and not only during yellow fever summers. Again, see Doerflinger, *Vigorous Spirit of Enterprise,* esp. chap. 1.

The interchangeability of poor farm boy servant and black slave has significant class implications. Re-fusing social distinctions based on racial difference,
it threatens to color all those dispossessed or marginal to Philadelphia's emerging capitalist economy. Is this the real threat the gruesome black monster poses
to Arthur and rural European Americans generally—that the new commercial
and fiscal capitalist economy will make economically displaced rural whites and
blacks interchangeable in the role of urbane middle-class Americans' feared
and detested negative Others? Is this what lies behind Arthur's cry: "To perceive, to fear . . . this apparition . . . were . . . one sentiment"? Time and
again, the novel positions the rural poor as grotesque, denigrates them as
"clowns," "simpletons," and "rustic," in contrast to the urbane and educated
bourgeoisie. Even hardworking farming families are represented as living in
"wooden hovel[s]" (34), which contrast sadly to the "loftiness" of the mercantile elite's urban mansions. (Arthur's own rural family consists of a feeble-
minded, alcoholic father who dies in debtors' prison, a stepmother-turned-
prostitute, genetically defective siblings, and a sister who has a child out of
wedlock.) Only in the city, Arthur insists, can a man "strengthen [his] mind
and enlarge [his] knowledge" (296)—in short, emerge as a republican gentleman. Although Mervyn occasionally expresses Jeffersonian platitudes about
the elevating nature of country life, he never remains in the countryside longer
than is absolutely necessary. He is, indeed, one of the first American characters
to celebrate urban life.[21]

Disdaining the rural poor, Mervyn goes on to represent urban laborers as
unthinking and inhuman wretches, useful only when subject to discipline and
control exercised by their social and economic superiors. Those hired during
the yellow fever epidemic to care for the sick in the hastily set-up hospital at
Bush Hill (tellingly, a former country estate) "neglect their duty and consume
the cordials which are provided for the patients, in debauchery and riot" (173).
They are "bloated with malignity and drunkenness," "depraved." "The cause of
it was obvious." They were hirelings, that is, wage laborers. "The wretches
whom money could purchase were, of course, licentious and unprincipled;

21. The divided nature of American ideology in the late eighteenth century is underscored by
Brown's (and Arthur's) deeply conflicted attitude toward the city. Men cannot develop intellectually in the country, the novel tells us. Yet it represents the city as ridden with dishonesty,
disease, danger, and decay. Is this why the novel ends with Arthur planning to flee the new
world with his rich, dark, Jewish bride? But will that marriage help him escape the dangers
wealth and commerce pose?

superintended and controlled they might be useful instruments, but that super-intendence could not be bought" (176). The message is clear. Wage laborers, the new urban working class, if unsupervised, would descend into anarchy and depravity (just as proslavery advocates argued African Americans freed from slavery would). Supervised by a virtuous republican gentleman, however (Arthur himself), they could be made to be orderly, productive "instruments." Instruments are tools, critical to the production process. But they are not autonomous agents or self-directed producers. They are not political subjects. Arthur Mervyn, and, through him, Charles Brockden Brown, has positioned the urban wage laborer exactly as defenders of slavery positioned the enslaved African American laborer. Both the wage laborer and the slave are represented as undisciplined, depraved, and immoral, requiring control and superinten-dence, incapable of republican political subjectivity—not fully human. The core distinction of free labor from slave labor erodes before our eyes.

Rereading these two mirror scenes yet again, we find that they undermine racial distinctions and social order in even more threatening ways, ways that question distinctions between the new ambitious and would-be upwardly mo-bile urban middling classes and the enslaved African Americans they so fre-quently own. Carefully examined, the graceful Arthur Mervyn, newly em-ployed as a gentleman's amanuensis, well dressed and ambitious, is as much an economic dependent as the tawny servant/slave. Both wear their mas-ters' clothing, eat their masters' food, live as dependents within their masters' houses, remain at their masters' beck and call. Indeed, only a few pages after Arthur gazes so admiringly at himself, he agrees to submit to Welbeck's re-quirement that he tell no man about his past life but rather assume the persona Welbeck creates for him—just as enslaved African Americans assumed the names, personas, and pasts white slaveholders constituted for them. As Toby L. Ditz points out, it was an eighteenth-century truism that the servant, the apprentice, and the clerk all owed absolute loyalty and obedience to their masters—just as the slave did.[22]

A "fearful dream" Mervyn describes having as a consequence of being knocked unconscious by the black servant underscores this connection between Mervyn-as—would-be refined gentleman and the monstrous servant figure. "I conceived myself lying on the brink of a pit whose bottom the eye could not reach," Mervyn reports. "My hands and legs were fettered, so as to disable me

22. Ditz, "Secret Selves, Credible Persons: The Problematics of Trust and Public Display in the Writing of Eighteenth-Century Philadelphia Merchants," in St. George, ed., *Possible Pasts*, 219–242, esp. 229.

from resisting two grim and gigantic figures, who stooped to lift me. . . . Their purpose . . . was to cast me into this abyss. My terrors were unspeakable" (148). The figures in reality were fellow Philadelphians who, believing Mervyn one of the fever dead, were preparing to bury him. But the dream powerfully suggests the horrors of the African slave trade and the Middle Passage, a parallel made more telling by sensationalist descriptions of the capture and enslavement of white Americans during the Barbary conflicts of the 1790s, common in the newspapers of the time. The white man and the black man both were subject to enslavement. What did Brown intend by so graphically connecting not only the white and black laboring poor but white gentlemen and enslaved blacks?

If we extend our vision slightly beyond the frame of Brown's novel, we will see another telling parallel between Arthur and Philadelphia's African Americans. *Arthur Mervyn* is a novel about appearances and representations. Its convoluted plot revolves around the question, Can we believe Arthur's self-representations as virtuous and benevolent?[23] Appearances are against Arthur. As already noted, at the height of the yellow fever epidemic, the still-impoverished Arthur, hearing that Philadelphians are abandoning their homes, flies to town in secret and at night. He does not tell a soul that he is going—or where. Later, when challenged, he claims he went to search for and succor a youth he scarcely knows: the very man who had treated him cruelly his first night in Philadelphia as a penniless naïf. Once in Philadelphia, Mervyn wanders through empty houses and is detected carrying off a chest he does not own. He claims altruism alone drives him, that he risks his life to nurse the sick, rescue orphans left by the epidemic, and deter those who robbed and defrauded the innocent. In return for all his good services, Arthur continues, he took in recompense only what was offered as reward for the return of stolen money. He is, he repeatedly insists, a truly selfless, virtuous, indeed, heroic republican. His whole life has been a noble battle against tyranny and injustice (as embodied by his father) and immorality (as embodied by his licentious stepmother). A host of angry voices, however, accuse Arthur of wantonness, fraud, deception, and robbery. Indulged by a too-fond mother, Arthur grew up a lazy and irresponsible youth, according to his rural neighbors. Rather than aid his father in

---

23. *Arthur Mervyn* has, not surprisingly, attracted an extensive body of critical literature focusing on just this point. See, for example, Patrick Brancaccio, "Studied Ambiguities: Arthur Mervyn and the Problem of the Unreliable Narrator," *American Literature,* XLII (1970), 18–27; William Hedges, "Charles Brockden Brown and the Culture of Contradictions," *Early American Literature,* IX (1974), 107–142; Emory Elliott, "Narrative Unity and Moral Resolution in *Arthur Mervyn,*" in Bernard Rosenthal, ed., *Critical Essays on Charles Brockden Brown* (Boston, 1981).

working the farm, he lolled about reading books and dallying salaciously with servant girls. When rebuked, Arthur refused to reform but set off secretly for the city, abandoning his aging father. In the city, Arthur is accused of participating in a conspiracy to defraud honest businessmen. He admits to witnessing a murder, helping dispose of the body, aiding the murderer's escape, and reporting the crime to no one. When a penniless farmworker, he courted a respectable young girl, only to abandon her when she loses her fortune. He disappears at suspicious moments. We have only his own word that he is virtuous, hardworking, and honest.

A bitter conflict divided Philadelphians during the yellow fever epidemic: a number of prominent white citizens charged Philadelphia's African American community with profiteering from the disaster, charging exorbitant rates to nurse the poor and then neglecting them, robbing the dead, vandalizing white homes. These citizens' chief spokesman, republican politician and publisher Mathew Carey, printed the allegations in his widely read *Short Account of the Malignant Fever*. Asserting that he had "aimed at telling plain truths in plain language . . . had taken every precaution to arrive at the truth" and that "most of the facts mentioned have fallen under my own observation," Carey reported that "the vilest of the blacks . . . extorted two, three, four, and even five dollars a night for attendance [on the sick as nurses], which would have been well paid by a single dollar. Some of them were even detected in plundering the houses of the sick." Stating that "many men of affluent fortunes . . . have been abandoned to the care of a negro . . . [and] no money could procure proper attendance," Carey equated black nursing with abandonment to no or improper attendants. Philadelphia's African American community, Carey appears to argue, seized upon the epidemic as an opportunity to enrich themselves while white men, women, and children suffered and died. They exemplified the most selfish, corrupt aspects of the new capitalism—aspects hitherto associated with corrupt and price-gouging merchants such as Robert Morris.'[24]

African American leaders, the Reverends Richard Allen, founder of the

24. Matthew Carey, *A Short Account of the Malignant Fever, Lately Prevalent in Philadelphia* . . . (Philadelphia, 1794), v–vi, 31, 76–77. We must note, as well, that the African American nurses that Carey accuses of abandoning their patients and robbing the dead are represented in much the same way as Brown depicted the tawny, misproportioned grotesque whom Arthur Mervyn accuses of hastening his master's death and pillaging his room—or the way Mervyn represented degenerate white day laborers working in Philadelphia's pesthouse. How multiple and fragmented are Philadelphians' representations of African Americans! At one moment, they are positioned the way great and corrupt merchants are positioned; at the next moment, as free day laborers were.

PLATE SEVENTEEN *The Revd. Richard Allen.* Engraving by J. Boyd after a painting by Rembrandt Peale, 1823. Allen was the bishop of the first African Methodist Episcopal Church in the United States. The Library Company of Philadelphia

American Methodist Episcopal Church, and Absalom Jones, the first African American to be ordained an Episcopal minister, angrily denounced Carey's charges. In a pamphlet they published defending Philadelphia's African American community, they pointed out that, early in the epidemic, Carey had fled the city, seeking safety in the countryside. Not only had Carey failed to sacrifice his self-interest for the general good; contrary to his assertion, he had not been in a position to directly observe very much about the epidemic. They, on the other hand, had never left the city. Closely associated with Dr. Benjamin Rush in his efforts to combat the disease, they had worked day and night to aid fever victims and to prevent the city from descending into total chaos. Under Rush's close direction, they had organized African Americans' nursing efforts. Philadelphia's blacks, they asserted, guided by Christian benevolence and a heroic republican willingness to sacrifice their lives for the general good, had faced the epidemic head-on. Week after week, they had nursed the sick, cared for abandoned orphans, and detected—and attempted to stop—those who sought to rob and defraud the sick and the helpless. They alone had buried the dead. Many refused compensation for their services. Others took only what they were offered. Many, Jones and Allen among them, had spent liberally from their own small purses to purchase coffins, hire grave diggers, and provide for the sick and orphaned—and had never been repaid.[25]

Carey, in contrast, they charged, had profited considerably from the sale of his history of the epidemic. Carey never asked who remained to care for poor, black fever victims or those left widowed and orphaned. He seemed to assume that African Americans, as a "natural" servile class, should "naturally" have assumed the role of nurse and grave digger. His attack thus contained the ill-concealed assumption of a social hierarchy based on race and shadowed by slavery, a hierarchy reinscribed by Brown's counterpointing of the noble Arthur and the murderous black servant.

Yet, is not Arthur, asserting his innocence in the face of charges of exploitation and robbery, positioned precisely as Philadelphia's African Americans were positioned in the city's larger debate about how to perceive virtue and evaluate truth—and precisely as the second mirror scene positions the servant/slave?[26] Like the African American community, Mervyn was accused of laziness, wantonness, deception, and robbing the fever dead. Like them, he could only assert that his intentions had been virtuous and selfless. Both within

<hr>

25. Absalom Jones, Richard Allen, and Matthew Clarkson, *A Narrative of the Proceedings of the Black People, during the Late Awful Calamity in Philadelphia in the Year 1793* (Philadelphia, 1794). For a discussion of this controversy, see, again, Powell, *Bring out Your Dead*, 95–101. Carey's assumption that it was their duty to remain in Philadelphia throughout the epidemic in service to afflicted whites offended them deeply, as did his failure to note how many African Americans died aiding their fellow citizens.

26. Following Allen and Jones's argument, one might well conclude that the servant, finding Arthur in his master's bedroom, had assumed Arthur was a robber and struck out against him for his master's sake.

Painted by I. Pole.   Engraved by W.R.Jones & I. Boyd.

THE REV.ᵈ ABSALOM JONES,

Rector of S.ᵗ Thomas's African Episcopal Church

in the City of Philad.

PLATE EIGHTEEN *The Revd. Absalom Jones.* Jones was the pastor of St. Thomas's African
Episcopal Church in Philadelphia. The Library Company of Philadelphia. Courtesy of the
Mother Bethel Church

and without the novel, we find telling parallels between white and black Americans. As yellow fever swept through Philadelphia, racial distinctions became ever more uncertain, contradictory, and confused. Virtuous white middle-class men and ruffian blacks shadowed, indeed doubled, one another. Black Philadelphians would not stay reassuringly Other; boldly, they asserted their claims to republican virtue and hence their centrality to the new Republic and its national identity. Does this confusion help explain the bitter, angry tone of Carey's denunciations? The question arises, not from a sense of ahistorical superiority to Carey. Rather, it reflects one of *This Violent Empire*'s central contentions—that racist violence (rhetorical as well as literal) emerges, in part, at least, out of frustration with the repeated erosion of difference.

But, as we have begun to see, the novel did not only destabilize racial distinctions when the whites were poor and marginal. It also erased them when representing wealthy players in the production of a European American bourgeois economy and culture. Arthur's own master, the elegant, educated, and wealthy nabob Thomas Welbeck, was, in fact, not the master of his own fortune. Quite the contrary, the fashionable attire and lifestyle that proclaim Welbeck's elite status had been secured with money stolen from a man who died of yellow fever. The genteel Welbeck and the dark servant are thus joined in a brotherhood of thieves. Indeed, Welbeck's great wealth, which impresses not only the innocent Arthur but Philadelphia's entire commercial community, was, like so many Philadelphia fortunes, made in the sugar and slave economy of the Caribbean. It was blood money produced by the sale of Caribbean slaves. Indeed, the key moment, from which all the events that shaped Arthur Mervyn's life followed, occurred not in Philadelphia or its environs but in Guadeloupe.[27] Brown's gothic tale revolves around the sale of a plantation and its slaves in Guadeloupe—and the resulting bills of exchange. The plantation owner, an Italian named Lodi, had falsely promised to free one of his slaves; the slave, enraged, murdered him. Lodi's son came to Guadeloupe to claim the bills of exchange from the plantation sale and to find his sister, who disappeared following their father's murder. Believing she had traveled to the United States, the son set sail for Baltimore, but, like so many who left the Caribbean

27. Ironically, Guadeloupe was the first of France's Caribbean colonies to mount a successful slave revolt—and the first to be reenslaved by Napoleon. Of course it was the slave revolt in Saint-Domingue that electrified European American imaginations during the 1790s and early 1800s. For the slaves' revolt in Guadeloupe, see Laurent Dubois, *A Colony of Citizens: Revolution and Slave Emancipation in the French Caribbean, 1787–1804* (Chapel Hill, N.C., 2004). For a telling fictional account of slavery and the slave revolt in Guadeloupe, see Alejo Carpentier, *Explosion in a Cathedral,* trans. John Sturrock (Minneapolis, 2001).

A

NARRATIVE

OF THE

PROCEEDINGS

OF THE

BLACK PEOPLE,

DURING THE LATE

Awful Calamity in Philadelphia,

IN THE YEAR 1793:

AND

A REFUTATION

OF SOME

CENSURES,

Thrown upon them in some late Publications.

BY A. J. AND R. A.

PHILADELPHIA : PRINTED FOR THE AUTHORS,
BY *WILLIAM W. WOODWARD, AT FRANKLIN's HEAD,*
NO. 41, CHESNUT-STREET.

1794.

PLATE NINETEEN Title page of *A Narrative of the Proceedings of the Black People, during the Late Awful Calamity in Philadelphia, in the Year 1793* (Philadelphia, 1794). The Library Company of Philadelphia

that year, he carried yellow fever with him. He is discovered alone and dying by Welbeck, who is, at that point in his career, penniless and dishonored. The dying man begs Welbeck to find his sister, Clemenza, and entrusts Welbeck with the bills of exchange to give to her. Welbeck appropriates the money and sets sail for Philadelphia. It is this stolen money, raised by the sale of human lives, that so impresses Philadelphia's commercial community, securing for Welbeck a life of elegant respectability. The irony is, of course, that Welbeck is in no way unique. The world of Philadelphia commerce, fashion, and respectability is financed, in large part, by the provision trade to the slave economies of the Caribbean. The novel provokes the reader to wonder—how much greater is Welbeck's guilt than that of other merchants involved in the provision trade? That Welbeck proceeds to find and then seduce Lodi's daughter and install her as his mistress in the mansion her father's fortune made possible only complicates these matters further. Within the white Atlantic imaginaire, the French Antilles were renowned for their black courtesans. Does Clemenza Lodi's position as Welbeck's mistress parallel those (other) French Caribbean courtesans, just as Mervyn and Welbeck mirror liveried blacks? Nor can we forget that, in the eighteenth century, the term "commerce" referred not only to trade but to prostitution—still one more doubling of the legitimate and illegitimate. In all these ways, the novel repeatedly asks where thievery (illegal commerce) ends and commerce (legal thievery, but also illegal sex) begins. What self-image does the novel encourage its aspiring European American middle-class readers, female as well as male, to internalize and enact?

By shifting our gaze from Mervyn to Welbeck, we have broadened our initial examination of middle-class subjectivity to explore the novel's deep-seated fears about the dangers commercial and fiscal capitalism posed to civic virtue—and the ways in which *Arthur Mervyn* invokes the yellow fever epidemic to symbolize those dangers. In all the novel's shifts and turns, blackness shadows the way. In a novel in which not one of the many commercial or fiscal transactions represented is honest or productive, virtually all occur in the dark of night. It is then that merchants plot to defraud one another, seduce innocent women, rob, murder, and bury their prey in unmarked dungeon graves. And it is at night that virtually every one of the novel's numerous defrauding merchants is cut down painfully by yellow fever—in one case, carried screaming to the pesthouse; in another, nailed into his coffin while still alive.

Yellow fever literally embodied Philadelphia's commercial ties to the slave economies of the Caribbean. Coloring our understanding of the nature of America's commercial economy, yellow fever constitutes an apt symbol for the ways the moral blackness of slavery seeped into the whiteness of the new

Republic and the new republican citizen. Think for a moment what yellow fever does to white men's bodies: it turns their skin yellow or coffee-colored. It fills them with black bile, which the victims compulsively try to rid themselves of, cannot, and die. The stench that then surrounds their bodies recalls the odor racist writers such as Edward Long claimed enveloped the bodies of African slaves during the Middle Passage. Read with eyes informed by Morrison's essays, it would seem that yellow fever provided Charles Brockden Brown with "a way of contemplating chaos and civilization"—and of problematizing, at the very moment he appeared to consolidate, the coherence and the virtue of the white American subject.

DARK HAGS AND MALE INGENUES

If *Arthur Mervyn* undercuts the apparently clear distinctions between free and slave labor, unveiling the servile and base components of bourgeois subjectivity, it makes distinctions between the white man of commerce and the genteel white woman equally uncertain. Ostensibly, *Arthur Mervyn* establishes the genteel woman as sentimental, innocent, and benevolent, submissive to the guidance of fathers and lovers—her one secret weakness, her vulnerability to the seductions of deceitful men.[28] But, having constituted Arthur Mervyn as the ideal middle-class subject, the American-Adam-as-every-capitalist, the novel proceeds to represent Mervyn as equally sentimental, innocent, benevolent, and vulnerable to the seductions of deceitful men. Mervyn, after all, was as much a victim of Welbeck's seductions as Clemenza Lodi. And, like so many of the women in the novel, Arthur Mervyn is without economic resources—as much as they, dependent on the support of successful men (Welbeck, Dr. Stevens, farmer Hadwick).[29]

This positioning is reinforced by self-representations. Throughout the novel, Mervyn represents himself in stereotypically feminine terms, underscoring the feminine and sentimental aspects of bourgeois subjectivity. Mervyn tells us that his most enjoyable times are spent in domestic conversation with groups of women, in which he is the only man. Concerning one such experience, he reported to Dr. Stevens (a.k.a. Benjamin Rush, who, we must remember, had

28. Numerous innocent and respectable young women are seduced in the course of the novel. Clemenza Lodi is the most obvious one, but so are Arthur Mervyn's sister and the young merchant Watson's sister.

29. The novel underscores the parallels between Mervyn and Clemenza Lodi. Welbeck finds both penniless, offers each a home, fine clothing, and a genteel appearance—all at the price of promising to tell no person of their real pasts.

married the daughter of a salonnière and was known for his support of women's education), "This intercourse was strangely fascinating. My heart was buoyed up by a kind of intoxication. I now found myself exalted to my genial element, and began to taste the delights of existence. . . . The time flew swiftly away, and a fortnight passed almost before I was aware that a day had gone by" (391). On another occasion, he tells Dr. Stevens, "My mind is ennervated and feeble like my body." "I cannot look upon the sufferings of those I love without exquisite pain. I cannot steel my heart by the force of reason" (393). "I enjoy," he notes another time, "fond appellations, tones of mildness, solicitous attendance" (17). He concludes, "I am in that respect a mere woman." Not surprisingly, we are also told that he was his mother's favorite child and, when young, was dressed by his mother in girls' clothing.[30]

In contrast to this depiction of the American Adam, the novel's critically important women are represented as decisive and forceful, economically self-reliant, ambitious for knowledge and worldly experience. Eliza Hadwick, Mervyn's first romantic interest, turns on him when he patronizes her. He treats her as his intellectual and social inferior, she argues, solely because she is a woman. Angrily, Hadwick demands, "Have I not the same claims to be wise, and active, and courageous as you?" (296). Equally significant, the text leads the reader to side with Hadwick.

Arthur Mervyn's most powerful, autonomous, and sophisticated character, in fact, is not one of the cast of ambitious and deceitful merchants—or Mervyn himself. It is a woman. Literary critics represent Ascha Fielding, his future wife, as the archetypal Oedipal mother, "Mama" to the desiring and youthful Mervyn. As a result, they downplay her phallic, "masculine" characteristics— unwisely. Fielding, the novel tells us, is "independent of controul, and rich" (432). Possessed of impressive capital resources, she is master of her own fortune. She is, moreover, socially autonomous, unencumbered by children, worldly, highly educated, and conversant with European politics. She is bold, unconventional, and intrigued by risk—in short, manly. Embracing Fielding, Mervyn assumes the role not only of adoring son but of dependent and clinging ingenue.[31]

---

30. Mervyn's experiences might also have paralleled Brown's experiences when participating in discussions with members of New York's Friendly Club and its women associates. See Teute, "'Republic of Intellect,'" in Barnard, Kamrath, and Shapiro, eds., *Revising Charles Brockden Brown*, 149–181.

31. So much the master of her own estate is she that, early in his relation with her, Mervyn pleads with her to employ him as her philanthropic factor or agent—a plea she rejects. An independent woman, she informs Mervyn, she can manage her philanthropic endeavors on her own.

Subverting distinctions between women and men, Ascha Fielding at the same time subverts distinctions between black and white. *Arthur Mervyn* envelops Fielding with the mysteries of the Orient. When we first see her, she is "arrayed with voluptuous negligence," reclining at her ease in a seraglio on the outskirts of Philadelphia (318)! We know nothing of her origins. Indeed, on first meeting her, Mervyn cries out, "Who, where, what are you? . . . Tell me, I beseech you!" (321).

We soon learn that Ascha Fielding is that archetypal liminal figure who spans East and West, black and white, outsider and insider. She is a Jew. Her father, born in Portugal, moved to London, where he became a wealthy and well-respected merchant. Her Semitic nature, however, makes her an outsider, indeed, a grotesque. "She is a foreigner," the quintessential spokesman for bourgeois respectability, Dr. Stevens, tells Mervyn, "unsightly as a *night-hag*, tawney as a moor, the eye of a gypsey, low in stature, . . . [and with] less luxuriance than a charred log" (432). In eighteenth-century imagery, this is to represent her as unmistakably black. Indeed, Stevens represents Fielding in this way when urging Mervyn to marry her—which Mervyn joyously does. As a result, his life changes radically. Mervyn abandons his plans to study medicine with Dr. Stevens so that he can dedicate his life to the service of his fellow men. Instead, Mervyn now plans to accompany Fielding back to England, where her wealth will permit him to assume the life of a leisured gentleman. The fantasies inspired by Mervyn's first glimpse of Welbeck's elegant surroundings—that Mervyn would be adopted by a wealthy and cosmopolitan Philadelphian from whom he would inherit the riches that so impress him—will now be fulfilled. Wealth, stability, and respectability will be his. Arthur will reemerge in this his third incarnation, a fashionable London gentleman. Thus concludes the career of the early American Adam.

What a relentlessly destabilizing text! A novel designed to expose the corruption that lies at the heart of commercial capitalism, it ends with its virtuous republican hero erotically entwined in the arms of that racist epitome of corrupt commerce—the Jew. (Eighteenth-century writers, Ditz reminds us, considered Jews "the craftiest of all Men . . . modern Seducers . . . so subtle and inventive, that they would, if possible, extract Gold out of Ashes.")[32] Ascha

---

32. In "Secret Selves, Credible Personas," in St. George, ed., *Possible Pasts*, 219, Ditz quotes from Giovanni Paolo Marana's *Eight Volumes of Letters Writ by a Turkish Spy Who Liv'd Five and Forty Years Undiscover'd at Paris . . .*, 9th ed. (London, 1730), VI, 17. A set of the eight volumes, Ditz tells us, was among the first acquisitions made by the Library Company of Philadelphia. The Library Company was founded by Benjamin Franklin's Junto. It was a popular and well-used lending library in late-eighteenth-century Philadelphia.

Fielding's fusion of the white middle-class American man's defining Others (women, blacks, and Jews) requires us to recognize not only the white middle-class man's desire for and dependence upon his constituting Others but the interdependence of those Others. Only by tracing the novel's complex layerings of similarity and difference, desire and disdain, will we begin to detect the contradictions that repeatedly destabilized the republican gentleman as the embodiment of a virtuous American subject. As *Arthur Mervyn* rends the distinctions separating white from black, free from servile, male from female, it forces us to think of the new American not as a compilation of opposing dyads but as a complex triangulation of multiple shifting relationships and roles held together by an unstable fusion of dread and desire.

NOVEL DISRUPTIONS: NOBLE BLACKS, HEROIC WOMEN, AND THE U.S. DILEMMA

If greed, deception, and pestilence threw their dark shadows over Philadelphia's industrious streets, rupturing European Americans' identities as virtuous republican gentlemen, how much darker was the shade they cast when projected onto a Caribbean island in the midst of a slave-led revolution? As we have seen, plantation slavery both tempted and repelled urban readers—economically, ideologically, and morally. Especially since, in the years following the American Revolution, the dark realities of slavery were proving increasingly difficult to ignore and deny. Abolitionist sentiment was steadily growing in both Great Britain and the northern states. Widely circulated abolitionist tracts and memoirs detailed the ways chattel slavery exploited and dehumanized its victims at the same time as they represented slaveowners as deceitful, sadistic, and sexually unrestrained.[33] In the summer of 1791, these tensions came to a head as slaves in Guadeloupe and Saint-Domingue, claiming inspiration from the American and French Revolutions, rose up in violent rebellion. Burning plantation after plantation to the ground, gruesomely murdering their oppressors, they declared the end of slavery and their right to life, liberty, and the pursuit of happiness. The line had been drawn. Liberal and republican principles faced their ultimate challenge.

None were more sensitive to the fast flow of events in the French Antilles than the new Republic's urban commercial and manufacturing classes. Would they side with their long-standing trading partners? Or, as new republicans,

33. See, for example, Paul Edwards, ed., *Equiano's Travels: The Interesting Narrative of the Life of Olaudah Equiano or Gustavus Vassa, the African* (Portsmouth, N.H., 1969).

would they embrace the radical implications of their own Declaration of Independence? As we have seen, it was not only the European American economy that depended on plantation slavery for its prosperity. European Americans had built their identities around a racist dyad that contrasted whiteness, virtue, civility, and productivity to blackness, savagery, licentiousness, and sloth. Furthermore, in the aftermath of their own western uprisings (Shays's Rebellion, the Whiskey Rebellion, vigilante activity along the frontier), fear of disorder and violence haunted urban America and especially its commercial classes. To embrace the rights of slaves to freedom and self-governance struck at the very heart of European Americans' racialized sense of self and social order. On the other hand, to deny the right of cruelly exploited slaves to freedom and self-governance undercut European Americans' self-image as virtuous, liberty-loving republicans.

These challenges swirled around Philadelphia as Charles Brockden Brown wrote his gothic melodramas. They were the secrets that *Arthur Mervyn* darkly hinted at. And they were the secrets another melodrama, Leonora Sansay's *Zelica, the Creole* brought to full light. On the pages of Sansay's novel, slaves' valiant struggles for freedom and dignity contested with the horrors many European Americans imagined would follow their recognition of a free black Haiti as a sister republic.

Zelica poses two interrelated questions. Can slavery, economic and political, ever be justified, or, because based on the exercise of absolute power, does it corrupt absolutely? Do Africans have the ability to govern themselves and assume the role of virtuous republican citizenship? Progressive Europeans had asked this latter question about European Americans at the beginning of their Revolution, a question European Americans felt they had answered affirmatively. But was the Haitian Revolution a legitimate successor to the American Revolution? Were European Americans and Africans similarly endowed? The novel forces readers to explore the ways a slave economy not only dehumanizes the enslaved but thoroughly corrupts all that participate in that economy. It pointedly asks, Who has the right to freedom and the pursuit of happiness? Afro-Caribbean slaves? White women? Only propertied white men? In attempting to answer these questions, the novel interweaves the three eighteenth-century political discourses we have explored so extensively—classic and commercial republicanism and Enlightenment liberalism.

As in *Arthur Mervyn*, the answers *Zelica* presents are riddled with ambivalence. Differences, repeatedly asserted, as quickly evaporate. Issues of race became inseparable from issues of gender and sexuality. But *Zelica*, far more than *Arthur Mervyn*, uses sexuality to aggressively destabilize both race and gender. Systematically complicating what racism would make simple, *Zelica* decenters identities and renders political distinctions uncertain. It represents black Haitians as both valiant freedom fighters and bestial animals bent on the rape of white women. It depicts Saint-Domingue's white creole elite as sadistic sybarites exploiting enslaved Africans and as pathetic victims of black savagery. French soldiers appear as enlightened advocates of equality and as the economic and sexual oppressors of creoles and blacks alike. Boundaries blur, distinctions evaporate. The sadist fuses with the victim, black with white, male with female. Ambivalence clouds Sansay's voice, reflecting the challenge black men's demands for political equality and white women's for a public voice posed for the United States' revolutionary generation. (Significantly, black women appear an absent presence in *Zelica*, as they had been in so much eighteenth-century literature.)

Who was this woman who chose to project the contradictions and confusions of her times onto a slave uprising in the richest plantation slave colony in the world? At times, Leonora Sansay referred to herself as "A Lady of Philadelphia." She was the daughter of a well-known tavernkeeper in that Revolutionary city, her father's establishment lying across the street from the Pennsylvania State House, where America's Independence and the universal promises of its Declaration were first proclaimed. It was here, within earshot of strident Revolutionary debates, that the young Leonora grew up. By the 1790s, she aspired to a writing career and had become the mistress of Aaron Burr. During these same years, she watched the opening events of the slave uprising in Saint-Domingue and heard the tales expatriated creole planters told of bloodcurdling atrocities perpetrated by barbaric slaves. In 1800, as Burr prepared to be sworn in as vice president and Toussaint L'Ouverture cemented his control over Saint-Domingue, she married a creole merchant from Saint-Domingue, Louis Sansay, and moved to Cape François, where she remained through Napoleon's efforts to reestablish slavery on the island and the final black uprising that resulted in an independent black Haitian state. In 1806, she returned to the United States and her involvement with Burr.[34]

Zelica, the Creole was the second novel Sansay wrote about a revolution whose extremes she knew firsthand.[35] Although she did not publish *Zelica* until

34. See an earlier novel by Sansay, *Laura: By a Lady of Philadelphia* (Philadelphia, 1809). For a discussion of Sansay's life, see Phillip S. Lapsansky, "Afro-Americana: Rediscovering Leonora Sansay," *The Annual Report of the Library Company of Philadelphia for the Year 1992* (Philadelphia, 1993), 29–46.

35. As already noted, Sansay first explored the Haitian Revolution in a book she published in 1808, *Secret History; or, The Horrors of St. Domingo, in a Series of Letters, Written by a Lady at Cape*

1820, it was still a product of the United States' Revolutionary generation. Religious enthusiasm, increasingly characteristic of nineteenth-century women's novels, plays no role in its vision, and, although the horrors of slavery are detailed, unlike classic nineteenth-century abolitionist tracts, Sansay never deploys the rhetoric of pathos and the sympathies to discuss the plight of the enslaved. Focusing on Saint-Domingue as the site of revolutionary struggle, Sansay explores the pros and cons of the slaves' determined struggle for freedom, independence, and self-governance in rhetoric that is decidedly political. But, at the same time, she asks, In the face of the horrors slavery breeds, how can whites maintain their virtue, sense of social order, and, most fundamentally, a coherent white identity?

Zelica begins at one of the most critical moments in the Haitian Revolution. After years of war and violence, Saint-Domingue has settled down to a period of relative calm and productivity. The French National Assembly has abolished slavery, and Toussaint L'Ouverture's military victories have secured black control of the island. Desirous of reestablishing trade with the United States, especially in much-needed munitions, L'Ouverture has encouraged the planter class to return, with the result that white creoles, like Sansay's merchant husband, have reestablished themselves in Saint-Domingue.[36] Productivity is on the rise. Trade with the United States is flourishing. It is at this moment that Napoleon, having established his military dominance in Europe, sends his victorious armies to invade Saint-Domingue and reestablish French imperial domination and, with it, slavery. As the novel begins, the sails of French ships cover the Atlantic as far as the eye can see. Crying, "Liberty or death!" Toussaint L'Ouverture's troops join together in determined resistance (I, 8–9). For ten years, they have enjoyed "their dearly-acquired freedom" and are resolved never to relinquish it (I, 8–9). The novel presents the black revolutionaries as classic republican heroes, Spartan in their asceticism, Roman in their bravery and love of freedom. They "had emancipated themselves and broke by their own efforts the fetters of bondage." In the face of what appears to be inevitable defeat, they "dar[e] . . . to oppose their undisciplined courage to the bravery of well-appointed troops, . . . warriors who had arrested the flight of the Austrian Eagle,—subdued the descendants of the Caesars" (I, 3). Their "nerves . . .

François, to Colonel Burr, Late Vice-President of the United States, Principally during the Command of General Rochambeau (Philadelphia, 1808).

36. See, for example, Gordon S. Brown, *Toussaint's Clause: The Founding Fathers and the Haitian Revolution* (Jackson, Miss., 2005). See, as well, Laurent Dubois, *Avengers of the New World: The Story of the Haitian Revolution* (Cambridge, Mass., 2004); and Madison Smartt Bell, *Toussaint Louverture: A Biography* (New York, 2007).

strung to resistance by a bitter recollection of their sufferings, . . . [they] had sworn never again to submit to the yoke they had thrown off whilst one arm possessed strength to wield a sword, or one heart palpitated in a breast warmed with the love of freedom" (I, 23–24). As one of their leaders asks: "Were men, who had enjoyed the blessings of liberty to be again loaded with chains? Men, who had raised their heads in proud defiance to their oppressors, were they to be again bowed beneath the galling yoke!" (I, 112). With these words, *Zelica* links Saint-Domingue's brave revolutionaries to European American patriots at Bunker Hill and Valley Forge.

Throughout the novel, Sansay is unstinting in her praise of the revolutionary leader Toussaint L'Ouverture, whom she presents as the quintessential virtuous republican, relentless in battle, wise in peace, a Cato reborn, a second George Washington. His soul "glowed with purest love of liberty." His greatest desire is "to emancipate permanently the people of colour from the bonds of slavery, and to establish them in the rights of which they had been deprived" (I, 209–210). Like Washington, he is an inspiring leader of men, as wise in peace as he had been brave in war. Under his guidance, plantations have risen from the ashes, and society has re-formed in the cities. Hope, even gaiety, is in the air. None but he can govern Saint-Domingue and secure its peace and prosperity.

Zelica presents General Henri Christophe, commander of the troops at Cape François, as second only to L'Ouverture in his love of liberty and his embodiment of republican virtue. We are told that his was "the finest form that was ever molded by the hand of nature—the finest face that was ever animated by the power of expression, giving in every graceful movement indicators of the superior soul by which it is informed" (II, 197). When the French general Charles Le Clerc demands that Christophe bow to French authority, Christophe angrily responds, "If you employ the force with which you menace us, we will oppose to it all our energy. You will not enter our city till it is reduced to ashes; and, on its smoking ruins you will find us still combatting" (I, 7–8). It is said that, if he could have, he would have summoned his soldiers "to make with their bodies a rampart to oppose the entrance of the French in the Cape" (I, 14–15). A well-trained soldier used to exercising self-control, however, Christophe defers to L'Ouverture's command that they withdraw to a more defensible location and burn Le Cap to the ground. So committed is Cristophe that he begins the conflagration by putting his own home to the torch. "The people of colour," Christophe assures the French, "will never submit to the dominion of the Europeans, whilst a single arm retained power to resist it. . . . The war between them would be one of extermination and if the troops from Europe were destined to gain the ascendency in the island, their empire should be held over mountains of ashes moistened with blood" (I, 4). Christophe steps forth a classic republican hero who has pledged his life, his property, and his sacred honor to the defense of freedom.

The determination to resist re-enslavement inflamed not only Saint-Domingue's men but its women. Sansay puts the following words in the mouth of Toussaint L'Ouverture's wife: "These monsters [the French]," she declares, "will employ all means to reduce you to the slavery from which you have escaped. . . . To preserve your freedom, you have but one resource, and that is war—eternal war with white men. . . . Let your cry be ever, Liberty or death!" (I, 206–207), a cry that echoed Joseph Addison's canonical republican play, *Cato: A Tragedy,* and the Revolutionary rhetoric of Patrick Henry and Nathaniel Hall. In these myriad ways, *Zelica* links the United States' and Saint-Domingue's revolutions.

Or does it? Although the novel begins by boldly praising the martial valor and republican virtue of Saint-Domingue's black soldiers, it suddenly undercuts that image with a counter and far more powerful one, that of suffering (white) creole "ladies" inhumanely driven from their homes by these same determined black soldiers.[37] As smoke from burning homes rises in the background, the ladies, dressed in white, struggle up a steep hill, prodded on their way by black, bayonet-wielding revolutionaries. Pathos saturates this picture of innocent suffering. We watch women, "some bearing their children in their arms—some supporting the feeble steps of aged relatives, their feet . . . torn to pieces . . . their steps marked with blood." "These creatures who had been nursed in the softest folds of luxury, . . . now exposed without shelter, . . . suffered excruciating torture." "But," the novel hastens to tell us, "their physical pains were forgotten in the more exquisite anguish of their moral torments. Every heart was torn with anxiety for some object of its dearest affection; trembled for a father, a brother, a husband, or a son, from whom they had been severed" (I, 16–17). Callously, General Christophe orders his men to blow up munitions hidden in the mountain. The resultant scene resembles the horrors of hell. "The mountain was strewed with severed limbs, blackened bodies, and disfigured heads. . . . Groans of agony, cries of anguish, and shrieks of despair resounded on every side. . . . Nothing was left them but unavailing sorrow and impotent regret" (I, 20–21).

With the entrance of the suffering creole ladies, the text shifts radically. Dropping its critiques of European imperialism and the excesses of Caribbean

---

37. Sansay uses the term "creole" to refer to white natives of Saint-Domingue, not to Afro-Caribbeans. This usage is particularly important when analyzing *Zelica's* role in the novel.

slavery, *Zelica* becomes a sexualized melodrama that repositions heroic black republicans as brutes who abuse weak and defenseless women. Even worse, it sexualizes rebellious slaves, presenting them as lusting for white female flesh. General Christophe, that emblem of Spartan severity and courage, in an instant is transformed into a potential rapist, panting after a creole woman, "the fairest of the race that he had devoted to destruction, and whilst his imagination rioted among heaps of slain and scenes of devastation, it pointed as the reward of his toils to some distant tranquil bower . . . where . . . he should devote his life to . . . the object of his idolatry" (I, 22, 23).

Christophe's fictional second-in-command, General Glaude, doubles Christophe. Initially represented as a republican hero, "among the first to hail the dawn of freedom," he dares to love a white woman, Clara, the U.S.-born wife of a wealthy creole merchant. For this outrage, the novel turns Glaude into a "savage" before our eyes. We are shown him gazing at Clara "with the admiration of a savage for its idol" (I, 80). "He burned with the fury of a tiger panting for his prey" (I, 101–102). He dreams of rape, his brute power overwhelming Clara's resistance. The fair Clara's response is predictable. Although she initially lavished praise on General Glaude's military prowess and love for liberty and defended his right to oppose the French invasion, when she discovers that he loves and desires her, she is "overpowered by the chill of terror." "To consider herself as the object of an unhallowed passion,—to be loved by a half-civilized negro" "was appalling." "She shuddered at his name" (I, 148–149). Indeed, never again does Clara utter Glaude's name.

It is not only "fierce chieftains" that the text transfigures as "monsters" and "half-civilized," "ruthless barbarians" but Haitians generally. They are represented as "slaves" to the savage superstitions of vodun. They "danced their savage dances," "crept like serpents," "perched like apes" on treetops (I, 22, 75–76, III, 276). They "panted" for freedom. They are "beasts of prey," "tiger[s] raging for blood." Sadists, they "resolved to destroy every white person that remains on the island" (III, 189, 215). Never again does the novel represent them as sentient and rational participants in the public sphere, never as educated or engaged in productive labor. Though *Zelica* ends with Saint-Domingue's revolutionary soldiers triumphant and their European enemies routed, the novel refuses to ever again praise them for battling overwhelming odds for their freedom.

Even more significant, it represents black soldiers as obsessed by their lust for white women and those white women as nobly resisting the blacks' "unholy feelings" with the last breaths in their bodies. As black soldiers prevail and the French are forced to scramble to safety on waiting ships, former slaves run

PLATE TWENTY *Revenge Taken by the Black Army for Cruelties Practised on Them by the French.* From Marcus Rainsford, *An Historical Account of the Black Empire of Hayti* (London, 1805). Courtesy of the William L. Clements Library, University of Michigan

wildly through Le Cap, raping and murdering. Possessed by satanic fury, they hang their victims by their necks from meat hooks, skin them alive, dismember them.[38] All that they meet are "sacrificed to a raging thirst for blood, which, like that of the tiger, became insatiable, and increased in proportion to the number of victims it devoured" (III, 217). Our last vision of Cape François is of a city again in flames, its streets littered with the blackened and dismembered bodies of innocent white women and children. The final condemnation of such unrestrained black cruelty is put in the mouth of one of the novel's most radical figures, De la Riviere, a creole planter selflessly dedicated to the cause of black freedom. Calling the pillage of Le Cap a slaughter, he continues, "It is an act of cruelty that . . . has deformed the image of Liberty, for which we fought, and that will eternally stain the annals of these people" (III, 264). *Zelica*'s message seems clear: no matter how much they desired freedom, no matter how valiantly they fought for it, black men could govern neither themselves nor their island. They could lay no claim to virtuous republican citizenship. They were not true heirs of the magnificent European American revolution.

But no sooner does the novel make this point than it unmakes it. Every act of black savagery, violence, and lechery is doubled by comparable acts committed by Saint-Domingue's white inhabitants. In this way, *Zelica*, like *Arthur Mervyn*, makes complex what race would make simple. Two groups of whites hold center stage in *Zelica*—Saint-Domingue's planter elite and the invading French army, come to reestablish slavery by the sword. As we have seen, northern European Americans tended to view both groups (planters and foreign soldiers) with suspicion. Let us explore the ways *Zelica* undercuts its presentation of Saint-Domingue blacks as whites' defining Others by complicating its representation of white victimization.

In *Zelica*, Saint-Domingue's planter elite, far from resembling the hardworking merchants and innovative entrepreneurs of Philadelphia or Boston, violated every republican norm and most liberal ones. Living off the labor of slaves they cruelly "oppress[ed] . . . to supply their extravagant enjoyments," they were absolute sovereigns "ruling [those] slaves with undisputed sway" (I, 23, 225). The only thing the creole elite could not master was themselves. Reason, self-control, and concern for the general good, so celebrated by European American republicans, found few devotees among those who were

38. See, for example, Sansay, *Zelica*, III, 217–236. Interestingly, the novel presents us with only three black women—one, an ancient, witchlike character, terrifying and intensely loyal to her white owners; the second, erotically represented as an "ebony Venus de Milo"; the third, a beautiful young woman whose bearing marks her as the child of noble parents but whose enslavement is never questioned.

"slave[s] of furious and ungovernable passions." Among them, "the senses only governed,—mind, soul, feeling, were powers wholly unknown" (I, 226–227). What was true of creole men was equally true of creole women. Many of those "ladies" the novel initially presented to us as helpless victims of black savagery were later re-presented as more savage than those who prodded them along with sharpened bayonets. Jealous of their husbands' many concubines, they resorted to sadistic revenge. One plantation mistress, angered by her husband's affair with one of his slaves, went so far as to cut off the unhappy woman's head and serve it to her husband for dinner.[39]

Famed for their sadistic impulses, the creole elite were equally famous for pursuing libidinous self-indulgences. "We were . . . the spoiled children of Fortune," one creole woman reported. "Pleasures, ever varied, ever new, followed our steps.—Our lives had no pursuit but happiness." Beautiful beyond belief, adrift in a sea of delight, Saint-Domingue "was the island of Calypso" (I, 225). But, as every virtuous republican knew, Calypso was an island of enchantment and seduction. There, men abandoned reason, responsibility, and duty to become the playthings of an enchantress. The Saint-Domingue Sansay describes was ruled by a multitude of such enchantresses. "Creole ladies," the novel tells us, "were ever remarkable" for their "voluptuous beauty," "rendered [more] interesting by an air of languor. . . . Almost too indolent to pronounce their words, they spoke with a slow and hesitating accent that always pleased, for their chief study was to say nothing but what was agreeable." They were "goddess[es], to whose slightest wishes every will bowed in obedience" (I, 233–234).

Certainly, that is how Sansay presents the seductive Madame Senat: "extended on a sofa, attended by three beautiful slaves: one was disposing her luxuriant hair into a thousand tresses; another gently agitated the air with a fan of plumes; and a third, with hands softer than the cygnet's down, rubbed the ivory feet of the voluptuous creole: St. Louis [her creole lover and the husband of Clara, the woman General Glaude desired] . . . played with a chaplet of pearls that was twisted around her arm" (187). "Pleasure was the deity she had ever worshipped," Sansay explains; "in its pursuit alone she lived—her life had no other object. . . . [She] represents, in her own person, all the charms combined in a seraglio" (I, 56). The theme of Oriental lasciviousness and decadence suggested here is confirmed when St. Louis explains to a visiting French officer: "We creoles are mussulmans in faith, and allow no souls to our

39. This was a common trope in descriptions of West Indian slavery.

women. We live for pleasure only,—pleasures that succeed each other like waves of a summer sea" (I, 57).

How different is this picture of Madame Senat—indeed, of all those other languid "goddesses"—from Sansay's initial representation of creole women: the weeping, pathetic ladies driven from their homes by black ruffians. Certainly, Sansay could not have expected her European American women readers, who had lived through the austere days of their own Revolution, to feel great sympathy for these sybarites, especially since Sansay's representations of them mimic representations of Saint-Domingue's legendary quadroon courtesans. Her depictions of their luxurious and voluptuous lives become even more puzzling when we think that the descriptions had the potential of seducing her northern readers, rendering them, in their desires, indistinguishable from corrupt creoles and quadroon courtesans. Again we find ourselves ensnared in a tangled web of disdain and desire.

If *Zelica*'s representation of the creole elite erodes rather than confirms racial differences, what about her depiction of the forces sent to reimpose French imperial power in the Caribbean and to restore slavery—men initially represented as "warriors who had arrested the flight of the Austrian Eagle,—subdued the descendants of the Caesars?" Far from assuming the role of ardent and virtuous republican, the French exceed the creole elite in corrupt self-interest, violence, and lechery. The opening pages warn us that Napoleon's army is "accustomed to conquest" and possesses a "restless spirit" (I, 1–4). Officers and men alike are arrogant and avaricious, seeing in Saint-Domingue the easy conquest of untrained savages and "the promise of a rich harvest of gold to reward their toils in less propitious climes" (I, 4). From the first moment, they seize possession of the island's richest estates, lay ruinous taxes on the planters, and extort money on threat of instant execution. Their "avowed intention" is "to make a fortune . . . and return to France to spend it" (shades of Thomas Welbeck and of the Lodi family from whom he stole his fortune) (I, 214, II, 150–152, 221).

French sadism surpasses that of both creoles and blacks. The Vicomte de Noailles (whose ball had so charmed Philadelphians, including, presumably, Sansay, a decade earlier) imports bloodhounds from Cuba to hunt black soldiers in the hills, half-starving the animals so that they will not only kill but eat those they catch. French generals order captured black revolutionaries to be hacked to pieces or burned at the stake. Far from aspiring to transparent republican virtue, they use duplicity to capture L'Ouverture and deport him to France and to his death. With L'Ouverture's capture, Saint-Domingue

PLATE TWENTY-ONE *The Mode of Exterminating the Black Army as Practised by the French.*
From Rainsford, *An Historical Account of the Black Empire of Hayti.* Courtesy of the William L.
Clements Library, University of Michigan

dissolves into chaos. Violence reigns. Plantations are destroyed. The French
are pushed ever back toward their last base in Le Cap.

Rather than meet these challenges with military valor, the French sink into a
sybaritic morass. From their first sight of Saint-Domingue, French troops have
been "impatient to luxuriate in aromatic bowers, and to find in the smiles of
voluptuous beauty the reward of their toils" (I, 5). The officers are no different.
General Rochambeau is noted for his "splendid balls, and brilliant fêtes," but,

creoles note with growing concern, "he neglects the army, and oppresses the inhabitants" (III, 36–37). Instead of meeting the enemy in open combat as the war enters its final stage, Rochambeau retreats into the inner recesses of his palace, where he plots not military resistance but sexual conquests. And whom does he most desire? None other than the beautiful Clara. Indeed, the very fantasies General Glaude was condemned for indulging in—that he could carry off Clara and force his desires upon her—General Rochambeau literally attempts, first trying to abduct Clara (a plot Glaude thwarts) and then luring her into his palace at the very moment that the black army, led by Jean-Jacques Dessalines and Christophe, breach Le Cap's defenses. "Whilst the din of battle was assailing his ears; whilst the interests of the country, that would probably be destroyed . . . were at stake, he thought only of Clara; . . . of receiving her yielding heart . . . of overpower[ing] [her] resistance" (III, 99–100). Once again, *Zelica* collapses differences. General Glaude and General Rochambeau are the same under the skin, savages "burn[ing]with the fury of a tiger panting for his prey."

Certainly, if uncontrolled passion proves blacks incapable of self-governance and virtuous citizenship, it must do the same for Rochambeau and the French, an observation pointedly made by none other than General Christophe. As he watches the French army prepare to invade and reestablish slavery, he wonders how, "after having raised the banners of liberty in France" and abolished slavery in all their domains, the French "had become in their own land the slaves of a stranger, and crouched beneath the throne of a despot" (I, 25). Abandoning their revolution's high ideals, they are only too ready to deprive others of the freedom they no longer seek to defend. From the perspective of each of the political discourses that inspired the United States' revolution—classic republicanism, commercial republicanism, and liberalism—the French have proved themselves incapable of virtuous citizenship. By the novel's end, the true nature of Calypso's island is revealed. Far from a site of republican virtue, it is home to rapine, sadism, and chaos.

PASSIONATE REPUBLICANS

Does this mean that not even one honest republican remains on the island? In a dramatic shift of plot, the novel celebrates two: the beautiful Clara and the equally lovely Zelica, our title character. What a striking move—celebrating women as the only virtuous republicans in a novel deeply informed by classic republicanism, a political discourse that resolutely proclaimed women incapable of civic virtue.

What does this privileging of two women's republican virtue tell us about the multiple understandings of freedom and virtue that circulated around the Revolutionary Atlantic world—and the roles women could be imagined playing in that world? Let us start with Clara. An ardent U.S. patriot, Clara celebrates her native land's commitment to liberty and independence. Although the wife of a wealthy creole merchant in the world's richest slave economy, Clara, like all true republicans, abhors artifice and deception. She longs to return to the United States, where "personal liberty is sacred, and all rights of man respected" (I, 31). Contrasting the French to the American Revolution, she holds up George Washington as the only true embodiment of republican virtue. Indeed, on seeing portraits of Napoleon and other French generals, she responds: "My ideas of a man who was destined to be the deliverer of a country was formed on a model that I can never hope to see equalled. The hero of my country received from nature a form worthy of the soul that animated it—the dignity of an elevated mind—the majesty of a superior soul . . . the glory of the human race, the immortal Washington" (I, 152). It goes without saying that in her eyes Napoleon was no Washington. Certainly General Rochambeau was not.

Celebrating the valor of her country's founding fathers, Clara epitomizes the virtuous republican wife. Zelica, in contrast, epitomizes the classic virile and freedom-loving republican himself. She is the novel's only truly masterful character. It is she who understands and controls the movements of black and white armies, she who is able to thwart the plans of French generals and black "chiefs." All to one end: to protect Clara, the woman she has sworn to keep safe from every danger. Rochambeau and Glaude alike threaten Clara's virtue and liberty. Zelica is determined to preserve both. To that end, she stains her skin black, disguises herself as a slave, slips through enemy lines, infiltrates Rochambeau's inner citadel, and puts her own liberty and life in jeopardy, all to save Clara's freedom and safety. Toward the novel's end, aware of Dessalines's intent to massacre the creole population, she urges Clara to "fly from this land of death . . . from this abhorred country that has been the seat of every crime" (III, 189–190). Zelica's message, which is also *Zelica*'s message, which is also the message of classic republicanism and of the American Revolution, seems clear: where there is no freedom, there is no virtue, no honorable life.

Ah, but what is Zelica's definition of freedom? Zelica's embodiment of republican virtue is far more complex than her assumption of manly courage and determination. Her story draws us into a labyrinth of ideological, racial, and sexual ambiguities. Leading us to explore the ways patriarchal privilege underlay classic republicanism, it simultaneously forces us to reexamine liberalism's commitment to universal equality. Step by step, let us trace our way through this labyrinth.

Shortly after meeting Zelica, readers learn that she is the creole woman General Christophe loves, "the fairest of the race that he had devoted to destruction" (I, 22). This early reference, along with the novel's title, *Zelica, the Creole,* suggest a close tie between her and the lascivious Madame Senat. But, far from accurate, these suggestions point to a deep ambivalence lying at the heart of the novel. Though fair and beautiful as the radiant sun, Zelica is not white—at least not by U.S. standards. She is a quadroon; her mother, "but one degree removed from black," was a slave on her father's plantation (II, 138). "My father," Zelica explains to the amazed Clara late in their relationship, "captivated by her beauty, and won by her merit, had resolution enough to combat the prevailing prejudices of his country, and married her." But, Zelica admits, "This union, that formed his happiness, has devoted me to indefinable misery" (III, 125). Why? Because Zelica has an irrepressible aversion to blacks (and, we must presume, an even greater aversion to thinking of herself as black. Significantly, never once in the novel does Zelica refer to herself as black). While she was still a child, her father, De la Riviere, the radical creole whom we have already met, sent her to France to be educated as a white woman.[40] When she returns to Saint-Domingue, she finds herself repulsed by the very sight of blacks. "Though their advocate, I am not their admirer," she tells a French soldier. "Whilst I think that they have an indisputable right to the freedom that they are struggling to obtain, I feel an involuntary sensation of horror at the sight of a black, and never behold one without shuddering" (I, 84).[41] Here, simply stated, is the conundrum that lay at the heart of so much

40. It is interesting that the name Sansay chose for the father character is that of one of the centers of revolutionary insurgency, Grand Reviere, on the Artibonite River plain between Le Cap and Port-au-Prince.

41. Zelica's comments at a relatively early stage in the novel perfectly capture tension many European Americans experienced between their hesitancy to justify slavery and their fear of emancipated slaves, and in particular of slave uprisings. "How little are you acquainted with the character of the people you thus dispose of," she remarks. "They may be swept from the surface of the earth,—they may be overpowered by numbers and perish, but they will never be reduced to slavery. Their souls are fired by a love of liberty; their arms are nerved by a desire of vengeance—a desire cherished and nurtured in their hearts' closest folds, for wrongs that have pressed on them for ages. You may exterminate, but you will never conquer, them" (I, 84). Nevertheless, Zelica cannot bring herself to truly support them. Her feelings do not simply reflect European ambivalence. They also reflect the deep animosity that marked mulatto/black relations in Saint-Domingue. Although many mulattoes did support the revolution, some sided

European American thought—and of this novel. Slavery corrupted all whom it touched, slaveowner as well as slave. At the same time, blacks, unable to govern themselves, must be excluded from white society and the virtuous white state.

From Zelica's perspective, her father's errors do not end with manumitting and marrying her mother. Throughout his life, De la Riviere has worked to ameliorate the conditions of Saint-Domingue's slaves, supported the slave uprising from its inception, and embraced as his beloved friend one of its principal military leaders, Henri Christophe. As Zelica tells Clara, her father "idolizes Christophe . . . [and] talks with enthusiasm of his unspoiled energy, the ardour of his untaught feelings, and the native grandeur of his soul" (III, 204–205). While Zelica is still in France, De la Riviere reaffirms his support of the revolution both by bequeathing his plantation to Christophe and by offering Christophe his own daughter in marriage—a proposal Zelica refuses in revulsion. Pronouncing death preferable to marriage to a black man, Zelica proclaims the absurdity of the radical political espousal of racial mixture (even though she herself is its product). She denounces her father's patriarchal acts as "tyrannical." Repeatedly, Zelica accuses her father of exercising despotic power and of retuning her, his beloved daughter, to the state of slavery from which he had rescued her mother (and from which he would rescue all other inhabitants of Saint-Domingue). She also asserts her determination to give her life to avoid that enslavement. "My father, with a despotism more cruel than that he had so energetically opposed, had decided my fate," she explains to a horrified Clara. "My blood still curdles with horror when I think of the moment when this fate was announced to me" (III, 129–130, 203). Time and again, she repeats this complaint, reaffirming her righteous defiance of his decree—and always in the charged rhetoric of classic republicanism. "Why, my dear father . . . is your unfortunate daughter the only creature whom you would deprive of that freedom of choice which you say is the inherent right of every human being?" (II, 202). She tells Clara: "He has broke the chain that bound a people, yet despotically disposes of my hand; . . . he leaves his wretched daughter no choice between that most abhorred slavery, mental bondage—and death" (III, 202). "Death would be a thousand times preferable," she angrily proclaims, adding, "My father . . . does not even suspect, that his daughter, all soft, all submissive, as I appear to be, inherits from him his own energy, and that I will sacrifice my life to save my feelings from violation" (III, 130, 204–205).

---

with French conservatives at key moments in the revolution. L'Ouverture's bloody war against the mulatto general in the south, Rigaud, exemplifies this hostility at its most violent.

PLATE TWENTY-TWO *Dragon, (Haïti)*. N.a., n.d. Watercolor drawing. Depicted here is a
white image of a tattered black revolutionary pictured in front of a hovel and a palm tree.
Courtesy of the William L. Clements Library, University of Michigan

De la Riviere's insistence that Zelica marry Christophe, coupled with Zelica's passionate refusal, constitutes the emotional heart of the novel. Its significance requires careful analysis. Not surprisingly, given the troubling ambivalences that destabilize the plot, there are several ways to read their contestation. One returns us to De la Riviere's and Christophe's loving relationship. De la Riviere, aiding and abetting the black revolution, plays a critical role in the transfer of the right to govern Saint-Domingue from the white creole elite, of which he is a member, to the black military, represented by Christophe. In the process, these two men engage in what Gayle Rubin calls "the traffic in women": upon handing political governance to Christophe, De la Riviere seeks to seal the transfer by handing over his daughter as well.[42]

Carole Pateman argues that the Lockean social contract, the bedrock of the liberal political state, presumes a sexual contract that confirms women's political inferiority and, consequently, their exclusion from the social contract. Zelica's marriage contract with Christophe thus not only marks the transfer of political power from white to black men; it reaffirms women's social, sexual, and political subordination within liberal republics, be these women black or white. Zelica insists that it is the forced subordination of women to male governance that she resents—as much as she resents her forced sexual connection to a black man. At this point, we realize that hiding at the very heart of a classic republican text is the assertion of a radical liberal political argument. While both father and daughter condemn slavery and celebrate freedom, "slavery" and "freedom" mean very different things to each of them. De la Riviere, speaking the language of pure classic republicanism, demands that Zelica sacrifice her personal preferences in service of the slave's glorious struggle for freedom. Zelica, in contrast, defines freedom in private, domestic terms—the right of a woman, resisting patriarchal authority, to choose her own husband. Proclaiming De la Riviere's support of the revolution to be "madness" and Zelica's resistance to the marriage to be noble, the novel affirms Zelica's position. It thus shifts from being a republican to a liberal text. But it is a liberal text inherently critical of the misogyny that lay not only at the heart of classic republican texts but of social contract texts as well. And so the discursive confusion we saw emerge in the novel's depiction of both blacks and whites as failed republicans multiplies. In pitting republicanism and liberalism against one another and then problematizing liberalism, it multiplies and destabilizes

42. Gayle Rubin, "The Traffic in Women: Notes on the 'Political Economy' of Sex," in Rayna Reiter, ed., *Toward an Anthropology of Women* (New York, 1975).

the meanings of liberty and virtue. What implications does this hold for the fabrication of a coherent U.S. national identity?[43]

These multiple fusions and confusions bring us what may be the most puzzling of *Zelica*'s many conundrums. Why did Sansay make Zelica a quadroon? If the novel's goal is to use Zelica's refusal of Christophe to fashion a female voice independent and critical of the misogyny embedded in both classic republicanism and classic liberalism, would not Zelica's forced marriage to Christophe be even more effective were Zelica, like Clara, unambiguously white? Miscegenation, after all, was an anathema in nineteenth-century white America. Reading Zelica against the novel's depiction of Clara's America may offer a further clue to the book's many riddles. Clara's America, you may recall, is represented as a country "where personal liberty is sacred, and all the rights of man respected." Most obviously, this representation of America obscures the denial of suffrage both to white women and the large body of enslaved African Americans resident in the United States, whose personal as well as political liberty is not sacred and whose economic and sexual rights are not respected. Enslaved blacks are as effaced from this representation of America as Zelica's black blood is effaced by her fair skin. Furthermore, as enslaved African Americans inspired hatred, fear, and revulsion among European Americans, so Zelica, as we noted, hates the very sight of blacks on Saint-Domingue. But this second analogy leads us to pause. It positions Zelica in relation to blacks as European Americans are so positioned. But Zelica, as a quadroon, is not a European American. However, might she not stand, even more significantly, for the new United States itself? Fusing black and white and refusing to admit that fusion, does Zelica not embody the United States in its racial—and ideological—complexities? Is she not the dark secret that shadows the new Republic, the pestilence stalking Philadelphia's dark streets, that the United States' claim to racial purity always obscures the blackness without which American is not whole?

CLARA AND ZELICA ARE women who passionately love one another. Early in the novel, we watch as, shortly after meeting, they turn from all others to wander romantically through a "wilderness of flowers." "They appeared not to remember that there was another being in the universe" (I, 43–44, 46, 93). "There was a sympathy of thought and feeling between these two lovely females that united their souls," Sansay tells us. "This sympathy did not require

43. Carole Pateman, *The Sexual Contract* (Stanford, Calif., 1988).

the slow movement of time to call it forth; a look discovered, a glance imparted, it" (I, 93). "Pressing [Zelica] . . . to her bosom," Clara thenceforth "considered this fair Creole as a blessing sent from heaven. . . . She would take her to her house and be incapable of living without her" (I, 76). Zelica returns Clara's affection. Calling her "dearest Clara," Zelica pours forth her love. "My sweet, my best-loved friend," "you, whom above all creatures, I love and honour" (I, 172–173). From their first meeting, Zelica devotes herself to Clara's well-being. "To Clara, all her attention was directed. She attended to her with unremitting assiduity" (I, 46–47). Long and dangerous separations did nothing to modify their feelings. After one such separation, we learn that Zelica, whose heart was "fond" and "affectionate," "whose love was idolatry,—whose friendship was passion, sighed to behold again the object that had awakened all its fondness. . . . She threw her arms around Clara, and pressed her to a bosom in which her image was enshrined." Passionately, Zelica cries out: "With my heart's fondest affection, I love you." Clara responds with tears (I, 170, 172, 176–177). The erotic epicenter of the novel lies not in Madame Senat's boudoir or General Rochambeau's palatial headquarters but in the glances these women cast toward one another. In contrast to their love for each other, their feelings for their male lovers fade into insignificance. Zelica's French fiancé is a dark figure in a night sea; Clara's husband is unfaithful, self-indulgent, and foolish; their would-be rapists evoke only disgust and rage.

Why does the novel make Clara and Zelica lovers? What relation does their love bear to republican virtue? Their love could, of course, simply exemplify women's loving friendships that many believe were commonplace in eighteenth- and nineteenth-century societies. But their love plays too central a role in the plot to be unremarkable. Unquestionably, it inspires Zelica's heroism and resolve in defense of Clara's liberty. Of equal significance, their homoerotic passion echoes that found at the center of one of the classic republican texts of the Augustan period: Addison's *Cato: A Tragedy*.[44]

Cato was one of the eighteenth century's most influential and frequently performed plays. Initially published in London in 1713, it quickly became one of the most politically significant dramas of the century. Repeatedly staged throughout the colonies in the years leading to and following the American Revolution, its influence on Revolutionary rhetoric is easily traced. Patrick

44. See, for example, Carroll Smith-Rosenberg, "The Female World of Love and Ritual: Relations between Women in Nineteenth-Century America," *Signs*, I (1976), 1–30. This section has been strongly influenced by Julie K. Ellison's pathbreaking study of Augustan theater, *Cato's Tears and the Making of Anglo-American Emotion* (Chicago, 1999), esp. 23–73.

Henry's cry, "Give me liberty or give me death!" was lifted almost verbatim from *Cato,* as was Nathan Hale's regret that he had only one life to give for his country. George Washington imagined himself as the virtuous and freedom-loving Juba. Indeed, Julie K. Ellison tells us, *Cato* continued to inform U.S. political discourses into the nineteenth century.[45]

At the play's heart lies the intense love that Cato, the last virtuous Roman republican, and Juba, a Numidian prince, feel for one another. The youthful Juba has modeled his life upon Cato's. In the words of Cato's two sons, "Behold young Juba, the *Numidian* prince! / With how much care he forms himself to glory, / And breaks the fierceness of his native temper, / To copy out our father's bright example." Cato gives Juba the ultimate compliment, telling him, "Thou has a *Roman* soul," and adds, "Thy virtue, prince, has stood the test of fortune, / Like purest gold, that, tortur'd in the furnace, / Comes out more bright, and brings forth all its weight." Juba, reduced to tears, responds: "What shall I answer thee? my ravish'd heart / O'erflows with secret joy: I'd rather gain / Thy praise, O *Cato,* than *Numidia*'s empire."[46]

Obvious parallels exist between the love Cato and Juba feel and that of De la Riviere and Christophe. Again we find the older white man and the youthful black soldier united by their love of liberty and devotion to the common good. Ellison tells us that at the core of Augustan republicanism lay "passionate masculine affection," an intimacy of love and devotion that grew out of their joint "intellectual resistance" to tyranny and dedication to freedom. Seen as elevating and pure, this form of masculine affection formed the basis of classic republican social cohesion. Their mutual love strengthened each in his dedication to liberty, the republic, and the general good. There were, of course, critical differences between this form of Augustan affection and what we see in *Zelica.* Mutual male love in the Augustan period occurred between men of property, education, and leisure, that is, among virtuous gentlemen. Christophe might have been nature's nobleman—certainly De la Riviere saw him as such—but he was scarcely De la Riviere's equal in wealth or education. On the other hand, his military successes positioned him as one of the Revolution's leading generals. In that sense, his courage and skill in battle rendered him De la Riviere's equal, just as Juba's courage in battle and dedication to Rome had given him a "Roman soul." Black and white love of liberty fuse.[47]

But the novel has already declared the love between De la Riviere and

45. Ibid., 41, 68–69.
46. [Joseph] Addison, *Cato: A Tragedy* (1734; rpt. Boston, 1767), 17, 59.
47. Ellison, *Cato's Tears,* 41–46.

Christophe a form of "madness." Furthermore, their love occurs offstage. We never see De la Riviere and Christophe together, never hear them express their affection for one another. Theirs is not the connection *Zelica* focuses upon. Rather, it is Zelica and Clara's love that doubles that of Cato and Juba. White and black, they, too, echo *Cato*'s racial configuration, as their embrace of virtue and liberty equals that of Addison's heroes. What a revolutionary move, substituting two women for the canonical Cato and Juba! What a powerful assertion of women's right to membership in the new virtuous republican body politic, to a place in the new political agora!

But, again, in this novel it is not wise to draw hasty conclusions. Nothing is ever as its seems to be. We have already identified Zelica as more liberal than republican in her sentiments, having refused to place the black revolutionaries' struggle for liberty above her personal romantic inclinations. Her father pleads with her to devote her life to the cause of freedom, tells her how her union with Christophe will advance the cause. A virtuous republican woman would not have refused such a sacrifice. In *Cato*, two virtuous Roman women, Marcia and Lucia, willingly make that sacrifice. In contrast, Zelica goes so far as to express regret that, because of French military ineptitude, the moment has been lost: "The blacks could have been made to yield to any terms . . . [but] it is now over, and they will never treat with white men, unless acknowledged as equals" (III, 199). She is certain that an independent black Haiti will bring destruction and desolation in its train. Desperately, she longs to flee Saint-Domingue and remove to a country where riotous blacks will not menace her and she can live in wedded bliss. The new liberal subject, Zelica adjures the political arena and virtuous republican sentiments. She has retreated into the private sphere of domesticity, sentimentality, and love.

Examined carefully, Clara's claims to republican virtue also emerge as highly suspect. The novel presents her bedecked in rich fabrics and diamonds, "fluttering among the giddy throng, the gayest where all were gay, even to the verge of folly" (II, 225). Her home is "a temple of elegance," "fitted up with all that . . . splendour could devise" (I, 141). Despite the National Assembly's abolition of slavery throughout the French Empire in 1793, slaves still serve at Clara's beck and call. "Their soft voices lulled her to repose, as she sunk on the silken sofa in noon-day slumbers." They draw "the perfumed bath [that] awaited her awaking" (I, 141–142). This is scarcely the traditional image of a virtuous republican matron, the Spartan-like mother of the Gracchi, for example, whose children were her jewels, or, closer to home, the equally Spartan Abigail Adams, raising her children alone through a trying revolution. Clara's claims to republican virtue become ever more shaky as we learn that one of these soft-voiced slaves was the daughter of an African prince, torn as a child from home and family and thrust into servitude. Despite yearning to return to her own homeland, where "personal liberty is sacred and all rights of man respected," Clara does nothing to secure this woman's return to her homeland.

SANSAY'S NOVEL ADDRESSES TWO of the most critical issues of her day: the challenges slavery posed to those who so proudly proclaimed all men endowed with inalienable rights and the dangers many feared emancipation posed to orderly and virtuous republics. *Zelica*, however, is unable to resolve those issues, as it is equally unable to project a coherent political persona. Confusion and ambivalence permeate this novel. Zelica is and is not white. Blacks are and are not valiant. White women are and are not helpless innocents. Saint-Domingue is an orientalist paradise and a land of death and despair. In the end, it seems that Sansay is unable to master a single coherent narrative voice. At times, she assumes the militant tones of Toussaint L'Ouverture's wife; at other times, the angry voices of slaveowning creoles condemning French corruption and cowardice; at still other times, the voice of the classic republican condemning creoles for their voluptuous lifestyle and cruelty to their slaves.

In these ways, *Zelica* and *Arthur Mervyn* echo one another. Both novels are obsessed with what it means to be a virtuous American. Both propose protagonists who celebrate republican ideals of love of liberty, honesty, and dedication to the common good. Both then plunge these protagonists into the dilemmas economic changes pose to the moral and political values of the new Republic. Both explore the disconnect between the educated gentleman's (and the creole planter's) life of luxury and privilege and classic republican asceticism; between fiscal capitalism and the republican culture of transparency and selflessness; between fear of women's potential to corrupt and women's demands for a political voice within the public sphere. And, most critically, both underscore the discordance between the Declaration of Independence's promise of universal equality and the Constitution's protection of chattel slavery.

Not one of their protagonists emerges from this maelstrom of promises betrayed and disdain laced with desire unscarred, much less triumphant—not Arthur Mervyn, the poor farm boy who would be the leisured gentleman; not Clara, staunch republican slave mistress and gay *socialiste;* not De la Riviere, whose "mad" love of blacks and black liberty destroys his country (Saint-Domingue); not Zelica, the colored celebrant of personal liberty who shudders at the sight of blacks.

Depicting the tempests that swirl through the infant United States, their dark and melodramatic pages starkly represent the dilemmas the virtuous Republic could not solve—and that so hampered the production of a coherent national identity. Resolutely, they seek to solidify their protagonists' divided selves by projecting a series of dark and deceptive Others. Repeatedly, the differences between those Others and the novels' virtuous Americans meld into destabilizing sameness. It would appear that the print culture of late-eighteenth- and early-nineteenth-century America offered no clear resolution for the moral dilemmas the fusion of capitalism and republicanism, slave labor and free trade, black and white or male and female citizenship presented to the new American bourgeoisie—any more than the political magazines had been able to pose a coherent, unified American subject.

Conclusion

It is impossible to assign us with any exactitude to a specific human family. . . . The European has mingled with the American and with the African, and the African has mingled with the Indian and with the European. Born from the womb of a common mother, our fathers, different in origin and blood, are foreigners; all differ visibly in the epidermis, and this dissimilarity leaves marks of the greatest transcendence.

—SIMÓN BOLÍVAR, Congress of Angostura (1819)

The white population of the United States (diverse, but of common European origin) exterminated the aboriginal population and thrust the black population aside, thereby affording itself homogeneity in spite of diversity. . . . Monstrous racial criteria . . . have accompanied the United States from its beginnings.—ROBERTO FERNÁNDEZ RETAMAR, Letters to Caliban

Throughout our history, these two visions of the United States have attracted and challenged us. The first imagines America as a country in which diversity, equality, and inalienable political rights are celebrated. The second refers to the United States' dark history as a white man's republic, jealously guarding its borders, suspicious of any who would darken its racial heritage. The first envisions us as emblems of liberty; the second justifies our determined march across the American continent and, from there, to wherever we feel our national interest requires. It justifies, as well, the marginalization of all within our borders who do not fit an image of the true American grounded on rigid systems of exclusion and marginalization. The drive for external dominance is thus tied to the refusal to accept our internal diversity and equality.

These two visions of the United States exist in bitter opposition. Yet both have strong popular appeal that relies on the denial of their incompatibility. Many U.S. citizens feel that relinquishing either of these visions would betray our nation's true identity—and power. *This Violent Empire* traces the origins of

465

these dueling visions, our collective denial of their incompatibility, and the ways that denial destabilizes both visions and thus our national identity. Our insistence on our right to seize American land compromises our assertion that all men are created equal. At the same time, our celebration of universal rights calls our imperial ventures into question. The result is an inherently contradictory, unstable national identity never quite at peace with itself. This is what I think of as the "U.S. dilemma."

This Violent Empire has focused on these fundamental antagonisms and instabilities—and on the complex relation between such instability and the violence that has long been seen as a key component of our national culture and nationalist expressions. It takes as its point of departure the contention that national identities, although appearing to offer points of commonality and collective belonging, a sense of "history and ancestry held in common . . . [of] some common origin," in fact are grounded on systematic patterns of exclusion. They derive their sense of cohesion less from their celebration of sameness than from their construction of a series of threatening Others whose fabricated differences overshadow the actual differences and contradictions dividing heterogeneous nations. As Stuart Hall argues, "Identities can function as points of identification and attachment only *because* of their capacity to exclude . . . to render 'outside,' abjected. . . . The unity, the internal homogeneity, which the term identity treats as fundamental is not a natural but a constructed form of closure . . . constantly destabilized by what it leaves out." Those left out constitute the boundaries of our national belonging.[1]

Such boundaries were particularly important in the formation of the United States. Deeply divided along religious, ethnic, economic, and cultural lines, the founding generation (and, indeed, all subsequent generations) had no common history to "stabilize, to fix . . . [or to] guarantee an unchanging oneness or cultural belongingness." The new Republic came into being at a time of radical change and uncertainty, of imperial rupture, popular uprisings, and unforeseen futures. This was, after all, the Age of Revolution, when political and economic discourses multiplied, new roles developed, meanings expanded and fractured. New men and new women strode forth, deploying new discourses—and old discourses newly interpreted—to demand new rights. Using Thomas Jefferson's ringing phrases, African Americans challenged the moral and constitutional legitimacy of slavery. Socially and politically marginalized sailors, day laborers, and hill-town and frontier farmers turned their ire against eastern

1. Stuart Hall, "Introduction: Who Needs 'Identity'?" in Hall and Paul Du Gay, eds., *Questions of Cultural Identity* (London, 1996), 1–17, esp. 5.

elites in phrases that same elite had taught them. The most radical ideological disjunction of all was, of course, that between an Enlightenment embrace of freedom and human brotherhood and a growing acceptance of the tenets of scientific racism. Cut off by their own volition from reassuring membership in one of the world's most powerful empires and rich Enlightenment cultures, clinging to the edge of a largely unknown and savage continent, the founding generation existed between, and thus outside of, the Enlightenment's stabilizing categories of metropole and native, European and savage, civilized and wild.[2]

In many ways, we continue to do so. We claim to be Americans, but we do not merge our identity with those of other American nations. Instead, we claim a racialized distinction between ourselves and nations lying south of us. They are the Others that establish our continued identity as European Americans, that is, as racially (and culturally) like Europeans. At the same time, we claim that being braver, more self-reliant, and more independent than Europeans marks us as Americans. Claiming to be exceptional, we are a liminal, uncertain people.

With so contrary a sense of national identity, we anxiously guard the boundaries of our nation and our sense of self. Busily, we manufacture figures to mark those boundaries—all those who are not "white," as we understand the category; those who do not celebrate Christ, as we claim to understand him; the poor, poorly educated, and unpropertied; gays, lesbians, and transgendered persons. The list goes on. But, as we have seen, the differences that mark the boundaries between our Others and ourselves continually dissolve. Our dangerous doubles, our (m)others, in Simón Bolívar's terms, our (br)others around the Americas and the world, figures we simultaneously dread and desire, will not remain other, external to the nation, different. Refusing difference, they destabilize us. And we turn upon them with rhetorical and literal violence. Out of the uncertainty of our sense of national belonging, out of the contradictions that destabilize our national discourses and compromise our embrace of our Declaration of Independence, comes our penchant for violence, our need to punish the Others who will not help us resolve our national, our U.S., dilemma.

I do not contend that we have never enthusiastically embraced our better, more universalistic self. We often have—during Reconstruction, especially as expressed in the Louisiana Constitutional Convention of 1868; in decisions by the Warren Court; in the civil rights, women's, and gay movements; in the 2008 presidential election. For the most part, however, these are individual occasions

2. Ibid., 4.

that have led to bitter, violent reactions. They have brought some changes, but they have brought the nation little ideological stability or consensus. As we stand at the beginning of the twenty-first century, how different is the United States from the late-eighteenth-century infant republic that simultaneously celebrated itself as an infant empire? How different, more stable, more coherent is our national sense of self? Our ability to resolve our national dilemma?

INDEX

Adams, Abigail, 184, 341, 411, 462; and political issues, 136, 143; and Revolutionary War, 140, 141

Adams, John, 7, 16, 347, 352, 360, 420; and effeminacy, 58, 88; and Benjamin Franklin, 73; and farmers, 95; and citizenship, 97, 116; and women, 140, 141, 143, 150, 167; administration of, 144; and fashion, 320; and food, 341

Addison, Joseph: *Cato*, 60n, 446, 460–461, 462

Africa, 398, 401, 408, 409–410, 417

African Americans, 12, 16, 51, 89, 466; as Other, 42, 43, 364, 378, 388–410, 411; and reparations, 394–395, 396; freedom suits by, 395–396; and sameness, 401–402; and difference, 402–405; ambivalence toward, 406, 410; and women, 411; and Charles Brockden Brown, 416, 422, 424, 425, 429, 433, 435, 440, 441; and "Africanism," 425, 426; political subjectivity of, 429; and Philadelphia, 431–435; and slavery, 466. *See also* Slavery

Africans, 12, 33, 38, 53, 389, 406; and slavery, 393, 394; as commercial subjects, 397–398; and difference, 402–404; and orangutans, 403, 405, 406; and Hottentots, 403–405; trade with, 405, 408; as victims, 408–409; and Leonora Sansay, 442, 443

Allen, Richard, 26, 431–432, 433; *Narrative of the Proceedings of the Black People*, 433, 436

Allen, William, 327, 361

American Magazine, 28, 36, 54, 80, 133, 237, 367; "Affecting Anecdote of the Late Charles Churchill," 80–82; and political representatives, 121–128; and Native Americans, 235; and women, 381

American Museum, 36, 245, 367, 368, 371, 386, 387, 399; and Constitution, 28, 57, 58n; subscribers to, 30; publisher of, 36; and classic republicanism, 61, 62, 63; and commercial republicanism, 68; and liberalism, 75, 78; and Shays's Rebellion, 105, 107, 109n; and political representatives, 124; and women, 156, 159, 161, 163, 165, 385; "Manner of Living of the Inhabitants of Virginia," 399–400; "Address to the Heart," 406–407, 408; and slavery, 406–408; "Slave," 407–408

American Philosophical Society, 30, 71, 367

American Revolution, 38, 47, 48, 68, 106, 218, 223, 239, 276–277, 279, 281, 339–340, 442; and western farmers, 14, 100, 101, 103; repayment of debt from, 58; and classic republicanism, 64; and commercial republicanism, 70; and popular sovereignty, 88, 119–120; and voting rights, 90; and extra-parliamentary committees, 119; and women, 137–150, 162–163, 187; and commercial profit, 349–350; and Leonora Sansay, 443, 445, 449, 451, 454

Ames, Fisher, 93, 104, 105, 117

Antifederalists, 15, 59n, 70n, 84, 107, 352, 414; and popular sovereignty, 119; and political representatives, 120; and Mercy Otis Warren, 147, 149, 167; social vision of, 343, 344

Articles of Confederation, 28, 47, 56–57, 85, 92, 119

Ball, Joseph, 350n

Bankruptcy, 10, 55, 335, 339, 357, 371, 384

Banks, 98, 350, 351, 352, 357, 362, 391, 426

Bannaker's New-Jersey, Pennsylvania, Delaware, Maryland, and Virginia Almanac, or Ephemeris, 25

Barlow, Joel, 37, 47, 71–72, 73, 174; *Vision of Columbus,* 367

Battle of Fallen Timbers, 216, 219

Bayard, Nicholas, 333

Beekman, James, 323, 338, 352

Beekman, William, 336

Belinda (former slave), 394–395, 396, 401, 404, 405, 408–409

Bingham, Anne Willing, 144, 184–186, 342, 344–346, 357, 359, 379, 411

Bingham, Thomas, 144

Bingham, William, 30, 89, 345, 347–349, 350n, 351–353, 356n

Black Legend, 281, 283

Blackness, 413, 414, 415, 442; and Charles Brockden Brown, 424, 426, 427, 428, 437; and Leonora Sansay, 459

Blacks: and Charles Brockden Brown, 417, 418, 419, 422, 425; and Leonora Sansay, 442, 443, 444, 446, 447, 449, 450, 451, 453, 454, 455, 456, 458, 459, 461, 462, 463. *See also* African Americans

Bland, Martha Dangerfield, 340

Blunt, Titus, 382–383

Body, 154, 162, 164, 180, 181, 247, 260; and Mary Rowlandson, 260–261, 264–265; and gentlemen, 310; and slavery, 393; and African Americans, 402–405; and Charles Brockden Brown, 422, 423, 424–425, 438

Boone, Daniel, 200n, 222, 267

Bourgeoisie, 15, 16, 17, 32–36, 57, 296, 320; and magazines, 27, 30, 38, 374, 377; and *Massachusetts Magazine,* 29; and novel, 40; and Native Americans, 42, 222; and Timothy Dwight, 50, 52; and classic republicanism, 64–66; and frontier, 70–71; and private property, 78; criticism of, 90; and western farmers, 91, 96, 100; and Shays's Rebellion, 105, 108, 110, 111, 112; and popular sovereignty, 116; and women, 134, 140, 143, 152–153, 163, 165, 324; and masculine systems, 150; and novel of seduction, 169; and

Hannah Foster, 183, 186; and republican court, 185; and western frontier, 220; and display, 235; and Pocahontas, 242; and Charles Brockden Brown, 277, 416, 422n, 424, 426, 428, 435, 438, 440; and Susanna Rowson, 284, 285, 286–287; and Benjamin Rush, 295, 296, 301–302; and national identity, 298–299, 376; and postcolonial anxiety, 303; and international respectability, 304; and social performance, 306; British, 310; and British gentleman, 315, 316; and American gentlemen, 319; and gentility, 319, 333, 334–335, 363; creole, 322; postcolonial, 340, 341, 353; and postcolonial financial crises, 357; and Protestant work ethic, 375; northern, 410

Boycott, 23, 94, 137–138, 139

Boylston, Nicholas, 320, 328n

Boylston, Thomas, 140

Bozarth, Elizabeth, 232, 267

Brackenridge, Hugh Henry, 28

Brontë, Charlotte: *Jane Eyre,* 250

Brown, Charles Brockden, 16–17, 39n, 41n, 215, 343, 367, 374n; *Arthur Mervyn,* 42, 416–442, 449, 463; *Edgar Huntly,* 42, 253, 268–280; and Susanna Rowson, 281, 282, 283; and gothic novel, 413–414

Buffon, Count de, 399

Bulfinch, Charles, 345

Burke, Edmund, 59

Burr, Aaron, 174, 378n, 390, 415, 443

Byrd, William, II, 241, 305

Byrd, William, III, 399

Byrd family, 319

Cadwalader, Anne, 321

Cadwalader, Elizabeth Wye, 321–322, 338, 390, 419

Cadwalader, John, 321–322, 328n, 336, 390, 419

Capitalism, 8, 65, 172, 183, 316, 348, 431; venture, 14, 130, 172, 209; commercial, 65, 332; and commercial republicanism, 71; and liberalism, 78; and western farmers, 103; and western frontier, 209; and Charles

Brockden Brown, 270, 416, 417–418, 420, 423, 428, 438, 440; and postcolonial elite, 358; and self-knowledge, 360
—fiscal, 14, 15, 18, 27, 65, 113, 332; and political magazines, 38; and western farmers, 99, 103; and citizenship, 113–114; and republican authority, 128–133; and Hannah Foster, 174, 178; denunciations of, 235; and postcolonial elite, 348–353; dangers of, 386; unease with, 414–415; and Charles Brockden Brown, 417, 428, 437, 463

Captivity narrative, 42; Native Americans in, 195, 222–233, 237, 248; and Mary Rowlandson, 251, 252, 254, 257, 258, 266, 267; and Charles Brockden Brown, 272; and Susanna Rowson, 281, 284, 286

Carey, Mathew, 75, 220, 272, 367, 387, 397; and press, 28, 30, 31; background of, 36; and commercial republicanism, 67, 68; and liberal citizen, 78; and women, 159–161, 163, 165–166; "Speech of Miss Polly Baker," 162–163; "Plan for the Establishment of a Fair of Fairs, or Market of Matrimony," 163; "On the Fear of Mad Dogs," 166; *Affecting History of the Dreadful Distresses of Frederic Manheim's Family*, 223, 226–227, 230–233; and Native Americans, 235, 247, 248–249; and education, 368; and slavery, 394–395, 401, 405, 408; and African Americans, 417; *Short Account of the Malignant Fever*, 431–433, 435

Caribbean, 9, 333, 340, 347, 349, 391, 420; and commerce, 373, 426; and Charles Brockden Brown, 417, 435, 437; and Leonora Sansay, 441

Carleton, Guy, 106

Charvet, Jean Gabriel: "Wallpaper Depicting Captain John Cook," 342

Chastellux, Marquis de, 341, 344, 348; *Travels in North America*, 399–400, 405, 407, 410

Chesterfield, Lord, 359

Churchman, George, 215, 277n

Citizen/citizenship, 94–96, 120–135, 138, 161, 163, 168, 169, 186–187, 438; rights of, 4, 38, 88; debate over, 8, 88–91; and identity, 10;

and need for nation, 18; and bourgeoisie, 33–34; and Others, 41, 87; republican, 41; and Timothy Dwight, 48–52; and property, 49, 63–70, 76–79, 89; and virility, 49, 60–62, 136; as *zoon politikon*, 49, 50, 60, 77, 78, 80, 85, 134, 151, 312, 358, 359; divergent views of, 59; and classic republicanism, 59–64, 360; and British gentry, 65; and fiscal capitalism, 65, 113–114; and British classic republicanism, 65–66, 69; and commercial republicanism, 66–74; and liberalism, 74–82; contrary view of, 82; and manliness, 85–86; and consent, 86, 89, 122, 132; as independent, educated, and cultured, 86; inclusion in, 88; and western farmers, 97, 100–103; and Isaiah Thomas, 102; and Shays's Rebellion, 105, 106, 110; and political representation, 112, 113, 122, 123–124, 125, 126, 128, 131, 133, 134; and sovereignty, 113, 122, 126; competency of, 116–118; and women, 140, 150–155, 167, 170, 187; and Abigail Adams, 143; and Native Americans, 207–208; John Corbly as, 231; and Benjamin Rush, 296; and confidence men, 358; and gentility, 360; and gentlemen, 378; and slavery, 388, 389, 393; and Leonora Sansay, 442, 449, 453, 461. *See also* Women: political subjectivity of

City, 34–35, 374; and Charles Brockden Brown, 418, 420, 424, 428, 431. *See also* New York City; Philadelphia

Clarkson, Matthew: *Narrative of the Proceedings of the Black People*, 436

Class, 15, 31–36, 42, 193, 242, 309–357, 368–377; and liberal subject, 76–77; and Shays's Rebellion, 106–110; and women, 152–153, 174–186, 321–327, 330–331, 340–346, 369–372, 378–380, 382–387; and Mathew Carey, 161; and Hannah Foster, 172–183, 185–186; and Native Americans, 197; and western frontier, 214–216, 368; and Charles Brockden Brown, 268–270, 275–276, 415, 417–418, 426, 428–429; and identity, 268n; and Benjamin Rush, 292–308, 338; and republican gentlemen, 304; and education,

368; and "Letter from Maria to Eliza," 369–372; and magazines, 375, 380; and consumerism, 379; in Virginia, 400

Classic republicanism, 18, 42, 58, 62, 284, 353; and Timothy Dwight, 49, 50; and virtue, 60–62, 64–65, 68–69, 73, 152–153, 170, 178, 180–181, 183, 339, 442, 444–446, 453; image of, 60–66; British, 64–66; and homogeneity, 65; and commercial republicanism, 68, 86; and Benjamin Franklin, 72, 73; and liberalism, 75, 77, 78–79, 81–82, 84; and manliness, 86; and western farmers, 99n, 100, 101, 103; and Shays's Rebellion, 109, 110; and representation, 112; and fiscal capitalism, 113, 235, 414; and Federalists, 128, 134; and service, 128; and commercial and fiscal actors, 129; and women, 150–152, 153, 170–171, 378, 380, 382, 383, 384; and Hannah Foster, 177, 179, 182, 186; and Native Americans, 201; and Susanna Rowson, 284; and gentility, 305, 311, 358–360, 361; and Robert Morris, 348, 355; and nostalgia, 360; social elitism of, 371; and consumer economy, 388; and Leonora Sansay, 442, 444, 446, 453, 454, 456, 458, 459, 460, 462–463; and Joseph Addison, 461; and Charles Brockden Brown, 463

Clinton, George, 343, 390

Clothes, 145, 153, 293, 295, 303, 312, 344; and Shays's Rebellion, 107–112; and western frontier, 213; and postcolonial anxiety, 303; and British gentleman, 313, 315; and portraiture, 329; and magazines, 377; and slavery, 391; and Charles Brockden Brown, 419, 421, 423, 425. *See also* Fashion

Clymer, George, 142

Coffeehouses, 30, 35, 59, 131, 314, 336, 362

Colden, Cadwallader, 32–33

Coleman, Benjamin, 393–394

College of Philadelphia, 71

Columbian Magazine, 28, 75, 77, 234, 246, 376, 405; publishers of, 37, 63; and Shays's Rebellion, 106; and political representation, 118; and romance, 371; and slavery, 397, 398, 401, 409–410, 411; "Observations on the Gradation in the Scale of Being between the Human and Brute Creation," 402–404

Commerce, 15, 30, 55, 58, 131, 134; and Britain, 8, 66, 312, 313, 315, 373; and farmers, 9, 10, 15, 98, 99, 103, 415; and consumerism, 9–10, 379; and East Coast, 14; and bourgeoisie, 31–34; and classic republicanism, 61, 359; and commercial republicanism, 67, 68; and Benjamin Franklin, 70, 387; and Shays's Rebellion, 92, 94, 108, 109, 110; and Isaiah Thomas, 101, 102; and satire, 111; and representation, 113; and popular sovereignty, 119; and Federalists, 128; and Native Americans, 201; and western frontier, 209, 211–212, 215; and agriculture, 215, 270; and Charles Brockden Brown, 270, 417, 418, 419, 420, 423, 424, 426, 428, 435, 437, 438, 440; and gentility, 305, 306, 311, 332, 333, 335, 336, 359, 360–362, 380; and Philadelphia, 321; and American Revolution, 340; postcolonial, 347, 353, 371–372; and wartime profits, 348–350; and Robert Morris, 351, 355; and magazines, 367, 372–377; as lifeblood of Republic, 373; as uncertain, 374; and women, 380, 384–385; and slavery, 390–392; and violence, 442. *See also* Merchants

Commercial republicanism, 58, 66–74, 81, 86, 128, 388, 405, 411; and Timothy Dwight, 49, 50; and corruption, 68; and Benjamin Franklin, 70–74; and liberalism, 75, 79, 82; and private economic sphere, 79; and Shays's Rebellion, 109; ideological contradictions of, 152–153; and women, 152–153, 378, 383, 386, 411; and Hannah Foster, 172–187; and gentility, 358, 360–363; and fiscal capitalism, 414; and Leonora Sansay, 442, 453

Commonwealth v. Jennison, 396

Constitutional Convention, 28, 30, 54, 57, 127, 352

Constitution of the United States, 27, 28, 34, 59, 129, 347, 414; ratification of, 4, 77; and Noah Webster, 54; and western farmers, 104; and Shays's Rebellion, 105; debates

over, 116; sovereign authority of, 119; and
women, 155, 380; and Native Americans,
196; and slavery, 392, 416

Consumerism, 303; and colonial America, 8–
10; and demographic differences, 14, 15;
and Charles Brockden Brown, 42n, 416;
and private property, 78; and women, 152,
170, 378–379, 380, 384, 386, 387, 388; and
Hannah Foster, 184, 186; and Native
Americans, 201; and gentility, 312, 329, 332,
360, 374; and British gentleman, 315, 316,
318; and colonial elite, 320; and John Cadwalader, 321; and American Revolution,
339; and postcolonial elite, 342, 344; and
Robert Morris, 355; and foreign trade, 373–
374; and fashion, 374, 379; and magazines,
374; and Noah Webster, 382; and Benjamin
Franklin, 387. *See also* Fashion

Continental army, 47, 56, 101, 342, 349

Continental Congress, 29n, 47, 52, 338, 341,
347, 363; and Articles of Confederation, 57;
and new constitution, 77; and western
farmers, 101; and women, 140; and merchants, 339

Contract, 94, 127, 128, 129–133, 398; social, 23,
75, 95, 128, 153–154, 420, 458

Cooper, James Fenimore, 212, 242, 246

Cooper, William, 246

Copley, John Singleton, 328, 329, 333, 343;
Mrs. Daniel Hubbard (Mary Green), 330;
Isaac Royall, 334; *Mary and Elizabeth Roy-
all,* 396

Corbly, John, 230–231

Cornwallis, Charles, 55, 106

Courtesy books, 309–310, 316

Coverture, 126, 286, 380

Coxe, Tench, 352, 356n, 373–374, 375, 376, 379

Craig, Margaret Murphey, 146

Creole/creolité, 212, 304, 305, 310, 404; and
gentility, 318–339, 322, 329, 333, 358; and
Leonora Sansay, 443, 444, 446, 449, 450,
451, 453, 454, 455, 458, 460, 463

Crèvecoeur, J. Hector St. John de, 37, 214, 235,
242

Critical Review, 365

Deane, Silas, 347, 348, 349

Declaration of Independence, 2, 63, 74n, 467;
and women, 143; and Hannah Foster, 175–
176; and slavery, 390, 393, 416; and equality,
402; and Charles Brockden Brown, 414,
463; and Leonora Sansay, 463

De Lancey, James, 334

De Lancey, Stephen, 333

De Lancey family, 319

Democracy, 5, 83, 94, 98, 242, 344, 358; excesses of, 3, 86; and western farmers, 41, 97,
103; as despotic, 103, 104, 119; and Charles
Brockden Brown, 269; and Benjamin
Rush, 295–296

Desire, 9, 21, 279, 341, 342, 360, 379, 387, 451;
and women, 170–171, 174, 176, 178, 184, 186,
380, 382, 385, 388; and Hannah Foster, 176,
182, 185, 186; and introjection, 200; and Native Americans, 200, 204, 205, 206, 240;
and Charles Brockden Brown, 279, 423,
424, 441; and magazines, 376

Dickinson, John, 141, 142, 336

Dickinson, Polly, 141, 336

Difference, 51, 154, 199, 233, 375, 435, 467; and
Native Americans, 204, 205, 208, 210, 212,
213, 214, 216, 219, 228, 241, 242, 248, 249,
263, 277; and western frontier, 212, 213; and
Mary Rowlandson, 266; and slavery, 393,
401; and African Americans, 402–405; and
Charles Brockden Brown, 427, 428, 441;
and Leonora Sansay, 451. *See also* Other

Diversity, 208, 209, 210, 211, 212, 220; and national identity, 2; of Americans, 51–52;
ideological, 82–83, 85; and liberalism, 84;
denunciation of, 84–85; celebration of, 465

Doubling, 197–205, 362; and Susanna
Rowson, 270–272, 274–275, 277–280; and
Charles Brockden Brown, 282–283

Drinker, Elizabeth, 141–142, 146, 337

Drinker, Henry, 141, 337, 351

Duer, Kitty Sterling, 144

Duer, William, 349, 350, 353, 415; as merchant
prince, 144, 340, 347; and speculation, 352,
356n, 376; fall of, 357

Dwight, Timothy, 37, 42, 84, 85, 207, 245, 414;

"Valedictory Address," 47–54; *Triumph of Infidelity*, 48

Economy, 7–9, 11, 29; and unrest, 8–9, 10, 55–56, 376; and bourgeoisie, 27, 32, 33; and Revolutionary War, 42; and slavery, 63, 389, 391, 398, 408, 442; and commercial republicanism, 67, 79; and fiscal revolution, 67, 109, 332; and fiscal speculators, 89; and farmers, 99n, 101, 103; and Shays's Rebellion, 108; and frontier, 210, 211; and King Philip's War, 255; and Susanna Rowson, 284; and American Revolution, 340; postcolonial, 350, 353, 357, 358, 371–372; and magazines, 367, 375; and women, 379, 383, 385

Education, 49, 172, 187, 285, 309, 388; and western farmers, 103; and women, 171, 323–325, 327, 368, 378, 379, 439; and British gentleman, 312, 316; and gentility, 368–369; and Charles Brockden Brown, 428, 463

Edwards, Jonathan, 47, 174, 197, 234

Effeminacy, 57, 58, 112, 165, 205, 230, 231; and commercial republicanism, 68, 86; and Others, 91, 375; and Shays's Rebellion, 107–112; and luxury, 151; and classic republicanism, 152; and women's influence, 154–155; and Native Americans, 203, 213, 247, 248; and gentility, 360; and Benjamin Franklin, 387. *See also* Gender

Eliot, John, 256, 263

Elite, 4, 76, 86, 118, 125, 145, 195; colonial, 6, 7, 193, 197, 306, 319, 322, 323, 329, 333, 334, 337, 338, 347, 353; and magazines, 29–32, 366, 374, 377; postcolonial, 56, 340, 341, 342–343, 347–358, 374, 421; and classic republicanism, 64, 83; and Benjamin Franklin, 73; and Shays's Rebellion, 94; and gentility, 361, 363; bourgeois, 363, 375, 377; and education, 368; Caribbean, 449, 451

Elliot, Andrew, 350

Enlightenment, 6, 26, 76n, 250, 283, 366, 442; and Timothy Dwight, 48, 50; and liberalism, 50, 75–79; and diversity, 84; and western farmers, 95; and women, 150, 168, 170–

171; continental, 154; and noble savage, 202–203, 233, 246; and Native Americans, 203; and Susanna Rowson, 269, 283, 286; and colonial elite, 331; and racism, 405, 467

Entrepreneurs, 6, 10, 65, 304, 374, 376, 378; and commercial republicanism, 67, 69, 71; and fiscal speculation, 350; and gentility, 361; and postcolonial economy, 371

Equality, 2, 243, 393, 401, 402, 465, 466; and liberalism, 74, 75, 76; and African Americans, 409

Faber, John, Jr., 330, 331

Farmers, 14, 52, 56, 89, 91, 134; frontier, 7, 59n, 125; and consumer culture, 8, 9; commercial, 9, 10, 15, 98, 99, 103, 415; and foreclosures, 10, 55, 91, 92; and British gentry, 33; and rebellion, 38, 41; of western Massachusetts, 41, 86–87, 94–112; and gender, 43; and commercial republicanism, 68; and Benjamin Franklin, 70, 387; vote for, 90; and Shays's Rebellion, 91–112; discontent of, 92–101; extralegislative actions by, 94, 95, 101, 102; and foreclosure, 99–100; representations of, 101–112; and agriculture, 106, 215, 247, 250, 367, 426; and popular sovereignty, 118; and political representatives, 120; and Jemimah Wilkinson, 161; and women, 165–167; activism by, 187; and manliness, 187; and western frontier, 209, 211; Native American, 218, 227, 228; and Native Americans, 222, 248–249; and Charles Brockden Brown, 270, 417, 418, 421, 427, 428, 431; and Susanna Rowson, 284; and Benjamin Rush, 296; and education, 368; and pastoral romance, 370; and "Letter from Maria to Eliza," 371; and romance, 371; and slavery, 389; in Virginia, 400; and economy, 415. *See also* Shays's Rebellion

Fashion, 10, 15, 30, 201, 329, 336, 369; and display, 66, 67, 179; and women, 87, 152, 386–387, 388, 411; and Shays's Rebellion, 109, 111; and elite, 110, 319, 415; and national identity, 309; and British gentleman, 311,

312, 314, 315, 318; Parisian, 342; and classic republicanism, 359; and magazines, 377; and consumerism, 379; British, 383; and Charles Brockden Brown, 419, 421, 427, 435, 437. *See also* Clothes; Consumerism; Gentlemen

Federalist Papers, 28, 84, 352

Federalists, 15, 124, 145, 347, 349, 352; and magazines, 29; and Timothy Dwight, 36–37, 48; and Noah Webster, 54, 121; and Benjamin Franklin, 72; and Thomas Jefferson, 84; and popular sovereignty, 117, 119; and representatives, 126; and political representation, 127, 131–132; and classic republicanism, 128, 134; and public creditors, 130; and state as private contractor, 131; contradictions of, 131–132; and money, 133; Judith Sargent Murray, 149, 167; social vision of, 343–344, 345

Ferguson, Elizabeth Graeme, 142, 325

Fielding, Henry, 311, 318

Filson, John, 200n, 222

Finch, Mary, Viscountess Andover, 330, 331

First Bank of the United States, 350, 354, 357, 414–415

Fisher, Joshua, 344

Fletcher, Andrew, 151

Fludyer, James, 338

Forts, frontier, 219, 220

Foster, Hannah, 41n; *Coquette,* 171–186, 267

France, 209, 276–277, 344, 351, 451; embassy of, 42, 338; and radicals, 52; and western frontier, 211; and Great Britain, 216, 217; and imperialism, 216, 217, 342, 462; ruling classes of, 298; and British gentleman, 315; and postcolonial era, 340; and slavery, 402n; and Leonora Sansay, 443, 444, 445, 449, 453, 454, 455

Franklin, Benjamin, 69n, 93n, 139, 379; and *American Museum,* 30, 36, 367; and magazines, 37; and commercial republicanism, 70–74; as model, 71; *Autobiography,* 72; and Lord Kames, 78n; self-presentations of, 79; and farmers, 98–99; and Shays's Rebellion,

107–108; and Native Americans, 204; *Narrative of the Late Massacres, in Lancaster County,* 222; and gentility, 300; and Masons, 327; on frugality, 376; and women, 385–387; and Charles Brockden Brown, 413, 417; and slavery, 426

Freedom/independence, 58, 60, 76, 132, 170, 339; and classic republicanism, 61, 62, 64; economic, 61, 64, 65, 152, 374; political, 61; and British republicanism, 65–66; and commercial republicanism, 68, 69; and Benjamin Franklin, 72; and liberalism, 74, 77; and governance, 77; diverse meanings of, 85; and frontier farmers, 94; and marriage, 127; and women, 139, 170; and gender, 156; and seduction novels, 171; and Hannah Foster, 173, 175–176, 177, 178, 179, 180, 181, 182, 183, 184, 186; and Native Americans, 200, 201, 205; and Mary Rowlandson, 252; and Susanna Rowson, 284; and republican gentlemen, 304; and British gentleman, 311; and gentility, 360; and African Americans, 389, 408; and slavery, 391–392, 393, 400, 401, 411, 415–416, 442; and Charles Brockden Brown, 425, 463; and Leonora Sansay, 442, 443, 444, 445, 446, 447, 449, 453, 454, 455, 458, 459, 460, 461, 462, 463; and scientific racism, 467

French Revolution, 35, 48, 145, 149, 276, 277, 343, 453, 454

Freneau, Philip, 352

Frontier, 203, 207–249, 281, 400, 466; western, 64, 208–209, 210; and Benjamin Franklin, 70, 71; Carolina, 93n; narratives concerning, 195, 222, 227; and Native Americans, 205, 217, 263, 269; conflict on, 208–209, 220, 239, 254, 255; forts on, 219, 220; and Charles Brockden Brown, 269, 270, 271, 274, 277. *See also* Settlers; Squatters

Frontiersmen, 42, 214–216, 233, 242; and Benjamin Franklin, 71; and Native Americans, 263; manliness of, 267; and Charles Brockden Brown, 271, 273, 277

Gadsden, Christopher, 137; "To the Planters, Mechanics, and Freeholders of the Province of South Carolina," 137–138

Gadsden, William, 384

Galloway, Grace, 142

Gender, 131, 134, 167–170, 262; and Others, 91; and Shays's Rebellion, 108, 110–112; and political creditworthiness, 132; and Abigail Adams, 143; and press, 155, 156–158; as disordered and dangerous, 161; and Hannah Foster, 175, 182; and captivity narratives, 230, 231, 232; and Native Americans, 247, 248; and Mary Rowlandson, 264–265; and frontier narratives, 267; and imperialism, 268; and Charles Brockden Brown, 279, 438–441; and magazines, 378–388; and African Americans, 410; and Leonora Sansay, 442–443. *See also* Effeminacy; Manliness; Sexuality; Women

Gentility, 15, 31, 304, 318–339; British standards of, 32, 318, 339, 369; and women, 158, 378, 384, 385; and Benjamin Rush, 291, 296, 299–300, 302; and balls, 299, 322, 363, 415; and national identity, 299; cultivation of, 300–301; culture of, 306–307, 310–318; and courtesy books, 310; and architecture, 313–314, 316, 319, 321; contradictory meanings of, 318; and American gentleman, 319; and John Cadwalader, 321; and salons, 323; and American Revolution, 339; and postcolonial era, 340–345; and republican courts, 345; and taste, 359; and ideological confusions, 361; and commerce, 373, 380; and consumerism, 374; and magazines, 374, 379, 380; and Charles Brockden Brown, 424, 438

Gentleman's Magazine, 30, 365

Gentlemen, 35, 305, 307, 339; and bourgeoisie, 34; British, 42, 65, 66, 304, 311–318, 332, 336; republican, 42, 304, 306, 309, 358, 361, 368, 378, 388, 411, 412, 415, 424, 427, 428, 429, 441; and Timothy Dwight, 50; landed, 64, 311, 316, 318; and Benjamin Rush, 296, 299; and postcolonial anxiety, 303; evolution of, 307, 309–318; American vs. British, 318–319;

colonial, 318–339; fashionable, 320, 321, 325, 329, 341, 342, 343, 345–353, 358, 359, 360, 361, 362, 380, 387, 422, 440; and magazines, 365–372; and Charles Brockden Brown, 422–424, 427–430, 440, 441, 463. *See also* Fashion

Gentry: British, 32–33, 310, 317, 325, 328, 329, 333, 355; country, 65; pseudo, 315, 318–319, 358; parish, 316–317

Gerry, Eldridge, 347

Girard, Rene, 204, 205, 216

Godwin, William, 146

Great Britain, 64, 209, 315, 345, 401; and imperialism, 5, 59, 69, 216, 217, 261–265, 267, 270, 276, 278, 279, 317, 353; and national identity, 22; and political discourse, 58; tyranny of, 60, 64, 339; and classic republicanism, 64–66, 69; gentry of, 65; Augustan and Enlightenment, 85; and Shays's Rebellion, 102, 106, 107; and popular sovereignty, 114–115; and trade restraints, 177; and France, 216, 217; and colonialism, 243–244; and Proclamation Lines of 1763 and 1770, 244; and Mary Rowlandson, 252, 262; and Susanna Rowson, 269, 282; and gentleman, 332; and postcolonial bourgeoisie, 341; emulation of, 343, 383

Greene, Nathaniel, 62–63

Grotius, Hugo, 75

Haitian Revolution, 35, 42, 276, 277, 416, 442–460

Hale, Nathan, 60n, 461

Half-Way Covenant, 257

Hall, Nathaniel, 446

Hall, Prince, 26

Hamilton, Alexander, 7, 88, 208, 350, 351, 415; and class, 33; and diversity, 84–85; and sovereignty, 115; ambition of, 309, 340, 347; and speculation, 352, 357

Hamilton, James, 327

Hancock, John, 16, 89, 95

Hemmings, Sally, 411, 415

Henrick, Caesar, 397

Henry, Patrick, 60n, 136, 446, 460–461

Herbeson, Massey, 232
Hill, Deborah, 335
Hill, Richard, 335, 339
Hobbes, Thomas, 154
Hobbesian world, 79, 96, 214, 220, 420
Home, Henry, Lord Kames, 77–78, 79
Hopkins, Samuel, 393
Hopkinson, Francis, 37, 234
Hudson Valley, 319
Hume, David, 79; *Treatise of Human Nature*, 80
Humphreys, David: *Life of Major-General Israel Putnam*, 223
Hutchinson, Anne, 260, 261
Hybridity, 134–135, 208, 212, 217, 241, 306

Identity, 10–11, 272, 274, 276, 280; British, 4, 281, 283, 314, 315, 317, 318, 329; contradictory, 17, 20; definition of, 17–18; formation of, 31, 43; and alterity, 38n; and western frontier, 212–216; and Charles Brockden Brown, 270, 274, 279, 421, 423, 424; and Leonora Sansay, 443, 444. *See also* National identity
Imperialism, 17, 207, 251, 255, 268, 353, 465–466; British, 5, 59, 69, 216–217, 261–265, 267, 270, 276, 278, 279, 317, 353; and Timothy Dwight, 48, 52–53; American, 196, 204, 207, 208, 209, 215, 222, 233, 239, 270, 275, 278; and Mary Rowlandson, 252, 261–265, 267, 269; and Charles Brockden Brown, 269, 270, 278, 279; and Susanna Rowson, 281, 282, 286; and Leonora Sansay, 446
Inchbald, Elizabeth: *Everyone Has His Fault*, 149
Intolerable Acts (1774), 94, 339
Ireland, 270, 275, 276, 277
Irish, 271, 275, 278

James I, 241, 243
Jay, Elizabeth, 359
Jay, John, 7, 192, 347, 352, 390
Jay, Sarah Livingston, 144
Jefferson, Thomas, 16, 347, 352, 357, 420, 466; and magazines, 30, 37; and Mathew Carey, 36; and Timothy Dwight, 48, 51; followers

of, 52, 343, 352, 428; as model, 63, 66, 72; and slavery, 63–64, 392; Federalist attacks on, 84; and republican court, 184, 185; and Native Americans, 192, 204, 237, 238, 239–240, 399; *Notes on Virginia*, 237, 238, 367, 399; and Susanna Rowson, 286; as gentleman, 305, 342; and Charles Brockden Brown, 413; and sexuality, 415
Jews, 51, 417, 440, 441
Johnson, Samuel: "Fountains," 381–382
Jones, Absalom, 26, 432, 433, 434; *Narrative of the Proceedings of the Black People*, 433, 436

King Philip's War, 252–267, 281, 282, 283
Knox, Henry, 14, 93, 347, 356n

Lacan, Jacques, 423, 424
La Luzerne, Anne-César, Chevalier de, 340, 357, 363, 402; ball of, 291, 296, 300, 301, 303, 310, 353
Land, 49, 66, 215, 216, 240, 357, 466; and speculation, 3, 6, 13, 216; and classic republicanism, 64–66; western, 97, 100, 103, 207, 209, 210, 214, 215, 216, 351; and Hannah Foster, 183; and Native Americans, 199, 200, 201, 216, 222, 228, 233, 247, 250, 263; and King Philip's War, 254; and Puritans, 256, 258, 262; and Charles Brockden Brown, 270, 273, 274, 275, 276, 278; and Susanna Rowson, 281, 282; and gentleman, 305, 311, 315, 317, 318, 319, 358; and gentility, 323, 333, 335
Latrobe, Benjamin, 354–355, 414–415
Laurens, John, 62, 63, 66, 72
Lawyers, 30, 35, 49, 50, 51, 96, 306
Le Clerc, Charles, 445
Lee, Ann, 159–160
Lee, Arthur, 338, 344, 345, 349, 377, 392
Lee, Richard Henry, 338
L'Enfant, Pierre Charles, 354
Lenni-Lenapes, 193–194, 270, 274
Liberalism, 58, 75, 128, 154, 158, 371, 405; Lockean, 14, 18, 75, 77, 79, 121, 215, 216; aspects of, 74–82, 83, 84; and property, 77, 78; and sympathies, 79–80; and women, 153–155, 170–171; and Hannah Foster, 175, 176, 182,

183; and Leonora Sansay, 442, 453, 454–455, 458, 459, 462

Livingston, Henry, 338

Livingston, Robert, 333, 347

Livingston, Sarah, 347

Livingston, Walter, 334–335, 349, 352, 415

Livingston family, 319

Lloyd, Thomas, 335

Locke, John, 96, 157, 215, 216, 235, 420; and liberalism, 14, 18, 75, 77, 79, 121, 215, 216; and social contract, 95, 153–154; and representatives, 126, 127n; *Thoughts concerning Education,* 312; and slavery, 394, 395

Logan, James, 93n, 193–194, 335

Logan (Mingo chief), 237–238, 239–240, 243, 245, 246, 399

London Magazine, 30

Long, Edward, 406, 438; *History of Jamaica,* 402–404

Lord Dunmore's War, 218, 239

Louisiana Constitutional Convention, 467

L'Ouverture, Toussaint, 443, 444, 445, 451–452; wife of, 446, 463

McGuffey's Readers, 237, 239–240

Maclay, William, 345

Madison, James, 85, 104, 119, 127, 347

Magazines, 27–40, 58–59, 70, 85–86, 132, 235; London, 30, 365, 366; and Constitutional Convention, 57–58; and classic republicanism, 60, 61, 64, 66; and commercial republicanism, 67, 68, 69; and liberalism, 74, 75, 76–77; and national identity, 82, 86, 464; and Shays's Rebellion, 101–112; and political representation, 116–128; and women, 150, 156–166, 366, 377–388; and Native Americans, 223, 233, 240, 247, 249; and gentility, 363, 365–372, 374, 379, 380; and commerce, 367, 372–377; and pastoral romance, 369–372; and American Revolution, 375; young readers of, 376–377; and African Americans, 389, 397–411; and slavery, 394–395, 397–410. *See also* Press

Manheim, Christina, 232

Manheim, Maria, 232

Manigault, Mrs. Gabriel, 344

Manigault family, 319

Manliness, 71–73, 91, 132, 134, 274, 380, 388; and citizenship, 59–62, 85–86; and civic virtue, 59–62, 135; and classic republicanism, 59–62, 78, 112; and Benjamin Franklin, 72; and Shays's Rebellion, 87, 109–111, 127; and women, 150, 155, 166–167; and ideological conflicts, 186–187; and Native Americans, 200–203, 205, 247; and western frontier, 214; and frontier, 230; and gentility, 360, 361. *See also* Gender

Marriage, 126–127, 151, 297; market for, 132, 134, 172; and Hannah Foster, 172, 173, 175, 176, 177, 180, 181; and miscegenation, 240, 241–242, 284, 285, 410, 459; and Native Americans, 241–242; and Charles Brockden Brown, 270, 277, 278, 439, 440; and Susanna Rowson, 282, 285, 286; and African Americans, 410; and Leonora Sansay, 456, 458, 459, 460, 462

Masculinity, 58, 110–111, 135, 201. *See also* Manliness

Mason, George, 127

Masonic order, 76, 99n, 327–328, 361

Massachusetts, 94, 99, 100, 101, 104, 254, 260; constitution of, 89, 95, 96–97; and Shays's Rebellion, 91–92; General Court of, 93, 98, 103; General Assembly of, 101; and slavery, 389, 394–396, 409. *See also* Farmers; Shays's Rebellion

Massachusetts Magazine, 29, 37, 145, 156, 371, 372, 389; and gentility, 367; and education, 368–369; "Letter from Maria to Eliza," 369–372, 406; and commerce, 372–377; and Protestant work ethic, 375; and Africans, 404–405; and poverty, 406

Massachusetts Spy, 28, 101

Mather, Cotton, 256, 257

Mather, Increase, 255, 256, 257, 259, 262, 263

Meade, George, 347

Melodrama, 169, 170, 447

Merchants, 6, 30, 79, 193, 295; and consumerism, 9, 10, 379; and British gentry, 33; and

Timothy Dwight, 49, 51; and British republicanism, 65, 69; British exclusion of, 65–66; and commercial republicanism, 68; elite, 88–89, 144, 341, 343, 357, 374, 415; and Shays's Rebellion, 92, 108, 110; and western farmers, 100; and Isaiah Thomas, 101–102; and popular sovereignty, 118; and Federalists, 128; and women, 139–140, 152, 187, 378, 384–385; and salons, 145; and Tammany Society, 192; and western frontier, 209; and Native Americans, 220; and Charles Brockden Brown, 268, 418, 419, 421, 426, 437, 439; and Susanna Rowson, 284; and republican gentlemen, 304, 358; and British gentleman, 313, 315, 316, 317; and Philadelphia, 321; and colonial gentility, 323; and gentility, 333–339, 355, 359–363; British, 338; as undercapitalized, 338–339; and American Revolution, 339–340; postcolonial, 343; and postcolonial elite, 347; and wartime profits, 348–350; and postcolonial economy, 371; and magazines, 374, 377; and slavery, 390, 391; and Leonora Sansay, 444, 447, 454. *See also* Commerce

Middle class: and popular sovereignty, 118; and women, 166; and Hannah Foster, 179, 180, 182; and Charles Brockden Brown, 270, 273, 276, 277, 278, 422n, 425, 426, 428, 437, 438, 441; and Susanna Rowson, 284, 286; and gentleman, 309; and British gentleman, 317

Middling classes, 27, 34–36, 86, 276, 284, 286; *Massachusetts Magazine*, 29; and magazines, 30, 366, 375–376; and political magazines, 38; and novels, 40, 169; and Constitutional Convention, 57; and private property, 78; and women, 143, 152, 165; and Hannah Foster, 174, 186; and republican court, 185; and Tammany Society, 192, 194; and Native Americans, 195, 199; and imperialism, 268; and Charles Brockden Brown, 275, 429; and Susanna Rowson, 285; and Benjamin Rush, 295; as gentlemen, 306; and British gentleman, 317; and gentility, 360–361; and Chevalier de La

Luzerne, 363; and republican gentlemen, 363; in Virginia, 400; and economy, 415

Milton, John, 419

Mobs, 64, 86, 89, 93, 101, 103, 369

Mohawks, 218

Money, 14, 98; hard currency/specie, 94, 98, 99, 101, 133, 370; paper, 94, 98, 112, 113, 131, 133, 362

Monthly Magazine, 374n

Moore, Hannah, 335

Moore, Milcah Martha: "The Female Patriot," 138–139

Moravians, 210, 211, 214, 217, 220

Morni (enslaved African), 406–407, 408, 409, 411

Morris, Gouverneur, 127, 347, 352

Morris, Mary White, 144

Morris, Mrs. Robert, 354

Morris, Robert, 30, 144, 300, 357, 376, 411, 431; and speculation, 6, 89, 347–352, 354–355; home of, 354–355, 356

Morris, Robert Hunter, 327

Murray, Judith Sargent: *Gleaner,* 149, 167

Narragansetts, 250, 254

Narrative of the Adventures of Capt. Isaac Stuart, 223

Narrative of the Captivity and Sufferings of Benjamin Gilbert and His Family, 223

National identity, 17–23, 26, 270, 277, 279, 292, 343; formation of, 2–3, 18–22, 61, 62, 69, 74, 85, 88; and magazines, 29, 31, 82, 86, 366; and Timothy Dwight, 48–53; conflicting visions of, 59, 82, 85, 186–187, 465–468; and classic republicanism, 60, 66; pragmatic-fractured, 82–87; and Shays's Rebellion, 87, 105, 110, 111; destabilization of, 134, 135, 417; and Native Americans, 191–206, 219, 220, 223, 233, 239, 244, 247; and western frontier, 207, 208; and captivity narratives, 230–233, 253; and American Revolution, 239, 339; postcolonial, 242–243; and women, 250, 378; and Charles Brockden Brown, 275, 278, 464; and Susanna Rowson, 280–281, 282, 286; and gentility, 291–307; and bourgeoisie, 298–299, 341, 376; and republican gentlemen, 304, 411, 412; and gentility, 309, 319, 358, 361, 411; and slavery, 398–399, 401; and African Americans, 405, 435; and Leonora Sansay, 459, 464. *See also* Identity

Native Americans, 43, 51, 295, 302; as savages, 6, 10, 198, 205, 218, 222, 223, 224, 225, 230–232, 233, 237, 247, 248, 250, 251, 256, 266, 267, 268, 271, 272, 273, 277, 284, 303; and *Cherokee Nation v. Georgia,* 6n; as Other, 38, 41–42, 187, 244, 245–247, 253, 256–259, 263, 266, 267, 268; and Shays's Rebellion, 105–106, 110; treaties with, 191–206, 193; representations of, 195, 222–238, 247–249, 251–259, 262, 263, 267; war with, 195, 198, 204, 205, 207, 216–233, 254, 273; as noble savages, 202, 203, 220, 227, 233–238, 245, 246, 281, 286; exclusion of, 207–208, 213, 219, 239, 243, 244, 256; and western frontier, 209–212; as inferior, 213–214, 245–247; as satanic, 214, 256, 258, 262; and religion, 217, 220, 256, 277; Conestogas, 218, 220, 227, 277; and cannibalism, 225–227, 256, 263, 403; as vanishing race, 236–240; and Mary Rowlandson, 251–259, 262–263, 266–267, 272; and King Philip's War, 255; and Susanna Rowson, 269, 280–286; and Charles Brockden Brown, 271–276, 278, 279

Nesbit, J. M., 347

New England, 9, 115, 203, 253, 258, 262, 333, 426

New Jersey, 13, 29, 47, 426

New Jersey Magazine, 29

New York, 11, 14, 29, 54, 107, 211; ratification debates in, 28; colonial society in, 33; and gentility, 333, 336; and wartime profits, 349; and slavery, 408

New York City, 47, 191, 194, 390–391, 426

Nicholson, Hannah, 379

Nicholson, John, 6, 357

Noailles, Vicomte de, 451

Nonimportation agreements, 52, 69, 137–138, 140, 187, 339, 384

Norris, Isaac, 335n

Northwest Ordinance (1787), 195n, 219

Old Whigs, 122, 124, 125. *See also* Radical Whigs; Whigs

Ortiz, Tomaso, 263

Other, x–xi, 40, 41, 43, 135, 272; constitution of, 20, 21; and magazines, 38, 86, 377–378; and slavery, 42, 407, 411; women as, 42, 87, 133, 150–155, 156, 162, 165–167, 378–388, 411; and Shays's Rebellion, 86–87, 103, 105–106, 107; Native Americans as, 187, 197, 204, 205, 220, 227–229, 233, 244, 245–247, 253, 256–259, 263, 266, 267, 268; and surrogacy, 202; and western frontier, 212–213; and Charles Brockden Brown, 274, 278, 416, 425, 427, 428, 441, 464; African Americans as, 364, 378, 388–410, 411, 435; and Leonora Sansay, 449, 464. *See also* Difference

Otis, James, 95, 167

Paine, Thomas, 28, 51, 120–121, 122, 146, 392

Passion, 59–60, 61, 376, 450, 453; and Hannah Foster, 176, 178, 180, 182, 185, 186; and Leonora Sansay, 447, 453, 459–460

Paxton Boys, 208, 220, 227, 263, 277

Peale, Charles Willson, 321, 328, 329

Peale, Rembrandt, 432

Pemberton, Mary, 142

Penn, Thomas, 193–194, 197, 322

Penn, William, 13, 335

Pennsylvania, 28, 77, 104, 203, 213, 239, 426; diversity of, 12–13; and Native Americans, 106, 217–218, 223, 227, 263; western, 268, 273; and Charles Brockden Brown, 270, 271; and Susanna Rowson, 284; and gentility, 333, 335; slavery in, 390

Pennsylvania Gazette, 217–218

Pennsylvania Magazine, 28

People, the, 18, 88, 89n, 96n, 97n, 114n, 115, 116, 119, 120, 196, 296, 297

Performativity, 72, 73, 110, 134, 321, 328–329, 343; and national identity, 20, 22–23; and Tammany Society, 191–206; and Benjamin Rush, 291–307; and gentility, 309–314, 318, 322–323, 327–328, 329, 331, 340–341, 345, 355

Pettit, Charles, 350n

Philadelphia: and press, 29, 107; and Robert

Morris, 354; and slavery, 389–390, 401, 408, 415–416; and Charles Brockden Brown, 416, 418, 419, 420, 422, 426, 430, 431; African Americans in, 416–417, 431–435

Philips, Adolph, 333

Pinckney, Charles, 57

Pleasure, 424, 450; and Hannah Foster, 175–178, 180, 182, 185. *See also* Desire; Sexuality

Pocahontas, 240–244, 264, 284

Pollard, William, 353

Powel, Elizabeth Willing, 144, 184, 344, 345

Powel, John, 411

Powel, Samuel, 322, 335, 336, 341, 344, 345

Powers, Eliza, 361

Press, 22–23, 26–36; and newspapers, 22, 35, 59; bourgeois, 33, 86, 103, 104, 128, 135, 232; and Constitutional Convention, 57; urban, 57, 104, 110, 129, 133, 134, 143, 155–167, 174, 182, 184, 186–187, 220, 222, 223, 244, 245, 299, 304, 319, 379, 380, 424, 426; and commercial republicanism, 68; and western farmers, 95–96, 103, 104; and Shays's Rebellion, 104, 110; commercial and fiscal actors in, 129; and money, 133; and women, 143, 155–167, 379; and gender, 156–158; and Elizabeth Whitman, 174; and Hannah Foster, 182, 184; and ideological conflicts, 186–187; and Native Americans, 223, 244, 245; and settlers, 229; and captivity narratives, 232; and state balls, 299; and postcolonial anxiety, 304; and republican gentlemen, 304; and American gentleman, 319; and merchants, 340; and Charles Brockden Brown, 424. *See also* Magazines

Print/print culture, 22–23, 26–36, 96, 134, 178, 268, 319, 424

Public, the, 129, 130, 131, 134

Pufendorf, Samuel, 75

Pultney, William, 351

Puritans, 15, 19, 176, 203, 250, 258, 280; and Mary Rowlandson, 252, 253, 255, 256, 261, 262, 267; and Susanna Rowson, 282, 283, 284

Quakers, 29, 213, 215, 255, 268, 297, 392; and Native Americans, 218, 220; and Charles

Brockden Brown, 269; and Susanna Rowson, 282, 284; and economy, 415

Quebec Act (1774), 244

Race/racism, 26, 38, 251, 252, 304, 306; and Native Americans, 195, 197–198, 203–205, 217–219, 222, 229–233, 239, 245–247; and frontier, 207, 208, 212, 213; and science, 245, 402–406, 467; and Mary Rowlandson, 262, 266, 286; and Charles Brockden Brown, 269–270, 420–435, 438, 440; and Susanna Rowson, 283, 285, 286, 287; and African Americans, 388–412; and Leonora Sansay, 442, 443, 451, 456, 459. *See also* African Americans; Difference; Native Americans; Other

Radical Whigs, 89n, 116, 120–124. *See also* Old Whigs; Whigs

Rainsford, Marcus, 448

Regulator Movement, 92, 96n, 99, 100

Representation, 135, 230–233; political, 112–128, 131, 133; metaphoric, 123, 124, 133; mimetic, 123, 124, 126

—rhetorical, 112–113, 123, 131–132, 150, 240, 271, 287; of women, 150, 155–167; of Native Americans, 222–238, 247–249, 251–259, 262, 263, 267; in captivity narratives, 224–233

Republican court, 184–185, 186, 342–343, 345, 352, 357

Revenge Taken by the Black Army for Cruelties Practised on Them by the French, 448

Revere, Paul, 19, 136, 252, 389

Revolutionary War. *See* American Revolution

Reynolds, Sir Joshua, 346

Rights: of citizen, 2; and Great Britain, 3; and colonial press, 23; natural, 75, 78; and citizenship, 88; and Massachusetts constitution, 89; and western farmers, 97, 103; of women, 153–155, 314; and Hannah Foster, 175; and Native Americans, 196, 239, 250; and surrogacy, 196; and frontier, 207; and republican citizens, 371; and slavery, 393, 397, 408, 416, 442; and African Americans, 396, 406, 408, 410; and Leonora Sansay,

454, 459, 463; celebration of, 465; as universal, 466

Rochambeau, Count, 300, 303

Rogers, Robert: *Reminiscences of the French War,* 222

Rolfe, John, 241, 243

Romance, 222, 380; and political discourse, 171; and Hannah Foster, 181, 182; and Logan (Mingo chief), 238; and Susanna Rowson, 284, 286; pastoral, 369–372, 406, 409

Ross, John, 337, 347

Rousseau, Jean-Jacques, 75, 154–155, 157, 158, 165

Rowlandson, Joseph, 254

Rowlandson, Mary White, 270, 271; *Sovereignty and Goodness of God,* 251–269; and Charles Brockden Brown, 272–274, 279, 280; and Susanna Rowson, 281–284, 286

Rowson, Susanna, 41n, 268; *Reuben and Rachel,* 42, 253, 269, 280–287; *Charlotte Temple,* 149, 171, 281; *Slaves in Algiers,* 149

Rush, Benjamin, 7, 37, 73, 184, 377; and Native Americans, 246–247; and gentility, 291–302, 304, 306, 315, 338, 339, 358, 363; and *American Museum,* 367; and education, 368; and slavery, 390, 392, 394; and yellow fever, 420; and Philadelphia epidemic, 433; and Charles Brockden Brown, 438–439

Rush, Julia Stockton, 146, 338

St. Clair, Arthur, 219

Salon, 144, 184, 202–203, 323. *See also* Republican court

Sameness, 393, 398, 401, 402, 406, 466

Sansay, Leonora, 41n; *Zelica, the Creole,* 42, 416, 442–460; *Secret History,* 416

Sansay, Louis, 443

Schuyler, Elizabeth, 33, 347

Schuyler, Philip, 347, 349, 352, 375, 415

Sedgwick, Theodore, 151

Settlers, 208, 220, 229, 240, 241, 276; and western frontier, 210, 211, 213; and Native Americans, 218, 219, 229; and land speculators, 351. *See also* Frontier; Squatters

Seven Years' War, 216, 217, 223, 235, 243

Sexuality, 73, 214, 242, 271, 285, 415; and women, 159, 162–164, 169–171, 174, 181, 428, 447, 450, 459–460; and Hannah Foster, 179–182; and Native Americans, 247, 248; and Mary Rowlandson, 265, 267; and Charles Brockden Brown, 269, 274, 279, 418, 431, 437, 438; and homosexuality, 279, 460; and romance, 369, 371; and Africans, 403, 405; and African Americans, 410, 411; and Leonora Sansay, 442–443, 447, 449, 450, 451–455, 458–462. *See also* Gender

Shays's Rebellion, 91–112, 220, 352, 370, 414; anxiety over, 3, 442; and magazines, 28, 38; and Others, 41, 86–87; and popular sovereignty, 116, 117, 125; and manliness, 127, 214; and Mathew Carey, 161. *See also* Farmers

Shippen, Alice Lee, 324–325, 327, 339, 399

Shippen, Nancy, 324–325, 327, 341, 344, 377

Shippen, William, II, 324–325, 327, 338, 341

Sinclair, William, 326

Slavery, 9, 18, 26, 244, 285, 319, 332; and Other, 42, 411; and classical republican ideal, 63; and citizens, 86; and western frontier, 208; and Native Americans, 222; opposition to, 287, 392–401, 406–410, 441, 444; and republicanism, 388–389, 442; northern, 389–392; reparations for, 394–395, 396; trade in, 397–398, 406–407, 409, 430; and freedom, 415–416; and Charles Brockden Brown, 416–417, 421, 425–430, 433, 435, 437, 463; and yellow fever, 420; and economy, 426, 442; Afro-Caribbean, 442; and Leonora Sansay, 442–460, 462, 463; challenges to, 466. *See also* African Americans

Smith, Elihu Hubbard, 343

Smith, John, 240, 241, 242–244, 263–265, 267, 284; *History of Virginia,* 262

Smith, Malancton, 120

Smith, William, 327

Sovereignty, 74, 196; popular, 2, 3, 64, 88, 95, 103, 113–128

Spectator, 29

Speculation, 103, 130–131, 173, 391, 414; in commercial paper, 14; and classic republicanism, 61; and British republicanism, 66; and Shays's Rebellion, 92; and Massachusetts General Court, 98; and western frontier, 100, 209, 210, 213; fiscal, 132, 134, 335, 348–353, 357; land, 194, 210, 214, 216, 218, 220, 239, 244, 333, 351, 352, 355, 357, 415; and Native Americans, 218, 220; and postcolonial elite, 347, 348–353, 355; and Revolutionary War, 349

Spotsworth, William, 37

Squatters, 3, 15, 218, 220, 242, 274; and western frontier, 208, 209, 213, 214, 215, 216. *See also* Settlers

Stepan, Nancy, 76

Sterling, Kitty, 357

Stiles, Ezra, 245, 246

Stockton, Annis Boudinot, 146, 147

Story, Joseph, 238–239

Stuart, Gilbert, 328, 329; *Joseph Brant,* 221

Sullivan, James, 97

Sullivan, John, 218

Surrogacy, 191–206

Swan, James, 397

Sympathies, 15, 79–82, 228, 236, 238, 258; and Native Americans, 235–237, 240; and Mary Rowlandson, 258; and African Americans, 405–410; and Leonora Sansay, 446

Tammany Society, 42, 191–206, 279

Taste, 312–313, 316–318, 367, 377

Taxes, 339, 395, 451; land, 91, 94; poll, 91, 94, 103; and western farmers, 97–98, 99, 103; and Shays's Rebellion, 370

Thomas, Isaiah, 220, 389, 404; publication by, 28–29; career of, 37; and Shays's Rebellion, 101–104, 106, 370; and women, 112, 138, 171; and Mary Wollstonecraft, 145; and captivity narratives, 235–237; and novel, 367; and gentility, 369; and economy, 371, 372; and commerce, 372; and Protestant work ethic, 375; and slavery, 406

Thomson, Hannah, 141

Tilghman, Molly, 344

Trenchard, John, 37

United States Magazine, 28

Van Cortlandt, Stephanus, 333

Van der Straet, Jan, 264

Van Rensellear family, 319

Vassall, Anthony, 397

Violence, xi, xiii, 21, 208, 256, 269, 442, 466; and identity, 2, 22, 208, 467–468; and western frontier, 213–215; and Native Americans, 217–233, 237, 239, 248, 254, 256; and Charles Brockden Brown, 273–274, 425; and difference, 435; and Leonora Sansay, 447, 449, 451, 452, 456

Walking Treaty, 193, 217, 274, 278

Warren, James, 7, 95, 167, 347

Warren, Joseph, 97

Warren, Mercy Otis, 147, 148, 149, 167, 343; *History of the Rise, Progress, and Termination of the American Revolution,* 147

Washington, George, 55, 141, 142, 144, 197, 399, 420; and empire, 5–6; and land, 14; and magazines, 30; and Constitution, 56–57; as model, 62, 63, 66, 71, 72; and Native Americans, 191, 195, 218, 220, 233; and Whiskey Rebellion, 208; and gentility, 309, 322, 335, 336, 338; and elite, 347, 352; and Robert Morris, 354; and Leonora Sansay, 445, 454; and freedom, 461

Washington, Martha, 142, 144, 184, 342–343, 345, 357, 359

Wayne, Anthony, 195n, 219

Webster, Noah, 36–37, 54, 57, 71, 80, 133, 366; and publication, 28, 31; on political representation, 121–128; and state as contractor, 129–130; and Native Americans, 220, 234–247; and gentility, 303, 336, 354, 367; and women, 381, 382

Wedgwood, Josiah, 315

Welbeck, Thomas, 451

Whigs, 89, 90, 91, 119; as lawyers, 88; defined, 89n; and western farmers, 95, 96, 97, 100,

103; and Massachusetts constitution, 96–97; and Isaiah Thomas, 101–102; and women, 137, 143. *See also* Old Whigs; Radical Whigs

Whiskey Rebellion, 93n, 208, 220, 414, 442

White, John, 254

Whiting, William, 100

Whitman, Elizabeth, 174, 180

Wilcocks, John, 347

Wilkinson, Jemimah, 159–161

Willett, Marinus, 192

Williamson, Peter, 231, 233, 275

Willing, Thomas, 30, 144, 347, 352, 353

Wilson, James, 6, 88, 127, 347

Winthrop, John, 262

Wollstonecraft, Mary, 149, 168, 174, 180; *Vindication of the Rights of Women*, 145–146, 147, 367

Women: and factories, 9; and magazines, 35n, 366, 379–388; as Other, 41, 42, 87, 91, 135, 136, 150–155, 156, 162, 165–167, 378–388, 411; rights of, 41, 149, 314; and classic republicanism, 82, 359, 378, 380; and Revolutionary War, 90, 141, 142–143, 187; and suffrage, 97, 459; satire about, 111–112, 161–167, 382–384; and political representation, 126–128; and misogyny, 128, 387–388, 458, 459; and commerce, 131, 152, 380, 384–385; political subjectivity of, 132, 139, 140–150, 163–164, 166–168, 175–178, 183, 184, 186, 250, 251, 258–260, 262, 265, 281, 284, 286, 287, 343, 344, 345, 346, 352, 359, 462, 463; bourgeois, 136, 143, 152–153, 378–388; middling, 136, 143, 187, 378–388; and public sphere, 136, 143–145, 146, 149, 159, 163, 165, 167, 168, 171, 250, 251, 298, 314, 322, 343, 344, 345, 346, 352; economic agency of, 137–138, 139, 141; elite, 138, 143, 144, 383; household and estate management by, 141–142; tory, 141–142; and salons, 144–145, 323, 327; as dangerous, 151, 153–155, 157–161, 164, 165, 378, 380–382, 384–387; and sexuality, 151, 159, 162–164, 169–171, 174, 181, 378, 428, 447, 450, 459–460; male governance of, 151–154, 157, 165, 380; and domestic sphere, 152, 153; exclusion of, 153–155; and farmers, 165–167; as republican wife and mother, 168–169, 171, 178; as writers, 170, 249, 250–287, 379, 444; and desire, 170–171, 174, 176, 178, 184, 186; and republican court, 184–185, 344–345, 352; and captivity narratives, 230, 232, 233; Native American, 238, 247, 250, 258, 264; and imperialism, 250, 251; and Native Americans, 250–287; as victims, 251, 267, 269; and Massachusetts Bay Colony, 260; and Charles Brockden Brown, 271, 273, 274, 275, 278, 279–280, 416, 438–441, 463; and national cohesion, 297–298; and state balls, 299; and education, 302, 323–325, 327, 368, 378, 379, 439; and British gentleman, 313; and tea rituals, 322, 327, 385; and gentility, 359, 360, 378, 384, 385, 411; and romance, 371; middle-class, 378, 382; and consumerism, 378–379, 380, 387, 388; and desire, 380, 382, 385, 388; and Samuel Johnson, 381–382; and fashion, 382–383, 385, 386–387, 388, 411; Hottentot, 403; African American, 410, 411; and rape, 447, 449, 453. *See also* Gender

Woodmason, Charles, 214, 229, 242

Worcester Magazine, 28, 37, 101–102, 106–107, 111, 112, 371

Yellow fever, 420–422, 424, 427–428, 430, 437–438